Literacies

Second edition

The second edition of *Literacies* continues to provide a comprehensive introduction to literacy pedagogy within today's new media environment. It focuses not only on reading and writing, but also on other modes of communication, including oral, visual, audio, gestural, tactile and spatial. Increased coverage of grammar, phonics and spelling has been integrated into this edition along with a comprehensive discussion of topics such as Multiliteracies and critical literacy.

Current Australian Curriculum content, such as achievement standards and language, literature and literacy curriculum strands, is integrated throughout, and the US Common Core State Standards are also included. In addition, a new chapter addressing cross-curricular priorities of the Australian Curriculum (Aboriginal and Torres Strait Islander histories and cultures), and a new chapter on literacies standards and assessment that incorporates assessment technologies, have been included. 'Making written meanings' is further explored in two separate chapters that cover both reading and writing.

New features include:

- coverage of the latest curriculum developments
- learning outcomes for each chapter
- additional practical classroom activities
- activities integrated with the text's website.

Videos and additional activities are provided on the book's website at literacies.com.

Literacies features the experiences of both teachers and students and provides a range of methods that teachers can use with students to develop their capacities to read, write and communicate. This book is a contemporary and invaluable resource for primary and secondary pre-service teachers and literacy students.

Mary Kalantzis is Dean of the College of Education at the University of Illinois.

Bill Cope is a Professor in the Department of Education Policy, Organization and Leadership at the University of Illinois.

Eveline Chan is a Senior Lecturer in the School of Education at the University of New England.

Leanne Dalley-Trim is Dean and Acting Head of School in the School of Education at James Cook University.

second edition

LITERACIES

MARY KALANTZIS

BILL COPE

EVELINE CHAN

LEANNE DALLEY-TRIM

CAMBRIDGE
UNIVERSITY PRESS

CAMBRIDGE
UNIVERSITY PRESS

477 Williamstown Road, Port Melbourne, VIC 3207, Australia

Cambridge University Press is part of the University of Cambridge.

It furthers the University's mission by disseminating knowledge in the
pursuit of education, learning and research at the highest international
levels of excellence.

www.cambridge.org
Information on this title: www.cambridge.org/9781107578692

First published 2012
Reprinted 2013, 2014, 2015
Second edition 2016

Cover designed by Ryan Taylor, Pounce Creative
Typeset by Aptara Corp.
Printed in Singapore by C.O.S. Printers Pte Ltd

A catalogue record for this publication is available from the British Library

A Cataloguing-in-Publication entry is available from the catalogue of the National
Library of Australia at www.nla.gov.au

ISBN 978-1-107-57869-2 Paperback

Additional resources for this publication at literacies.com

Contents

Acknowledgements

The authors and Cambridge University Press would like to thank the following for permission to reproduce material in this book.

Figure 1.2: Yolngu.net; **1.4**: Mary Kalantzis and Bill Cope; **1.6**: © Lindsay Holmwood. Reproduced under Creative Commons Attribution-ShareAlike 2.0 Generic License; **1.7**: Courtesy of the National Museum of China; **1.8**: © 1991–1996 Unicode, Inc. All rights reserved; **2.2**: Modern Museum of Art/Film Stills Archive, New York City; **2.3**: The Henry Ford Museum; **4.1**, **9.12**: Rudolf Flesch. 1955. *Why Johnny Can't Read, And What to do About It.* New York: Harper. pp. 142, 168; **4.2**: E. Fletcher and T.V. Cooke. 1966. *Enjoying English, Grade 5.* Sydney: Whitcome and Tombs. p. 7; **4.3**: New South Wales Department of Education. c. 1955. *Seaside Story.* Sydney: NSW Government Printer, pp. 18–19; **4.4**: Claire Kinsella. 1969. *Modified Cursive Copybook: Book 1.* Hong Kong: Real Books. p. 30; **4.5**: W.G. Lake. c. 1965. *Planned Composition, Book 3.* Sydney: Aidmasta Productions; **5.1**, **9.10**: Scott, Foresman and Company. 1951. *Dick and Jane: We Play.* New York: Grossat and Dunlap. pp. 8–9; **5.2**: Reprinted with permission from *Phonic Phacts* by Ken Goodman. Copyright © 1993 by Kenneth S. Goodman. Published by Heinemann, Portsmouth, NH. All rights reserved; **5.4**: Maria Montessori. 1917. *The Montessori Elementary Material.* New York: Schocken Books; **7.1**: Barbara Comber, Pat Thomson and Marg Wells. 2001. 'Critical Literacy Finds a "Place"; Writing and Social Action in a Low-Income Australian Grade 2/3 Classroom'. *The Elementary School Journal* 101:451–64. University of Chicago Press. Reproduced with permission; **8.1**: © Babbletrish; **8.7**: Gunther Kress. 2003. *Literacy in the New Media Age.* London: Routledge. p. 42. Reproduced with permission from Taylor & Francis; **8.12**: Courtesy of Kathy Mills; **9.14**: Gunther Kress. 1999. *Early Spelling: From Convention to Creativity.* London: Routledge; **11.15**: © 2011 Google; **12.2**: © Phillip Kalantzis-Cope, **12.4**. © Shutterstock.com/Shawn Hempel; **12.5**: Kress, Gunther. 1997. *Before Writing: Rethinking the Paths to Literacy.* London: Routledge. p. 31. Reproduced with permission from Taylor & Francis; **12.6**: Courtesy Pippa Stein and Denise Newfield; **12.7**: David McNeill. 1992. *Hand and Mind: What Gestures Reveal About Thought.* Chicago: University of Chicago Press. p. 150; **12.8**: Ohio Library Council; **12.10**: Courtesy David Andrew and Joni Brenner; **12.11**: Gunther Kress, Carey Jewitt, Jon Ogborn and Charalampos Tsatsarelis. 2001. *Multimodal Teaching and Learning: The Rhetorics of the Science Classroom.* London: Continuum. By kind permission of Continuum International Publishing Group, a Bloomsbury Company; **13.4**: © Getty/Lambert/Archive Photos; **14.7**: © Joel Abroad <http://www.flickr.com/photos/40295335@N00/4840412198/>; **14.8**: Courtesy Ambigapathy Pandian and Shanthi Balraj; **15.1**: Photograph by White House Photographer Frank Wolfe. Source: LBJ Library & Museum; **15.2**: Courtesy of Karen Martin; **15.3**: Courtesy Mario E. Lopez-Gopar.

Every effort has been made to trace and acknowledge copyright. The publisher apologises for any accidental infringement and welcomes information that would redress this situation.

INTRODUCTION

The work of learning and teaching literacies

Old basics and new

This book offers a 'Multiliteracies' approach to literacy. We coined this term together with our colleagues in the New London Group during discussions in which we were trying to capture some of the enormous shifts in the ways in which people made and participated in meanings (Cope & Kalantzis 2009; New London Group 1996). The Multiliteracies approach attempts to explain what still matters in traditional approaches to reading and writing, and to supplement this with knowledge of what is new and distinctive about the ways in which people make meanings in the contemporary communications environment.

The two 'multis' of Multiliteracies

The term 'Multiliteracies' refers to two major aspects of meaning-making today. The first is *social diversity*, or the variability of conventions of meaning in different cultural, social or domain-specific situations. Texts vary enormously depending on social context – life experience, subject matter, disciplinary domain, area of employment, specialist knowledge, cultural setting or gender identity, to name just a few key differences. These differences are becoming ever more significant to the ways in which we interact in our everyday lives, the ways in which we make and participate in meanings. For this reason, it is important that literacy teaching today should not primarily focus, as it did in the past, only on the rules of a single, standard form of the national language.

Communication increasingly requires that learners are able to figure out differences in patterns of meaning from one context to another and communicate across these differences as their lives require. A doctor reads different things and speaks differently depending on whether they are with a patient or another doctor, yet doctor and patient need to relate. A salesperson is an expert about a product who can make sense of technical manuals, but also needs to be able to explain something to a customer who may find reading an instruction manual difficult. An interaction between two school friends on Facebook will be very different from the history essay they write for school. All the time, we move between different social spaces, with different social languages. Negotiating these language differences and their patterns or designs becomes a crucial aspect of literacy learning.

The second aspect of meaning-making highlighted by the idea of Multiliteracies is *multimodality*. This is a particularly significant issue today, in part as a result of the new information and communications media. Meaning is made in ways that are increasingly multimodal – in which written-linguistic modes of meaning interface with oral, visual, audio, gestural, tactile and spatial patterns of meaning. Writing was once the main way of making meanings across times and distances. Today, written modes of meaning can be complemented by, or replaced by, other ways of crossing time and distance, such as recordings and transmissions of oral, visual, audio, gestural and other patterns of meaning. This means that we need to extend the range of literacy pedagogy beyond alphabetical communication. It also means that, in today's learning environments, we need to supplement traditional reading and writing skills with multimodal communications, particularly those typical of the new, digital media. Our approach here is to expand traditional understandings of the function and form of the written word. We want to explore the broader range of ways in which literacy works in contemporary society.

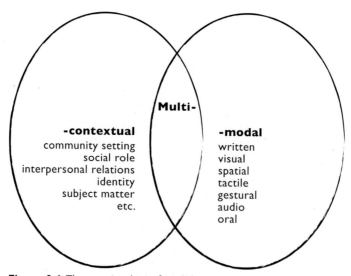

Figure 0.1 The two 'multis' of Multiliteracies

Agendas of literacies

Our key questions in this book are:

- How do we enable all learners to make and participate in meanings that will develop their capacities, as children and later as adults, to be effective and fulfilled members of society; to make a contribution to society according to their interests and abilities; and to receive in return the benefits society offers?
- How do we redress the ongoing and systemic inequalities in literacy learning and broader educational outcomes for learners from different backgrounds and with different dispositions?
- What and how do we teach in the context of enormous changes in the modes and media of communication?
- How do we promote understandings about literacy relevant to our contemporary times when our ways of making meanings are changing so radically?
- If literacy has traditionally been understood to be two of the three 'basics' (the proverbial three 'R's of reading, writing and arithmetic), what might be considered 'basic' today?
- What is the continuing role of the traditional basics, and how do these connect with 'new basics'?
- How might these new basics engage more effectively with a broader spectrum of learners?

The basics of old literacy learning involved elementary phonics to translate the sounds of speech into the symbolic images of writing, and reading as a process of decoding the meanings of written words. It focused on textual formalities, such as 'correct' spelling and grammar. It privileged a particular form of speech and writing in the national language that was held up as the unquestioned 'standard' or 'educated' form. It had students read to appreciate the style of 'good writing', first in school 'readers' and later in canonical texts considered to be of 'literary' value. Reading meant 'comprehension' of meanings that were thought, in a straightforward way, to be intrinsic to texts and as intended by their authors. 'Knowledge' and 'skills' were demonstrated in tests as the successful acquisition of these elements of literacy, by writing correctly or showing that one had read the 'correct' meanings written into texts by giving the right answers in multiple choice comprehension tests.

The old basics shaped the development of people who were literate in a certain sense and for a particular kind of society. However, from the perspective of today, this traditional or heritage conception of literacy is in many respects too narrowly focused. At worst, it seems decontextualised, abstract, rule-bound and fragmented into formal components, such as phonics, grammar and literature. In its most rigid forms, this kind of literacy learning produced (predictably for those times) compliant learners: people who would accept what was presented to them as correct, and who passively learned knowledge that could not easily be applied in different and new contexts.

If they did well at school, the students of this era became knowledgeable in the sense that they recognised received rules and conventions. They learned complicated spelling rules, or the grammar of adverbial clauses, or the lines of great poets. This was a kind of knowledge – a moral lesson about complying with the directives of received authority. It may well have worked for the social settings of the time in which unquestioning compliance was regarded as a good thing. A lot of students, however, didn't do so well at this kind of schooling, and when they found jobs that were unskilled or menial, they could have blamed themselves and their 'abilities' for not having done better at school.

These heritage literacy teaching practices are not adequate on their own to meet the needs of the today's society and economy. This is not to say that phonics, grammar and literary texts are unimportant – in fact, as we will make the case in this book, they are just as important as ever. However, what was taught was for some students sometimes not enough, and at other times not terribly relevant or the highest priority for learning given today's functional, communicative needs. Nor, as we will see later in this book, are some 20th-century attempts at reform, such as progressive education or 'authentic' literacy pedagogy. For all their optimistic idealism, many such pedagogical innovations have had a negligible impact on the systemic inequalities reinforced by education.

The more contemporary terms for the traditional three R's are 'literacy' and 'numeracy'. Certainly, traditional mathematics, reading and writing are today as important as ever – perhaps even more important. However, literacy and numeracy can either stand as substitute words for the old basics, or they can capture a broader understanding of communication and a more active approach to learning.

We use the term 'new basics' to catch the flavour of a more contemporary, relevant and inclusive approach to knowledge. Literacy is not simply a matter of correct usage. It also is a means of communication and representation of meanings in a broader, richer and all-encompassing sense. If this is the case, the new communications environment presents challenges to heritage literacy teaching practices, in which the old habits of literacy teaching and learning need to be reconsidered and supplemented. For example, we have to consider how we learn grammar and spelling in writing environments supported by checking routines in writing software. Also, contemporary sites of writing, such as email messages, text messages and social media posts, are more fluid and open, creating new literacy conventions.

In fact, the messages in these new writing spaces are often more like speaking than writing. Some have even developed new and quirky conventions that we learn as we go – abbreviations, friendly informalities, emoticons and cryptic 'in' expressions – all of which take their place in the new world of literacy. Increasingly, contemporary texts involve complex relationships between visuals, space and the written word: the tens of thousands of words in a supermarket; the written text around the screen on the news, sports or business program on the television; the text of an ATM interface; websites full of visual icons and active hypertext links; the subtle relationships of images and text in glossy print magazines; news and

Table 0.1: Old and new basics

Old basics	New basics
• Reading and writing are two of the three 'R's	• Literacy and numeracy as fundamental life skills
• Phonics rules	• Multiple 'literacies' for a world of multimodal communications
• Correct spelling and grammar	• Many social languages and variation in communication appropriate to settings
• Standard, educated English	• 'Kinds of people' who can innovate, take risks, negotiate diversity and navigate uncertainty
• Appreciating texts of prestige 'literary' value	• A wide and diverse range of texts valued, with growing access to different media and text types
• Well-disciplined 'kinds of people'	• People who can negotiate different human contexts and styles of communication

information delivered to e-book readers; and the hybrid oral-written-visual texts of instant messaging and social networking sites.

Written texts are now designed in a highly visual way, and meaning is carried as much multimodally as it is by the words and sentences of traditional literacy. This means that teaching the traditional forms of alphabetical literacy today needs to be skilfully supplemented by rigorous learning about the multimodal design of texts.

We now have to learn how to navigate the myriad different uses of language in different contexts: this particular email (personal, to a friend) in contrast to that (applying for a job); this particular kind of desktop publishing presentation (a newsletter for your sports group) in contrast to that (a page of advertising); different uses of English as a global language (in different English-speaking countries, by non-native speakers, by different subcultural groups) in contrast to formal settings where certain 'educated' forms of the language are still used (such as scientific reports); in indexes to reference books in contrast to web searches; or in writing a letter in contrast to sending an email. So the capabilities of literacy involve not only knowledge of formal conventions across a range of modes, but also effective communication in diverse settings and the use of tools of text design that are multimodal, rather than a reliance on the written mode alone.

These are the reasons why we have chosen to title this book 'Literacies' in the plural. In the past, 'literacy' seemed enough. Today we need to be able to navigate 'literacies'.

Communication and representation

So far, we have mainly been speaking about communication, or the passing of a message from person to person. However, literacies are more than that; they are also about thinking, or a phenomenon that we want to call 'representation'. We use literacies to make meanings for ourselves – silently, as we talk to ourselves using the concepts that language provides us, as we formulate arguments in our heads, as we write notes, as we create mental images, as we conceive things in diagrams, as we make models. Nobody need ever hear or see what our representations are. However, we are nevertheless using literacies to think and to make meanings for ourselves, to make sense of our worlds. Literacies in this sense come together as an extension of our minds.

More than simply being a business of communicating competently and appropriately in contemporary social settings, the new basics are also about what we have called a 'new learning' (Kalantzis & Cope 2012). Literacy, for instance, involves rules and their appropriate application. Literacies are additionally about the challenge of being faced with an unfamiliar kind of text and being able to search for clues about its meaning without the barrier of feeling alienated by it and excluded from it. They are also about

Figure 0.2 Representation and communication

understanding how a text works so you can participate in its meanings (engaging its own particular 'rules'). They are about working out the particular context and purposes of the text (and here you will find more clues about its meaning to the communicator and to you). They are about ways of seeing and thinking (representation) as much as they are about creating meaningful and effective messages (communication). Finally, literacies are about approaching communication in an unfamiliar context and learning from your successes and missteps as you navigate new social spaces and encounter new social languages. These are some of the more expansive and more flexible elements of the 'new basics'.

In the most general of senses, education is always about creating 'kinds of people'. The old basics were about people who learned rules and obeyed them; people who passively accepted the answers to the questions of the world that had been provided to them by 'authorities', rather than regarding the world as many problems to be solved; and people who carried supposed correct information and rules in their heads. The new basics enable new 'kinds of people': people better adapted to the kind of world we live in now and the world of the near future. These people will be flexible and collaborative learners. They will be problem-solvers, broadly knowledgeable and capable of applying divergent ways of thinking. They will be more discerning in the context of much more and ever-changing complexity. They will be innovative, creative risk-takers.

Forming people with these capacities requires not just new contents for literacy teaching but also new pedagogies, or ways of teaching. In fact, it is the contention of this book that literacy learning will increasingly need to focus on enabling these kinds of people – namely, people who are able to move comfortably between the many literacies of work, public and community life, and know how to communicate through multiple and changing media – and not just people who are in command of only their own specific dialect or social language, nor a rigid and culturally specific body of rules for 'proper' communication that in the past was called 'literacy' in the singular.

These kinds of people will be able to navigate change and diversity, learn as they go and communicate effectively in a wide range of settings. They will be flexible thinkers, capable of seeing things from multiple perspectives. They will have an expanded range of ways of making meaning – a broad communicative repertoire, so they can make and participate in meanings in a wide variety of social and cultural settings. They will be capable, in other words, of negotiating 'literacies' in the plural.

Literacies as tools for meaning

An ability to work across literacies in the plural opens paths to social participation, ideally enabling learners from different cultural, social, gender and socio-economic backgrounds to make meaning and succeed. Underlying this book are three key agendas for the individual and public good:

- *personal enablement*, or the ability to lead a life with full capacities for self-expression and access to available cultural resources
- *civic-economic participation*, including communicative capacities for work, informed engagement in political processes and community participation
- *social equity*, including capacities to access education, opening access to social and material resources.

What kinds of literacies learning will enable students to be effective, self-reliant and actively participating community members, citizens and workers? And how will literacies contribute to the project of equity, giving learners from historically marginalised groups opportunities that have not always been, or are not reliably, available to those groups? And how will we know when a learner's potential has been realised and that their learning has contributed to transforming them into creative and socially effective makers of meaning?

The story of social mobility in the modern world is not uncommon; it has been the goal of immigrants and less-educated people with aspirations for their children. For the world's billions, however, mobility is the exception rather than the rule. The social position of one generation by and large predestines the social position of the next. And when mobility opportunities do arise, the reason for the opening most often is education.

We live in a grossly unequal world, and even the most strident defenders of an unequal status quo argue that the system gives everyone at least one best chance. This chance is education. Doing well at school offers 'equality of opportunity'. The reality, of course, is that not all schools are as well resourced as others. And some students from some kinds of backgrounds find the culture of conventional schooling less congenial than others. As a general rule, students succeed who find schooling congenial and who go to schools well enough resourced and thought to be 'good'; those who are not provided such conditions, fail. This is how, despite its promise, education reproduces inequality.

We want to formulate a proposition about this situation, and a programmatic challenge, as follows:

> All schools can be congenial to learners. All schools, even less well-resourced schools, can provide powerfully engaging and effective learning experiences for all learners. And because they can, they must.

More boldly and more contentiously, we believe that, for the first time, the promise of education can be made real for all. Our reason for believing this is based on an optimistic view of the potentials offered by the conjunction of new technologies of meaning-making with an epochal shift in what we call the 'balance of agency'. The old cultures of command and compliance are being displaced by cultures of contribution and creative collaboration. We will elaborate on this argument in the chapters that follow. The raw material for our general argument is going to be literacy learning, one of the most significant things that schools provide. If we, as educators, allow learners more agency, and we use whatever technological resources are available to support new relationships between learners and their learning environments, we may be able to achieve something that has not so far been achieved in the modern history of mass-institutionalised education – greater equity of outcomes. In this book, we want to examine the ways in which such a utopian objective may be achieved through literacies pedagogy.

This book, then, is about realising one of the key promises of democracy. Despite changes in pedagogical fashion, content emphasis and classroom organisation, teacher preparation and professional learning, the inequalities of learner outcome between different social groups are at best staying the same or at worst widening. We need to change this situation and, where we are slipping back, turn things around. Literacies, understood broadly as tools for meaning, are a key to success for all curriculum domains in school and for self-realisation in life beyond school.

New literacies, new schools, new teachers

Today's learners

Schools everywhere in the world are today facing larger challenges than they ever did in the past, given the diversity of classrooms, the pace of technological and social change, and a crisis of public and private resourcing for education. The challenge to sustain and expand the historical practices of literacy pedagogy is but one piece in a larger context of educational change.

Let's start with our students. In our schools, we see a new generation of learners. We'll call them Generation 'P', for 'participatory'. These learners have different kinds of sensibilities from the students of our recent past. They have at hand ubiquitous smart devices, connected to the new social media and allowing them to communicate with people at a distance from them at any time of day and anywhere.

An earlier generation of learners may have been more used to being passive watchers of stories at the cinema or on television; this was intrinsic to the producer-to-consumer dynamic in the 'mass media'. Generation P, however, have become used to being characters in the stories of video games, where they play a part in how the story ends. An earlier generation used to listen to the 'top 40' songs from playlists selected by a radio station. Members of Generation P make their own playlists for their mobile music players, and if you ask the students in any class what is on their playlists, they are all going to tell you something different depending on their preferences.

An earlier generation expanded their habits of literacy by reading in their spare time, and more so than they did by writing. Generation P do as much by writing as reading in their spare time – and reading and writing are fused as integrated practices in social network sites and text messaging. An earlier generation passively watched TV programming that others considered good for them, tuning in to a handful of available channels. Generation P 'channel surf' hundreds of channels, or the millions of videos that are on the World Wide Web, or make their own videos – on their cameras or on their phones – and upload them to the Web.

An earlier generation received much of their learning within the formal context of schooling. Generation P learn more in semi-formal and informal settings and from a variety of sources – in the self-learning routines of electronic devices and software applications, for instance, and in social interactions in expert communities, such as networked gaming and interest communities on the Web.

The world of communication and meaning-making has changed. The members of this generation are showing signs of being frustrated by an old-fashioned literacy curriculum that expects them to be passive recipients of knowledge deemed by their elders to be good for them. The children of Generation P do not necessarily take well to being given rules that they have to apply. Nor do today's workplaces and other community settings necessarily require impassive, compliant dispositions. The most productive workers and most effective community members today are not those who just take orders from the boss or uncritically follow instructions issued by leaders. They are the ones who actively participate, who solve problems, who innovate, who take calculated risks and who are creative. In sum, they ideally give the best of their innovative and creative selves to the groups and organisations to which they belong.

New kinds of school environment and new kinds of literacy learning designs are already emerging that aspire to cater for the next generation of learner. The curricula of such new schools encourage learners to be actively and purposefully engaged in their learning by setting them real intellectual and practical challenges. Teachers and learners are required to make meaningful choices about what and how they learn in order to meet new, higher standards of performance and student wellbeing.

Here are just a few examples of the kinds of work students do in the new school contexts: researching information using multiple sources and reporting upon their findings in an extended web project report; tackling real-world problems, which they have to try to solve; documenting hypotheses; performing trial interventions; reporting on results; analysing issues from different perspectives; working in groups to create a collaborative knowledge output; and working in internet and other multimodal new media spaces that bring together writing, image, sound and video. These more engaging and more varied learning spaces are more relevant to the kind of world that Generation P already inhabits in their everyday lives. The new learners take greater responsibility for their learning, in part because they are given greater autonomy and scope for self-control. They are knowledge-producers, drawing together a range of available knowledge resources, instead of being knowledge-consumers fed from just one source – the reader or textbook – like students in the classrooms of the recent past. They work effectively in pairs or groups on collaborative knowledge projects, authoring knowledge to be jointly constructed or shared with peers. They continue to learn beyond the classroom, using social media to continue their reading, writing and learning anywhere and at any time. This phenomenon is called 'ubiquitous learning'. They critically self-assess and reflect upon their learning. They give feedback on their peers' writing in 'social networking' interactions. They are comfortable players in environments where intelligence is collective and writing is collaborative. They no longer draw on the sum of things that can be retained in just one individual's head; they have the capacity to source knowledge online or from other students or from experts, parents and community members.

Tomorrow's teachers

These are big changes, indeed. However, none of these can be achieved without a transformation of the teaching profession. If we are to have 'new learners' we need nothing less than 'new teachers'. The new teachers are designers of learning environments for engaged students, rather than people who regurgitate the content of the textbook. They are professionals who are able create the conditions in which learners take more responsibility for their own learning. They remain authoritative sources of knowledge without being authoritarian. They are comfortable with internet learning design and delivery platforms – learning spaces that are not just lesson plans, nor textbooks, nor student workbooks but are all these things, with a look and feel more like social networking or blogging sites. The Scholar digital literacies platform that we have created is one such example of this kind of workspace (https://cgscholar.com). We will speak more about Scholar at the end of this Introduction.

This evolution of teaching practices involves a big shift in professional identity, as teaching increasingly moves from being the talking and testing profession to becoming a hybrid documenting, data-driven profession. The online environment expands the reach of learning across time and space, beyond the walls that confine students to a classroom and a bell that constrains chunks of learning within the set number of minutes for a 'lesson'.

Table 0.2: New learning

New learners	New teachers
• Research information, using multiple sources and media	• Engage learners as active knowledge-makers
• Analyse ideas from multiple perspectives	• Design learning environments rather than just delivering content
• Work in groups as collaborative knowledge-makers	• Provide learners with opportunities to use the new media
• Tackle difficult questions and solve problems	• Use new media for learning design and to facilitate student access to learning at any time and from any place
• Take responsibility for their learning	• Are able to 'let go' as students take more responsibility for their learning
• Continue their learning independently beyond the lesson and the classroom	• Offer a variety of learning paths for different students
• Work closely with other learners in an environment that nurtures collective intelligence	• Collaborate with other teachers, sharing learning designs
• Critically self-assess their own thinking and learning	• Continuously assess student learning and progress, using that information to create the most appropriate learning experiences for different students

Instead of closing the door of the classroom and doing their own thing, new teachers are collaborative professionals, sharing their learning designs with other teachers online, reusing and adapting others' learning designs, jointly writing learning designs in teams, peer-reviewing others' learning designs, team teaching in classes that can sometimes be smaller than normal and at other times bigger than normal – in other words, immersed in a professional culture of mutual support and sharing.

The new teacher manages multifaceted learning environments in which not every student has to be on the same page at the same time. In fact, different students may be working on different things depending on their learning levels, needs and interests. And their work will be seamlessly integrated across time as well as space, as learning interactions continue out-of-hours and between home and school. Instead of waiting until the test at the end, the new teacher continuously assesses students, tracking progress and differentiating their instruction all the time in order to make sure their teaching is right for each learner's needs. The new teachers take a greater degree of control of their professional lives.

How can these enormous changes be negotiated, extended and supported? One answer is from the bottom up – the solid and sustainable difference that 'users', 'consumers' and 'producers' make when they are driving change rather than reacting to externally imposed change. With the expanding habits of collaboration and the increasing use of online tools, teachers grow accustomed to creating engaging learning tasks and learning environments, more suitable for what we have earlier in this Introduction called 'Generation P'. In turn, these organic practices create practical professional retraining opportunities for teachers, where they learn and deploy new learning design skills and ways of engaging learning and use evidence of observable learner performance to track and modify the impact of their choices on learner outcomes.

Another direction of reform comes from the top down, in the form of a reframing of learning objectives of the whole education system, subject by subject. This requires new educational standards and objectives for education. Our times are changing rapidly, and nothing less than a revolution is needed in educational objectives and systems. However, resource constraints and political ambiguity often make top-down change difficult to achieve.

government education policies
educational standards
whole school plans
curriculum designs
teacher professional stance
teacher-created learning designs
learner activities
learner interactions with each other

Bottom-up

Top-down

Figure 0.3 Sources of change in education

Meaningful and lasting change requires the support of all sectors of the community. Teachers need to become a new kind of professional, interacting with community stakeholders to explain the changes they are making to the design of learning environments and to engage others in producing outcomes. Students need to learn how to learn in new ways. Parents need to participate in and support new kinds of learning, media and learning environments; these will be very different from the schooling of their childhood memories.

The transition from learning 'literacy' in the traditional sense to learning 'literacies' is required by the communication demands of the 21st century. This is but one area of change in a larger frame of educational and social reference; just one aspect of the ongoing transformation of our learning processes and educational systems.

How this book is organised

This book is an introduction to literacy teaching and learning. It is a distillation of the main ideas at the core of a school subject area called 'literacy' in many parts of the world and 'language arts' in others. Sometimes the area is named after the national language – 'English', for instance. The body of knowledge in this subject area has historically concerned itself with learning to read and write. We will argue that the agenda of 'literacies' in the plural should still be reading and writing, but also more.

In this book, we attempt to give a comprehensive account of major approaches to literacy pedagogy. On our journey, we weave between a big-picture reconceptualisation of the field and grounded stories of the experiences of learners and teachers, in the past and recently. At the same time, taking a forward-looking perspective, the book attempts to present, in a concise way, the Multiliteracies theory of meaning. It also offers a pedagogical framework, mapping the range of moves that teachers can make as they work with learners to develop their capacities to mean and to communicate.

Guiding narrative

This book is an outline of the broad dimensions of an area of learning historically called 'literacy', but which we have chosen to call 'literacies' because we want to cover all that has normally been covered by 'literacy' and more.

Part A of the book consists of two chapters exploring the 'why' of literacy learning.

- *Chapter 1* discusses the arrival of literacy on the human scene some thousands of years ago, and its chequered consequences. It takes a quick tour of our meaning systems on a scale of reference as wide as our existence as a species: our human natures before the rise of writing, the impacts of writing and, most recently, human possibilities in the rise of the new media.
- *Chapter 2* looks at the purposes of literacy learning since the growth of mass, compulsory, institutionalised schooling. We examine the changing purposes of literacy learning – changes so significant, in fact, that they warrant a shift in focus from literacy in the singular to literacies in the plural. In this chapter we focus on the communicative purposes of literacies in the rapidly changing worlds of work, citizenship and public life. We then look at their changing ways of making meaning in the new, digital media.

Part B is a series of chapters that describe and analyse the approaches or reasoning that underlie the four major paradigms for literacy teaching and learning that have emerged since the beginning of modern schooling. All four pedagogical approaches remain alive and well today. In fact, we want to suggest ways in which we may continue strategically to deploy revised aspects of all of them.

- *Chapter 3* starts with some concrete examples of contemporary literacies pedagogy at work, then examines the four major activity types that are to be found in a well-rounded literacies pedagogy.
- *Chapter 4* explores the founding paradigm of literacy in the modern history of schooling, a 'didactic' approach in which students learn the formal rules of official or standard versions of the national language, read texts to 'comprehend' what the author (supposedly) 'really' says, and learn to appreciate a high-cultural literary canon.
- *Chapter 5* examines an 'authentic' approach to literacy that emerges as a serious alternative to didactic literacy in the 20th century. It focuses on the learners' own meanings, the texts that are relevant to them in their everyday lives, and supports a process of natural language growth that begins when a child learns to speak.

- *Chapter* 6 investigates a 'functional' approach to literacy, which has students deconstruct and reconstruct textual genres of educational success and social power.
- *Chapter* 7 discusses 'critical' literacy pedagogies that explore differences in language and social power, address real-world challenges, help students develop their voice for active citizenship and support them in taking control of their own lives.

Part C analyses the 'what' of literacies in the plural as a more expansive, multimodal version of something that, in an earlier era, was called 'grammar '.

- *Chapter* 8 introduces some key concepts that help us understand the basic features of meaning-making. Representation is meaning-making to ourselves, or sense-making. Communication is representation that has been communicated to another, a message that they have interpreted. Representation and communication are design processes in which we make choices among available resources for meaning, never simply to reproduce them but to make a new meaning. The chapter also explains multimodality, and the ways in which we can learn by switching from one mode to another.
- *Chapter* 9 begins a journey through the first of several modes of meaning explored in the remaining chapters of this section: the written mode. It examines the nature of reading and the relationships between the sounds of speech (phonemes) and the images of writing (graphemes). It also explores the processes and strategies of learning to read for meaning.
- *Chapter* 10 examines the dynamics of learning to write. It addresses the key question: how is learning to write different from learning to speak? It also outlines several major grammars of language – traditional grammar, transformational-generative grammar and systemic-functional grammar – as well as suggesting a Multiliteracies grammar of writing whose most basic questions can also be applied to other modes.
- *Chapter* 11 explores the ways in which meanings are represented in images, and the ways in which perception (seeing) is connected with visualisation (image-making) and imagination.
- *Chapter* 12 explores the dimensions of spatial, tactile and gestural meaning, from the sensuous materiality of meanings embedded in lived contexts to the potentials of the tactile mode to express the full symbolic range of language through Braille and the gestural mode through sign language.
- *Chapter* 13 explores audio and oral meanings, contrasting the important differences between speaking and writing that are often neglected by literacy pedagogy, compared to 'literacies' pedagogy in the plural.

Finally, Part D examines the 'how' of learning literacies, or pedagogy.

- *Chapter* 14 draws on the ideas introduced in Parts B and C to explore the role of literacies, not just as a defined subject area but as a basis for thinking and learning in all subject areas.

- *Chapter 15* speaks practically to the ways in which literacies pedagogies can address the varied learning needs of students in diverse school populations.
- *Chapter 16* explores the translation of literacies pedagogies into 'standards' mandated by systems, and assessments that record individual student progress and the progress of groups of students.

Supplementary web materials and the Scholar workspace

The guiding narrative in this book is supplemented by a website at literacies.com. Frequent links are made to this website in this book. This site includes videos, key texts by thinkers and researchers, a glossary of terms used in this book, lists of additional readings, and links to supplementary resources, including learning modules and literacies applications.

In this book, the link 'See literacies.com Learning Modules' takes the reader to sample resources created by teachers that illustrate literacies themes introduced in a particular chapter. The link '#edtech Literacies Applications' provides access to examples of literacies learning and teaching using educational technologies.

Figure 0.4 The literacies.com website

It is also possible to deliver the contents of the book as a course through the Scholar learning platform. Scholar supports classroom discussion in its Community space, multimodal writing and formative assessment in its Creator space, assessment data for learners and teachers in its Analytics space, and a wealth of curriculum resources in its Bookstore space. Lecturers and professors using this book in their literacies classes may choose to use Scholar as a delivery platform.

Figure 0.5 The Scholar online learning platform: cgscholar.com

The medium supports the message as course participants become involved in multimodal web writing, and a very social writing experience including peer review of works-in-progress and the kind of online discussions that are typical of social media.

To view the two Literacies Learning Modules that support this book, visit https://cgscholar.com > Bookstore > Higher Education Modules > Learning Design and Leadership. Chapters 1–7 of the book are covered in the Learning Module 'Literacy Teaching and Learning: Aims, Approaches and Pedagogies'. Chapters 8–16 can be found in the Learning Module 'Multimodal Literacies: Communication and Learning in the Era of Digital Media'. These Learning Modules include discussion starters, student surveys, and student projects with peer review rubrics. One of the projects is to design a literacies learning module! Also in the Bookstore are Literacies Learning Modules and Learning by Design Modules that we have designed for delivery in Year/Grades 4–12. To get started in Scholar, just visit https://cgscholar.com and set up an account.

PART A

The 'why' of literacies

CHAPTER 1

Literacies on a human scale

Overview

This chapter focuses on how we humans have made meaning in three historical moments. We will start with what we call 'first languages', the languages used before we had writing as we know it. We will then discuss some consequences of the development of writing, which began about five millennia ago, and how this culture of writing intensified with the mass application of printing after the 15th century and continues into modern times as more and more of the world's peoples learn to read and write. Finally, we will consider aspects of the new cultures of meaning-making that emerged during the late 20th and early 21st centuries, supported initially by photographic technologies and more recently by technologies for the electronic production and distribution of meaning.

It has been established by philosophers and scientists of language that writing is no mere transcription or writing down of thought. It is not even a direct record or copy of speech. It is a 'technology' or 'artefact' developed for a specific way of thinking and being. The ways of thinking and the everyday experiences of people who live in cultures where speaking is the main form of communication are very different from those whose cultures are dominated by writing. This has great relevance as we consider what is appropriate literacy teaching and learning in our contemporary times.

 See literacies.com Deutscher on The Unfolding of Language (Deutscher 2006).

Three globalisations

Our narrative in this chapter centres around a brief history of human systems of meaning. For this purpose we will measure historic time on a scale of 100 000 years, which is the approximate period that the human species has existed. We will look at the first 95 000 years, then at the 5000 years since the first appearance of writing, and finally the most recent half century, commencing in the third quarter of the 20th century, which has brought such radical changes in our human communications. Our three moments occur sporadically and involve long and short transitions: we want to call them 'the three globalisations' (Kalantzis & Cope 2006). In this chapter we only have space to picture these schematics in the broadest of brushstrokes.

First languages

Human beings are global creatures. From the moment we emerged as a species, we became the first sentient beings to fill virtually every habitat. This happened during the first globalisation, a process led by the speakers of what we want to call 'first languages'.

Starting out from sub-Saharan Africa, an initially small population filled the earth. We became different peoples speaking different languages because, in the relative isolation of one tribe from another, our ways of speaking drifted in varied directions.

 See literacies.com Edward Sapir on Differences in Language and Culture (Sapir 1921).

This is one part of the story. We want to suggest, however, that the differentiation of languages in the first globalisation was a more integral and systematic process than if it were simply caused by accidental drift and isolation.

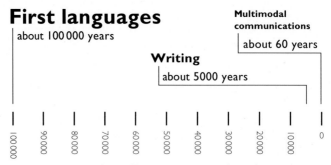

Figure 1.1 A timeline of human systems of meaning

The languages of the first globalisation – how and why they are so different

We can get a glimpse of the character of first languages because they are still spoken by indigenous peoples around the world. Among the thousand or so speakers of Yolŋu Matha, a first language of North Eastern Australia, people speak a whole range of very different language forms – baby language, adult language, women's language, old men's sacred language, and the dialects of different clan or family groups. They are all intentionally different, because the differences say something about each individual and their world. What you call a place or a person tells you who and what you are in relation to that place or person. Add to this complexity the fact that the same word may be used to signify a totem (a sacred animal), a place and a living person, because these are so closely connected in the cosmology and **epistemology** of the people. You might name a place differently from the way someone else would name it because your ownership relationship to it is different from theirs. When a person dies, their name cannot be spoken again and so the whole world, with its places and totems, has to be renamed as a mark of respect.

Epistemology: A way of knowing, or a philosophy or theory of how you come to know

Our peculiarly symbol-making human species ended up covering the globe with perhaps 10000 symbol systems, if one takes language as the measure. In fact, language diversity is far wider and deeper than that, taking into account – as one must – the seemingly wanton peculiarities of dialect and social language.

However, it was not just cultural practices like these and the natural drift of language that made languages different. **First languages** were specially designed to differ, often in ways that we find hard to comprehend today. The result was an extraordinary number of languages for what was, until the last few millennia at least, a species with a relatively small total population.

First language: An indigenous language and a culture that originally represented and communicated meanings in ways that did not need or use an alphabetical or character-based writing system

The decline and death of first languages

There are about 7000 languages in the world today. This number is rapidly diminishing. Of the 1000 languages in Brazil a century ago, only 200 are left today. Of the 500 Australian languages at the moment of British colonisation at the end of the 18th century, probably only a dozen will survive into the middle decades of the 21st century. Of what were probably myriad languages in Europe, only 60 remain today after four millennia of literate civilisation, and many of these are relatively modern derivatives of Latin, Germanic or Celtic languages (Crystal 1997: 286). This fact is one of the main things we want to examine in this chapter: our population as a species has grown hugely over the past centuries, but the number of languages we speak has gone into rapid decline.

See literacies.com Abley on Threatened Languages (Abley 2003).

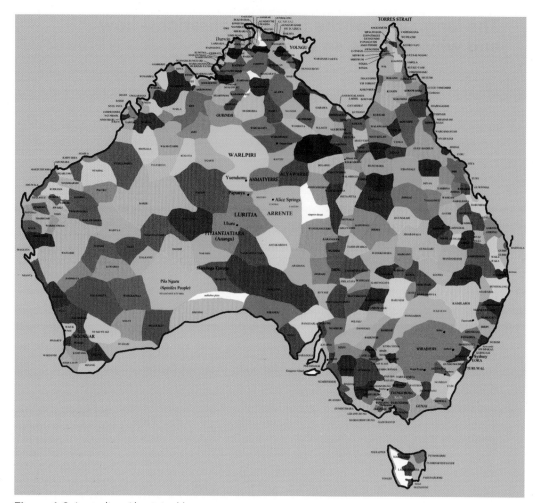

Figure 1.2 Australian Aboriginal language map

The emergence of the culture of writing is one of the main reasons for this decline. Ninety-six per cent of the world's population now speak one of the top 20 languages, and these are all languages of writing (McWhorter 2001). Only 283 of today's languages have more than one million speakers and only 899 have more than 100 000 speakers (Crystal 1997).

The ancestral homes of the speakers of small and rapidly disappearing languages are Australia, Melanesia, the Americas, Siberia and Arctic Europe. The languages that displaced them were first brought by farming societies that used writing as an instrument of elite control. This control took the form of religious hierarchy, bureaucratic regulation and privileged knowledge. The displacement of what we call 'first languages' began with the Indo-European and Celtic languages brought into Europe by invading farmers from the East; Greek and Latin and their derivatives in Europe; the languages of the African kingdoms, as was the case with

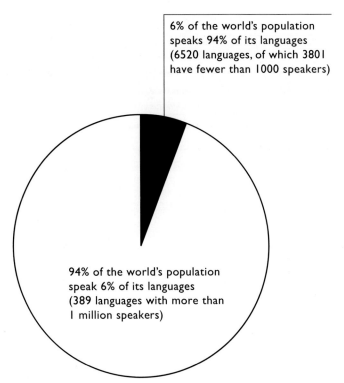

6% of the world's population
speaks 94% of its languages
(6520 languages, of which 3801
have fewer than 1000 speakers)

94% of the world's population
speak 6% of its languages
(389 languages with more than
1 million speakers)

Figure 1.3 Large and small languages

the Bantu languages; the languages of the Maya, the Aztecs, the Olmecs and the Incas in Mesoamerica; and the Chinese languages and their derivatives in East Asia. More recently, industrial societies have used literacy in 'standard' or national forms of their languages as an instrument of mass citizenship.

We know that the populations speaking first languages were, by subsequent standards, small. A rough estimate of their average size might be 1000 speakers per language. So, if the world's population was 10 million by the time the habitable world was populated at about 10 000 BCE (excluding New Zealand and the Pacific), there may have been 10 000 spoken by perhaps 10 million people. If these estimates bear scrutiny, then perhaps half of the world's first languages still exist.

What is it about first languages that makes them so different from those of literate humanity?

 See literacies.com Everett on the Pirahã Language of Brazil (Everett 2005).

Exploring the differences between first languages

We want to mention several features of first languages: their diversity, their tendency to diverge or to maintain and develop their differences, their dynamism and their inherent **synaesthesia**.

Synaesthesia: Switching between modes to express meaning

The range of language forms among first languages is nothing less than staggering, reflecting the enormous capacity of human beings to invent meanings. To take something as fundamental as the nature of human agency, the relationship of subject, verb and object varies dramatically. For example, the Northern Australian languages Warrgamany and Dyirbal use a case system – called 'ergative-absolutive' by linguists – which is used by its speakers to intertwine subject and object in a common structure of action (Dixon 1972; Dixon 1980).

 See literacies.com Whorf on the Hopi Language (Whorf 1956).

First languages differed in another remarkable way, not just in the existence of differences but also in their continuous and active process of making new differences. From a contemporary point of view, the rate and frequency of divergence between and within first languages makes little sense. Why would small, neighbouring groups speak different languages at all, let alone languages that were often so vastly different from each other? One answer is that these groups grew progressively more different from each other because they were isolated, and because there was not much need to communicate with neighbours.

All the evidence, however, points the other way. Speakers of different first languages communicated with each other regularly and frequently, and certainly to a greater degree than the neighbours in a modern city apartment block. In fact, the speakers of first languages managed language diversity with a degree of sophistication rarely found today. Individuals were almost invariably **multilingual**, speaking up to perhaps five or more languages. Also, they had developed shared forms of communication, such as gesture language.

Multilingualism: People in a society speaking many languages

So why go to all this seemingly needless trouble? The answer, it seems, is in an inherent logic of divergence. In first-language societies, a word may refer to a bird, a place, a religious totem and a person's name. In the next language group, the same bird/place/totem/person is named differently, and that is essential, because it defines the precise relation of a particular person to a particular place. Meaning occurs in complex overlapping ways that connect closely to shared understandings of place and people's relations to place and to each other.

 See literacies.com Levi-Strauss on the 'Savage Mind' (Levi-Strauss 1966).

There is a tendency within first languages to add more complexity because of 'internal divergence': clan or family groups speak different dialects; women develop their own languages; and adults learn ever more arcane secret and sacred languages as they get older and progress towards becoming elders. Differences in language use are ongoing, evolving and difficult to pin down in any time or place.

This world of different languages and dialects had little to do with 'evolutionary drift' or with isolation. People did not live in completely isolated groups. Meanings were transmitted over long distances and quite rapidly, despite the differences between symbol systems. The peoples of the Australian desert knew about whales seen from the shore, thousands of kilometres away. The peoples of the first **globalisation** dealt with difference by being hugely multilingual and developing special ways of communicating across language gaps.

Globalisation: Social and historical processes in which the whole world becomes a frame for human action

We also want to note the dynamism of first languages. The languages of the first human communities are characteristically flexible and changing. It may be that, on a person's death, their name cannot be spoken, in which case the whole metaphorically layered world to which their name refers has to be renamed. Or meanings are renegotiated in ceremonial moments when different groups tell their histories, religion and law to each other. What is distinctively 'first' is not the language one happens to encounter today, but a peculiarly dynamic and always rapidly changing meaning system (Christie 1992).

First languages and multimodal communications

First languages had many sophisticated, graphical and multimodal ways of representing meaning. Over the course of the 20th century, linguists and historians

Figure 1.4 Multimodal communication: Yolŋu Garma Festival, Yirrkala, Northern Australia

Table 1.1: From first languages to writing

First languages	Written languages
• Small populations	• Much larger populations speaking the one language, displacing small languages
• Large differences, even between languages that are close together	• Strong family relations between languages, such as Indo-European and Chinese language groups
• Important internal differences: by age, gender, clan	• Pressures towards monolingualism, learning large and powerful languages
• A great deal of multilingualism and special lingua francas or special languages of shared communication	• A dependence on consistent and stable meanings so strangers – even distant strangers – can understand what we mean
• Meanings that are changing all the time; language that is dynamic	• Written meanings given higher prestige than other modes of meaning
• Multimodal meanings using language, image, gesture and spatial and tactile understandings	

attempted to describe the features of human communication before **writing**, but did so in terms of the absence of writing in its modern forms. They graduated from using terms of negative comparison, such as 'illiterate' or 'preliterate', and began instead to use more positive terms, such as 'orality' (Ong 1982). For all their attempts to avoid negativity, however, orality is still assumed to be 'lesser' than the orality-plus-literacy of modern existence.

Writing: The use of alphabetical symbols (representing sounds, such as English) and characters (representing concepts, such as Chinese) to record language

We want to use the term 'synaesthetic civilisation' in an attempt to account more accurately for the fullness and complexity of first languages, involving a multimodal overlay of word, image, gesture, sound and space. By 'synaesthesia', an idea we explore in detail in Chapter 8 of this book, we mean a capacity to make meanings in more than one mode – language, image, gesture, and spatial and tactile understandings – and to switch backwards and forwards between these modes.

 See literacies.com Cope on Indigenous Australian Language Change (Cope 1998).

Starting to write

A second globalisation

During the second globalisation, people started to write. Some languages were written with alphabetical symbols (such as English) and others were written with character-based language symbols (such as Chinese). Writing emerged in four different places – in Mesopotamia about 5000 years ago, and later in India, China and Central America. There may have been no direct connection between these four events, although each happens in the moment of urban settlement supported by farming.

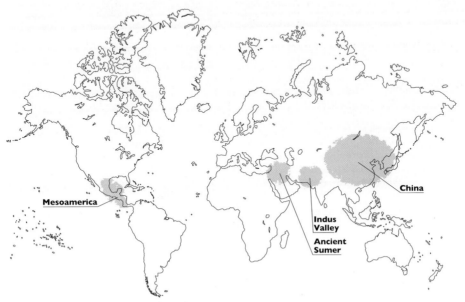

Figure 1.5 The birthplaces of the first writing

See literacies.com Diamond on the Origins of Writing (Diamond 1999).

We of modern societies have developed the habit of calling this moment 'the beginning of history' or 'the dawn of civilisation'. The long period before that was 'prehistory', inhabited by 'uncivilised' peoples. In taking such a view, we forget that this moment was also the beginning of the end of another kind of history.

With these new societies came inequalities of a kind never experienced in the first globalisation. Farming brings the possibility of accumulating wealth and using surpluses for projects that are no longer linked just to the basic needs of everyday life. The monumental ruins of older civilisations stand as a testament to, and over-whelming reminder of, the scale of that inequality. To take one of the touchstones of this transition: writing was used from the start as an instrument of elite control; as a medium for maintaining inventories of ownership; for keeping records so that surpluses could be taxed or taken as rent; as an instrument of bureaucratic gov-ernment; and in sacred religious texts that helped reconcile slaves to their fate in an unequal social order.

See literacies.com Childe on Writing in Ancient Sumeria and Egypt (Childe 1936).

Figure 1.6 Cuneiform script, Pergamon Museum, Berlin

A measure of the spread of the second globalisation is the mass displacement of the languages of the first globalisation. This was achieved by Indo-European languages across a span from Europe to central India and by the Chinese languages and their derivatives in East Asia. The languages of the invading farmers displaced the many spoken languages of the first globalisation. Writing cemented their supremacy. Modern imperialism only accelerated this process, by which powerful countries conquered large parts of the world and spread their languages as they did so, including the Chinese, Arabic, Spanish and, most recently, English empires.

 See literacies.com Crystal on Language Death (Crystal 2000).

The coming of writing

In the societies of the second globalisation, systems of meaning were stabilised, standardised, homogenised and generalised.

This second globalisation came to span the whole earth, and remarkably quickly. It brought not just the sameness that is to be found within large language groups, 'world religions' and 'civilisations'; there was also a sameness across and between these groups: the handful of domesticable plants and animals that spread like wildfire right across the globe; the religions that even shared common ancestral figures, like the Abraham of the Jews, the Christians and the Muslims; and

Figure 1.7 Early Chinese writing

the inventions that were so quickly swapped and copied, such as the plough, the wheel, monumental architecture and writing. There were subtle differences, to be sure, and as tourists wandering today through the ruins we pay our respects to these. In the larger scale of things, however, the differences between the languages of the peoples of the second globalisation were small compared to the differences between the world of meaning of the first globalisation and the world of meaning influenced by writing of the second.

See literacies.com Ong on the Differences between Orality and Literacy (Ong 1982).

Modernity arrived near the end of this second globalisation. Its key features were European colonisation or conquest of large parts of the world; industrialisation or the establishment of the modern factory system; and commodity production and global economic integration through which goods were traded around the world. On four continents – the two Americas, Australia and Africa – most people became speakers of a European language as a common language or lingua franca, if not as a first language.

Modernity: A time, beginning at about 1500, when there emerged new manufacturing technologies (such as printing), new ways of thinking (such as science and secular reasoning) and new social relationships (such as urban and industrial work)

How writing affects human life

The emergence of writing within this historical mix had a huge impact on the ways in which humans lived and thought. In its founding moments, Socrates lamented what he considered to be the negative effects of writing on human thinking capacities.

 See literacies.com Socrates on the Forgetfulness that Comes with Writing (Plato c. 399–347 BCE).

For most of its millennia, writing has been a way of maintaining ownership and wealth; a tool of state bureaucracy to communicate rules; and a medium of religious power. In this functional sense, the 'quipu' or knotted strings used by Inca rulers to store information were a form of writing, telling of authoritarian power, redistribution of wealth and religious conformism. So writing became a means, not only for increased 'collective learning', but also for the institutionalisation and maintenance of inequality. Its emergence was one sign of the end of the relatively egalitarian ways of life of first peoples.

 See literacies.com Levi-Strauss on the Functions of Writing (Levi-Strauss 1955 (1976)).

Then a new phase began in the history of writing, beginning with Gutenberg's invention of printing in 1450 and extending to about 1900. Literacy became a way of recording and ordering the world. It underpinned a fundamental social logic in industrialised societies, propagated by mass-institutionalised education. So what was this way of thinking, this sensibility of the literate cultures of the second globalisation?

 See literacies.com Goody on the Differences between Orality and Literacy.

Literate cultures create languages that both expand our collective knowledge and hugely simplify the many things that are subtle and complex in first languages. For example, hundreds of pronouns in some indigenous languages can be contrasted with the handful in modern English. Literate languages emphasise other things, such as vocabulary. The number of words in English has become so large that literate users of the language have to rely on a dictionary.

Literacy and social pressures to uniformity

Literate languages also tend to standardise and homogenise meanings. People are expected or required to use written text in the same way; hence the spelling or pronunciation rules, the definitions of vocabulary words and the grammatical conventions that come to be taught in school.

One of the main purposes of schooling is to have all citizens speaking, reading and writing a common language. Achieving the homogeneous nation-state in which everyone speaks, reads and writes the same language becomes an ideological and practical project of modern **nationalism**. The modern state assimilates outsiders – the indigenous peoples or migrants who need to be able to speak a common language to assume roles in the larger social machine. In response to their needs, the state provides education and other services, all in the one language.

 See literacies.com Gellner on the Logic of Nationalism (Gellner 1983).

Nationalism: A period in which the power of nation-states grows and strong governments take control of geographic areas with clearly defined borders. Nationalism is the ideology that supports this process, often insisting on standardisation (such as every student being taught the one, national language) and the related phenomena of assimilation (people who are different changing their language and culture to fit in) and homogenisation (making all citizens more or less the same).

In less benign moments, fascist or communist leaders take it upon themselves to force their visions of the universal, homogeneous citizen on their populations. In these modern lifeworlds, people learn to take on board received truths. The ideal learner in the classroom of modern, mass-institutional education quietly absorbed received facts and disciplinary knowledge. The ideal wife and the ideal child subjected themselves to the discipline of the head of the household. Such was the predisposition towards sameness of the command society, with its work by command, politics by command and culture by command. We discuss the pressure for homogeneity in greater detail in Chapter 2.

Literate languages tend to fix words to written symbols in such a way that language drift comes as a surprise, serving only to confound the best-laid plans of dictionaries and grammar textbooks, and of curricula delivering learning in the one, official language. 'Get rid of that terrible new colloquialism!' a stern teacher may say, when a student writes a 'hip' or 'geeky' word in their essay. 'Don't speak that language in the classroom,' they may say to a student talking to another student in their shared home language. 'Speak properly,' they may say to a child speaking in dialect or informal community vernacular.

Writing becomes a privileged mode of meaning

Literate cultures also tend to separate the modes of meaning. Modern literacy separates written word from image, gesture and sound. This results in part from the very way in which we manufacture each mode of communication: the separation of image and font in typesetting and letterpress printing, and the separation of the oral from other modes in later technologies, such as telephone and radio.

The cultural effects of writing

The mastery of reading and writing becomes a key to entering the new worlds that have been created in recent centuries, worlds of great material progress and cultural richness. The more capable you are in reading and writing, the greater the possibility that you can negotiate a better life for yourself.

 See literacies.com Febvre and Martin on the Coming of the Book (Febvre & Martin 1976).

However, reading and writing have also produced new constraints. By fixing meanings in these rigid forms of writing, literate cultures become less capable of dealing with change than the peoples who spoke first languages. We have to obey the rules of language and life. We have to say things in standardised ways so strangers will understand what we mean. We use reading and writing to maintain fixed power hierarchies. Our anxieties about change are more notable than our capacities to deal with change in our lived realities.

 See literacies.com Rose on the Idea of the Author (Rose 1993)

So here we have the ways of being and thinking that began with scribal (hand-written) culture and then, later, became part of print cultures. Writing tends to standardise and homogenise forms of meaning. It tends to abstract or separate modes of meaning from each other. It comes in a social and cultural context that affords less scope for the negotiation of meanings, so diminishing our capacity for human agency and our ability to deal with change.

 See literacies.com The Origins of Modern Textual Architectures

New media, new literacies

The third globalisation

In the last part of the 20th century and the first part of the 21st, changes occurred in the way we humans communicate – changes in the technologies of communication, the balance of written and other modes, the ways in which language differences are negotiated and the broad accessibility of new communications media. These changes have been so sweeping that they perhaps deserve to be labelled a 'third globalisation'.

The rise of new communications technologies

In the 20th century, there was a series of transformations in the ways meanings were produced and reproduced. Initially these were connected with photography. Lithographic printing, film and analogue television brought image and text closer together. Then the pace of change was quickened with the widespread application of digital technologies to the communication of meanings in the last quarter of the 20th century and the opening decades of the 21st.

 See literacies.com Kress on Writing and Image Culture (Kress 2003).

After five millennia when the written word was a source of power in many so-cieties, then half a millennium in which this power was multiplied by the printing

Table 1.2: The three globalisations

First globalisation	Second globalisation	Third globalisation
Earlier phases:		
• The spread of human settlements over almost the whole habitable earth	• The first farming	• Written, visual and oral meanings beginning to come together with lithographic printing technologies, analogue television etc.
• The harvesting of wild foods	• Monument building	• Digital communications and internet technologies that speed the process of easily accessible and affordable multimodal communications for all
• Societies in which people have relatively equal access to material and cultural resources	• Surpluses and inequality	• Multilingualism, supported by new technologies
• Multimodal and synaesthetic civilisations	• The invention of writing, used only by elites in a scribal (handwritten) culture	
Later phases:		
	• Colonisation or conquest of much of the world by imperial powers	
	• Rapid spread of major world languages and decline in small and indigenous languages	
	• Industrialisation; many people moving from farming life into cities	
	• Invention of the printing press and then modern schooling, which brings reading and writing to a growing percentage of the population	

press, photographic means of representation began to restore power to image. Then, from the third quarter of the 20th century, digital technology accelerated this process as the elementary modular unit of manufacture of textual meaning was reduced from the character to the pixel.

Letterpress printing technology, invented in the mid-15th century, used letters as its smallest units of manufacture, laying them out one by one on the printer's forme. Digital letters are made of lots of little dots, which are now the smallest units in the manufacture of writing. Digital pictures are made of the same thing – pixels or picture elements. As images and fonts are now made of the same raw materials, they are more easily combined. By the turn of the 21st century, we had television screens that streamed more and more writing over image. We had magazines and newspapers in print or e-book formats, which with great ease layered image and text in a way that was never easily achievable in the era of letterpress printing. Back then, the pages of alphabetical type had been separated from the pages of 'plates' or images.

 See literacies.com Jenkins on Collective Intelligence and Convergence Culture (Jenkins 2006b).

Writing loses its privileged place

We also have a return to the aural and the oral. New overlays of oral and written modes emerge as email and text messaging more closely resemble the fluidity of speaking than the earlier literate forms of letters and memoranda. This represents a return to **multimodality**. Writing has lost its special place as the most effective way to convey meanings across time and space, now that we have these other technologies to record and transmit oral, audio, visual and gestural meanings. As a consequence, we find ourselves constantly engaged in mode-switching.

Multimodality: The use of different and combined modes of meaning: written, visual, spatial, tactile, audio and oral

Language differences become important again

After an era of standardisation, homogenisation and assimilation, even the global-imperial language of the modern world, English, is diverging internally. The social languages of subcultures, peer cultures, communities of fashion, fad and fetish, diasporic communities of second-language speakers and communities speaking local and regional dialects – each of these forms of English is becoming more different from the other. They are spoken through the seemingly endless number of television channels, streamed radio, Web communities and person-to-person. Underneath this are new logics of identity and senses of belonging. Today's communities increasingly defy the neatly homogenising efforts of the nation-state. We are returning to a deep logic of divergence and diversity.

These ways of meaning also paradoxically create the conditions for a return to radical multilingualism. For example, we have call centres that run in tens – and why not hundreds or thousands? – of languages. As machine translation gets better, it reduces the language-boundedness of a particular meaning. When it comes to writing, the universal scripting system Unicode is entirely agnostic about alphabetical and ideographic meanings because all are manufactured of the same stuff and rendered to the same media. Ironically, these modern textual techniques make the maintenance and revival of peripheral first languages an easier and more achievable task.

See literacies.com Crystal on the Multiplicity of the English Language (Crystal 2005).

Linear B		Cypriot	
da	𐀅	*ta*	𐠭
na	𐀙	*na*	𐠙
pa	𐀞	*pa*	𐠞
ro	𐀫	*lo*	𐠒
se	𐀮	*se*	𐠩
ti	𐀴	*ti*	𐠯
to	𐀵	*to*	𐠰

Figure 1.8 Linear B and ancient Cypriot scripts, as represented in Unicode

New media accessibility

The new media are also more accessible than the printing presses of the era of print literacy – cheaper to access and more manipulable by amateurs. As long as you can get access to a computer or a mobile recording device like a phone with a camera, you can create a video and publish it to a blog or a social media feed. Digital media also are becoming less expensive to access. People can create and distribute content in the 'creative commons' of 'social production' without having to have the weighty capital of publishers or media corporations behind them. They can even build their own content manipulation and delivery platforms using freely available open source software code.

See literacies.com Lankshear and Knobel Remix Lessig (Lankshear & Knobel 2008).
Benkler on Social Production (Benkler 2006).
Raymond on Open Source (Raymond 2001).

So here we are, 5000 years after the invention of writing. The historical narrative we have told is a story of partial return to synaesthesia, divergence, multilingualism and deep diversity. But in important ways, it's not really a return at all. It's something that is, once more in human history, very new and its consequences are hard at first to predict. We can be sure of one thing only: that the future will be like none of our pasts. We want to suggest, however, that as we imagine our human futures we may at times have much to learn from the ways of meaning embodied in first languages and their cultures of representation and communication.

See literacies.com Eight Aboriginal Ways of Learning.

Summary

First languages: the first globalisation	Starting to write: the second globalisation	New media, new literacies: the third globalisation
• Extraordinary language differences; a range of ways of making meaning	• Language simplified in many respects; narrow social functions of writing to serve elites	• Meanings differing increasingly with the rise of 'diversity' in the new, global cosmopolis
• Divergence: language differences by design	• Meanings standardised and homogenised	• Divergences between social languages; globalised multilingualism
• Dynamism, or constant language change	• Conformity required to generate stabilised, official versions of standard languages	• More accessible media, supporting divergence in cultures and social languages
• Synaesthetic civilisation, using multiple modes of meaning	• Separation of modalities of meaning and privileging of the written word	• A return to multimodality with photographic, then digital technologies

Knowledge processes

For an introduction to, and overview of, the knowledge processes, visit Chapter 3. For additional learning and discussion activities, access the Literacies Learning Module in the bookstore at https://cgscholar.com

experiencing the new

1. Research a threatened 'first language' or indigenous language. What are the sources of the threat to this language? What might be lost if the language were to fall into disuse?

conceptualising by naming

2. Look at a linguist's account of a first language in an article or a book. How do linguists describe languages? What concepts do they use to highlight the distinguishing features of a language? Make a list of the main concepts and define them.

experiencing the new

3. Choose one ancient writing system and describe the early stages of its early evolution. What were the initial uses of writing?

analysing critically

4. Debate Socrates' proposition about the forgetfulness that comes with writing.

conceptualising with theory

5. Define 'standardisation', 'homogenisation', 'nationalism' and 'assimilation'. Combine these words into a theory of how earlier modern societies exerted pressures to conform. Mention language and schooling in your theory.

experiencing the known

6. Create a timeline of the changes that have occurred in the communications environment during your lifetime. Or interview your parents and grandparents to create such a timeline. What are the consequences of these changes?

CHAPTER 2

The purposes of literacies

Overview

In this chapter, we take a look at contemporary social changes, including the changing purposes of literacies in everyday life. One of the primary functions of schools is to prepare learners for this 'real world' of communication – for work, citizenship and contemporary community life. In the world of work, the emergence of a 'knowledge economy' dramatically changes the objectives of school, away from a very basic notion of literacy as a set of rules and mechanical procedures for reading and writing the right way, to literacies in the plural where workers can navigate a variety of modes of workplace communication and customer interactions, and using a multimodal range of means of communication. In the world of citizenship, the purpose of the old literacy in the singular was that everyone learned the one, standard form of the national language. Today, the forces of globalisation and cultural and social diversity mean that we don't just belong to a nation-state, but many overlapping civic spaces, reflecting levels of participation and civic responsibility, from the very local to the global. Each one of these spaces has its own, peculiar way of communication and modes of interaction. Then, in the third area that we investigate in this chapter, community life, digital and online media position users in a more participatory role than the old mass media of television, radio or magazine. In this chapter, we examine the response of the Australian Curriculum and invite readers in other countries to explore their curriculum frameworks for evidence of changing educational objectives.

Why literacies?

Literacies and opportunity

Why 'literacies'? Or even more fundamentally, why education – in which literacy is considered to be one of the 'basics'?

Education provides access to opportunities in the form of better-paid employment, an improved chance to participate in civic life, and personal growth. It also promises deeper understandings of the world and ways of being in the world, enabling people to do more for themselves and make a contribution to the lives of others. Literacies are central to these fundamental educational objectives.

Education is a key site of social opportunity, even if the scales of opportunity are often unevenly balanced. Equity is a value that matters in a fair society, a principle that requires equivalent opportunities to be available to all, irrespective of their social origins or cultural background. A more ambitious goal of education may be for it to contribute to greater equality. Sometimes, all that it seems to achieve is an ongoing struggle to reduce the gap between the haves and the have-nots – hence, for example, the compensatory literacy programs, the remedial reading programs for children who have been 'left behind', and the special efforts made in schools in poor neighbourhoods and in schools with sizable indigenous and immigrant student populations.

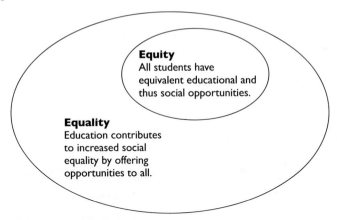

Figure 2.1 Educational objectives

What is the role of literacies learning in the knowledge society? How is that tug-of-war playing out in reality as well as in teaching and learning practices? To answer these questions, we will look at what is happening in the public lives of citizens and in people's everyday lives.

Changing literacies for changing times

The changes that are occurring – and rapidly – in our communication environment prompt a reconsideration of our approaches to literacy teaching and learning. In our analysis, we want to focus on the growing significance of two dimensions of 'literacies': the multilingual and the multimodal. Multilingualism is an increasingly significant phenomenon, which requires a more adequate educational response in the case of minority languages and world languages in the context of globalisation. However, in a broadened interpretation of multilingualism, language takes many different forms in the burgeoning variety of what Gee (2000) terms 'social languages'. These language differences are visible in professional, national, ethnic, subcultural, interest or affinity group contexts, many of which are hard for outsiders to each particular social or cultural context to understand. The everyday experience of communication increasingly requires that people negotiate the different ways in which they use language at home, at work and in their community lives. There is not just one set of rules about how to use language (the older idea of 'literacy' in the singular), but many different kinds of language use in many different contexts (the newer idea of 'literacies' in the plural that we explore in this book).

There is also a question of what Gee (2000) calls the 'kinds of people' who find themselves comfortably at home in this new environment. These people can move in and out of, navigating within and across, different social contexts and communicate equally well in all of them. How does education shape, or fail to make a contribution to, the development of these 'kinds of people'? This is not just a question of developing new social practices of communication through literacies; these literacies will be essential in creating new or transformed forms of employment, new ways of participating as a citizen in public spaces, and new forms of community engagement. If our learners become good at navigating across different contexts of language use, they will be good at living in a highly interconnected, globalised, multicultural world.

See literacies.com Gee on Social Languages (in Chapter 15).

Table 2.1: The purposes of literacies

Communications	Representations
• Literacies for the new workplace	• Literacies to make sense of the world
• Literacies for public participation	• Literacies for thinking and learning
• Literacies for personal and community life	• Literacies for identity

Literacies for work

It is frequently argued nowadays that our education systems are not geared to the needs of a rapidly changing economy and society. There is concern that young people entering today's workforce are not equipped with the skills deemed necessary for the global, competitive society in which we now live. Tony Wagner interviewed employers whose enterprises typify the modern economy. He did not find people asking for workers who had learned basic literacy skills or who knew the right answers to things as measured by standardised tests. Instead, they wanted people for their workforces who were good at critical thinking, problem-solving, and collaborating with and influencing others. Such people would be agile and adaptable, take initiative, be entrepreneurial, know how to access and analyse information, be curious and imaginative, and have effective oral and written communication skills (see Table 2.2).

Table 2.2: Workers of the past and today

Industrial-era employees	Knowledge-era employees
• Well-disciplined and reliable	• Able to take responsibility
• Able to understand and take orders	• Able to solve problems and innovate
• Basically literate and numerate	• Able to collaborate with and influence others
	• Able to access information as needed and to communicate effectively in a variety of settings – professional, technical, cultural, social

See literacies.com Wagner on New Workplace Capacities.

Literacies for the 'knowledge society'

Trends over recent decades point to the emergence of what has been called a 'knowledge society': a society that values the dispositions and capacities that Wagner identifies.

One key aspect of these socio-economic transitions is the increasing economic significance of knowledge systems. These are now accessed through the reading and writing spaces of computing devices. The interfaces of these devices require multimodal literacies and shape almost every aspect of the production of goods and services today. This in turn affects product design, service quality, reputation, brand, customer loyalty, business systems, intellectual property creation, technology use and human resource management. The overall result of these changes is variously called the 'information society' or the 'post-industrial economy'.

Of all the formulae designed to guide our economic destiny, the one that seems to be most prevalent today is 'knowledge-based growth'. This concept is rooted in an economic theory called 'endogenous growth theory', or the concept of growth that comes from within an economy based on the knowledge, skills and capacity of its population. According to this theory, 'endogenous development' is built upon the direct economic benefits of learning and higher levels of knowledge (McMahon 2009). This transformation is affecting every sector, kind of work and relationship between producer and user – including

Knowledge economy: An economy in which information, communication, cultural and service industries play a significant role and provide a relatively large proportion of jobs, and in which traditional manufacturing and agricultural sectors require the use of information and other advanced technologies

the transformations occurring in the agricultural and manufacturing sectors. In this way, the term '**knowledge economy**' highlights the important connections between education and economic growth. Computer-mediated forms of representation and communication are at the heart of these changes and the multimodal 'literacies' these embody.

What happens to people who don't have the capacities to operate effectively in these new economic settings? We have reason to redouble our efforts to develop a dynamic and innovative knowledge-based economy, to take a leap in which the knowledge qualities of our people, products and services contribute to productivity and economic growth.

Table 2.3: From the industrial economy to the knowledge economy

Industrial economy	Knowledge economy
• An economy dominated by the heavy industrial and manufacturing sectors	• Growth of the service, information and knowledge sectors of the economy
• Most jobs low-skilled, with relatively few technical and professional jobs requiring higher levels of education	• Decreasing demand for low-skilled jobs
	• Increasing communication demands in all jobs, along with higher-level literacies
	• Near-universal use of computers and computing devices in work, operated though multimodal interfaces

See literacies.com Barton on Literacy and Economic Development.

The post-Fordist workplace

Post-Fordism: A system of work that requires multiskilling, teamwork and contribution to corporate culture

The ways in which people live their daily lives in workplaces have changed dramatically. The trends behind these changes have been collectively termed '**post-Fordism**', or the 'new capitalism'. Post-Fordism replaces the old hierarchical command structures epitomised in Henry Ford's development of mass-production techniques.

See literacies.com Ford on his Car Factory.

The old capitalism was a system of rigid hierarchy, driven by a top-down discourse of discipline and command: bosses passed memos down to factory-floor supervisors, who shouted orders to workers, who often did not need to be able to read and write. A fine division of labour systematically deskilled workers. A few did the engineering and management work and this required literacy. However, the bulk of the workforce did process work, spending all day inserting and tightening

Figure 2.2 A still from Charlie Chaplin's *Modern Times*

one particular screw in one particular place before the product they were making moved down the production line to the next person.

See literacies.com Taylor on Scientific Management.

In these earlier industrial times, most schools taught no more than the rudimentary 'basics'. Literacy was the first two of the 'three R's': reading, writing and arithmetic. Children memorised spelling lists and correct grammar. School was a universe of straightforwardly right and wrong answers, authoritative texts and authoritarian teachers. The underlying lesson of these basics was about the social order and its sources of authority.

See literacies.com Heath on Work and Community Literacies.

Figure 2.3 Assembly line work

Figure 2.4 The traditional classroom

Since the arrival of post-Fordism, more work organisations are opting for a 'flattened hierarchy'. Commitment, responsibility and motivation are won by developing a 'workplace culture' that encourages the members of an organisation to identify with its 'mission'. The old vertical chains of command are replaced by the horizontal relationships of 'teamwork'. A division of labour into its most minute, deskilled components is replaced by 'multiskilled' all-round workers who are flexible enough to be able to do complex and integrated tasks (Cope & Kalantzis 1997a). These changes have enormous impacts on the nature and extent of workplace communication.

 See literacies.com Peters and Waterman on Business Excellence.

Table 2.4: The changing workplace

The Fordist workplace	The post-Fordist workplace
• Strict organisational hierarchy: written memos from managers, oral orders from supervisors	• Shared responsibility in teams
	• Multiskilling
• Fine division of labour, requiring minimal skills for the majority of workers	• Vision, sense of a mission and of belonging to the corporate culture
• Minimal knowledge and skills: the rudimentary basics of 'reading, writing and arithmetic' plus a capacity to be disciplined and accept rules	• Informal oral and written workplace communications
	• Training, mentoring and continuous learning in an always-changing job

The new language of work

With a new work life comes a new language. A good deal of this change is the result of new technologies, such as the iconographic-, text- and screen-based modes of interacting with fellow workers and even controlling the machines that make things. The communicative demands placed upon workers have changed greatly, and a large part of the reason for this is the new social relationships of work. Whereas the old 'Fordist' organisation depended upon formal systems of command, such as written memos and the supervisor's orders, effective teamwork depends to a much greater extent on informal, interpersonal discourse. This informality translates, for example, into informal, quasi-oral written forms, such as email or instant messaging.

Our challenge as educators is to develop a pedagogy that will work pragmatically for the new economy, and for the most mundane of reasons: it will help students get a decent job, particularly if the dice of opportunity seem to be loaded against them. Education is, after all, a site of social – and economic – opportunity.

Facing challenging futures

Equally plausible, however, is a bleak reading of today's economic realities, the global convulsions of our times. For instance, the language of teamwork, vision and mission and corporate culture may actually be about getting people to work harder and be less critical. Everyone is supposed to personify the enterprise; to think, act and will the enterprise. The 'entrepreneurial self' is prioritised within contemporary discourse, within these 'new times', in which we live and work. However, beneath its seemingly more pleasant surface the old hierarchies persist, and with them their vast disparities of power and wealth. There is evidence, in fact, that work inequalities are in some respects getting worse. The new workplace, in this pessimistic view, might be regarded as a place where the more you are lulled into feeling you belong, the greater the inequities become.

A lot of people are left out of the new economy: the home healthcare workers; the service workers in hospitality and catering who wash dishes and make beds; the undocumented immigrants who pick fruit and clean people's houses; and the people who work in old-style factories in China or call centres in India. For these people, the old pedagogies of literacy may continue to perform the functions they always did. This, in fact, may in part explain their persistence.

In the heart of the new economy, those who do not speak the nuanced language of corporate culture may find that their aspirations to social mobility hit a 'glass ceiling'. To counter this, our literacies pedagogy has to go one step further and help foster a critical understanding of the discourses of work and power. We need to consider the kinds of learning and literacies that would nurture more productive and more egalitarian working conditions.

See literacies.com Sennett on the New Flexibility at Work.

In responding to the radical changes in working life that are currently underway, we need to tread a careful path. We need to give students the opportunity to develop skills for access to new forms of work through learning the new language of work. However, at the same time, our role as educators is not simply to be technocrats. Our job is not to produce docile, compliant workers. Students need to develop the skills to speak up, to negotiate and to be able to engage critically with the conditions of their working lives. Indeed, the twin goals of access and critical engagement are not incompatible.

 See literacies.com Gowen on Workers' Literacies.

Communications skills for the new workplace

So, moving from the general needs of a new economy to the specific dynamics of literacies pedagogy, what should we, in practical terms, do? Here we suggest some broad-brushstroke items to contribute to a literacies agenda for the new workplace – whether our objective is to enhance the individual's prospects of employment, or to improve the profitability of the enterprise, or to support the development of a region, or to strengthen the competitiveness of a nation, or to change the system so the benefits of economic progress are more equitably shared.

- *Participant communicators:* At every level of employment, our workplaces need people who are meaning producers as well as meaning consumers; who are active listeners and capable of speaking up; who are problem-solvers and knowledge-makers; who communicate their knowledge and contribute their best through their active participant communication.
- *Thoughtful communicators:* We need people who can carefully read and interpret multiple sources of information; who can balance perspectives; who can articulate their individual values as well as the corporate ethos; who can temper personal judgement with broader and divergent interests; and who can think critically.
- *Reflexive communicators:* Workplaces need people whose high-level communicative abilities also reflect capacities to think at a high level; to articulate thoughts and to engage in processes of metacognitive reflection: in other words, effective workers who will be critically self-aware of their own thinking about thinking, and communicating about communicating.
- *Boundary-crossing communicators:* We live in a society and economy where every customer is different; where global markets are as subtly varied as local niche markets; where each affiliated organisation and each division in an organisation has its own peculiar culture; and where contemporary work teams represent every shade of ethnicity, gender identity, network affinity, life experience, knowledge base and perspective. Effective workplace communication in these settings is a matter of boundary-crossing, about reading relevant communication differences and communicating effectively across these **differences**.

Differences: Social categories that describe the differences between individuals and groups of individuals, such as class, locale, family, age, race, sex, sexuality, physical and mental abilities, language and ethnicity

- *Multimodal communicators:* Workplaces need people who can operate across multiple modes of communication, reading and writing about the world through the oral, written, visual, gestural, tactile and spatial modes, shifting between modes as and when necessary. This is particularly the case given the role of information and communications technologies in contemporary workplaces.

This list reflects deep shifts in the human capacities valued in work. It is incumbent upon educators to expand the literacy standards that should underpin a knowledge economy. Indeed, we need to rethink the types of learning required by the kinds of people who will be the most productive workers, capable of contributing to the enterprise at the same time as contributing to the quality of working and community life for all.

Present and future gazing: workforce and learning skills in the here and now and into the future

What constitutes work and the skills needed to undertake such work in contemporary contexts and the foreseeable future are markedly different from the definitions and requirements of the past. And it is the case that there have been a number of 'drivers' that have brought about change, albeit emergent change to date in some instances, and that will continue to bring about such change over the course of this, the current, decade. Six key drivers of change – disruptive shifts that are likely to reshape the landscape (i.e. both the contemporary and future 'workscape') – have been identified:

Driver 1 – *Extreme longevity* i.e. increasing global lifespans change the nature of careers and learning

Driver 2 – *Rise of smart machines and systems* i.e. workplace automation nudges human workers out of rote, repetitive tasks

Driver 3 – *Computational world* i.e. massive increases in sensors and processing power make the world a programmable system

Driver 4 – *New media ecology* i.e. new communication tools require new media literacies beyond text

Driver 5 – *Superstructed organisations* i.e. social technologies drive new forms of production and value creation

Driver 6 – *Globally connected world* i.e. increased global interconnectivity puts diversity and adaptability at the centre of organisational operations (Davies, Fidler & Gorbis 2011).

As would be expected, while each discrete driver will serve to have impact, it is the convergence of these drivers operating simultaneously that will produce significant disruption.

In view of these six drivers, 10 'skills' relevant to and required of workers in the present and future workscape have also been acknowledged. These skills are as follows: sense-making, social intelligence, novel and adaptive thinking, cross-cultural competency, computational thinking, new-media literacy, transdisciplinarity,

Table 2.5: Ten skills for the future workforce and relationship to drivers

Skills for the future workforce	Definition of skill for the future workforce	Relationship to drivers
Sense-making	Ability to determine the deeper meaning or significance of what is being expressed	Driver 2 – Rise of smart machines and systems
Social intelligence	Ability to connect to others in a deep and direct way, to sense and stimulate reactions and desired interactions	Driver 2 – Rise of smart machines and systems Driver 6 – Globally connected world
Novel and adaptive thinking	Proficiency at thinking and coming up with solutions and responses beyond that which is rote or rule-based	Driver 2 – Rise of smart machines and systems Driver 6 – Globally connected world
Cross-cultural competency	Ability to operate in different cultural settings	Driver 5 – Superstructed organisations Driver 6 – Globally connected world
Computational thinking	Ability to translate vast amounts of data into abstract concepts and to understand data-based reasoning	Driver 3 – Computational world Driver 4 – New media ecology
New-media literacy	Ability to critically assess and develop content that uses new media forms, and to leverage these media for persuasive communication	Driver 1 – Extreme longevity Driver 4 – New media ecology
Transdisciplinarity	Literacy in and ability to understand concepts across multiple disciplines	Driver 5 – Superstructed organisations Driver 1 – Extreme longevity Driver 3 – Computational world
Design mindset	Ability to represent and develop tasks and work processes for desired outcomes	Driver 3 – Computational world Driver 5 – Superstructed organisations
Cognitive load management	Ability to discriminate and filter information for importance, and to understand how to maximise cognitive functioning using a variety of tools and techniques	Driver 3 – Computational world Driver 4 – New media ecology Driver 5 – Superstructed organisations
Virtual collaboration	Ability to work productively, drive engagement, and demonstrate presence as a member of a virtual team	Driver 5 – Superstructed organisations Driver 6 – Globally connected world

Source: Adapted from Davies, Fidler & Gorbis (2011).

design mindset, cognitive load management and virtual collaboration. These skills and their relationship, by way of particular relevance, to the drivers are captured in Table 2.5.

So, what 'kinds of people', and with what proficiencies and abilities, are required and valued in the contemporary world of work? 'Success' as a worker in the present and conceivable future demands a fresh and extensive repertoire of knowleges and skills that go beyond traditional academic skills. Clearly, one will need to be in command of the 'new(er) language of work' and the multiple and complex literacy demands permeating such. While basic reading and writing skills – and indeed basic technology skills – remain essential, they are not sufficient in the 21st century. Given this, we must equip students with '21st-century skills'; bearing in mind, too, that 'the world economy no longer pays for what people know but for what they can do with what they know' (Andreas Schleicher, OECD Deputy Director of Education, cited in The Economist Intelligence Unit 2014: 7).

Literacies for citizenship

Literacy in the era of nationalism

In the era of the strong nation-state, literacy was about making students the same: learning to read and write in standard forms of the national language, obeying its rules and respectfully giving the right answers, and learning to revere its literary high culture. It was, in other words, citizenship of a peculiar kind. Modern nationalism brought together communities so they could be governed within defined geographical borders. The people within those borders had to be made homogeneous, speaking a common language and sharing a single communal story.

See literacies.com Anderson on the Nation as Imagined Community.

In the era of nationalism, schools played a critical role in these processes of linguistic and cultural assimilation; hence the agenda of literacy teaching that all students learn the formal rules of the standard form of the national language. The pressures to develop linguistic and cultural homogeneity were intense, going to the heart of the relationship of state to **civil society** in the modern era.

Civil society: Self-organising communities and social groups, such as families and cultural organisations

See literacies.com Gellner on the Logic of Nationalism (in Chapter 1).
Cope and Kalantzis on the Assimilationist Culture of the Modern Nation.

Globalisation and diversity

The last decades of the 20th century represent a turning point in the history of the nation-state and the nature of the relationship of states to citizenries. The cultural and linguistic trajectory of the modern state was altered. The reasons for this change are deep and many and include the forces of globalisation, which expand the geographic reach of economic, social and political power; the diversification of local communities through mass migration; and the increasingly vocal claims to linguistic and cultural rights by minority, indigenous and immigrant communities.

The changing status of government in society

Perhaps the most important structural force influencing citizenship has been the shrinking size and diminishing significance of **the state**. In the middle of the 20th century, the welfare state was the capitalist world's answer to communism. Capitalist states felt they had to afford a program of redistributive justice and become large and expensive 'nanny' states, blunting their sharper edges and ameliorating their worst inequalities.

The state: Government in control of law-making, courts, policing and the military

Neoliberalism: An ideology that seeks to make the state as small as possible, believing that the market and the corporation are better forms of social organisation and more productive than the state

In the last decades of the 20th century, however, states began a conscious program of retreat, shrinking the size of government and reducing the scale of welfare programs. They developed policies of deregulation, which allowed business and professional communities to create their own standards of operation. They privatised formerly public assets, selling them to private shareholders and corporations. This trend, often called '**neoliberalism**' by academic commentators, was associated with the idea that society was created through the market, and that the state should stay out of social and economic affairs to as great an extent as possible.

See literacies.com Harvey on Neoliberalism.

These developments have been experienced in schools in the form of shrinking government funding, pressure for teaching to become a self-regulating profession, self-managing schools that are run more like businesses or corporations, and increasing numbers of private community schools and even privately owned for-profit schools. Education is conceived more as a market than as a service provided to citizens by government. In the context of the shrinking state, its role has been at times reduced to the most basic of basics – literacy as phonics and cheap, mechanised comprehension tests. The assumption is that, for those who can afford the tuition fees and find value for their money, the private education market can do the rest. Some parents have even pulled their students out of school as the home schooling movement has grown.

Today's state of affairs can be interpreted in several ways. One interpretation is bleak: the spread of the ideology and practices of the market exacerbates inequality.

There is another interpretation, however: one that regards this as a moment of opportunity. As the state shrinks, we witness the rise of self-governing structures in civil society. The internet, for instance, is governed not by any state or coalition of states but by the World Wide Web Consortium, a group of interested experts and professionals who cohere around elaborate processes of consensus-building and decision-making. Across the internet, self-regulating communities flourish. We also encounter struggles for control when community and corporate interests find themselves at loggerheads. Mostly, governments stay out of these spaces and do not participate in these struggles.

For better or for worse and to varying degrees, the general trend seems to be that the old top-down relationship of state to citizen is being replaced by multiple layers of self-governing community, from the local to national and global levels.

To the extent that these self-governing spaces in civil society are opened up by government retreat and tax cuts, they may be doomed to penury and failure. They may also contribute to a dangerous fragmentation into a not-so-civil society. This is the basis of the case against neoliberalism, whose long-term success as a strategy for governance is by no means assured. And whether it succeeds on its own terms or not, its desirability is vigorously debated.

New literacies for new citizenship

Either way, the old literacy is no longer adequate, either to support decentralised governance along neoliberal lines or to support a civil society capable of making reasonable demands of its state. We need instead a literacies pedagogy for active and informed citizenship, centred on highly literate learners as agents in their own knowledge processes and capable of contributing their own ideas as well as negotiating the differences between one community and the next. Meanwhile, some of the 'back-to-basics' people are arguing for a return to the rigours of nationalism, however futile this may be, given the deeper structural trends.

> **Diversity:** The social relationships and organisation of human differences, operating sometimes productively, and other times in discriminatory or inequitable ways

 See literacies.com Street on Literacy and Nationalism.

Just as global geopolitics has shifted, so do schools have to service linguistic and cultural **diversity**. Their fundamental role has changed. The meaning of literacy pedagogy has changed. Local diversity and global connectedness not only mean that there can be no single, universal standard; they also mean that the most important skill students need to learn is to negotiate differences in **social languages**, dialects, code-switching and hybrid cross-cultural discourses. In this way also, access to wealth, power and symbols should be possible no matter what one's **identity** markers – such as language and dialect – happen to be.

> **Social language:** The particular way of communicating of a social group – for instance, an ethnic group, an age or peer group, a profession, an affinity or interest group, or a group sharing an understanding of a certain kind of technology. The vocabulary the group uses, the way its members express their ideas, the ways of communicating that may seem strange or difficult for outsiders to understand.

In this context, cultural and linguistic diversity is not only a social resource in the formation of new civic spaces and new notions of citizenship. Just as powerfully, diversity can be used as a classroom resource. This is not just so that educators can provide a better 'service' to 'minorities'. Rather, such a pedagogical orientation

> **Identity:** Who a person feels him/herself to be, as an individual and as a member of various social groups

will produce benefits for all. For example, there is a cognitive benefit for all children in a pedagogy of linguistic and cultural pluralism, including 'mainstream' children. When learners juxtapose different languages and patterns of meaning-making, they gain abilities to think about their thinking (**metacognition**) and to think about their language use (metalinguistic awareness).

Metacognition: Thinking about thinking; one example of this is metalinguistic awareness, or a capacity to think and communicate about one's communications

The current Australian Curriculum provides an example of one education system's endeavour to address cultural and linguisitic diversity – and indeed other capacities deemed essential for 21st-century learners. We present this here as an example of the kinds of expectations that are typical of modern curriculum frameworks all around the world. For instance, in the United States, the Common Core State Standards put in place expectations of a similar order. So, if you are reading this book in another country, consider the similarities or differences in contemporary curriculum where you are.

In the Australian Curriculum seven 'general capabilities' are explicitly addressed in the learning – or discipline – areas comprising the curriculum document (Australian Curriculum, Assessment and Reporting Authority [ACARA] 2015a). These are literacy, numeracy, information and communication technology (ICT) capability, critical and creative thinking, personal and social capability, ethical understanding, and intercultural understanding (ACARA 2015i).

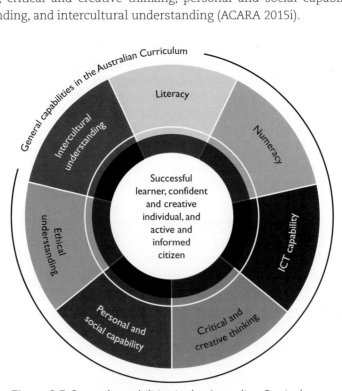

Figure 2.5 General capabilities in the Australian Curriculum

In addressing the last of these general capabilities, namely 'intercultural understanding', the Curriculum espouses the following position:

In the Australian Curriculum, students develop intercultural understanding as they learn to value their own cultures, languages and beliefs, and those of others. They come to understand how personal, group and national identities are shaped, and the variable and changing nature of culture. The capability involves students in learning about and engaging with diverse cultures in ways that recognise commonalities and differences, create connections with others and cultivate mutual respect.

Intercultural understanding is an essential part of living with others in the diverse world of the twenty-first century. It assists young people to become responsible local and global citizens, equipped through their education for living and working together in an interconnected world (ACARA 2015h).

In addition to these general capabilities, the curriculum specifies three 'cross-curriculum priorities' that are again embedded in all learning – discipline – areas, namely 'Aboriginal and Torres Strait Islander histories and cultures', 'Asia and Australia's engagement with Asia' and 'Sustainability'. With the specific intent to focus upon the notion of cultural and linguistic diversity, we draw attention at this point to the 'Aboriginal and Torres Strait Island histories and cultures' and 'Asia and Australia's engagement with Asia' priorities.

Table 2.6 details the ways in which these two cross-curriculum priority areas are presented in the Australian Curriculum.

Table 2.6: Cross-curriculum priorities in the Australian Curriculum relating to cultural and linguistic diversity

Aboriginal and Torres Strait Islander histories and cultures	Asia and Australia's engagement with Asia
The Aboriginal and Torres Strait Islander priority provides opportunities for all learners to deepen their knowledge of Australia by engagement with the world's oldest continuous living cultures. Through the Australian Curriculum, students will understand that contemporary Aboriginal and Torres Strait Islander communities are strong, resilient, rich and diverse (ACARA 2015e).	… An understanding of Asia underpins the capacity of Australian students to be active and informed citizens working together to build harmonious local, regional and global communities, and build Australia's social, intellectual and creative capital. It also builds understanding of the diversity of cultures and peoples living in Australia, fosters social inclusion and cohesion and is vital to the prosperity of Australia. This priority will ensure that students learn about and recognise the diversity within and between the countries of the Asia region. Students will develop knowledge and understanding of Asian societies, cultures, beliefs and environments, and the connections between the peoples of Asia, Australia, and the rest of the world. Asia literacy provides students with the skills to communicate and engage with the peoples of Asia so they can effectively live, work and learn in the region (ACARA 2015f).

The language – and, arguably the philosophical intent – of the Australian Curriculum, as evidenced in the 'intercultural understanding' general capability and two of the three 'cross-curriculum priorities', clearly constructs cultural and linguistic diversity as a social resource for individuals and communities alike, and as a mechanism for producing particular kinds of civic spaces and citizens. Furthermore, it visibly positions cultural and linguistic diversity, and engagement with such diversity in the context of the classroom, as a resource that serves to benefit *all* students.

Literacies for contemporary community life

Literacies and diverse identities

We live in an environment where cultural differences – varieties of identity and affiliation – are becoming more and more significant. Gender, ethnicity, generation and sexual orientation are just a few of the markers of these differences. Some of these differences are accidents of birthplace, appearance and socio-economic circumstance that are the basis of historic inequalities and patterns of discrimination. We explore these dynamics in detail and in relation to literacies pedagogy in Chapter 15.

For those who yearn for a homogeneous community with agreed cultural norms and universal 'standards', this diversity seems to be evidence of a distressing fragmentation of the social fabric. Indeed, in one sense it is just this: a historical shift in which singular, assimilating and homogenising national cultures have less hold than they once did. Adding to this dilemma are the effects of government pulling back from welfare responsibilities in the interests of individualism and choice, and blaming victims of discrimination, inequality and poverty for their fate.

Affinity space: A place where informal learning takes place. It can be either virtual or physical in nature. It is a space in which participants are afforded the opportunity to learn with others who share a common interest, goal or endeavour – as opposed to a shared race, class, culture, ethnicity or gender.

To illustrate one dimension of contemporary diversity dynamics: one of the effects of less regulated, multichannel digital media systems is that they undermine the concept of collective audience and common culture. They promote the opposite: an increasingly accessible and expanding range of subcultural choices and the growing divergence of specialist and subcultural discourses. The **affinity spaces** (Gee 2004b) in the new, social media have the same effect on identity formation, promoting variety and divergence more than convergent sameness.

 See literacies.com Kalantzis and Cope on New Media Literacies.

The 'balance of agency' in the new communications environment

A key reason for the rise of this kind and level of diversity, we would argue, is a profound shift in what we call 'the balance of agency'. As workers, citizens and persons, we are more and more required to be users, players, creators and discerning consumers rather than the spectators, delegates, audiences or quiescent consumers of an earlier era. Even though it is only happening in fits and starts, the hierarchical command society is being displaced by the society of peer-to-peer reflexivity.

 See literacies.com Wark on Gamer Theory.

Take, for instance, something as ordinary and pervasive as narrative. In everyday family and community life, the narratives of gaming have now become an even bigger business than Hollywood. From the most impressionable of ages, children of the Nintendo, PlayStation, Xbox, iPod/Pad/Phone or Android generation become habituated to the idea that they can be characters in narratives, capable of determining or, at the very least, influencing the story's end. They are content with being no less actors rather than audiences, players rather than spectators, agents rather than voyeurs, users rather than readers of narrative. Not content with programmed radio, children build their own playlists on their smartphones and tablets. Not content with programmed television, they read the narratives on DVDs and internet-streamed video at varying depths (the movie, the documentary about the making of the movie) and dip into 'chapters' at will. Not content with the chosen perspectives of sports telecasting on broadcast television, they choose their own camera angles, replays and statistical analyses on interactive digital TV.

 See literacies.com Knobel and Lankshear on the New Literacies.

Old logics of literacy and teaching are profoundly challenged by this new media environment. Traditional, didactic literacy is bound to fall short. This not only disappoints young people, whose expectations for engagement are greater, but also fails to direct their energies in the direction of the kinds of people required for the new domains of work, citizenship and community life.

 See literacies.com Gee on What Video Games Have to Teach Us About Learning and Literacy.

In the transition from the old 'popular culture' of broadcasting to the new world of 'narrowcasting', consider what has happened to one of the media: television. Instead of being subjected to pressures to conform, pressures to shape ourselves in the image of the mass media, we now have cable or satellite television with its thousands of channels packaged in any number of ways. Television now caters not to the 'general public' but to ever more narrowly defined communities. For example, the 'international' channels are broadcast in any number of different languages; there are channels catering to particular sporting interests; others present particular genres of movie. Add to these interactive TV, video internet streaming and video upload services like YouTube and Vimeo. These new broadcast media extend choice by genre and by language to millions of titles with infinitely nuanced tones of voice and hues of culture.

See literacies.com Shirky on Creativity in the New Media.

As a part of this process, the viewer becomes a user. Transmission is re-placed by user-selectivity. Instead of being passive receptors of mass culture, we become active creators of information and co-designers of our own enter-tainment. We find places of cultural engagement that precisely suit the subtle-ties of who we are and the image in which we want to fashion ourselves. The new media even turns the traditional mass media communicative relationship around the other way. Instead of just watching video, you can shoot and edit your own video on a device as ubiquitous as your phone, then broadcast it to the world through the internet. Social networking and resource sharing sites, such as Facebook, Twitter, YouTube, Instagram and Flickr, open up new ways in which to participate as active creators of information and through which to construct and (re)present one's self in the world.

See literacies.com Jenkins on Participatory Media Culture and Youth.

Living and communicating in diverse communities

As a consequence of this development, another type of differentiation has become pivotal in today's lifeworlds, and much more profoundly and pervasively so than the straightforward demographic groupings that underwrote an earlier identity politics of gender, ethnicity, race and disability that had evolved as a response to exclusionary social systems and practices. The moment more scope for participation and **agency** in communications becomes available, we face layers upon layers of difference. The result is actually existing agencies in the massively plural.

Agency: A person's capacity to act; the degree of control they have over their own actions and of responsibility for their actions

These changes go far deeper than the simple demographics captured in census categories, school enrolment forms or school data management sys-tems. Deep differences are uncovered – of experience, interest, orientation to the world, values, dispositions, sensibilities and social languages. Insofar as a person inhabits many lifeworlds (home, school, professional, interest, affilia-tion), their identities are multilayered. Personhood can barely be understood as a singularly unified identity. In ourselves, we are many cultures. We speak many social languages. Indeed, diversity has become a paradoxical universal in our times.

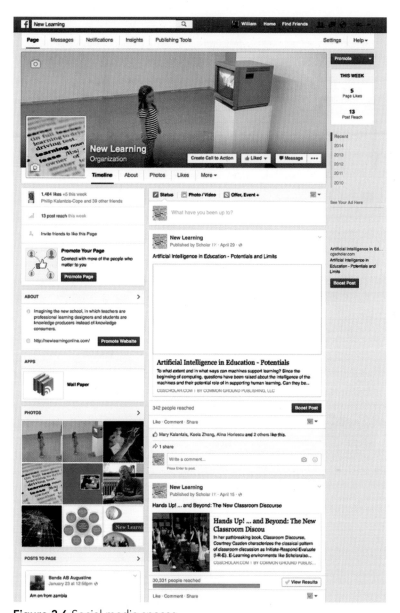

Figure 2.6 Social media spaces

Language and other modes of communication become a crucial marker of life-world differences – one's accent, vocabulary and styles of meaning-making, or the images one communicates on social media, for instance. As lifeworlds become more divergent and their boundaries become more blurred, the central fact of language becomes the multiplicity of meanings and their continual intersection. Just as there are multiple layers to everyone's identity, there are multiple discourses

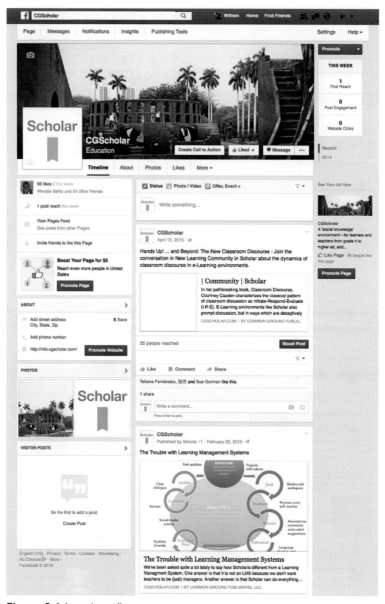

Figure 2.6 (*continued*)

of identity and images of the self to be negotiated. We have to be proficient as we negotiate the many lifeworlds each of us inhabits and the many lifeworlds we encounter in our everyday lives. This creates a new challenge for literacies pedagogy.

See literacies.com Haythornthwaite on Participatory Transformations.

Figure 2.6 (*continued*)

New literacies for changing times

The ramifications for teaching and learning are enormous. A literacies pedagogy can be agnostic about the stance that learners and teachers may wish to take in relation to changing social conditions – provided this does not inadvertently facilitate harmful exclusion or discrimination. Learners may take either the route of compliance or that of critique. If they take the former route, education can help them develop capacities that will enable them to access the new civil society and share in its benefits. Or they may reject its values in the name of an emancipatory view of education's possibilities. Either way, their choices will be more explicit and open to scrutiny. And either way, education has a fundamental responsibility to provide learners with tools for effective meaning-making – hence the concept of literacies.

Figure 2.6 (*continued*)

We are living in transitionary times. The trends we observe today are contradictory at every level of society and the media through which we make meanings. For every moment in which agency is passed over to users and consumers, power is also centralised in ways that can be disturbing. The ownership of commercial media, communications channels and software platforms is becoming alarmingly concentrated. Moreover, to what extent do the new media provide an escape from reality more than they provide social access? Debates about the value of gaming versus the exposure of children to it display this tension. On top of this, for every dazzling new opening to knowledge and cultural expression in the 'gift economy' of free content on the internet, there are disturbing new possibilities for the invasion of privacy, cynically targeted advertising and control over knowledge sources and media.

See literacies.com Galloway on Protocol.

There are huge variations in the ways that literacies teachers have responded to these changes, from 'makeover' practices that bolt the new onto the old, to breakthrough learning relationships that are genuinely innovative and authentic. Whatever the path, we cannot afford to ignore the trajectories of change and we need to be able to justify whatever pedagogical paths we choose to take.

Table 2.7: New literacies

Literacies for work	Literacies for citizenship	Literacies for contemporary personal and community life
• Multimodal computer and other machine interfaces • A range of formal and informal texts, from emails to reports, websites and management information systems • Multimodal meanings in team, customer, corporate and training, including oral, written, visual, gestural, spatial	• Many levels of citizenship, from self-regulating interest or community groups, to corporate citizenship, local government and issues of national and international concern • 'Reading the signs' at each of these levels of participation, as well as contributing to debate and thoughtful decision-making	• Using the new, digital and multimodal media to access culture and express identity • Negotiating diversity in everyday interactions in families, neighbourhoods, on the internet etc.

Summary

	Early industrial society	Developed industrial society	Knowledge society
Work	• Value in fixed capital, not the skills of workers, who are mostly unskilled • Minimal, predictable, stable work expectations • A premium placed on discipline and workers reliably taking orders	• New technologies, recognition of the value of 'human capital' • Higher levels of skill, communicative competence and interpersonal capacity required in the workplace	• Value in human skills and relationships, intangible organisational knowledge and service values • Complex and changing expectations that require flexibility, creativity, innovation and initiative
Civics	• Citizens expected to be passive and loyal to leaders • A homogeneous citizenry, or one at the very least where people are expected to become the same • Uncritical loyalty to leaders expected	• Weakening of the nation-state as a consequence of neoliberal contraction and the forces of globalisation	• An active, aware, multicultural citizenry • Many levels of civic participation and responsibility (community organisations, global and local networks, internet communities, local, national, regional and global levels of governance)
Community life	• Ideally, compliant personalities, accepting of established structures and values, respectful of authority figures, taking orders • The nuclear family as the model, and the gender relations that go with it	• Greater importance attached to identity and diversity • Multichannel media supporting more diverse communities	• Multilayered identities, social networks, tolerance, community ethics, responsibility, resilience

	Early industrial society	Developed industrial society	Knowledge society
Media and literacies	• A few channels of mass media (e.g. no more than several newspapers) • The relative separation of different modes of meaning • Didactic literacy pedagogy, teaching the rules of writing in the standard form of the national language	• An early trend to multimodality in photographic and print technologies • First-generation digital texts that retain traditional visual design principles • First-generation e-learning systems that reproduce the knowledge relations of the traditional classroom	• Read/write media, blurring the boundaries of writers/readers, producers/ consumers, creators/ audiences • Increasingly integrated multimodality of texts • New literacies pedagogies that focus on multimodality and the different kinds of meaning that happen in varied social and cultural contexts

Knowledge processes

experiencing the known

1. Create a map of the social languages of your life. How are they different? What are their modes of communication (text, image etc.)? How do these languages reflect the multiple layers of your identity?

experiencing the new

2. Interview a person who has recently retired or who is near retirement. How has work changed over the course of their working life? How has workplace communication changed? How have such changes impacted on their work and their sense of being a 'worker'?

experiencing the new

3. This chapter has briefly examined the ways in which the Australian Curriculum has endeavoured to address the issue of, and engage with, the cultural and linguistic diversity of learners in schools. Examine if, and how, the curriculum of another

country has made similar changes. Or if you are not in Australia, how has your curriculum addressed the changes described in this chapter? Has it succeeded? Or is there further way to go?

conceptualising with theory

4. Take the following terms, and use them to create a short theoretical statement on the influence of social changes on our communications environment over recent decades.

   Asynchronous messaging Messages that are not communicated live, in real time, but are recorded for another person to receive at another time

   Cosmopolitanism An ideology and practice of valuing differences and managing diversity

   Fordism The system of production-line industrial work that Henry Ford played a large part in inventing

   Hypertext A computer link from one place in a digital text to another text or place in that same text

   The virtual Life-like communications across distances

analysing critically

5. Choose a site of 'citizenship crisis' and analyse the dilemmas in the changing nature of nations and states – for instance, the question of immigration or struggles over government funding for services. Use recent media reports to describe the dimensions of the crisis. What are the implications of this crisis for education?

applying creatively

6. Design a lesson plan that illustrates to students one important aspect of the new media environment. Specify the learning level, discipline area etc. You may wish to use the web planner we have provided at L-by-D.com

PART B

Approaches to literacies

CHAPTER 3

Literacies pedagogy

Overview

This chapter begins with some classroom examples that illustrate contemporary literacies pedagogy at work. It then goes on to develop a framework for classifying the range of activity types that make for a productive and purposeful literacies **pedagogy**. These 'knowledge processes', or 'things you do to know', consist of a variety of activity types: experiential ('experiencing the known' and 'experiencing the new'), conceptual ('conceptualising by naming' and 'conceptualising with theory', analytical ('analysing functionally' and 'analysing critically') and applied ('applying appropriately' and 'applying creatively'). Expert teachers have always woven backwards and forwards between these different activity types, or ways of knowing and learning. The knowledge processes are also deeply rooted in traditions of literacy pedagogy that in the next chapters of this book we will call 'didactic', 'authentic', 'functional' and 'critical'. Over these chapters we will explore these traditions, while also focusing on the question of the kind of literacies pedagogy that is appropriate to our times.

Pedagogy: A sequence of activities designed to facilitate learning

Literacies pedagogy in action

Meet Pip, whose Year 6 students in a small rural school were creating interest-based 'passion projects'. Pip has her students weave between 'experiencing the known' and 'experiencing the new'. She asks them to bring in familiar texts, and in the passion project itself to work on something closely connected to their identities. They also explore new websites. They develop concepts that describe the design elements of websites, including 'icons' and 'links' ('conceptualising by naming'). They develop theory that connects these concepts in generalisations about how people navigate their way through websites and the design of websites compared to newspapers ('conceptualising with theory'). They critically analyse the features of more and less successful website designs ('analysing critically'). They apply what they learn in the creation of a passion website and a class newspaper ('applying appropriately' and 'applying creatively'). The purpose of this weaving between knowledge processes is to harness each learner's identity in a double way: as personal interest, and to evolve expertise in expressing those interests in a web environment. As well as requiring a lot of reading and writing, the work also explicitly aims at expanding learners' technical knowledge about the web and the most effective ways of deploying its affordances to make meanings (Cloonan 2010b; Cloonan 2015).

Figure 3.1 Passion projects

 See literacies.com van Haren, Passion Project.

To Greece now, where Anna Fterniati uses a knowledge process approach to analyse Year 6 Greek language textbooks produced by the Ministry of Education. She finds a considerable amount of 'experiencing the new', as measured by introducing students to authentic texts; but little 'experiencing the known', where students are introduced to texts familiar to them. There is considerable 'conceptualising' in which the design elements of various texts and genres are described. But there is a relative lack of 'analysing critically' in which the social and cultural purposes of texts are interrogated. However, she does find a good deal of 'applying', in which students produce new texts, both of a conventional written kind and multimodal. This 'knowledge process' analysis suggests areas in which the textbooks might be supplemented by teachers (Fterniati 2010).

Next, to another Year 6 class: an English language class in Singapore. A public school serving mainly working-class families, this school is located in an industrial neighbourhood. There are 18 Malay and three Chinese students in the class. English is a challenge for students, who have limited access to the language outside school. In the words of researcher Jennifer Pei-Ling Tan, the main challenge teachers face is to enhance these students' motivation to learn and improve their English language proficiency, which the students perceive to have limited relevance to their everyday lifeworlds other than in the school context. Given this, she notes that 'the tendency [is] for teachers to resort to even more prescriptive methods of skilling-and-drilling' (Tan 2007: 146).

It is in this context that the School Fun Fair project was developed, a 10-week long unit of work to plan the school fete. 'Experiencing' activities include reflections on personal experiences of fairs, interviews with previous fair participants and a field trip to a fair. 'Conceptualising' activities include creating a plan for the design of the fair, and discussion of the design elements of the various textual materials to support the fair. 'Analysing' activities include identification of potential problems, critiquing previous years' efforts and evaluating the success of the event once it was over. 'Applying' activities involve creating banners and decorations, flyers, fun-fair coupons, how-to-play instructions, DJ presentations on the Fun Fair day, and a post-day website presentation with written and photographic reports (Tan 2007).

In Australia, Kathy Mills describes the pedagogical weaving of a Year 4 teacher in a public school in a low socio-economic locality. The teacher introduces blogging to the class by showing them blogs on a Disney fan site. The students react with 'oohs' and 'aahs' as they respond to familiar imagery and narratives from the media and popular culture. This is framed by the teacher as an example of 'experiencing the known'. The teacher asks the students to define a blog and to name its parts – 'conceptualising by naming' and connecting the concepts, in other words 'conceptualising with theory'. In another activity, she introduces the children to photo manipulation software, but with minimal introduction – 'experiencing the new'. She allows students in pairs to experiment with the software. In a mood of great hilarity, they explore positioning themselves in images and modifying images to funny effect. In 'applying' activities, the children create their own blogs, following the conventions of blog construction – 'applying appropriately'. However, the blogs also show considerable variety in design and content from one blog to the next – 'applying creatively' (Mills 2015).

Literacies teacher and researcher Anne Cloonan has created an early literacy learning module centred around the children's television series *Hi-5*. The activity sequence starts with finding out which television programs the children watch, and what they like about them – 'experiencing the known'. In 'experiencing the new', the children watch an episode of *Hi-5* that most of them have not seen. In 'conceptualising by naming', the students name the design elements of the program – character, logo, sound effects, caricature, segments. In 'conceptualising with theory', they build storyboards that explain the program's structure. In 'analysing functionally', they work out the different roles that are played by the various characters, and also use the concepts to analyse their favourite children's television program. In 'analysing critically', they examine the purposes of the accompanying fan website. In 'applying appropriately', they create a storyboard for their own program, and 'applying creatively' they act out and film an episode.

Figure 3.2 Analysing a children's television phenomenon

 See literacies.com Cloonan and Cope, Analysing a Children's Television Phenomenon: Using *Hi5* as a Teaching Resource.

In a secondary English class in a Chicago high school, Anna McBride is teaching the novel *The Hunger Games*. In 'experiencing the known', students discuss the reality television programs that they watch, exploring the motivations people have to participate and the ways in which they are manipulated. In 'experiencing the new', the students begin to read the novel, using a 'patterned partner reading' strategy. 'Conceptualising by naming' now, they play the 'nail that character' game in which they create words for character traits ('impulsive' or 'strategic') and then find evidence in the text to support their generalisations. 'Analysing functionally', the students draw generalisations about how character interacts with plot to reveal themes. 'Analysing critically', they link the themes of the novel with problems and issues in contemporary society, and compare these to the ways in which similar problems arise in reality television. 'Applying appropriately', the students write a character description of one of the principal characters in the novel, and 'applying creatively', they create a multimodal tribute to *The Hunger Games*.

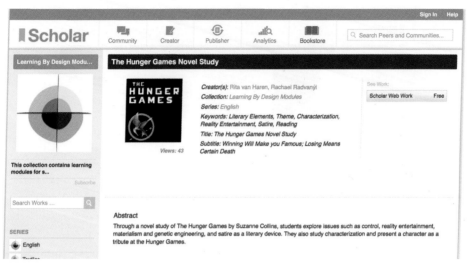

Figure 3.3 *The Hunger Games*

See literacies.com Gill, Radvanyi, Nott, Keogh and van Haren, The Hunger Games Film Study

And now an example of literacies in another curriculum area: history. Prue Gill, Jennifer Nott, Jessie-Kate Watson, Rita van Haren, Stephen Ahern, Rachael Radvanyi and Matthew Sandeman have created a history unit on the Black Death for their classes at Lanyon High School in Canberra, Australia. In 'experiencing the known', students share their views about infectious disease in a 'round robin exercise'. They 'experience the new' by immersion in texts about Medieval Europe and the arrival of the plague. They 'conceptualise by naming' as they make a distinction between primary and secondary sources in history. They 'conceptualise with theory' by considering the concept of bias in primary and secondary texts. They 'analyse functionally' by considering how information or explanatory texts are organised. They 'analyse critically' to discuss the causes of plague, and the way these are represented in the sources. They 'apply appropriately' by writing an information/explanation text on the effects of the plague on 14th-century Europe. Then, 'applying creatively', they develop a text about a different infectious disease at another time in history.

See literacies.com Gill, Nott, Watson, van Haren, Ahern, Radvanyi and Sandeman, The Black Death

In these brief descriptions, we have for clarity's sake presented the knowledge processes used in the activities in the same order. However, the actual order was different and the learners came back to many of the knowledge processes several times. The key is to justify the mix, and to work on transitions from one knowledge process to another that prove to be effective pedagogical moves.

Figure 3.4 The Black Death

Rita van Haren works across a cluster of five schools in Canberra. Here she is talking with a student who has been learning in a school setting in which teachers design student learning using the 'knowledge process' approach.

Researcher Do you like school?

Student F1 Depends on what you are doing. If you are doing something interesting like big projects or debates, seeing different points of view and asking questions. If I feel connected to it and know what it's getting at – what the point is … It is easier to understand why you are doing it and you can actually put it into your life now; not finding out later.

van Haren (2015) concludes:

> The evidence indicates that when teachers gave up control and scaffolded the agency of students through the knowledge processes, students took up this opportunity for autonomy and their learning was transformed. This transformation is more than assimilation and just moving to what the teacher wanted the students to learn.

 See literacies.com Morgan on the Knowledge Processes in Practice (Morgan 2010).

Things you do to know

The historical roots of literacies 'knowledge processes'

Educators teach literacy – and for that matter develop learners' knowledge in other school discipline areas as well – in a number of different ways. We outline and analyse these in this chapter and the following chapters of Part B. We want to suggest that there are valuable lessons to be taken from all the approaches to literacy we are about to explore – didactic literacy in Chapter 4, authentic literacy in Chapter 5, functional literacy in Chapter 6, and critical literacy in Chapter 7. When each of these approaches is somewhat one-sided in its methods, we need to supplement it with aspects of the other approaches. We also believe that we need to recalibrate our approaches to literacy teaching to align with contemporary conditions for meaning-making – including multi-modality and the diverse forms of communication that we encounter in the wide range of social and cultural contexts in our daily lives. We can only do this by refining and extending the pedagogical traditions upon which our profession is founded.

We will classify four orientations to literacies teaching and learning as follows:

- experiencing (the known, or the new)
- conceptualising (by naming, or with theory)
- analysing (functionally, or critically)
- applying (appropriately, or creatively).

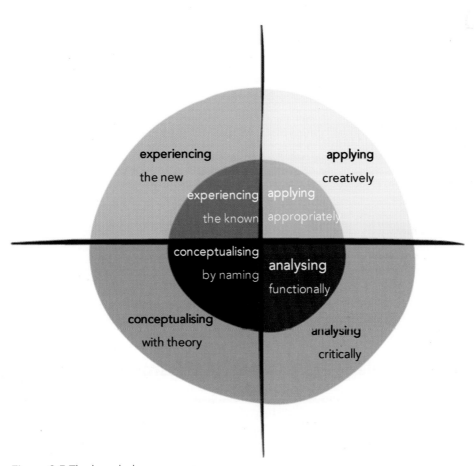

Figure 3.5 The knowledge processes

We call these 'knowledge processes': foundational types of thinking-in-action, or four things you can do to know (Cope & Kalantzis 2015d). We do this because we want to shift the emphasis of pedagogy away from the stuff that happens to have found its way into children's heads – their thinking and understanding – to epistemology, or the things they are able to do in the world in order to know. The knowledge processes also capture the range of different types of activities that students can undertake as part of their literacies learning.

Table 3.1 shows the historic roots of these knowledge processes, although of course, excellent pedagogy has always involved a balanced and appropriate mix of activity types.

Table 3.1: A summary of the historic roots of the four knowledge processes

Didactic literacy	... relies extensively on 'conceptualising by naming', or teaching abstract concepts that can be applied in general contexts; in the case of literacy learning, starting with phonics rules, moving through grammar, and later examining canonical literacy devices and styles. And when it comes to literary texts, didactic literacy does encourage one kind of immersion – 'experiencing the new'. (Chapter 4)
Authentic literacy	... places a strong emphasis on 'experiencing the known', starting with the learner's own interests, experiences and motivations. In the case of literacies, whole language and process writing are good examples of this approach, with their focus on student self-expression in writing and meaningful enjoyment of reading. (Chapter 5)
Functional literacy	... is very much concerned with 'analysing functionally', or working out how literacy texts are structured to serve different purposes, and 'applying appropriately', or learning how to create meanings that will be powerfully efficacious. (Chapter 6)
Critical literacy	... focuses on 'analysing critically', interrogating the motivations behind communicated meanings and creating texts that engage with the world in a critically reflective way; also 'experiencing the known' when it comes to expression personal and social identities and 'applying creatively' when it comes to making innovative and new media texts. (Chapter 7)

The 'knowledge processes' in classroom terms

Table 3.2 divides each of the four knowledge processes into two sub-processes, describing the way these general ideas translate into classroom activities. Used as a checklist of activity types, this schema provides teachers and learners with more control over their instructional choices and their learning outcomes.

Table 3.2: Checklist of activity types

Experiencing	△ *the known* – learners bring to the learning situation perspectives, objects, ideas, ways of communicating and information that are familiar to them, and reflect upon their own experiences and interests
	△ *the new* – learners are immersed in new situations or information, observing or taking part in something that is new or unfamiliar
Conceptualising	△ *by naming* – learners group things into categories, apply classifying terms, and define these terms
	△ *with theory* – learners make generalisations by connecting concepts and developing theories
Analysing	△ *functionally* – learners analyse logical connections, cause and effect, structure and function
	△ *critically* – learners evaluate their own and other people's perspectives, interests and motives
Applying	△ *appropriately* – learners try their knowledge out in real-world or simulated situations to see whether it works in a predictable way in a conventional context
	△ *creatively* – learners make an intervention in the world that is innovative and creative, distinctively expressing their own voices or transferring their knowledge to a different context

These knowledge processes were originally formulated by the New London Group for the Multiliteracies framework as *situated practice, overt instruction, critical framing* and *transformed practice*. In subsequent application of these ideas to curriculum practices in the 'Learning by Design' project, we have reframed these ideas and translated them into the more immediately recognisable 'knowledge processes' tags for planning, documenting and tracking learning (Cope & Kalantzis 2009).

'Learning by Design' formulation	**Original Multiliteracies formulation**
Experiencing	Situated practice
Conceptualising	Overt instruction
Analysing	Critical framing
Applying	Transformed practice

The 'Learning by Design' terms are words that can be used with learners in the classroom. At the same time they capture some profound differences in kinds of ways of knowing or 'epistemic moves'. They are also meant to be familiar to teachers, building, as we shall demonstrate in the following chapters, on major pedagogical traditions. They are not a sequence. You might start with concepts, then attempt to apply them, then connect them to personal experience. Nor do they require 'balance'. Some subject matters or learning situations might call for a lot of conceptual work, others for more experiential work. The knowledge processes require instead that teachers reflect purposefully on the mix and ordering of the epistemic moves they make in their classrooms and are able to justify their pedagogical choices on the basis of learning goals and outcomes for individuals and groups.

KNOWLEDGE PROCESSES

Experiencing…

the known - **bring in, show or talk about** something/somewhere familiar or 'easy' - listen, view, watch, visit

the new - **introduce something less familiar, but** which makes at least some sense just by immersion - listening, watching, viewing, visiting

- write an explanation, create a flow diagram, draw a technical diagram, create a storyboard, make a model.

– identify gaps and silences, analyse purposes (what a piece of knowledge is for), predict and discuss consequences, hold a debate, write a review.

Conceptualising…

by naming - define terms, make a glossary, label a diagram, sort or categorise like and unlike things.

with theory - draw a diagram, make a concept map, or write a summary, theory or formula which puts the concepts together.

Applying…

appropriately - write, draw, act out in the 'usual way', solve a problem.

creatively - use the knowledge you have learned in an innovative way, take an intellectual risk, apply knowledge to a different setting, suggest a new problem, translate knowledge into a different mix of 'modes' of meaning.

Figure 3.6 The knowledge processes – examples of literacies activities

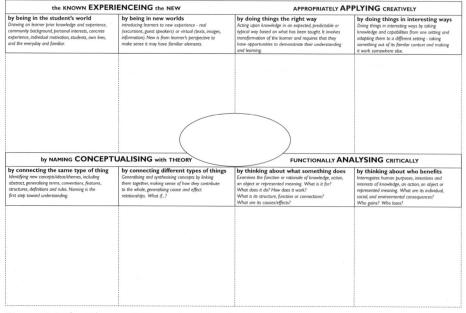

the KNOWN **EXPERIENCEING** the NEW		**APPROPRIATELY APPLYING** CREATIVELY	
by being in the student's world	**by being in new worlds**	**by doing things the right way**	**by doing things in interesting ways**
Drawing on learner prior knowledge and experience, community background, personal interests, concrete experience, individual motivation, students, own lives, and the everyday and familiar.	introducing learners to new experience - real (excursions, guest speakers) or virtual (texts, images, information). New is from learner's perspective to make sense it may have familiar elements.	Acting upon knowledge in an expected, predictable or typical way based on what has been taught. It involves transformation of the learner and requires that they have opportunities to demonstrate their understanding and learning.	Doing things in interesting ways by taking knowledge and capabilities from one setting and adapting them to a different setting - taking something out of its familiar context and making it work somewhere else.
by NAMING **CONCEPTUALISING** with THEORY		FUNCTIONALLY **ANALYSING** CRITICALLY	
by connecting the same type of thing	**by connecting different types of things**	**by thinking about what something does**	**by thinking about who benefits**
Identifying new concepts/ideas/themes, including abstract, generalising terms, conventions, features, structures, definitions and rules. Naming is the first step toward understanding.	Generalising and synthesising concepts by linking them together, making sense of how they contribute to the whole, generalising cause and effect relationships. What if…?	Examines the function or rationale of knowledge, action, an object or represented meaning. What is it for? What does it do? How does it work? What is its structure, function or connections? What are its causes/effects?	Interrogates human purposes, intentions and interests of knowledge, an action, an object or represented meaning. What are its individual, social, and environmental consequences? Who gains? Who loses?

Figure 3.7 The 'Placemat' Curriculum Planning Tool

The 'knowledge processes' in learning theory

Now, to discuss the knowledge processes in theoretical terms. Learning to mean is a process of weaving backwards and forwards across and between different ways of knowing – experiential, conceptual, analytical and applied.

Experiential literacies learning

'*Experiencing the known*' engages learners in reflection upon their own life experiences. It brings into the classroom familiar knowledge and ways of representing the world. An old pedagogical adage says to 'start where the learner is at'. In literacies learning, experiencing the known does this in a very direct way by asking students to bring to the classroom textual artefacts and communicative practices that demonstrate the meanings they make in their everyday lives. In this way, learning connects with learners' cultural backgrounds, identities and interests. Experiencing the known involves the explicit articulation of everyday experience that often lies implicit in practices. It prompts self-reflection about the sources of one's interests and perspectives. By means of these types of activity, not only do learners introduce their invariably diverse experiences into the classroom; teachers and other learners also begin to get a sense of each student's prior knowledge.

'*Experiencing the new*' occurs with immersion in new situations, information and ideas. In the case of literacies, this will mostly involve engaging with new texts or texts of an unfamiliar variety – reading written texts, listening to spoken texts or sounds, observing gesture, looking at visual texts or moving about in spaces. In this way, learners are exposed to new meanings, outside of their everyday experiences. However, this will only work as a learning experience if it is within a zone of intelligibility and safety – sufficiently close to their own life experiences to be within what Vygotsky calls their 'zone of proximal development' (Vygotsky 1962 (1978); see further Chapter 14). **Experiential learning** of these kinds has been articulated at length within the tradition we will in Chapter 5 call 'authentic pedagogy', from Jean-Jacques Rousseau to John Dewey, Maria Montessori and beyond – learning that is relevant to and connected with a learner's life experience. It is the main theoretical basis of immersion models of literacy, such as whole language and process writing. Learning is most effective, according to experiential theories of learning, when it is socially situated, when it connects with learner identities and when it is meaningful to them. However, as a stand-alone pedagogy, it has also come under attack and found itself in retreat in recent decades. Again, more on this in Chapter 5.

Experiential learning: Learning by immersion in texts, activities, physical settings and social situations

Conceptual literacies learning

'*Conceptualising by naming*' involves classification by general or common properties. It entails drawing distinctions of similarity and difference, categorising and naming the constituent elements of the thing to which the concept refers. In literacies learning, concepts form a metalanguage, or language about language. This might include traditional textual concepts, such as 'noun' or 'narrative', and also concepts that describe visual and new media designs, such as 'eyeline' or 'hyperlink'. The renowned theorist of child development, Lev Vygotsky, traces the development of conceptual thinking through developing the meaning of symbols from 'complexes' in the young child to 'conceptual' representations in later childhood (Vygotsky 1934 (1986)). However, even for younger children, the symbols they learn to use in school represent proto-concepts, on their way to becoming full concepts through the transformational effects of education. These evolving conceptual understandings can be represented in different modes and multimodally, including, for instance, the use of words, diagrams, objects and spaces.

Students end up learning school disciplines that consist of specialised, disciplinary knowledge based on more precise conceptual distinctions than those made in everyday language in the course of casual experience. The terms used by academic disciplines are more technical in character and less ambiguous than 'natural' language. The kinds of distinctions they encapsulate are typical of those developed by bodies of academic knowledge (science or history or literary studies, for instance) and by expert communities of practice (professionals or enthusiastic hobbyists, for instance). In the case of teaching literacies, using this knowledge process, students develop metarepresentations with which to describe the design elements of texts, starting with phonics and picture generalisations in early childhood learning and in later education being able to analyse literary styles or the grammar of texts. Didactic pedagogy has a big emphasis on teaching the technical language of a discipline: nouns and verbs; scenes and denouements; and the rules and conventions of literacy in the standard form of the language. Its mode is to tell, then to test students to see whether they have learned what they have been told. However, in a more active literacies pedagogy we could do more than this with conceptualising by naming. Students are asked to look at a text or consider something in the world in order to create their own conceptualisations – naming and classifying according to general features. It may be a text that they are familiar with, or something they experience in the world – but that they now consider conceptually in terms of its general characteristics, and give that general phenomenon a name – 'planet' or 'narrative' or 'hyperlink', for instance. This is an example of the 'weaving' that can productively occur between different knowledge processes; in this case there has been a particular reality (this planet or this text) and the abstract, generalising concept. Weaving like this between knowledge processes deepens learners' cognitive capacities. Vygotsky conceives this as a movement between the world of everyday or spontaneous knowledge and the world of systematic academic concepts (Vygotsky 1934 (1986)). Piaget conceives this as a transition during a child's intellectual development from concrete and abstract thinking (Piaget 1923 (2002)). There will be more about this in Chapter 14.

'*Conceptualising with theory*' means making generalisations by putting concepts together into interpretative frameworks. This is how learners build cognitive models or knowledge representations. Experts in a subject domain typically organise knowledge into schemas and make sense of new information through processes of pattern recognition. Such knowledge representations are useful tools for understanding, knowledge-making and knowledge communication (Bransford, Brown & Cocking 2000). Theories can connect concepts in a number of different ways – in a conclusion that makes a generalising statement, in the definition of a term in relation to other terms (as a subset of a parent term, or by distinction with sibling terms) or in a diagram or concept map, for instance. This knowledge process sits within a tradition of didactic pedagogy that focuses on teaching through explicit or direct instruction, starting with generalisations and requiring that students apply them, and teaching that privileges theory as the conceptual essence of a discipline (see Chapter 4). It also reaches beyond didactic pedagogy when, instead of telling learners the theory then testing to see whether they can remember or apply it, students are asked to help build the theory for themselves. A conceptual approach to literacies pedagogy involves the introduction of an explicit, abstract, conceptual framework of meta-representations in order to describe the underlying structures of meaning. This will include not only written texts, but multimodal texts such as the navigation paths of the internet, or the design of videos, or the forms of interaction shaped by physical spaces. Chapters 9 to 13 of this book introduce the Multiliteracies conceptual framework for describing multimodal meaning.

Analytical literacies learning

'*Analysing functionally*' encompasses processes of reasoning, drawing inferential and deductive conclusions, establishing functional relations (such as between cause and effect) and analysing logical connections. Learners develop chains of reasoning and explain patterns in knowledge and experience. In the case of literacies learning, students learn to explain the ways in which texts work to convey meaning, or the way their design elements function to create a whole, meaningful representation. This is one of the main emphases of functional literacy, to be analysed in detail in Chapter 6.

'*Analysing critically*' suggests evaluation of the perspectives, interests and motives of those involved in knowledge-making, cultural creation or communication. By this means, learners interrogate the interests behind a meaning or an action. This requires interpretation of the social and cultural context of an expression of meaning or a piece of knowledge. This is the primary focus of the critical literacy paradigm that we explore in Chapter 7. One key aspect of analysing critically is to reflect metacognitively on the influence of one's own perspectives and processes of thinking. Thinking is also more efficient and effective when accompanied by the process of metacognition or monitoring and reflecting upon one's own thinking – an integral part of which is weaving between the new knowledge one encounters in the other knowledge processes and self-reflection about one's own knowledge background and thinking processes (Bransford, Brown & Cocking 2000).

Applied literacies learning

'*Applying appropriately*' entails the application of knowledge and understandings in predictable or 'correct' ways. To take a literacies example that sits within the pedagogical tradition of functional literacy, a student might write a science report or a narrative in a way that shows they have mastered report or story genre. Applying appropriately involves taking knowledge or text type back to realistic situations of application in the real world or the simulated spaces of education as if you were a scientist, or a short story writer. Such an approach to literacies builds on traditions of literacy teaching and learning that emphasise communicative practice. It draws upon a tradition of **applied learning**, or learning by doing, in which learning occurs through a process of transfer of generalisable knowledge to practical settings, weaving between the conceptual and the applied. Functional literacy pedagogy (Chapter 6) places a very strong emphasis on appropriate application.

Applied learning: by using or creating things – texts, objects or social arrangements

'*Applying creatively*' suggests a more innovative application of knowledge. For instance, in the terms of functional literacy pedagogy, it might involve recombining design elements to create a hybrid text, or the construction of a multimodal text, or ironical play upon a canonical text type. It may involve the transfer of knowledge or text type from its current or predictable setting to a distant context, subject matter or setting. Or it may bring to bear the learner's interests, experiences and aspirations in such a way that the application is uniquely or distinctively 'voiced'. Applying creatively is a process of making the world anew with fresh forms of action and perception. This is commonly an aspiration of critical pedagogy (Chapter 7).

The knowledge processes as a teaching and learning repertoire

By reframing and building upon the foundational traditions in pedagogy, the knowledge processes are intended both to align with and to extend our experiences as learners and professional experiences as teachers. They describe a repertoire of 'epistemic moves', or things students can do to know. Our purpose in articulating them in this way is to suggest that teaching can be made more powerfully effective when teachers and learners have an explicit and deliberate framework for naming the range of epistemic moves they are making. Explicit naming may suggest to teachers that they frame their pedagogical repertoires in purposeful ways and justify the range of activity types they use in order to meet particular teaching and learning goals.

In this conception, pedagogy is a careful process of choosing a suitable mix of ways of knowing and purposeful weaving between these different kinds of knowing. Education is a process of broadening learners' capacities to make knowledge for different disciplines and different purposes. Our aim here is not to supply a formulaic sequence of steps for pedagogical action, but to expand both teacher and learner repertoires of knowledge-making actions. In this view, pedagogy is the design of knowledge action sequences in ways that suit different academic and social domains: choosing activity types, sequencing activities, transitioning from one activity type to another and determining the outcomes of these activities. In the everyday practicalities of pedagogy, talking about the sequencing of knowledge processes becomes a way for the teacher or learner to say explicitly, 'Now I am using this particular way to know, and now I am using that other way, and here is the reason why I did this, then that.' This is also a way of identifying the range of knowledge outcomes that the learners have demonstrated. The teacher thus can show an alignment between instructional inputs and learner outcomes.

By indicating and documenting the epistemic moves they make, teachers may also realise in retrospect that they have been unreflectively caught in a rut, using a narrow range of knowledge processes or a mix and sequence of knowledge processes that do not in practice align with the stated goals of learning. It is useful to be able to unpack the range of possible knowledge processes in order to decide upon and justify what is appropriate for a subject or a learner, to track learner inputs and outputs, and to broaden the pedagogical repertoires of teachers and the knowledge-making capacities of learners. If teachers and learners use a broader range of knowledge processes, they may find that powerful learning arises as they weave between a more varied mix of knowledge processes in a carefully planned way. They might also consciously select the range and sequence of knowledge processes that is most appropriate to a discipline area, a topic, a school context, or a learner or group of learners.

See literacies.com Learning Modules

See literacies.com #edtech Literacies Applications

Summary

These, then, are the knowledge processes as a series of pedagogical principles.

Experiencing:

- Human cognition is situated.
- It is contextual.
- Meanings are grounded in the real world of patterns of experience, action and subjective interest.
- One key pedagogical weaving is between school learning and the practical out-of-school experiences of learners.
- Another is between familiar and unfamiliar texts and experiences. These kinds of cross-connections between school and the rest of life Cazden calls 'cultural weavings' (Cazden 2006).

Conceptualising:

- Specialised, disciplinary knowledges are based on finely tuned distinctions of concept and theory, typical of those developed by expert communities of practice.
- Conceptualising is not merely a matter of teacherly or textbook telling from the texts of legacy academic disciplines, but a knowledge process in which the learners become active conceptualisers, making the tacit explicit and generalising from the particular.
- In the case of literacies teaching and learning, conceptualising involves the development of metarepresentations (or representations of representations) to describe 'design elements'.

Analysing:

- Powerful learning also entails a certain kind of analytical capacity.
- 'Analytical' can mean two things in a pedagogical context – it can describe analysing functions or being evaluative with respect to human purposes and motivations.
- In the case of literacies pedagogy, this involves analysing text functions and critically interrogating the interests of participants in the communication process.

Applying:

- Applying entails the appropriate and creative application of knowledge and understandings to the complex diversity of real-world situations.
- It involves production capacities with the design elements for a wide variety of different text types and communication purposes.
- In the case of literacies, this means making texts and putting them to use in communicative action.

Knowledge processes

experiencing the known

1. Describe one striking moment of learning in your life (in school or out of school) that illustrates each of the knowledge processes.

analysing functionally

2. Take a chapter of a textbook or a unit of work created by a teacher. 'Parse' or 'mark up' the learning activities according to the 'knowledge processes' presented in this chapter.

analysing critically

3. What biases or limitations would you identify in terms of the range and sequence of knowledge processes in this unit of work? What recommendations would you make?

applying creatively

4. Using the Learning by Design 'placemat' (see Figure 3.7), map out two or three lessons that use all eight knowledge processes. (The placemat is also available to download as a printable PDF from the Chapter 3 webpage of literacies.com.) Then consider the order in which might sequence these knowledge processes. What kind of weaving do you anticipate?

conceptualising with theory

5. Write a theory of learning in terms a parent might understand, using the concept of 'knowledge processes' introduced in this chapter.

CHAPTER 4

Didactic literacy pedagogy

Overview

Pedagogy: A consciously designed sequence of learning activities

Comprehension: Understanding the meaning of written texts, as intended by the author

Literary canon: Written texts regarded as the best writing and highest cultural expressions of a society and its language – and because of this, worthy of appreciation through learning

Didactic literacy **pedagogy** was the founding approach to reading and writing when mass, compulsory, institutionalised education was first introduced in the 19th century. It is still an approach that is widely advocated publicly and applied in schools today. A didactic approach to literacy requires learning the rules of the ways in which sounds and letters correspond. It involves learning the formal rules of what is presented as the one, correct way to write. It is about **comprehension** of what authors are really supposed to mean. It is about learning to respect the high cultural texts of the **literary canon**. Its syllabi tell you what is to be learned. Its textbooks follow the syllabi. Teachers are expected to follow the textbooks. And, if they are to score well, students have to give the right answers when it comes to the test.

On the paradigms of literacies

In the remaining chapters of this part of the book, we look at the thinking that lies behind four major approaches to literacy, which we call 'didactic' (this chapter), 'authentic' (Chapter 5), 'functional' (Chapter 6) and 'critical' (Chapter 7). Of these, didactic literacy has been around in its current form since the beginning of modern times, a period that roughly stretches from the invention of the printing press in the 15th century. Later, in the 19th century, it became the basis for mass compulsory education. Authentic literacy, which takes a child-centred or naturalistic learning approach, has some old intellectual roots too – in the ideas of the 18th-century philosopher Jean-Jacques Rousseau, and later the educational theories and practices of 'progressive' early 20th-century educators, such as Maria Montessori and John Dewey. Both functional and critical approaches are to a large extent products of the second half of the 20th century.

Table 4.1: A timeline of literacies pedagogies

Approximate timing	Pedagogical paradigm	Some leaders
Since about 1500	Didactic pedagogy (Chapter 4)	Petrus Ramus
Since about 1900	Authentic pedagogy (Chapter 5)	John Dewey Maria Montessori
Since about 1975	Functional pedagogy (Chapter 6)	Michael Halliday
Since about 1975	Critical pedagogy (Chapter 7)	Paulo Freire Michael Apple

So there is a rough chronological logic to these chapters. However, we also have a methodological rationale behind the way we are introducing these ideas and practices. They map against the 'knowledge processes' that we introduced in the previous chapter.

We want to argue that there are aspects of each of these pedagogical traditions that we may want to keep, extend and strengthen. In fact, at various times in the process of literacies learning, we may find it necessary to make pedagogical choices that have their roots in each of these approaches.

See literacies.com A Tale of Two Classrooms (Kalantzis & Cope 1993: 262).

Education historian Larry Cuban quotes a 1914 report critical of the way high school reading and writing were taught in Buffalo, New York.

> It is composed largely of such work as copying, composing, and correcting short illustrative sentences, selecting single types from constructions from sentences frequently too easy for the pupil, completing elliptical sentences, memorizing terms and definitions, diagramming and parsing in a routine fashion (Cuban 1993: 29).

Table 4.2: The 'knowledge process' emphases of various literacies pedagogies

Literacies pedagogy	Main 'knowledge process' emphases
Didactic (Chapter 4)	*Experiencing the new:* reading literary texts of high cultural value
	Conceptualising by naming: learning grammatical terms, literary concepts
	Conceptualising with theory: learning the rules of phonics, spelling, grammar, literature appreciation
Authentic (Chapter 5)	*Experiencing the known:* exploring personal voice in writing, following interests in reading
Functional (Chapter 6)	*Analysing functionally:* a focus on how different kinds of texts serve different social purposes
	Applying appropriately: mastery of socially powerful genres of writing
Critical (Chapter 7)	*Experiencing the known:* developing personal identity and voice
	Analysing critically: working out the social agendas and biases of texts
	Applying creatively: designing texts, including innovative new media texts, that express students' identities, interests and perspectives

Since the beginning of mass, institutionalised education in the 19th century, literacy teaching has often been like this. **Didactic teaching** of this kind is to be found still in many of the classrooms around the world, even though teachers are expected to prepare learners for the complex realities of the 21st century.

Didactic teaching: Spelling out learning content explicitly, such as the facts and theories of a discipline, with the expectation that learners will memorise the content they are presented. This approach is often also called 'transmission pedagogy' or 'direct instruction'.

We are going to explore the dimensions of didactic literacy pedagogy – how it works and what it does – by making an analytical tour that takes us past some real examples. It is notoriously hard to see into the classrooms of the past, even the recent past. Historically, classrooms have been places where, after teachers have shut the door, the primarily oral discourse of teaching slips into the air, unrecorded. (This changes with the use of technologies for representation and communication that ubiquitously record e-learning interactions – something we will explore later in this book.)

One way we can get a glimpse into classrooms of the past is to look at the textbook materials teachers and students used. These were often written by teachers, or by teacher-trainers, professors and professional textbook writers who would want to suggest idealised ways of teaching. These texts tell us something about the content to be taught and the way the teachers were expected to speak to their students. So, to reconstruct the shape of teaching and learning in the didactic classroom, we are going to return to textbooks of the mid-20th century and tell the story of the literacy classroom that they reveal. Some of these textbooks are the ones we used when we were at school. Others we have since collected as teachers and literacy researchers.

We describe didactic literacy pedagogy in quite a degree of detail in this chapter, covering the range of literacy contents and lesson activity types because the details are themselves fascinating. Chapters 9 and 10, and the online resources that accompany them, will provide you with the theories of didactic literacy in the form of **phonics** and traditional **grammar**. In this chapter, we will illustrate the ecology of the didactic literacy classroom, the way the classroom is organised and what happens in it. Our aim will be to provide a graphic portrayal of the cultural values, habits and purposes of this kind of classroom community.

Phonics: The connections between the sounds of speech and the formation of words from the letters of the alphabet and punctuation

Grammar: The way in which words are connected to make meanings in sentences, including changes in word forms to indicate number or time and the ordering of words in sentences

We do not do this in order to simply dismiss didactic literacy pedagogy as old-fashioned. In the first instance, we just want to understand it. There are some aspects that may remain relevant today, in some community contexts if not others, for some learners if not others, and for some aspects of the process of learning literacies if not others. And once again, we are referring to literacies now in the plural – including not just a single approach, but a mix of different literacy pedagogies.

In fact, if we look at today's curriculum frameworks, we find many examples of literacy learning outcomes that suggest a didactic approach to pedagogy – see Table 4.3.

Table 4.3: Literacy learning outcomes suggesting didactic pedagogy in Australia and the United States

Australian Curriculum	US Common Core State Standards
• *Text structure and organisation:* Recognise that different types of punctuation, including full stops, question marks and exclamation marks, signal sentences that make statements, ask questions, express emotion or give commands (Year 1). • *Sound and letter knowledge:* Recognise most sound-letter matches, including silent letters, vowel/consonant digraphs and many less common sound-letter combinations (Year 2). • *Text structure and organisation:* Understand how the grammatical category of possessives is signalled through apostrophes and how to use apostrophes with common and proper nouns (Year 5).	• *Reading foundational skills – phonics and word recognition:* Know and apply grade-level phonics and word analysis skills in decoding words (Grades K–5). • *Reading informational text – integration of knowledge and ideas:* Trace and evaluate the argument and specific claims in a text, assessing whether the reasoning is sound and the evidence is relevant and sufficient to support the claims (Grade 7). • *Language – conventions of standard English:* Demonstrate command of the conventions of standard English grammar and usage when writing or speaking (Grades K–10).

(continued)

Table 4.3: Literacy learning outcomes suggesting didactic pedagogy in Australia and the United States (*continued*)

Australian Curriculum	US Common Core State Standards
• *Examining literature:* Identify, describe and discuss similarities and differences between texts, including those by the same author or illustrator, and evaluate characteristics that define an author's individual style (Year 6). • *Examining literature:* Identify and evaluate devices that create tone, e.g. humour, wordplay, innuendo and parody in poetry, humorous prose, drama or visual texts (Year 8). • *Examining literature:* Compare and evaluate how 'voice' as a literary device can be used in a range of different types of texts, such as poetry to evoke particular emotional responses (Year 10).	• *Language – vocabulary acquisition and use:* Acquire and use accurately general academic and domain-specific words and phrases, sufficient for reading, writing, speaking, and listening at the college and career readiness level; demonstrate independence in gathering vocabulary knowledge when considering a word or phrase important to comprehension or expression (Grades 9–10). • *Reading literature – key ideas and details:* Analyse how complex characters (e.g. those with multiple or conflicting motivations) develop over the course of a text, interact with other characters, and advance the plot or develop the theme (Grades 9–10). • *Reading literature – integration of knowledge and ideas:* Demonstrate knowledge of 18th-, 19th- and early-20th-century foundational works of American literature, including how two or more texts from the same period treat similar themes or topics (Grades 11–12).

For the purposes of comparison across this and the following three chapters, we analyse these paradigms, approaches or models of literacy pedagogy – didactic, authentic, functional and critical – across four dimensions (Table 4.4).

Table 4.4: A framework for analysing classroom learning ecologies and literacy pedagogy

Dimension 1: The **contents** of literacy knowledge	• Its subject matter, or what learners are meant to learn
Dimension 2: The **organisation** of literacy curriculum	• How the subject matter is arranged
Dimension 3: Learners **doing** literacy	• The ways in which learners are intended to learn to make meanings
Dimension 4: The **social relationships** of literacy learning	• The relationship of learners to literacies knowledge, learners to other learners and learners to teachers

The contents of literacy knowledge – traditional topics and approaches

The bell rings and the students begin to file into the classroom. Mrs Plato's desk is on a small, raised platform at the front of the class. Behind her is the blackboard. In front of her are four rows of desks, eight children sitting in each row.

Sophia is a good student, so she's sitting towards the back of the class. Mrs Plato has put the students whose attention tends to wander at the front of the class so she can keep a close eye on them.

You'll have to suspend your judgement about the kinds of students in Mrs Plato's class, because one minute she seems to be teaching younger children and in another she seems to be teaching older children. And the year? Probably in the 1950s, but it could be the 1920s or even the 2010s. Also, our Sophia is unbelievably wise. At times, she seems to know more about language than Mrs Plato and, as you'll see, Mrs Plato knows a lot.

'Good morning, children.'

'Good morning, Mrs Plato,' all the children respond in sing-song unison. The starting notes for the class are always the same; something like the chord that chimes when you start up a computer, thinks Sophia, who in addition to her other strangely insightful qualities seems to have come from a later era.

Synthetic phonics

'Now, children,' says Mrs Plato, 'we know that letters stand for sounds and words are made up of letters. This is how we read, by putting the sounds of letters together into words and words into sentences.

'We've learned the sounds of all the letters of the alphabet already, but now we're learning the sounds of some combinations of letters that are joined, *qu*, *th* and *wh*. Let's read through our word list for today.'

The children get back into their sing-song unison: 'smith, this, squint, that, quit, then, quick, this, squint, thick, with, think, with, then, thrush, thrift, whack, whip, think, broth, thrash, whiff, whim, when, smith, broth, whip, thrill, moth, thrift, whim, when, thing, quiz, cloth, whack, then, thrush, thrill, cloth, quilt, whiff, quiz, whack, whim, that, thing, cloth, quill, that, whiff, thank, whip, thin, thick, thrift, when, them, thump, quilt, them, quack, quill, whisk, thrush, smith, them, whip, thump, whisk, quit, quiz, quill, quack, whisk, quick, thank, moth, thrash, quit, thank, thin, thump, broth, thrill, quack, think, quick.'

Wow, what a pile of words, Sophia thinks to herself. They went past so fast. And I wonder what 'thrush' and 'whim' are? It doesn't matter, I suppose, as long as we know how the sounds come together into words.

Also, funny – when I listen to myself, the *th* in 'thing' sounds different from the *th* in 'that' and the *th* in 'cloth' … and I know we haven't got to longer words yet, but it's different again in 'clothing'.

Then, if I listen hard, I can hear the *h* in 'when' … or is it a silent letter? It's so hard to tell.

And another thing, when the boy from New Zealand says 'whisk', the *i* sounds to me like *oo* in 'look'. Poor thing, how is he ever going to learn to spell properly?

'Now, children,' says Mrs Plato, 'I want you all to learn these words for our spelling test tomorrow.'

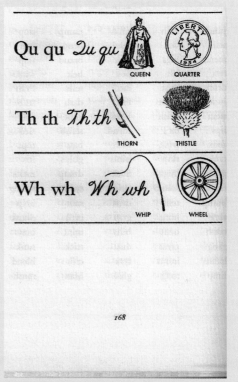

Figure 4.1 Some digraphs, or pairs of letters that represent a single phoneme (a unit of sound in spoken language)

Mrs Plato is using an approach to teaching rudimentary reading called '**synthetic phonics**'. This means that students start with the smallest components of spoken language, sounds or phonemes. They learn the letters or letter combinations that go with sounds, then put these sounds together into words. This is also sometimes called a bottom-up approach to learning to read. This approach starts with an emphasis on coding; that is, categorising words by their features, rather than their meanings. Reading starts with recognising spelling patterns in words, and later progresses to putting words in order to make meanings in sentences and paragraphs. Putting together sounds is a key to reading words (Chall 1967 (1983): 29–33).

Synthetic phonics: An approach to learning to read and write by starting with the sounds of letters, then putting them together into words (as contrasted with analytic phonics, where you start with the look of meaningful whole words, then take apart their sounds)

 See literacies.com Meyer Describes a Phonics Lesson (Meyer 2002).

A rigorous phonics and a complete set of spelling rules is complicated in all alphabetical languages, but especially so in a language like English with multiple roots (in Germanic and Latin languages), borrowings and exceptions. In fact, it is so complicated that it is hard to know how much phonics is just enough, and how much is too much (see Chapter 9). The more they want to teach, the more dependent teachers often find they become on highly structured textbooks and programs.

 See literacies.com Engelmann on 'Making up for What Amy Doesn't Know' (Engelmann 1992).

Traditional grammar

'Today, children, we are going to learn more about the parts of speech.'

Another day, another of Mrs Plato's lessons. The work is harder today, so Sophia must have been miraculously transported to another grade or year level.

'To be good writers we must study language in detail – the ways in which words and sentences are built, and the rules and customs that govern English.

'Imagine how difficult it would be to understand lessons in woodwork or domestic science if you did not know the meanings of words such as 'chisel' and 'omelette'. How could anyone discuss the working of a motor car unless he knew the names of the various parts and how they fit together?

'The English language is made up of many parts. There are rules to be obeyed and mistakes to be avoided. For parts of language, there are special names. Unless we are familiar with them, we cannot talk about the language intelligently; neither can anyone else explain clearly to us where we may have gone wrong. This is why we have to learn the names for the parts of language we need to know to be able to write and speak good English.'

Mrs Plato does not normally explain herself very much as she teaches. Didactic pedagogy is a practical thing. The teacher just sets the exercise and the children do the work. However, this is the beginning of the school year, and besides she is repeating what the foreword to the textbook says.

I suppose this makes sense, Sophia thinks to herself. To be able to do something well, you need to know a lot about it; you need to know how it works. But, funny thing – I've been using language since I was about one or two, and it has worked for me just fine even though I never knew how. But if this is what Mrs Plato wants us to learn, I want to get good marks.

'Now, children,' says Mrs Plato, 'look at the sentence I am writing on the board.'

Mrs Plato turns her back to the class and writes this sentence, underlining some of the words:

At the concert a very young girl sang two beautiful songs.

'This sentence is about a girl and her actions. The sentence is made up of naming words, action words, describing words and words that tell us about time and relationships. We will look at them all together first and then find out how they work to make meaning in this sentence.

'The word *very* tells how young she is; therefore it is an adverb.

'The word *young* describes the girl; therefore it is an adjective.

'The word *sang* tells what the girl did; therefore it is a verb. The verb shows that the girl did something to some other thing; therefore it is a transitive verb.

'The word *at* begins the phrase *at the concert* and governs *concert* in the objective case; therefore it is a preposition.'

See literacies.com Parsing a Sentence.

OK, Sophia thinks. So now I know the names of these parts of speech … but how does that help me use language?

As if she has read Sophia's thoughts, Mrs Plato goes on.

'Now, let me tell you an important rule about proper sentences. Proper sentences must always have a verb.

'If a person says *I am on my way home* we know perfectly well what he means, but if he suddenly says *On my way home* we wait to hear what else he is going to say. *I am on my way home* is a sentence, because it makes sense and has a complete meaning. It needs to have a verb, or a "doing word". *On my way home* is not a whole statement; it is called a phrase. It has no verb, which is why it is not a sentence.'

Hmm, thinks Sophia. What a strange word *am* is. It's not really about doing at all. Besides, there seems to be just as much doing in *on my way home* as *I am on my way home*.

Mrs Plato explains how people sometimes write sentences that are incorrect because their verbs are missing.

'Some journalists, trying to appear brisk and conversational, avoid long sentences in which several phrases are separated by commas. They put them between full stops as though they are sentences. For example: *The Government should act now. Before it is too late.*

'This is thoroughly bad English, and you should not imitate it in your own writing.

'Another kind of bad English also leaves out the verbs, because that is what we sometimes do in conversation. For example: *Quite a good idea.*'

See literacies.com Writing Correct Sentences.

That's funny, thinks Sophia. I see sentences without verbs everywhere, when a person wants to emphasise a point, or write like speaking, or in advertisements. But now I know that writing like this is not the right thing to do at school.

'Now, children,' says Mrs Plato, 'turn to page 9 and do the exercises. Change these incorrect sentences without verbs into proper sentences.'

> Silence falls over the class as the students take the ten sentences that their textbook tells them are incorrect and try to rewrite them correctly in their exercise books.

So here's another lesson of didactic literacy learning. It is important to know how to recognise and name the parts of sentences, such as nouns and adjectives, objective cases and transitive verbs. Parsing a sentence into its 'parts of speech' is just the beginning of the rules of grammar. And the more you get into it, the more complicated it becomes. Indeed, the complexity seems to be never-ending. The more rules you learn, the more exceptions come up. We will come back to the question of how language is structured in Chapter 10, with an overview of traditional grammar as well as a couple of other modern grammars: transformational and systemic-functional grammar. We will also suggest a new synthesis of what we call the 'design elements' of written language in Chapter 10.

But getting beyond the details of traditional grammar, details like those that Mrs Plato is teaching to her class, there's a more important underlying lesson, one which you need to learn quickly, and that is that there is only one way of writing correctly at school. Other ways are incorrect, even if in real life you encounter a lot of language use that would be incorrect in school. This is a deeper and more important rule than all the complicated details about the rules. It's the rule about the rules. In the end, obeying the rules is what is tested.

'Correct' usage

And why this emphasis on 'rules' and 'correctness'? We'll let Mrs Plato explain.

> Sophia is thinking of putting up her hand to ask, but Mrs Plato comes up with an answer that beats her to the question.
>
> 'You can tell an educated person by the way they use speech correctly,' says Mrs Plato. 'You see, listen to this.
>
> '*She remembered the actress who she had seen in a previous play.* That doesn't sound educated, does it? That's because it breaks a rule.
>
> 'You see, children, care must be taken to use *who* in the nominative case and *whom* in the objective case. *Who* should be *whom* because it is objective after *had seen.*
>
> 'Here's another sentence that breaks the rule:
>
> '*He is the boy whom I believe was chosen to represent his school.*
>
> 'In this sentence, *whom* should be *who*, as it is nominative to *was chosen.*'
>
> Gee, I never realised that, Sophia thinks to herself. I don't think I've ever used the word *whom*. I'd better try to learn this rule so I can sound educated like Mrs Plato.
>
> 'Now, children, fill in the gaps in the sentences in page 23 of your book. Remember the rule and put the right word in each sentence, *who* or *whom.*

'And now, another rule,' says Mrs Plato, relentless in her pursuit of potential error.

'I want to tell you about adjectives. Keep in mind that the comparative degree should be used when comparing two things only; thus we say *the taller of two girls. Little* refers either to size or to quantity, for example, *a little apple* and *a little news. Less* and *least* refer to quantity only: *less moisture* and *least trouble.* As *less* indicates quantity, we ought not to say: *There were less spectators here today. Fewer,* which indicates number, should be used. You see, you can tell that *less spectators* shows that you are less educated.'

See literacies.com Common Errors.

Funny, thinks Sophia, who often watches sport on television with her Dad. TV sports commentators must be less educated. I wonder how they got such good jobs?

So here's the next rule of didactic literacy pedagogy. Applying the rules is a marker of the kind of person you are. Powerful and better-educated people speak correctly. Other people speak incorrectly, and when you meet a new person you can tell pretty quickly the kind of person they are by the way they speak. 'I ain't got no …' is a double negative, and there's a rule about that. ('Never use a double negative.') It's colloquial, so it doesn't sound educated. However, as the linguist William Labov would point out, it's correct in 'Black English Vernacular' and, in that context, speaking the 'educated English' of school would be decidedly funny if meaning and social relations were what mattered most – more about this in Chapter 7 (Labov 1972).

Naming language structures

On now to our next lesson in Mrs Plato's class.

'Children, I'm going to put the present indicative first person singular verb on the board, and you tell me the past indicative first person singular and the past participle.'

Mrs Plato draws a neat table on the board.

'Tell me the past tense indicative of *see. I see* becomes, when it refers to something in the past … ?'

Nearly everyone in the class shoots up a hand, even the kids in the front row whose attention tends to stray. This is an easy question and it's still only the beginning of this lesson. Mrs Plato starts to fill out the table.

Present indicative first person singular	Past indicative first person singular	Past participle
see	saw	seen

What strange big names for such ordinary little words, Sophia thinks.

'Next, *sew*,' says Mrs Plato, looking for answers from the class, 'and *seek*, and *shake*.'

Present indicative first person singular	Past indicative first person singular	Past participle
see	saw	seen
sew	sewed	sewn, sewed
seek	sought	sought
shake	shook	shaken

See literacies.com Grade 9 Verbs.

That's strange, Sophia says to herself. I thought that word was spelt 'sow'. And how can there be two correct past participles for it? Also, I can't see a pattern here; these words seem all over the place.

She looks down the big list of past participles in her textbook.

'Next,' says Mrs Plato, 'we're moving on to perfect participles, a special kind of past participle. Listen to these two sentences:

'*The traveller filled his waterbags. He continued his journey.*

'We can use a perfect participle to combine these sentences.

'*Having filled his waterbags, the traveller continued his journey.*

'*Having filled* is called the perfect participle. It is formed by adding the past participle *filled* to the word *having*.'

What a funny thing to do, thinks Sophia. This idea sounded better before it was changed with a perfect participle.

'What are the perfect participles of these verbs? *Write … having written; hear … having heard; do … having done.*

'Now write down these sentences and then combine the two,' Mrs Plato tells the class. She slowly dictates the sentences to the students.

'*Marco Polo travelled across Asia. He reached Cathay.*

'*The Arab reached Mecca. He felt contented.*

See literacies.com Perfect Participles and Noun Objects.

'Having travelled across Asia, Marco Polo reached Cathay,' Sophia writes in her book.

She is sure she has all her answers right. But what peculiar things to say, she thinks.

She hands her answers to the teacher and, sure enough, when she gets her work back the next day, she's got them all right. Mrs Plato has written at the bottom of the page, 'Excellent work, Sophia.'

So here's the next underlying lesson of didactic literacy pedagogy. It's a game of naming the parts of language by learning and applying technical definitions. You can work out the kind of word by creating a generalisation in your mind about the function of the word. This learning is not so much about what you actually do with the word in real life. It's more about learning how to think technically and abstractly. Then, even if you end up creating some strange sentences that seem to float aimlessly in the world, at least you learn how applying the rules forms a logical system, connecting one kind of word with another. Of course, the meanings always matter, even for didactic literacy pedagogy, but at least one part of learning is to just think about technical names, rules and formal systems.

The challenge is that, the more you study grammar, the more labels you need to describe the extraordinary range of ways in which words, phrases and clauses are connected in sentences. You need to memorise more and more names, more and more rules, more and more examples and more and more exceptions. After a while, it becomes unclear whether learning more of the technical language about language actually helps you become a better writer and reader. The question then is: how much is just enough and not taking up too much time?

Extending vocabulary

'Next, children …' Mrs Plato says loudly, because the class seems to be getting restless, 'we're going to look at the meanings of words.

'There are all kinds of people in the world. Some are pleasant and some are unpleasant but all too often we use only two words in describing them: *nice* and *nasty*. This is a pity, for there are many, many words that we could use instead to help us describe what they look like, how they behave, and so on.'

Sophia hopes Mrs Plato thinks she is nice. Surely Mrs Plato must think children who have to sit in the front rows are nasty, given the way they misbehave when their attention wanders.

'Now, children, turn to page 23 of your books and choose a suitable adjective from those given in the left-hand column to suit the people mentioned in the right-hand column. Write them out like this: *a welcome caller*. No adjective may be used twice.'

graceful	*visitor*
haughty	*prince*
generous	*villain*
sinister	*dancer*
handsome	*princess*

See literacies.com People Vocabulary.

Sophia is a bit puzzled. She knows there can be only one right answer. This is an important lesson about doing English she has already learned, and learned well. In her imagination, she thinks of movies she's seen, or imagines scenes in movies that may be made with a graceful visitor, a graceful prince and yes, of course, a graceful villain.

But I wonder what Mrs Plato means me to answer? she wonders. The best way to tackle this question is to work out the connections most likely made by a person like Mrs Plato.

I can imagine a haughty dancer, she thinks. But Mrs Plato would probably think a dancer to be graceful, so I'll start by crossing off *graceful* and *dancer* …

Here we've reached the next lesson of literacy. There can be only one best meaning for things, and this is what the teacher or the textbook writer would think, rather than allow the range of possibilities that you might imagine as a reader.

Reading comprehension

'Next, children, comprehension. Turn to page 107 and read this week's passage, "Mother Kangaroo and her Joey". Let's read it as a whole class.'

The students know what this means. One after the other reads a sentence at a time, starting from the front of the class and moving back. A student stumbles over a word.

'Now sound out the letters, one letter at a time,' says Mrs Plato. 'Remember, writing is just the sounds of words spelt out on the page.'

When the reading has finished, Mrs Plato tells the students to answer the comprehension questions. In fact, Sophia can't quite remember what the passage said because there were so many interruptions as one student and then another stumbled over a word that needed to be sounded out. So she quickly reads the passage again.

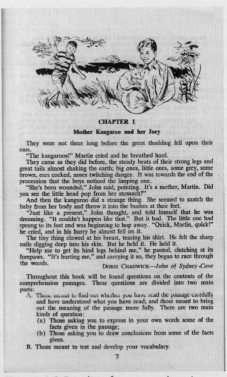

Figure 4.2 Reading for comprehension

She starts answering the questions, which are mostly quite easy, until she reaches question 7.

7. John thought he was dreaming because:
    a. He heard the noise made by the animals.
    b. The mother seemed to throw the baby at him.
    c. The kangaroo had been wounded.
    d. The little kangaroo ran towards him.

See literacies.com A Comprehension Exercise.

Actually, thinks Sophia, there could be some truth in all of these statements. John could easily have been dreaming because the little kangaroo ran towards him. (Sophia knows that kangaroos mostly run away from you.) Or the noise may have seemed dreamlike to John. Or the kangaroo's wounds may have scared John to the point where he thought he was in a dream.

But I think the answer should be (b) because the word *throw* comes near the word *dreaming* in the text. Actually, I don't quite get this, because John could hardly think he was dreaming in the middle of all that noisy fuss. Sophia is uncertain.

This raises some issues about the notion of truth in text that underlies didactic pedagogy. Texts can only be about one thing, and that is what the author meant them to be about. As we can't ask the author what they really meant, we have to guess what they must have really meant. Multiple choice questions leave no room for interpretation, but that's the easiest way to calculate a score to represent a student's reading ability. However, all meaning is in the interpretation, a relationship between an author's text and readers with a range of different perspectives that may lead them to see different things in the text. And, of course, authors can often mean more than one thing in their texts. Getting the meaning of the text right is not so simple.

Reading fluency

'Open your Helen and John reader,' Mrs Plato tells the class next. 'Let's go around the room again, one child reading a sentence at a time.'

Mrs Plato starts with those troublesome students in the front row.

Student 1: 'Helen and John spent happy days playing in the rock pools, paddling in the waves, and building sand castles.'

Student 2: 'Sometimes they sat on bright rugs, while mother and father told them stories.'

See literacies.com A Third Grade Reader.

Then, sentence by sentence, student by student, the story heads around the class. After about the fourth or fifth student, the change of voice and faltering reading of some students mean that the troublesome students' attention has wavered and they are beginning to shuffle. These are the ones who don't relate to an idealised story of the comfortable-looking family of mother, father and the two children with their big car, because their families are not like that. They don't get to the beach much and some of the students, in fact, have never been to the beach. As for reading books to children on the beach, who would do that? For one of the children who's never been to the beach, the only place they have encountered books being read is at school.

18

Happy Days.

Helen and John spent happy days
playing in the rock pools,
paddling in the waves,
and building sand castles.

Sometimes they sat on bright rugs,
while mother and father told them stories.

Mother had a new book, " Story Time."
The children loved this book,
for they could read every story in it.

Helen liked
" The Little Black Pussy-cat " best,
and John " The Little Coal Truck."

Read the stories,
and see which one you like best.

Story Time.

Figure 4.3 Seaside story

Literature appreciation

'Be quiet, you children,' Mrs Plato insists.

'Now, listen carefully. We read stories in order to instil into your minds a love of literature that will last beyond schooldays and be an unfailing source of profit and delight. A child who has gained the habit of reading for the sake of the pleasure and the profit that it brings will continue his self-education after he has left school. The stories you are reading will afford a compendium of useful knowledge as well as a treasury of beautiful thoughts. I want you to learn to appreciate what is meant by an author's style. Such appreciation, accompanied by the judicious imitation of good models, should lead to an improvement in your own methods of composition.'

Mrs Plato didn't often explain the purposes behind what was happening in the classroom, but these were the sentiments expressed in the introduction to the school reader that Sophia and her classmates were reading from.

 See literacies.com A School Reader.

Here we encounter yet another aspect of didactic literacy pedagogy: the idea of reading good books for the value of literature. As students get older, they will start to read great books in order to appreciate the literary canon.

This is an old idea, expressed in the 19th century in the words of Matthew Arnold as 'learning the best that has been thought and said' (Arnold 1869). In the late 20th century, Yale University English literature professor Harold Bloom became one of the promoters of what he calls 'The Western Canon'. For Bloom, the canon consists of those texts that are 'authoritative in our culture'. He selects canonical authors and their texts 'both for their sublimity and their representative nature. ... One breaks into the canon only by aesthetic strength: mastery of figurative language, originality, cognitive power, knowledge, exuberance of diction.' For Bloom, nobody stands ahead of Shakespeare in the Western literary canon. As for the cultural products of the present day:

> Sometimes I try to visualize Dr Johnson or George Eliot confronting MTV Rap or experiencing Virtual Reality and I find myself heartened by what I believe would be their ironical, strong refusal of such irrational entertainments (Bloom 1994, 1–2, 29, 517).

 See literacies.com Matthew Arnold on Learning High Culture (Arnold 1869). Bloom on the Western Canon (Bloom 1994.

Others have expressed regret about what they perceive to be the decline of reading traditional literature in the electronic age, given the competition for people's attention and time presented by the new media. E. D. Hirsch, a professor of English at the University of Virginia, is one of these people. He promotes a traditional vision of the cultural and literary canon for schools. 'Only by piling up specific, communally shared information can children learn to participate in complex and cooperative activities with other members of their community,' he says. He contrasts his vision with the multicultural **curriculum** in which different students learn different things that are supposedly relevant to them. Hirsch advocates an agenda for teaching that he calls 'cultural literacy which involves all students grasping the common, core culture of a nation'.

Curriculum: A tying together of the micro-sequences of pedagogy into larger frameworks of courses, subjects and disciplines

> For nation builders, fixing the vocabulary of a national culture is analogous to fixing a standard grammar, spelling and pronunciation. ... [N]ational culture ... transcends

dialect, region, and social class. ... The traditional materials of national culture can be learned by all citizens only if the materials are taught in a nation's schools (Hirsch 1988).

See literacies.com Reading in an Electronic Age (Birkerts 1994).
Hirsch on Cultural Literacy (Hirsch 1988).

In this aspect of didactic literacy pedagogy, students are expected to read things that are good for them – well-written stories for young learners, which lead them into appreciating the literary classics as they become older learners. The broadcast media are not literature. Popular cultural practices, such as playing video games, are not literature. The internet is not literature. Multicultural writings, relevant to the lives of varied groups of students, are not literature. Literature consists of 'the greats' and we can forge a shared, common culture if we all read the same things and appreciate their greatness. This is literacy in the unambiguously singular; a body of canonical texts, at least some of which everyone should read if they are to have a shared experience of the high culture of the nation or language.

Back in Mrs Plato's class, she wants to teach her pupils some of the literary devices great writers use, and to contrast these with a few decidedly unliterary errors of expression and style that some writers make.

'A naval instructor who found one of his cadets completely entangled in a rope said to him, "Very pretty! Very pretty! All we want now is a little dab of sealing wax." What figure of speech was he using?'

Mrs Plato directed the class to the textbook in which this and a number of other examples had to be lined up with these items: sarcasm, high-flown English, double negative, spoonerism, redundancy, mixed metaphors.

See literacies.com Figures of Speech.

'These are examples of expression and names for things that are considered poor style. You'd never find such literary missteps in great writers.'

Sophia knows the game. Find the literary misstep in each sentence and give it a name.

Table 4.5: Mrs Plato's pedagogical choices (1)

Dimension 1: The contents of literacy knowledge	Its subject matter, or what learners are meant to learn
• Synthetic phonics	
• Traditional grammar	
• 'Correct' usage	
• Naming language structures	
• Extending vocabulary	
• Reading comprehension	
• Literature appreciation	

The organisation of literacy curriculum – following the syllabus, the textbook and the teacher

Delivering structured and sequenced knowledge

Mrs Plato is a diligent teacher. The Department of Education syllabus says to do this in week 1, to do that in week 2, to do something else in week 3. So she does. She is helped by the textbook, whose expert author has written it to fit in with the syllabus, chapter by chapter, week by week.

It is now week 3, or Chapter 3 of the textbook. The reading comprehension passage for this week is Aesop's fable 'The Sick Lion'. The grammar for this week is subject and predicate. And of course, there are spelling words for the week that the students can learn for the weekly spelling test.

Sophia looks at the table in the front of the book every now and then, looking ahead to future topics. Wow, I wonder what that means? That looks hard.

But she also knows that when you reach the end of the year and are looking back, the work you did months before always seems so easy. Isn't it odd how hard it seemed at the time? At the end of every term, there is a test so you can see how much you have learned or, in the case of those troublemakers in the front row, how some students haven't learned as much they should have.

 See literacies.com 'Enjoying English': Grade 5 Year Overview and Term 1 Test.

Arranging knowledge in this manner is a feature peculiar to modern, literate cultures and formally institutionalised pedagogies. The 16th-century French scholar Petrus Ramus has been credited as the inventor of the modern textbook, one of the most distinctive aspects of didactic pedagogy (Ong 1958). A century after Gutenberg's invention of the printing press, Ramus carried the cultural logic of the mechanical reproduction of the written word to its pedagogical conclusion. He produced detailed expositions of knowledge that shifted the centre of gravity of learning and knowledge away from the scholar-teacher and Socratic dialogue.

 See again literacies.com Socrates on the Forgetfulness that Comes with Writing (in Chapter 1), this time not only for what Socrates is saying but also for the way Socrates the teacher interacts with his students).

Ramus, unlike Socrates, directed learners towards the printed text, held in an identical copy by every student. His textbooks – running, remarkably, to some 1100 editions and spreading across much of the intellectual world of early modern

Europe – dealt with dialectic, logic, rhetoric (persuasive communication), grammar and mathematics.

In addition to the fact that they were mostly in Latin, the lingua franca of intellectual life across Renaissance Europe, the Ramus texts were profoundly classicist in their contents, looking back as they did to the ancient European past. They had no new knowledge in them. Rhetoric or dialectic (argument backwards and forwards), for example, were considered important because they were part of the cultural legacy of classical Greece and Rome. Ramus simply rearranged and reproduced the thoughts of classical authors. The learning of grammar was no more than learning the grammars of Latin and Greek. This, incidentally, continues in traditional English grammar, a grammar better suited to describe Latin and Classical Greek than a language like English, which relies for meaning more on word order than on Latin or Greek, and which has many more irregularities.

See literacies.com Kalantzis and Cope on Petrus Ramus.

However, the Ramus texts did not just look back. Their content may have been backward-looking, but their method was not. Never before had rhetoric and dialectic been formalised and laid out in didactic text on a page. In the societies to which the texts referred – societies that had existed 2000 years earlier – both disciplines had been learned through practice, rather than through a set of rules to be memorised. Now knowledge was associated with the silent, visual world of the printed page. The Ramus texts were very modern things, in other words, even though their subject matter referred way back into the past. One new feature of the textbook was to arrange knowledge into a formally ordered spatial page layout. This text, as found now in the printed textbook, required a peculiar economy in the way it represented knowledge.

See literacies.com Ong on Petrus Ramus (Ong 1958).

Applying objective thinking

A new logic was applied to the way information was arranged: a logic that proceeded, to use Ong's words, 'by cold-blooded definitions and divisions leading to still more definitions and more divisions, until every last particle of the subject had been dissected and disposed of' (Ong 1958: 134–5). There were numerous sections, divided into subsections and subsubsections; granules of knowledge ordered and marked by a multilayered structure of headings and subheadings. Teachable knowledge was thus set out in a systematic, logical unfolding, starting from the easier granules and moving on to the harder. The space on the page translated into units of time in the class timetable. Each granule of the printed text was a 'lesson' or several lessons, the one following the other until the program for the term or the year was finished. If the textbook in this pedagogical system became a key artefact in knowledge transmission, the teacher became a conduit for print knowledge, dutifully following its logic in the organisation of the classroom and the delivery of the curriculum.

'Finally, children,' says Mrs Plato in bringing the sequence of lessons to a close, 'let's see what you have learned. Turn to page 48 and take the term 2 test.'

After these many weeks of turning the pages lesson by lesson, and the chapters week by week, it was time to see how much the pupils had learned. Did they know their parts of speech? Could they form nouns from verbs or adjectives? Could they turn indirect into direct speech? After the test, the teacher read out the answers and the students added up their scores … as, in fact, they had been doing every week. In this way, learning can be boiled down to little numbers, laid out in a progress grid in the peculiar game of schooling.

See literacies.com Keeping Score.

Table 4.6: Mrs Plato's pedagogical choices (2)

Dimension 2: **The organisation of literacy curriculum**	**How the subject matter is arranged**
• Delivering structured and sequenced knowledge	
• Applying objective thinking	

Learners doing literacy – copying, repetition, memorisation and applying rules

Copying

'Now, children,' says Mrs Plato, 'I want to tell you that handwriting is an essential skill in written communication. Every individual needs the ability to write easily, legibly and rapidly to meet the demands of school, social or business activities. I want to help you develop *good* writing characterised by legibility and style. At the same time, training in writing must ever aim at useful speed.

'The best means of obtaining the necessary speed with legibility and style will be found in constant vigilance on the part of you, the pupil. I will never accept slovenliness and illegibility. Good handwriting is a mechanical skill gained by constant practice by the pupil and effective supervision by me, your teacher.'

See literacies.com Beginning Handwriting.

At the start, Mrs Plato has the students do 'printing'; that is, writing with letters that are not connected. Next comes 'running writing'.

'Sit erect but not rigid with feet apart and resting flat on the floor, the part of the legs below the knees being vertical; hips well back on the seat; shoulders level and parallel with the desk; chest forward but clear of the desk; head

> 30
>
> *Sunday   Monday   Tuesday*
>
> *Wednesday   Thursday*
>
> *Friday   Saturday   Sunday*
>
> *Spring   Summer   Autumn   Winter*
>
> | MARKS | |
> |---------|---------|
> | Student | Teacher |
> | | |

Figure 4.4 A cursive copybook

inclined slightly forward towards the paper but not turned sideways (the movement should be forward from the hips); eyes not less than a foot from the writing paper.'

Hmm, thinks Sophia. My favourite place for reading or drawing or writing is lying on the floor of my room at home, or sitting on the lounge in the living room.

The children shuffle a bit to try to get into the right position to begin their first cursive writing exercise. However, those children in the front row never seem to be able to sit still long enough to get their posture exactly right.

'Turn to page 8, children, and do the first exercise. Cursive writing has a slope and you need to get the slope right.'

Dot to dot, a hundred times, the class silently begins its journey into running writing.

See literacies.com Handwriting.

How boring is this? thinks Sophia. By the end of the page she is sick of it. She glances ahead in the book and admires the days of the week beautifully written on page 30. But she knows she won't be up to this page until she's copied all the lines on the other pages.

Here is the next underlying lesson of didactic pedagogy: you learn by copying, not just once, but many times, by repetition. The more you repeat the copying, the better you are likely to learn what you have copied.

Formulae and repetition

'Next, open your exercise books. We are going to write a composition.

'Now let me remind you, children, every composition has a *beginning*, a *middle* and an *ending*. The middle is by far the longest part, but the beginning and the ending are just as important as the middle, if not more important.

'The *beginning* should be brief. If your composition is about some kind of an outing, it is not necessary to write half a page on rising early, having breakfast, preparing the lunch basket or backing the car out of the garage. There is no reason why a composition about an outing, for instance, should not begin at the actual scene of the beach, park, zoo, harbour or wherever it may be. Similarly, the *ending* should finish the composition quickly, clearly and fittingly. This not only rounds off your story, but it can often add that "finishing touch" which makes the difference between an ordinary composition and a good one.

'The *middle* of the composition comprises the bulk of the story and may consist of three or four paragraphs. It should not contain anything that does not concern the particular story being told and should move on from one point to the next as each happens or is described.

'In order to avoid mistakes and to use the best words and phrases, each sentence should be carefully thought out before putting pen to paper. Try to avoid writing the first thing that enters your mind, but do not wait too long for ideas. Once you have begun, keep straight on until the story is ended. Do not make false starts by crossing out or ruling off and starting all over again. When you have finished a composition, read it right through and see how it sounds to you. Correct any mistakes in grammar or punctuation.

'Now, today's composition assignment is to have the title "What the World Will Be Like in a Hundred Years". Write this as a heading at the top of a new page in your composition exercise books.

'Of course, in writing about the future you're going to have to use the future tense a lot. Remember, the things in your composition will not *have* happened, nor *are* they happening; they *will* or *may* happen, *will be* happening or occurring, and so on.

'Here are the paragraphs you are to use:

1. More of everything – people, houses, shops, motor cars, factories, farms, dams, power plants, and so on.
2. Differences in fashion – dress, clothing, hairstyles, motor car design, building structures – wider roads – overhead pedestrian crossings and footpaths at the level of the first floor of high buildings in cities, etc.
3. New towns and industries in the country – new irrigation schemes based on new dams and canals – new hydro-electric schemes – more people in country and closer farming settlements.
4. Development and advancement of poorer countries and increasing trade and travel between the countries.
5. Things that may lead to war and disputes – things that could lead to peace and agreement – communications and talks, meetings and games – rich countries and poor – education, medicine, religions and beliefs.'

 See literacies.com Writing a Composition about the Future.

WRITING ABOUT THE FUTURE

Remember, things have not happen**ed**, nor **are** they happen**ing**; they **will** or **may** happen, **will be** happen**ing** or occur**ring**, and so on.

Figure 4.5 How the world of 2060 looked to Mrs Plato

Sophia tries to match Mrs Plato's advice about the beginning, middle and end of the composition to these paragraphs, but it doesn't seem to work. It would be possible to start or end with any of these paragraphs. Not to worry. Sophia starts writing: 'In the future there will be more of everything. There will be more people …'.

Compositions are about writing things 'in your own' words. Sophia is going to write what Mrs Plato wants, but will change the words here and there so it really is her own work.

Figure 4.5 (*continued*)

> 2. **What the World Will Be Like in a Hundred Years.**
>
> Paragraphs:
> 1. More of everything—people, houses, shops, motor cars, factories, farms, dams, power plants, and so on.
> 2. Differences in fashion—dress, clothing, hair styles, motor car design, building structures —wider roads—overhead pedestrian crossings and footpaths at level of first floor of high buildings in cities, etc.
> 3. New towns and industries in country—new irrigation schemes based on new dams and canals—new hydro-electric schemes—more people in country and closer farming settlement.
> 4. Development and advancement of countries to the north of Australia—New Guinea, Indonesia and Malaysia, China and India, Vietnam—Burma and Pakistan—the Philippines—Japan—increasing trade and travel between the countries.
> 5. Things which might lead to war and disputes—things which could lead to peace and agreement—communications and talks, meetings and games—rich countries and poor —education, medicine, religions and beliefs.

Figure 4.5 (*continued*)

So here's the next lesson of didactic pedagogy. Sometimes copying is the name of the game. But at other times didactic pedagogy means doing your own work, in your own words, while conforming to scaffolds of correct or good usage – repeating formulae, in other words.

Memory work

'Today is Friday, class, the day we have our weekly spelling test,' Mrs Plato announces.

Sophia has been trying to memorise the week's words each night. Last night, she asked her mother to test her and she got nearly all of them right.

'Ambiguous, a-m-b-i-g-u-o-u-s, ambiguous.'

And again, and again.

Now the test is on and Mrs Plato says, '*Ambiguous*. The sentence was ambiguous. *Ambiguous*.'

Sophia writes down the word; she's pretty sure she's got it right. Then amelioration, amenable, amethyst, anaesthesia, analogous, analyst, anonymous, antagonise, antithesis, apoplexy, apparel, apparition, arraign …

See literacies.com Senior Spelling.

Here is yet another lesson of didactic pedagogy: memory work. You have to make sure you can remember things. Spelling is a good example. You learn to spell by memorising lists of individual words.

See literacies.com My Spelling.

And you learn to spell by learning spelling rules.

'Listen to me say this word, children: custom, custom.

'You hear, this word has two syllables? And the pattern goes consonant-vowel-consonant-new syllable-vowel-consonant-vowel; you hear that?

'When a syllable has only one vowel and ends with a consonant, we say that it is a closed syllable. The vowel is usually not long and hard to hear,' Mrs Plato explains.

Sophia has been working hard at her spelling rules, and here is another one – they certainly are getting harder. Strange thing, though, she can hear the *u* more clearly than the *o*, and this new rule does not try to explain that, or how she is going to learn the spelling of this word when some children in the class from different countries seem to pronounce *u* like the *ar* in *car* and others like the *oo* in *look*.

See literacies.com Spelling Rules.
Rules, rules and more rules, all to be remembered.

'And now, today's grammar rule,' says Mrs Plato. 'Remember the rule: "Do not use a past participle for a past tense, or a past tense for a past participle." Turn to page 143 and correct the faulty sentences.

'Let's do the first one together.

'*He swum across the river.* Of course, this is incorrect.

'The correct form of the past tense is *swam. Swum* is the past participle. *He swam across the river* is correct.'

See literacies.com Grade 9 Verbs.

The students set to work correcting the faulty sentences in the list. Luckily, the textbook says they were faulty, so Sophia knows she has to change at least something in the sentence. Some of the sentences sound pretty OK – the way you hear people normally speak. Sophia has a secret rule of her own when she does these kinds of exercises. She asks herself, 'How would Mrs Plato say this?' as she says the sentence silently in a pretend version of Mrs Plato's sternest, teacherly voice.

Table 4.7: Mrs Plato's pedagogical choices (3)

Dimension 3: Learners doing literacy	The ways in which learners are intended to learn to make meanings
• Copying	
• Formulae and repetition	
• Memory work	

The social relationships of literacy learning – authority in language knowledge

Testing literacy

'Pick up your pens and start a new page in your exercise books. Write at the top of the page, "Dictation Test". Listen carefully as I read this passage to you one sentence at a time.

'"Aunt Jane likes to tell her young *relatives* about her visit to *foreign* lands. We are *interested* in each *adventure* and are *eager* to learn about those *distant continents*. We like to *imagine* that we are *travelling* with our aunt and are seeing those *strange* lands."

'Now turn to your textbook and correct your exercise by comparing it with the copy in the book. What score did you get out of 10?'

See literacies.com Dictation.

Sophia, excellent student as she is, loves counting up her score. Only nine out of 10 this time; *traveling* is wrong but she's sure she's seen it somewhere spelt with one *l*. But much better than many of the other children in the class, some of whom rarely get more than five or six right. Mrs Plato always has these dictation tests on Fridays, to cap off the week's spelling work.

'Next, students, we're going to punctuate a letter. Have a look at the letter on page 176 of your textbook. Notice the arrangement and the punctuation.

'The first part is the writer's address. "Riverview", which is the name of his house, begins halfway across the page. The second line of the address begins slightly to the right under the first, and the third line begins slightly to the right under the second. The words in these lines all begin with capital letters. The address must always be carefully punctuated. Notice that inverted commas are placed around the name of the house and that a comma is then placed at the end of the line. A full stop or period is placed after 'st' because it is the shortened form of 'street'. A comma is always placed at the end of this line. A full stop is placed after the name of the town, because it is the end of the address. In the date, a comma is placed after the name of the month and a full stop is placed after the year; that is, at the end of the date.'

See literacies.com Punctuating a Letter.

Sophia has seen many letters that do punctuation differently, sent by relatives in different parts of the world, or letters with advertising material that have come through the mail, or letters that have been printed out from a computer. She's also heard some people call a 'full stop' a 'period'. Still, she is going to get this exercise right, so she copies the punctuation pattern into a letter of her own.

'And now, children, for our last exercise for today, let's match sentences. In the first panel below, you'll find 10 sentences, each of which means the same thing as one of the 10 sentences in the second panel. Write each sentence from the first panel, then write below it the sentence from the second panel that has the same meaning.'

See literacies.com Matching Sentences.

Sophia has always enjoyed this kind of work, particularly at the end of a big school day during which she has had to remember so many things and has had to put her mind to so many difficult rules. She slowly and carefully copies the sentences, one by one. What a sense of satisfaction she feels at the end – a whole two-and-a-half pages of her neatest writing. When Mrs Plato collects the books, she writes on this page 'Excellent work, Sophia.'

Valuing conformity

Historian Harvey Graff describes the role of literacy teaching in the establishment of a new, mass, institutionalised schooling system in the 19th century. Literacy, he says, was used as an instrument to inculcate 'punctuality, respect, discipline, subordination; … a medium for tutelage in values and morality'. Literacy helped shape 'a controllable, docile and respectful workforce, willing and able to follow orders' (Graff 1979: 262). Mass education using didactic literacy pedagogy was, in other words, an important cultural tool in the construction of modern society (Graff 1987).

See literacies.com Graff on Literacy Learning in the Nineteenth Century (Graff 1979).

In these ways, the modern social order is realised through the spatial order of the classroom (students facing the teacher and not each other), the temporal order of the school timetable (this time strictly for literacy learning, and other times for each of the other subjects), and the overall curriculum (taking one little literacy step after another, in preordained sequence).

Table 4.8: Mrs Plato's pedagogical choices (4)

Dimension 4: The social relationships of literacy learning	The relationship of learners to literacies knowledge, learners to other learners and learners to teachers
• Testing literacy	
• Valuing conformity	

See literacies.com Reading and Writing in Time and Space.

There is another aspect we would call epistemological – that is, concerned with ways of knowing. There are objective language facts. These can be described either as rules to be learned or, in the case of things not susceptible to rules (such as irregular spellings, grammar or the meanings of **vocabulary**), learned by memorisation. There is one correct, standard English of schooling, which happens to be closer to the vernacular of wealthier and more educated people and native speakers than the dialects of poorer and less educated people, immigrants and indigenous peoples.

> **Vocabulary:** A person's or a culture's stock of words and their meanings

At the heart of didactic literacy pedagogy is the printed textbook: formalistic, authoritative, non-negotiable. The textbook is not just a metaphor for a system of social order in which the written text assumed a place of unprecedented importance. It is a crucial medium for socialising children into modern society. Didactic pedagogy represents an enormous break from the whole of human history to this point, in which, with the occasional and partial exception of literate elites, the majority of the population functioned mostly by interacting with each other using more fluid, inter-subjective, oral texts. Before compulsory schooling, socialisation for the majority of the population occurred only informally during the course of growing up in communities. Didactic pedagogy, in other words, has a very particular, and quintessentially modern, rhyme and reason. It inducts masses of young people into a new social order, making them into the kinds of people needed in this social order. Indeed, it changes the world.

In the 21st century, didactic pedagogy is still going strong – in some schools, in the practices of some teachers, and for some groups of students. No longer does it enjoy the unrivalled dominance it did in the first century or more of mass, institutionalised education, but it is still a very powerful cultural force. Indeed, since the closing decades of the 20th century we have been through a very public reactionary (using this word literally rather than pejoratively) phase in which vocal advocates have argued for a return to 'back to basics'.

For instance, explicit instruction and direct instruction approaches have been advocated, particularly for 'at risk' students. Didactic pedagogies are alive and well in some forms of religious teaching, such as Koranic learning. These contemporary practices place the teacher firmly and authoritatively at the centre of the 'instructional' process, as a direct counterpoint to the more student-centred or authentic pedagogies we describe in the next chapter. These approaches have also come in for considerable criticism in what have been called the 'literacy wars' (Schoenfeld & Pearson 2009; Snyder 2008).

See literacies.com Goeke on Explicit Instruction (Goeke 2009).
Carnine et al. on Direct Instruction (Carnine, Silbert, Kame'enui, Tarver & Jungjohann 2006).
Rosowsky on Koranic Literacy (Rosowsky 2005).

And to take another series of 'wars' – the so-called 'culture wars' – the concept of a canon has come to prominence again, particularly in debates about the objectives of education. Starting in the last decades of the 20th century, there were the pronouncements of Ronald Reagan's Secretary of Education, William Bennett, about what he supposed to be the growing neglect of 'our' cultural legacy (Bennett 1984). Diane Ravitch and Chester Finn rhetorically asked what it was of the Western tradition, substantively, that students had learned by the time they left school (Ravitch & Finn 1988). Allan Bloom wrote *The Closing of the American Mind*, a best-seller arguing that 'Great Books' and the classics were truer and more valuable than other texts (Bloom 1987). E. D. Hirsch wrote another best-seller, arguing that in order to acquire 'cultural literacy' all Americans needed to learn the culture represented by standard English (Hirsch 1988). In other countries, similar debates continue to rage.

See literacies.com Cope and Kalantzis on the Struggle for the Western Canon (Cope & Kalantzis 1997b).
Donnelly on Back to Basics (Donnelly 2008).

Larry Cuban's more sanguine analysis, in his sweeping historical overview of classroom practices in the United States over the past century, is that American schools have changed less in the way they have operated pedagogically in that period than either enthusiastic progressivists, who support authentic pedagogy, or the 'back-to-basics' prophets of doom would like to have us believe (Cuban 1993: 2). If often only in a watered-down form, didactic pedagogy lives on. We can only conclude from this that, unlike the stage-coach, which was irretrievably consigned to the dustbin of history by the railway, didactic curriculum contains some workable and enduring insights into the nature of modern life and the functions of mass, institutionalised schooling as an instrument of socialisation.

Exploring connections between the 'knowledge processes' and didactic pedagogy

What can we learn from didactic pedagogy? Often, in the past and still today, didactic pedagogy has plainly worked. Students have learned things, even if some educators might want to criticise it from the perspectives of the other pedagogical traditions, such as the authentic, functional and critical literacy traditions that we outline in the following chapters. What, then, are the insights of didactic pedagogy that we might want to retain in a more rounded or holistic pedagogy?

One of the strengths of didactic pedagogy is its focus on what we call, in the Multiliteracies pedagogy, the 'knowledge processes' of conceptualising. Such a focus often involves explicit instruction, unveiling the academic schemas that are the backbone of a discipline – its concepts and their meaning, factual instances that illustrate the concepts, the characteristics of these concepts, and the relations between concepts. In these ways, 'conceptualising' connects with the old traditions of didactic pedagogy, including its more modern variants, such as 'direct instruction'. Such learning environments are regarded as academic knowledge-centred, rather than student-centred, learning environments. But there remains a place for structured academic knowledge, and this may not be an objective that is necessarily at odds with a balanced focus on the learner.

Typically in didactic pedagogies, the work is highly individualised and knowledge is regarded as principally cognitive – the stuff in one's head, such as the things that a student can absorb and retain in memory and reasoning that will generate correct answers. The orientation of such teaching is often 'skill and drill', to use a popular caricature or, to be derogatory, 'drill and kill'. Behaviourist psychology accounts for the acquisition of academic concepts and facts in didactic teaching with its theory of stimulus–response or reward–punishment. Behaviourist educators develop curricula that are carefully sequenced, with one-concept-at-a-time progress towards 'mastery' of a content or discipline domain. When there is little immediate motivation in the knowledge itself, other motivations of reward and punishment are established in the form, for instance, of teacher responses in question and answer dialogue ('no, that's not right', or 'well done!') or test scores ('room for improvement' or 'great score!'). These are called extrinsic rather than intrinsic motivators.

Despite these well-known criticisms of didactic pedagogy, those advocating this primarily conceptual approach still frequently take aim at the proponents of experiential learning – the main emphasis of authentic pedagogy, which we will explore in the next chapter. The proponents on either side in this debate remain as vehement as ever. In a return to this discussion in the pages of a leading educational psychology journal, Kirschner and colleagues argue that novice learners should be provided with direct instructional guidance in the form of information that fully explains the concepts and procedures that learners are expected to learn. The authors draw upon cognitive science to make their argument, claiming that problem-based, experiential learning places an unrealistic load on short-term memory as the student deals with novel information. Committing facts, laws, principles and theories of a discipline to long-term memory, they argue, supports more enduring learning. They conclude that 'to achieve expertise in a domain, learners must acquire the necessary schemata or conceptual structures that allow them to meaningfully and efficiently interpret information and identify the problem structure' (Kirschner, Sweller & Clark 2006: 83).

To these arguments, we also need to add the cultural argument that immersive environments, such as those of experientially oriented, authentic pedagogies, often tend to favour students whose home cultures and sensibilities are closer to the culture of schooling. For students whose lifeworld experience is more distanced from the culture of schooled literacies, explicit teaching may at times be more effective. Add to this the case for efficiency – that it may at times be more efficient to spell out disciplinary concepts and theories than to have students reinvent the epistemic wheel, sifting through the mountain of facts and

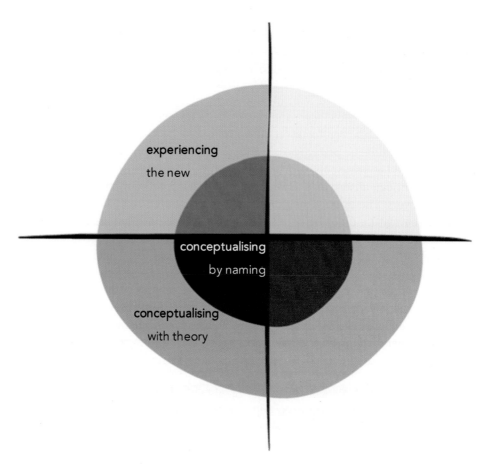

Figure 4.6 The emphases of didactic pedagogy

rediscovering disciplinary procedures. Finally, whereas the experiential learning knowledge processes that underpin authentic pedagogies favour inductive reasoning (from the particular to the general), conceptual learning values deductive reasoning (making sense of the particular because the general already makes sense). The latter is certainly a time-effective way to get a big-picture, overview sense of a body of knowledge.

Another knowledge process that we need to mention in a discussion of didactic literacy pedagogy is 'experiencing the new'. If didactic pedagogy neglects the texts of students everyday lives (home cultures, media texts, or popular culture, for instance – in other words, experiencing the known), it nevertheless does encourage students to experience new and often unfamiliar texts considered to be of high literary value – and by immersion in these texts, students will be inducted to the national culture.

So, for all its faults, there is still a place in our pedagogies for some of the insights, methods and activity types of didactic pedagogy. However, we would advocate a more balanced pedagogy that complements conceptual knowledge processes with other experiential, analytical and applied knowledge processes. For the seasoned teacher whose pedagogical practices have mainly been didactic, this may simply be a matter of expanding their pedagogical repertoire by bringing a broader range of activity types into their classroom.

See literacies.com Learning Modules

See literacies.com #edtech Literacies Applications

Summary

	Didactic literacy pedagogy
The contents of literacy knowledge	Formal rules, correct usage, reading for one meaning and appreciating the literary canon
The organisation of literacy curriculum	Following the syllabus, the textbook and the teacher
Learners doing literacy	Copying, repetition, memorisation and applying rules
The social relationships of literacy learning	Authority in language knowledge

Knowledge processes

conceptualising by naming

1. Start a wiki defining key concepts in the literacies pedagogy: important terms in the analysis of the ways in which communication and language work, and the ways in which they are learned. Maintain and extend this wiki as you work through this and the remaining chapters of this book.

experiencing the new

2. Locate a source from which you can get a concrete sense of the dynamics of didactic literacy pedagogy. Your source may be an old textbook or an interview with a retired teacher. Write your own analysis of the dimensions of didactic literacy around:
   a. the contents of literacy knowledge
   b. the organisation of literacy curriculum
   c. learners doing literacy
   d. the social relationships of literacy learning.

experiencing the known

3. Describe a learning moment in which you have experienced didactic pedagogy. How did that moment feel? In what ways was it an effective or ineffective learning moment?

applying appropriately

4. Over this and the following three chapters, you will engage with the theory and practice of four major approaches to literacy – didactic, authentic, functional and critical. Choose a literacy topic that might be taught in one lesson and that

exemplifies the didactic approach. Script hypothetical teacher–student talk in the course of this lesson.

analysing critically

5. Debate St Benedict's proposition about the ideal conditions of learning (see http:// newlearningonline.com/new-learning/chapter-8/st-benedict-on-the-teacher-and-the-taught).

analysing functionally

6. Discuss the learning conditions under which didactic pedagogy is most and least appropriate.

analysing critically

7. Consider a particularly appropriate application of didactic pedagogy (for a particular subject matter or learning context) and develop a lesson plan illustrating this application whose primary (though not necessarily exclusive) focus is didactic.

CHAPTER 5

Authentic literacy pedagogy

Overview

Authentic pedagogies were first formulated as a direct counterpoint to didactic pedagogies. They became well known and influential from the beginning of the 20th century, initially through the work of John Dewey in the United States and Maria Montessori in Italy. When it comes to reading and writing, authentic pedagogies promote natural growth, a continuation of processes of language learning that began with learning to speak. Authentic literacy pedagogy recommends immersion in personally meaningful reading and writing experiences, with a focus on processes of reading and writing rather than the formalities of rules and adherence to conventions. It calls its approach learner-centred and aims to provide space for self-expression. In terms of the Multiliteracies 'knowledge process' terminology, authentic pedagogies focus mainly on experiential knowledge processes.

It's a new school year and Vincent has a new teacher. From the minute he walks into Mr Joyce's classroom, Vincent knows things are going to be different. Last year, he had been in the same class as Sophia, Mrs Plato's class. Like Sophia, Vincent is a strangely wise student. And like Mrs Plato's class, Mr Joyce's class is strangely all-over-the-place. In one moment, it could be for a lower class or grade level; in another, a higher level. The first thing Vincent notices is the arrangement of the desks, clustered in little groups with the students facing each other. This is very different from the set-up in Mrs Plato's class.

'Welcome to a new school year,' says Mr Joyce cheerfully, 'and what a wonderful year I am sure it is going to be.'

The contents of literacy knowledge – authentic meanings

Analytic phonics

'Let's read,' says Mr Joyce excitedly. He hands every child a little Dick and Jane reader titled *We Play*.

He starts to read, and the children follow him in turning over the pages.
Oh, Father.
See funny Dick.
Dick can play.
Oh, Mother.
Oh, Father.
Jane can play.
Sally can play.
Oh, Father.
See Spot.
Funny, funny Spot.
Spot can play.
'Now, let's read together.'
The class reads the little story again.

Mr Joyce then pulls out his flash cards. On one side of these are written the words 'Mother', 'Father', 'Dick', 'Jane', 'Sally' and 'Spot'. On the other side are pictures of Mother, Father, Dick, Jane, Sally and Spot. He shows each picture and flips the corresponding card to show the word – which the whole class says in unison. Then again, but this time just the word. Then the class reads the story yet another time.

What a boring story, Vincent thinks. Not at all interesting or exciting like *The Three Little Pigs* or *Little Red Riding Hood*.

And what a silly way to speak. I've never heard anyone speak this way about playing. Besides, my family doesn't look like Dick and Jane's. They seem like they are from a movie or something.

If synthetic phonics puts together sounds to make words, **analytic phonics** does things the other way around. It starts with whole words. If and when children get to discuss phonics at all, it is to take whole words apart. It is often said that analytic phonics works from the top down, whereas synthetic phonics works from the bottom up. Or, to demonstrate the contrast in another way, analytic phonics has a meaning focus and synthetic phonics has a coding focus (Chall 1967 (1983)).

Analytic phonics: An approach to learning to read and write by starting with the look of meaningful whole words, then taking apart their sounds (as contrasted with synthetic phonics, where you start with the sounds of letters and then put them together into words)

Oh, Father.
See funny Dick.
Dick can play.

Figure 5.1 We play

To teach whole words, the Dick and Jane books juxtapose words with images so that the story can be told almost entirely from the pictures. They have lots of repetition of words. They support word-guessing; if you know some words in the sentence but not others, you can probably guess the ones you don't know from the overall pattern of the sentence. They are about ordinary, familiar things – or at least they are supposed to be – so that children can read into the words things that jell with their own life experiences.

The Dick and Jane readers date from the 1930s, when the 'look-say' approach to learning reading came into vogue in the United States and other countries. There is no explicit phonics in them, just authentic reading for meaning. The starting point is the meaning of whole words, linked together into simple sentences. There are no drills to be memorised or phonics rules to be learned.

The analytic phonics approach does contain some important insights about the nature of reading. When we read for meaning, we read whole words or even groups of words, not the sounds of letters. If we were to sound out every letter as we read, the reading process would be painfully slow and the sense hard, if not impossible, to capture. We become fluent readers, not by reading every word laboriously, but by going with the flow of language, skipping across its alphabetical details. This is why teachers in the past often told young readers not to move their lips during silent reading. And this is why, when you proofread a piece of writing, typos are often hard to notice.

According to the advocates of analytic phonics, it is only when students learn to make meanings from words – perhaps after they have learned at least 50 'sight words' – that they may be considered ready to start to take words apart and to analyse sounds and letter patterns. Even then, phonics is a limited stratagem, of use only to help decode words that a reader may have heard before but has not previously seen. If they have not heard the word before, sounding it out is unlikely to help their reading.

One version of analytic phonics is the '**whole language**' approach to reading developed by Kenneth Goodman. 'Instead of word attack skills,' he says, 'the program must be designed to build comprehension strategies ... Children learning to read should see words always as parts of larger, meaningful units' (Goodman 2005: 3). Phonics, according to Goodman, is just too complicated to teach because its rules are so many. Even if we learn a lot of rules, they never really apply consistently and neatly. We will look at just how complicated phonics is in Chapter 9 and its companion web material.

> **Whole language:** A focus on learning to read and write by starting with real meanings in whole texts, and incidentally addressing formalities and conventions, such as phonics, grammar and the literary devices

'Phonics is learned best in the course of learning to read and write, not as a prerequisite,' says Goodman (1993: 50). So, for example, rather than allow students to be hindered by spelling, we should let them use invented spellings, at least in first drafts. They may check their spellings later or learn spellings as they encounter these words in published texts. Reading is a process of making sense of meaning, not uttering the sounds of letters. Some phonics is fine, but it needs to be analytic rather than synthetic. Phonics should never be taken out of the meaning-context of real words and sentences. Language is not an abstraction; it is meaningful expression (Goodman 1993). As we will see later, protagonists on the other side of the battle lines in the 'reading wars' disagree.

Table 5.1: Synthetic and analytic phonics

Synthetic phonics	Analytic phonics
• Putting letters representing sounds together to make words	• Starting with whole words and analysing the sounds of their letters
• Phonics rules	• Repetition of sight words
• Correct spelling	• Invented spelling, to get the meaning across in first drafts
• A focus on the mechanics of reading and writing	• A focus on meaning in reading and writing

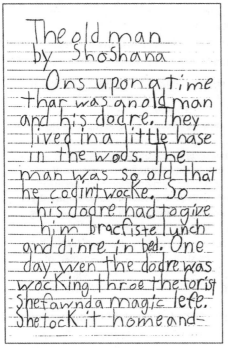
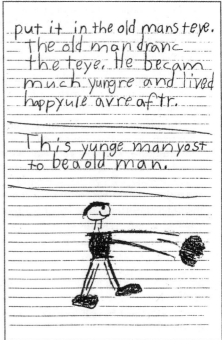

Figure 5.2 Invented spelling

Pen to page

Today the class is learning handwriting. But you'd never know it. Mr Joyce does not have the students copying out writing as Mrs Plato did, starting with up-and-down lines in their copybooks and eventually copying out that incredible sentence that has every letter of the alphabet: 'The quick brown fox jumps over the lazy dog.' Vincent will never forget that sentence. It was an odd thing to do and he wrote it so many times.

Mr Joyce has lots of things around the room so that learners can see and feel letters. He has boxes of letters you can touch and form into words. He has pictures around the classroom of animals with names that start with a particular letter and which have funnily curled themselves into the shape of that letter, such as a snake in the shape of a letter 's'.

See literacies.com Montessori on Handwriting (Montessori 1912 (1964)).

Mr Joyce has a drawing time every day, and with the drawing he always tells the kids to use words that say what the drawing is. Some kids' labels are very hard to read, Vincent thinks. But every now and then Mr Joyce says, 'That's lovely writing' or 'What's that letter, there? Let's make that letter the best we can.'

See literacies.com Graves on Handwriting (Graves 1994).

Process, conference or workshop writing

It's dreamily all-over-the-place, Mr Joyce's class. Sometimes it feels like a secondary class; sometimes it feels like a class for early literacy learners. Don't forget, like Sophia in our previous chapter, Vincent is a magically multi-aged student; at one moment in a class that seems to be for a lower grade or level, at the next moment in a higher-level class.

'Today, we're going to start our first writing for the new year,' says Mr Joyce. 'Now, in my class you get to choose your own topic. I want you to be writing about things you feel strongly about or that really mean something to you.'

Smart as he is, Vincent finds this hard. Mrs Plato never asked them to do that. Oh dear, he thinks, what am I going to write about today? What can I say about anything?

After quite a bit of agonising and some prodding from others, he decides to write about his holidays.

'It's going to take us a few weeks to write our stories,' says Mr Joyce, 'because in my class we use a process, conference or workshop writing approach. This means we are going to go through a number of steps in our writing. Step 1, we'll think about our ideas, do some research, collect some notes. Step 2, we'll write drafts. Step 3, we'll conference or talk about our drafts. And finally, in Step 4, we'll publish our finished work in a little book we'll make just for that one piece of writing.'

See literacies.com Parry and Hornsby on Conference Writing.

That sounds like a lot of work for one piece of writing, Vincent thinks to himself. Mrs Plato had us getting through our writing much faster than that.

Vincent and his classmates start working. The classroom becomes a noisy hum as they talk with each other.

'What are you going to write about?' Vincent asks the child on the other side of the little cluster of desks.

'Dunno,' he says.

Wasn't he one of the students Mrs Plato had put at the front of the class last year? Vincent wonders.

Mr Joyce is now wandering around the classroom, watching the children get started on their writing project. He has already noticed that the boy opposite Vincent is just staring out of the window.

'So what would you like to write about? Tell me something that's surprised you lately, or pleased you lately, or that you've enjoyed lately.'

'We won at the footy last week?' grunts the boy. His father has taken him to watch their local team play a home game.

'There you go; you can write about your team's exciting football victory,' suggests Mr Joyce, reframing what he said in words that sounded more like writing.

Meanwhile, Vincent's writing about his holidays is starting to take shape.

'On our holidays, we …'. He's made a little list of things he can remember: why his family went on holidays, who came along, where they went, how they travelled, how long they were away. He also tries to remember some of the interesting things that happened.

His first draft is pretty messy, but Mr Joyce says, 'Don't worry about that.'

The boy opposite has stopped again. He is stuck on a word.

'How do you spell "hooligan"?' he asks. Apparently there was some trouble at the game.

'Don't worry about that now. Just write the word down as you imagine it might be like for the moment,' says Mr Joyce. 'We don't want something like spelling to get in the way of the flow of your ideas for now. Also, don't worry too much about punctuation; we can also get that right later.'

Reread, revise, edit, proof, rewrite. First draft, second draft, final draft. This is a busy class indeed. All this time, Mr Joyce keeps walking around the room, chatting with students.

'How's the writing going?' 'What's the story about?' 'What are you going to say next?' 'Do you need any help?' He is full of questions. Mr Joyce calls this his 'roving conference'.

'Now children, we are going to have a peer conference,' Mr Joyce announces once the class has finished drafting. 'I want everyone at your table to read another student's writing and give them feedback. Use my IOU formula:

'I stands for *information* ('meaning'). Is there enough here to satisfy the reader? Is it specific, descriptive, interesting …?

'O stands for *organisation* ('structure'). Is there a well-sequenced development of ideas? A good 'lead' (opening)? An effective ending? Will readers get an impression of order unity? (coherence/logic).

'U stands for *use of conventions* ('surface features').

Words: wide and appropriate vocabulary? correct spelling?

Sentences: lively, varied, well-linked, punctuated, correct?

Paragraphs: well-developed, not tediously long, smoothly linked?'

 See literacies.com Dwyer on Process-Conference Writing.

Vincent finds himself reading about the hooligans at the football match; not a very interesting story for him, because he's never been to a football match. His family follow basketball. And he doesn't know how to spell 'hooligan', either. However, by this time the other boy has looked the word up in a dictionary and added it to his personal spelling list.

Meanwhile, Mr Joyce works his way around the class, holding a publishing conference with one student after another.

'Have you checked your information, spelling, punctuation and grammar?' he asks. 'Remember, the best way to do this is to read your writing aloud to yourself to see whether it reads nicely, and to look up the dictionary to check any words you're unsure of.'

The classroom hum gets louder and louder.

Then, on to the most fun aspect of process-conference writing, Vincent thinks: publishing. Everyone turns their writing into a little book, with a cardboard cover, nicely illustrated and stapled at the edge. It's been a few weeks of hard work, but worth it, Vincent thinks.

But what will we do next? he wonders. You always knew what was going to come next in Mrs Plato's class, because if you were just finishing Chapter 3, you could glance ahead to see what was in Chapter 4.

For today at least, his question is soon answered by Mr Joyce.

Self-directed reading

'Next thing, it's reading hour.'

In Mrs Plato's class, they'd all read the comprehension passage that began each chapter of their textbook. Or they'd all be reading the same little storybook, which was called the class reader. They'd even read together as a class, or listen as one student after another read out one sentence after another.

But Mr Joyce has a reading centre in one corner of his classroom. Here he has a whole range of books, ranging from easy to hard; not school readers, but the kinds of books you find in a children's bookstore.

Group by group, Mr Joyce asks the students to go over and choose a book. This is the first reading lesson of the year. After that, students get a new book whenever they have finished the previous book, depending on how long it has taken them to read it.

'It's up to you; I've grouped the books into easy, average and hard. Choose whichever type of book you would like to read. Also, choose the kind of story you enjoy or information topic you would like to read about.'

Every now and then, Mr Joyce asks a person to tell their group, or even the whole class, about a book they have particularly enjoyed.

See literacies.com Walshe on Individualised Reading and Writing.

Mr Joyce is practising an approach to schooling that emerged around the turn of the 20th century, an approach that we have called authentic pedagogy. It is also often called 'progressive pedagogy', but we have chosen the word 'authentic' because it captures the sense of naturalness and relevance with which this kind of pedagogy attempted to distinguish itself from didactic pedagogy. John Dewey in the United States was one of the path-breaking exponents of this new philosophy of curriculum. Although his ideas can be taken as typical of the whole movement, he was certainly not alone. Other educators, including Maria Montessori in Italy, were coming up with a broadly similar critique of didactic pedagogy.

Mr Joyce's reading and writing classroom is arranged in this spirit. Instead of abstract and formal concepts, instead of the discipline of learning the rules of correct usage, instead of having every student on the same page at the same time, the focus of this approach is on authentic meanings. Topics are chosen that really interest and engage the students and the learner is an active, creative, free writer, reader and thinker.

Active meaning-making

Just as much as didactic pedagogy was a product of its times and places, and in this sense a cultural product, authentic pedagogy was also a cultural product. From its beginnings, it reflected an emerging view of the sort of education appropriate for the modern society of the 20th century. At its heart was an ideology of change and progress. Dewey's *School and Society* opens with a chapter entitled 'The school and social progress', based on a lecture he first gave in 1899 and published in book form in 1915. One aspect of this progress was to celebrate modern technological society's mastery of nature.

> [The earth] is the great field, the great mine, the great source of the energies of heat, light and electricity; the great scene of ocean, stream, mountain and plain of which all our agriculture and lumbering, all our manufacturing and distributing agencies [are created] ... [This is how] mankind has made its historical and political progress ... [The earth is] the home to whose humanizing and idealizing all his humanity returns (Dewey 1915 (1956): 19).

This worldview had important implications for school pedagogy. It meant that there was a singular cultural purpose in curriculum, and this could be traced to a confidence in the inevitable progress of modern, industrial society. For this reason, Dewey developed a focus on practical activities and experiences, instead of the bookish learning of didactic teaching. At school, children should learn the practical knowledge they required to become 'cooks, seamstresses, or carpenters'. Classrooms should be 'active centres of scientific insight into natural materials and processes, points of departure whence children shall be led into a realization of the historic development of man' (Dewey 1915 (1956): 19).

Progress was not a value that, in Dewey's view, sat well with textbooks pre-occupied with 'lore and wisdom handed down from the past', which dictated fixed 'standards of proper conduct' and which consequently anticipated that 'the attitude of pupils must be one of docility, receptivity and obedience'. Progressiv-ist education, in Dewey's conception, was a direct response to the inappropriate-ness of a didactic curriculum that imposed knowledge from above and outside. In Dewey's alternative vision:

> To imposition from above is opposed expression and cultivation of individuality; to external discipline is opposed free activity; to learning from teachers, learning through experience; to acquisition of isolated skills and techniques by drill is op-posed acquisition of them as a means of attaining ends which make direct vital ap-peal; to preparation for a more or less remote future is opposed making the most of the opportunities of present life; to static aims and materials is opposed acquaint-ance with a changing world (Dewey 1938 (1963): 3, 5–6).

Dewey was also concerned that a traditional didactic curriculum was one that 'imposes adult standards, subject matter and methods'. This was enforced as a matter of sheer necessity, he thought, because the contents of the curricu-lum, in their nature, were 'beyond the reach of the experience young learners already possess' (Dewey 1938 (1963): 4). He considered this to be a pedagogy that was nothing short of brutal, and one that verged on being meaningless to its students.

> Textbooks and lectures give the results of other men's discoveries, and thus seem to provide a short cut to knowledge; but the outcome is just a meaningless reflecting back of symbols with no understanding of the facts themselves (Dewey & Dewey 1915: 14–15).

The traditional classroom was arranged for listening, thus teaching 'the depend-ency of one mind upon another' (Dewey 1915 (1956): 31–2).

 See literacies.com Dewey on Progressive Education (Dewey 1915 (1956); Dewey 1938 (1963)).

Table 5.2: Mr Joyce's pedagogical choices (1)

Dimension 1: The contents of literacy knowledge	Its subject matter, or what learners are meant to learn
• Analytic phonics	
• Pen to page	
• Process, conference or workshop writing	
• Self-directed reading	
• Active meaning-making	

society and government rested on citizens. This had implications that went all the way through to the micro-politics of the classroom. 'The function of the teacher must change from that of a cicerone and dictator to that of a watcher and helper' (Dewey & Dewey 1915: 172, 297, 303, 304).

Dewey's contemporary, Maria Montessori (1870–1952), was Italy's first female doctor. Montessori helped establish the Casa dei Bambini or 'Children's House' in 1907, a preschool in a poor area of Rome designed to cater for children whose parents were both at work. Montessori believed that the chief role of educators was to assist children to teach themselves in a free, but structured, environment. She also believed that the separation between school and home (or community) should be reduced as much as possible.

See literacies.com Montessori on Free, Natural Education (Montessori 1912 (1964)).

She taught sentence formation and, only incidentally, grammar. Rather than take given sentences apart, she had the students forming sentences of their own, arranging words printed on cards into sentences laid out in the compartments of boxes.

'How different grammar will seem to the young pupil, if, instead of being the cruel assassin that tears the sentence to pieces so that nothing can be understood, it becomes the amiable and indispensable help to "the construction of connected discourse"!' (Montessori 1917 (1973)).

See literacies.com Montessori on Grammar.

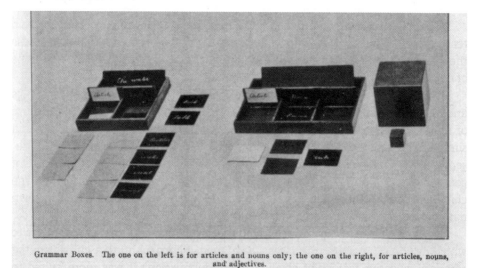

Grammar Boxes. The one on the left is for articles and nouns only; the one on the right, for articles, nouns, and adjectives.

Figure 5.4 Learning sentence formation in the Montessori system

Progress was not a value that, in Dewey's view, sat well with textbooks pre-occupied with 'lore and wisdom handed down from the past', which dictated fixed 'standards of proper conduct' and which consequently anticipated that 'the attitude of pupils must be one of docility, receptivity and obedience'. Progressiv-ist education, in Dewey's conception, was a direct response to the inappropriate-ness of a didactic curriculum that imposed knowledge from above and outside. In Dewey's alternative vision:

> To imposition from above is opposed expression and cultivation of individuality; to external discipline is opposed free activity; to learning from teachers, learning through experience; to acquisition of isolated skills and techniques by drill is op-posed acquisition of them as a means of attaining ends which make direct vital ap-peal; to preparation for a more or less remote future is opposed making the most of the opportunities of present life; to static aims and materials is opposed acquaint-ance with a changing world (Dewey 1938 (1963): 3, 5–6).

Dewey was also concerned that a traditional didactic curriculum was one that 'imposes adult standards, subject matter and methods'. This was enforced as a matter of sheer necessity, he thought, because the contents of the curricu-lum, in their nature, were 'beyond the reach of the experience young learners already possess' (Dewey 1938 (1963): 4). He considered this to be a pedagogy that was nothing short of brutal, and one that verged on being meaningless to its students.

> Textbooks and lectures give the results of other men's discoveries, and thus seem to provide a short cut to knowledge; but the outcome is just a meaningless reflecting back of symbols with no understanding of the facts themselves (Dewey & Dewey 1915: 14–15).

The traditional classroom was arranged for listening, thus teaching 'the depend-ency of one mind upon another' (Dewey 1915 (1956): 31–2).

 See literacies.com Dewey on Progressive Education (Dewey 1915 (1956); Dewey 1938 (1963)).

Table 5.2: Mr Joyce's pedagogical choices (1)

Dimension 1: The contents of literacy knowledge	Its subject matter, or what learners are meant to learn
• Analytic phonics	
• Pen to page	
• Process, conference or workshop writing	
• Self-directed reading	
• Active meaning-making	

society and government rested on citizens. This had implications that went all the way through to the micro-politics of the classroom. 'The function of the teacher must change from that of a cicerone and dictator to that of a watcher and helper' (Dewey & Dewey 1915: 172, 297, 303, 304).

Dewey's contemporary, Maria Montessori (1870–1952), was Italy's first female doctor. Montessori helped establish the Casa dei Bambini or 'Children's House' in 1907, a preschool in a poor area of Rome designed to cater for children whose parents were both at work. Montessori believed that the chief role of educators was to assist children to teach themselves in a free, but structured, environment. She also believed that the separation between school and home (or community) should be reduced as much as possible.

 See literacies.com Montessori on Free, Natural Education (Montessori 1912 (1964)).

She taught sentence formation and, only incidentally, grammar. Rather than take given sentences apart, she had the students forming sentences of their own, arranging words printed on cards into sentences laid out in the compartments of boxes.

'How different grammar will seem to the young pupil, if, instead of being the cruel assassin that tears the sentence to pieces so that nothing can be understood, it becomes the amiable and indispensable help to "the construction of connected discourse"!' (Montessori 1917 (1973)).

 See literacies.com Montessori on Grammar.

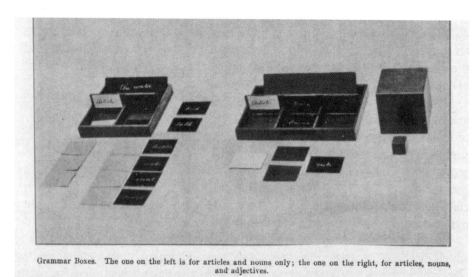

Grammar Boxes. The one on the left is for articles and nouns only; the one on the right, for articles, nouns, and adjectives.

Figure 5.4 Learning sentence formation in the Montessori system

Progress was not a value that, in Dewey's view, sat well with textbooks pre-occupied with 'lore and wisdom handed down from the past', which dictated fixed 'standards of proper conduct' and which consequently anticipated that 'the attitude of pupils must be one of docility, receptivity and obedience'. Progressivist education, in Dewey's conception, was a direct response to the inappropriateness of a didactic curriculum that imposed knowledge from above and outside. In Dewey's alternative vision:

> To imposition from above is opposed expression and cultivation of individuality; to external discipline is opposed free activity; to learning from teachers, learning through experience; to acquisition of isolated skills and techniques by drill is opposed acquisition of them as a means of attaining ends which make direct vital appeal; to preparation for a more or less remote future is opposed making the most of the opportunities of present life; to static aims and materials is opposed acquaintance with a changing world (Dewey 1938 (1963): 3, 5–6).

Dewey was also concerned that a traditional didactic curriculum was one that 'imposes adult standards, subject matter and methods'. This was enforced as a matter of sheer necessity, he thought, because the contents of the curriculum, in their nature, were 'beyond the reach of the experience young learners already possess' (Dewey 1938 (1963): 4). He considered this to be a pedagogy that was nothing short of brutal, and one that verged on being meaningless to its students.

> Textbooks and lectures give the results of other men's discoveries, and thus seem to provide a short cut to knowledge; but the outcome is just a meaningless reflecting back of symbols with no understanding of the facts themselves (Dewey & Dewey 1915: 14–15).

The traditional classroom was arranged for listening, thus teaching 'the dependency of one mind upon another' (Dewey 1915 (1956): 31–2).

 See literacies.com Dewey on Progressive Education (Dewey 1915 (1956); Dewey 1938 (1963)).

Table 5.2: Mr Joyce's pedagogical choices (1)

Dimension 1: The contents of literacy knowledge	Its subject matter, or what learners are meant to learn
• Analytic phonics	
• Pen to page	
• Process, conference or workshop writing	
• Self-directed reading	
• Active meaning-making	

Courtesy of Miss Elizabeth Irwin, Public School 61, New York

THE NEW AND THE OLD IN EDUCATION

Above: Freedom! Pupil initiative! Activity! A life of happy intimacy
— this is the drawing-out environment of the new school. *Below:* Eyes
front! Arms folded! Sit still! Pay attention! Question-and-answer
situations — this was the listening régime.

Figure 5.3 Frontispiece of *The Child Centered School*, written by colleagues of John Dewey

The organisation of literacy curriculum – process pedagogy and natural language growth

Natural learning

Dewey expressed his alternative view through the metaphor of organic growth. Don't interfere from an adult standpoint: 'give nature time to work.' This would require a transformation of curricula and classrooms and going to the root of the way knowledge is appropriated, even to the extent of questioning the status of facts.

> So, teachers, instead of having their classes read and then recite facts from the textbook, must change their methods. Facts present themselves to everyone in countless numbers, and it is not their naming that is useful, but the ability to understand them and see their relation and application to each other (Dewey & Dewey 1915: 172).

Instead of being a passive receiver of facts, in Dewey's pedagogy the child would assume the role of questioner and experimenter.

Dewey's more authentic approach set out to remedy three evils that, in his view, marked didactic curriculum. The first was the lack of organic connection with the child's life. Without such connections, knowledge and learning were purely formal and symbolic. Dewey did not deny that the symbol was important. He considered it to be a product of past reality and a tool for exploration. However, he felt that it had to symbolise in an active and meaningful way. It had to have a meaning to the child. Facts, such as the language facts of grammar, had to have an evident meaning and purpose. Otherwise they remained no more than mere symbols, dead and barren.

The second evil was that didactic teaching, in Dewey's view, gave students no reasons to be motivated. 'An end which is the child's own carries him on to possess the means to its accomplishment.' Curriculum was most successful in conditions of equilibrium of 'mental demand and material supply'.

Thirdly, he argued that a typical method of didactic pedagogy, to simplify things and make them logical, removed the more complex and thought-provoking nature of reality. Dewey saw a world that was much more interestingly complex than a simplifying curriculum and its textbooks might have us believe. Having been presented with 'facts' and synthesis, the child was not made 'privy to the nature of generalisation'. Knowledge was presented as memorisation, not reasoning. 'The child gets the advantage neither of the adult logical formulation, nor of his own native competencies of apprehension and response' (Dewey 1902 (1956): 24–6).

Dewey felt there was a politics to didactic pedagogy, and this was a politics to which he could not subscribe. It was, he argued, a curriculum that cultivated 'the colorless, negative virtues of obedience and submission'. It was more 'suited to an autocratic society' than to a society in which responsibility for the conduct of

society and government rested on citizens. This had implications that went all the way through to the micro-politics of the classroom. 'The function of the teacher must change from that of a cicerone and dictator to that of a watcher and helper' (Dewey & Dewey 1915: 172, 297, 303, 304).

Dewey's contemporary, Maria Montessori (1870–1952), was Italy's first female doctor. Montessori helped establish the Casa dei Bambini or 'Children's House' in 1907, a preschool in a poor area of Rome designed to cater for children whose parents were both at work. Montessori believed that the chief role of educators was to assist children to teach themselves in a free, but structured, environment. She also believed that the separation between school and home (or community) should be reduced as much as possible.

 See literacies.com Montessori on Free, Natural Education (Montessori 1912 (1964)).

She taught sentence formation and, only incidentally, grammar. Rather than take given sentences apart, she had the students forming sentences of their own, arranging words printed on cards into sentences laid out in the compartments of boxes.

'How different grammar will seem to the young pupil, if, instead of being the cruel assassin that tears the sentence to pieces so that nothing can be understood, it becomes the amiable and indispensable help to "the construction of connected discourse"!' (Montessori 1917 (1973)).

 See literacies.com Montessori on Grammar.

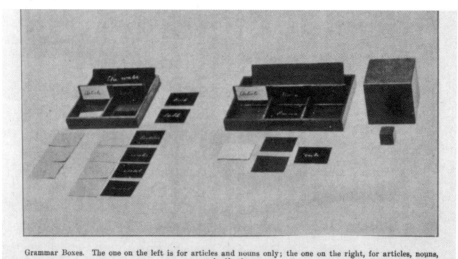

Grammar Boxes. The one on the left is for articles and nouns only; the one on the right, for articles, nouns, and adjectives.

Figure 5.4 Learning sentence formation in the Montessori system

Learning to mean

Mr Joyce now has his class working on an integrated unit of work that he has planned. He does not use a textbook. The subject the students are studying is science.

This unit of work is going to take four weeks to complete. Fortunately, Mr Joyce also teaches reading and writing to Vincent's class. Combining literacy and science lessons gives the students more time to get the work done. Of course, there has to be lots of reading and writing in a major science project like the one the class is about to undertake.

'Now class, we're going to study ecosystems. I want you to choose an ecosystem to study – forest, sea, pond, desert, savannah, whatever interests you. In fact, if you like, you could do this work in groups, join a table of students working on an ecosystem that you are all interested in. That way you can share resources and give each other feedback on the drafts of your ecosystems report.

'You'll need to collect books from the library. You'll need to search the internet. You'll need to take notes from reference books. You'll need to draw a diagram that shows the connections in your ecosystem and label it. Then I want you to write up a project describing the way your chosen ecosystem works. Remember, it is a closely interconnected *system*; that's why we call it an *ecosystem*. All the time you'll need to be reading in order to write, writing about what you're reading, and reading each other's writing. And all this to be able to do science well!'

 See literacies.com Debra Goodman's Class (Goodman 1996).

What a lot of work, thinks Vincent. And a lot of time just to figure things out when some of the other students in our class are not as focused as me on doing well at school. I wonder how this will come together so we understand what actually happens in a pond?

This was the ecosystem he had chosen. However, by the end, he realised he'd learned how to search and discover information. He had participated in a really helpful class conference with Mr Joyce about how a science report was different from the account of his holiday that he had written. Also, he had very much enjoyed laying out his project, which he presented in the form of a poster. Mr Joyce put up all the posters on the wall of the classroom, and it was interesting to see all the other finished projects, because even when they were all describing different ecosystems, the models everyone drew looked quite similar.

Why learn like this? We return to the phrase coined by Kenneth Goodman: 'whole language'. Te xt remains meaningful and purposeful only when it is considered at the level of 'whole language'. Goodman uses as an analogy the way children learn oral language: a developing process in the meaningful interplay of adults' and children's oral texts. As written and oral languages, he believes, have all the same basic characteristics, children should learn how to use written language through schooling in a way directly analogous to the 'natural' way young children learn oral language. Immersion, lots of active reading and writing and doing it for a reason that fits in with the child's own interests, experience and intentions, he argues, are the best ways to learn. The learning must be focused on relevance, purpose, respect, meaning and power. The student should be in control of the meanings, feel some degree of power as a knowledge-maker, be involved in purposeful work, and be respected for their contribution. (Goodman 2005).

A 'whole language' curriculum, as a consequence, will draw on a range of 'authentic resources' instead of textbooks, and on student experience and communicative intentions rather than formal language facts to be ingested. This is how a whole language approach will be relevant. It will encourage students to use language for their own purposes. It will focus not on language in the abstract, but on the meaning the children want to communicate. It will respect the individuality of learners and their different life experiences. By giving students a sense of control and ownership of their own language, in broader political terms, it will also give them a sense of their potential power as social actors.

See literacies.com Goodman on Whole Language (Goodman 2005).

Vincent explains his reading and writing process.

'At first I read through a short book on the life cycle of a fresh-water pond, then I looked up an encyclopaedia entry. Then I made out a list of topics. I kept on thinking, "Is there one more topic I should put?" Now I have six: plants, animals, food chain, photosynthesis, nutrients, pollution.

'I wonder if it's too many; but I have a lot of information, so now I think it's OK. So I'm going to at least look in two more books before I start my drafts, because I need more information.

'Also, we have a pond in the nature reserve down the street. Let me think about the things I have seen there.'

Vincent finds he has a patchwork of notes, drawings, ideas and headings.

Gradually, he starts to pull his work together into a science report. By his third draft he has clear headings:

1. Introduction: why we study ecosystems
2. The parts of a pond ecosystem
3. How a pond ecosystem works
4. Damage to the ecosystems
5. Conclusions: how to look after our ecosystems.

See literacies.com Graves on the Craft of Writing (Graves 2003).

Donald Graves calls writing a 'craft'. He and Donald Murray are the best-known promoters of the notion of '**process writing**'. In contrast to older traditions of teaching writing, Murray argues, process writing keeps student interest and intent at its core. Teacher-set assignments, he says, inhibit what students have to say.

In this spirit, Mr Joyce set one broad parameter in Vincent's class, and that was the science concept 'ecosystem'. However, beyond that:

Process writing: Learning to write as a series of steps, like the steps adult and professional writers use: planning, drafting, conferencing, rewriting, publishing

> The student finds his own subject. It is not the job of the teacher to legislate the student's truth. It is the responsibility of the student to explore his own world with his own language, to discover his own meaning. The teacher supports but does not direct this expedition to the student's own truth (Murray 1982: 16, 129).

Children, says Graves, must choose their own topic in order to gain a sense of ownership. From this starting point, 'the writing process has a driving force called voice.' The teacher is not there to impart knowledge, but must wait to give help when it is needed as the child struggles for control. 'Teachers who have waited find that children give them the energy, the energy of control and ownership.' As a result, student-initiated topics and information are primary, not writing conventions. Writing in the classroom is conceived, not as a matter of learning and correctly applying conventions, but as a number of steps (the process, open to any contents): prewriting, drafting, conferencing, editing, publishing (Graves 2003: 9, 21, 87–8, 227, 244).

Table 5.3: Mr Joyce's pedagogical choices (2)

Dimension 2: **The organisation of literacy curriculum**	**How the subject matter is arranged**
• Natural learning	
• Learning to mean	

Learners doing literacy – active learning and experiential immersion

Different learners see and do things differently

'Reading hour now,' says Mr Joyce.

Around the classroom, students are sitting at their group tables or lying on the carpet reading books. Vincent notices that the girl opposite him is reading a book he read a few weeks back. He really enjoyed that book, a story about a boy who noticed that a swimmer was in some trouble at the beach and three girl lifeguards who went out to save the swimmer.

Vincent and the girl start to talk about the book.

'I really liked the three girls. Imagine going out into those big waves to save the swimmer. How brave were they?' she said.

'I reckon the boy in the story was the real hero,' says Vincent. 'He noticed the swimmer was in trouble and alerted the lifeguards. Besides, there were three of them and they were all wearing safety gear. Not that brave at all, really.'

The above vignette raises an important point about reading. Different readers read different things into a story, depending on their interests and experiences. What is read is not simply a matter of what the author says. It is also a matter of interpretation. A reader does not, when they read well, read the truth in the text. They read their own meanings into the text. Reading is a process of active meaning construction, not a neutral conduit for communicating comprehensible facts. This makes reading tests that have multiple choice answers seem quite limited in the kinds of understandings they can test.

See literacies.com Goodman on the Construction of Meaning in Reading (Goodman 1996).

'Who was the hero? a) the boy was the hero; b) the girls were the heroes; c) the ambulance people were the heroes; d) there were no heroes here; everyone was just doing their job.' All four answers could be correct.

These are the most interesting kinds of questions and Mr Joyce certainly wouldn't expect a right or wrong answer. Instead, he asks, 'What meaning did you make of the text?'

Of course, there could be a right or wrong answer to the question, 'What day did this happen? a) Saturday; b) Sunday; c) Wednesday; d) the author does not tell us the day of the week.'

It's just a matter of scanning the text and looking for the names of days of the week. Anyhow, Vincent had been so moved by the flow of the story that he hadn't noticed what day it was. If Mr Joyce had asked this question, it might have been possible to answer correctly, but it was not very important to the story. To answer a question like this, Vincent would have to look back over the text to see whether he could find mention of a day. Fortunately he didn't, and Vincent and his fellow student have quite a good discussion about what makes a hero.

See literacies.com Graves on Testing Reading and Writing (Graves 2002).

> At the end of the conversation, even though Vincent and the girl opposite have come to different conclusions about the story, they both feel good that each other's interpretation has been valued and respected. Reading is an enjoyable activity that affirms their identities, rather than telling them they are right or wrong, and whether they are a 58 per cent or an 85 per cent kind of person.

 See literacies.com Hayes and Bahruth on Reading to Write (Hayes & Bahruth 1985).

Generating motivation

When it came to the specific question of literacy, Dewey's principles of motivation, experience and activity translated into practices that marked a dramatic break from didactic teaching. Dewey regarded language as a social, purposeful thing rather than something that was abstract and formal. The most effective language learning involved students 'having something to say rather than having to say something'. Language teaching, in other words, should be 'done in a *related* way, as the outgrowth of the child's social desire to recount his experiences and get in return the experiences of others' (Dewey 1915 (1956): 55–6).

One notable example of the adoption of this principle was Dewey's report that many schools were installing printing presses, not so much to teach the printing trade but so that the children themselves could print some of the pamphlets, posters or other papers the school needed. They were motivated to do this, not just because they found setting the type enjoyable and interesting, but because there was a good reason to be producing the copy for print.

In a similar vein, the experience of Mr Wirt of Gary, Indiana was cited by Dewey as evidence of the way language learning is more powerful when linked to practical purpose. In a number of schools under Mr Wirt's superintendency, 'application periods of English' were conducted – in carpentry and cooking, for example. These lessons 'correct from the language point of view any written work done as part of their other activity'. A pupil in one of these classes, who had been corrected for a mistake in grammar, was overheard saying, 'Well, why didn't they tell us that in English?' to which his neighbour answered, 'They did, but we didn't know what they were talking about' (Dewey & Dewey 1915: 83ff).

And yet, even if the method differed in authentic pedagogy, there was a singular cultural end to teaching: the 'correct' acquisition of the standard English that seemed to be required for practical purposes in a modern, industrial social setting.

> Type setting is an excellent method of drilling in spelling, punctuation, paragraphing and grammar, for the fact that the copy is going to be printed furnishes a motive for eliminating mistakes which exercises written by a pupil for his teacher never provide (Dewey & Dewey 1915: 84).

Summarising the value to the student of 'application' English lessons, Dewey said that these 'give him a reason for writing, for spelling, punctuating, and paragraphing, for using his verbs correctly, and improvement becomes a natural demand of experience' (Dewey & Dewey 1915: 85).

This conception of language made no concession to the fact that students' experiences of language outside school might be very different, be they native speakers of languages other than English or speakers of non-standard dialects. There were new cultural assumptions at work in this pedagogy. Motivated student activity was a pedagogical tool in the interest of progress and modernity. However, even if their methods of teaching and learning were different, these cultural assumptions were as powerfully single-minded as those of didactic pedagogy. This extended to the point of sharing with didactic pedagogy some of the same objectives – 'correct' grammar, for example – even if these objectives were now to be achieved by another means.

Mr Joyce's curriculum is a bit like that, too. All the students will eventually read the same books: the ones that are good for them. Though using a kinder, gentler pedagogy, Mr Joyce ultimately wants all the students to appreciate the same good literature, and learn the universal characteristics of good story writing. Along the way, he hopes they will also pick up correct spelling and the habits of good grammar.

Table 5.4: Mr Joyce's pedagogical choices (3)

Dimension 3: Learners doing literacy	The ways in which learners are intended to learn to make meanings
• Different learners see and do things differently	
• Generating motivation	

The social relationships of literacy learning – self-expression in a learner-centred pedagogy

Valuing authenticity

There is a moral economy to authentic pedagogy, to use a phrase coined by historian E. P. Thompson (Thompson 1971). By 'moral economy', following Thompson, we mean the social norms governing person-to-person and group relationships – in our case, the relationship between teachers and learners as they learn to read and write.

In authentic literacy pedagogy, the interests and motivations of the learner are the focus of reading and writing, rather than the expectations of set readings, comprehension of supposed facts in text, learning language rules and correct usage of standard, 'educated' forms of the language. Teachers become autonomous, professional sources of learning, instead of being intermediaries in a tightly governed relationship of syllabus–textbook–test. They are responsible for constructing an environment more in tune to the processes of learning rather than to their being authority figures who transmit non-negotiable learning contents. More than anything, they are responsible for the creation of a welcoming environment that affirms and nurtures the whole person.

 See literacies.com Walshe on the Role of the Teacher.

At the same time, authentic pedagogy opens up horizontal lines of communication between learners. Their lines of sight are directed to each other and not just to the teacher's eyes at the front of the classroom and the teacher's handwriting on the blackboard. They talk a lot with each other, not only when the teacher asks them to put up their hands to talk, as was normal with didactic pedagogy, and not only one at a time. Students learn by working together, not just by listening to the teacher. Reading and writing become sociable activities.

 See literacies.com Boomer and Davis on Co-operative Writing (Boomer & Davis 1980).

It is also possible – desirable even – to create individualised instruction, appropriate to the needs of students at different stages of learning development. Students can work at their own pace. They can work individually or in groups. They do not all have to be on the same page at the same time.

 See literacies.com Blackburn and Powell on Individualised Instruction (Blackburn & Powell 1976).

However, authentic pedagogy is not without its limitations, and later pedagogical innovations, such as functional and critical literacy pedagogies, try to compensate for these. The first limitation is that the underlying cultural assumptions of authentic pedagogy are often less open than they seem. In Dewey's case, a particular view of progress motivated his views of language and literacy learning. In this view, cultural difference was something that schools needed to erase.

> There is in a country like our own a variety of races, religious affiliations, economic divisions. Inside of the modern city, in spite of its nominal political unity, there are probably more communities, more differing customs, traditions, aspirations, and forms of government or control than existed in an entire continent in an earlier epoch (Dewey 1916: 25).

As a necessary remedy to this situation, there was 'the assimilative force of the American public school'. Only through public schooling, Dewey argued, 'can the centrifugal forces set up by the juxtaposition of different groups within one and the same political unit be counteracted' (Dewey 1916: 25).

The curriculum itself was a critical instrument for the creation of a culturally uniform, modern nation. 'Common subject matter accustoms all to a unity of outlook upon a broader horizon than is visible to the members of any group while it is isolated' (Dewey 1916 (1966): 21–2). So, for example, the Howland School, a Chicago public school in a 'foreign district', staged a large festival play: a pageant illustrating the story of Columbus to which 'a few tableaux were added about some of the most striking events in pioneer history, arranged to bring out the fact that this country is a democracy'. The whole school took part. The pageant had 'value as a unifying influence in a foreign community' and, indeed, a value to the nation 'greater than the daily flag salute or patriotic poem'. Dewey contrasted this school's approach to teaching history and civics with the 'dry ... facts of a routine textbook type' (Dewey & Dewey 1915: 129–31). However, the objectives of this teaching had not significantly changed, and these were to create a homogeneous citizenry that would work well together in modern industrial enterprises.

Literacy for the modern world

Needless to say, there were some quite pragmatic social reasons why didactic curriculum was no longer considered appropriate in 20th-century education. 'The world [had] been so tremendously enlarged and complicated', not just by transport and communications, but by continual scientific discoveries. It was a world where things were changing all the time, and there was so much that could be learned that cramming facts was becoming counter-productive. This only served to highlight further the increasing irrelevance of didactic pedagogy – the 'hopelessness of teaching with lists of facts' (Dewey & Dewey 1915: 171–2).

Setting literacy learning in the context of these large historical changes, authentic literacy pedagogy represented a shift from what Cook-Gumperz calls a 19th-century concern with literacy as a tool of social stability and a newly emerging 20th-century emphasis on literacy as a fundamental technology upon which dynamic and constantly changing modern societies are built (Cook-Gumperz 2006: 33).

Student-centred curriculum thus became one of the central devices of authentic pedagogy. However, one of the things Vincent had noticed, once the textbook was taken away, was that he was less clear about where the curriculum was going. Also, the discourse of the classroom tends to shift from the teacher telling students things, to students trying to determine 'correct' answers to questions by guessing

Table 5.5: Mr Joyce's pedagogical choices (4)

Dimension 4: **The social relationships of literacy learning**	**The relationship of learners to literacies knowledge, learners to other learners and learners to teachers**
• Valuing authenticity	
• Literacy for the modern world	

the answers in the teacher's head. The game of learning remains a game of getting things right. The difference is that, rather than drilling the right answer, the teacher tries to lead the students to the right answer through questioning.

See literacies.com Delpit on Power and Pedagogy (Delpit 1988).
Kalantzis and Cope, Debating Authentic Pedagogy.

Table 5.6: Literacy learning outcomes suggesting authentic pedagogy in Australia and the United States

Australian Curriculum	US Common Core State Standards
Responding to literature: Discuss characters and events in a range of literary texts and share personal responses to these texts, making connections with students' own experiences (Year 1).	*Language – vocabulary acquisition and use:* Use words and phrases acquired through conversations, reading and being read to, and responding to texts, including using adjectives and adverbs to describe (e.g. When other kids are happy that makes me happy) (Grade 2).
Creating literature: Create literary texts using realistic and fantasy settings and characters that draw on the worlds represented in texts students have experienced (Year 5).	*Reading literature – range of reading and level of text complexity:* By the end of the year, read and comprehend literature, including stories, dramas, and poetry, at the high end of the Grades 4–5 text complexity band independently and proficiently (Grades 4–5).
Literature and context: Make connections between students' own experiences and those of characters and events represented in texts drawn from different historical, social and cultural contexts (Year 6).	*Writing – research to build and present knowledge:* Recall relevant information from experiences or gather relevant information from print and digital sources; take notes and categorize information, and provide a list of sources (Grade 4).
Creating texts: Plan, draft and publish imaginative, informative and persuasive texts, selecting aspects of subject matter and particular language, visual, and audio features to convey information and ideas (Year 7).	*Reading literature – integration of knowledge and ideas:* Compare and contrast the experience of reading a story, drama, or poem to listening to or viewing an audio, video, or live version of the text, including contrasting what they 'see' and 'hear' when reading the text to what they perceive when they listen or watch (Grade 6).
Responding to literature: Reflect on, extend, endorse or refute others' interpretations of and responses to literature (Year 10).	*Reading literature – range of reading and level of text complexity:* By the end of Grade 9, read and comprehend literature, including stories, dramas, and poems, in the Grades 9–10 text complexity band proficiently, with scaffolding as needed at the high end of the range (Grade 9).
Investigate and reflect on different ways of reading literary texts, including the differences between initial personal responses and more studied and complex responses (Years 11–12).	*Writing – text types and purposes:* Write narratives to develop real or imagined experiences or events using effective technique, relevant descriptive details, and well-structured event sequences (Grades K–12).

Nevertheless, there are some many important insights we may want to take away from authentic pedagogy and apply in a broader and more balanced approach to pedagogy. Table 5.6 provides examples of literacy learning outcomes in the Australian Curriculum and US Common Core Standards that suggest an approach in the spirit of authentic pedagogy.

Exploring connections between the 'knowledge processes' and authentic pedagogy

Authentic pedagogy focuses on what we have called in Chapter 3 'experiential' knowledge processes. Its movements have at various times included discovery learning, inquiry learning, problem-based learning and project learning. Authentic pedagogy is process-oriented and learner-centred. The most mentioned recent version of this pedagogy is called 'constructivism', in which students construct their own meanings, internalising knowledge by rebuilding it for themselves with the scaffolding or support of a knowledgeable teacher. Its emphasis is on motivation, participation and grounded learner activity. In the case of children's learning, constructivist learning is framed by the unfolding and natural development of the brain through a number of stages. It involves the psychological processes of assimilation of new meanings into existing cognitive structures, or the accommodation of new meanings that require adjustment of existing cognitive structures (Piaget 1923 (2002); Windschitl 2002).

In constructivist classrooms, learners are often given the opportunity to play an active role in determining the area of focus, formulating questions and selecting activities.

- They face intellectual challenges in which they have to figure things out for themselves using raw information or drawing upon their experiences of everyday life.
- Learning occurs in an environment of immersion, with loose guidance by the teacher. Students are encouraged to interact with each other, and engage in collaborative talk.
- They learn in a 'community of practice', in which a premium is placed on trust and an atmosphere of safety has been established.
- Content is culturally appropriate, and sensitive to students' interests, needs and backgrounds. Identity is the starting point for the self-construction of meanings.
- Learning will be intrinsically motivating if it engages with learner interests, if it makes personal sense to the learner and if it expects them to be an active knowledge-maker.
- Guiding questions are diagnostic, and students are supported in self-explanation, and in offering an account of their prior understandings and knowledge as a starting point for learning. Learners take a degree of ownership of their learning and assume a measure of responsibility.

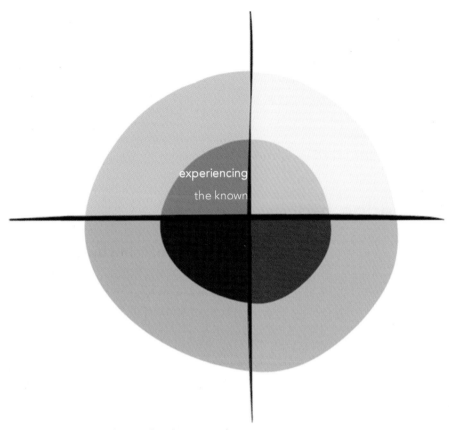

Figure 5.5 The emphasis of authentic pedagogy

As a general rule, this involves a shift in the role of the teacher from the days of didactic pedagogy, from 'the sage on the stage to the guide on the side', or 'leading from behind'. However, few accounts of authentic pedagogy leave it as just that. Many suggest a strategic move to didactic teaching every now and then, as the teacher offers mini-lessons 'just in time' and 'just enough' at strategic moments of direct instruction or conceptualising.

In this chapter, we have sketched the dimensions of authentic literacy pedagogy, exploring the thinking of some of its founders and illustrating its practices with examples. The message of this book is that there are strengths and weaknesses in each of the four major approaches to literacy pedagogy that have emerged since the rise of mass institutionalised education in the 19th century. The case we make through the 'knowledge process pedagogy' is that we can learn lessons from all four approaches.

See literacies.com Learning Modules

See literacies.com #edtech Literacies Applications

Summary

	Authentic literacy pedagogy
The contents of literacy knowledge	Authentic meanings
The organisation of literacy curriculum	Process pedagogy and natural language growth
Learners doing literacy	Active learning and experiential immersion
The social relationships of literacy learning	Self-expression in a learner-centred pedagogy

Knowledge processes

conceptualising by naming

1. Add entries to your wiki defining key concepts in the literacies pedagogy: important terms in the analysis of the ways in which communication and language work, and the ways in which they are learned. Maintain and extend this wiki as you work through this and the remaining chapters of this book.

experiencing the new

2. Locate a source from which you can get a concrete sense of the dynamics of authentic literacy pedagogy. Your source might be a curriculum resource: a whole language or process writing program, or perhaps the literacy dimensions of *Man: A Course of Study*, a program from the 1970s (see http://www.macosonline.org/). Or your source might be an interview with a teacher who believes in or practises authentic pedagogy. Write your own analysis of the dimensions of authentic literacy around:

   a. the contents of literacy knowledge
   b. the organisation of literacy curriculum
   c. learners doing literacy
   d. the social relationships of literacy learning.

experiencing the known

3. Describe a learning moment in which you have experienced authentic pedagogy. How did that moment feel? In what ways was it an effective or ineffective learning moment?

applying appropriately

4. Over the four chapters in this section of the book, you are engaging with the theory and practice of major approaches to literacy. Choose a literacy topic that might be taught in one lesson that exemplifies authentic pedagogy. Script hypothetical teacher–student talk in the course of this lesson.

conceptualising with theory

5. Write an account of the learning theory behind whole language or process writing. Choose one main theorist as your reference point, such as Ken Goodman, Frank Smith or Donald Graves.

analysing critically

6. Debate Jean-Jacques Rousseau's proposition about the ideal conditions of learning (see http://newlearningonline.com/new-learning/chapter-2/jean-jacques-rousseau-on-emiles-education).

analysing functionally

7. Discuss the learning conditions under which authentic pedagogy is most and least appropriate.

analysing critically

8. Consider a particularly appropriate application of authentic pedagogy (for a particular subject matter or learning context) and develop a lesson plan illustrating this application whose primary (though not necessarily exclusive) focus is authentic.

CHAPTER 6

Functional literacy pedagogy

Overview

Functional approaches to literacy focus on students learning to read and compose the kinds of texts that enable them to succeed at school and to participate in society. Their aim is for learners to understand the reasons why texts exist and how this affects the shape of texts. Unlike didactic approaches to literacy, which break language into its parts in order to learn formal rules, functional approaches start with the question, 'What is the purpose of this whole text?' and then move on to the next question, 'How is the whole text structured to meet these purposes?' Reading and writing are closely linked activities as learners explore the ways different kinds of texts work to make different meanings in the world.

This orientation to literacies pedagogy focuses on the knowledge processes of analysing and applying. Functional pedagogies equip students to work out how texts are organised to achieve different purposes, and to learn how to use these texts in real-life contexts to enact socially powerful meanings. To illustrate how functional approaches to literacy learning work, this chapter explores one example: the 'genre' approach.

> This year, Mary is in Ms Derecho's class. Like Sophia and Vincent in the previous two chapters, Mary is a strangely wise girl, who not only does very well at school but also thinks a lot about the ways things happen there.
>
> Ms Derecho starts her first lesson for the year by telling the class that they will be doing 'genre literacy' for an integrated reading and writing program.

The contents of literacy knowledge – learning the genres of school success and social power

The purpose of texts

'Written language is all around us,' announces Ms Derecho with all the seriousness you would expect of a language teacher. 'Tell me about some of the kinds of written language you come across every day.'

'Newspaper reports,' says one student.

'Storybooks,' says another.

'Instructions, recipes, poems, information books, magazines ...'; the students in the class come up with a long list.

'How is each different? Why are they different?' asks Ms Derecho.

Ever the keen student, Mary responds: 'They're different because they are about different things.'

'That's right, Mary; a newspaper report is different from a recipe and a storybook is different from a poem, not only in its meaning and topic but also in the way it is organised and written. In the **genre** approach to understanding writing, we look at the way in which different genres of text have different purposes.'

Genre: A kind of text that serves a particular social purpose

Functional approaches to literacy focus on meaning-making and how language is used in different contexts to achieve social goals. Genre-based pedagogy makes explicit the ways in which different types of text are structured to serve different purposes. For example, a report is different from a recipe, which is different from a fairy story, which again is different from a news story, which is different from a scientific explanation. Each of these purposes produces a different kind of writing, each with its own pattern of organisation. The starting point for learning in the genre approach is the purpose of the whole text; then the structural stages of the text (or macrostructure); then, only after that, the language patterns (or microstructures) within each stage, at the level of sentences, clauses, groups within the clauses and words, that give the text its distinctive characteristics.

Table 6.1: Different text types, different purposes

Types of text	Purposes
News article	• Presentation of information and reporting from different perspectives
Fable	• A story with a moral
Recipe	• The ingredients needed and the steps used to cook food
Science report	• Factual information about something in the natural world

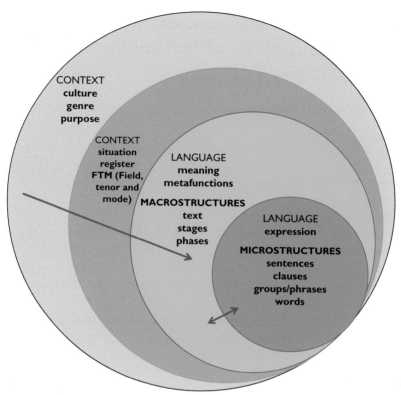

Figure 6.1 A model of text in context – focus on meaning and function

In this way, it is the opposite of traditional grammar, which starts with the separate parts of texts and, with these, assembles the larger parts – from sounds to words (phonics), from words to clauses and sentences (grammar), from sentences to paragraphs, and from paragraphs to whole works of literature. The kind of didactic pedagogy associated with traditional grammar is often formal and abstract, where learning about language at times seems to be for the sake of learning the rules just because rules are there to be learned. In contrast, functional pedagogy focuses on the communicative intentions and reasons for producing the text in the first place; in other words, the social purposes of language – language for action and reflection in the real world.

See literacies.com Lock on Functional Grammar.

'Today, class, we are going to start work on one of the most important written genres we use in school as we move up the levels of schooling as well as in society: the factual genre that we call a "report". What do we use reports for?'

Mary has seen a report that her mother brought home from work. She has heard mention of government reports on the news. She has also heard about scientists who have written reports describing their discoveries. But so far she's never read a report in school.

'Most reports give information about the world and they can be used to document and store information about different subjects,' Ms Derecho explains.

'Reports classify and describe living things like plants and animals, and non-living things like volcanoes, tsunamis and the stars. They also classify and describe issues that affect society, like the way people organise the government; the education system; and technological developments in computers, television or satellites, for instance. Some reports are written for experts who work in a special **field**, some for beginners who are just beginning to learn about something and some for people with special interests and hobbies.

'Now, we are going to write our own information report for a science unit about sea mammals that I want us all to undertake,' announces Ms Derecho.

Field: Subject matter or topic ranging from everyday, commonsense topics to highly specialised topics that might involve technical vocabulary, and special conventions for writing.

The stages of a genre

'The stages of an information report usually include a *general classification* of a subject and a *description* of the appearance, the behaviours, and the special or interesting habits of the subject.'

She writes this scaffold on the board to guide the students' conversation:

Genre	Stages
Information report on sea mammals	• General classification
	• Description – appearance
	• Description – behaviours
	• Description – habits

'To show you how reports work, we are going to do a joint construction of a report on whales first. "Joint construction" means that we are going to write the text together, as a whole class. You will come up with the ideas together for each stage and you'll tell me what to write, and I'll write them down on the board.

'But first, I am going to give you some reports to read about all kinds of whales, including Baleen Whales. Also, see what information you can find in the library or on the internet. As you read this material, look carefully at the type of information that has been selected and how it is organised for each report.'

After reading and research time, Ms Derecho brings the class together for their joint construction.

'OK, what do we now know about the Baleen Whales? How about the way they look …?'

'Oh Miss, Miss …'. The students in the class are really keen to tell Ms Derecho what they have learned from the reports they have read and the research they have done.

'Remember what we have read about Baleen Whales?'

Ms Derecho reads from one of the information books she has collected as a special class resource collection for this report writing exercise. In **functional literacy**, there is a lot of reading, but it is not reading by itself – it is reading closely interconnected with writing. The students are looking for language patterns and choices as well as developing content knowledge through their readings that they can use in their own written texts.

'"They are two-toned in colour", it says in this book. What shall we put down here?'

The boy who sits opposite Mary is the first student Ms Derecho asks to contribute. He tends to be a bit unfocused, even disruptive at times, so getting him involved early seems a good idea.

'But they've really only got one colour,' he says. He's been reading about this topic and already has learned some things about whales he did not know before.

'What is it?'

'Grey. Grey-blue.' More than one student chimes in at this point, to get the mix of colours right.

'Grey-blue?'

'Yes, it's blue but it's got a bit of grey in it,' says another student.

'All right.' Ms Derecho is writing on the board now:

Baleen Whales are grey-blue in colour.

'Yes?'

'Miss, are we going to have to know how the Baleen Whale eats?' The boy opposite Mary is particularly interested in that.

'We're going to have that in the – what part of the report?' asks Ms Derecho. The class chorus: 'Behaviours.'

'OK, let's compare the way the two of them look now … great answers. All right, we've added that. What about the important thing? What makes them all Baleen Whales?'

'They have baleen instead of teeth.' Mary is at last given a chance to answer one of the teacher's questions. It's OK that she had to wait, because she's one of the best students in the classroom.

'Right. Do you know what baleen is?'

Quite a few students answer this question at the same time, so it is hard to hear the answer. So Ms Derecho pushes on.

'Right, like a filter which helps them …?'

'Filter food,' a student calls out.

'Good,' Ms Derecho keeps writing.

They have baleen instead of teeth, which helps them filter food from the water.

What else do we know about them?'

'The size – they're larger than the Toothed Whales.' Back to the boy opposite Mary.

'Yes, and who belongs in this group?'

'Baleen Whales,' several students call out.

'No. We know it's the Baleen group. But who belongs in this group?' The students have not quite answered in the way that Ms Derecho had wanted. Baleen Whales are the group; not the different kinds of whales within that group.

'The Blue Whale', says Mary, who has caught onto Ms Derecho's pattern of thinking. Ms Derecho can rely on getting the answer she wants from Mary, which is why she was not asked her to answer the first few questions.

'Yes. And what is the Blue Whale?'

'The largest whale,' say a number of students, for whom this piece of information has stood out in their readings.

'Is it just the largest whale, or is it something else?'

'It's the largest creature,' answers Mary, who knew that, even though the Blue Whale is the largest whale, Ms Derecho was looking for a different answer at this point.

'Right.'

It's the largest living creature on earth.

Ms Derecho is writing on the board again. 'Having the … – which whale?'

The class chorus: 'The Blue Whale.'

Ms Derecho keeps writing. 'As a member of their …?'

The class chorus: 'Group.'

The boy opposite Mary has dropped out of the chorus. His mind has wandered, perhaps because he's lost interest in whales by this point. Mary thinks things are going rather slowly too, while they wait for the teacher to write each new little idea on the board.

'And how big does the Blue Whale get?'

'10 metres?' '32 metres?' There is some uncertainty in the class about the measurement. Several students reach for some information books to help clarify this piece of information.

'OK, so,' Ms Derecho writing again, 'It grows to a size of …?'

The class chorus: '32 metres.'

'And?'

'150 tonnes.'

'Right.'

By the end of the joint construction, this is what Ms Derecho has written on the board:

WHALES

Whales are sea mammals and are warm-blooded. They belong to the Cetacea Order and they can be divided into two groups: the 'Toothed' and the 'Baleen' Whales. They are grouped together according to whether they have teeth or not.

Whales have smooth skin. All whales have a layer of fat called 'blubber'. It is used to keep them warm when they dive deep. Their bodies are streamlined. This means they are long and slim, enabling them to move through the water. They have a few bristly hairs on their snouts. A whale's tail is called a fluke. It helps it to move forward in the water. Whales also have two flippers to help them steer left and right and to balance.

Their eyes are on the sides of their heads. Because of this, they don't rely on their eyesight for swimming. Instead, they rely on radar or sound waves. The whale's nose is called a 'blowhole' and is situated on top of its head. The blowhole is used to get air for the whale's lungs. The females of the species are called 'cows', the males are called 'bulls' and the babies are called 'calves'.

<u>Toothed Whales</u>: These are two-toned in colour, dark on top and lighter on the bottom. They have teeth. They have rounded snouts or pointed snouts. Some have long dorsal fins on their backs to stop them rolling over. They are fast swimmers. Toothed Whales are smaller in size compared to Baleen Whales. The Dolphin is the smallest whale. It ranges in size from 2 to 3 metres and can weigh up to 95 kilos.

<u>Baleen Whales</u>: These are grey-blue in colour. They have baleen instead of teeth, which helps them to filter food from the water. They are the largest group of living things. The Blue Whale is a member of the Baleen family. It grows up to 32 metres long and weighs 150 tonnes. It is known as the largest living creature on earth.

Whales come to the surface for air. They spout old air out through their blowholes and take new air in. The Baleen Whales surface two to three times per minute unless they are in danger, or catching food. They live in salt water. In summer, whales migrate to the cool waters of the Poles and in winter they migrate to the warmer waters of the Equator. Toothed Whales eat squid and fish and Baleen Whales eat krill and plankton. The Blue Whale's heart beats at one beat per minute and it lives for 90 years, while smaller whales live for 35 to 40 years. The cow can reproduce at the age of between five and 10 years and is pregnant for two years. The calf is born alive, tail first. It drinks its mother's milk and the mother cares for it until it is old enough to hunt for itself. The small whales hunt in pods or schools and the larger whales hunt in pairs or individually. They communicate by singing, clicking or squeaking.

Whales are known as 'friendly giants'. They are playful and friendly towards other whales and humans. They jump out of the water and this is called 'breaching'. A pod of whales sometimes beach themselves. It is thought they do this when the leader or the smallest one is sick.

Source: Macken, Kalantzis, Kress, Martin, Cope & Rothery (1990).

Report: A genre of text that provides information

'Can you see the structure of a **report**?' asks Ms Derecho. 'We start with a general classification, then we have a series of paragraphs each describing some aspect of whales.'

See literacies.com Macken et al. on Reports.

Mary understands what reports are, but she is a little puzzled by the structure of the report Ms Derecho has written on the board. Some parts of the general classification paragraph are description: for instance, they describe the facts that whales are warm-blooded and that some have teeth while others don't. The second paragraph does make sense as a description, because it tells about the parts of the whale's body. But then the next two paragraphs, the ones about Toothed Whales and Baleen Whales, seem to be about putting whales into groups, or classifying them, the job that the first paragraph was supposed to do. The second-last paragraph seems to be about so many different things that it is hard to say what kind of paragraph it is. The last paragraph is more than a description. It seems to be an evaluative paragraph about why we like whales.

Language structures and language functions

I've learned a lot of interesting things about whales from writing this report, Mary thinks to herself. But this genre thing is a bit slippery.

When it comes to understanding text, Mary, our imaginary student, is perhaps too critically observant for her years.

Ms Derecho pushes ahead.

'The next step in our genre writing is independent construction. You can use the scaffold of a report that I put on the board to guide you as you write. I want you to choose a different sea mammal, like the dolphin or the seal, and independently construct your own text.'

General classification, description, description, description, description – paragraph by paragraph Mary writes a report on dolphins, one of her favourite species. She saw dolphins when she and her family visited Sea World.

A functional approach to literacy is explicit about the ways in which language works to make meaning. It is direct and open about the way that different genres are designed to create different kinds of meaning for different social purposes. Language functions produce language structures. First we consider our meaning purposes; then we consider the ways we can use language to realise these purposes.

For example, let's say Mary wanted to write a text describing a scientific experiment. She would construct a text that used the features of the explanation genre, rather than the **narrative** genre or the argument genre. The point here is not just the information in the text, but also the most effective and successful way of organising and communicating that information.

Narrative: A genre of text that tells a story

Linguistic features and Range of Achievement

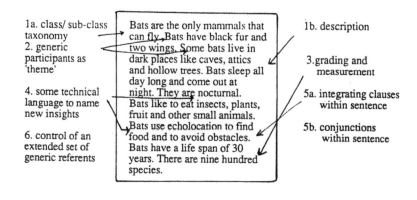

Figure 6.2 A Year 2 information report

Functional literacy pedagogy engages students in the role of apprentice as they work with the teacher – who assumes the role of language expert – to develop an understanding of language system and function. The pedagogical scaffold (Table 6.2) is designed so that the responsibility for text construction is gradually transferred from teacher to the student through the teaching learning cycle.

Table 6.2: Pedagogical scaffold

- Modelling and deconstruction
- Joint construction
- Independent construction

It makes visible the structure and sequence of text – the steps that a learner goes through in order to become a good writer of those genres that are valued in educational and wider social settings. This involves the explicit teaching of grammar – but a grammar that starts with the whole text, then the stages in that text, and then examines the details of the ways in which words in clauses are connected in sentences to contribute to the meaning of the whole text. The conferencing method is used here also, individually and in groups during the independent construction stage, to assist students with spelling, punctuation, vocabulary, and sentence and paragraph structure.

See literacies.com Martin and Rothery on Grammar: Making Meaning in Writing.

Functional literacy pedagogy is the application of Michael Halliday's systemic-functional linguistics to literacy learning (Halliday 1975; Halliday 2004). Variations on the genre theme are a distinct aspect of literacy pedagogy in many places around the world. Among the proponents of genre pedagogy, differing views emerge on the nature of language and on viable or worthwhile pedagogy. However, common to those working within the functional approach, genre is a category that describes the relation of the social purpose of text to language structure. It follows that, in learning literacy, students need to analyse critically the different social purposes that inform patterns of regularity in language: the whys and wherefores of textual conventions, in other words.

See literacies.com Halliday on Learning How to Mean (Halliday 1975).

Field, tenor and mode

'We are going to study one of the greatest plays of all time, Shakespeare's *Hamlet*.'

Ms Derecho is introducing the next unit of work and Mary seems to have been miraculously transported from primary science to secondary English from one lesson to the next. But then again, she is only an imaginary girl, following us on a journey into these pedagogical spaces.

'Here are three of the basic functions of language,' says Ms Derecho, 'and I want you to find these functions at work in *Hamlet*.

Tenor: Nature of the relationships between the writer and the reader – how well they know each other, whether they are of equal status in their relationship and how involved they might be affectively or emotionally

Mode: The role language plays in the organisation of text, and the channel or medium of communication, where language can be more spoken-like in quality to quite written-like

'Text is about something. We call that "something" the *field*. It has a certain **tenor**, or particular way in which it ties people together. And it takes a particular form or **mode**, which is the form of the text and the way the text holds together.'

Ms Derecho is a marvellous teacher, Mary thinks. Shakespeare can be hard and boring, but she always makes things so interesting.

The students look at scenes from several different *Hamlet* movies. They reorder the jumbled plot of *Hamlet* in an animated storyboard. They divide the board into two sides with a line and debate 'Ghosts are real', 'Revenge is understandable' and some other contentious propositions. They create a sociogram showing the relationships of the characters in *Hamlet*. They put their own family members into the roles in *Hamlet*, and ask 'How would you feel if …?' They perform some scenes from *Hamlet*. Then they start to work on a retrieval chart.

Field	**Tenor**	**Mode**
(subject matter or content of communication)	*(relationship of participants in communication)*	*(channel of communication or form of expression)*
	Act 1, Scene 1	
	Act 1, Scene 2	

'The field includes the action,' explains Ms Derecho as she presents another set of features of the genre approach to understanding text: what's going on, the characters, themes, topics, settings and processes.

'The tenor is the way in which the characters and audience respond to each other with feelings such as empathy, suspense, judgement and humour. The mode is the channel of communication and the devices used to express meaning.'

See literacies.com Radvanyi et al. on Hamlet, Madness and Revenge.

Table 6.3: Ms Derecho's pedagogical choices (1)

Dimension 1: **The contents of literacy knowledge**	**Its subject matter, or what learners are meant to learn**
• The purpose of texts	
• The stages of a genre	
• Language structures and language functions	
• Field, tenor and mode	

Whether it be writing a report or doing Shakespeare, the focus of functional literacy is on the genres of school success and, directly or indirectly, social power. It is explicit about the purposes of those texts, the way texts are ordered or staged, and how aspects of the context of language use, such as field, tenor and mode, influence patterns in the grammar (Halliday & Hasan 1985). These distinctions are made in functional linguistics in order to explain how the choices a writer makes come together to make meaning.

The organisation of literacy curriculum – reading genre models and writing within generic frameworks

Locating the functional approach

During the 20th century, many educators began to reject the traditional didactic literacy pedagogy. This was mostly from the point of view of a paradigm that we have called authentic pedagogy, a paradigm that every now and then exercised official and institutional dominance in education. This progressive approach was founded on the concerns with traditional curriculum espoused by Dewey and Montessori at the turn of the 20th century. At various times, the teaching of literacy through formal conventions was de-emphasised – for instance, by the whole-word 'look-see' approach to beginning reading in the second quarter of the 20th century, and the 'process writing' and 'whole language' approaches in that century's third quarter.

The process approach was modelled on how expert writers write – the cognitive processes they engage in, and it was learner-centred. The starting point for writing was the student's topic of interest but critics argued that it paid little attention to explicit knowledge about language. This meant that for students who came from literate backgrounds, it was an engaging and effective approach, but for those without this knowledge about language and how it works, there was little systematic input or direct instruction to guide them. The whole language approach emphasised the importance of meaning and the use of 'whole language' (rather than isolated sentences, words, sounds) in teaching students to read and write. However, like process writing, this approach did not offer systematic instruction about text features or explicit knowledge about language.

Following Dewey, students whose classroom experiences were designed according to the authentic approach were now to be active learners – to learn by doing; to learn through practical experience rather than learn facts by rote. Learning was to be meaningful rather than formal. The most effective learning, it was assumed, would take place when it was relevant to the individual rather than institutionally imposed. Curriculum was to stress process over content. Textbooks that, in their nature, seemed to dictate content, were to be cast aside or redesigned so they could be dipped into as an instructional resource rather than provide a program of study. In the area of learning to read and write, an analogy was drawn between the way children learn oral language and the way they learn literacy in school. Authentic resources, things that students wanted to read and write and that were of relevance and interest to their own lives, would be used instead of textbooks. The focus of the reading and writing curriculum would no longer be on language in the abstract but on the meaning the child wanted to communicate.

See literacies.com Snyder on The stories that divide us: Media (mis)representations of literacy education.

Far from being part of the 'back-to-basics' movement or even taking sides in the 'reading wars' and 'grammar wars', the functional approach to literacy takes to task both the didactic and the authentic approaches. From the point of view of the advocates of functional literacy, authentic pedagogy so often fails in practice to improve learner outcomes. Failure persists, even if the dynamics of how failure occurs have changed.

Genre-based literacy pedagogy in the functional approach originated from research conducted on the kinds of texts children need to write to succeed at school. Linguists working in collaboration with teachers identified a number of different genres that children wrote for various purposes and developed a teaching cycle that included explicit teaching about text features (Callaghan & Rothery 1988; Martin 1986). They aimed to develop a 'visible pedagogy' to improve the educational outcomes of students marginalised by mainstream schooling (Cope & Kalantzis 1993).

The genre approach has since been implemented in curricula in Australia and later around the world in various forms. In the text-based pedagogies that followed, the focus on the features of language at text, paragraph, sentence and word levels, and the explicit teaching of these, addressed the limitations of earlier process and whole language approaches, which were popular during the 1970s and 1980s when the formal teaching of grammar was dropped from school curricula.

The idea of 'genre'

'Genre' is used in functional literacy pedagogy to connect the relatively stable forms of text types with variations in social purpose. Texts are different because they do different things. So any literacy pedagogy has to be concerned, not just with the formalities of how texts work, but also with the living social reality of texts in use. How a text works is a function of what it is for. Genres are social processes (Martin 1997). Texts are patterned in reasonably predictable ways according to patterns of social interaction in a particular culture. Social patterning and textual patterning meet as genres.

Genres are textual interventions in society. They are not simply created by individuals in the moment of their utterance. They represent familiar patterns of meaning that have been socially created for particular communicative purposes. Different genres, moreover, can give their users access to certain realms of social action and interaction, or particular spaces of social influence and power. Take lawyers' language, or chess players' language, or academic language. We know these are social realms from which a lot of people are excluded, and this pattern of social exclusion is marked by the language used in each setting. Learning new genres, and expanding the range of genres we can use, gives us the power of choice and the linguistic potential to join new realms of social activity and social power. This is not a matter of having to replace the language and genres we learned in the communities of our birth. Rather, it's a matter of expanding our capacities and thus our social opportunities, so we can choose from a broader range of language options and genres.

In the world outside schooling, immersion in the social practice of a genre is sometimes sufficient to 'pick up the language', so to speak, although there are obviously other institutional barriers that may still make this impossible, or all but impossible. This is not to imply that language users need to be significantly aware of the linguistic 'how' of their activity, even if they are largely aware of the social 'why' of a particular discourse in use. You do not have to know about language to be able to use language. It is not necessary to know your linguistic 'hows' to be able to put text into social use and realise its potential 'whys'.

In school, however, there are two sorts of impulses that pull language away from this usual condition. The first is the social role (and inherent limitations) of institutionalised schooling. School is the most significant of all sites of potential social mobility. Expressed in terms of language, schooling has the potential to prepare students to use a range of genres with a wide range of potential social applications. However, it cannot do this by immersion alone; nor would that be an efficient use of resources.

School is a rather peculiar place. Not only is its mission peculiar; so are the discursive forms or the ways the texts of learning speak to students. It is at once a reflector of the outside world and discursively quite different from the outside world. Because school needs to concentrate the outside world into the generalisations that make up school knowledge, it is epistemologically (the way it knows) and discursively (the way it speaks) different from most of everyday life in the outside world. For example, it makes sense to use generalising concepts and abstractions that can be transferred into many contexts, rather than just 'pick things up' by immersion.

Table 6.4: Genres at school

School subjects	Examples of typical genres for reading and writing	Textual purposes and features
Science	Report	Provides structured information about the natural world, based on information or observation
English	Narrative	Tells a story, with an orientation to characters and setting, a complication that is the point of the story, and a resolution that brings the story to an end
History	Argument	Provides evidence and alternative perspectives on that evidence, and draws interpretative conclusions

Developing a metalanguage

As a site of cultural reproduction with an extremely broad charter, schooling is typically conceptual in its orientation, concentrating knowledge into generalisations and framing knowledge of the world in coherently articulated subjects or disciplines. When it comes to speaking about language itself – how language is used in school and in the outside world towards which school is oriented – schooling necessarily uses a **metalanguage**, a language with which to make generalisations about language.

> **Metalanguage:** Language for talking about language – specific terminology that allows us to identify and talk about different features of text, including grammatical terms

This is just a matter of efficiency and a matter of school's peculiar relation to the world: of, but not in, the world. The argument of the functional literacy pedagogues against those who favour authentic literacy pedagogy runs like this: 'Let's not abandon the metalanguage; education is the only social site where grammar as metalanguage is really important.' Against the didactic pedagogues, the genre theorists' argument is: 'Let's always explain the metalanguage in terms of social purpose; if the project of school is social access and part of that is access to genres of a variety of realms of social power, let's make that connection of structure and purpose explicit.'

The 'hows' of language need also to be brought to the fore in education as a consequence of the unique social mission of schooling to provide all students, including historically marginalised groups, equitable access to as broad a range of social options as possible. This may include groups marginalised by reason of culture, gender, socio-economic background, or the prejudicial social meanings ascribed to 'race', 'dialect', 'ability' and even 'behaviour' or 'appearance'.

Schooling in a democratic society at the very least boasts that it creates equality of opportunity. As educators, we are duty bound to take this at its word. However, those outside the discourses and cultures of certain realms of power and access often find that acquiring these discourses requires explicit explanation – the ways in which the 'hows' of text structure produce the 'whys' of social effect. If you live with the 'hows', if you have a seventh sense for how the 'hows' do their social job by virtue of having been brought up with those discourses, then they will come to you more or less 'naturally'. Students from historically marginalised groups, however, need explicit teaching more than students who seem destined for a comfortable ride into the genres and cultures of mainstream power.

Table 6.5: Dimensions of metalanguage

Metalanguage or a language for talking and thinking about language	<ul><li>Finding ways to think about, and words to describe, the context of communication</li><li>Finding ways to think about and describe the organisation of the whole text 'genre'</li><li>Finding ways to explain how the text is structured to make meaning, including its macrostructures (stages) and microstructures (word choices and arrangements)</li></ul>

See literacies.com Schleppegrell on The role of metalanguage in supporting academic language development.

Writing an explanation text

Back in Ms Derecho's classroom, we find the students about to start a unit of work on climate change.

'Climate change is a very difficult issue for us humans in the world today,' says Ms Derecho in the serious intellectual voice that she, as a teacher, often assumes.

'Some people think that climate change is a hoax. Others think it is one of the most critical challenges facing us today. I'm not going to ask you what you think today, because I want you first to think like a scientist about these issues. Scientists don't rush to judgement without first studying the evidence very carefully. Writing explanations is one way scientists present us with their evidence. More than this, writing explanations is not just a way of telling; it is also a way of thinking about the evidence.'

OK, this is going to be a serious business, Mary silently says to herself, to think the way a scientist does ...

'We're going to start our learning with modelling. I want you to read some scientific explanations written by others of why climate change is a fact, or not. Here's an information book on climate change. And here's the executive summary of a report on climate change, not too technical, written to be read and understood by a wide audience. Here's a website that presents climate science research findings. Here are some links to blogs that discuss evidence of climate change.'

Ms Derecho has collected a lot of examples of scientific text, and asks the students to search for more.

'To write well,' she tells the class, 'you need to read a lot, not just to pick up the ideas and information you need, but to get a feel for how real texts work in the subject area you are writing about.

'So you can see, there's a lot of information available about climate change, much of it using the explanation genre. Here are some newspaper opinion pieces by the climate change sceptics, the people who don't believe human actions are affecting our climate, and here are some counter-arguments by people who believe that the science points to the damaging effects of humans on our climate. Whichever side of the debate they are on, people use scientific explanations to support their case.'

Ms Derecho is exposing students not only to the scientific debate and the evidence used to support the case, but also to authentic scientific texts through which people lay out their arguments. In fact, writing things down like this helps them think through their case. She gets the students to do lots of reading of real texts, the writings of actual scientists, discussions of serious consequence.

This makes me feels very responsible, Mary thinks to herself. Some day, I'd like to be a scientist like one of these writers.

Ms Derecho is immersing children in the field, including a lot of new vocabulary about climate change. She exposes them to texts representing a number of modes, from newspaper opinion pieces to websites. She is getting the students to recognise the sense and tenor of this kind of scientific writing.

On this last point she comments: 'Notice that these writers rarely use "I". They try to make the facts they have collected speak for themselves. Though, of course, you can see that the two sides of the debate have selected facts that suit their case. The "I" of the scientist is always there, but cleverly hiding behind the facts they have chosen! They want the facts they present to appear strong enough to make their case.

'So how does the explanation genre work? What are its stages? Have a look at this scientific explanation.'

Ms Derecho points the class to a text written by one of the world's best-known climate scientists; not too technical, because he wrote it as an opinion piece for a respected newspaper. The starting point for understanding text is to identify the **schematic structure** of the genre. She has prepared another scaffold outlining the parts of the explanation genre.

Schematic structure
Macrostructure of a text – its stages and phases.

'Explanations describe "how" and "why", and this is how they do it: they begin with a description of the event or phenomenon, then paragraph by paragraph they provide one explanation after another of the "how" and "why" of the phenomenon.

'Sometimes the steps in an explanation are connected by what we call an "implication sequence": if step 1, then step 2; if steps 1 and 2, then step 3; if steps 1, 2 and 3, then step 4; and so on.

'See how this text works.

'*Phenomenon*: "Climate change is …" (the concept introduced and defined)

'*Explanation paragraph 1*: "Climate change is caused by humans creating more carbon dioxide and …" (causes explained)

'*Explanation paragraph 2*: "The effect of carbon dioxide on climate is …" (immediate effects explained)

'*Explanation paragraph 3*: "If the temperature rises by …" (broad view of a range of impacts on different ecosystems)

'*Explanation paragraph 4*: "The impacts of these environmental changes will be to …" (human impacts, impacts on animal and plant life)

'*Explanation paragraph 5*: "Ways to address climate change include …" (suggestions of some courses of action to reduce the harmful effects of humans)

'Then finally, a *generalisation* paragraph that draws conclusions from the evidence: "This evidence points conclusively towards …".

'You see how one paragraph logically connects with the next? And how the case builds up by explanation from the scientific evidence?'

Very convincing, thinks Mary, but the climate sceptics play the same kind of game in their writings, and the two sides of the argument can't be both right. She's too wise for her age, this Mary.

'Next,' says Ms Derecho, 'we're going to do a joint construction of a climate text.'

Mary is familiar with this process – it is not long since the class jointly constructed the 'whales' text. But that was a report. This time the class is jointly constructing an explanation.

Ms Derecho starts to work her way through a new climate change text on the electronic whiteboard. She's gone very modern since she did the last joint construction on whales. Students chime in with suggestions for sentences and, when Ms Derecho stops in the middle of a sentence, the next word.

Phenomenon, explanation 1, explanation 2, explanation 3 … then she stops at a sentence.

'I want us also to think about the grammar in this sentence. This is a very typical sentence in an explanation. The sentence began the fourth paragraph, linking the theme defined in the phenomenon and the explanation about to be presented in this paragraph with the explanations in the previous paragraphs.

'"The impacts of these environmental changes will be to …"

'Now, a lot is being said in just a few words. "These environmental changes" would make no sense if you had not read the preceding paragraphs already. Just three words ask you to cast your mind back to a whole argument. "Environmental change" is a nominal group. "These" is a diectic or pointer, which connects this idea at this step in the explanation with the earlier steps.

'Also, we could say "The environment is changing", but this would not sound so convincingly like serious science. Instead, we capture a process or action in a nominalisation. Scientists do this all the time. "I discovered" becomes "the findings indicate". "I understand" becomes "this understanding is". We turn a process into a thing in order to make it sound as if the thing speaks for itself. Here, the nominalisation is "environmental change", a single participant that packs in a lot of processes.

'Then the whole rest of the sentence is about "The impacts of these environmental changes". We could have turned the sentence around the other way and said "Rising sea levels will … have an impact …" and this may have been a perfectly good sentence. But when the participant-actor is put at the end of the sentence and the participant-recipient is put at the beginning, it makes the text sound more detached and scientific, don't you think? It's a bit like the grammar checkers on your computer, which tell you that you shouldn't use the passive voice, now that advice is not helpful when you want to downplay the role of the actor-participant.'

Table 6.6: Explanation genre

Context	Macro-structures	Micro-structures
Genre: scientific explanation Purpose: to convince a reader about the comprehensiveness and accuracy of an account of a natural phenomenon	• Name phenomenon • Explanation/evidence • Explanation/evidence • Explanation/evidence • Concluding generalisation	• Specialised vocabulary, carefully defined • Nominalisations: giving names to processes • Third person and passive voice 'objectivity' • 'Pointers' that connect one part of the explanation with another

Wow, I think I'm getting this grammar, Mary thinks. I can see how one sentence sounds more scientific than the other, but I don't think I can use these hard technical words to explain the reason why.

'Now it's independent construction time,' says Ms Derecho as she reaches the end of the jointly constructed text on the electronic whiteboard.

'Write your own explanations of climate change. Read some more. Collect your evidence. Define the phenomenon. Plan the stages in your explanation. Start drafting. Discuss the evidence and issues that come up as you write. Review your draft. How can you make your explanation more convincing? Share your drafts and check spelling, word choices and sentence and paragraph structure. Produce a final version and publish it so we all can read it.'

See literacies.com Callaghan, Knapp and Noble on The Genre Curriculum Cycle or 'Wheel'.

'So class, now we're done, what's the purpose of the explanation genre? And how does it work to achieve that purpose?'

Mary thinks it is time to say something of what she has been thinking.

'Explanations, Ms Derecho, try to convince us of something, and they do this by trying to have the facts speak for themselves, as if it's not just the author's opinion but is simply true. But my worry is that here we have two sides of the argument using the same genre, and using it very effectively. How will we ever know the truth about climate change?'

Table 6.7: Ms Derecho's pedagogical choices (2)

Dimension 2: The organisation of literacy curriculum	How the subject matter is arranged
• A focus on genres for school success	
• Examination of macrostructures: genre, overall organisation of texts	
• Examination of microstructures: words, sentences, grammar	

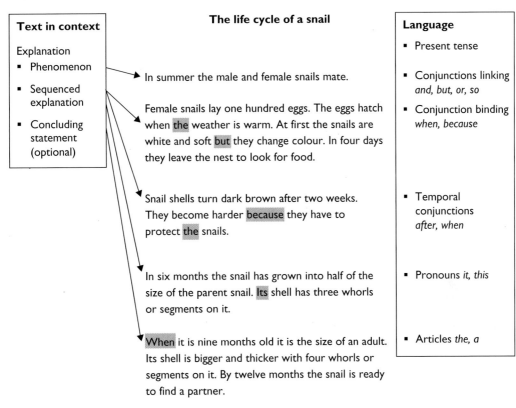

Text in context

Explanation
- Phenomenon
- Sequenced explanation
- Concluding statement (optional)

The life cycle of a snail

In summer the male and female snails mate.

Female snails lay one hundred eggs. The eggs hatch when the weather is warm. At first the snails are white and soft but they change colour. In four days they leave the nest to look for food.

Snail shells turn dark brown after two weeks. They become harder because they have to protect the snails.

In six months the snail has grown into half of the size of the parent snail. Its shell has three whorls or segments on it.

When it is nine months old it is the size of an adult. Its shell is bigger and thicker with four whorls or segments on it. By twelve months the snail is ready to find a partner.

Language
- Present tense
- Conjunctions linking and, but, or, so
- Conjunction binding when, because
- Temporal conjunctions after, when
- Pronouns it, this
- Articles the, a

Figure 6.3 The explanation genre: 'The life cycle of the snail'

essay writing is functional literary pedagogy. & writing course on the outdrop.

Learners doing literacy – genre scaffolds and independent construction

Writing a narrative

'And today, class, we're going to write something different. This time it is going to be a story. What do people know about the story genre? What are your favourite stories? Where do we find stories? What are their purposes?'

The class discusses all the places they encounter stories – in books, at the movies, on television – and also the true stories told in the news, or the stories we tell each other when we recount a sequence of events that we have experienced.

'Well, among these different story genres, today we are going to start working on narrative genre. Let's all go away first and read a narrative.'

Ms Derecho has collected a whole lot of models of narratives for students to read, compare and discuss.

Modelling – joint construction – independent construction. Mary has got used to the genre of genre by now!

Part way through the independent construction stage, Ms Derecho explains:

'A narrative deals with events that are problematic and that lead to a crisis or turning point of some kind. The complicating events are usually resolved by a main character. Aspects of setting and details about characters and situations are important for orienting the reader. Any part where the writer attempts to bring out the significance of the events in a particular stage is an evaluation. In the final part of the narrative there is some kind of resolution stage, where the problems or complicating events that were set up in the earlier part of the text are resolved for better or worse. So here are the stages of a narrative: *orientation – complication – evaluation – resolution* – and possibly also a *reorientation* or *coda*, like a moral to a story.'

But the last movie I saw started with a flashback, not a once-upon-a-time orientation, thought Mary. And it ended without a resolution, making you imagine the end of the story. I'll try to do my narrative the way Ms Derecho says, but it seems narratives don't always do that.

Mary started to write her story, 'True Love'.

Ms Derecho is impressed by her final text. She writes on Mary's final draft:

'In terms of the genre you exploited all the relevant stages of the genre including that of evaluation (e.g. "Now this boy had a problem …"). With regard to the tenor, the dialogue is well framed. In terms of field, the activity sequences are exploited to point up the significance of the events for Mergertroyd. In terms of the written mode, you have command of the textual resources necessary to create a possible world for the reader via written text alone. Well done, Mary.'

See literacies.com Macken et al. on Story Genres.

Table 6.8: Narrative genre

Context	Macro-structures	Micro-structures
Genre: narrative Purpose: to tell an imaginary story for entertainment or as a lesson	• Orientation • Complication • Evaluation • Resolution • Reorientation/coda	• Characters • Setting • Interpersonal tenor • Time represented in activity sequence • Dialogue

Table 6.9: Ms Derecho's pedagogical choices (3)

Dimension 3: Learners doing literacy	The ways in which learners are intended to learn to make meanings
• Modelling and deconstruction	
• Joint construction	
• Independent construction	

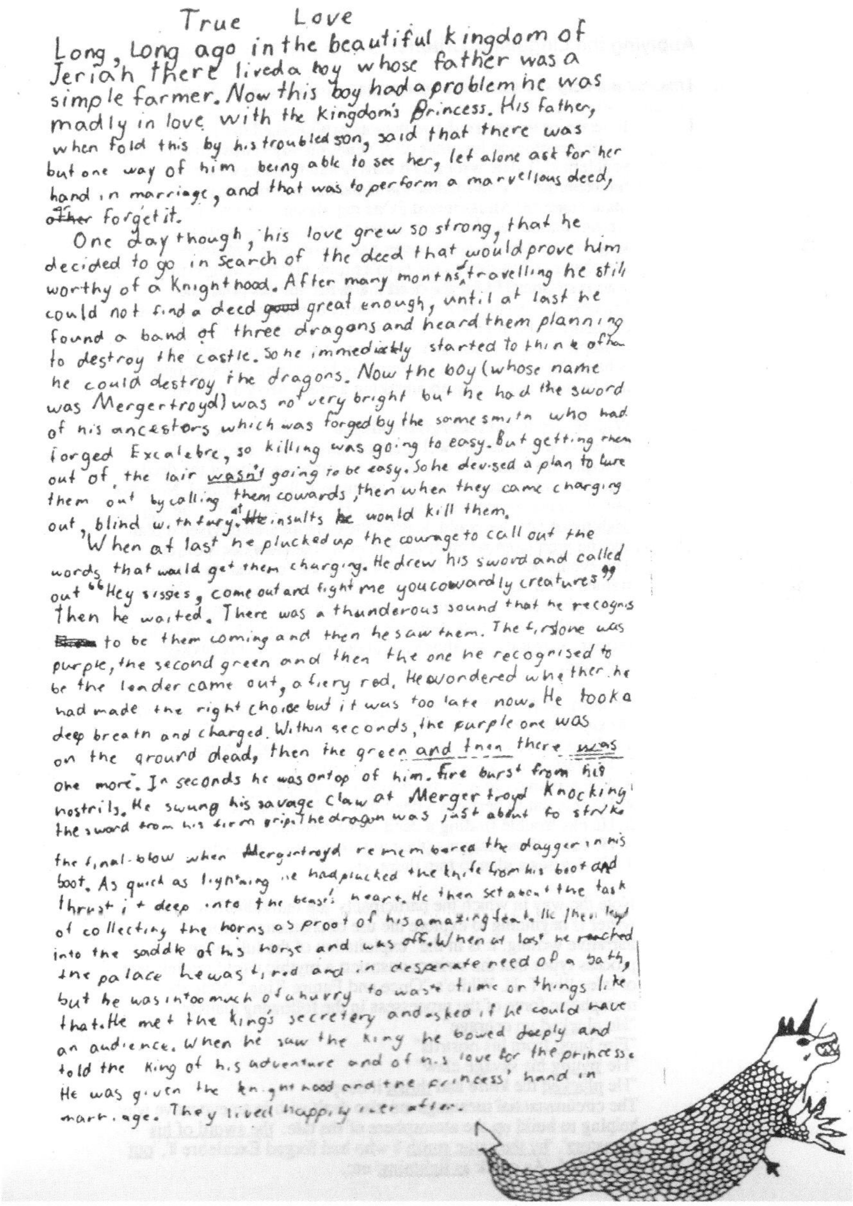

True Love

Long, Long ago in the beautiful kingdom of Jeriah there lived a boy whose father was a simple farmer. Now this boy had a problem he was madly in love with the kingdom's Princess. His father, when told this by his troubled son, said that there was but one way of him being able to see her, let alone ask for her hand in marriage, and that was to perform a marvellous deed, either forget it.

One day though, his love grew so strong, that he decided to go in search of the deed that would prove him worthy of a knighthood. After many months, travelling he still could not find a deed good great enough, until at last he found a band of three dragons and heard them planning to destroy the castle. So he immediately started to think of how he could destroy the dragons. Now the boy (whose name was Mergertroyd) was not very bright but he had the sword of his ancestors which was forged by the same smith who had forged Excalebre, so killing was going to easy. But getting them out of, the lair wasn't going to be easy. So he devised a plan to lure them out by calling them cowards, then when they came charging out, blind with fury. the insults he would kill them.

When at last he plucked up the courage to call out the words that would get them charging. He drew his sword and called out "Hey sissies, come out and fight me you cowardly creatures" Then he waited. There was a thunderous sound that he recognis ed to be them coming and then he saw them. The first one was purple, the second green and then the one he recognised to be the leader came out, a fiery red. He wondered whether he had made the right choice but it was too late now. He took a deep breath and charged. Within seconds, the purple one was on the ground dead, then the green and then there was one more. In seconds he was on top of him. fire burst from his nostrils. He swung his savage claw at Merger troyd knocking the sword from his firm grip. The dragon was just about to strike the final blow when Mergintroyd remembered the dagger in his boot. As quick as lightning he had plucked the knife from his boot and thrust it deep into the beast's heart. He then set about the task of collecting the horns as proof of his amazing feat. He then leapt into the saddle of his horse and was off. When at last he reached the palace he was tired and in desperate need of a bath, but he was in too much of a hurry to waste time on things like that. He met the king's secretary and asked if he could have an audience. When he saw the king he bowed deeply and told the king of his adventure and of his love for the princess. He was given the knighthood and the princess' hand in marriage. They lived happily ever after.

Figure 6.4 A Year 5 narrative

The social relationships of literacy learning – benefits of learning powerful text forms

The uses of genres in school

Functional literacy pedagogy is about learning to mean in a social environment and educational context where mastery of particular genres is valued. It is centred around expert-designed, teacher-introduced scaffolds and functional grammar, followed by independent construction of texts that, more or less successfully, exemplify these genres.

Among the key genres of schooling are those with the main purpose of engaging – recount, narrative, anecdote, exemplum, news story; informing – historical account, explanation, report, procedure; and evaluating – arguments (exposition and discussion), text responses (personal response, review, interpretation). To give some extremely synoptic content to just a few of these examples:

- *Reports* are factual texts that describe the way things are: they can be about natural phenomena, social phenomena or technical phenomena (their functions). They are frequently used in school in social studies and science (their educational context). As texts, they usually start with general classification that locates the phenomenon, followed by successive elements contributing to a description, such as types, parts and their functions, qualities, uses or habits and so on. The focus in reports is on generic participants, without temporal sequence and mostly using the simple present tense. Considerable use is made of 'being' and 'having' clauses (**lexico-grammatical features**).

> **Lexico-grammatical features** Patterns of words and grammar that give a text its distinctive characteristics

- *Procedures* are factual texts designed to describe how something is accomplished through a sequence of actions or steps. They are more about processes than things (functions). In school they are frequently used in art, cookery and science, for example (educational context). Procedures mostly commence with a statement of the goal, followed by an ordered series of steps (schematic structure). They usually centre on generalised human agents, such as 'you' or 'the experimenter'; use the simple present tense; link the steps in the procedure with temporal conjunctive relations, such as 'then', 'now' or 'next'; and mainly use material/action clauses (lexico-grammatical features).
- *Recounts* retell events for the purpose of informing or entertaining. They include diaries, personal letters, descriptions of events and so on (functions). In school, children's first writings are usually recounts, and the genre continues to have currency throughout schooling: for example, reporting on science experiments and some forms of 'creative' writing (educational context). Recounts characteristically begin with a contextualising orientation, followed by a series of events, and often conclude with a reorientation (schematic structure). The focus in recounts is on individual participants, with the text sequenced temporally, often in the past tense (lexico-grammatical features).

Table 6.10: Some school genres

Genre	School context	Macro-structures	Micro-structures
Report: Factual text describing natural, technical or social phenomena	• Science reports • Social studies reports	• General classification • A series of descriptions of aspects, parts, functions or qualities	• Generic participants • No temporal sequence • 'Being' and 'having' clauses • Processes turned into things • A focus on general states
Procedure: Text that describes how things are done, step by step	• A write-up of a science experiment • A recipe • Technical instructions	• Goal • Ordered sequence of steps	• Generalised human actors • Temporal conjunctions • Action clauses, connection of persons with things
Recount: Text that retells events and experiences	• Recounting personal experiences • Recounting what happened in a lesson	• Contextualising orientation • A series of events • Tying the events together into a meaningful conclusion	• Individual participants, first person • Temporal sequence
Narrative: Does not pretend to be factual, even though it may connect with the author's experience	• Creative writing	• Orientation – contextualises participants in place • Complication – something surprising or important happens • Evaluation – tries to make sense of the complication • Resolution – deals with the consequences of the complication	• Specific individual participants • Tense and time sequence progressions • Mental processes as participants react to events or contemplate them

- *Narratives* are texts that do not pretend to be factual, even though they may be closely linked to actual or vicarious experience. They set out to amuse, to entertain or to instruct (functions). In school, narratives are frequently expected in 'creative writing' (educational context). Narratives begin with an orientation that introduces and contextualises the participants. This may be followed by an evaluation, which foreshadows the general direction of the story. The narrative develops via one or more complications. These then come to a resolution, and possibly a reorientation that returns to the scene that was set in the orientation and evaluation (schematic structure). Characteristic language features include specific individual participants, use of the past tense, temporal conjunctions and the use of material or action processes in the complication and resolution stages particularly, compared to relational and mental processes in the orientation and evaluation stages (lexico-grammatical features).

Table 6.11: Overview of typical genres in curriculum areas

English	observation, literary description, recount, narrative, news story, feature article, personal response, review, character analysis, thematic interpretation, critical response, exposition, discussion, challenge
History	biographical recount, historical account, news story, site interpretation, explanation, exposition, discussion, challenge
Geography	factual description, factual recount, explanation, exposition, discussion
Creative arts	description, response, review, interpretation, report, procedure, procedural recount, design brief, exposition, discussion, challenge
Science	factual description, protocol, procedural recount, demonstration, research article, classifying report, explanation, discussion, challenge
Personal development, health and physical education	factual description, protocol, procedure, procedural recount, report, explanation, exposition, discussion, challenge

Source: Christie & Derewianka (2008); Humphrey, Droga & Feez (2012).

See literacies.com Christie on Learning to Mean in Writing.

The expectation to link social purpose to text structure leads to an understanding of language very different from that of traditional grammar. Starting with the question of purpose, analysis of the text proceeds by looking at the structure of the whole text. Only then does it account for the progress of the whole text in terms of what happens in sentences and clauses. Unlike traditional grammar, which starts with words as 'parts of speech' and rarely gets further than dissecting clauses and sentences, genre analysis is concerned primarily with whole texts and their social functions. Sentence and clause analysis is performed in order to explain the workings of the whole text and how it realises its social purpose.

Learning to use socially powerful texts

What then of the social relations of learning? We've seen the phases of learning writing and reading in practice in the examples given in this chapter. There are three. In the first, the modelling phase, students are exposed to a number of texts that exemplify the genre in question. If the subject is science and the topic is dolphins, for example, students may read texts on sea mammals from various sources. Generically, these texts are most likely to be reports. This could lead to a discussion of what the texts are for (functions), how the information in the reports is organised (schematic structure) and aspects of the way the text 'speaks' (words and their sequence).

Phase two involves joint negotiation of a class text. The first element in this stage is study of the field (specialised knowledge) and the context (where events are happening) of the genre: students observe, research, interview, discuss, take notes, draw diagrams and so on. This is followed by joint construction of a class text, in which students participate in the process of writing a report, guided by the teacher. The teacher acts as a scribe as the students contribute to a jointly constructed text that approximates the structure of report genre and employs the key word choices and sequences characteristic of reports.

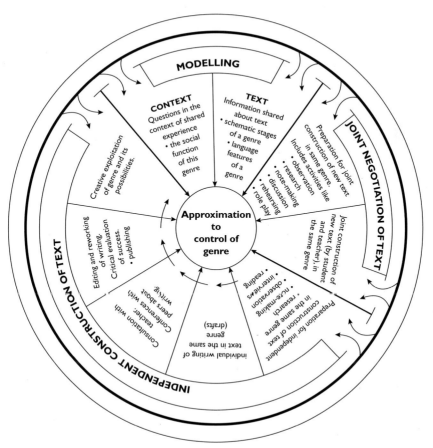

Figure 6.5 The teaching learning cycle: phases of reading and writing in a genre approach

See literacies.com Rossbridge and Rushton on The critical conversation about text: joint construction.

In the third and final phase, students independently construct their own reports: preparing with more work on the substantive field; drafting their own reports; conferencing with peers and the teacher about their individual writing efforts; critically re-evaluating their texts as they edit for publication; and then, perhaps, creatively exploiting the genre to represent other fields. The cycle can then be repeated, working on progressively more sophisticated aspects of the report genre.

See literacies.com Teaching learning cycle – Ross on YouTube.

Thinking broadly in terms of the social purposes of this learning, we see parallels between the language demands of different stages of science education and the language demands of different occupational positions in science-based industries. Moving from personalised recounts to more professional genres of report or explanation tracks a progression from commonsense knowledge and everyday texts to texts that are increasingly technical and formal. These texts are meant to be read by strangers, often far removed from those who wrote them. They become public texts for public purposes.

Students today are moving into a workforce in which there are increasing demands to use and create documentation. Written texts, such as reports, procedures and persuasive writing, are becoming an increasingly important element of working life, not to mention well-informed public life when it comes to thinking about contentious issues, such as climate change, stem cell research or human reproductive technologies. The functional approach to literacy aims to put structure and content back into literacy teaching.

See literacies.com Humphrey on Creating effective persuasive texts within and beyond schooling.

See literacies.com Kalantzis and Cope on Debating Functional Literacy.

Table 6.12: Ms Derecho's pedagogical choices (4)

Dimension 4: The social relationships of literacy learning	The relationship of learners to literacies knowledge, learners to other learners and learners to teachers
• The uses of genres in school • Learning to use socially powerful texts	

Exploring connections between the 'knowledge processes' and functional literacy pedagogy

Functional pedagogy focuses on knowledge processes that we have called 'analysing functionally' and 'applying appropriately'. It is derived from an analysis of what people do through language and a principled relationship between language form and function. Its emphasis is on making meaning. Learning to mean is seen as a social process – language is learned in interaction with more capable others.

This view of learning brings the functional approach into close alignment with the concept of the zone of proximal development at the heart of Vygotsky's sociocultural psychology (described further in Chapter 14): the zone between what a child can achieve alone and with assistance. Supported by the scaffolding provided by the teacher throughout the teaching learning cycle, students learn to explain the ways in which texts work to convey meaning effectively. They then apply their knowledge of language and meaning-making resources in real-life social contexts to participate in and enact, or indeed to challenge, the discourses of their schools and communities.

 See literacies.com Learning Modules.

 See literacies.com #edtech Literacies Applications.

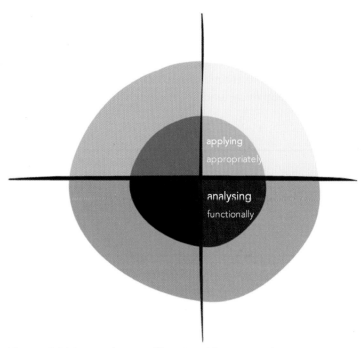

Figure 6.6 The emphases of functional literacy pedagogy

Summary

	Functional literacy pedagogy
The contents of literacy knowledge	Learning the genres of school success and social power
The organisation of the literacy curriculum	Reading genre models and writing within generic frameworks in the context of subject area learning.
Learners doing literacy	Students gradually take on more responsibility for constructing texts as they move through the teaching-learning cycle from teacher-directed modeling, teacher-guided joint construction to scaffolded independent construction.
The social relationships of literacy learning	Learning powerful text forms for educational success and social access

Knowledge processes

conceptualising by naming

1. Add entries to your wiki defining key concepts in the literacies pedagogy: important terms in the analysis of the ways in which communication and language work in social contexts, and the ways in which they are learned. Maintain and extend this wiki as you work through this and the remaining chapters of this book.

applying appropriately

2. Choose a text type (genre) that might be taught in one lesson. Design a lesson that exemplifies the genre teaching-learning cycle based on functional literacy pedagogy. Script hypothetical teacher–student talk in the joint construction stage of this lesson.

conceptualising with theory

3. Write an account of the learning theory behind functional approaches to literacy. Refer to the work of 'genre theorists' or linguists, such as Michael Halliday and Gunther Kress.

analysing functionally

4. Discuss the learning conditions under which functional literacy pedagogy is most and least appropriate.

applying creatively

5. Consider a particularly appropriate application of functional literacy pedagogy (for a particular subject matter or learning context addressing the needs of a particular student group) and develop a lesson plan illustrating this application whose primary (though not necessarily exclusive) focus is functional.

CHAPTER 7

Critical literacies pedagogy

Overview

Critical pedagogies generally acknowledge that literacies are in the plural. They recognise the many voices learners bring to the classroom, the many sites of popular culture and the new media, and the differing perspectives that exist in real-world texts. They support learners as meaning-makers, as agents, as participants and as active citizens. They use the learning of literacies as a tool to enable students to take more control over the ways that meaning is made in, and about, their lives, rather than allow them to be alienated, swamped or excluded by unfamiliar texts – or simply to be confused or grudgingly compliant. More recently, **critical literacies** have also become sites for the interrogation and creation of media and **new media** texts. In this chapter we will explore the contents of critical literacy knowledge, see how literacy and identity are connected and understand the organisation of critical literacy curriculum.

Critical literacies: Approaches to literacy that focus on texts that communicate student interests and experiences and address challenging social issues, such as discrimination and disadvantage

New media: Communications media utilised since the rise of digitisation and the internet, now easier and cheaper to access and supporting wider social participation, with more people acting as creators of textual content

Another student, another teacher. Kosta's teacher is Ms Wheelbarrow, who calls her approach to teaching reading and writing 'critical literacy'. Like the children in the previous chapters, Kosta is preternaturally wise, and it's hard to pick the learning level of his class. Sometimes it seems to be a class for younger learners; at other times for older learners.

The contents of literacy knowledge – learning about social differences, and popular and new media cultures

Critical thinking through literacies

'Now, class,' Ms Wheelbarrow sets the tone with one of her serious voices, 'we are going to look at how our own local community works.'

'Tell me what you know or like best about our community, and also the biggest problems you think we have.'

'I like the basketball courts,' says the boy opposite Kosta.

'And the public library,' adds Kosta, 'with all the cool events they have for children.'

'And the biggest problems?' asks Ms Wheelbarrow.

'The creek stinks,' says another student. 'It's full of rubbish and the factories along the sides of it empty smelly grey stuff that comes from their drains.'

After quite some discussion, the class agrees that the creek is the worst thing about their community. So the class decides to use the creek as a subject for a problem-solving unit of work as part of their integrated science and literacy program.

'Let's start by documenting the state of the creek,' Ms Wheelbarrow suggests to the children. 'Let's look at these Google Earth images. What surrounds the creek?'

The class notes the names of nearby factories and the streets whose run-off is likely to end up in the creek. They research water pollutants by looking at books in the library and searching websites. They consider scientific explanations of how creek ecologies work; their plant, fish, bird and animal life; and how these ecologies are affected by pollutants. Then they prepare a checklist of things they will be looking out for when they make a visit to the creek.

After several weeks of preparation, the day of the creek inspection arrives. Ms Wheelbarrow has divided the class into groups to document different things, with a camera for every group and every student with a checklist on their clipboard. One group will document litter and dumped rubbish. Another will document drains that run into the creek; still another, surrounding factories and housing, and a last group, evidence of the effects of pollution and rubbish on the ecosystem of the creek.

Back in class, each group writes a report of their findings using the new technical terms they have learned. Then they organise their observations in a structured way. They create and present PowerPoint slideshows of their findings.

'Who's responsible?' asks Ms Wheelbarrow.

'The factories that allow polluting run-off,' says one student.

'The householders who wash their cars and allow the chemicals to run into the street drain,' says another.

'It is a big problem,' she says, 'as your reports tell us. Actually, we're all responsible,' says Ms Wheelbarrow. 'As a community, what can we do about this?'

After some discussion, the class comes to the conclusion that the local city council is the main responsible authority, and that the class will send a compilation of the different groups' reports on the creek to the Mayor, and a copy to the city's Environmental Protection Department.

'Dear Mayor,' begins the covering letter, 'Our class is concerned about the state of our local creek …'.

Later the class visits the city offices and makes a presentation to the Mayor and representatives of the Environmental Protection Department. Kosta leads off with the class PowerPoint slideshow, a compilation of key points from the various presentations they created earlier. One student from each group speaks to several slides that their group has contributed to the overall case. Then they formally hand a final version of their report to the Mayor.

I wonder whether they were just being polite to us because we are students, Kosta thought to himself, or will they take us seriously and actually do something about the creek? It's been like this for so long …

See literacies.com Comber, Thomson and Wells on Critical Literacy.

If you could have 3 wishes what would you wish for? Draw them.

Figure 7.1 Children's critical literacy

This is one version of critical literacy, the substance of which is to tackle real-world issues by creating authentic texts that address questions of concern and interest to learners and their communities.

Michael Apple calls this 'democratic curriculum', not because it exhibits the formal processes of democracy as a political system (such as periodically voting for representatives), but because it is grounded in what he calls 'democratic values'. These are based on a 'faith in the individual and collective capacity of people to create possibilities for resolving problems'. A democratic curriculum requires 'critical reflection and analysis to evaluate ideas, problems, and policies' (Beane & Apple 2007: 7).

 See literacies.com Apple and Beane on Democratic Schools.

In the same spirit, William Ayers (2010: 150–1) draws a distinction between true education and mere training. Education, he says, 'is bold, adventurous, creative, vivid, illuminating – in other words, education is for self-activating explorers of life, for those who would challenge fate, for doers and activists, for citizens'. Training, on the other hand, is something 'for loyal subjects, for tractable employees, for willing consumers, for obedient soldiers'. For Ayers, 'education tears down walls; training is all barbed wire'. 'Education', he suggests, 'will unfit anyone to be a slave'. The result of education is personal and social transformation, no less. We find life as given; we experience moments of discovery and surprise and gain energy from remodelling and refashioning; then we achieve 'new ways of knowing and behaving, expanded horizons and fresh possibilities'.

 See literacies.com Ayers on Teaching for Democracy.

Paulo Freire and Donaldo Macedo (1987) also talk of transformation. Specifically in the case of literacy, this is a process of reading and writing about the world in which literate citizens become 'subjects' instead of the passive 'objects' of texts; 'agents' of texts instead of the 'victims' of texts. Literacy is not a matter of acquisition of technical communication skills. It is a process of learning how to make meanings that place individuals in the world, that change the world. Literacy is, as such, political; and critical literacy is an emancipatory practice in which one not only reads the 'word' but also the 'world'.

 See literacies.com Freire and Macedo on Emancipatory Literacy.

This is the first of several aspects of critical literacies pedagogy that we will highlight in this chapter: an orientation to texts that exemplifies and requires **critical thinking**. The other aspects, which we will come to shortly, are a concern for the varied identities of learners and studying the popular, mass and new media.

Critical thinking: Learning to see the world from multiple points of view, not assuming that things are exactly what texts say they are. Learning to question texts and interpret the human interests expressed in texts

Critical literacies pedagogy does not focus on mechanical skills or learning facts or rules separated from their use. These are kinds of the narrow focus in didactic pedagogy that critical literacies pedagogy highlights by way of contrast. Critical pedagogy involves students as social actors, raising questions of local or personal concern, or of wide and pressing human concern. It has learners identify problems and challenges of the moment. It addresses difficult issues to which there may be no easy answers; which may be contentious, and/or political. It does this, not to be political for politics' sake, but in order to exercise and nurture certain kinds of purposeful and reflective habits of mind and action.

The aim of critical literacies is to help learners understand the ways things are constructed in the world by people's values and actions. Its assumption is that the world of learning is not simply a series of rules to be obeyed, facts to be learned and knowledge authorities to be followed. In textual terms, a critically literate person identifies relevant and powerful topics, analyses and documents evidence, considers alternative points of view, formulates possible solutions to problems and perhaps also tries these solutions, comes to their own conclusions and makes well-reasoned arguments to support their case.

Table 7.1: Contrasting pedagogical values

Critical literacies	Didactic literacy
• Democratic values – acting upon real issues and problems in the world	• Formal rules, dry facts, mechanical skills
• Active, participatory	• Passive, compliant
• Education	• Training
• Personal and social transformation	• Social reproduction

Literacy and identity

Another kind of focus in critical literacy pedagogy comes with a recognition that all representation and communication involve human identities. Literacy and **identity** are inextricably interconnected. The 'possession' and 'use' of literacy – of particular literate practices – inscribes the identity of the user; the 'who' and 'what' they are. This type of critical literacy pedagogy also recognises that these human identities differ.

Identity: A person's ways of thinking, communicating and being, based on their life experiences and aspirations

William Ayers (2010) recounts a lesson in which African-American activist Stokely Carmichael contrasts Black Vernacular with the English of power, bell hooks (1994) sees Black Vernacular as a language of resistance. A teacher describes the way in which he brought rap lyrics into the classroom, comparing traditional poetry texts with rap texts and affirming the literary knowledge and talents of students who otherwise would be regarded as failures in school, and who might have been uninterested in conventional literacy content (Duncan-Andrade & Morrell 2008).

See literacies.com
Ayers on Teaching for Democracy.
hooks on the Language of Power.
Duncan-Andrade and Morrell on Teaching Hip Hop.

Sometimes this version of critical literacy is named 'postmodern education', bringing a rich cacophony of student voices into the classroom and validating popular ways of speaking and identities. Here, students – positioned as subjects who have agency – determine which meanings are important to them and the curriculum starts with these. Critical literacy creates a space for modes of expression that have historically been suppressed and devalued. Aronowitz and Giroux (1991) call this a 'border pedagogy', which 'confirms and critically engages the knowledge and experience through which students author their own voices and construct social identities' (128–9).

See literacies.com Aronowitz and Giroux on Postmodern Education.

This focus on critical literacy also requires at times a certain kind of introspection about one's own stances and attitudes towards the different 'Other': students who are disabled, or of a different sexual orientation, or of a different ethnic or racial group.

See literacies.com Ware on Teaching about the 'Other'.

Addressing discrimination and disadvantage

Ms Wheelbarrow comes into the classroom with another one of those 'let's-get-serious-because-we-are-about-to-start-a-new-unit-of-work' looks.

'I want you all to listen to this scenario,' she starts off, 'a story about two fictional friends, Heather and Ellen. They might be two people in my group of friends.

'One day Heather decides she doesn't like Ellen any more. It seems that someone told her something Ellen had said, and this has upset her. Heather tells all their friends that they should ignore Ellen and not let her into their group any more. I don't know what to do. I only know I don't want to be like Ellen. So every time Ellen comes near us, we walk away giggling and ignoring her. We've all defriended her from Facebook and Heather has started a mean group about her that we've all joined.'

Ms Wheelbarrow gives everyone a 'Common Connections' table to start their critical thinking about this scenario and its possible relationship to their own lives.

The part about …
Reminded me of …
Because …

'Now, I don't want you to name names,' says Ms Wheelbarrow. 'Change any names so real people in your Common Connections table cannot be identified.'

Pairs share their stories. They watch a video on bullying. As they watch the video, they fill out a wins/loses analysis for the target (the person who experiences **discrimination**), the perpetrator (the initiator of discrimination), the bystander (who doesn't act, just watches) and the ally (who comes to the aid of the target).

Discrimination: Systematic exclusion of a person or group of people based on negative attitudes towards them, and practices or habits of exclusion

'Now I want you, in each of your groups, to role-play a bullying situation in which you each take one of these roles. Write a script for your role-play, because later you are going to present it to the class.'

Groups select a variety of areas of discrimination for their bullying role-plays: sexual harassment, discrimination on the basis of sexuality, racism, age discrimination, disability discrimination. They work away at their scripts, then they perform them.

So many kinds of discrimination, thinks Kosta. It's a wonder we don't completely tear ourselves apart. What a jungle!

The class then listens carefully to the lyrics of some popular songs that deal with discrimination. They talk about the modes of persuasion in these lyrics. They watch videos of some famous speeches pleading for an end to discrimination, including Martin Luther King's 'I have a dream' speech. They each write the script of a speech to the others in the school designed to inspire students to take a stand against discrimination and bullying.

'All We Want Is a Fair Go' is the title of Kosta's speech about racism. It's one of the best, and selected for presentation to the whole school assembly.

See literacies.com Dunn et al. on Values of Social Justice and Inclusion.

Another area of focus in critical literacy pedagogy is popular and new media: what we refer to as popular culture. Also called the 'culture of the people' and the 'culture of the masses', popular culture takes various forms, including popular literature and music, television, film, comics, graphic novels, magazines, the internet and video games. In an older, didactic pedagogy, the mass and popular media were regarded as mere entertainment, not the stuff of serious literacy learning.

Aesthetics: Refers to the idea or study of design and art

They were considered to be junk culture rather than the 'high' culture of a literary canon; devoid of **aesthetics** and moral worth, and associated with the 'vulgarities' of popular taste; sites of non-standard forms of the vernacular rather than the standard forms of language used by government, academic discourse and 'serious' public discussions.

See literacies.com Buckingham on Media and Identities.

Given the globalised world that our students now inhabit and the proliferation, sophistication and powerful 'pull' of popular culture texts, there is a clear rationale, an imperative, for bringing popular culture into the classroom. As Giroux (1997: 32) notes: 'Learning in the postmodern age is located elsewhere – in the popular spheres ... culture.' Giroux (1996: 67) comments, too, that:

> Schools need to redefine curricula within a postmodern conception of culture linked to the diverse and changing global conditions that necessitate new forms of literacy, a vastly expanded understanding of how power works within cultural apparatuses, and keener sense of how the existing generation of youth are being produced within a society in which mass media plays a decisive, if not unparalleled, role in constructing multiple and diverse social identities.

And so, perhaps now more than ever, it is seemingly necessary that we equip our students with the critical tools needed to 'read' texts, to 'read' the world, and to endow students with the capacity to transform their world and their place in it.

There are many reasons why a teacher might want to bring popular culture and media into the classroom. First, to connect with learners' identities. Second, to start with the known before moving on to the new. Students bring to learning powerful symbolic resources that are derived to a significant degree from the media and popular culture, so this is a way to start 'where the students are at'. Such an approach facilitates the building of connections between students' out-of-school literacy practices and 'expertise' and the literacies required in the context of school, as well as the mobilisation of their existing cultural knowledges and practices. Third, media and popular culture encompass texts of our time that carry enormous emotional affect and social effect. These are powerful sites of meaning-making activity, very different in their form and substance from the world of earlier generations and traditional curriculum. And students take undeniable pleasure in popular culture; pleasure that can be harnessed to engage students. Furthermore, a critical literacy pedagogy that draws on popular culture texts can serve to engage students who are 'struggling' with literacy and to motivate students who are considered 'at-risk' learners.

In the case of the new, digital media, the teacher may want to introduce students to the latest 'can do' media as a project of empowering learners to access cultural and knowledge resources, and to cross the 'digital divide'. Some students, by virtue of their levels of access, are more able to use the new media than others. Now we are definitely speaking of literacies in the plural, the many modes and spaces of contemporary media, and the extraordinarily varied range of identities and interests expressed in these spaces.

Noting that 'popular culture itself has ... become a focus of the new work on digital media and learning' (Gee 2010: 12), James Paul Gee (2007) analyses video games: a multimodal site of literacy in which students navigate narratives as powerful as any in the literary canon. They do this as characters, as players, as actors in the narrative. They negotiate text and image. By comparison, the levels of textual and cognitive interaction in traditional schooling are decidedly wanting.

Table 7.2: Gee's analysis of video games as learning environments

Active learning	Learner as producer, not just consumer; a strong sense of ownership and agency; the learner is offered and makes choices
Interactivity	Play as a form of simultaneous 'reading' (interpreting) and 'writing' (producing)
Learner as mentor	Teaching others at the same time as learning oneself; horizontal knowledge relationships
Engagement	Compelling reasons to engage; getting drawn in; making an emotional commitment; 'projective identity' creating motivation for extended engagement
Identity	Attentional economy based on the development of strong identities in the game; a trigger for a deep investment on the part of the player
Empathy	Talking, thinking and acting as if you are in the game; simulation that invites emotional investment
Community	An affinity space, a place for sharing and collaboration
Multimodality	Extensive use of visual, linguistic, audio (on the screen), tactile (hand and eye), gestural and spatial (as represented on the screen) modes, with a redundancy; different modes repeating and reinforcing each other's meanings
Risk	Lowering of real-world consequences; 'psychosocial moratorium'; you can always start again, which lowers the cost of failure
Reward	Visible outcomes, with achievement possible at different levels, relative to the level of mastery
Critical	Looking for deceptions built into the game and trying to find ways to outwit the game
Conceptual	Working out the game's design and design principles; building mental models to master the game
Metaknowledge	Tells you current capacities and potential capacities; assesses previous knowledge and supports players to make decisions for themselves
Staging	Cycles of new learning, staged mastery and progressive competence; cycle of challenge → routinise → challenge. Also, building up intuitive and tacit knowledge, creating incremental generalisations that remain fruitful in later stages of learning; basic skills are transferable, not learned in isolation or out of context

See literacies.com Gee on Video Games and Learning.

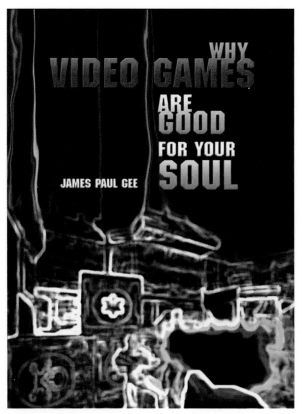

Figure 7.2 James Paul Gee on video games

We call upon students to undertake 'interrogative' work – to interrogate texts – when we engage them in critical literacy pedagogy. In doing so, they come to 'unveil', to expose, the worldviews and the ideologically invested assumptions, values and attitudes that serve to inform – and are (re)presented in – the text. They come to recognise that texts are constructs tied to social and cultural practices; that texts are value-laden, never neutral. They form alternative positions and multiple points of view and, in this way, demonstrate 'critical reflexivity'. They are thus positioned to engage in acts of textual intervention and transformation.

In textual terms, critical literacy practices might involve, for example: asking in whose interests particular texts work, examining multiple and conflicting texts, examining the historical and cultural contexts of discourses in texts, reading texts against one another, comparing the vocabularies and grammars of related texts, investigating how readers are positioned by the ideologies in texts, making multiple passes through texts, and transforming and redesigning texts (Luke & Freebody 1999).

Table 7.3: Interrogating texts: questions for students to ask

Some questions for younger readers	Some questions for older readers
• What is this text about? How do we know? Who would be most likely to read it and how do we know?	• What is the subject matter or topic?
	• Why might the author have written this text?
	• Who is the intended audience? How do you know?
• What does the author want us to *know* (about the world and the people in it)? What do the pictures suggest? What do the words suggest? Does this 'match' what you know (about the world and about people)? Why/why not?	• What worldview and values does the author assume that the reader holds? How do you know?
	• What knowledge does the reader need to bring to this text in order to understand it?
• What does the author want us to *believe* about the world and the people in it? What suggests this to us? Does this 'fit' with what *you* believe about the world and about people? Why/why not?	• Who would feel 'left out' in this text, and why; and is it a problem? Who would find that the claims made in this text clash with their own values, beliefs or experiences?
	• How is the reader 'positioned' in relation to the author (e.g. as a friend, as an opponent, as someone who needs to be persuaded, as invisible, as someone who agrees with the author's views)?
• How could we rewrite this text so that it 'matches' more closely all of our experiences and fits more effectively with what we know about the world and about people?	• Are there 'gaps' or 'absences' or 'silences' in this text? If so, what are they? For example, is there a group of people missing who logically should be included? Are different groups talked about as though they belong to the same, seamless group? Does the author write about a group without including *their* perspective on things or events?

Source: Knobel (1998: 97–8).

Ms Wheelbarrow is about to start a study of the media within an early literacy unit of work. Kosta is in the class still, though never sure whether this is a flash-back to when he was younger or, for that matter, what grade he is in. He is a strangely easygoing boy. 'What children's television programs do people like?'

Ms Wheelbarrow lists them on the board: *Sesame Street*, cartoons, *Hi-5* … A lot of children seem to like *Hi-5*, which Ms Wheelbarrow personally detests for its kitschy commercialism. However, she does a quick survey of the class and it seems *Hi-5* is most popular.

'OK, let's watch *Hi-5*,' she says. 'Tell me about the characters. What are their names? What are their cartoon icons? What are their signatures? Which character do you like best? Let's do a survey.'

Ms Wheelbarrow has created an online survey in which students select their favourite characters and give the reasons for their preferences.

Hmm, thinks Kosta, after a group discussion of the survey results. The boys seem to like Ainsley and Tanika but the girls like Mary and Dayen.

'Next, let's create a storyboard of another *Hi-5* program. What are the parts of the program? How is it organised?

'Now let's go to the *Hi-5* website. What do you find here?'

'Lots of things to buy,' calls out the boy opposite Kosta, 'and my mother gets cranky when I keep asking for the toys that go with *Hi-5*.'

'So why do you think *Hi-5* has a website?' asks Ms Wheelbarrow.

'To sell us things,' says the boy, 'to hook us into being connected with the story and the products in as many ways as possible.'

Ms Wheelbarrow pauses to discuss this point with the whole class, wanting to bring out her concerns about the manipulative side of commercial TV and children's shows.

'And now, class, in groups I want you to design and film your own children's television program. Create a storyboard outlining the sections, then each write a section of the script. We'll then play out the script in a rehearsal (and it's not too late to improve the script), film your program and play our programs to the class.'

See literacies.com Cloonan on Analysing a Children's Television Phenomenon.

It is clearly important to incorporate popular culture texts into the curriculum and to utilise them in our classrooms in pedagogically productive, critically oriented ways. In order to do this, teachers need to understand contemporary literacies in their broadest sense; be aware of the kinds of texts and out-of-school literacies with which our students engage; and value the rich linguistic, social and cultural

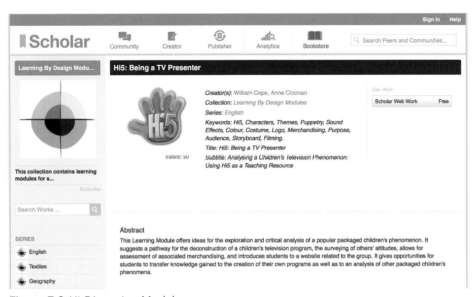

Figure 7.3 *Hi-5* Learning Module

Table 7.4: Ms Wheelbarrow's pedagogical choices (1)

Dimension 1: The contents of literacy knowledge	Its subject matter, or what learners are meant to learn
• Addressing issues and problems, developing critical thinking skills	
• A focus on learner identities	
• Addressing discrimination and disadvantage	
• Using popular culture and new media	

expertise that students bring with them to school. And, while it is important to engage in critical work, teachers must also be mindful when objectifying and opening up popular culture texts to analysis, making their construction apparent and questioning such – and calling upon students to do the same – that they also acknowledge the appeal of these texts, the personal and affective investment students have in them and the pleasure they draw from them (Dalley-Trim 2012).

The organisation of literacy curriculum – a focus on voice and agency

Finding voice

Critical literacy pedagogies are organised around the **voice** and agency of learners. For Peter McLaren (2015: 179), voice is the stuff of 'the stories that people tell'. It consists of the forms of expression people use to articulate their experience and represent their background knowledge. It is the means that people have at their disposal to 'be heard' and to define themselves and be present in the world. It is also grounded in one of the principles of democracy: that people are free to have their say in the processes of governance that affect their lives. It is an aim of critical literacy that:

Voice: The way in which a person expresses their identity

> students can acquire the pedagogical courage and moral responsibility to participate in democratic life as critical social agents, transforming themselves into authors of their own histories rather than being written off as the passive victims of history (McLaren 2015: 27).

 See literacies.com McLaren on Student Voice.

'We are what we say and do, says Ira Shor.

> The way we speak and are spoken to help shape us into the people we become. Through words and other actions, we build ourselves in a world that is building us. ... *Literacy* is understood as social action through language use that develops us as agents inside a larger culture (Shor 2009: 282).

See literacies.com Shor on Critical Literacy.

Finding a voice does not necessarily mean identifying oneself with all or any of the texts of the world around us, still less acquiring the voices presented in popular culture and the media just because they are everywhere. Rather, one can resist, and indeed reject, the voices and 'storylines' on offer. Anne Hass Dyson (2001) tells of Tina's reaction to the less active roles of females in Ninja narratives. At first she, like the other girls in her class, steered away from Ninja stories because they seemed to be for the boys and not the girls. In a twist of the narrative, however, Tina reconstructed one of these stories to have a female superhero. The stuff of voice is a matter of varied interpretations, ambiguity, ambivalence, complexity, contradiction and flux.

See literacies.com Hass Dyson on Critical Literacy and Gender.

Being creators in the new media

Digital media add another layer of pedagogical opportunity for teachers by creating a contemporary space where student voices can be expressed. New technologies provide spaces for students to express themselves in the form of video, podcast, blog sites or wikis, which are no different from the tools that mature or professional users have. Lankshear & Knobel (2006: 196) point out that these technologies facilitate '"authentic" rather than "pretend" versions of the social practices in question'.

As Gee (2010: 12) notes: 'Digital tools have allowed "everyday people" to produce and not just consume media.'

See literacies.com Lankshear and Knobel on Pedagogy for i-Mode.

Ms Wheelbarrow wants the members of the class to be expert users of the new media. So she asks students to find five examples of personal profile blogs.

'What are they saying?'

'They're telling the world the things people really like or believe in,' says the girl opposite Kosta.

'And how do they work? What are their parts?'

The class begins a blog technical glossary: 'hyperlinks', 'icons', 'navigation', 'tags' …

Then everyone begins a blog with what Ms Wheelbarrow calls a 'passion project', a blog post on their biggest interest (Cloonan 2010b). The boy opposite Kosta starts a blog on 'Big Rigs'. His father is a truck driver. Kosta creates his passion project on mythological creatures. He reads fantasy novels.

When the blogs are finally published to the Web, the range of topics, and also the range of blog designs, is amazing, Kosta thinks. All the students have put so much work into these blogs because they have been writing on things they really care about. And the students' blogs look every bit as good as the 'real' blogs they have found on the internet; in fact, just as real.

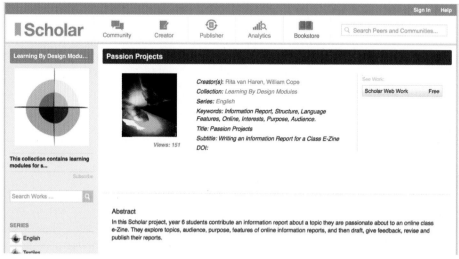

Figure 7.4 Passion Project Learning Module

 See literacies.com van Haren, Passion Project (in Chapter 3).

'Postmodern' concerns

Critical pedagogy has been heavily influenced by what is sometimes termed a '**postmodern**' concern for different identities. This version of critical literacies pedagogy has its roots in the authentic pedagogy of Dewey and shares many of its most basic assumptions – about student activity, motivation and experience, for instance. Much of the time, it mounts critiques of didactic pedagogy that deploy the same repertoire of arguments as did Dewey at the beginning of the 20th century.

Postmodern: A social orientation and orientation to learning based on the idea that there is no single way of being human and no universal truth. There is just a wide range of perspectives based on different life experiences, histories, cultures and interests.

However, today's critical pedagogies also part company with Dewey's authentic pedagogy in some important ways. If Dewey's emphasis was on the singular culture of industrial modernity, the emphases of the new pedagogy are on difference, discontinuity and irreversible cultural and linguistic fragmentation. That is, society is believed to be too complex to predict or shape, so all we can do is listen to each other; the future will take care of itself if we just do this. Those who promote the new pedagogy frequently make direct links with broader intellectual movements, such as feminism, gay rights and anti-racist movements that have become more vociferous and effective since the last decades of the 20th century: movements that have focused on recognising and respecting socio-cultural differences and identities.

The critical pedagogy we are trying to capture in this chapter is founded in newly prevailing senses of the world, often encapsulated in the word 'postmodernism'. Modernist grand narratives of progress are no longer valid, they say. They reject the idea that the whole world is heading in one direction towards the one preferred future of economic development, private enterprise capitalism and social freedom in which all individuals should be treated the same way. Instead, they see enormous social and environmental problems arising from these economic models. Western culture, which is at the heart of the idea of progress and the economic system of capitalism, does not deserve to be credited as the democratic liberator of all societies. Nor is the Western canon all that we should be learning about in school. We should also learn from other cultural traditions and their texts. In this way of thinking, all ways of speaking and thinking are as good as each other and appropriate to their social and cultural contexts. There is no one correct way of being or of speaking, or one correct interpretation of a text – it is all a matter of perspective. There is no one truth, just points of view. And we should revel in our differences instead of wanting everyone to be the same.

Aronowitz and Giroux (1991) point to the 'decay of master narratives' or common stories that explain our world, and 'metadiscourses', or explanations that aim to present universal knowledge that will be good for everybody. They allow 'no privileged place' to Western culture; to that 'by which Western culture legitimates itself' (Aronowitz & Giroux 1991: 13). Their intention is 'to legitimate [the] subaltern' discourses [the ways of speaking of disadvantaged groups] as equal (Aronowitz & Giroux 1991: 14). Language positions the author or reader according to race, class and gender.

Accordingly, the primary task of curriculum is to be relevant to individual learners – to connect to their personal lives and experiences. A critical pedagogy of postmodernism and difference builds on the insights of authentic pedagogy

Table 7.5: Perspectives on society and knowledge

Modern perspectives	Postmodern perspectives
• A belief in social progress based on private enterprise	• Uncertainties about progress, with many social problems: poverty, environmental degradation etc.
• Individual freedom and an idea of equality in which every individual is treated in the same way	• All people fundamentally different, based on group identities; e.g. gender, ethnicity
• Valuing the 'greats' of the Western literary and cultural canon	• Valuing the different cultural voices of people from different backgrounds
• Knowledge a matter of truth and facts	• Knowledge a matter of perspective; no fixed truths or definite facts

regarding the value of curriculum as an active thing, in the hands of students and driven forward by their motivation. This pedagogy advocates a radical devolution of curriculum control and, consequently, an inevitable diversification of its contents according to the variety of student experience and student interest. In, for example, a postmodern high school, say Aronowitz and Giroux (1991), students and teachers have the final authority in making curriculum decisions. There are no requirements imposed from above. Students plan their own courses of study. Teachers may well try to persuade students, but in the last analysis it is up to the students. They may choose courses that are offered, but if these are not to the students' tastes they may choose independent study. Even within a class or a course, different groups will be working on different things.

Garth Boomer (1982: 3) carries this sense of the openness of the ideal curriculum right through to the dynamics of classroom discourse; that is, even the ways in which teachers and students talk and relate with one another:

> The teacher rarely tells the student what he thinks they ought to know ... He [also] recognises that the act of summary or 'closure' tends to have the effect of ending further thought. If a student has arrived at a particular conclusion, then little is gained by the teacher's restating it. If the student has not arrived at a conclusion, then it is presumptuous and dishonest for the teacher to contend that he has ... Lessons develop from the responses of students and not from a previously determined 'logical' structure. The only kind of lesson plan, or syllabus, that makes sense to [the good teacher] is one that tries to predict, account for, and deal with the authentic responses of learners to a particular problem ... We have discovered in our attempts to install inquiry environments in various schools that great strides can be made if the words 'teach' and 'teaching' are simply subtracted from the operational lexicon.

This means there can be no pre-set curriculum. The teacher is like the mother of a small child learning oral language, with the 'uncanny knack' that Jerome Bruner (1986) observed mothers have of being one step ahead of their children. Given classroom constraints, in the nature of this sort of curriculum students will, much of the time, need to communicate with each other in teacherless groups (Mayer 1990).

What does this mean for language teaching and learning? For a start, there is a sustained critique of teaching the closed repertoire of 'Great Books'. In much the same spirit as Dewey, Donald Murray (1982: 14) criticises English teacher training for its obsession with literature, finished writing, and language as it has been used by authors: 'And then, fully trained in the autopsy, we go out and are assigned to teach our students to write, to make language live.' John Mayer (1990) reads a conception of education as transmission into Matthew Arnold's (1869) well-worn dictum about teaching 'the best that has been thought and said in the world'. The products rather than the processes of literary analysis are presented, and formulaic interpretations have to be rote-learned by students so they can be tested by teachers. In the end, 'nothing questioned means nothing gained'. Literacy becomes a medium for elitism and tracking, an icon marking as separate those deemed worthy to be the inheritors of higher education and higher culture.

Multiple 'Englishes'

Critical literacies pedagogy also questions the value of teaching '**standard English**'. Its supporters have become uncomfortable with the idea that any form of language should be regarded as normal or superior. Instead, the language labelled 'standard' is seen to be just one culturally specific dialect in a world of dialect differences where no one culture, language or dialect can be regarded as superior.

Standard English: The version of English used by the more powerful, dominant groups in society

In his celebrated study of urban 'Black English Vernacular', Labov (1972) argues that, by comparison, 'standard' middle-class English is deficient in some important ways. Middle-class English is cumbersome and verbose when describing central human subjects, such as death. As found in academic discourse and technical or scientific books, standard English is 'simultaneously over-particular and vague', lacking the logical clarity and even grammaticality of Black English Vernacular (Labov 1972: 222). To deny Black English Vernacular a legitimate place in school, then, is not only to condemn a cultural resource born of students' experience that is demonstrably an effective, living, working, cultural tool. It is also to do a serious disservice to its speakers by incorrectly assuming that their language and background are cognitively and linguistically deficient. The problem for speakers of Black English Vernacular is not in their language, but in the school's prejudiced view of their language.

See literacies.com Labov on African-American English Vernacular.

The solution to these dilemmas, from the perspective of critical literacies pedagogies, is for schools to view all dialects – indeed all ways of using language in society – as linguistically equal. The focus should be on language differences not language deficits. Schools must 'reject negative, elitist, racist views of linguistic purity that would limit children to arbitrary "proper" language', says Goodman (2005: 25). Let's not fall into the trap of teaching a traditional grammar, which condemns 'non-standard' dialects, say Aronowitz and Giroux (1991). 'The successful usage of the students' cultural universe requires respect and legitimation of students' discourses, that is, their own linguistic codes, which are different but not inferior,' say Freire and Macedo (1987: 127); 'in the case of Black Americans, for example, educators must respect Black English'. Likewise, within the Australian context, as another example, Aboriginal and Torres Strait Islander languages and dialects should be acknowledged and respected. Conceiving the same bent in language education in larger political terms, a critical approach to literacy adds up to a 'pedagogy of voice', a narrative for agency, says Giroux. It is part of 'a moral and political project that links the production of meaning to the possibility for human agency, democratic community and transformative social action' (Giroux 1987: 10).

In the frame of reference of postmodern critical literacy, then, schools have to assume that there are no literary truths or universal, stable language facts. There is just language variation, with functions appropriate and relative to cultural – and social – experience.

Table 7.6: Ms Wheelbarrow's pedagogical choices (2)

Dimension 2: The organisation of literacy curriculum	How the subject matter is arranged
• Finding student voice	
• Being creators in the new media	
• 'Postmodern' concerns	
• Multiple 'Englishes'	

Learners doing literacy – engagement with real-world issues and active citizenship

Building on lived experience

A group of students in a crumbling public school in a Chicago housing estate brainstorm problems in their community. The list is long. Then Dyneisha shouts: 'Most of the problems on that list have to do with our school building bein' messed up. Our school is a dump! That's the problem.'

Soon the discussion reaches a critical point, that they need a new building, and 'How's we 'posed to get this new school?'

So the class decides to assemble the evidence they need, and to make their case for a new school by writing to a state senator, describing the conditions in which they are meant to learn and how these can be improved (Schultz 2007).

 See literacies.com Schultz on Democratic Curriculum in a Chicago School.

On the other side of the world, Pippa Stein (2001) describes the subtleties of what she calls 'linguistic reappropriation' as students in a South African classroom create bilingual stories, based on African storytelling traditions but full of contemporary politics and acute irony. Here's the beginning of a story told by 13-year-old Nobayeni Ndebele:

> Once there lived Mandela [the first black president of South Africa], Gatsha [the Zulu leader of the Inkatha Freedom Party] and De Klerk [the last president of apartheid South Africa]. Mandela visited Gatsha in his house and he and Gatsha agreed that they would add a potion to De Klerk's food to win him over to their side. Off they went to De Klerk's house, with pots of pap [a thick porridge made from maize, the staple diet of the majority of Black South Africans] and meat. On their arrival there, they said to De Klerk, 'Today we have cooked deliciously. Let's eat together now.' So they all sat down at the table and Mandela cut the meat. He cut, cut, cut carefully and then laid it out on the table artistically.

> But De Klerk was not used to eating pap. Mandela said to him, 'Well we don't
> know what to do now because you do not eat pap. We, on the other hand, are men.
> We eat pap. You, I'm afraid, will never be strong.'
>   Then Gatsha said, 'OK, let me go and buy De Klerk some bread.' ... [In-class trans-
> lation from Zulu]

A tale of trickery and political intrigue ensues, with one student translating the
text into English for those in the class who are not speakers of Zulu. Stein (2001)
calls this a process of creating an 'alternative canon', introducing text forms and
languages not historically valued in literacy curriculum. Students work with this
canon to analyse the social purposes of text production, discuss the complexities
of translation, unpack the multiple layers of meaning and consider the many possible interpretations.

 See literacies.com Stein on Linguistic Reappropriation.

In both of these cases, learners are engaging with issues that are close to home.
They bring their identities and interest, their lived experiences, to bear in the work
of literacy learning. They engage with the texts of their own lives. They are involved
in a participatory process of meaning-making. This active participation, starting
with the voice of persons and communities, becomes a basis for taking students
into new, personally and socially relevant and more expansive domains of motivation, meaning and participation.

Table 7.7: Dimensions of critical literacies

Connect with lived experience	Introduce texts from students' own lives
	View from multiple perspectives and unpack multiple layers of meaning
Think critically	Identify problems, voice concerns, assemble evidence from a variety of sources, make a case
Take action	Offer solutions, make others aware, participate

Working in the new, participatory media

Many educators now see opportunities for expanding the possibilities of participation in the new, digital media. Henry Jenkins (2006a) observes that a large proportion of young people participate in online media, and the less privileged sometimes
to the same – or even a greater – extent than the privileged. This is the basis for
what he calls a 'participatory culture' where the barriers to community engagement are low; where you learn by doing and by informal mentorship; where the
means of creative expression are readily accessible; where people feel that their
contributions matter; and where social connections and bonds are formed.

 See literacies.com Jenkins on Participatory Culture.

James Paul Gee speaks of forms of active engagement and learning that are intrinsic to video games. 'Video games are largely just problem-solving spaces' and show 'many of the learning principles that contemporary research in the learning sciences has argued work for deep and effective human learning' (Gee 2010: 11). Video games create powerful frameworks for learning because they support active participation. Whether it be those observing communities of young people at work with wikis, blogs or digital media production tools and web repositories, 'nearly everyone who has come to this issue has been impressed by the ways in which popular culture today is using digital tools and other devices to engage in powerful, deep, and complex thinking and learning outside of school' (Gee 2010: 11–12).

See literacies.com Gee on the New Digital Media.

Meaningful participation, then, is a touchstone of critical literacy, and the new media may create the cultural, not to mention technological, conditions for learning that is more powerfully participatory.

Table 7.8: Ms Wheelbarrow's pedagogical choices (3)

Dimension 3: Learners doing literacy	The ways in which learners are intended to learn to make meanings
• Building on lived experience	
• Working in the new, participatory media	

The social relationships of literacy learning – literacies as a tool for taking control of one's life

Investigating challenging social issues and moral dilemmas

Ms Wheelbarrow has moved on to teaching Japanese history with a unit on the Second World War, and how it ended with the explosion of two nuclear weapons, destroying the cities of Hiroshima and Nagasaki. It's a topic that is far away in time and space, but she wants to bring some very difficult historical questions close to home for the learners in her class. She also wants to integrate this unit strongly into her literacy-across-the-curriculum approach.

'Let's start,' says Ms Wheelbarrow, 'by using our "hot potato" strategy to record everything we already know about Japan.'

The class divides into groups, and Kosta ends up being the scribe for his.

'Food', 'language', 'anime', 'manga', 'technology', 'the Second World War'. Everyone in the group takes turns to describe something they already know about Japan. Kosta is surprised just how much his group already knows from the media, general knowledge and work that some of them have done at school in other classes.

'Next, I want each group to do a jigsaw activity about Hiroshima today, in which different members of the group collect information about some aspect of life in Hiroshima: geography, public places, historical sites, education. Do your individual research, then we'll get into expert groups to share knowledge among people who have looked at the same aspect of today's Hiroshima, and then we'll get back into our original groups to put together a complete picture.'

There's lots of note-taking, making collages of text and image, and plenty of talk.

'Next lesson,' says Ms Wheelbarrow, 'we're going to see what happened one terrible day in 1945, so I want you to come into the classroom ready to be serious and respectful observers.'

Next time they come to class, the students find that Ms Wheelbarrow has covered the classroom walls with confronting images and texts. She has a video clip playing on the electronic whiteboard. The images all depict the atomic bomb hitting Hiroshima.

As the students come into the room, Ms Wheelbarrow says: 'I want you to enter the room in silence and take a walk around the room, absorbing all the images. Think about how you feel about these images and what facts you can learn by looking at the images and texts.'

There is an unusual quiet to the class. Some of the pictures are shocking.

'Now, share with a partner and decide what comment you will contribute in circle time.

'Next, I want you in groups of four to read the transcript of an interview with Mitsuo Tomosawa, a survivor. To help you with your reading, you will be given one of the following reading roles:

'Illustrator – you will draw some images, some things that you could picture or imagine while reading this interview. At the end you will share and explain it to your group.

'Codebreaker – you will make a list of unusual words. These could be words you haven't seen before, or words you just aren't too sure of. These will be discussed at the end.

'Investigator – you'll pretend you are going to interview Mitsuo Tomosawa and make a list of questions to ask him.

'Discussion manager – you'll get your group talking about the interview you just read by asking them some interesting questions about Mitsuo Tomosawa's experience.'

This is the beginning of a unit of work that lasts for several weeks. Students write empathetic letters to survivors. They write a critical analysis of the role of atomic weapons in ending the Second World War. They research and report upon the way the local Japanese community in their country was treated during the Second World War, and debate the justice of this treatment.

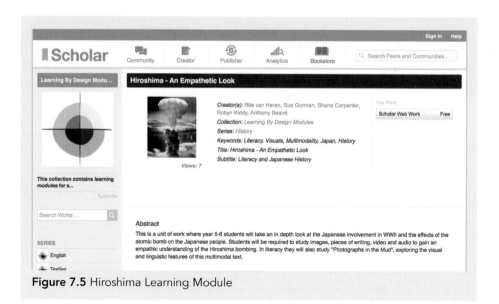

Figure 7.5 Hiroshima Learning Module

 See literacies.com van Haren et al. on Hiroshima – An Empathetic Look.

Here, the subject matter is distant from students' experience, but the teacher uses a number of strategems that prompt the learners to be active participants in knowledge. She starts by finding out what the children know. She gets them to contribute different aspects of knowledge into a holistic picture. She engages them emotionally, joining fact with affect. She connects distant events with local events. She positions students as text producers as well as text analysers.

Behind critical literacy is a 'moral economy' of learning, in which the balance of agency shifts from the vertical model of teacher-to-student knowledge transmission in didactic pedagogy to a horizontal student-to-student model of collaboration in which knowledge is co-constructed in a community of learners. These are the conditions in which students will be able to use literacies to take greater control over their own lives.

Human differences and social justice

There are two main strands to critical literacies – not so identifiable in separate schools of thought, because both strands are often intertwined. One is a generalisable orientation in which critical literacy, in Paulo Freire's terms, consists of processes of thinking and activities of reflection on social reality. This stands in direct contrast to a didactic pedagogy in which 'a narrating Subject (the teacher)' stands in relation to 'patient, listening objects (the students) … Narration (with the teacher as narrator) leads the students to memorize mechanically the narrated content. Worse yet, it turns them into "containers", into "receptacles" to be filled by the teachers' (Freire 2015: 71–2).

See literacies.com Freire on Education Which Liberates.

Another orientation is one we might call 'postmodern' or, in Giroux's (1996: 73–4) words, a meeting of minds with:

> a new kind of student forged within organizing principles shaped by the intersection of the electronic image, popular culture, and a dire sense of indeterminacy ... finding their way through a de-centred cultural landscape no longer caught in the grip of a technology of print, closed narrative structures, or the certitude of a secure economic future ... new hybridized cultural practices inscribed in relations of power that intersect differently with race, class, gender, and sexual orientation.

In other words, this is a world of extraordinary and irreconcilable differences.

 See literacies.com Giroux on Postmodern Education.

By the first decades of the 21st century, critical pedagogy has moved in the direction of the second of these two strands, towards a theory of cultural and linguistic difference. No longer, for this approach, is there is a superior literary canon and official standard form of the national language. There are only different literary, discursive and cultural traditions. Nor are there fixed language facts, only language and dialect variation that is relative to different cultural needs and interests. Central to this critical vision of literacies in the plural is the concept of student 'voice' – which in practice, in any one classroom, means 'many different voices'. The teacher, then, is only a facilitator who gives students space to voice their own interests in their own discourses.

However, on some occasions this approach appears to go so far as to mean a live-and-let-live approach to patterns of difference, which, not coincidentally, align with patterns of educational and social outcome. In other words, not all differences are equal. Leaving differences the way they are can also mean leaving inequality the way it is.

Of course, this is a world of cultural diversity, of multiple gender identities, of many different types of family, of subcultures and styles and fads and fetishes. It is a world where there are thousands upon thousands of blogs speaking in specialist tongues and where the television channels and YouTube downloads are endless, reaching into the souls of aficionados of every manner of peculiar discourse, from

Table 7.9: Ms Wheelbarrow's pedagogical choices (4)

Dimension 4: The social relationships of literacy learning	The relationship of learners to literacies knowledge, learners to other learners and learners to teachers
• Investigating challenging social issues and moral dilemmas	
• Exploring human differences and social justice	

Table 7.10: Literacy learning outcomes suggesting critical literacy pedagogy in Australia and the United States

Australian Curriculum	US Common Core State Standards
• *Language variation and change:* Understand that spoken, visual and written forms of language are different modes of communication with different features and their use varies according to the audience, purpose, context and cultural background (Year 2).	• *Reading literature – integration of knowledge and ideas:* Compare and contrast two or more versions of the same story (e.g. Cinderella stories) by different authors or from different cultures (Grade 2).
• *Examining literature:* Recognise that ideas in literary texts can be conveyed from different viewpoints, which can lead to different kinds of interpretations and responses (Year 5).	• *Reading literature – craft and structure:* Describe how a narrator's or speaker's point of view influences how events are described (Grade 5)
• *Language for interaction:* Understand the uses of objective and subjective language and bias (Year 6).	• *Reading informational texts – craft and structure:* Determine an author's point of view or purpose in a text and analyze how the author acknowledges and responds to conflicting evidence or viewpoints (Grade 8).
• *Literature and context:* Explore the ways that ideas and viewpoints in literary texts drawn from different historical, social and cultural contexts may reflect or challenge the values of individuals and groups (Year 8).	• *Writing – research to build and present knowledge:* Gather relevant information from multiple print and digital sources, using search terms effectively; assess the credibility and accuracy of each source; and quote or paraphrase the data and conclusions of others while avoiding plagiarism and following a standard format for citation (Grades 6–8).
• *Language for interaction:* Understand how language use can have inclusive and exclusive social effects, and can empower or disempower people (Year 10).	• *Reading literature – craft and structure:* Analyse a particular point of view or cultural experience reflected in a work of literature from outside the United States, drawing on a wide reading of world literature (Grades 9–10).
• Investigate the relationships between language, context and meaning by analysing and evaluating how responses to texts, including students' own responses, are influenced by purpose, taking into account that a text's purpose is often open to debate, personal, social and cultural context, and the use of imaginative, persuasive and interpretive techniques (Years 11–12).	• *Speaking and listening – comprehension and collaboration:* Evaluate a speaker's point of view, reasoning, and use of evidence and rhetoric, assessing the stance, premises, links among ideas, word choice, points of emphasis, and tone used (Grades 11–12).

Pentecostalism to pornography. It is a world where a dozen or more languages might be spoken on one city block, while the television brings live coverage to that same block of what is happening at the ends of the earth. So what else can we do but create a pedagogy that gives voice to each child's cultural proclivities and to the bewildering kaleidoscope of dialects and discourses?

See literacies.com Kalantzis and Cope on Debating Critical Literacy.

Modern curriculum standards often include aspects of critical pedagogy. Table 7.10 provides some examples from the Australian Curriculum and the US Common Core State Standards.

Exploring connections between the 'knowledge processes' and critical literacies pedagogy

Linking this chapter back to the knowledge process schema we introduced in Chapter 3, critical pedagogy frequently aligns with the knowledge process of 'experiencing the known', where students develop personal identity and voice. Critical

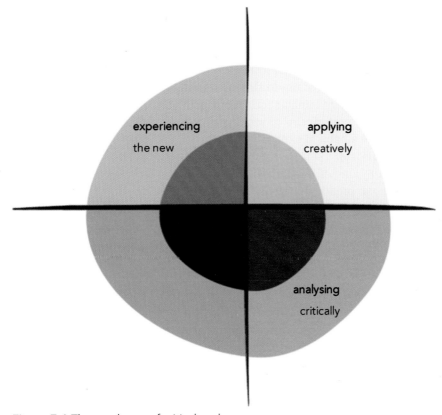

Figure 7.6 The emphases of critical pedagogy

pedagogy also aligns strongly with the knowledge process of 'analysing critically' insofar as it interrogates the purposes of knowledge and texts, and engages in critique and inspires learners to consider themselves to be agents of change. It prompts learners to regard their ways of seeing things, thinking about things and expressing themselves as a product of their vantage points or perspectives and, for that reason, often quite different from others. Finally, critical pedagogy suggests that students become engaged in 'applying creatively', designing texts, including innovative new media texts, that express their identities, interests and perspectives.

Towards a robust literacies pedagogy

It has not been our purpose in this book to take sides in the perennial pedagogy wars. Various aspects of didactic, authentic, functional and critical pedagogies may each have their place in learning. The knowledge process schema that we introduced in Chapter 3 highlights the range of activity types that a teacher might put to pedagogical work. These different activity types are typical of each of the pedagogies we have described in the past four chapters. (See Table 3.1 for an overview.)

It is not the aim of the knowledge process schema to prescribe a correct pedagogical path. Rather, it is to provide teachers with tools to map the paths they take. This may involve focusing more or less on one pedagogical approach, with justifiable reasons.

The knowledge process schema can also be used to connect with a wide range of pedagogical practices via crosswalks or equivalences. Each of the orientations to knowing and learning captured in the knowledge processes stands in relation to major traditions in education. In this sense, the four knowledge processes are descriptive of the range of familiar educational pasts and living teaching practices, more than they are prescriptive of scope and sequence. The difference for us is that teachers make a habit of explicitly reflecting on the impact of their choices on knowledge outputs.

Rarely does any one of the pedagogical approaches we have described in this section of the book predominate without at least some drawing upon aspects of one or more of the other three. For instance, in a celebrated article, Brown and Campione argue for a middle ground of 'guided discovery': 'On the one hand, there is considerable evidence that didactic teaching leads to passive learning. But on the other, unguided discovery can be dangerous' – for example, when students invent misconceptions or waste valuable school time discovering things that could more directly have been presented to them (Brown & Campione 1994: 230). Rather than 'balance', which suggests that we water down different approaches in the interests of moderation, we recommend purposeful weaving between different epistemic moves for explicitly targeted outcomes – each of which, in its place and in its most robust forms, has its place. In this way, our 'crosswalk' approach seeks to make links with productive heritage pedagogical practices.

Crosswalks, in a more general sense, can also be made to schemas of educational objectives that purport to be comprehensive. Here we will provide just one

Table 7.11: Bloom's Taxonomy of Educational Objectives

Knowledge process	Bloom's taxonomy equivalents (A–D are 'knowledge objectives' and 1–6 are 'cognitive objectives')	Literacies examples
Experiencing the known	D. Metacognitive self-knowledge 1. Cognitive processes of remembering: recognising and recalling	Awareness of one's resources for meaning-making, the relevance of personal knowledge and experiences of texts, and a sense of 'voice'
Experiencing the new	A. Factual knowledge of specific details, elements and terminology 2. Cognitive processes of understanding: inferring, summarising	Making sense of new meanings in (not too) unfamiliar texts
Conceptualising by naming	B. Conceptual knowledge of classifications and categories 2. Cognitive processes of understanding: classifying, exemplifying, comparing	Concepts for metarepresentation that generalise about design elements
Conceptualising with theory	B. Conceptual knowledge of principles, generalisations, theories, models and structures 2. Cognitive processes of understanding: explaining	Connecting concepts to explain how a kind of text works to make meaning, in general terms
Analysing functionally	C. Procedural knowledge of subject-specific skill, algorithms, techniques and methods 4. Cognitive processes of analysing: differentiating, organising, attributing	Explaining how a specific text works, applying or testing the theory in practice
Analysing critically	D. Metacognitive knowledge about cognitive tasks 2. Cognitive processes of understanding: interpreting 5. Cognitive processes of evaluating: checking, critiquing	Interpreting the purpose of a specific text, including the human interests involved
Applying appropriately	C. Procedural knowledge of criteria for determining when to use appropriate procedures 3. Cognitive processes of applying: executing, implementing	Creating a text appropriate to a genre or that is workable in a predictable context of use
Applying creatively	D. Metacognitive, strategic knowledge 6. Cognitive processes of creating: generating, planning, producing	Creating a hybrid text, or transferring one's knowledge of text to a different context

example: a mapping of the knowledge processes to one of the most famous and widely used of such schemas, Bloom's Taxonomy of Educational Objectives (Anderson & Krathwohl 2001). The product of a project sponsored by the American Educational Research Association and first published in the 1950s and updated regularly since, the taxonomy has provided a guide to those planning and delivering learning experiences and designing assessments.

See literacies.com Learning Modules.

See literacies.com #edtech Literacies Applications.

Summary – Part B: Approaches to literacies

	Chapter 4: Didactic literacy pedagogy	Chapter 5: Authentic literacy pedagogy	Chapter 6: Functional literacy pedagogy	Chapter 7: Critical literacies pedagogy
Dimension 1: The contents of literacy knowledge	Learning the formal rules; the one correct and proper way to write; reading what texts 'really' say; appreciating the literary canon	Relevant, authentic, realistic meanings expressed in reading and writing	Learning the genres of school success and social power	Learning a critical orientation to the world; learning about differences in language and power; learning about popular culture and new media
Dimension 2: The organisation of literacy curriculum	Student follows teacher who follows textbook that follows syllabus	Process pedagogy; integrated units; teacher-planned units of work; natural growth	Reading genre models; writing of own content within genre frameworks	Supporting learner agency; focus on purpose in meaning-making
Dimension 3: Learners doing literacy	Copying, repetition, memorisation of rules and conventions; getting the answers 'right'	Active learning; immersion in reading and writing experiences; inquiry pedagogy	Expert-designed, teacher-introduced scaffolds and functional grammar; student independent construction	Engagement with real-world issues; experiences of active citizenship; creating texts that engage with the world
Dimension 4: The social relationships of literacy learning	Authoritative knowledge of objective facts; authoritarian teacher; the discipline spatial order of the classroom and temporal order of the instructional program	Self-realisation, learner-centred pedagogy; the values of the expressive individual	Learning to mean in a social environment and educational context where mastery of particular genres is valued	Using literacies to take control over the conditions of one's life; being an adept meaning-maker in the new media

Knowledge processes

conceptualising by naming

1. Add entries to your wiki defining key concepts in the literacies pedagogy: important terms in the analysis of the ways in which communication and language work, and the ways in which they are learned. Maintain and extend this wiki as you work through this and the remaining chapters of this book.

experiencing the new

2. Locate a source from which you can get a concrete sense of the dynamics of critical literacy pedagogy. Your source might be a curriculum resource (see, for example, McLaughlin & DeVoogd 2004), or it might be an interview with a teacher who believes in or practises critical pedagogy. Write your own analysis of the dimensions of didactic literacy around:

   a. the contents of literacy knowledge
   b. the organisation of literacy curriculum
   c. learners doing literacy
   d. the social relationships of literacy learning.

experiencing the known

3. Consider your own schooling and reflect on what experience you had of engaging with popular culture and new media texts. Was it an enjoyable experience? Do you consider it to be a 'valuable' learning experience?

   How has this experience 'shaped' the ways in which you now think about the possibility of, and possibilities for, using such texts in your classroom?

experiencing the known

4. Describe a learning moment in which you have experienced critical pedagogy. How did that moment feel? In what ways was it an effective or ineffective learning moment?

applying appropriately

5. Over the four chapters in this section of the book you have been engaging with the theory and practice of major approaches to literacy. Choose a literacy topic that might be taught in one lesson that exemplifies critical pedagogy. Script hypothetical teacher–student talk in the course of this lesson.

conceptualising with theory

6. Write an account of the learning theory behind whole language or process writing. Choose one main theorist as your reference point, such as Paulo Freire, Henry Giroux, Peter McLaren or Donaldo Macedo.

analysing functionally

7. Analyse a video game, using James Gee's framework. Find examples of each kind of learning in the game. How do the game's learning principles compare with the classroom of didactic pedagogy?

analysing critically

8. Discuss the learning conditions under which critical pedagogy is most and least appropriate.

applying creatively

9. Consider a particularly appropriate application of critical pedagogy (for a particular subject matter or learning context) and develop a lesson plan illustrating this application whose primary (though not necessarily exclusive) focus is critical.

applying creatively

10. This chapter has explored critical literacies pedagogy and placed particular emphasis on the use of such an approach in relation to popular culture and new media texts. Critical literacies pedagogy is, nonetheless, applicable to an examination of the full gamut of texts. In shifting the emphasis from popular culture and new media, you are to select a picture book (i.e. a literary text; a work of children's 'literature') used in contemporary classrooms, consider the following scenario and prepare the task at hand.

    Scenario: The school in which you are employed is committed to staff peer-to-peer professional development and, as such, it is a requirement of all staff to present a 'Staff Professional Development Session'. It is now your turn to present to the staff in your school. In undertaking this task, you are required to prepare a PowerPoint presentation focusing on implementing a critical literacies pedagogical approach to the teaching of your chosen picture book.

PART C

The 'what' of literacies

CHAPTER 8

Literacies as multimodal designs for meaning

Overview

Meaning-making is a process of representation (sense-making) and communication (in which a message prompt is interpreted by another person). This chapter analyses the design process through which people take available resources for meaning, and use these as building blocks for designing new meanings. Although they are often similar, newly made meanings are never quite the same as any previous meanings. These 'redesigned' meanings then enter the world. At this point the world has been transformed, even if in the smallest of ways. Then the cycle of meaning-making can start over again. Even though in the schools of our recent past and still today we have separated out literacies as a singular subject that deals with the mechanics of reading and writing, our processes of meaning are always at least to some extent multimodal, bringing together written, visual, spatial, tactile, gestural, audio and oral modes. This is particularly true in the contemporary era. The new, digital **media** are intrinsically multimodal. This chapter suggests an approach to 'design analysis'. It is a prelude to the six chapters in this section of the book that outline a multimodal grammar, one that will help us describe and understand meaning-making across different modes.

Media: The materials used to make meaning

Meaning-making in representation and communication

Meaning-making today

Morgan: You get Garado, he's a water Pokémon. A big one. You get that in Shootport City. It's overseas. You need to dive to get there. You need to dive down and there's like an opening underwater. So you go through there.

Researcher: That's an [above sea] city, or is it underwater?

Morgan: No it's not underwater, it's on top. You go under water. You press speed. You go up then you ... that way and then you find you are in it.

Researcher: So it is lucky that you found that or did you know to go there?

Morgan: I know to go there. In the old game I went through it. I went through the whole thing and I actually went through and I didn't get the big Pokémon ...

Researcher: When you are playing this game, do you feel like you are in the game playing it or do you feel like you are outside the game?

Morgan: Outside the game. Yeah, but sometimes I wish that this was the Pokémon world, but it doesn't come true (Clancy & Lowrie 2005: 143–4).

Morgan is 10 years old and an avid Pokémon player. He is talking here with new media literacies researchers Sue Clancy and Tom Lowrie about one of the best-selling games ever. Pokémon is available not only for hand-held game devices but also for console video games, manga comics, movies, board games, storybooks, guidebooks, cheat sites, trading cards and other merchandise. Playing the game, Morgan navigates his way through different landscapes in a journey or a quest where he may encounter many of the hundreds of species of Pokémon. He engages in a wide variety of literacies: visual, spatial, audio, written and gestural. Note, for instance, the ways in which words and images represent space, and how Morgan quite tangibly feels a kind of physical presence in the Pokémon space.

Clancy and Lowrie (2003) show how Morgan's thinking when playing this game is organised through narratives. They identify two kinds of narrative:

> [The] internalised narratives are those that players construct as they move through the actual game processes, while the externalised narratives are those that players construct when they are talking to each other about aspects of the games (at 1129).

Representation: Making a meaning for oneself, using a sign system to 'make sense' of the world

Communication: Signs that are made, which another person may at some time receive

The internalised narratives we call **representations**. These are the thinking processes that Morgan uses to make sense of the game, understandings about the nature and purpose of the game and its characters that allow him to make meaningful choices about where to go and what do to next. The externalised narratives occur when he explains the narrative to someone else, in this case the researchers. We call this **communication**.

Table 8.1: Representation and communication

Internalised narratives, or	*Representations*	The thinking processes we use to make sense of things and actions
Externalised narratives, or	*Communication*	The expressions of meaning we make to someone else

Figure 8.1 Pokémon

Sign systems and semiosis

Literacies are processes of *meaning-making*, sometimes called 'semiosis', or the process of using signs. **Semiotics** is the study of how we use signs. This is a multidisciplinary academic endeavour, which traces the connections between a signifier (a word, for example) and the things it signifies (the things it refers to), and between signifiers in systems of signs (for example, languages).

Semiotics: The study of sign systems

Take the sentence 'We walked the dog down the street.' *We*, *walked*, *the dog* and *the street* are all signifiers: words we use to represent things that exist (that is, the things that they signify). However, these signifiers do not make a lot of sense separately from each other. They fit together into a meaningful sentence based on the systematic relationship between words. The grammar or structure of the sentence tells us that the dog is not walking us; we are walking the dog.

In addition, there is a larger set of unspoken meanings in the language: 'we' means 'not I' or 'not just one of us'; and 'walked' means 'not ran' or 'will walk tomorrow', to mention several contrasting alternatives. The sentence makes sense, not as a collage of separate signifiers but as a closely interconnected set of meanings that fits into the hugely complex meaning system that is the whole of language. Also, the reality we live is not an arbitrarily thrown-together set of things signified. Experienced meanings come together into patterns that make sense in our everyday reality. When they contradict our intuitions – for instance, when an enthusiastic dog walks *us* – we laugh.

In a **sign system**, the meanings we create between signifiers are designed to correspond with the connections between the things we are experiencing. Our symbolic meanings (signifiers) form a coherent system. Our experienced meanings (signified) are just as coherent. When things are going well, when things are making sense, the connections between our signifiers seem to us to correspond nicely with the connections we are experiencing in the world.

Sign system: A series of interconnected signifiers (symbols), which stand for a series of interconnected signifieds (things that can be experienced in the world)

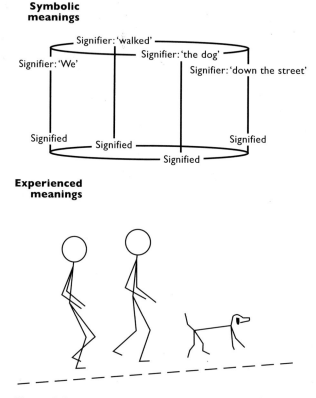

Figure 8.2 A sign system

See literacies.com Saussure on Signs.

The connections between signifiers and signified are matters of convention, and vary from language to language. We may all know about dogs, but it is a convention of our culture to connect the word 'dog' with that animal. In Greek, the word is 'skili', but the sounds or look of this word are meaningless if you don't know the conventions of Greek as a sign system.

In this book, rather than use the words 'semiosis' or 'semiotics' to describe the study of sign systems, we are going to stay with the more plain-speaking concept, *meaning-making*. Meaning-making occurs when we put signifiers together into a coherent system that more or less corresponds with the sense of the world of our experienced meanings, or what is signified.

Representation

We have seen Morgan making meaning in and about his Pokémon space. Put this way, this book is about how school can help children become capable adult meaning-makers at a time when our meaning-making environments are dramatically changing. It is also about the ways in which the meaning-making capacities nurtured by literacies can help learners in all subject areas, not just the areas traditionally called 'English' or 'language arts'. We have been making the case in this book that the changes in our communications and learning environments are so significant that we need to expand our frame of reference beyond 'literacy' to 'literacies'. More than reading and writing – the traditional stuff of literacy in the singular – we also need to focus on multimodal meaning-making as an expanded framework for literacies in the plural. This is the basis for the theory of Multiliteracies that we have developed with colleagues over a number of years and that we will now outline in Part C of this book (Cope & Kalantzis 2009; New London Group 1996).

There are two primary ways in which we make meaning. We make meaning for ourselves, called *representation* (Morgan's internalised narrative), and we make meanings that we use in our interactions with others, called *communication* (Morgan's externalised narrative). Of course, these two kinds of meaning-making are closely connected. For instance, we often think through what we are going to say (representation) before or as we say it (communication). Representation is not only a key aspect in the process of what we communicate orally through speech or in writing, for instance. We also represent to ourselves communicated meanings that we hear and read. This is called **interpretation**. Teaching and learning in all subject areas require us to know and understand the distinctive processes involved in representation and communication and their overlapping natures.

Interpretation: The sense one person makes of a message communicated by another person

Representation or thinking starts with our interest, something that has for the moment captured our attention or to which we have directed our mental focus. We may be thinking about something, looking at something, making sense of

Table 8.2: Representation, communication and interpretation

Representation	or telling yourself
Communication	or telling others
Interpretation	or telling yourself what you think others mean

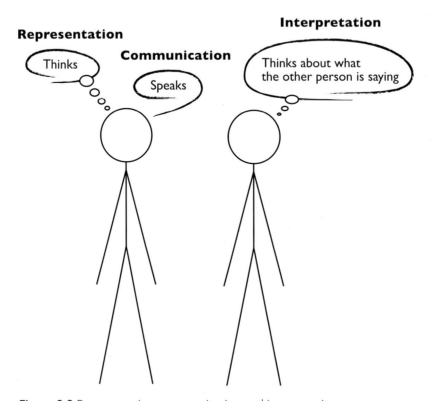

Figure 8.3 Representation, communication and interpretation

something we are experiencing, talking silently to ourselves about something, or rehearsing in our own minds what we may say to another person.

Of course, pre-existing conditions support this process of representation, such as our ability to see meaningfully (to make out things that we can see and to know what these things mean); to hear meaningfully (listening, for instance, to speech or music); or to use language as a tool for thinking as well as communicating (speaking and writing). These are all things we have all learned, which allow us to make sense of the world. In other words, they allow us to make meaning for ourselves. Literacies are tools for representing that meaning to oneself. Representation is the cognitive work that individuals do with their minds. It is the raw material of thinking.

Representation is also very fluid. It is not simply a matter of applying the rules of language, or the conventions of image recognition. Meaning-makers do not just see things as they are; they also, to a certain extent, see things in their minds' eyes in ways that suit them, which fit their preconceptions. To this extent, they are always (re)constructing their worlds, seeing them in new ways, thinking new thoughts, envisioning things from fresh perspectives and imagining new possibilities. This is the source of human creativity and innovation.

Communication

Communication occurs when a person creates a message that serves as a prompt that impacts upon the meaning universe of another person or persons. This message-prompt might be a spoken utterance, a written text or an image, for instance. A prompt suggests a response, even if this takes the form of a silent or anonymous response, such as listening, reading or viewing, and even if the person responding is not someone you know, or not someone you even expected to receive the prompt and react to it.

Communication is a reciprocal thing, in which one person's meaning-action prompts another person's representation (at least), and possibly also a communication from them. It is a meaning-exchange between speaker and listener, writer and reader, or image maker and viewer. Representation is individual and cognitive; communication is social and interactive. Representation is in a person's thinking; communication is in people relating around each other's thinking.

Communication requires the creation of a prompt in the form of something that may be taken to be a message by someone else (such as a spoken utterance,

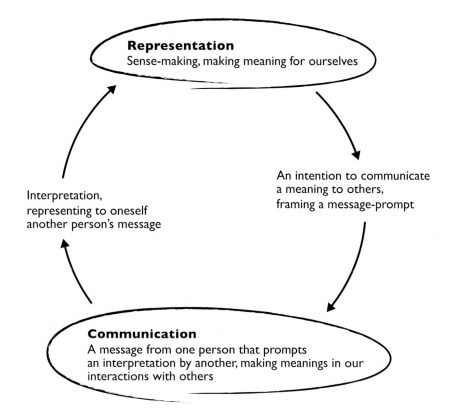

Figure 8.4 The cycle of meaning-making

a gesture or a presented image). However, there has been no communication until someone has connected with that message. The connection, moreover, is never just a matter of receiving the message, as a simple transmission model of communication might suggest: meaning-maker makes message → sends message → audience gets message. It is also the business of interpretation. Listeners, readers and viewers have to do some representational or thinking work of their own in order to have the message speak to them. They have to interpret the message so it makes sense to them. And their interpretations can always vary depending what they are inclined to see or hear in the message.

In fact, no two interpretations of a communicated prompt can ever be quite the same, because no two people have quite the same perspective on the world. When Person A asks, 'Can I help you?' Person B may think to themselves, 'Fantastic, we'll get the task done faster'. But hearing the same message, Person C may think to themselves, 'Don't they think I can do this myself?'

The interpreter does not absorb the message as if the message could speak for itself. Rather, they take the message on board on their own terms. In other words, the interpreter only ever receives a message filtered through the prism of the ways they have learned to represent the world to themselves, coloured by their own experiences, interests and identities. People only hear or see what they are able to hear and see or want to hear and see.

There is no avoiding the task of interpretation, or making sense of a prompt for oneself. This is not to suggest that listeners are always so preoccupied by their own interests that they are insulated from hearing something new. Nor are they trapped in their own perspectives – even though many communicators sometimes find themselves thinking that, in frustration. Listeners, readers and viewers are to a greater or lesser degree moved and changed by the meaning-prompts they encounter.

Sometimes, communication involves cycles of clarification – for instance, repeating things, repairing misunderstandings, or qualifying things that were perhaps said too simply at first. 'Now, am I correct in thinking you are saying ...?' This may lead to a closer alignment of the message and the re-representation of the meaning in the listener's interpretation. But sometimes these cycles will only demonstrate a wider misalignment of meanings than originally thought. 'I can't believe you're really saying that,' you may say to yourself, but not out loud so you don't offend the other person. Whatever the social-interactive outcome, the point is that communication is a matter of give and take, a reciprocal process involving interpretations as well as prompts.

 See literacies.com Kress on Representation and Communication.

Meaning-making as a dynamic process

This model is a departure from the assumptions of heritage, didactic literacy pedagogies. The emphasis of didactic literacy is on consistent stable meanings and their direct transmission – the correct meanings of words, proper grammatical usage, the meaning of a sentence, or what the author is saying, for instance. The process of representation is a matter of 'getting' meanings as if they were static and intrinsic. It is as if meanings were in a kind of code waiting to be decoded by listeners, readers and viewers. If language were indeed an objective code, all we would have to do would be to decode its meanings and let them speak for themselves. A Multiliteracies approach, by contrast, focuses on the inevitable fluidity of meanings, their different interpretations and the necessity to negotiate meanings socially. In other words, we continuously and actively reshape meanings. We are always making sense of the world in new ways, our own ways. We always have to work at our meanings, re-representing a communicated meaning so that it makes sense to us. Sometimes this process of interpretation is silent, in our own heads; sometimes it is out loud, or visible, prompting a response from the communicator of the meaning or someone else who happens to be nearby.

For these reasons, the process of communication is not only one of 'understanding', or 'comprehension'. Rather, what the reader or listener or viewer represents to themselves as they interpret a message is not what the message transparently says, but what they make of the message, the particular way they hear or see the message – even if, sometimes only subtly, this will vary depending on the listener-reader-viewer's own interest and own way of re-representing a message to themselves. Person A might say 'I like your work'. Person B might appreciate the recognition. Person C might fear that Person A will copy it now. Person D might think that Person A is just saying it to make them feel better, but doesn't really mean it.

This fluidity in meaning-making, incidentally, contradicts the key assumptions of reading tests that attempt to measure 'comprehension' by seeking right and wrong answers to multiple choice questions. Reading is not only a question of what the author really said. It is also a matter of interpretation. In fact, in reading, the most important questions are the ones that are more open to interpretation. We can go searching for a day of the week in a story to find out when the action happened. This may not be open to much interpretation. But it is not a very interesting thing to know. The more important question is the kinds of characters involved in the story, and this is very much a matter of interpretation – and much more significant to the text. Here's a much more interesting question that no reading comprehension test can ever ask: 'Which character do you identify with and why?' From reader to reader, the answer is going to be different. Of course, this is not to say that anything goes, and that everything is a matter of subjective interpretation. However, interpretation is always a part of the equation, and the more profound the issues at stake, the more room there is for argument about alternative interpretations.

See literacies.com Roland Barthes on the Death of the Author.

Meaning-making as a design process

Using resources for meaning

Jason Ranker uses the Multiliteracies idea of 'design' to analyse eight-year-old John's writing processes – the way he is communicating and the representations or thinking processes that shape these communications. John is a former student of his, an infrequent and uncomfortable writer. John is creating a comic based on the story of the Grim Reaper.

> **Jason:** Where did you get the idea for having a character called the Grim Reaper? Was that from a television show or a book or something? Or did you make him up?
>
> **John:** I made him up sort of. I don't know.
>
> **Xavier:** (seated nearby and overhearing our conversation) Grim. You know, in *Grim and Evil*.
>
> **John:** Oh, yeah. It sort of comes from that. In fact, I guess it is from that …
>
> **Jason:** What parts of your comics come from *Grim and Evil*?
>
> **John:** *Grim and Evil* hardly ever has other monsters in it. It's practically not about the Grim Reaper. He's just one of the characters.
>
> **Jason:** What other kinds of shows have other monsters in it?
>
> **John:** With the Grim Reaper? None. It's more like an action comic. Like Marvel. Sort of like a Marvel comic.
>
> **Jason:** What happens in those?
>
> **John:** Well … it's just like a superheroes comic. The superheroes battle.
>
> **Jason:** Do you read superhero comics much?
>
> **John:** Yeah. I have some at home. Like *Spiderman* and *The Hulk* (Ranker 2007: 418–9).

John's Grim Reaper story, and the medium of the comic that he uses to communicate his story, is based on a wide range of resources drawn from his world of meaning: story characters, images, motifs and kinds of dialogue. But it is by no means a copy of these resources. In fact, John is drawing from a wide variety of resources for meaning, including comics, the World Wide Web, television and video games. He ends up creating six drafts of the comic, each one transforming these meanings further as he presents his particular reworking of the story.

Two meanings of 'design'

How, then, does one make meaning? What are the processes that people like John go through? The Multiliteracies theory of meaning-making expands on more static frameworks for understanding representation and communication such as 'traditional grammar' and 'the literary canon', suggesting a more dynamic conception of meaning-making as a process of **design**. We chose this word 'design' because it has a fortuitous double meaning. On the one hand, it exists in all things in the world, patterns and structures that exist in natural and human-made things – the design of a wind-up clock, or the design of the leaf of a plant. This is something we call 'morphology'. Things have designs.

Design: A pattern in meaning and a process of making meaning

Intangible things have designs, too, including abstract things like knowledge. Messages also have designs. The parts of messages can be identified, and also the way these parts fit together. Design in this sense is the study of form and structure in the meanings that we make. This is 'design' used as a noun.

See literacies.com Fairclough on Discourse.

On the other hand, design is also a sequence of actions, a process motivated by our purposes. This is the kind of design that drives representation as a process of thinking and message-making as a process of communication. It is something you do, an act of representation or communication, making a prompt in sound or image to which someone else may respond. This meaning takes the word back to its root in the Latin word *designare*, or 'to mark out'. Design in this sense refers to a certain kind of agency. It is something you do. This is 'design' used as a verb.

We want to use this duality in meaning for the term 'design' to highlight two closely related aspects of design: design as meaning-structure (the parts that make up a sentence, song, book or video, along with the particular connections holding those parts together) and design as socially influenced and socially directed agency (our intention to communicate, the message we make and its interpretation by another). Figure 8.5 shows how design works as a process of meaning-making in action.

Table 8.3: Meanings of 'design'

Design	Verb	• A sequence of actions, such as representation → communication → interpretation
	Noun	• The form and structure of something, such as the components of meaning and how they are connected – in written text, a spoken text, or an image, for instance

(Available) designs

We live in a world of designs: patterns of meaning available to us in the form of our cultural and environmental heritage – the conventions of language, imagery, sound, gesture, touch and space. We have heard, seen and felt these designs. We have lived with them since we were born. We have learned how to use them to make meaning for ourselves and to interact with others. Designs are available to us as meaning-making resources, at once meanings-in-the-world (the 'sense' or order

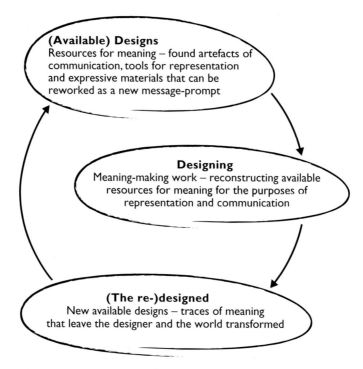

Figure 8.5 The meaning-design process

in the universe that makes experiences coherent) and meanings-for-the-world (the meanings we make of the world in our 'sense-making' or interpretation). These available designs are our resources for meaning.

Designing

Using the meaning-making resources in available designs, we engage in acts of designing. In designing, the meaning-maker creates a new design. However, in putting available designs to use, the meaning-maker never simply replicates or copies found designs, even if the raw materials they use seem to have been largely reproduced from well-established patterns of meaning-making. The meaning-maker always creates a new design, a design like no other ever made before. Their design is inevitably an expression of their voice, which draws upon the unique mix of meaning-making resources: the codes and conventions they happen to have had available in their contexts and cultures.

This moment of design is a moment of transformation, remaking the world by designing it afresh. Designing is the act of doing something with available designs of meaning, be that representing the meaning to oneself through the active, interpretative processes of reading, listening or viewing, or communicating to others by creating message-prompts to which others may respond, such as writing, speaking or making pictures.

This is the reason why, when we design, we never simply replicate available designs. We always rework and revoice the world as found. No two stretches of oral or written language, and no two photographs, no two things we make by hand, are ever quite the same, even when those meanings are seemingly of the most predictable or even clichéd kind.

Here's a remarkable thing. The last few hundred words of the text you have just read have never been written this way before, and the last few hundred words you have spoken have never been said this way before. We have all learned a whole lot of words and a whole lot of grammatical structures, and we can put these words together into intelligible patterns. But never before have these words been assembled in quite this way. For sure, we draw upon building blocks for meaning that we have inherited from our culture, resources we have for meaning. To this extent our meanings are derivative. However, every time we work with these building blocks we put them together in a way that has never been done before – not in quite this way, anyhow. We use the resources for meaning available to us, but we always add something of ourselves as we express these meanings as our own. We always re-create the world in a way that says something of who we are – a way of speaking, a style of thinking, a timbre in our voice, a nuance in our stance, a tone of argumentation, all speaking to the kind of person we uniquely are. You can always hear or see the subtleties of personality coming through – something that makes their meanings as clearly distinctive as the differences between people's faces.

When language or imagery or space-making are understood to be design processes, each act of meaning never merely repeats or reproduces available design resources. Designing always involves an injection of the designer's guiding interests and cultural experiences, their subjectivity and identity. Everyone's experiences are different, reflecting an always unique mix of personal attributes, material (social class, locale, family), corporeal (age, race, sex and sexuality) and symbolic (language, ethnos, gender); more on this in Chapter 15. This can been seen and heard in the sometimes subtle, and at other times unsubtle, stuff of designer voice or style.

Having conceived meaning-making in this way, it follows that differentiation, creativity and innovation are normal parts of our natures as thinking and communicating creatures. We could just look back from the point of communication to work out the meanings in the words or images, the structure of their composition and the syntax of their connections. We could just conduct an archaeology of meaning as if our resources for meaning were given to be used, fixed and unchangeable. However, we want to suggest a prospective or forward-looking view of meaning-making. In this view, we are interested not just in the meanings that we find, but also in the work we do with these meanings, which always changes the meaning resources we have inherited, at least to some degree.

This is a view that puts imagination and creative reappropriation of the world at the centre of representation and communication, and thus learning.

(The re-)designed

The process of designing, of making a meaning in the world, often leaves a tangible, communicated trace, such as an image, an object, an oral utterance or a written text. As the design process draws to a momentary close, the world has been transformed, no matter in how small a way, because the trace that has been left behind is unique. This trace may affect another person if and when they receive the redesigned meaning as a message-prompt.

But even if no one is ever touched by a person's meaning, if no one hears or sees their message-prompt, it will still have left the representer transformed; it will have helped them to think things through afresh or to see things in a new way. Communication may occur immediately or at some later point if and when a person encounters the message-prompt. This is because the redesigned has joined the repertoire of available designs, so providing openings for new designs. The re-designed – something heard, pictured, written – is returned to the world, and this return leaves a legacy of transformation. Indeed, for having been through this process of transformation, neither the designer nor their world will ever be quite the same again.

The redesigned is a residue, a trace of transformation that is left in the social world of meaning. The texts of designing become the redesigned, new resources for meaning in the open and dynamic play of subjectivities and meanings. One person's designing becomes a resource in another person's universe of available designs. This is how the world is left changed.

Designing is transformational work. In the life of the meaning-maker, this process of transformation is the essence of learning. The act of representing the world and others' representations of the world transform the learner. Communicating those representations back to the world also transforms the learner. The act of designing leaves the designer redesigned.

As the designer makes meanings, they exert their subjectivity in the representation and communication processes. As these meanings are always new (insights, expressions or perspectives), the designer remakes themselves through their design work. This is one of the key propositions of Multiliteracies theory: that a theory of meaning as transformation or redesign is also the basis for a theory of learning (Cope & Kalantzis 2000; Kalantzis & Cope 2013; Kress 2000a).

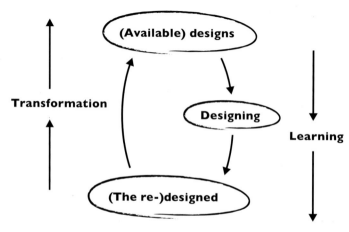

Figure 8.6 Learning and transformation

Design in practice

Ranker (2007: 422) concludes his analysis of John's Grim Reaper comic by analysing his 'redesigned' meaning.

> [This is] the outcome of designing new meaning by assembling parts of previous meanings … Rather than producing a straightforward replication of popular-cultural sources that interested him, John designed and redesigned meaning through each successive comic.

John has transformed the available resources for making meaning, making a unique meaning in the world. He has also transformed himself, having shaped narrative in a way he never has before.

To reiterate these generalisations with another concrete example, let's consider a young child learning to write and read. And let us consider that writing and reading are design processes, representing and communicating a meaning via the peculiar visual and linguistic modes of literacy.

The following example is what might be regarded as proto-writing. A child sits on his father's lap, and this is what he says: 'Do you want to watch me? I'll make a car … got two wheels … and two wheels at the back … and two wheels here … This is a car.' Kress reads this double sign to consist of circles signifying 'wheel' and wheels signifying 'car': 'Circles are apt forms for meaning wheels … and wheels here is a metaphor for car.' These are what he calls 'motivated signs': 'it is the interest of the sign-maker at the moment of making the sign that leads to the selection of the criteria for representing … "wheel-ness" and "car-ness"' (Kress 2003).

By recognising this as a design process, we grant agency to a young sign-maker. This work may not, however, be noticed as early writing or pre-reading in a literacy learning context where a teacher or a parent is anxious to tell young learners conventional, formal literacy things that they do not yet know. However, from a design perspective, the available resources for meaning can be traced to what the

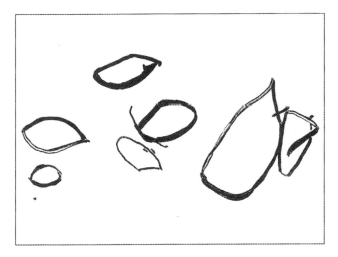

Figure 8.7 'This is a car'

child does know and can do as a designer, grounded in his life experiences of cars, wheels, circles and drawing. The child designs. The result is a (re)designed meaning, which he makes on paper as proto-writing and decodes as pre-reading. Designing is this ordinary, and this extraordinary.

See literacies.com Kress on Design.

Design pedagogy

In a pedagogy of Multiliteracies, all ways of meaning, including language, are regarded as dynamic processes of transformation rather than processes of reproduction. That is, meaning-makers do not simply replicate design conventions. Take the conventions of poetry. A student does not just apply the rules or conventions of poetry when they write a poem. The written words they use and the poetry rules they use to connect them may be quite ordinary. However, they reshape words and rules to make up their poem in an always unique way. Meaning-makers, in other words, do not just use what they have been given; they are fully makers and remakers of signs and transformers of meanings.

The pedagogical implications of this shift in the underlying conception of meaning are enormous. A pedagogy of Multiliteracies requires that we recognise the pivotal role of agency in the meaning-making process. Through this recognition, it seeks to create a more productive, relevant, innovative, creative and even emancipatory pedagogy. Literacy teaching is not only about skills and competence; it is also aimed at creating a kind of person, an active designer of meaning, with a sensibility open to differences, problem-solving, change and innovation. The logic of Multiliteracies recognises that meaning-making is an active, transformative process. A pedagogy based on that recognition is more appropriate for today's world of change and diversity.

A pedagogy of Multiliteracies speaks to the question of conventions or design patterns in meaning, not so students might learn their morphology or structures in a formalistic fashion, but in order to connect the conventions with their social purposes. The conventions always have purposes, and the purposes always have a cultural and situational basis. The regularities and patterns are the reason why we can make sense of them. Their unfamiliarity is what we need to deal with when we cross into new situations or social spaces.

It will never be practical to teach the structures, forms, modalities, genres or discourses of every conceivably relevant social space, because in today's world especially, this can only open up the receding horizons of complexity and diversity. However, we can create learning experiences through which learners develop knowledge and strategies for reading the new and unfamiliar when they encounter it. You can't necessarily predict the rules of meaning in the next social space you encounter. But you can learn how to look for patterns, to negotiate the unpredictable, to begin to interpret designs of meaning that may not at first make sense. Multiliteracies pedagogy aims to develop these skills and sensibilities by first asking the question of design form and function, or how meanings are made differently for different purposes, and then how they are further transformed by the particular interests of the communicator and the interpreters of their message-prompts.

 See literacies.com Bakhtin on Genre.

Designing and learner identities

Chandler-Olcott and Mahar introduce us to 13-year-old Rhiannon, who publishes her fan fiction on her 'Fanmania' website. Fan fiction is particularly conscious about the resources of available design upon which it draws. It reuses characters taken from cartoons or video games and writes new stories using these characters. In this instance, Rhiannon is drawing from the Japanese tradition of animation, anime.

This is how Rhiannon introduces herself to the wider fan fiction community on her website:

Birth Date: 06/21/–

Favourite Foods: Orange Chicken. Steak and Eggs, RICE, and … PIZZA!

Least Fav Foods: Spinach, Squash, and grins Cavier. (I hate it so much I dun even know if that's how u spell it …) Oh, and sardines, too!

Fav Music: I like Rock, Techno/Dance

Least Fav Music: ACK! POP!! Like Spear Britney … And the Backstreet Bums, and NSTYNC … BLAH!

Hobbies: Drawing, building webpages, writing songs and fanfics, and stories. Hanging out with my buds, and my …

Boyfriend: Of course!! My bestest friend …! Scott!! (Chandler-Olcott & Mahar 2003b).

Rhiannon's fan fiction stories mostly have romantic themes. They also meld the characteristics of a number of genres including science fiction, fantasy and 'teen buddy' movies. Being an avid fan and immersed in the genre provides her not only with designs for meaning in terms of characters and narrative she can rework, but also visual, linguistic, spatial and gestural designs for meaning.

Rhiannon has downloaded 'bishonen' images. 'Bishonen' is a Japanese word that fans use to describe characters they find attractive. Her bishonen gallery includes two pictures of Scott, with the comment that she thinks he looks like Squall, hero of the game *Final Fantasy*. Recognising the sources of images by attribution and naming the sources and the original creators is important in these online environments as a way of explicitly marking that an image or character is drawn from available designs of meaning. However, this is not just a site where Rhiannon reproduces the available designs she has found. She is also a designer of meanings, telling her own stories in a highly innovative way, leaving the world redesigned for the readers who visit her website (Chandler-Olcott & Mahar 2003a).

Multimodality

New media and multimodality

West Oakland, California, as researchers Hull and Nelson (2005: 230) tell us, is:

> an isolated community that has fallen on very hard times, with high rates of job-lessness and crime, a deteriorating infrastructure, struggling schools, and few of the ordinary resources that most communities take for granted, such as supermarkets, bookstores, restaurants, and banks.

The people who live there today are mostly 'long-time African American residents joined by recent immigrants from Southeast Asia, Mexico, and South America'. People are trying to find ways to reclaim a sense of community, one of which is a centre called DUSTY, or 'Digital Underground StoryTelling for You(th)'. Digital storytelling combines still and moving images, with music, written and spoken text. Oakland is known as the birthplace of many famous rappers, so digital music-making seems to have evolved naturally as a companion to digital storytelling.

> At DUSTY, aspiring wordsmiths as young as 9 and 10 can be seen writing their lyrics, practising their freestyles, and deeply and undistractably engaged in sophisticated software that allows for the creation of digital beats (Hull & Nelson 2005: 231).

Here we find Randy Young creating a digital storytelling piece he has titled 'Lyfe-N-Rhyme'. Just over two minutes long, this story combines original rap lyrics with still images, written text and music. It combines autobiography within the local neighbourhood with wider social commentary, using images and textual references to connect the personal and local with world issues.

> Randy lays bare intimate, troubling aspects of his life and world, inviting audiences to do the difficult work of reflecting on the intimate concerns they hold for themselves, for those they care about, and for the larger community (Hull & Nelson 2005: 238).

It is also a tightly coordinated multimodal presentation, using written text, spoken poetry, image and music.

 See literacies.com Randy Young, Lyfe-N-Rhyme.

Hull and Nelson (2005: 238–9) conclude:

> Lyfe-N-Rhyme is not just a powerful story but also a transcendent synthesis of form and meaning across a variety of semiotic modes. Yes, we are at once touched and

Figure 8.8 'Life N Rhyme' on YouTube

disturbed by the words Randy speaks. Yes, the montage of images that he lays out is arranged to an arresting effect: now soothing, now shocking, and so on. And yes, we feel the pulse of the music and verse thump in our chests and minds. Crucially though, we emphasize that the power felt from this piece is not tantamount to the simultaneous, additive experience of the aforementioned effects, as one might suppose. Again, the full import of the semiotic tapestry that Randy crafts is not merely in but also in between the warp and the weft.

This is the kind of highly innovative meaning-design work schools should encourage in learners. It is motivating work because it is powerfully expressive of the meaning-maker's identity and involves the development of communication skills that are highly relevant and transferrable in today's workplace, community and educational settings. This work requires sophisticated mastery of some of the most powerful processes and media of expression of our contemporary times. It is evidence of the power of what we call '**multimodality**'. Multimodality is not new. It has always been an essential part of human meaning-making, no matter how hard traditional schools may have tried to separate out the formalities of alphabetical literacy. Multimodality, however, is much more insistently significant in the era of the new, digital media.

Multimodality: Using more than one mode in a text or a meaning-making event

The nature of multimodality

In the Multiliteracies theory, we identify seven modes of meaning: *written, visual, spatial, tactile, gestural, audio* and *oral*. *Multimodality* is the theory of how these modes of meaning are interconnected in our practices of representation and communication.

We use a stratagem we call *design analysis* to describe these interconnections. We also use this phrase to get around the limitations of the term 'grammar' in literacy studies, which is often associated too narrowly with alphabetic literacy and a traditional theory of its syntax.

No matter how hard we may try to separate out the written mode for the purposes of didactic literacy teaching – learning to read and write – all representation and communication is intrinsically multimodal. For example, when using written language, there is a stage of visualising things and talking to oneself about what one is writing. Then there is a stage of putting pen to paper or typing text on a screen, which is a visual as well as a linguistic process. When we read, the same thing happens – we re-represent meanings in silent mental speech; we imagine how the things in the writing look or feel; we talk to ourselves about tangential thoughts prompted by our interpretation of what we are reading. In each case, what we re-represent to ourselves is never quite the same as what is written. This switching from one mode to another is integral to our processes of re-representation and transformation in our designs of meaning.

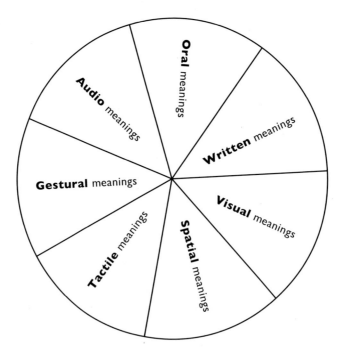

 Figure 8.9 Modes of meaning in a multimodal theory of representation and communication

Nor is it desirable to stay within the neatly separated domains of reading and writing, given the kinds of mode-shifting that help us all to represent meanings, to communicate and to learn. It helps us to visualise something in an image, as well as to have it described in words. The two meaning-making processes are quite different, but swapping backwards and forwards between modes helps us make meanings for ourselves and others. This is why, instead of 'literacy' (reading and writing), our focus in a Multiliteracies approach is 'literacies' (meaning-making as multimodal processes of representation and communication). All forms of representation and communication are multimodal.

 See literacies.com Kress and van Leeuwen on Multimodality.

We also need to take into account our ever-changing contemporary communications environments, full of developments such as speaking devices that are also writing and image-making devices (such as mobile phones), media devices that represent and prompt interactive gestures (such as game consoles), and books that show movies on which you can also create finger art (e-book readers). Of all the changes in the environment of meaning-design since the 20th century, one of the most significant challenges to the old literacy teaching is the increasing multimodality of our media for the representation and communication of meanings. Traditionally, literacy teaching has confined itself to the forms of written language. The new media mix modes more powerfully than was culturally the norm, or even technically possible, in the earlier modernity dominated by the book and the printed page.

Modes of meaning

Table 8.4 shows the modes of meaning that are increasingly coming together, literally, in our devices for writing and reading, speaking and listening, image-making and image-viewing.

We have arranged the modes by the resemblances or practical connections they have with their neighbours. The written is expressed visually, and images and text can easily be put together (more easily in fact, in digital media, than ever before). The experience of space is visual, and can be represented visually in plan or image. The tactile is a bodily encounter with objects in space. Gesture is a bodily relation to space, and a representation with a close affinity to touch. Audio is a kind of bodily gesture, bodily felt as well in the form of hearing and vibrations. Gesture also often overlays speech, bringing into action two simultaneous and closely interconnected modes. Written, visual, spatial and gestural modes use our bodily sense of sight. Oral and audio modes use our sense of hearing. The tactile mode uses our bodily senses of touch, smell and taste. Gestural and tactile modes use our senses of kinaesthesia or bodily presence.

For all the crossovers and connections, however, we have classified the different modes into distinct categories because each represents a place where discrete human meaning-making systems occur – such as the distinction between

Table 8.4: Modes of meaning

Written meaning (more in Chapters 9 and 10)	Reading (representing meaning to oneself as one interprets the written message-prompts of others – Chapter 9); and writing (communicating written meanings in traces that may be found by another as a message-prompt – Chapter 10)
Visual meaning (more in Chapter 11)	Making still or moving images (communicating meanings in traces that might be seen by another as a visual message-prompt); viewing images, vistas, scenes (re-representing found visual meanings to oneself, depending upon perspective and focal points of attention and interest)
Spatial meaning (more in Chapter 12)	Positioning oneself in relation to others, creating spaces and ways of moving around in spaces (which others may experience in communication as a message-prompt); and experiencing spatial meanings (re-representing spatial meanings to oneself as, for instance: proximity, layout, interpersonal distance, territoriality, architecture/building, streetscape, cityscape and landscape)
Tactile meaning (more in Chapter 12)	Making experiences and things whose effects can be felt as touch, smell and taste (tactile communication) and the re-representation to oneself of tactile meanings in the form of the meanings one gives to bodily sensations, such as feelings of touching and being touched. Forms of tactile communication and representation include skin sensations (temperature, texture and pressure), grasp, manipulable objects, artefacts, aromas, and cooking and eating. For those without the bodily capacity to see, written language can be translated in its entirety into tactile meaning, for instance in the form of Braille
Gestural meaning (more in Chapter 12)	Communication using movements of the body: hands and arms, expressions of the face, eye movements and gaze, demeanours of the body, gait, clothing and fashion, hairstyle, dance, action sequences, manifesting in many forms, including ceremony and ritual
Audio meaning (more in Chapter 13)	Communication that uses music, ambient sounds, noises, alerts (meaning in social interaction); and hearing and listening (an individual re-representing the audio meanings they encounter to themselves, or imagining sounds)
Oral meaning (more in Chapter 13)	Communication in the form of live or recorded speech (representing meaning to another); and listening (re-representing oral meanings one encounters to oneself, talking to oneself or rehearsing intended speech)

Mode of meaning: A way of making meaning: written, visual, spatial, tactile, gestural, audio and oral

Mandarin as a spoken language and Chinese script, which works for a number of languages because it is not phonically based; and the differences in **mode of meaning** between photography, music, sign language or architecture.

Each mode has its own systems of interconnecting the component parts of meaning. Moreover, different modes of meaning and different combinations of modes will use different media, which we define here as the materials, tools and practices we humans use to represent and communicate meanings: pens and paper, keyboards and touch screens, oils and canvases, cameras and phones, voice and sound recording devices, videos and game consoles that capture gesture, and tools to give the things we make texture, taste and smell.

The process of synaesthesia

Even though they are printed in black, Mirabelle experiences colours when she sees numbers. When Esmeralda hears the note C-sharp played on a piano, she sees blue. Mirabelle and Esmeralda are two of neuroscientist V. S. Ramachandran's research subjects. They have a condition called **synaesthesia**, a phenomenon that is not regarded as a neurological disorder as such, but rather as a 'surreal blending of sensation, perception and emotion'. Synaesthesia in the quite narrow, diagnostic sense is something that only a few people experience. However, Ramachandran (2011: 75–6) argues that it not only 'sheds light on normal sensory processing', but also sheds light on 'some of the most intriguing aspects of our minds – such as abstract thinking and metaphor'.

Synaesthesia: Switching between modes

He describes the underlying neurological process of synaesthesia as 'cross-activation', something we all experience when we associate one kind of sensation with another. 'Cross-sensory synthesis' is:

> a grand junction where information about touch, hearing and vision flow together to enable the construction of high level precepts. For example, a cat purrs and is fluffy (touch), it purrs and it meows (hearing), and it has a certain appearance (vision) and fishy breath (smell) (at 97–9).

So the abstract concept of 'cat' ties together a number of sensations through this process of 'cross-sensory' synthesis, which is something we all experience. Metaphor, Ramachandran 2011: 104) says, is a similar process.

> Just as synaesthesia involves making arbitrary links between seemingly unrelated perceptual entities like colours and numbers, metaphor involves making non-arbitrary links between seemingly unrelated conceptual realms.

We use the word 'synaesthesia' in this book in a broader sense than is commonly the case in psychology and neuroscience. We do so on the basis of fundamental cognitive mechanisms we all share, mechanisms that underlie synaesthesia. More specifically, we want to define synaesthesia as a process of shifting backwards and forwards between different modes of meaning.

Synaesthesia is the process of expressing a meaning in one mode, then another. You can describe a scene in words or you can paint a picture of the same scene. The person interpreting your meaning will envisage a scene differently when they hear what you say in words compared to when they see a picture of the scene,

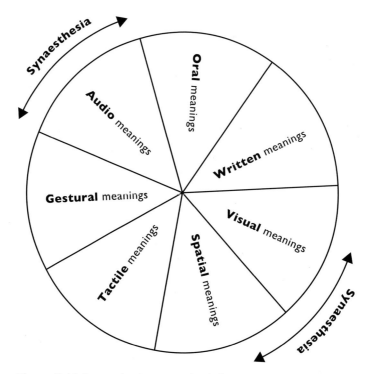

Figure 8.10 Synaesthesia, or mode-shifting

even though these are both attempts to represent and communicate the same thing.

Synaesthesia and learning

Synaesthesia can be a powerful way to support and deepen learning. You may express something in words, or it may make more powerful sense to you as an image or a diagram. Knowing how to represent and communicate things in multiple modes is a way to get a multifaceted and, in this sense, a deeper understanding of these things. A synaesthetic approach can be used as a pedagogical support for learning to read and write, through the juxtaposition and transposition of parallel or complementary modes of meaning. The pictures in a children's book are a good example of this, or the diagrams in a science textbook, or an oral discussion of the meaning in a written text.

A science teacher is introducing electric circuits to her eighth-grade students in a Learning by Design research project. She asks the students to create a simulation of a blackout after a hurricane (experiencing the new). What would happen if there were no electricity for a while? She introduces the students to textual material that introduces electricity and circuitry in images, circuit diagrams and explanatory theoretical text (conceptualising by naming and with theory). She has the students create a burglar alarm, using all the tactile and gestural modes of prototype building (applying appropriately). She asks them to create wiring instructions

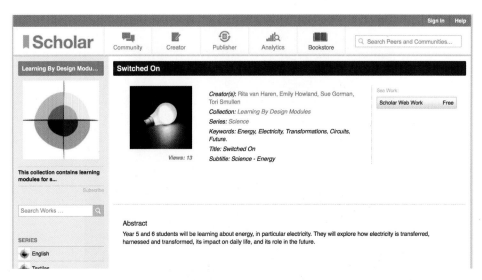

Figure 8.11 Electricity Learning Module – Literacies Across the Curriculum

for an electrician, and use instructions for a layperson (analysing functionally). Finally, she has students reflect orally on the difference between selling your parents on the idea of installing a burglar alarm and providing a technician with clear and accurate wiring instructions (analysing critically).

See literacies.com van Haren, Howard, Gorman and Smullen, Analysing Electricity.

Why this focus on multimodality in literacies, and on the power of synaesthesia? The answer in part is because it was always there, and neglected in some pedagogies, to the detriment of what might have been possible in the quest to create engaging and effective learning environments for children. The most insightful educational theorists and practitioners have known this for a long time, including Friedrich Froebel, the 19th-century initiator of the idea of 'kindergarten' and Maria Montessori, who designed her highly tactile learning 'contraptions' at the turn of the 20th century.

See literacies.com Froebel's Kindergarten.

Kathy Mills is a researcher working in a school in a low socio-economic locale in Brisbane, Australia. There are 35 nationalities in the school, as well as Indigenous Australians – Aboriginal and Torres Strait Islander children. The Year/Grade 6 class whose literacy learning she is researching is streamed, consisting of 23 of the lowest-performing students in the grade (Mills 2010). The students today are creating a 'claymation' animation in which clay models are manipulated, image by image, to create a moving sequence of images in movie software.

Figure 8.12 Manipulating the claymation figure

Paweni is a student who migrated to Australia only a year before and who speaks only Thai at home. She and her fellow students are at the storyboard, or planning, stage before the claymation is shot. They are drawing a road, which a claymation figure will cross when they come to shoot the story. Sean, David and Rhonda are other students in Paweni's group, working together on a joint storyboard.

> **Paweni:** That's more big. [starts to erase drawing] Here. Here. [Paweni gets a ruler and measures a wider, straighter road.]
>
> **Sean:** Hey, I'll do the lines.
>
> **David:** Paweni – that road's too big.
>
> **Sean:** Very … big.
>
> **Rhonda:** Way, way, way, way, way, too big! …
>
> **Paweni:** Wait – too big! [rubs out the lines as the others watch].

In the juxtaposition of gesture, drawing and spoken words, Paweni's peers scaffold her to change 'more big' to 'too big'. 'Paweni's language,' concludes Mills, 'was an invitation to other children to anticipate with her in sense-making, to achieve solidarity with her – and they readily accepted this invitation' (Mills 2006: 142–3). Crucially, mode-shifting between visual, gestural and spoken modes supported this process. Synaesthesia is this simple and this profound.

Towards multimodal literacies

Today, there is a greater urgency than ever to expand the idea of literacy to multimodal literacies. One reason relates to disciplinary contents beyond the literacies

Table 8.5: Multimodal literacies

Multimodal literacies	
	• Expand the idea of literacy beyond reading and writing
	• Include the literacies of the new, digital media
	• Recognise the powerful learning opportunities as a consequence of synaesthesia or mode-shifting
	• Recognise learners as designers of uniquely voiced meanings
	• Focus on meaning-making as transformation, which changes the meaning-maker and their world

classroom itself, or the uses of literacies across the curriculum. A local history project may include not only writing but photographs, a timeline and a video oral interview. A science report of an experiment will include not only a write-up of hypotheses, methods and results. It will also include diagrams, tables and perhaps also a video recording gesturally (showing and pointing) the experiment itself. The best kind of history project and the best-documented science experiment may be those whose processes are communicated multimodally. Digital recording devices and writing environments make this more possible than ever before. We now have readily accessible ways to record and share the synaesthetic realities of knowledge representation and communication.

Indeed, considering communications in general, the range of our media for representation has enormously expanded since the late 20th century, most significantly with the rise of digital media. This is the consequence in part of a series of transformations over the course of the 20th century in the means of production and reproduction of meaning, beginning with photography and its derivatives, and also telephony and recorded sound and their derivatives. However, there has been a substantial quickening of the pace of change since the widespread application of digital technologies from about the beginning of the third quarter of the 20th century.

New literacies emerge, centred around the affordances of these new technologies for hybrid and multimodal expression. Visual and written modes of meaning had relatively separated by virtue of the invention of printing. In old books, the 'plates' were in different sections of the book from the printed word, because different technologies were used for typographic printing (letterpress) and the printing of images (lithography). Already from about the mid 20th century, photo type setting and photolithography begin bringing text and image closer together on the printed page. With digital technologies, even for printing on paper, image and text become again even more closely intertwined. The practical consequences are enormous, as more written text appears in traditionally visual media and truly integrated multimodal media emerge. From the mid-1990s, the World Wide Web takes this even further with its blurring of the boundaries and overlaying of written text, icon and image, as well as with its extensive use of spatial and architectonic metaphors associated with site navigation. These technologies also include the capacity to overlay audio because, ultimately, sound too can be made into the same digitally recordable stuff – binary encodings. The effect of all of these changes over the past half-century, picking up pace with digitisation, has been to reduce the privileged place of written language in Western culture, progressively bringing the visual and other modes to a par. The project of learning, teaching and assessing literacy needs to take these changes into account, if it is to maintain a vital connection with the everyday lives of people in our contemporary world.

A growing literature describes the wide range of multimodal literacies practices emerging in schools. David Cole and Darren Pullen, in their book *Multiliteracies in Motion*, bring together a wide range of authors from around the world and include rich descriptions of bringing multimodal learning into the literacies curriculum (Cole & Pullen 2010). Annah Healy's edited collection, *Multiliteracies and Diversity in Education*, presents vivid examples of the ways in which multimodal teaching and learning practices can support the needs of diverse learners (Healy 2007). Michele Anstey and Geoff Bull provide a highly practical guide in their *Teaching and Learning Multiliteracies* (Anstey & Bull 2006) and Len Unsworth's *Teaching Multiliteracies Across the Curriculum* includes a wealth of examples of teaching multimodal literacies (Unsworth 2001). Our own *Pedagogy of Multiliteracies* also offers a range of examples of multimodality at work in curriculum practice (Cope & Kalantzis 2015a).

Design elements

Describing meaning in order to think about meaning

In traditional alphabetical literacy learning, we have relied on what has been called a metalanguage or a language to speak about language. This takes the form of a set of conventions, which traditionally have taken the form of rules about spelling, grammar and the like. This is a process of describing meaning in order to think about meaning. We want to retain this idea, if not the traditional static ways of describing language.

Young children learn to speak by immersion in language, engaging with the community of people into which they are born – listening, copying, repeating, trying out words and being corrected. Learning to read and write at school, however, is different. Students come to school with oral language and with this the capacity to generalise about meaning. This means that classrooms can be more explicit, direct and thus more efficient by teaching general patterns that can be reapplied in different places. This capacity needs to be used by teachers to build on the language and meanings students bring with them. To do that, they need a language to describe the meanings they make.

We need a metalanguage to describe multimodal meanings, a way of talking explicitly for the purposes of learning about the form, structure and social purpose of meaning-making. Instead of 'grammar' as explained above, we call this description a metalanguage of design elements. In the Multiliteracies approach we want to value a range of modes of meaning. We use 'design analysis', because it is a broader idea than traditional metalanguages such as grammar and phonics. It includes these ideas, of course, and more.

Elements of a design analysis

What, then, are the basic design elements, the building blocks of meaning, such that we can ask the same questions about meaning, no matter which mode we are talking about? Of all the modes of meaning what are the aspects of meaning we might cover in design analysis?

Each mode means in a different way, engages different human senses and uses different combinations of media. Examining the design elements of meaning in this way allows us to ask the same questions about meaning, regardless of the mode. Following are five questions about meaning that we might ask of any meaning, in any mode. These are questions learners can ask as they undertake design analysis. They provide a common metalanguage for working with both the similarities and distinctiveness of each of the modes of meaning.

- *To refer:* What do the meanings describe?
- *To dialogue:* How do the meanings connect the people who are interacting?
- *To structure:* How does the overall meaning hold together?
- *To situate:* How are the meanings shaped by their context?
- *To intend:* Whose purposes and interests are these meanings designed to serve?

All meaning-making, across all modes, operates at five levels of meaning that these questions address. We *refer* to things, events, processes and abstractions. We *dialogue* with ourselves and others. We *structure* our meanings in ways that are both conventional and always innovative to the extent that every new design uniquely recombines available designs and leaves a redesigned meaning.

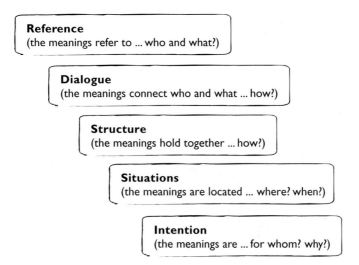

Reference
(the meanings refer to ... who and what?)

Dialogue
(the meanings connect who and what ... how?)

Structure
(the meanings hold together ... how?)

Situations
(the meanings are located ... where? when?)

Intention
(the meanings are ... for whom? why?)

Figure 8.13 Design elements

We *situate* our meanings in contexts, or at least find that they are situated in a context. And we *intend* when we position and or encounter meanings in webs of purpose or agency that express our interest. Here are some of the ways in which these five questions about meaning play out across the different modes.

What do meanings refer to? Referring may delineate particular things, in writing or speaking in the form of nouns to represent things or verbs to represent processes. In images, particular things may be delineated with line, form, and colour; in space by volumes and boundaries; in tactile representations by edges and surface textures; in gesture by acts of pointing or beat. Referring may also be to a general concept for which there are many instances: a word that refers to an abstract concept; an image that is a symbol; a space that is characterised by its similarity with others; or a sound that represents a general idea. Referring can establish relations: prepositions or possessives in language; collocation or contrast in image. It can establish qualities: adjectives or adverbs in language; or visual attributes in images. It can compare, including juxtapositions or metaphors of all kinds, in words, image, sound or space.

These are some parallels. 'The mountains loomed large', says the sentence, then the image provides an entirely similar yet entirely different expression of the same thing – complementary, supplementary, or perhaps disruptive. As much as we want to point out the parallels, we also want to highlight the irreducible differences that account for the variations and disruptions, and offer evidence of the complementary value of multimodality. Writing, for instance, consists of sequential meaning-elements, moving forward in English one word relentlessly at a

Figure 8.14 Mountains in written and visual modes

time, left to right, line to line. It requires of us a composing and reading path that prioritises time, because the progression of the text takes us through time. The image, by contrast, presents to us a number of meaning-elements simultaneously. Its viewing path prioritises space. When we do both, we may attain a fuller, more nuanced meaning, or for that matter, a less settled meaning.

How do meanings connect the participants in meaning-making? Here we establish roles: speaker/listener, writer/reader, designer/user, maker/consumer, gesturer/observer, sound-maker/hearer. We direct or encounter orientations: in language first/second/third person and direct/indirect speech; in image, placement and eye-lines; in gesture, pointing to self, others and the world. We also encounter agency: in language, voice, mood and transitivity; in image, focal planes of attachment and engagement; in space, openings and barriers. And we discover a range of interpretative potentials: open and closed texts; realistic and abstract images; directive or turn-taking gestures; spaces that determine flows deterministically and others that allow a range of alternatives.

How does the overall meaning hold together? In response to this question, we analyse the devices used to create internal cohesion, coherence and boundedness in meanings. Each mode composes atomic meaning units (morphemes, picture elements, physical components, structural materials in the built environment, strokes in gesture) in a certain kind of order. This order is both conventional (using what we call 'available designs' for meaning) and inventive (the process of 'designing'), as a consequence of which no two designs of meaning are ever quite the same. There are internal pointers: pronouns or connectives in language; keys and arrows in images; wayfinding markers in space; cadence and rhythm in sound. There is idea arrangement: sequence in text; positioning of picture elements in images; the functional mechanics of tangible objects. And there are the tangible forms of media: handwriting, speaking, drawing, photographing, making material objects, building, making music, or gesturing.

Where is the meaning situated? Meaning is as much a matter of where it is, as what it is. To the extent that context makes meaning, it is a part of the meaning. A label on a packet points to the contents of the packet, and speaks to the supermarket where it is for sale. A text message speaks to the location of the conversants and the images that are posted with it. A kitchen relates to living areas in a house that in turn fits into larger patterns of everyday suburban life. Bells and electronic 'dings' can mean all manner of things, depending on their context. Across all modes, meanings are framed. They refer to other meanings by similarity or contrast (motif, style, genre). They assume registers according to degrees of formality, profession, discipline or community of practice.

Finally, whose interest is a meaning designed to serve? Now we interrogate the meanings we encounter or make for evidence of motivation. How does rhetoric work, in text, image or gesture? How does subjectivity and objectivity work in written and visual texts? In these and other explorations of interests, we might interrogate meanings for their cross-purposes, concealments, dissonances, or a variety of failures to communicate. We can explore the dynamics of ideologies, be these explicit or implicit, propagandistic or 'informational'. For this we need critique, or the

Table 8.6: A grammar of multimodal meaning

Reference … raises the question, *'what do the meanings refer to?'*	What is the reference point? What does it denote? What is its subject or subjects? – remembering of course that answers to this question may be fluid, ambiguous and a matter of interpretation.
Dialogue … raises the question, *'how do the meanings connect the people who are interacting?'*	How do happenings appear, who/what makes them happen, and what are the effects of their happening? How are the people interacting connected? What interpersonal relations, person-to-thing or thing-to-thing relationships do the meanings try to establish? – remembering of course, that the social participants may not see the social connections in the same ways.
Structure … raises the question, *'how does the overall meaning hold together'?*	What makes a meaning cohere? What is its composition? What are its parts, and how do the parts fit together? What are its organisation and structure as a whole? What is its structure? – not that everyone will necessarily feel that their own meanings or the meanings they encounter are always totally coherent, or that you can ever get to the bottom of everything that is meant.
Situation … raises the question, *'in what context are the meanings located?'*	How is the meaning connected into its surroundings? How does the meaning fit into the larger world of meaning?
Intention … raises the question, *'what are the purposes of these meanings and whose interests do they serve'?*	Why are the meaning makers involved in meaning-making activities? What motivates them? How does the meaning, its context and its reception reveal the interests of those involved? How does the communicator regard their audience? Who is more and less powerful? The interests of different message-makers always vary, depending on who they are, and interpreters of these messages always bring their interests and identities to bear in what they make of the meaning.

methods used in critical literacies pedagogies to uncover interests that may have been left unstated or deliberately concealed in text, image, gesture, sound or space.

So, how might these questions translate into pedagogical practice? Anne Cloonan asked these five 'design element' questions of an early literacy unit by Robyn, centred around the story of *Rosie's Walk*, available both as a storybook and an animated video. 'Rosie the hen leaves the chicken coop', begins the book's blurb, 'and sets out for a little walk. Right behind her is the fox, slyly trying to catch up with her.' She showed the video without sound and had the children act out what they saw as gestures, then listen to the video with the audio storyline, identify the characters in the picture book version of the story, create a 'story map' and make a video in which they recreated the story (Cloonan, Kalantzis & Cope 2010).

See literacies.com van Haren and Cloonan, Rosie's Walk.

Over the course of a number of lessons, Robyn had the students address each of the design elements.

- *To refer:* Who and what are in the story? (Rosie the hen and the fox) How are they represented in words, images, sound, space and gesture? What action is portrayed? (Rosie's journey)
- *To dialogue:* How is the producer of the meaning connected with the recipient? (The author as storyteller, the book illustrator, the video maker – we are not part of the story the way we are in games, for instance.)
- *To structure:* How does the story hold together? (We mean the way the sentences are presented on the pages of the book, each part of the story on a new page.) How are the pictures in the book connected with the text? What does each example of writing and picture tell you that the other does not? How is the video ordered like a storyboard?
- *To situate:* Where is this text to be found? Where would we read the book, or watch the video? Why?
- *To intend:* What are the interests and motivations of the characters? (For example, Rosie vs the Fox.) How are we positioned? (What do we know that Rosie does not know, and the fox does not know? What is the moral of the story?)

In these ways, the students begin to develop a metalanguage to describe the design elements of these multimodal texts.

Multimodal writing using new media

In the era of digital media, numerous writing platforms are available that support multimodal writing. One such platform is Scholar, created by the first two authors of this book. You will find case studies of other multimodal writing platforms in the '#edtech Literacies Applications' page for this chapter at literacies.com – and please consider submitting your own case studies for possible publication on this page, via the e-Learning Ecologies Case Studies community in Scholar.

 See literacies.com Multimodal Web Writing

In Figure 8.15 we find ourselves in Janet Austiff's Year/Grade 7 class at Manteno Middle School. The students are writing a biography as part of the 'Ordinary People, Extraordinary Lives' Learning Module in Scholar. Here we see a student in Scholar's Creator space writing up the story of Rosa Parks, who during the civil rights struggles in the 1960s in the United States, refused to sit at the back of the bus in seats designated for Blacks. Not only is the student able to add images. In the spirit of multimodality, she could, if she wished, embed inline video, audio, documents, live links … and if the subject was technical or scientific, include dynamic data, diagrams, animations, simulations, mathematical formula, computer code … in fact,

Figure 8.15 Multimodal web writing

any number of digital objects. These are the expanded dimensions of multimodal writing in digital and online media.

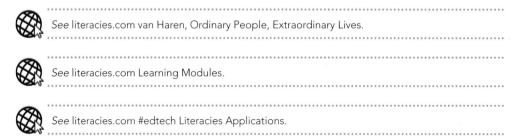

See literacies.com van Haren, Ordinary People, Extraordinary Lives.

See literacies.com Learning Modules.

See literacies.com #edtech Literacies Applications.

Summary

Representation: making meanings for ourselves, including interpretations of the meanings of others			
Communication: making meanings for others, received by others as messages, and interpreted by others according to their interests and perspectives	*(Available) designs:* resources for meaning from which we can choose *Designing:* creating new meanings by reworking available resources The *(re-)designed:* the new meaning created by designing		
		Multimodality: making meanings in more than one way *Synaesthesia:* making meanings in one way, then another; shifting between one mode and another	
		Modes of meaning: • *Written meanings:* writing and reading • *Visual meanings:* perception and image • *Spatial meanings:* location and positioning • *Tactile meanings:* touch and bodily sensation • *Gestural meanings:* body language	

			• *Audio meanings:* sound and music
			• *Oral meanings:* speaking and listening
			Design elements:
			• *To refer:* who, what, how?
			• *To dialogue:* how the meaning-maker connects with the receiver of the message
			• *To structure:* how the meaning holds together
			• *To situate:* where the text is to be found
			• *To intend:* whose interests the text serves, and how

Knowledge processes

conceptualising by naming

1. View one or more of the videos illustrating Multiliteracies in practice at http://newlearningonline.com/multiliteracies/videos/. Identify the similarities and differences between this and traditional literacy pedagogy.

conceptualising with theory

2. Create a mind-map illustrating your understanding of the concepts of representation and communication.

analysing functionally

3. Undertake a design analysis of an everyday text, such as a newspaper article or a video. Identify the design elements of the text using the five questions about meaning introduced in this chapter.

applying creatively

4. Develop a lesson plan that uses all modes of meaning and requires synaesthesia. You might consult the Scholar lvearning platform to write up your work – go to L-by-D.com.

CHAPTER 9

Making meaning by reading

Overview

The next two chapters examine written language, beginning in this chapter with a discussion of different approaches to learning about the connections between the sounds of speaking and the written representation of these sounds. The aim in this chapter is to explore approaches to reading, or making sense from **written meanings**. Chapter 10 goes on to discuss alternative approaches to describing how written language works, from the traditional grammar of didactic pedagogy, to Chomsky's transformational-generative grammar, to Halliday's functional approach. We end that chapter with our own Multiliteracies approach, specifically its treatment of what we call the 'design elements' of written texts.

Modes of meaning

Over the course of this and the following chapters, we lay out and explain the conceptual tools and metalanguage for analysing the designs of modes of meaning: written, visual, spatial, tactile, gestural, audio and oral. We start with written meaning in Chapters 9 and 10 for no other reason than that this has been the traditional focus of literacy teaching and learning. We then move to outline some tools for the **design analysis** of visual meanings in Chapter 11, because writing and image share important common features: both are apprehended by our sense of sight. Today, visual and written designs are more closely overlaid than ever. After working our way through a design analysis of spatial, tactile and gestural meanings in Chapter 12, we will look at the closely connected audio and oral modes in Chapter 13. These last two modes are grouped into the one chapter because they share the sense of hearing as their primary mode of apprehension.

Design analysis: A process of analysing the design elements of a written meaning or multimodal meaning

We have deliberately separated oral and written meanings, placing them at opposite ends of our design analysis in order to highlight their important differences. Although, of course, written and oral modes are closely related through the phenomenon of language, there are some important differences that we need to be aware of in literacy studies. Indeed, we want to argue that written and oral meanings are as different from each other as each of the other modes and, for that matter, just as closely related as all modes – intrinsically, in the nature of multimodality.

Table 9.1: Dimensions of design analysis

Design analysis Naming the design elements or components that go together to make patterns of:	1. Answering the five questions about meaning:
	'What do the meanings refer to?' (Reference)
Written meaning	*'How do the meanings connect the people who are communicating?'* (Interaction)
Visual meaning	
Spatial meaning	*'How does the overall meaning hold together?'* (Composition)
Tactile meaning	*'Where are the meanings situated?'* (Context)
Gestural meaning	*'Whose interests do these meanings serve?'* (Purpose)
Audio meaning	
Oral meaning	2. Seeing how designs are made, differently all the time:
	From *(Available) designs*
	to *Designing*
	to *(The re-)designed*

In the written mode: learning to read

Before we get into the technicalities of reading, let's look into the practicalities of some classes where learners are at different stages of learning to read.

Wombat Stew by Marcia Vaughan is a classic Australian Story about a dingo (a native Australian dog) that catches a wombat and wants to cook him in a stew. As most students in the Year/Grade 1 class have not read the book, the teacher starts with a pair-share predicting strategy: in pairs, they discuss what they think the book is going to be about. Next, the children read the book and share their response with their partner. In the activities that follow, students develop vocabulary by linking words to images (Figure 9.1), use phonemic strategies for unfamiliar words, analyse language features of the text, such as repetition and rhyme (Figure 9.2), and use multimodal literacies strategies to connect text to image and gesture (Figure 9.3).

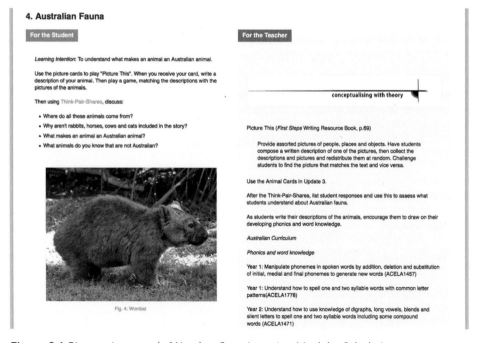

Figure 9.1 Pictures into words (Wombat Stew Learning Module, Scholar)

See literacies.com van Haren and Gorman, Wombat Stew.

In the learning module that they are currently doing, 'Diving into Books', students in Grade/Year 3 analyse the ways in which narratives work: at the sentence level in the use of action and description words; and at the level of the whole text, in terms of the stages of orientation. These are the beginning of the narrative, the sequence of events that follows, and the closing evaluation (Figure 9.4). They make their generalisations about the ways in which narratives work by comparing

5. Language Mode

For the Student

Learning Intention: To think about the word choices of the author and how they add to the book.

Let's re-read the story. You can read along.

1. Language in *Wombat Stew*

Why is the platypus ambling rather than walking?

Platypus Journey by Max Moller

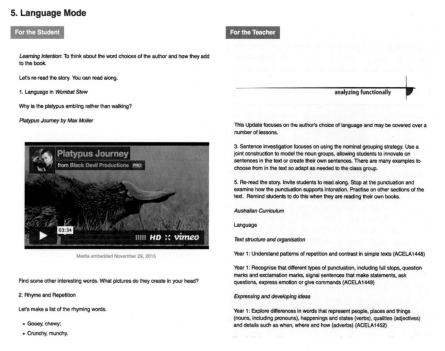

Media embedded November 29, 2015

Find some other interesting words. What pictures do they create in your head?

2. Rhyme and Repetition

Let's make a list of the rhyming words.

- Gooey, chewy;
- Crunchy, munchy.

For the Teacher

analyzing functionally

This Update focuses on the author's choice of language and may be covered over a number of lessons.

3. Sentence investigation focuses on using the nominal grouping strategy. Use a joint construction to model the noun groups, allowing students to innovate on sentences in the text or create their own sentences. There are many examples to choose from in the text so adapt as needed to the class group.

5. Re-read the story. Invite students to read along. Stop at the punctuation and examine how the punctuation supports intonation. Practise on other sections of the text. Remind students to do this when they are reading their own books.

Australian Curriculum

Language

Text structure and organisation

Year 1: Understand patterns of repetition and contrast in simple texts (ACELA1448)

Year 1: Recognise that different types of punctuation, including full stops, question marks and exclamation marks, signal sentences that make statements, ask questions, express emotion or give commands (ACELA1449)

Expressing and developing ideas

Year 1: Explore differences in words that represent people, places and things (nouns, including pronouns), happenings and states (verbs), qualities (adjectives) and details such as when, where and how (adverbs) (ACELA1452)

Figure 9.2 Rhyme and repetition (Wombat Stew Learning Module, Scholar)

6. Visual and Gestural Modes

For the Student

Learning Intention: To analyse the pictures and the gestures of the characters in *Wombat Stew.*

Look at the images of the dingo in the story.

With a partner, find an image where the dingo is:

- happy
- sad
- surprised
- angry

The gestures tell you how dingo is feeling. Gestures include face expressions, and the position of body and hands. With your partner, discuss the gestures that tell you how dingo is feeling.

Look at the pictures of each animal. Now act out how each animal is feeling. Your teacher will call out an animal. Use your facial expressions and your hands and body.

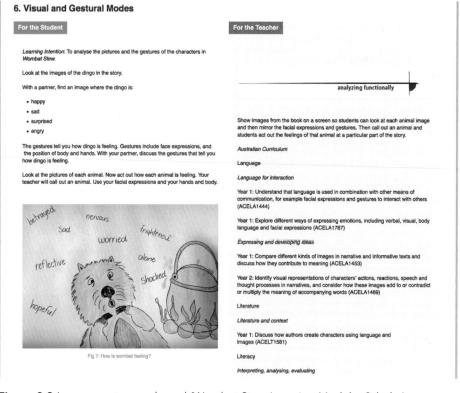

Fig 7: How is wombat feeling?

For the Teacher

analyzing functionally

Show images from the book on a screen so students can look at each animal image and then mirror the facial expressions and gestures. Then call out an animal and students act out the feelings of that animal at a particular part of the story.

Australian Curriculum

Language

Language for interaction

Year 1: Understand that language is used in combination with other means of communication, for example facial expressions and gestures to interact with others (ACELA1444)

Year 1: Explore different ways of expressing emotions, including verbal, visual, body language and facial expressions (ACELA1787)

Expressing and developing ideas

Year 1: Compare different kinds of images in narrative and informative texts and discuss how they contribute to meaning (ACELA1453)

Year 2: Identify visual representations of characters' actions, reactions, speech and thought processes in narratives, and consider how these images add to or contradict or multiply the meaning of accompanying words (ACELA1469)

Literature

Literature and context

Year 1: Discuss how authors create characters using language and images (ACELT1581)

Literacy

Interpreting, analysing, evaluating

Figure 9.3 Image, gesture and word (Wombat Stew Learning Module, Scholar)

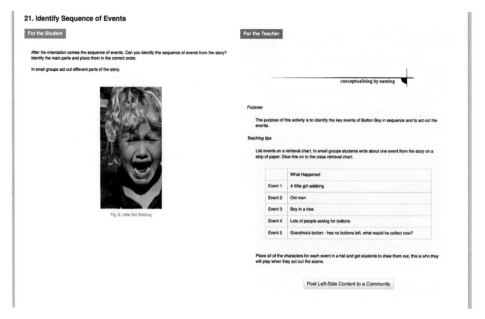

Figure 9.4 Identifying a sequence of events (Diving into Books Learning Module, Scholar)

three different story books. Then, they apply their generalisations by writing a narrative.

See literacies.com Doykas, Gray, Marsden, Queripel, Kiddy and van Haren, Diving into books.

Now we are in a Year/Grade 7 class, where the students are studying the novel *Trash*, by Andy Mulligan, about children who live in a rubbish dump. Early in the process of analysing the novel, students imagine what it would be like to live in a rubbish tip, and watch online documentaries that describe the reality of that experience (Figure 9.5). Before they start to read, they predict what the novel might be about (Figure 9.6). Using a partnered reading strategy, they then read the novel chapter by chapter, retelling and summarising as they go, and discussing language features of the narrative, such as the ways in which tension is created.

See literacies.com Radvanyi, Gill, Nott and van Haren, Trash: A novel study.

Next, we are in a Year/Grade 10 class, studying George Orwell's *Animal Farm*. This learning module starts with the knowledge process of 'experiencing the known', with students discussing their experiences of power (Figure 9.7). The updates that follow invite students to explore Orwell's biography, the Russian Revolution, Stalinism and the nature of allegory. In terms of our questions of meaning, *Animal Farm* can hardly be understood just in terms of what is said in the text. To make sense, it must be situated in historical and social context.

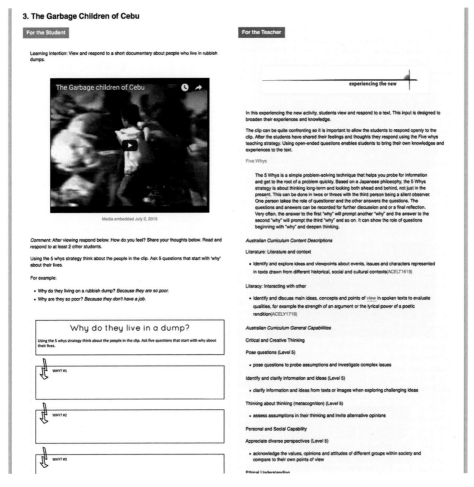

Figure 9.5 Immersion in new experience (Trash Learning Module, Scholar)

 See literacies.com Nott, *Animal Farm.*

These examples illustrate a range of strategies in reading pedagogy. Now for the underlying theory …

Working at reading

We can think of reading as making sense of written meanings. From a Multi-literacies point of view, meaning-making in reading is about interpreting messages communicated in the written word, or more precisely, representing meaning to oneself as one interprets the written message-prompts of others. Reading multi-modal texts is about interpreting messages frequently communicated visually via written word and images – in this age of digital text design, reading and viewing

Figure 9.6 Predicting as a reading strategy (Trash Learning Module, Scholar)

have become inextricably entwined. In the written mode, readers interpret what is signified in written language. This is more than decoding the signs and symbols of writing. In this process, readers make their personal representations about the meanings communicated by the writer. Meanings are exchanged between writer and reader, though often distant in time compared with face-to-face spoken inter-actions where communication or meaning exchange is more immediate. This view of reading makes some very different assumptions about language, meaning and meaning-making from those underlying some of the other approaches to literacy introduced in this book, such as the phonics of didactic pedagogy or the 'whole language' approach, an example of authentic literacy pedagogy. The rest of this section of the chapter explores the varying emphases in reading pedagogies as-sociated with didactic and authentic approaches, while the second main section, 'Connecting the sounds of speech with the visuals of writing', considers more inte-grated approaches to reading.

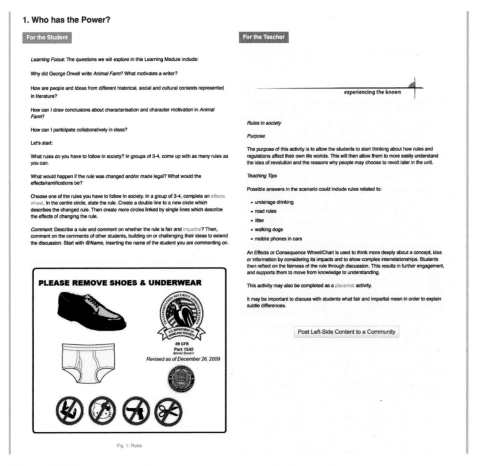

Figure 9.7 Experiencing the known, as an entry point into understanding a new text (Animal Farm Learning Module, Scholar)

Synthetic and analytic phonics

Didactic literacy pedagogy tends to address the task of learning to read the written word by focusing on sound–letter correspondences, or the ways in which the sounds of speaking are transcribed in alphabetical writing. Reading, in this conception, is principally a decoding exercise. Students decode the letters (**graphemes**) of a word into sounds (**phonemes**); they 'sound out' the word vocally or silently, then connect the sight of the word with the sound of the word and its meaning – assuming they know its meaning in spoken language in the first place.

Grapheme: A visual representation of a sound (in an alphabetic language, such as English) or an idea or word (in a language that uses logograms, such as Chinese)

Phoneme: A sound of speech that can be represented in writing

So when children learn to read English, they learn that its code runs from left to right, that the sounds of words can be broken up into distinguishable parts, and that these parts can be represented as letters or clusters of letters. But not all written codes follow these conventions; there is, for example, Arabic, which runs the other way from right to left; Hebrew, which leaves out vowels; Chinese, which mostly represents ideas, rather than sounds, in its characters; and English, which has characters that are logographic – that is, they represent an idea rather than its sounds (for example, 8, + and @) in a similar way to Chinese logograms. In a didactic approach to literacy, phonic decoding is a first step in the mechanics of reading in English. A child has to learn phonics by rote because there is no obvious connection between the letter *a* and its sound, and the letter *b* and its sound. The oldest of didactic reading pedagogies left things mostly at this point. Children were good readers if they could read aloud, clearly and fluently, or even eloquently.

This is called a **synthetic phonics** approach to learning to read (refer also to Chapter 4). The teacher starts with teaching students letter names and sounds, often beginning with consonants followed by short vowels, so that children can read and spell monosyllabic words, such as *cat* and *dog*. Consonant blends, diagraphs and long vowels are then introduced so children can read words such as *plant*, *chip*, *rain* and *game*. Somewhere along the way students also learn about diphthongs, unique sounds made from combining two vowel sounds (e.g. *soil*, *cloud*); words with more than one **syllable**; the connections between spelling rules (such as having a long vowel before a single consonant – 'later' – and a short vowel before a double consonant – 'latter'); and punctuation. This letters-to-words approach came to be softened somewhat in the 20th century by a words-to-letters approach, in which early readers were asked to sound out words, identifying their component sounds and aligning these with their spelling. This was called an **analytic** (in contrast to a synthetic) approach to phonics (Schoenfeld & Pearson 2009).

> **Synthetic phonics:** Learning to read and write by putting the sounds of letters together into words
>
> **Syllable:** A sound unit within a word consisting of a vowel (or vowels) and often also a consonant (or consonants)
>
> **Analytic phonics:** Learning to read and write by taking apart the sounds of meaningful whole words

Synthetic phonics	Start with the sounds **c-a-t**	...and then make the word **cat**
Analytic phonics	Start with the meaningful word **cat**	...and then take apart its sounds, **c-a-t**

Figure 9.8 Approaches to phonics

 See literacies.com Chall, Debating Phonics.

Reading as decoding and meaning-making

In the first quarter of the 20th century, didactic literacy pedagogies added a second major step to the decoding process to include comprehension. At this level of

The Author's Coding	The Reader's Decoding
It was raining on Wednesday afternoon, so John and Betty decided to go the movies ...	What day did John and Betty go to the movies? A. At the weekend B. On Wednesday C. A Wet Day D. Today

Figure 9.9 Comprehension as decoding

decoding, learners put words into sentences to make sense of the author's meaning. It is as if the reader can hear the author speaking (all being well) clearly and directly. This additional decoding step became an important part of the repertoire of didactic pedagogy with the introduction of the multiple-choice reading comprehension test.

From the 1920s to the 1960s, authentic reading pedagogies established themselves as a major alternative to didactic approaches with a new focus on meaning and real-life, authentic texts. What ensued was an ongoing battle, which continues until this day. Authentic approaches managed to manoeuvre themselves into the ascendancy several times over the course of the 20th century, but by the first decades of the 21st century didactic reading pedagogies were once again in a position of institutional dominance in the form of 'phonemic awareness' programs for early literacy learners and the application of standardised comprehension testing as a proxy for reading ability. No matter which position is temporarily in the ascendency, the 'reading wars' never seem to go away. The focus of authentic pedagogy is on meaning. Its proponents claim that learning to read through phonics, strictly speaking, is impossible, and that too much teaching of phonics gets in the way of the purpose of reading, which is meaning.

 See literacies.com Schoenfeld and Pearson on the Reading Wars.

In spoken English, there are approximately 5000 different syllables, each with its own peculiar mix of sounds and letters when represented in written form (Snow, Burns & Griffin 1998: 22). Berdiansky, Cronnel and Koehler (1969) examined over 6000 one- and two-syllable words from school reading books that children between the ages of six and nine ought to be able to identify. They found 69 grapheme units (representing a single sound, such as 'th') connected with 38 different sounds in 211 different ways. They found 166 different rules (patterns of sound–letter correspondence that occurred in at least 10 different words) and 45 exceptions (sound–letter correspondences that happened only once or a very few times). They found that vowels could be pronounced in 79 different ways. Phonics, concludes psycholinguist Frank Smith, is incredibly complicated – too complicated, in fact, to be taught (Smith 2004: 143–6). Not even the computers that use speech recognition today can make sense of sounds alone – they have to put sounds in words in meaningful sequences.

The 'look–say' approach to reading

An early attempt to get around these problems with phonics was what came to be called the 'look–say', or whole word, method of teaching reading. Whole words were learned by sight. Items were labelled around the classroom – 'table', 'chair', 'window', 'door' – and the children came to associate the meaning of the whole word with the thing it labelled. Children read story-readers that had been carefully designed for meaning in an early version of multimodal communication and synaesthetic learning. Here there was a picture of Dick and Jane running with their dog, Spot. Beside the picture were the large, clear words 'See Spot run!' This now famous sentence comes from one of the first early reading series, the Dick and Jane books, published in the 1930s and republished for many decades after that. Only after students had started to read whole words was a 'focused analysis' of phonics introduced, which had the teacher grouping words with similar sounds (such as 'farm', 'fun', 'family', 'fine' and 'first') so that the students could identify similarities.

Oh, Father.
See funny Dick.
Dick can play.

Oh, Mother.
Oh, Father.
Jane can play.
Sally can play.

Figure 9.10 The look–say approach in a Dick and Jane reader

The proponents of authentic reading pedagogies argue that an overemphasis on phonics can get in the way of the purpose of reading, which is meaning. When we read for meaning, we don't look at the letters and sound them all out. We get to know the look of whole words. Our eyes move along the line in 'saccades', or small, rapid, jerky movements of the eye as it jumps from looking at one little group of words to another.

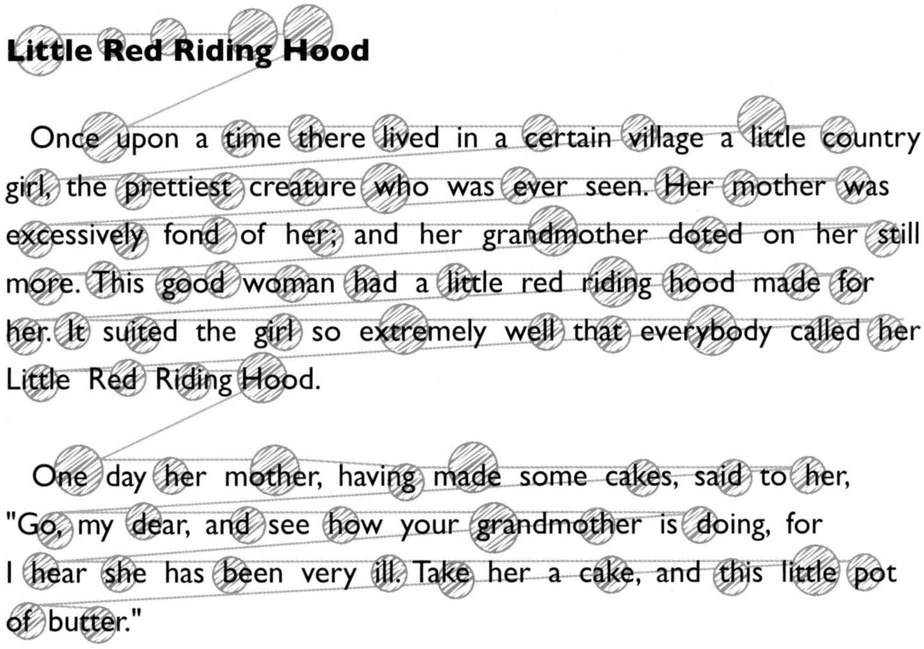

Little Red Riding Hood

Once upon a time there lived in a certain village a little country girl, the prettiest creature who was ever seen. Her mother was excessively fond of her; and her grandmother doted on her still more. This good woman had a little red riding hood made for her. It suited the girl so extremely well that everybody called her Little Red Riding Hood.

One day her mother, having made some cakes, said to her, "Go, my dear, and see how your grandmother is doing, for I hear she has been very ill. Take her a cake, and this little pot of butter."

Figure 9.11 Reading saccades

We don't look closely at every word or give all words the same attention. Our minds can fill in many of the words just because we know what words will be in the gaps. Sometimes, when the meaning does not gel, we move back to look over a word or cluster of words. When we get stuck on a word, we guess at its meaning from the context or by thinking of similar words. Almost the last thing we do is sound it out. This is laborious, and it gets in the way of the thinking processes of meaning.

According to this perspective, learning to read can be as natural as learning to speak. Just as a young child picks up speaking because they need to participate in the social world of spoken meaning, so later they will pick up reading. They can do this in the same way: by immersion. As the rules of sound–letter correspondence are too numerous, varied, untidy and boring, the child will learn to read by immersion in written meanings by developing their written meaning understandings. Says Smith (2004: 3, 5):

> 22 pairs of facial muscles are constantly orchestrated to display at least four thousand different expressions, all produced and universally understood without any instruction at all. Some basic expressions of emotion – like fear, anger, surprise, disgust, sadness and enjoyment – may be instinctive, but the majority are learned early in life ... When was anyone taught to interpret all this, to read faces? ... Reading print is as natural as reading faces.

This naturalistic approach prescribes learning to read by immersion in lots of 'authentic texts', starting with easier texts and moving on to harder ones – including exciting stories, interesting information and functional signs. One of its

Whole language: A 'naturalistic' approach to learning to read and write in which students are immersed in authentic texts that interest them and experiences of making meaning through reading and writing

key ideas, and a phrase that has at times come to be the name of the entire movement, is '**whole language**'. The whole language approach, which focuses on strategies for finding meaning, stands in direct contrast to synthetic phonics, which may require students to sound out decontextualised letters and clusters of letters, and spell isolated words.

Table 9.2: Synthetic and analytic phonics compared

Synthetic phonics	Analytic phonics
• Piecing together whole words from the sounds of their letters	• Taking apart whole words that are known from sight, then looking for patterns in the letters
• Learning phonics rules in order to apply them; and rote-learning spelling, including exceptions to phonics rules	• Inferring phonics rules by repeated exposure to examples
• Writing is coding; reading is decoding of meaning, or 'comprehension'	• Writing is the creation of meaning; reading is the interpretation of meaning
• Requires a metalanguage to describe patterns in language, or conceptual thinking	• Immersion, in written language, is enough to learn to read and write
• Learning to read and write is quite different from learning to listen and speak	• Reading and writing can be learned naturally, in the same way as listening and speaking

 See literacies.com Goodman on Reading.

Reading and mental models

The theoretical rationale behind this approach is based in psycholinguistics, a subdiscipline at the intersection of psychology and linguistics that focuses on the psychological factors that influence language learning and use. Reading is not a sounding process. It is a thinking process. Let's start with words. 'Table' only means something because we have an experience of tables. We have categorised some very different-looking things (dining-room tables, coffee tables and table-tennis tables) around their distinguishing features, or similarities in how they look and what they are for. We have done this for the practical purposes of making sense of these objects when we see them and putting them to use in our lives. If I come across the word 'orrery' in a sentence but have never experienced an orrery in the real world or seen a picture of one in a book, sounding out the letters would do me no good. It would not help me with its meaning. (If you don't know what an 'orrery' is, look it up, but more important than finding the definition, find some pictures of the actual thing, and the meaning will likely stay with you.) The meaningful readability of the words 'table' or 'orrery', in other words, is connected to my experiences of tables or orreries. With the help of my powers of perception, language and culture, I need to have a category of objects in my experience in order for these objects to be meaningfully nameable.

The category of 'table' also fits into my mental models of the world or of schemas. Schemas tie together a number of related concepts. These include furniture (including a working theory of how tables relate to chairs) and restaurants (with many tables and chairs, and a peculiar pattern of social relations in which these tables and chairs are configured). We use our mental model of restaurants to negotiate the next restaurant we visit, which we manage to do successfully even though we have never been to this one before. We also apply mental models to our reading. So when we read 'We arrived at the restaurant, and then were taken to our table and seated by the waiter', we apply our mental model to making sense of this written meaning. If we have never been to a restaurant or seen an arriving-at-a-restaurant scene in a movie, this sentence will be hard to understand, no matter how good we may have become at phonics. Reading for meaning is about predicting from our experience. We read 'We arrived at the restaurant, and then ...' and before we even start to read the rest of the sentence we can anticipate predictable endings for that sentence. Completely unpredictable endings do not make sense. Surprises may make sense ('I tripped over on the way to the table ...') because they come from the range of reasonable alternatives and our understanding of the 'complications' that are the reason why we tell stories. But '... and this is the reason two and two make four' makes no sense as an ending to this sentence, because it does not fit with the range of sensible meaning possibilities that are predictable from our mental models of the experience of arriving at a restaurant.

For these reasons, the authentic reading pedagogues argue that the best strategy to determine the meaning of an unfamiliar word is to work it out from context, to apply your mental models of coherent experience to the text and to try to fill in the gap of meaning represented by a difficult word. You predict the meaning of the strange word from the meanings of the words around it. You compare it in your mind to a similar known word. Or you skip the word, hoping that the text will make enough sense without it. Smith (2004: 55) calls this 'mediated word identification'.

Reading, then, is a relationship between a text and our thinking. We read meanings into texts by connecting them with our knowledge, experiences and interests. When we read for meaning, we apply mental models or cognitive structures kept in our long-term memory to the text we see (Anderson & Pearson 1984). From one reader to the next, our mental models are never quite the same. This is why every act of reading comprehension is a process of interpretation, or bringing our own meanings to bear on the text. The truth that we make of the text, and from person to person, is thus never exactly the same.

More recent approaches to teaching comprehension extend this cognitive view of reading to include the explicit teaching of reading comprehension skills and strategies that readers use to bring meaning to and extract meaning from texts (e.g. Harvey & Goudvis 2007; Paris & Stahl 2005). Paris (2005) distinguishes between constrained reading skills that can be mastered in a relatively short timeframe (e.g. letter knowledge and decoding skills) and unconstrained reading skills (e.g. vocabulary and comprehension), which develop over one's lifetime in various contexts.

So reading, as thinking, involves readers engaging in deliberate, situated strategies (in contrast to automated, context-free skills of decoding). These include connecting prior knowledge to new information in text, identifying literal information explicitly stated in the text, making inferences based on information in the text and their own prior knowledge, questioning or predicting by creating mental images, and summarising and synthesising information from a text.

See literacies.com Dougherty Stahl on Constrained and Unconstrained Reading Abilities.

Reading as the design of meaning

At this point we would like to reframe this reading process as 'design'. This is because we believe our design approach allows us to capture the complexities and dynamism of meaning-making. To reiterate the concepts we introduced in Chapter 8, our 'available designs' are the categories of meaning we have, and the mental models of the world that tie these categories together. Available designs are meanings that we recall and connect to the text as we read. Some of these recollections take the form of visual, spatial, gestural and other meanings: for example, restaurants we have seen in pictures and movies, or actual restaurants where you have been shown to a table by a waiter.

As we read the text 'We arrived at the restaurant ...', we apply our categories and mental models to it, giving it a meaning based on our experience. This is never quite the same as the next reader's meaning, and that is because our particular experiences have been different. If we've mostly been to fast-food restaurants, the mental model we bring to the sentence will be different from that of someone who is used to going to fancy restaurants with tablecloths and table waiters who meet you at the door. In such a situation, the experience of this reading leaves our world and transforms us because it stays in our memory as a new meaning – we may never have been to a fine dining restaurant or heard the words 'degustation menu' before, but we learn something about these meanings and words from the new

Table 9.3: Making meaning through reading – reading as design

Reading as 'design'	(Available) designs	We've seen the word, phrase or genre of text and we've experienced its meaning – or at least, we have enough clues for it to make sense even if some parts of it are unfamiliar.
	Designing	As we read the text, we are helped along by the mental images it creates. We make sense of the text in our own particular way based on our experiences and interests.
	The (re-)designed	We are left with our interpretation of the text, our memory of what it says and how it says it. Our meaning-world is transformed in however small a way by the text we have just read.

reading or from watching a movie. The textual experience ends in an incremental extension to the range of our understandings of restaurants, which we may recall in our next visit to a restaurant or our next piece of reading or writing about a restaurant.

Hybrid approaches to reading

Although the advocates of authentic literacy have some powerful arguments, which we have recast here in terms of a Multiliteracies design approach, they have also been criticised for the limitations in their approach, and not just by the advocates of didactic pedagogy but also by people who are sympathetic to many of their intentions.

The more rigorously consistent of the authentic reading pedagogues argue against metalanguages of any kind. 'There is no evidence,' says Smith (2004: 48), 'that making text structures explicit improves comprehension'. However, to return to the general arguments outlined in more detail in Chapter 5, the immersion model is neither necessary nor efficient in schools. It is not necessary because, unlike children learning to speak, children have a resource for categorising and mental-model-making that they didn't have when they learned to speak, and that is language itself. If we can generalise about language, it will help learners to understand how to use language, and to do this in a more efficient way than by repetition of examples. Moreover, the immersion approach works better for students who 'get' the meaning of written meaning instinctively, because they come from environments that use a lot of writing and in which the value of reading and writing is self-evident. In other words, it has a bias towards learners with certain kinds of prior experience. It also has a bias towards certain kinds of texts: those, according to people who make it their business to judge such things, considered to be of literary value. Finally, it tends to neglect the power of reading–writing connections of the kind described in the analysis of functional literacy approaches in Chapter 6.

As a way of overcoming the polarities that emerged in teaching reading, Richard Anderson proposed a 'balanced approach'. In a path-breaking report, he says that the common view that reading is a process in which:

> pronunciation of words gives access to their meanings, then sentences, then texts ... is only partially correct. A text is not so much a vessel containing meaning as it is a source of partial information that enables the reader to use already-possessed knowledge to determine the intended meaning. Phonics is not to be dismissed, but its aims should be broader than learning an endless list of rules. ... 'The goal of phonics is not that children be able to state the "rules" governing sound–letter relationships. Rather, the purpose is to get across the alphabetical principle, the principle that there are systematic relationships between letters and sounds' (Anderson, Hiebert, Scott & Wilkinson 1985: 8, 35).

See literacies.com Anderson on a Balanced Approach to Reading.

In a similar spirit, Allan Luke and Peter Freebody (1997, 1999) developed a 'Four Resources' or 'Four Roles' model (Freebody 2007). Firstly, effective readers are 'code-breakers', picking up on the spirit of phonics and extending it, able to recognise the connections between sounds and the spelling of words, but also able to identify larger structural conventions in texts. Secondly, they are 'meaning-makers' in the sense in which authentic literacy advocates suggest and more, participating in making sense of texts by connecting them with meanings recollected from their own mental models. Thirdly, they are 'text users', able to get things done by reading and writing texts – something very much in the spirit of the functional approaches described in Chapter 6; they read to learn and learn how texts are used to achieve purposeful social and cultural goals. Finally, effective readers can be 'text analysts', interrogating a text for the points of view and interests it represents, and comparing these with their own and others' interpretations of experience. In a functional approach to reading, analysis of model texts provides the pathway for teachers to apprentice students into becoming adept decoders, participants and users of texts. There are also strong resonances in this fourth perspective with the critical literacies approaches that we outlined in Chapter 7.

Table 9.4: The Four Resources Model

Code-breaker	**Meaning-maker**
Coding competence: to break the code of written texts by recognising and using fundamental features and architecture, including alphabet, sounds in words, spelling, and structural conventions and patterns	*Semantic competence:* to participate in understanding and composing meaningful written, visual and spoken texts, taking into account each text's interior meaning systems in relation to the reader's available knowledge and their experiences of other cultural discourses, texts and meaning systems
Text user	**Text analyst**
Pragmatic competence: to use texts functionally, by knowing about and acting on the different cultural and social functions that various texts perform inside and outside school, and understanding that these functions shape the way texts are structured, their tone, their degree of formality, and their sequence of components	*Critical competence:* to analyse critically and transform texts by acting on knowledge that texts are not ideologically natural or neutral; that they represent particular points of views while silencing others and influence people's ideas; and that their designs and discourses can be critiqued and redesigned in novel and hybrid ways

Source: Adapted from Freebody (2007); Freebody & Luke (1990); Luke & Freebody (1999).

Learning to read

Cumming-Potvin (2007) describes the experience of Nicholas, a Year/Grade 7 boy participating in a reading circle, which encourages the habit of reading and promotes the use of literacy skills. In his own estimation, Nicholas finds reading difficult; he describes it as 'spelling the letters'. Evidently, phonics lessons earlier in his school life have left a lasting impression. The class is reading a novel, *Tuck Everlasting*, an adventure in which the hero ends up helping a person who has committed a serious crime. To connect the story's main theme with students' lived experiences, and to develop their engagement with its most difficult and contentious meanings, the teacher asks Nicholas' reading circle to discuss the nature of crime. Crime is not just a word to be decoded; it is also an idea that this novel explores with depth and subtlety. The way the word is used, the central meaning of the novel, may challenge and extend the mental models of crime that the students bring to the reading. 'Is it a crime to ride your bicycle without a helmet?' asks Mrs Parker, Nicholas' teacher. It is illegal in Nicholas' state, but children do it and even though they may realise that it is foolish, mostly they don't consider it to be a crime.

The topic Mrs Parker sets for discussion in the reading circles is 'Everyone who commits a crime should be punished'. The researcher joins the discussion in Nicholas' group.

Art: What would ... if you like just rode [by bicycle] to your friend's house not wearing a helmet?

Researcher: OK Is that a crime?

Nicholas: Yeah –

Martin: No ...

Nicholas: Yes, yes it is ...

Researcher: You think that's a crime ...

Kevin: Because it's the law ...

Researcher: Because it's against ..., because it's illegal? It's against the law. OK, so that's a crime. What about if you threw a ball into ... by accident, you were playing on say ... your front lawn and you threw the ball and it hit the neighbour's window by accident and broke the window?

Martin: (Laughs). I've done that –

Kevin: That's not a crime –

Nicholas: No! No! That's an accident.

Researcher: No? Why? That's an accident?

Nicholas: But then you would have to pay for it.

Researcher: OK, so ...

Nicholas: It's not like you wanted to get into the house and take some stuff.

This discussion scaffolds the most important meanings in the novel, meanings that are matters of subtle interpretation and not reducible to the ABCD answers of comprehension tests. It also makes a connection with reader identity that gives the reading greater depth of purpose, even for a struggling reader like Nicholas.

In another moment, in another classroom, a teacher, Janelle, is working over a digital learning object with her class on her electronic whiteboard. She passes over the words 'ace' and 'photon torpedoes' and 'knuckle', words that many of her students didn't know. Sounding out the words would not help, in part because these words do not sound out in an obvious way, but also because the students have never heard them before. But their meanings are hyperlinked, just a click away – an important stratagem for tackling new meanings in texts with live hyperlinks (Kitson, Fletcher & Kearney 2007).

Connecting the sounds of speech with the visuals of writing

Introduction

We want to reframe the essence of the didactic perspective on literacy as 'conceptual' and the authentic approach as 'experiential'. The most effective way to learn to read is to weave between conceptual and experiential 'knowledge processes' – ideas we have already introduced in Chapter 3.

We don't want to take sides in the reading wars. Our reason for this is not because we want to take a neutral or half-way position. The conceptually focused stance of didactic pedagogies is completely correct (but by itself not sufficient). The experientially focused stance of authentic pedagogies is completely correct too (but also by itself not sufficient). Despite the, at times, emotively ideological posturing of the combatants in the reading wars, the best of didactic approaches supplement their primary focus on conceptual knowledge processes with experiential knowledge processes, and the best of authentic approaches supplement their primary focus on experiential knowledge processes with conceptual knowledge processes. If they don't, they're simply not as effective as they might otherwise have been. Excellent teachers have always mixed and matched different activity types or knowledge processes.

Current curriculum documents also recognise the importance of both the conceptual and experiential aspects of literacy. For example, in the Australian Curriculum: English (see ACARA 2015g), achievement standards for each school year include linguistic, cognitive, social and multimodal dimensions of reading and viewing, characteristic of balanced or hybrid approaches. While there is a greater emphasis in the early years on technical skills of decoding, the development of intellectual and cultural reading practices around meaning-making and participating in texts are also explicitly addressed. So, by the end of the first year of formal schooling (Foundation year):

> students use predicting and questioning strategies to make meaning from texts. They recall one or two events from texts with familiar topics. They understand that there are different types of texts and that these can have similar characteristics. They identify connections between texts and their personal experience.

They read short, decodable and predictable texts with familiar vocabulary and supportive images, drawing on their developing knowledge of concepts of print, sounds and letters and decoding and self-monitoring strategies. They recognise the letters of the English alphabet, in upper and lower case and know and use the most common sounds represented by most letters. They read high-frequency words and blend sounds orally to read consonant-vowel-consonant words. They use appropriate interaction skills to listen and respond to others in a familiar environment. They listen for rhyme, letter patterns and sounds in words (ACARA 2015g).

[By the end of the Year 10 there is a greater emphasis on the role of readers as text analysts.]

By the end of Year 10, students evaluate how text structures can be used in innovative ways by different authors. They explain how the choice of language features, images and vocabulary contributes to the development of individual style.

They develop and justify their own interpretations of texts. They evaluate other interpretations, analysing the evidence used to support them. They listen for ways features within texts can be manipulated to achieve particular effects (ACARA 2015g).

A similar balance of approaches can be found in the US Common Core State Standards (Common Core State Standards Initiative [CCSS] 2010) and modern curriculum standards documents in many other countries.

Beginning reading

In moments of teaching and learning when we take a conceptual approach, teachers need to know the following things about the connections between the sounds of speech and the visuals of writing. As soon as children are able to grasp these concepts, it is good to name them explicitly and have students generalise about how spoken language and written language are connected. This is often called the '**alphabetical principle**' – but, as we shall see, there is more to this principle than the sounds of the letters of the alphabet.

Alphabetical principle: Letters of written words roughly follow the sounds of the same word, spoken. This contrasts with languages such as Chinese, which are principally logographic, and whose characters represent ideas

Table 9.5: A phonics snapshot

1.	*Phonemes*: Letters of the *alphabet*, by themselves ('a', 'b', 'c') or in groups ('ou', 'th', 'ed'), represent sounds or *phonemes*.
2.	*Vowels and consonants*: There are two kinds of phonemes: *vowels*, or sounds that are made when your vocal chords are vibrating (a, e, i, o and u) and *consonants*, which are made when you use your mouth or tongue to obstruct the sound (b, c, d, f, etc.).
3.	*Syllables*: Syllables are single sound units, which always have a vowel and may include one or more consonants (e.g. 'clever', 'running' each have two syllables).
4.	*Words*: Words can have one or more syllables. You can recognise words by the spaces around them.

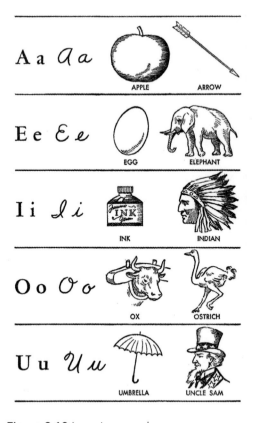

Figure 9.12 Learning vowels

An overview of phonics concepts

Here is the short version of the story of how to translate the sounds of speech into the visuals of writing.

Phonics and cognition

Children need to know this stuff to be able to read and write. It looks deceptively easy, but it is actually hard. In fact, it is so hard that one can only marvel at the dazzling representational capacities of the human species that learners in their early years of school can learn something this hard. Here is how hard it is: the relationship of 'a' and 'b' to their respective sounds is purely abstract. There are no contextual clues to help learning. The word 'dog' is an abstraction, too, but you learn it by the repeated juxtaposition of word and animal in the world of experience. There is nothing about the relationship between 'a' and its sound to help you, other than the strange experience of reading, writing and literacy pedagogy. As Snow, Burns and Griffin (1998: 22) say in their influential report on reading: 'letters of the alphabet are referentially meaningless and phonologically abstract.' This is a generalisation that is in fact true of all phoneme (sound) to grapheme (writing)

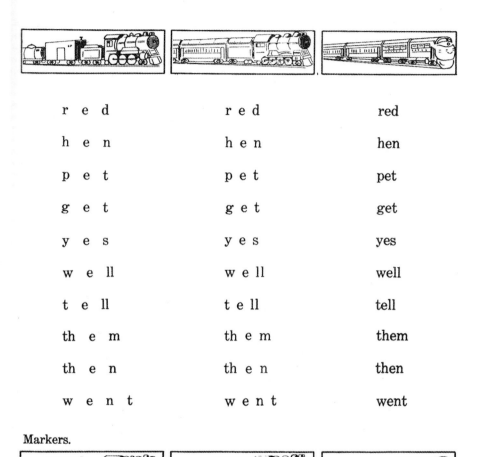

Run your train under these words.
Sound the letters as you go.

r e d	r e d	red
h e n	h e n	hen
p e t	p e t	pet
g e t	g e t	get
y e s	y e s	yes
w e ll	w e ll	well
t e ll	t e ll	tell
th e m	th e m	them
th e n	th e n	then
w e n t	w e n t	went

Markers.

Figure 9.13 From letters to words (a page from a 1955 phonics book)

relationships. Young learners have to learn a lot of these abstractions to be able to read, with no clues in the writing itself. It's amazing that they do, and at such an early age.

Then there's another layer of abstraction. It's helpful to be able to use abstract concepts, such as 'alphabet', 'syllable', 'word', 'vowel', 'consonant' and even 'phoneme', as you learn to read and write. You didn't need a metalanguage or language about language to learn to speak at home. But it's very helpful to have tools for design analysis or metalanguage about written language when learning to read and write in school. Literacy researcher Jeanne Chall (1967(1983): 25) calls this kind of learning 'the formal, abstract aspects of language'. This kind of learning helps you think conceptually and makes your learning more efficient because you are able to generalise and transfer these generalisations from one instance of language use to another.

This short story of the connections between the sounds of speaking and the visuals of writing is already extraordinary but true. To recap, children need to learn these key conceptual distinctions as they become readers and writers, and these distinctions are in all probability more conceptually challenging than anything they have encountered so far in their short lives. In fact, they may even be the biggest conceptual challenge they face in their whole lives. To reiterate the conceptual scheme, around the other way this time:

1. *Words.* Written meanings are expressed in *words* or groups of *words* in the form of *phrases* or *sentences*.
2. *Syllables.* Words are made up of sound units called *syllables*.
3. *Vowels and consonants.* Syllables connect the two sound types, *consonants* and *vowels*.
4. *Phonemes.* Phonemes are sounds that correspond with their written representation as *graphemes*.

Whether teachers choose to use all of these concepts in their teaching, and whether they emphasise them by naming them explicitly or allow the concepts to come out during experiential immersion in reading and writing, the conceptual challenge is the same.

The complexities of phonics

If this wasn't hard enough, there is an even more complicated version of the story. Learning to read would be enough of a conceptual challenge if we could just learn these four concepts. However, there is no way of keeping to these rules. The rules work more or less some of the time, but for an awful lot of the time they don't work or become too numerous and complicated to be worth committing to memory or learning in school. For every rule, we'd have to learn the thousands of times when the rule doesn't work or the times when another rule is needed. In sum, there are important relationships between the phonemes of spoken language and the graphemes of written language, but they are complicated, subtle, numerous and hard to learn.

See literacies.com Meyer on Spelling Rules that Work Only Sometimes.

The key question for educators is how much phonics is appropriate and enough. The only thing that is certain about phonics is that no one can learn everything, in part because the variabilities are endless. On the other hand, it still helps to know a fair amount, and this can only be learned in the form of abstract rules – because that's what sound–letter meaning patterns are: abstractions. No matter how good a reader and writer becomes, no matter how many rules they learn, they will still

Table 9.6: Phonics is complicated!

1. **Phonemes**. The sounds of language, *phonemes,* do not neatly or consistently match *graphemes* (the letters and clusters of letters in an alphabetic language like English). In one count, English has 47 phonemes, represented by of single letters and digraphs or pairs of letters. But:

   - If only spelling were as simple as learning the letters that go with these 47 sounds, but each sound can be spelled many ways. For instance, to take just one of the 47, the long 'a' sound can be spelt at least 19 different ways (ate, steak, veil, obey etc.). So there are many hundreds of spellings of the 47 sounds.

   - Add to these the 'blends', where two letters fuse into a single blended sound (such as 'br' in 'broom', and the number of sounds jumps from 47 to hundreds.

   - So do 'silent' letters that may have been sounded at some time in the history of the language, but no longer are – the 'g' in 'light', and how wrong is the spelling 'lite'? And how simple is the silent 'e' that changes the sound of the 'i' two characters earlier? (Not very!)

   - Dialects add another layer of difficulty – 'merry' might sound like 'Mary' or 'marry', depending on your dialect.

2. **Vowels and consonants.** *Consonants* can't happen without *vowels,* and consonants and vowels are modified by each other in always-fused sound units.

   - Collections of sounds are often treated as a single perceptual unit – consider the vowel plus 'r' sound at the end of 'fear' and 'Cuba' – some people will hear it as a separate phoneme, others not.

   - Nasal sounds are partially absorbed by the preceding vowel or following consonant. (Could you tell the difference between 'at' and 'ant' if the sounds of these words were cut out of the sentences where it is clear from the meaning that 'at' is not 'ant'?)

   - Some consonant sounds are very hard to distinguish, such as the 'ch' or 'j' sounds (technically called 'affricatives') that commence the words 'train', 'drum', 'jump' and 'church'.

   - Aspiration (the amount of air with a sound) varies. Some consonants sound quite different when they are at different places in the word, such as the 'p' and 't' sounds in 'pit' and 'tip' … it's easy to write 'pig' for 'pick' and 'cub' for 'cup'.

   - Vowels blend with consonants – from a phonemic point of view, how wrong is it to write 'brid' for 'bird'?

   - The sounds of language are also very variable, and most of the time it doesn't matter. Different people may sound things in different ways. At the micro level of consonant–vowel fusing, the one person might pronounce something in a peculiar way – just this time or all the time when they speak – without affecting the meaning. For instance, when some people speak, you may hear the 't' in 'counted' or 'wanted', and you may never notice whether it is there or not. The difference between 'ladder' and 'latter' may be noticeable, or it may not.

   - Spoken language is never heard sound by sound, least of all at the rate at which letters flow past, and never at a level at which there is any purpose in distinguishing consonants from vowels – these are always heard as a single unit.

(continued)

Table 9.6: Phonics is complicated! (*continued*)

3. **Syllables.** You can hear *syllables* in a spoken word, but you can't see them in a written word. And there are about 5000 syllables in English – in other words, 5000 different sound clusters.

   - In fact, a lot of audible information in spoken language is lost because informationally important sounds are not recorded in writing, such as stress on one syllable in a word, and intonation patterns in a word. '?', '!', ',', '...' and '.' only present a very limited amount of information about intonation.

4. **Words**. *Words* run into each other in speech, so their beginnings and ends are nearly impossible to hear. Nor do they correspond with units of meaning or *morphemes*. In other words, there is no easy rule to apply to work out where a word starts and ends, either by listening to its sound in speech or by thinking about it from the perspective of meaning.

   - Where words begin and end is a matter of writing convention rather than either sounding or meaning. Some pairs of words are a single morpheme, such as 'railway station'. Other words have two or more morphemes – 'un-think-able' has three. Sometimes two morphemes are to be found in one syllable – 'walked', for instance.

   - Sometimes English spelling follows sounds (when 'life' becomes 'lives'), but other times it follows meaning (the 'c', when 'electric becomes 'electricity').

   - Then there are homophones, or words that sound the same but have different meanings ('read', 'red'); homographs, or words that look the same but have different meanings (and dictionaries try to sort out these differences – look up 'set', which is the hardest word in the English language if you were to use the measure of the largest number of alternative meanings).

encounter words they have not seen before, or heard before. Or they will need to write words that they know how to say but don't know how to spell. In these circumstances, phonics strategies and phonics knowledge are essential.

Thus there are no neat or reliable rules that help you learn words. You just have to learn a lot of words – connecting the way they look, with the way they are spelled, with they way they sound, with what they mean (Gunning 2008: 110, 158–61; Goodman 1993: 6, 24).

The priority of graphemics over phonics in written meanings

If there is one important overall generalisation about phonics, it is that graphemics (letter combinations of the written word) rules, not phonics (the sounds of speech). Children learning to write have an ingenious ear for the sounds of language. But writing is not about sounding conventions, or recording the sounds of language. It is about alphabetic conventions, the ways people have agreed that words should be written. These agreements are recorded in dictionaries. What children write in the form of 'invented spelling' is a marvellous and educationally invaluable first approximation of a word. However, the dictionary will tell us that many of these

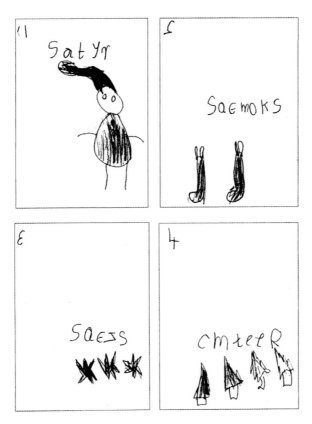

Figure 9.14 A six-year-old gets the phonics right in a Christmas book: (1) Santa; (2) some socks; (3) stars (writing reversed); (4) Christmas trees

approximations are errors, even though they may contain wonderful insights about the sounds of speech. What should we do with these errors?

In the first instance, we should not call these errors, because they are spellings based on exactly what the children have heard and have been taught to do as they learn phonics – to focus on the correspondence of written letters and spoken sounds. Later in their writing (a second draft) or later in their learning (not to interrupt their train of thought or meaning expression for the moment), they can move away from the sounds of language to the conventions of writing. These, as we have seen, deviate in so many ways from the sounds of speech. In any event, the connections between the sounds of speech and the look of writing are so subtly variable that they can't be accurately captured in a manageable or sufficiently comprehensive set of phonics rules.

As adults, we do much the same thing as we put spelling approximations in the sentences we are typing, not wanting to interrupt the flow of our thoughts but knowing that the spellchecker will make suggestions and so our spelling of a word can later be changed so it is the same as the spelling of others writing in our language. Our first approximation is not wrong, because it serves us very well for the moment, in recording a thought that might otherwise escape our short-term memory. It is better to get it down wrongly for the moment than to look up the word and lose our train of thought. In fact, this is exactly the way we adult writers work today with grammar checkers in computer writing spaces or suggestive text on our phones.

At the end of the day, writing is not about getting the phonics right. It is about getting the graphemics or written text right. And in reading, it is the formal patterning of writing that gives you a rough enough indication of the sounds of language, not the other way around. Graphemics rules! There is also a broader cultural logic to this in a society that, for the past few centuries at least, has privileged writing over speaking and other modes of meaning.

Learning written meaning both ways

None of the complexity of phonics should be taken to imply we should not learn its rules and focus instead just on graphemics, or the sight recognition of words. What if we were just to learn lots of words and their correspondences – their look, sounds and meanings at the whole word level? This, more or less, was the look–say method of the 'Dick and Jane' readers. Such an approach, by itself, makes learning English a bit like learning Chinese, in that one would be memorising the look of thousands of sight words. This is just as daunting a task as learning phonics rules, either in the simpler version that we presented above, or the more complicated version.

In fact, we eventually read by knowing a lot of sight words. As mature readers, we only sound out words that we don't already recognise as whole words or whose meanings are not obvious from context. Phonics becomes a rarely needed and limited strategy for competent readers – for instance, when encountering an unfamiliar word or proper noun that for some reason needs to be spoken. However, it is very useful for students learning to read and write, because in English we happen to have an alphabetical language. It helps to have some simple generalisations, and school needs to use these generalisations to make learning processes more efficient than immersion or experience-only approaches. There are some useful phoneme–grapheme relationships, even though they become more complicated the more you learn, and even though they are ultimately quite unreliable and of very limited value to mature readers.

So, we should do phonics and do it well, because it is helpful in early literacy learning. The generalisations of phonics are powerfully useful, and the further we delve into the arcane depths of the partial and non-correspondences of the sounds and visuals of writing, the more expert readers and writers we will become. Phonics is indeed of some – if limited – use later in life as one of several strategies we can use when we encounter unfamiliar words. But to return to a key point we made earlier: developing and applying concepts that relate something as abstract as the relations of meanings to phonics to graphemics is one of the great cognitive challenges of every child's life. It is a challenge that, almost miraculously given its scale, early schooling is designed to address. Teaching the phonics concepts explicitly can assist learners to make this conceptual leap.

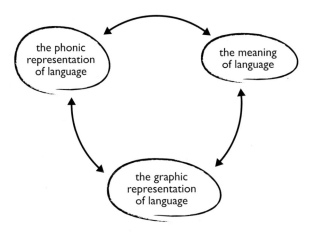

Figure 9.15 Reading and writing, conceptually speaking

However, the look–say people are also right. Even when we do phonics, we need to learn a lot of words by repeated exposure, one by one. Take 'yacht', for instance – there are no phonics rules that will ever help us with this word. Because written words, not their sounds, are the substance of reading and writing, and the sounds are sometimes so unreliably connected to their graphic representations we need to learn these representations and then the sound that is connected with them. In other words, we need to learn the look of the word whose letter combination is an unforgiving marker of literacy; the corresponding sound of the word (taking into account that looks and sounds only roughly correspond and only some of the time at that); and the meaning of the word (taking into account that words do not correspond with units of meaning, or **morphemes**). It is nothing less than a marvel that humans can master so strange, abstract and untameably irregular an artefact as writing, and at such an early age.

Morpheme: A meaning unit within a word or that combines several words

For these reasons, we would suggest a both-ways approach to beginning reading and writing, combining the conceptual bent of didactic literacy pedagogies with the experiential bent of authentic literacy pedagogies.

Developing vocabulary, comprehension and critical reading

Beyond deciphering the alphabetic code, reading involves comprehending, interpreting, evaluating and reflecting on the meaning of texts. To make meaning in the written mode, effective readers engage a range of deliberate, goal-directed strategies to process words and other visual symbols to derive meaning from texts (Afflerbach, Pearson & Paris 2008). By repeated reading and exposure to a wide range of textual experiences, students begin to recognise the most frequently occurring words in a language by sight – by the time they are in Year/Grade 3 they need to be able to recognise several hundred high-frequency words automatically.

But in order to tackle unfamiliar, complex or multisyllabic words, children need to be equipped with deliberate strategies or problem-solving techniques. Many words cannot be decoded phonically so students need a range of strategies for word recognition that draw on contextual, semantic and grammatical as well as phonic cues. These text processing strategies enable readers to predict, recognise words, work out unfamiliar words, monitor their own reading, identify and correct errors, read on and reread (ACARA 2015g). Because these strategies involve conscious, learned behaviours, they can be taught through modelling, metacognitive instruction about how and why to use strategies, and eventually by scaffolded and guided practice (Afflerbach, Pearson & Paris 2008; Harvey & Goudvis 2007; Paris & Stahl 2005).

In the early years, young readers can be taught to decode phonetically regular single-syllable words by using strategies such as:

- sounding out
- associating new words with words they already know ('decoding by analogy') using knowledge of onset and rimes and word families, and
- applying phonic rules.

Teachers can model strategies to help younger readers learn to associate letter shapes, names and sounds – for example, pointing out the first letter of a child's name, drawing attention to letter shapes and names through games and hands-on activities, and singing the alphabet song. Strategies for letter identification, decoding, oral reading and comprehension can be meaningfully embedded in dialogic reading and talk around text. Authentic texts need to be carefully selected to engage children in rich literary experiences that connect with their lived experiences. Wall charts and word banks of high-frequency words can be displayed around the classroom to support sight vocabulary.

In the primary years students continue to build their word identification skills by using a range of strategies alone or in combination. These include:

- phonic analysis – students use their knowledge of phoneme–grapheme correspondences, phonics rules and spelling patterns
- decoding by analogy – students use their knowledge of phonograms to deduce the pronunciation or spelling of an unfamiliar word
- syllabic analysis – students break words into syllables and decode each syllable using their knowledge of phonics
- morphemic analysis – students apply their knowledge of root words, prefixes and suffixes to read new words (Tompkins, Campbell & Green 2012).

More experienced readers also use their knowledge of grammatical function, text structures and context as cues to facilitate word recognition and comprehension.

The goal of explicit strategy instruction is to lead students to independent practice and fluency in their reading so that they can become successful text participants and users. Snow and colleagues spell this out:

> Comprehension can be enhanced through instruction focused on concept and vocabulary growth and background knowledge, instruction about the syntax and

rhetorical structures of written language, and direct instruction about comprehension strategies such as summarising, predicting, and monitoring. Comprehension also takes practice, which is gained by reading independently, by reading in pairs or groups, and by reading aloud to (Snow, Burns & Griffin 1998: 7).

In contrast to traditional didactic approaches that teach decoding as an isolated skill using controlled texts, such as those in commercial phonics programs, balanced, hybrid approaches currently adopted by education and curriculum authorities emphasise an integrated, situated approach to decoding. Making sense of print is important from the very beginning. Explicit teaching about breaking the code is best taught in the context of reading authentic children's literature and information texts as part of the larger literacy program across the curriculum. When selecting texts, teachers should consider the overall purposes for learning, key concepts that the text embodies, type of text and its features, readability and suitability for the teaching focus.

See literacies.com Wendy Cowey on Literate Orientation.

To prepare students for reading, teachers design a range of activities across the curriculum to build prerequisite background knowledge and to introduce unfamiliar or specialised and technical vocabulary before introducing the new text. Teachers need to demonstrate how words and images work together to construct meaning. As primary school children learn to identify the main ideas in a text, to skim and reread, teachers explicitly teach decoding and comprehension strategies. They model (e.g. by thinking aloud to demonstrate their reasoning), explain and scaffold appropriate reading strategies so that students can be aware of and monitor their own comprehension and reading strategies. Some key reading strategies are summarised in Table 9.7.

Engaging further with texts

This is only part of the story of making meaning from reading. In contemporary conceptions of reading literacy, one cannot ignore the contexts in which children engage in reading. The image-saturated, multimodal texts found in the online digital environment are very much a part of the early literacy experiences in which children learn to read and read to learn. A number of features of the online environment contribute to a more complex task for readers – hyperlinked information structures, interactivity and game-like formats, a wide variety of navigational prompts and icons, still and moving images or multimedia in various combinations with written and spoken language. Additional skills are needed for the successful location, integration and evaluation of information, particularly when attempting to integrate meanings from across different modes of meaning.

Features of web-based texts, their layouts and design principles have spilled over into print-based texts. Reading and its cognate process of viewing are inseparable when children engage with texts that incorporate a variety of visual cues and

Table 9.7: Comprehension strategies and reading processes

	Strategies for comprehension
Activating, expanding and refining prior knowledge	*Connecting* – text to self, text to text, text to world to access what we already know to help understand new information *Expanding* and *refining* prior knowledge
Making predictions about the text	*Predicting* – using clues such as the cover, title, author, illustrations and text type to predict likely future events in a text
Monitoring of comprehension	*Questioning* – helps us understand the text *Clarifying* the content *Self-correcting* and *re-reading* – and other repair strategies
Retrieving information	*Identifying* literal information explicitly stated in the text *Visualising* – creating mental images of elements in a text *Organising* – information from a text
Interpreting text	*Making inferences* – based on meanings implied in the text and our own prior knowledge *Interpreting* the text and reading between the lines *Determining importance* – finding the most important ideas in a text *Summarising* – creating a short version of the main ideas in the text *Synthesising* – integrating ideas and information from the text with what is known to develop new ideas and understandings
Reflecting on text	*Critically reflecting* on content, structure, language and images used to construct meaning in a text

pictorial elements that have shifted the way readers engage with and process text. We return to the notion of the design of meaning in the chapters to follow.

 See literacies.com Learning Modules.

 See literacies.com #edtech Literacies Applications.

Summary

Didactic reading pedagogy	Authentic reading pedagogy	Literacies pedagogy and design analysis
Phonics: Learning sound–letter correspondences *Comprehension:* Getting the right answers about what texts 'really' say	*Meanings:* Learning the meaning of whole words, making sense of words from context *'Whole language':* Natural learning, immersed in meaningful texts	*Understanding patterns in meaning:* Not every rule of sound–letter correspondence but the general idea that there can be correspondences *Whole-text patterns:* Being able to navigate through whole texts by understanding their social purposes and architectures

Knowledge processes

experiencing the known

1. In terms of the reading pedagogies described in this chapter, how would you describe your own experience of learning to read? Which approaches have you personally found most effective?

experiencing the new

2. Read a highly scripted 'direct instruction' or basal reading program lesson. What do you find appealing or alienating about this approach to learning to read?

analysing critically

3. Debate the proposition that synthetic phonics is the most effective path to early reading for students from poor and disadvantaged families. In preparation, read sample texts of proponents of both sides in this debate.

conceptualising by naming

4. As you work through this chapter, keep a running log of concepts about language. Define these concepts in a glossary. Perhaps this could take the form of a collaborative wiki, in which different students:

   a. name and define a concept
   b. provide examples
   c. suggest teachable moments when this concept might be used in learning to read.

conceptualising with theory

5. Create a concept map linking the terms defined in the previous activity.

analysing functionally

6. Take a section from a piece of children's literature that creates the setting for the story. In groups of four, have each person design question probes to help students engage in one of the four roles of the reader. Now come together as a group and look at the repertoire of reading practices that students need to engage in these four roles. What aspects of each role would be most useful for EAL/D (English as an additional language or dialect) readers?

applying appropriately

7. Develop a lesson plan that applies the concepts of design analysis to activities for scaffolding reading for students with a range of learning needs. Design lesson activities to provide differentiated learning experiences for students struggling with literacy and multilingual students with EAL/D.

CHAPTER 10

Making meaning by writing

Overview

This chapter continues to examine written language, this time from the perspective of representing and communicating meaning by writing. We begin by looking at how making meaning in the written mode develops with a discussion of how speaking and writing differ. We then explore alternative approaches to describing how written language works, from the traditional grammar of didactic pedagogy, to Chomsky's transformational-generative grammar, to Halliday's functional approach. We end the chapter with our own Multiliteracies approach, which describes what we call the 'design elements' of written texts.

Learning to write

Brielle Riley and Michelle Hodge have been teaching a learning module that they have created together for their Year/Grade 2 classes. 'Experiencing the known', students talk about the different things that water is used for in their lives, sorting the words for different uses into categories (conceptualising with theory). 'Analysing function-ally', they write down what water feels like, looks like, smells like and tastes like. 'Analysing critically', they discuss water and survival in pairs. 'Applying creatively', they create a poster that persuades others to save water.

See literacies.com van Haren, Riley, Hodge and Gorman, The Wonder of Water.

In a Year/Grade 5/6 class, Emily Howland's students are writing a narrative, inspired by the allegorical tale *The Island*. They read the text (experiencing the new), then examine the features of narrative, including orientation, complication, resolution and coda (conceptualising by naming). They explore specific language features of a narrative, such as figurative language, circumstances expressed in adverbial phrases, participants in noun phrases, and the use of complex sentences (more conceptualising by naming). They analyse how all these things work to-gether to create an allegorical tale (analysing functionally). Then they write their own allegorical tale (applying creatively).

See literacies.com van Haren, Anne Dunn and Robyn Kiddy, The island: An allegorical tale.

Meanwhile, students in Prue Gill's Year/Grade 8 writing class are about to write a biography as part of a learning module, 'Ordinary People, Extraordinary Desti-nies'. As part of the pedagogical move 'exploring the known', they discuss what might make an ordinary person extraordinary. 'Experiencing the new', they watch some TED talks and CNN heroes videos (Figure 10.1). They read the biography of Eddie Mabo, an ordinary Australian of Torres Strait Islander descent who dared to challenge the law of the land that said he and his people didn't own their tra-ditional lands, finally winning his case in court and establishing land rights for Indigenous Australians. 'Analysing functionally', the students explain the ways in which information texts in general, and biographies in particular, work to commu-nicate relevant aspects of a life history. 'Conceptualising by naming', students dis-cuss the language features of a biography; then 'conceptualising with theory', they analyse the overall design features of an information text. Moving on to 'applying appropriately', they start to write the biography of a person of their choice, whose beginnings may have been humble but who went on to make an extraordinary contribution. The peer review rubric created by the teacher-authors of this learning module highlights notions of formal style, information description, text organisa-tion, transitions and referencing. Students have already identified these features in the sample Eddie Mabo text. 'Analysing critically', they peer review each other's writings, offering critical and constructive feedback to their peers.

Figure 10.1 Exploring the nature of 'extraordinary' (Ordinary People, Extraordinary Destinies Learning Module, Scholar)

 See literacies.com Gill, Nott and van Haren, Ordinary people, extraordinary destinies.

In a final example for the moment, students in Prue Gill, Rachael Radvanyi and Jennifer Nott's Year/Grade 10 classes are studying *Hamlet*. Starting with 'experiencing the known', the module asks students to reflect on moments of 'crossing the line' in family relationships (Figure 10.2). 'Experiencing the new', students discuss a video about how the English language has changed over time (Figure 10.3), and view *Animated Tales of Hamlet*. 'Conceptualising by naming', they examine the nature of characterisation in the person of Hamlet. 'Analysing functionally', they discuss the role of the ghost scene in the narrative. 'Applying appropriately', they write a literary criticism essay exploring the themes of revenge or madness in *Hamlet*. 'Analysing critically', they peer review each other's essays. 'Applying creatively', they develop an oral presentation on the development on of one character in the play.

 See literacies.com van Haren, Gill, Radvanyi and Nott, Hamlet – madness and revenge.

So, what's happening in these writing classrooms? What is writing and how do we do it?

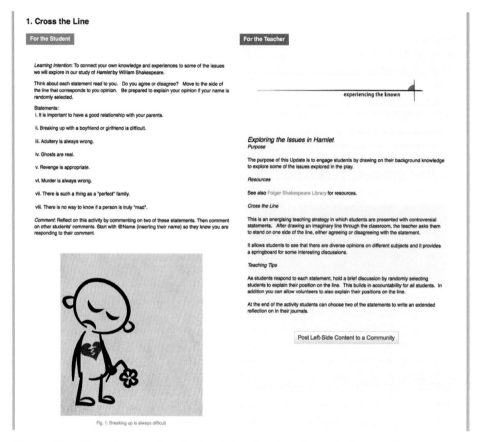

Figure 10.2 Discussing crossing the line in families (Hamlet – Madness and Revenge Learning Module, Scholar)

Working at writing

Speaking and writing

Writing is hard and, in some senses, unnatural work. It results in the production of an artefact for use in communications for which the writer and reader may not be present in the same space or time. This artefact needs to be intelligible to those involved in the meaning exchange even more so because the written artefact mediates this exchange.

Writing requires authors to choose from among the meaning resources available to them in their systems of writing, transforming their oral language into writing through a process of synaesthesia, or mode-shifting. Although of course linked to spoken language, writing is surprisingly unlike speaking, something that we explore in greater depth when we discuss oral meanings in Chapter 13. It's a big jump from talking to others or silently to oneself, to creating written text whose

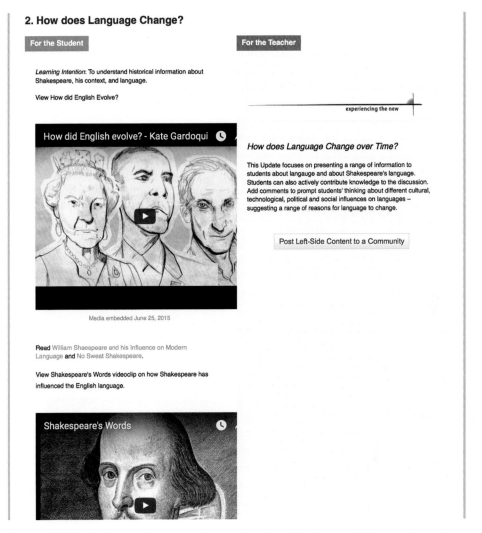

2. How does Language Change?

For the Student

For the Teacher

Learning Intention: To understand historical information about Shakespeare, his context, and language.

View How did English Evolve?

How did English evolve? - Kate Gardoqui

experiencing the new

How does Language Change over Time?

This Update focuses on presenting a range of information to students about language and about Shakespeare's language. Students can also actively contribute knowledge to the discussion. Add comments to prompt students' thinking about different cultural, technological, political and social influences on languages – suggesting a range of reasons for language to change.

Post Left-Side Content to a Community

Media embedded June 25, 2015

Read William Shaespeare and his Influence on Modern Language **and** No Sweat Shakespeare.

View Shakespeare's Words videoclip on how Shakespeare has influenced the English language.

Shakespeare's Words

Figure 10.3 Reflecting on language change (Hamlet – Madness and Revenge Learning Module, Scholar)

meanings will be received in communications where the author has no immediate feedback or capacity to respond. We often think that writing is just a transcription of speech, but it is not. The process of synaesthesia required to shift from the oral mode to the written mode is much more complicated work than that. It is more like 'learning to hear and think about one's language in a new way' (Olson 1998: 32). Writing and speaking also entail quite different mental processes.

Making choices in writing is sometimes an agonising business. 'Is this quite what I mean?' we may ask ourselves as we search for a word that may capture our meaning better than the one we have just written. We find ourselves making changes to our text all the time, working over it, crafting it until we are more or less happy with it and consider that it can stand on its own without our presence to explain its meaning.

One of the more important differences between oral and written language is that regular speaking is spontaneous and interactive. If you want to change something you have just heard yourself say, you can say it again differently. You can't go back and remove what you've just said, as you can in writing. You can reframe, correct or restate, but you can't delete it once it has been heard. This is one of the reasons why oral language is full of repetitions, a flow in which you say something one way then another, until you think you have said more or less what you want to say the way you want it said. Also, oral language does not have some of the foundational, carefully ordered idea-units that written language does: conventionally spelt words, punctuation, the sentence, the paragraph, the section, the subheading, the title, and a sign-off of authorship – all of which are specifically designed to frame written meaning. These all take a lot of time and mental effort to get into a well-ordered shape.

For instance, the mechanics of writing using conventional spelling in English and other alphabetic writing systems is a far from a natural process. It requires learned, conscious understandings about the writing system and the resources available to make meaningful marks. Words in English are constructed through representations of both their sounds and meaning – it is a *morphophonemic* language (Adoniou 2014). Spelling words conventionally involves making use of multiple sources of knowledge about: how sounds are organised in the language (*phonology*), understanding what letter sequences will work and what graphemes to use, especially as there is often not a simple correspondence between the phonemes and graphemes of English (*orthography*), knowing about parts of words, such as root forms, suffixes and prefixes, that carry particular kinds of meanings (*morphology*), and how these are influenced by the origin of a word (*etymology*) – words in English originate from many different languages. Finally, a visual knowledge that enables one to identify the visual pattern of a word, as emphasised in look-and-say approaches to reading, is also important in spelling.

 See literacies.com Adoniou on What teachers should know about spelling.

The meaning production process is also very different from speech. We start by carefully planning a written text – what to write in the first, middle and last sections. Then we go backwards and forwards over a written text a number of times to get the structure and tone right, to make the sentences tight, and to be sure we have chosen the best words to serve our meaning-making purposes. We go out of our way to avoid unnecessary repetition. Writing is a tightly structured product, the stuff of careful deliberation in all directions across the text. It is a multilinear process. We might make several drafts as we refine the text. Speaking, by comparison, is a linear, one-way flow – albeit a messy, and often hesitant, repetitive, discursive and transactional flow that unfolds in real time. Speaking is driven by our mind, voice and emotions in the moment of engagement with others.

The impact of technologies on the writing process

Our technologies for working over written text have radically changed since the last decades of the 20th century. They have made it easier for us to do the methodical backwards-and-forwards work that writing requires. In the days when people wrote everything in handwriting or typed on a manual typewriter, changes made a mess of the page. It was time-consuming and laborious to go over multiple drafts, and to have to write or type them again from beginning to end in order to have a clean revised copy. Until about the 1980s, before the rise of the personal computer and other digital devices as near-universal tools for writing, this is what people did.

Something significant happened to the way we write with the arrival of the personal computer and, specifically, word-processing programs. Making changes became as easy as delete and retype, or cut and paste. We can make as many changes as we wish and, unless we want another person to see the changes we have made by turning on the review or tracking function, we can change a text as often as we like and it still looks as neat as a finished product. When we work on a computer or other electronic device, we have a lot more flexibility to move backwards and forwards in the multilinear processes of drafting and revision. There are no resistances to making changes, and there is none of the extra work we had to do in the past to produce a clean copy of a new draft. This gives us more opportunities than we have ever had to work carefully over a written text, to make it more and more like what is special and unusual about writing, and so less and less like speaking. It makes writing more distinctively writerly. Today, we also have the writing supports of spelling and grammar checkers, thesauruses, templates and styles definitions: formal tools for writing that we don't need for speaking; and we have changes tracking and annotation tools to assist in collaborative authorship of a shared text.

At the other end of the spectrum, more recent technologies of social media have facilitated new forms of writing, such as emails, text messages and social media dialogue. In many ways, these are more akin to speech in their immediacy and potential for interaction than to the deliberate, conscious effort required of conventional types of writing emerging from print and word-processing technologies. But even these are still interestingly different from speaking, including features such as suggestive text that help make the message more writing-like. We will discuss the phenomenon of quasi-oral text further in Chapter 13.

Errors and changes in written text

In order to analyse the design elements of written language, we are going to focus on the choices we make and particularly on the kinds of changes we might incorporate as we work over a draft. In the Multiliteracies approach that we have been outlining in this book, we recognise that language performs differently in different places for different purposes. So there are no immediately certain errors. There are, of course, errors in the looser sense that a writer may not know some of the writing conventions that could most effectively assist with purposeful meaning-making in a particular situation. A young child's early attempt to make meaning through drawing and writing (Figure 10.4) illustrates this point.

Figure 10.4 Young child's drawing and writing

Our approach is to focus on the choices that are available to writers to ensure that what is intended is communicated and that they are mindful of what makes sense to which audiences and for which specific purposes.

So, rather than talk about something as rigid and definitive as error, we want to suggest the ideas of change and improvement that characterise the writing process. The first attempt to write something down may be perfectly suitable as a first approximation – there may be a spelling to check later, a tone that could be made more appropriate to a context, or another word that captures a meaning more effectively. There are always options and changes that can be made as the writer struggles to find words and craft word orders that progressively get closer to the meaning they want to express and that better fit the purposes or conventions of the particular context.

This means that we put an emphasis on preparing writers to work effectively on their choices of meaning for the variety of purposes that matter to them and that will be most effective in particular contexts. We do this because we believe activating agency, motivation and creativity matters significantly in formal school learning contexts, where the artefacts of writing have tended in the past to be linked with the culture of school and its subjects and at times its overly rigid ideas of what is correct and what is not. In the real worlds of citizens, workers and community members, people work at making things better rather than getting them right from the start.

Effective writers, in schools as well as in everyday life, know how to work over their texts carefully, making changes as they give shape to their meanings. They think explicitly about the reasons why they make these changes, based on the purpose of their writing. For example, possible changes you might make as you reread a draft of your own writing may include rewording something you think you can express better, or a change suggested by the machine's spelling or grammar checker, or a change that a reader suggests you should make (for instance, in a suggestion or comment they make via changes tracking). You may agree and make the change. Perhaps, though, you may disagree with the spell checker or reader's suggestion. That word they thought was a spelling error is in fact the name of a place, or a transcription of the sound of a dialect. That sentence they thought was grammatically flawed because of its passive construction is in fact exactly what you want to say because you want to de-emphasise the role of the actor. In these cases, what may have been considered an error or poor style from one perspective is in fact proven to be a matter of varying judgement, perspective and interpretation.

Our **design analysis** of the features of writing is not a catalogue of rules of correct usage or potential errors. It is a taxonomy of design options that allows for different types of textual change and a list of questions that you as an author may ask as you work over a text, or that a proofreader may ask of you as you reshape your text so it serves its purposes most effectively. Your response as a writer to your own questions of yourself, or your reader's questions of your text, or the machine suggestions – perhaps – will be to make a change. Whether you make that change or not is a matter of your own understanding of the meaning you want to make and the choice you have made to express that meaning, at least until you can find a way that better suits your intention, or you discover that you have not been understood. The question invites deliberation, suggests alternative choices and allows that choices may be justifiable for particular purposes. There are no inevitable and universally right and wrong choices in meaning-making. However, we can assume that when an author creates a text or makes a change to a written text, they have made it for a reason that says something about their knowledge of how language and communication work, the context for the communication, their preferences, or the design elements they want in their writing. They have made the change in order to improve their text and make it more effective.

> **Design analysis:** A process of analysing the design elements of a written meaning or multimodal meaning

Written meanings: a design analysis

Further into this chapter, we offer a brief outline of a taxonomy of design options for written language. These are choices that a writer may make in the first instance but that, on reflection or at the suggestion of a reader, they may change because they agree that the change will strengthen their meaning. The assumption is that most of the time, if you have made the change, it is because you consider the changed text a closer approximation to your intended meaning than the text was originally, because the change will better serve your meaning-making purposes in a particular context and because it will be interpreted accurately, as intended. But first, we want to mention several other paradigms for understanding the structures of written and spoken language: traditional grammar, transformational grammar and systemic-functional grammar.

A traditional grammar of English

Parts of speech in traditional grammar

Traditional grammar consists of the labels that describe the forms and structural relationships of words in written language. Here is a brief outline.

In traditional grammar, words form a *vocabulary*, or the range of words a user has at their disposal for writing, reading, speaking and listening. Word forms can vary – for instance 'has', 'have'

> **Traditional grammar:** A theory of language that names parts of speech and the formal grammatical connections between these parts of speech in a sentence (syntax)

and 'had' are forms of the verb 'to have' – according to number, person and tense. Words can also be connected with each other in different ways by means of devices such as word order. 'John hit Mary' means something different from 'Mary hit John', even though both sentences use the same three words.

Words can also be categorised into a number of different *parts of speech*, each performing a particular role in the sentence.

- A *noun* is a word that names a person, place, thing, or manner of being ('boy', 'home', 'deer', 'anxiety').
- A *pronoun* is a word that stands in for a noun in a sentence, assuming that noun has already been mentioned before in the sentence or that the noun referred to will be understood by a listener or reader if it is missing from the sentence ('he', 'there', 'it').
- An *adjective* is a word that adds an attribute to a noun or a pronoun ('blue', 'fast', 'six').
- A *verb* is a word that describes an action or state ('run', 'stays', 'is').
- An *adverb* adds an attribute to a verb and other parts of speech, except nouns, explaining 'how' ('slowly', 'well', 'very').
- A *preposition* is a word that begins a small cluster of words to show connections between things in a sentence and in the world ('in', 'with', 'for').
- A *conjunction* is a word that connects sections of text – words, phrases, clauses or sentences ('and', 'or', 'however').
- An *interjection* is a word that expresses emotion, often in the form of one-word sentences ('hello', 'sorry', 'oh').

This makes eight parts of speech – until we scratch beneath the surface, that is, where each part of speech becomes more ambiguous and complicated than you might at first think. Here's a more complete version of traditional grammar, describing finer distinctions between parts of speech and their interconnections.

- *Proper nouns* have a capital letter, and refer to particular person or place (Mary, Chicago); *common nouns,* with no capital letter, refer to ordinary or general things (girl, city).
- *Personal pronouns* refer to people and things ('she', 'it', 'theirs'); *relative pronouns* connect people and things ('who', 'that'); *interrogative pronouns* ask questions ('who?', 'where?'); *demonstrative pronouns* point to things ('these', 'that'); *reflexive pronouns* refer back to a person or thing ('itself', 'myself'); *indefinite pronouns* refer to non-specific people or things ('you', 'something').
- Adjectives can be *positive* ('good'), *comparative* ('better') and *superlative* ('best'). Articles are special kinds of adjectives that must be connected with common nouns, be that a *definite article* for something specific ('the') or an *indefinite article* for instances of something general ('a', 'some').
- Verbs can be *transitive,* which means they connect an actor with the thing acted upon ('kicks' in 'The girl kicks the ball'); and they can also be *intransitive* when the actor acts, but nothing can be directly acted upon by this kind of action ('laughed' in 'The boy laughed').

- Adverbs can be *positive* ('fast'), or *comparative* ('faster') and *superlative* ('fastest').
- Prepositions do so many important connective things that the range of their uses almost defies classification, adding different kinds of meaning to almost every part of speech ('in', 'of', 'at', 'before').
- Conjunctions can be *coordinating* ('and', 'but'), *subordinating* ('because', 'while') and *correlative* ('either … or'; 'not only … but').

These parts of speech can be varied and recombined in many different ways to say an infinite range of things.

- A *morpheme* is the smallest unit of meaning. For instance, 'unbelievable' has three units of meaning or *morphemes*: the *prefix* 'un', the *stem* 'believe' and the *suffix* 'able'.
- Nouns can vary if they are *singular* ('dog'), *plural* ('dogs') or *possessive* ('dog's/dogs').
- Pronouns vary depending on whether they are *first person singular or plural* ('I', 'me', 'we'), *second person* ('you') or *third person male, female or neuter singular or plural* ('he', 'she', 'it', 'they'); they can also indicate possession ('my', 'our', 'your', 'her', 'his', 'their').
- Verbs can vary in their *tense* depending on whether they are *past perfect* ('walked'), *past continuous* ('was walking'), *past pluperfect* ('had walked'), *present* ('walks'), *present continuous* ('is walking'), *future* ('will walk'), *future continuous* ('will be walking'), *future perfect* ('will have walked') or *infinitive*, which refers to any time ('to walk').
- They also have different *moods: indicative* ('You are well'), *imperative* ('Be well!'), *interrogative* ('Are you well?') and *subjunctive* ('If you are well').
- Finally, verbs can also be in the *active voice*, where an actor directly acts upon someone or something ('Mary kicked the ball'), or in the *passive voice*, where the thing being acted upon and the action are given priority ('The ball was kicked by Mary').

Syntax in traditional grammar

There is an endless range of choices we can make in syntax – so expansive, in fact, that no two stretches of several hundred newly created words are ever the same.

Syntax is the combination of different parts of speech into *phrases*, *clauses* and *sentences*.

- A *phrase* is a cluster of words functioning as a group, such as a *noun phrase*, which acts like a noun ('the lazy dog'), a *prepositional phrase*, which begins with a preposition ('in the garden'), and a *verb phrase*, which is like a verb ('run quickly').
- A *clause* has a *subject* (someone or something that acts) and a *finite verb* (the action; an *infinite* verb does not act, nor do some other parts or kinds of verbs that cannot act, either, such as *past participles* ('walked'), and *gerunds* ('walking'). A clause often also has a *predicate*: the thing or person that the thing or person in the subject is acting upon.

- A sentence is an *independent clause* because it can stand on its own ('The cat sat on the mat'). *Dependent clauses* connect with other parts within a sentence. *Noun clauses* stand for a noun ('What I can see' in 'What I can see is something large and green'); *adverbial* clauses describe a verb ('When the party was over' in 'When the party was over, we went home'); and *adjectival clauses* describe a noun ('that we went to' in 'The party that we went to was fantastic').
- Sentences can be *declarative* statements ('The cat sat on the mat'), *imperative* commands ('Please sit on the mat'), *interrogative* questions ('Is the cat sitting on the mat?') or *exclamatory* expressions of feeling ('Oh my goodness, the cat is sitting on the mat!').
- As we assemble sentences, we need to make sure that related words, whose forms can vary, are in *agreement* (which they are not in 'She cat are sitting') and that they are in the right *order* (which they are not in 'Sitting her are cat').

This is just the beginning. Traditional grammar can get so much more complicated than this because making meaning is rich, complex and varied.

We have created this summary because those of us who work in literacy education need to know these basic terms. They come up all the time, particularly from people who have learned to read and write in a didactic literacy pedagogy, or who have studied another language in the traditional way. The ideas behind these terms can also be useful to readers and writers from time to time.

 See literacies.com Strauss Demonstrates Traditional Grammar.

Complexities and challenges in traditional grammar

The reason why grammars get so complicated is because language is such a fluid and complex thing. In its fullness, language defies simple definitions and classifications. We may say a noun is a person, place or thing (the old schoolbook definition), but nouns also include happenings and states that often seem very like verbs ('running' in 'Running is good for you'). In fact, it's not hard to change many verbs into nouns, in order to sound more objective ('Our investigation revealed …' instead of 'We investigated …'), through a process called *nominalisation*. Likewise, adjectives can become adverbs (when 'quick' becomes 'quickly').

Prepositions, meanwhile, are so all over the place that they defy subclassification. In English we have thousands of combinations of prepositions with particular ideas in phrases, and because their use is so varied, any one preposition can be used in an incredible number of quite different ways ('in the room', 'in trouble', 'in itself'). As for pronouns, imagine putting 'he' and 'any' into the same category – these words express such different kinds of meaning.

Then there's a challenge with the most basic definition of ideas as units to be labelled. A sentence, we are told in some grammar books, expresses a complete thought. So does a morpheme, a word, a phrase, a paragraph and a whole text. It just depends on how big and multifaceted the thought you want to express. And for that matter, big and complex thoughts can be jammed into few words. We can take the easy way out and say a sentence starts with a capital letter and ends with a stop punctuation mark ('.', '?', '!'). But that's not to describe how it's made, just how it looks after it has been made. We might say that a sentence must always have a verb (an old-fashioned grammar rule), but we've just seen how hard it may be to find verbs, and many perfectly good sentences do not have a verb. Not that this knowledge is irrelevant or unimportant. If you want to sound formally correct, sentences should indeed have verbs. But not always. There are some contexts – the previous sentence, for instance – where not having a verb works perfectly well.

When we move on to parts of speech, we can try to define them by the things they do. For instance, nouns name things. But we can have word clusters such as noun phrases and noun clauses that include verbs, prepositions and adjectives, and that in combination act like a noun. So the distinction between nouns and verbs becomes less clear. Also, verbs describe actions. But we have word clusters such as verb phrases and verb clauses that include nouns, prepositions and adverbs, and that in combination act like a verb. In other words, different parts of speech can have different functions depending on where they occur in the structure of a sentence, clause or phrase. So a knowledge of word-class distinctions is useful only to a point.

The more seriously you take traditional grammar, the more complicated it gets and the more qualifications to the rules are needed. The more you study this kind of grammar, the more obvious it is that language does not just fit into neat categorisation and classification. Computer scientists in a field called 'Natural Language Processing' (NLP) use computational linguistics to try to read computer-like logics into the connections between words in texts, and they have found it incredibly hard. Compared with the subtlety and fluidity of language, even the smartest computer programs in the world are very simple, mechanical things. Often the best they can do is to collect large bodies of text, called 'corpora', and try to predict patterns statistically from the masses of word uses and word combinations.

The pedagogy of traditional grammar

So how does traditional grammar work in didactic pedagogy? The answer is to teach a lot of rules, then give a piece of writing a mark based in part on how many 'errors' it has. Here, however, are a few old-fashioned grammar rules, along with a counter example of when an apparent error may not really be an error. (Some of these are handy to know, by the way, for when you are writing something that someone else may, wrongly perhaps, consider an error.)

1. A sentence must have verb. (But not when it's a title, or a headline, or an advertising slogan, or you want to be emphatic.)
2. Always put the subject at the beginning of a sentence. (But that does not always happen – 'It's me', for instance … and by the way, because it is the subject, 'me' is grammatically incorrect; this sentence should be 'It is I'. However, you would only say 'It is I' when you wanted to sound old-fashioned and formal. Most of the time, 'It's me' will be correct.)

3. Never use a double negative. ('I ain't got no ...', but of course this is correct in some vernaculars.)
4. Never split an infinitive. ('To boldly go' – but of course this has become common nowadays.)
5. Never end a sentence with a preposition. ('That's what it's for!' – except when you want a certain kind of emphasis.)
6. Don't mix mass and unit. ('Fewer apples' and 'less pie' are right. 'Less apples' is supposed to be wrong, but is so commonly used today that this old grammatical distinction is fading away.)
7. 'That' introduces essential clauses ('The house that Jack built'), while 'which' introduces non-essential clauses ('Jack built a house, which is located in Central Australia'), although there is a fair bit of latitude to use 'that' and 'which' interchangeably.
8. Use commas to separate phrases and semicolons to separate clauses. (But it's not always this simple.)

These rules are mostly about little things, and not logically derived from the core ideas of traditional grammar. So what do we do with traditional grammar in didactic literacy pedagogy? We name parts of speech. We learn rules in order to show in our writing and speaking that we know them. However, knowing parts of speech and rules takes a lot of effort compared to the relatively small contribution this makes to knowing how to write.

Moreover, traditional grammar does not have a lot to say about the design of written text beyond the sentence. The main point of traditional grammar, then, is a certain kind of schoolish formalism. It may help you become a certain type of recognisably 'educated' user of the language (Carter & McCarthy 2006). However, there has been much debate about the effect of this type of teaching on the practical business of learning to read and to write.

 See literacies.com Myhill and Watson on The Role of Grammar in the Writing Curriculum.

Language choices and change types

These are the reasons why we have suggested the ideas of 'language choice' and 'change type' for the design analysis we want to use in a Multiliteracies approach to crafting meanings. This replaces the starkly unequivocal idea of 'correct' and 'incorrect' grammar that is characteristic of traditional grammar teaching. As we write, we are faced with myriad choices related to our purposes. More than one alternative may be right, or more right for one text in one context than for another text in another context. Reviewing a first attempt at a written expression, and replacing it later with something that seems to work better, is a matter of refining the choice of design elements in relation to the purpose for meaning-making. A hastily typed, phonically accurate representation of the word is correct for its purpose, and can be changed later with the help of a spell checker. A word that is for the moment the best word you can find to capture a meaning is correct as a first approximation, until you change it later on to a word that works better.

Such choices and changes may occur either in representation (making sense to yourself, silently thinking 'should I say this or that?') or in communication with others (as someone annotates your written text, or asks for clarification, for instance). In other words, the process of designing and changing a text could take the form of a debate an author has in their own mind as they write in a private drafting and revision session, typing one wording and then replacing it with another that seems better suited to their purposes, or an audience of potential readers, or that is more clearly, precisely or vividly expressed. Or it could be a point for discussion in the very sociable world of writing in which a copy editor, or teacher or critical friend, makes a suggestion for a change.

Nothing in writing is necessarily or always wrong. Writing is provisional, always open to discussion when an author makes changes they may consider an improvement. This results in a changed text that the writer considers more apt to their purposes in representation and communication. And on review, the change may be changed again. A change is only ever provisionally an improvement on the text it replaces.

Transformational-generative grammar

The deep structures of meaning and surface structures of language

Transformational-generative grammar began its life in 1957 with the publication by linguist Noam Chomsky of his book *Syntactic Structures*. Chomsky (1957 (2002)) felt that traditional grammar did not do a good job of explaining how language worked at a deep, structural level. For instance, traditional grammar cannot distinguish between grammatically identical sentences that have very different meanings. The grammar of 'John is eager to please' is the same as 'John is easy to please', but in the first sentence John is acting (pleasing others), while in the second he is being acted upon (others are pleasing him). Traditional grammar can do nothing to highlight this highly significant difference in meaning. Nor can traditional grammar explain how the same sentence can have radically different meanings, such as 'Visiting relatives can be tiresome'. Nor can it explain how two very different sentences may have the same meaning. 'John painted the picture' means the same thing as 'The picture was painted by John' (Herndon 1970: 121, 173, 167). In other words, Chomsky argued that traditional grammar cannot explain some important aspects of meaning in language.

Chomsky came to the conclusion that there are deep structures of meaning underlying sentences. The sentence itself is only at the surface level of these features. The process of turning deep structures of meaning (the way you think) into the surface features of language (what you say and what you hear) was called by

Transformational-generative grammar: A theory of language, invented by the linguist Noam Chomsky, that analyses the deep structures of meaning common to all languages

Chomsky 'transformational' or 'generative'. That is, a logic deep in your brain transforms meanings into language, or generates language. To put it another way, the surface structures of language are generated from the structures of meaning located deep in your mind. The task of **transformational-generative grammar** is to unpack the underlying structures of meaning.

Chomsky's grammar

As in traditional grammar, Chomsky's basic unit of analysis is the *sentence* (S). But his sentence is not simply described as having a subject and object and needing a verb. Chomsky's sentence descriptions include a *noun* (N), *noun phrase* (NP), *pronoun* (Pron), *auxiliary* (Aux), *determiner* (D), and a *verb*, which can either be *transitive* (Vt), *intransitive* (Vi) or a *linking* verb (Vl) – for example, the verb *be* (be). This is just the beginning of his analysis – there is a lot more.

Sentences can then be mapped in a tree diagram called a 'phrase marker' in order to show their structure (Figure 10.5).

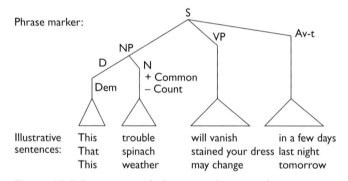

Figure 10.5 Sentences with the same phrase marker

Beneath this sentence there are a number of rules, just one of which is shown in Figure 10.6.

Chomsky's aim was to create a set of general rules from which it would be possible to generate every grammatically correct sentence in that language, and no grammatically incorrect ones. This way of representing linguistic meanings has its roots in mathematics and formal logic. Chomsky's aim in developing these abstract tools was to show the ways in which the structures of human thought are represented in language. Each type of meaning unit (a word or phrase, that is, a meaningful cluster of words) could be filled with any existing content you want. ('Cat' and 'dog' are both nouns, and their differences are not relevant to the deep structures of meaning. One word can easily be substituted for the other and the grammatical structure of the statement will stay exactly the same – although, of course, the specific meaning will change.) Words can be recombined in any way you like, applying the grammatical rules to their connection, such that no two stretches of more than a few words are ever exactly the same.

S	→	{ (Emph) (Q) (Neg) }	NP	VP	(Av-p)	(Av-t)	(Agt)	(S)
Sen- tence	may be rewritten	optional elements	necessary elements		optional elements			
	either *or* *or* *or*	Emphasis Question Negative a combina- tion of Question and Negative	Noun phrase	Verb phrase	Adverb of place	Adverb of time	Agent	Added sen- tence

Figure 10.6 A phrase structure rule that applies to the sentences in Figure 10.5

In this approach, language consists of word types and mental calculations, cognitive-computational procedures that correctly connect words together – we consider the whole utterance, not its parts. Traditional grammars, by contrast, work on the assumption that there is value in naming and learning single words, word order and sentence structures.

Chomsky's approach tries to explain how we manage to put words into grammatical order when we correctly apply general rules. In this sense, the underlying rules produce or generate meanings; even particular meanings that could never have been thought or said before ('The green dog waltzed upside down across the thorny sky'). In the set of rules of his 'generative grammar', Chomsky shows how we humans are capable of producing any number of novel variations on underlying cognitive structures as we transform these in the 'surface structures' of language and the infinite range of its particular meanings.

Culture and learning in the Chomskian view

Chomsky draws some important conclusions about culture and learning from his theory. On the subject of culture, he believes that all human languages have the same deep structures to make meaning. That is, the brain of every human is wired the same way, even if the surface expressions of these brain functions are different from language to language. In other words, the surface features of each different language may be different (its vocabulary, word order, or grammar, for instance), but the underlying kinds of meaning units (nouns, verbs and the like) and the logical rules for their interconnection are always the same in all human languages. This is why he and his followers have often called their grammar 'universal grammar'. The words come out in different ways in different languages, but the underlying structures are always the same.

See literacies.com Chomsky on Language and Nature.

On the subject of learning, he argues that the logical structures of language are so complicated that they could not possibly be learned in the short time that a baby takes to learn oral language. Famously, using this argument he demolished the learning theories of behaviourist psychology in his 1959 article (Chomsky 1959). The behaviourists believed that language was a behaviour that was acquired by immersion in an environment where that behaviour could be taught and learned. Chomsky argued that there must be a language organ of sorts in the body, a set of innate concepts hard-wired into the brain. Then the child fills this capacity with the particular sounds that constitute the words of the language they are born into. The deep structures of universal grammar are transformed into the surface levels of the particular language that the child happens to learn, by accident of circumstance given the group into which they are born.

We have included this very brief outline of transformational-generative grammar in this chapter because it has become a major paradigm for understanding human meaning-making capacities and processes. However, it has not proven to be particularly useful for educators – not that it was ever intended to be. It may seem strange that a theory that claims to explain how language works and how it is learned cannot readily be applied to education. In fact, the reasons why it cannot be easily applied to education are important. They tell us what not to do as we try to analyse the designs of meaning, or at least not if we want to do it in a way that will advance our theories of learning and practices of pedagogy.

For a start, the theory is abstract and formal. It gets more and more complex the further it delves into the intricacies of language. This is a problem for all systems that aim to develop comprehensive, let alone universal, rules. They become more and more complicated as more of their details are elaborated. In fact, not only has the transformative-generative system become increasingly complicated over the decades as details are added at its periphery, but some of the fundamentals have been proven not to work and have had to be changed. The distinction between deep and surface structures proved hard to maintain, so it was replaced by the ideas of 'logical form' and 'phonetic form', and then 'internal' and 'external' languages. Later still, any attempt to make this kind of distinction was abandoned. 'Rules' came to seem a too rigid and deterministic idea, so this was replaced by the more malleable idea of 'principles'. Some have even gone on to argue that a heavy system like this in time begins to collapse in on itself as it deals with the human complexities of something like language (Searle 2002).

What is the useful lesson we might take from the history of transformational-generative grammar? Language is incredibly complex. This complexity makes the teaching of its necessary rules also too complex. This is not to say, however, that we should revert to the position of the authentic literacy pedagogues, who say 'Let's just do a lot of language' (by, for instance, doing lots of reading and writing in school), and 'We'll learn through the doing.' In fact the sort of language experience a child gets by using it in the first few years of their life cannot be replicated in class time and the comparatively short periods of time devoted to literacy learning in the school timetable. Laying out general patterns in language – which is what a grammar does – becomes a convenient pedagogical shortcut. An immersion approach is also difficult when the incessant 'talk' that is such an important foundation to language learning in the child's first years is discouraged or limited in school time.

For practical reasons, we do need to talk about language openly and explicitly to help us learn to write in school. However, we cannot talk only about language in a way that claims to represent strict rules and think that this approach can be true of every language, or even every way of using a language. In other words, we need a broader language to speak about language, or a *metalanguage*. Or, to cast this in the wider frame of reference of multimodal meaning-making, we need an explicit and generalising 'design analysis', capable of describing 'design elements' and how they work to make meaning.

Then there's the question of Chomsky's argument about the inborn nature of language, or its innateness. If language is innate – already built into a person's natural skillset – then what do we do in schools? How do we explain different types and levels of use of any language by a learner? This is not so terribly unlike the question 'If differences in intelligence between learners are innate or inbuilt, then what do we do in schools?'. There is a danger in this sort of thinking that can lead to learners being labelled negatively or streamed too soon.

We do know that identity and social conditions have an enormous impact on skills, knowledge and comfort with formal school learning. Because we can do things to address these factors, we should. On the question of language, we must not commit the error of thinking one person's 'language organ' (if there is such a thing, and that is very much a matter of dispute) may appear more capable of making certain powerful meanings than another person's. Of course, Chomsky never intended to say this. However, this can be one unfortunate consequence of biological determinism.

We do know that people's spoken and literate capacities, and thus the practical expression of their abilities to think as well as to communicate, can vary enormously and that we can account for these variations in terms of social context, life history, motivations and opportunities to learn. Innateness arguments are neither provable nor a very helpful contribution to a pedagogical agenda. For these reasons, it is best that we concentrate on what we can do to help learners expand their ways of making and expressing meaning and thus to think in progressively broader, more effective and more powerful ways.

In discussion of Chomsky's linguistics, the question of individual or cultural difference also arises. As educators, we can view our learners and their cultures in one of two ways. We can say they are all fundamentally the same. In the final analysis, we can say, we all mean to mean the same things, but mean them in superficially different ways. We can dismiss our learners' differences as being on the 'surface'. Alternatively, we can regard their differences as important; at least as important as the similarities. People and cultures, for sure, are similar in significant respects, but they are different in other, equally significant ways. There is no point in trying to reduce every difference to an underlying similarity.

The interpersonal systems of pronouns (relationships), the temporal systems of tenses (time) and the action relations of transitivity (activities) are often very different between one language and another. We provided some examples of this from the 'first languages' we described in Chapter 1. The same could be said of the speaking or writing of individual students, the unique expression of their voices that comes through in the process of 'designing', and even things they write, that in the Chomskian scheme of things would be regarded as 'ungrammatical'. There is profound meaning in these differences, which is not to be simply ignored as voice or dismissed as error, nor subjected to deeper rules that seek automatically to make things that are so apparently different essentially the same.

Finally, there are some common features in both traditional and transformational-generative grammars. They both have 'parts of speech' that have the same kinds of problems of definition and distinction. Simply learning to name the label of a 'part of speech' – a noun, a verb, a preposition – does not help us know all the important things that an instance of that word does in making meaning. Moreover, they both try to find universal grammatical rules that connect these parts of speech correctly – such as time agreement, clauses and connectives. With both approaches it is difficult to move beyond the meaning unit of the sentence. The meanings at the level of whole texts are neglected, as well as the contexts that are needed for these texts to make sense. Furthermore, both are overly formal, giving things technical names and analysing underlying logics in ways that soon become too complicated to be of much use in the practical task of helping people learn to use language or to write more effectively.

Systemic-functional grammar

The key theorist of **systemic-functional grammar** is Michael Halliday. Like the traditional and transformative grammarians, he is interested in how language works as an integrated meaning system. However, he is also interested in what people do with language and how they mean using language – in other words, how language functions in settings for social interaction. At every moment of speaking or writing, we make choices between alternative ways of meaning in order to suit our meaning-making purposes. All meaning happens in settings or situations. Meanings make sense in the context of these situations as they are exchanged for various communicative purposes, and not just because there is an internal logic built into the meanings, as one might tend to assume from the strict emphasis on system in traditional and transformative grammars. Rather, the relationship between form and function is a principled one, oriented to meaning.

Functional grammar: A theory of language, invented by linguist Michael Halliday, that analyses differences in the structure of language according to its varied social purposes or functions

Halliday's grammar

Halliday describes grammar as 'a resource for making meaning ... [and one that] embodies a theory of everyday life' for making sense of our lived experiences

(Halliday 2009: 142). In Halliday's functional grammar, choices in the grammar allow us to fulfill three main functions or *metafunctions* of language (Halliday & Hasan 1985: 12):

- Language for expressing and connecting ideas enables us to talk about things and happenings and our experiences in the world. Halliday calls this the *ideational* metafunction (also termed *experiential*).
- Language for interacting with others enables us to establish and maintain social relationships and to communicate our feelings and attitudes towards people and experiences. This Halliday calls the *interpersonal* metafunction.
- Language for organising meaning to make internal connections within a text, and to refer to aspects of the situation in which the text is located, enables us to create cohesive texts through which we communicate about the world and our relationships in that world. This is the *textual* metafunction.

We can examine the structure of any whole text, or even a single sentence or clause, and see all three of these functions at work – 'every act of meaning embodies all three metafunctional components' (Halliday 2009: 265).

 See literacies.com Halliday on Meaning.

To develop this idea, meanings in situations are realised by texts in three ways, as shown in Table 10.1.

Table 10.1: Three ways by which meanings in situations can be realised by texts

Meanings in a situation	→ Meanings expressed through →	Meanings in a text
Field, or what is going on	*Ideational* metafunction	*Experiential* meanings
Tenor, or how the people who are taking part are connected	*Interpersonal* metafunction	*Interpersonal* meanings
Mode, or the role of language	*Textual* metafunction	*Textual* meanings

Source: Adapted from Halliday & Hasan (1985: 26).

This is a simplified overview of Halliday's systemic-functional grammar, which, like all grammars, becomes more complicated and heavily qualified the more it finds itself having to account for language in its totality. Also, all three metafunctions are perspectives on meaning that apply to every clause, without exception, in all their subtlety and complexity. Even the most seemingly ordinary of meanings in language is deceptively complicated because it is always doing all three things, and all at once. One can only marvel at human consciousness – that we can think of so much at the same time. We seem to know which aspects of meaning to keep an eye on during a particular instant of meaning because they are for the moment the most relevant, while leaving other things in the back of one's mind or in peripheral consciousness.

Table 10.2: Meaning and function in systemic-functional grammar

Metafunction	Examples
Experiential meanings (influenced by the *field* of discourse) bring together *participants* (who is involved), *processes* (what is happening) and *circumstances* (where, when, how and why it is happening). Grammatical resources for making meaning are patterned around *transitivity* – who or what does what to whom or what.	• *Participants* can have different roles, including actor (e.g. 'I' in 'I jump'), carrier ('I am tall'), sayer ('I say'), beneficiary ('him' in 'I gave him the present') and goal ('present' in 'I gave him the present'). • *Processes* connect participants through what is happening, including material processes (e.g. 'jump' in 'I jump'), verbal processes ('say' in 'I say'), relational processes ('have' in 'I have a present') and mental processes ('think' in 'I think'). • *Circumstances* elaborate about when, where, why and how, including, for instance, manner – (e.g. how? 'by train'), cause (why? 'for you'), accompaniment ('with you'). • The connections might be *receptive*, when a recipient can in fact have something done to them ('I gave him the present'), and others *operative*, when something I do cannot directly affect another person ('I wondered').
Interpersonal meanings (influenced by the *tenor* of discourse). Grammatical resources for making meaning are framed by choices in *mood* and *modality*.	• *Mood* many be declarative (e.g. 'I am walking'), interrogative ('Will you walk?') and imperative ('Walk now!'). • *Modality* refers to levels of certainty, which may be low (e.g. 'may', 'could', 'might'), median ('will', 'would') and high ('has to', 'must').
Textual meanings (influenced by the *mode* of discourse). Grammatical resources for making meaning are shaped by patterns of theme and cohesion.	• The *theme* is the topic of a clause (e.g. 'We' in 'We are walking down the street'); the *rheme*, which in English follows the theme, and contains new information ('are walking down the street' in 'We are walking down the street'). • *Cohesion* consists of connective devices that hold a text together as a coherent series of ideas, and also that point to things in the outside world: reference (e.g. 'she' refers to 'Mary' who has been mentioned in the text, or if she has not been mentioned, it is because the people in the situation will know who 'she' is); and conjunction ('and', 'meanwhile', 'although').

Source: Halliday (2002).

 See literacies.com Gerot and Wignell Demonstrate Functional Grammar.

Comparing Halliday's grammar with others

Whereas traditional and transformative grammars focus almost exclusively on the sentence or clause, systemic-functional grammar pays attention to multiple layers (*strata*) of language – from its expression forms in phonology and graphology, to patterns in the *lexico-grammar*, to the structures of whole texts and their social purposes. For instance, a newspaper report on a new medical discovery, a story about an illness and its cure or a doctor–patient conversation are all considered to be different genres or types of whole text. The term *genre* here is used to indicate the type of text structured to suit an overall meaning purpose, rather than its style, as in literary studies.

A *genre* has an overall social purpose; it is staged in the sense that it has a characteristic beginning, middle and end, and it is made up from clauses that take distinctive experiential, interpersonal and textual forms (Martin 1992: 546ff).

The written genre of a news item might be structured:

> Newsworthy event → background circumstances → elaboration on incidents and sources

... and it might focus on processes for describing the background and reporting the incidents, and verbal-on-verbal processes for reporting evidence from sources.

The written genre of story might be structured:

> Orientation → complication → resolution

... and it might focus on mental processes linked by temporal conjunctions.

The oral genre of doctor – patient conversation might be structured:

> Greeting and invitation to describe symptoms → description of symptoms → diagnosis → prescription → departing greetings

In each case, a purposeful social exchange of meanings produces a different structure and set of word choices.

Writing is a process of making choices that are most effective in the context of meaning. It may not be so effective to provide someone with a narrative about cooking a meal when it would be more effective to provide a written procedure in the form of a recipe. Or recounting your feelings about a scientific experiment may be less than helpful when you are expected to write a report about scientific causes and effects. In each case, the genre of the whole text will be a key to the effectiveness of the meaning-making.

Like the other grammars, the systemic-functional approach provides much more information than can usefully be directed to aid reading and writing, and learning literacy. Too much goes on in language to be able consciously disentangle every element. Linguists do this because that's their job. Their profession has all sorts of applications: from machine translation, to semantically informed search engines on the Web, to automated assessment of student writing. However, there are a lot of things about language that users of written or oral language just do not need to know. This is because much of the time they already intuitively know what they mean without needing technical explanations of how they do it.

It has sometimes been disputed whether knowing grammar has any benefits at all when it comes to the practical business of meaning. There have also been times in the past where the teaching of grammar in schools has been criticised as being meaningless and irrelevant to students' learning, particularly by the most single-minded advocates of what we have called authentic literacy pedagogy. For teachers in a constantly shifting landscape of practices and policies, it is important to understand these different emphases and approaches, which make different assumptions about language and learning that may underlie these issues.

As outlined earlier in this chapter, historically the study of grammar in schools involved the parsing of sentences and labelling of various grammatical categories or *parts of speech*. This is often referred to as teaching 'traditional grammar'. Students of foreign languages were taught grammar so they could understand the structure and patterns of the languages they were learning. However, such traditional approaches to the teaching and learning grammar often did not have much relevance to what students had to do with texts in their schooling or their everyday lives, travel and work.

Functionally oriented curricula, such as the Australian Curriculum: English, emphasise that the goal of teaching grammar should go beyond students' labelling of various grammatical categories. They recognise that a conscious knowledge about the meaning-making resources of grammar is important for children as they learn to write. Children need to know what language choices lead to clearer expression and logic, better arguments or more imaginative storylines. They need to be able to convert this knowledge about language into 'a resource for effective reading, listening viewing, writing, speaking and designing' (ACARA 2009: 6).

Many other countries today use a mix of approaches to learning to write. For instance, the US Common Core State Standards have a strong focus on language concepts, many of which are from traditional grammar. It also has a functional approach to text types, focusing on the different forms and purposes of three major types: information/explanation, opinion/argument and narrative (Common Core State Standards Initiative [CCSS] 2010).

Table 10.3 provides a brief comparison of different approaches to grammar and its teaching.

The functional approach is useful in several respects. For a start, it is pragmatic. It focuses on purpose and meaning in text, and situates text in its context (textual functions), rather just analysing the dry rules of textual systems. This functional orientation means that its focus is on the question of choices among alternatives. When speaking, the speaker has a specific purpose and is constantly reworking what they are saying: rephrasing things, correcting things that didn't come out right or saying them again or slightly differently in order to elaborate until they are more satisfied that they have achieved the meaning they intend to make. When writing, the author also has a specific reason and is constantly going back over a

Table 10.3: Different approaches to grammar

	Traditional	**Transformational**	**Functional**
View of language	Language is a set of rules	Language is rule-governed creativity	Language is a social process
View of grammar	Rules of formation and usage	An innate device in the human mind	A resource for making meaning in social contexts
Derivation	Ancient Greek and Latin	Theorising about universal principles of language	Analysis of what people do through language
Related disciplines	Philosophy	Philosophy; cognitive psychology	Sociology; anthropology
Form vs function	Mainly concerned with form	Emphasis on syntactic form; some interest in semantics	Principled relationship between form and function
Mode emphasis	Written mode	Not concerned with mode	Spoken and written modes
Unit of analysis	Parts of speech and their combination	Phonemes through to complex syntactic forms	Text, clause, group, word, phoneme
Key figures	Dionysius Thrax, Bishop Lowth	Chomsky	Halliday
Classroom implications	Overt teaching of rules, often as end in themselves	Teacher's knowledge of acquisition sequence guides selection of input	Discussion of relevant grammar point in context to heighten language awareness and appropriate use

Source: Adapted from Derewianka (2001: 264–5).

text and revising it so it more closely reflects their purposes. When reading, a person also is seeking a certain goal and may need to reread a word, or sentence, or longer stretch of text until it makes sense to them.

The focus here is not only on using the rules of a language system. It is not only about decoding rules for meaning. It is also a matter of understanding the relationship between rules or conventions and our purpose for speaking, listening, reading or writing. We face choices about the texts we produce and receive. As we suggested earlier, in the making or interpreting of meaning, we constantly rework to improve a text we are writing or to produce our understanding of a text that we are interpreting. In each case, we are always dealing with levels of approximation of meaning. This is why we find ourselves continuously going over texts as we try to get a better approximation. This fits better with our ideas of all being designers of meaning in which we make 'choices' and 'changes' instead of obeying 'rules' or making 'mistakes'.

The core texts of Halliday's systemic-functional grammar only 'do' language. However, unlike traditional or transformational-generative grammar, systemic-functional grammar certainly invites us to recognise that meaning is bigger than language – language is one system in a whole suite of meaning-making systems in a culture, which include visual, gestural, spatial and tactile modes as well. The tools of systemic-functional linguistics also allow us to investigate meaning in this broader frame of reference. In a very ordinary sense, you cannot do the experiential, interpersonal and textual things of everyday life except multimodally. Language never exists as a closed 'system' that is in any factual or analytical sense separable from the intrinsic multimodality of our human, sensory experience.

In the following excerpt from a transcript of a lesson on 'Minibeasts', Year/Grade 2 students talk with their teacher about the insects they found in nearby bushland during a class field trip. As they prepare to write a recount of their experiences, the teacher guides them in making the shift from their hands-on sensory experiences of the physical world to recreating these experiences in words and gestures.

Excerpt from Transcript 1

S1:   We caught three stinkbugs …

S2:   Pat caught the grasshopper

T1:   Show them how the grasshopper was going, Pat, when you tried to catch it.

Can you show us with your hand?

What was it doing before you tried to grab it?

S3:   Jumping

T1:   Good boy

And how high was he jumping?

Show us on the carpet with your hands how high he must've jumped.

S4:   We caught two ants – a bull ant and a normal ant

T1:   What's a normal ant? Can you describe it?

S4:   A small black one

T1:   Oh a small black one right

S4:   Yeah and it had three body parts and …

The talk around the children's first-hand observations is critical in helping the students to reconstrue these shared tactile experiences in language. A second shift into written language requires new ways of meaning and doing that involve an awareness of how language functions as a symbolic meaning system. Language becomes a tool for reflecting on experience and reconstruing it. In the classroom, it also involves the negotiation of a metalanguage to talk about how to mean through writing, as illustrated in the excerpt below.

Excerpts from Transcript 2

T1:   What's a recount?

S: Something that's already happened and you just write about it again

T1:   What's another word for recount?

S: Um, it's true

T1:   It is

        Is it imaginative writing or factual writing?

C: (It is) factual

T1:   Because it truly did happen

        Instead of saying recount, I could say re-?

S: Tell

T1:   Retell the story. OK. Good

T1:   What day did we go on the minibeast hunt?

C: Friday

T1 :   Right

        Who can give me a sentence?

        Perhaps you can put more than one piece of information in your sentence

        That would be really clever

T1:   Cameron

S: … we caught some minibeasts …

S: We went on Friday to a minibeast hunt

T1:   We went on Friday to a minibeast hunt

T1:   Good

T1:   Can someone change that?

T1:   The information's perfect

T1:   I think we might be able to just rephrase that

S: On Friday we went on a minibeast hunt

As the teacher and students jointly construct the recount, a shift is made from the multimodal spatial and tactile experiences of the field study and the spoken and gestural modes of the class discussion towards the written mode. The events around the minibeast hunt are reconstituted in a meaning space distanced from the physical and temporal locations in which they occurred. First-order experiences of the world are recontextualised in a linguistic context – in a second-order meaning-making space and time. In this new dimension, text is created as an object, an artefact, which can then be acted upon as an entity in its own right. The text object now has a name – a 'recount', with its own internal structure made up of 'sentences' and patterns of meaning that can be 'rephrased'. Teacher and students work together to negotiate this retelling of their experiences, with the teacher skilfully shaping the students' language by making explicit through talk the participants, processes and circumstances of the event, and how the information can be ordered.

Excerpt from Transcript 2

T1:   We've told our reader who went, where we went and why we went

T1:   Now we have to list what happened

T1:   When you are doing this part, are you allowed to write what happened last up here?

S: No

T1:   What is important to remember when you're saying what happened?

        It's really important otherwise someone's going to get so confused when they read it

S: It's supposed to be in order

T1:   Good boy. It must be in the order that it happened

Developing writing across the school years

The development of writing in young children may be viewed as a process involving a shift to a new way of making meaning with symbols and signs. Making meaning in writing involves a process of abstraction from material reality. In the early years, children's written language is speech-like in quality (Figure 10.7), and resembles the spoken language of their immediate social worlds.

However, the process of making meaning in the written mode involves a substantial conscious effort as young writers grapple with handwriting, typing and spelling as they re-represent their experiences on the page or screen (Figures 10.8, 10.9).

As they move through their formal schooling, children's encounters with the world become systematically ordered as school knowledge is increasingly represented in the written mode. Progression into the primary years is associated with an expansion of children's meaning-making resources to include a range of written text types used to construct knowledge in school subject areas – they learn to describe, explain, argue and tell stories in writing (e.g. Figures 10.10, 10.11, 10.12).

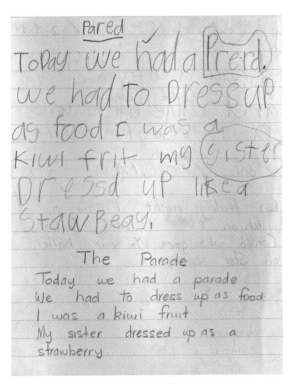

Figure 10.7 Early writing sample

Figure 10.8 Year/Grade 2 writing by hand – draft and review

Figure 10.9 Year/Grade 2 writing on computer – revised and published

By the middle and later school years, subject-based texts become more technical and abstract as the specialised knowledge of the discipline areas becomes more complex. Students' writing often includes precise, densely packed information characterised by the use of technical vocabulary (e.g. *Locrian mode, organum, fauxbourdon, first inversion, pedal point* in music Figure 10.13).

This is largely achieved in English through nominalisation, where an element or group of elements in a clause is made to function in the place of a nominal group. In Figure 10.14, for example, the processes ('*create*', '*sequence*') congruently

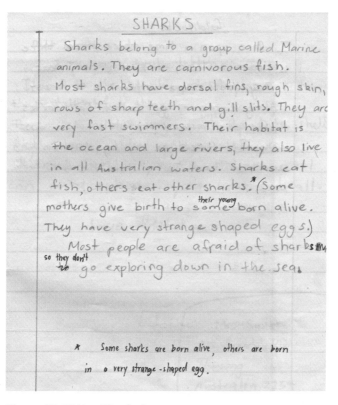

SHARKS

Sharks belong to a group called Marine animals. They are carnivorous fish.

Most sharks have dorsal fins, rough skin, rows of sharp teeth and gill slits. They are very fast swimmers. Their habitat is the ocean and large rivers, they also live in all Australian waters. Sharks eat fish, others eat other sharks.* (Some mothers give birth to some *their young* born alive. They have very strange shaped eggs.)

Most people are afraid of sharks *so they don't* go exploring down in the seas.

* Some sharks are born alive, others are born in a very strange-shaped egg.

Figure 10.10 Year/Grade 4 report

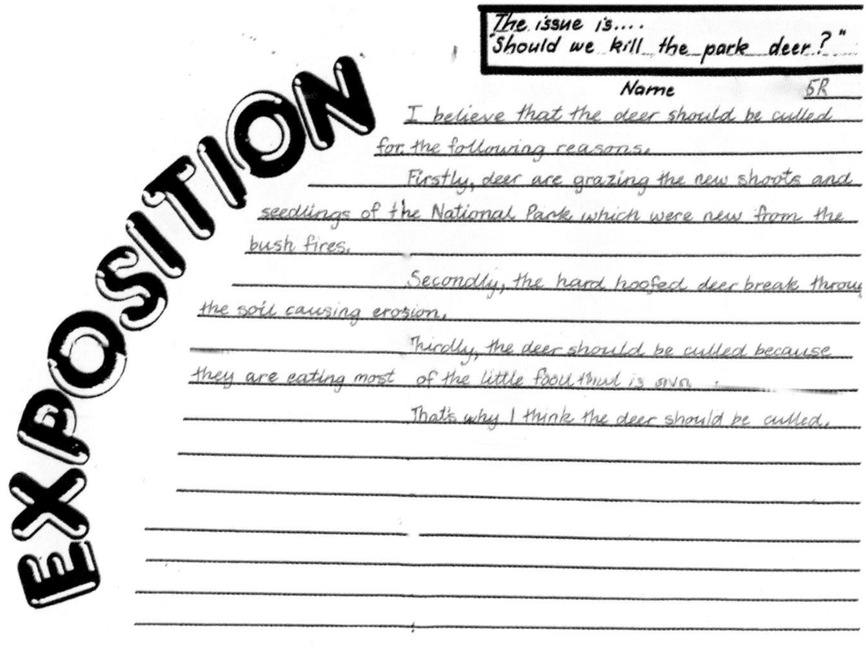

EXPOSITION

The issue is....
"Should we kill the park deer?"

Name _____ 5R

I believe that the deer should be culled for the following reasons.

Firstly, deer are grazing the new shoots and seedlings of the National Park which were new from the bush fires.

Secondly, the hard hoofed deer break through the soil causing erosion.

Thirdly, the deer should be culled because they are eating most of the little food that is own.

That's why I think the deer should be culled.

Figure 10.11 Year/Grade 5 expository writing

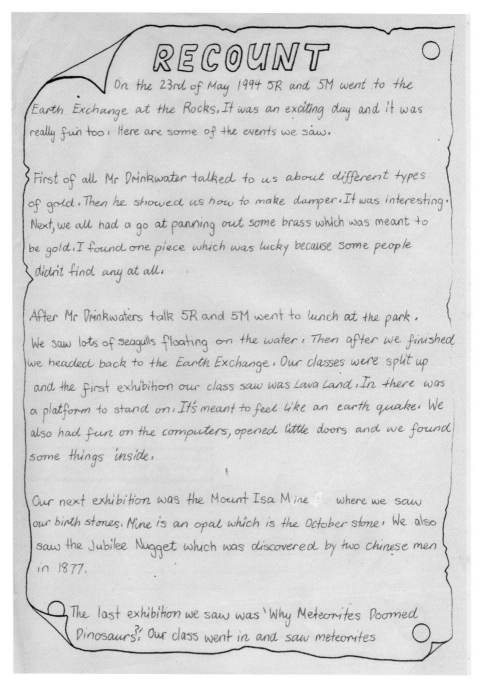

RECOUNT

On the 23rd of May 1994 5R and 5M went to the Earth Exchange at the Rocks. It was an exciting day and it was really fun too. Here are some of the events we saw.

First of all Mr Drinkwater talked to us about different types of gold. Then he showed us how to make damper. It was interesting. Next, we all had a go at panning out some brass which was meant to be gold. I found one piece which was lucky because some people didn't find any at all.

After Mr Drinkwaters talk 5R and 5M went to lunch at the park. We saw lots of seagulls floating on the water. Then after we finished we headed back to the Earth Exchange. Our classes were split up and the first exhibition our class saw was Lava Land. In there was a platform to stand on. It's meant to feel like an earth quake. We also had fun on the computers, opened little doors and we found some things inside.

Our next exhibition was the Mount Isa Mine where we saw our birth stones. Mine is an opal which is the October stone. We also saw the Jubilee Nugget which was discovered by two Chinese men in 1877.

The last exhibition we saw was 'Why Meteorites Doomed Dinosaurs?' Our class went in and saw meteorites

Figure 10.12 Year/Grade 5 recount

realised by verbs, are reworded as nouns ('the *creation* of maps', 'the *sequencing* of DNA').

The effect is the 'breaking down [of] the more natural relations between meanings and their realisation which characterises spontaneous spoken discourse. The

(iv) Briefly outline SIX (6) aspects or examples of Debussy's compositional style that were discussed in class.

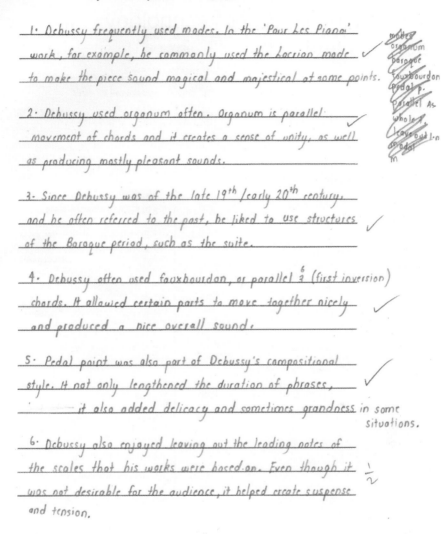

1. Debussy frequently used modes. In the 'Pour Les Piano' work, for example, he commonly used the Locrian mode to make the piece sound magical and majestical at some points. ✓

2. Debussy used organum often. Organum is parallel movement of chords and it creates a sense of unity, as well as producing mostly pleasant sounds. ✓

3. Since Debussy was of the late 19th /early 20th century, and he often referred to the past, he liked to use structures of the Baroque period, such as the suite. ✓

4. Debussy often used fauxbourdon, or parallel $\frac{6}{3}$ (first inversion) chords. It allowed certain parts to move together nicely and produced a nice overall sound. ✓

5. Pedal point was also part of Debussy's compositional style. It not only lengthened the duration of phrases, it also added delicacy and sometimes grandness in some situations. ✓

6. Debussy also enjoyed leaving out the leading notes of the scales that his works were based on. Even though it was not desirable for the audience, it helped create suspense and tension. $\frac{1}{2}$

Figure 10.13 Secondary-school writing – Year/Grade 10 music

result is a highly abstract form of argumentation' (Martin 1993: 240). In developing these abstract ways of meaning, children's writing becomes more efficient in compacting information into ideationally rich texts that structure knowledge in ways that enable them to engage in more specialised fields of discourse. The affordances of digital multimodal authoring opens up even more choices for the ways in which meanings can be represented, structured and communicated, as exemplified by the Year 12 student response to science fiction literature shown in Figure 10.15.

The science of gene technology: benefits and risks
By Year 12 student

The Human Genome project may help to save lives; but when it comes to our own moral and ethical viewpoints can we find a common ground?

Founded in 1990, the U.S. Human Genome Project (HGP) was a 13-year effort conducted by the U.S. Department of Energy and the National Institutes of Health. The projects goals included, identifying all of the 20,000-25,000 genes in human DNA and determine the sequences of the 3 billion chemical base pairs that make up human DNA. The project also improved related technologies and addressed the ethical, legal, and social issues (ELSI) that arose from the project. [1]

The techniques used in the Human Genome Project are characterized by two major components: first, the creation of maps of the 23 pairs of human chromosomes and secondly the sequencing of the DNA making up these chromosomes.

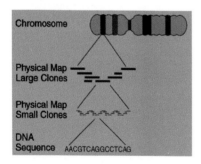

Geneticists will create either a genetic linkage map or a physical map; both depict the relative positions of the DNA markers, known as genes.

One of the most frequently used sequencing methods employed by the HGP is the Sanger method. Which sequences DNA by employing an enzyme that can

polymerize DNA and label nucleotides, the basic building blocks of DNA. [2]

Although the HGP began only 19 years ago, discoveries in the field of genetics, laid the foundation work that made the HGP possible.

1953	James D. Watson and Francis F. Crick found the double helix structure of the DNA
1966	The genetic code is deciphered.
1973	Herbert Boyer and Stanley Cohen prove that DNA that has been cut and recombined is active in a living cell.
1977	The first human gene is isolated; the gene for insulin
1985	Renato Dulbeco proposes the sequencing of the whole human genome.
1987	The Italian Human Genome Project (HGP) is started
1988	The Human Genome Organisation (HUGO) is founded
1990	The Human Genome Project is started officially in the USA with funding of 3 billion US dollars and a timespan of 15 years
1995	The French HGP is started. The German HGP is started
1996	90% of all human genes are identified
2003	99% of human sequence finished to 99.99% accuracy
	HGP completion in spring of 2003

Pro vs. Con

Similar to any new technology, the data obtained from the HGP will be both useful and controversial. Benefits from the HGP extend into a wide range of fields that include, molecular medicine, energy sources and environmental applications, risk assessment, bioarchaeology, anthropology, evolution, human migration, DNA forensics

Figure 10.14 An excerpt from a Year/Grade 12 biology report

and agriculture applications. [3] Interoperating the genome data is still in its initial stages, however we are beginning to see a new era emerge in the diagnosis of diseases. A shift from treating the symptoms of a disease to looking at the fundamental cause of the disease has occurred. This opens the door for earlier detection of genetic predispositions to specific diseases. Other beneficial ventures of the HGP are the production of disease/insect/drought resistant crops. From an economical standpoint there would be a reduction in the cost of produce and consumers would be provided with pesticide-free foods. [3]

Controversial or revolutionary?

Both of these applications are considered to be among the most controversial and debatable "benefits" obtained from the HGP. Hence, there are associated limitations outlined by the ELSI research, which represents the worlds largest bioethics program. The societal concerns arising from the new genetic technology include, privacy and confidentiality, psychological impact and stigmatization, reproductive issues, philosophical implications, health and environmental issues, uncertainties and commercialization of products. [4]

In terms of the examples mentioned above, testing for genetic predispositions to specific diseases comes with a bag full of limitations and moral and ethical considerations. Tests for adult on-set disorders and cancers are targeted to people of high risk due to their family medical history. The tests give only a probability for developing the disorder. One of the most serious limitations of these susceptibility tests is the difficulty in interpreting a positive result because some people will never develop the disease. [5]

Limitations regarding the second example of genetically modified crops range from potential human health impacts to the monopolization of world food production.

Do the benefits outweigh the limitations?

The data obtained from the HGP is also limited by the nature of DNA, some genes are found inside other genes, making identification difficult. 97% of DNA consists of non-coding regions, the use of 50% of these regions is still not known. [6] The nature of the HGP allows there to be associated benefits and limitations regarding the data obtained.

Impacts on society

The HGP has created the field of genomics, the study of genomes. Because the human genome, applies to everybody each individual will be impacted differently. It is difficult to give a clear cut, "one size fits all" answer to how the HGP has impacted society. Based on your race, moral, ethical and religious beliefs you may be inclined to a specific viewpoint regarding the HGP.

You must consider benefits of the HGP; most significant to the greater portion of society are medical applications. Does the thought of improved diagnosis of disease, earlier detection of genetic predispositions to disease, gene therapy and pharmacogenomics "custom drugs" sound appealing to you? Do these potentially life saving technologies erase your own fears of fairness, uncertainties and privacy issues?

The HGP has the potential to save lives.

It is important to note that The Genetic Information Nondiscrimination Act (GINA) became law in 2008. GINA prohibits U.S. health insurance companies and employers from discrimination on the basis of information derived from genetic tests. [7] Optimistically policy makers from other nations may follow in America's footsteps in creating a nondiscrimination act.

Gene therapy 101

To understand how the HGP will save lives, gene therapy one of the most beneficial and yet again controversial applications needs to be explored. But what is it? Gene therapy is a technique for correcting defective genes responsible for disease development. [8] Sickle cell mutation is a perfect example of how gene therapy has the potential to help the hundreds of the thousands of people affected by this genetic mutation.

In a recent article for New Scientist, Philip

Figure 10.14 (*continued*)

Cohen wrote that 'gene therapy has passed an important milestone with the first successful treatment of sickle cell mutation in a mouse model of the disease.' Sickle cell appears to be an ideal candidate for gene therapy, because it is caused by a mutation in a single DNA letter of the beta-globin gene. This tiny misspelling produces hemoglobin molecules that distort the red blood cells into a sickle shape. [9]

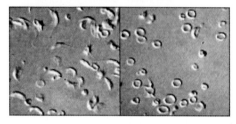

Sickel cell   Normal red blood cell

A team of scientists working at the Harvard Medical School inserted an intentionally mutated copy of the gene, known to interrupt the production of the faulty hemoglobin chains. [9]

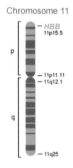

The team has produced amazing results in combating the sickle cell mutation within mice, it is expected within the next 2-3 years that we will begin to see human based trials. If successful within humans, gene therapy will be able to manage and treat the mutation that can have serve affects on its patients.

The future

The HGP has opened the door on "new genetics". The success of the project has enabled geneticists to create new gene testing, gene therapy and tailor made drugs that are specific to your own genetic makeup – pharmacogenomics. Over the next decade we will begin to see the widespread use of gene testing as a way to screen for the possible development or confirmation of specific diseases and disorders. Gene therapy will be an important treatment tool, as its versatility has the potential to manage a range of genetic diseases that affect the human population. Pharmacogenomics are anticipated to be better, safer and a more accurate method of treating an illness. All of these future directions of "new genetics" raise questions of moral and ethical dilemmas.

Should testing be performed when no treatment is available?
Should parents have the right to have their minor children tested for adult-onset diseases?
How does genomic information affect members of minority communities? [4]

A careful balance

Every individual will have unique concerns regarding the future of new genetics. Policy makers and government bodies must make considerations to accommodate for the populations variety in ethical and moral beliefs. The beneficial potential of new genetics is powerful and must not be overshadowed by unintended controversial effects. As we begin to realize the benefits of new genetics, maintaining a cautious approach will help minimize the risks. [10]

New genetics will introduce a new era of life saving medicine.

Figure 10.14 (*continued*)

References/ sources

Pictures

1.DNA question mark
http://www.istockphoto.com/file_thumbview_approve

2. Chromosome mapping
Unit 14: The Human Genome Project
European Biotechnology Education 1998
Pg 6

3. Sickle cell anemia chromosome pair
Unit 14: The Human Genome Project
European Biotechnology Education 1998
Pg 9

4. Sickle cell vs. normal red blood cell
http://www.newscientist.com/article/dn1690-sickle-cell-treatment-marks-gene-therapy-milestone.html

Content

[1] http://www.ornl.gov/sci/techresources/Human_Genome/project/about.shtml

[2] http://www.medilexicon.com/medicaldictionary.php?t=54859

[3] http://www.ornl.gov/sci/techresources/Human_Genome/project/benefits.shtml

[4] http://www.ornl.gov/sci/techresources/Human_Genome/elsi/elsi.shtml

[5] http://www.ornl.gov/sci/techresources/Human_Genome/medicine/genetest.shtml

[6] http://hsc.csu.edu.au/biology/options/genetics/3060/genetics_974.html#a2

[7] http://www.ornl.gov/sci/techresources/Human_Genome/publicat/primer2001/8.shtml

[8] http://www.ornl.gov/sci/techresources/Human_Genome/medicine/genetherapy.shtml#

[9] http://www.newscientist.com/article/dn1690-sickle-cell-treatment-marks-gene-therapy-milestone.html

[10] http://www.ornl.gov/sci/techresources/Human_Genome/publicat/judicature/article3.html

Figure 10.14 (*continued*)

Five questions about meaning

In this book, we adapt the basic principles of systemic-functional grammar, not only in order to create a comprehensive design analysis of multimodal meaning, but also to provide a framework that may help meaning-makers shape their meanings and learn to be better meaning-makers. This takes the form of the five

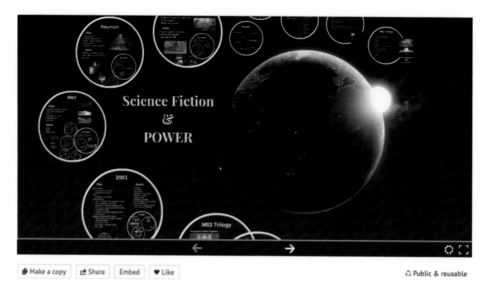

Figure 10.15 Grade/Year 12 multimedia presentation

relatively straightforward questions about meaning that will help us identify the design elements of a text in any mode or mix of modes:

1. What do the meanings describe? (To refer)
2. How do the meanings connect the people in the action and the people who are interacting? (To dialogue)
3. How does the overall meaning hold together? (To structure)
4. How are the meanings shaped by their context? (To situate)
5. Whose purposes and interests are these meanings designed serve? (To intend)

In the following chapters, we outline a design analysis of multimodality that draws upon and adapts the insights of systemic-functional linguistics for other modes: visual, spatial, tactile, gestural, audio and oral. One direct parallel between our multimodal design analysis and systemic-functional linguistics is that our concept of 'reference' (what a meaning is about) is roughly similar to the Hallidayian concept of 'field' or 'experiential meanings'. Our concept of 'dialogue' is like the Hallidayian concept of 'tenor' or 'interpersonal meanings'. And our concept of 'structure' is similar to the Hallidayian concept of 'mode' or 'textual meanings'. We have added to these three 'context' and 'purpose', to make a total of five questions that can always be asked about any meaning.

The writing process

So far in this chapter, we have focused on the substance of writing. Now it is time to turn to the writing process. Ideally, for extended pieces of writing this occurs in five phases: 1) plan; 2) draft; 3) review; 4) revise; and 5) publish. We outline these in Table 10.5, and provide examples from the Scholar learning platform – other digital writing environments have many similar features.

Table 10.4: A multiliteracies design analysis of written language

Reference *What do the meanings refer to?*	• *Something particular?* e.g. words such as 'David', 'is walking' – proper nouns, nouns referring to specific things and verbs that refer to specific actions. Includes: 　◦ *A person, who?* e.g. words such as 'her', 'David', 'the doctor'. 　◦ *A place, where?* e.g. words such as 'New York', 'the city'. 　◦ *A time, when?* e.g. words such as 'Monday', 'this evening' – connected with the tenses of verbs. 　◦ *An object of interest, what?* e.g. words such as 'David's exercise class', 'fitness'. 　◦ *Something general?* e.g. words such as 'people', 'to walk' – common nouns, verbs that refer to kinds of action. 　◦ *A characteristic?* e.g. words such as 'tall', 'fast', 'many'; singular or plural; 'the' or 'a', comparatives – adjectives to describe nouns and adverbs to describe verbs. 　◦ *A relation?* e.g. words that connect meanings to each other, such as 'is a kind of', 'is a part of', 'between', 'because' – prepositions in phrases or clauses; markers of possession.
Dialogue *How do the meanings connect the people who are interacting?*	• How are the *actors connected* through the action described in the text? e.g. words expressing active/passive voice; asking/suggesting/instructing; kinds of possibility, such as indicating definite/maybe/maybe if. • What are the *effects of the action?* e.g. who is the subject or object, direct or indirect objects. • What is the *writer's stance?* e.g. the formality or informality of the tone of a text; author commitment or affinity to the proposition; voice/mood. • What is the *position of the reader?* e.g. direct 'you' instructions, 'it' or 'she' in third party recount, more or less space for multiple interpretations; direct representation/ metaphor/allusion; framing of writer/reader interactivity.
Structure *How does the overall meaning hold together?*	• *Word choice* and positioning? e.g. how a word fits with the surrounding text, repetition/non-repetition; emphasis/consistency of reference/variety for style or deepening meaning. • *Within-text pointers* and their clarity/explicitness? e.g. thing-pointer words, such as 'this', 'that' or 'it'; time-pointer words, such as 'now' or 'then'; place-pointer words, such has 'here' or 'there'; person-pointer words, such as 'he' or 'she'. • *Clause and sentence flow?* e.g. narrative flow, logical connectives and argumentative clarity using subordinate clauses, conjunctions, subject/predicate, given/new. • *Sectioning?* e.g. commas, colons, semi-colons, long dashes and brackets for sections within sentences, punctuation for sentences, paragraphing, sections and section heads, lists, tables, the text title. • *Chaining?* e.g. the flow of sections. • *Media?* e.g. handwriting, typography.

(continued)

Table 10.4: A multiliteracies design analysis of written language (*continued*)

Situation *How are the meanings shaped by the context of their location?*	• *Outside-text pointers?* e.g. shared assumptions/explicitness about the social and physical setting. • *Comparison?* e.g. analogy, metaphor, simile. • *References* to other texts? e.g. allusion/explicit mention, quoting, informal/formal citation. • *Inclusions/exclusions?* e.g. things deliberately or unconsciously not mentioned. • *Genre* or resemblance to other texts? e.g. close adherence to genre/hybrid recombination of genres/departure from genre.
Intent *Whose interests do these meanings serve?*	• What is the *stance* of the author? e.g. directly/subtly, emotive/objective, explicit/implicit agendas. • How does the author *engage* or attempt to get the attention of the reader? e.g. narrative interest, rhetorical effect. • What are the *interests* of the writer that the text communicates? e.g. expressions of worldview/ideology/identity, visible/hidden biases. • What *roles* does the reader have? e.g. directive/open navigation paths, such as a novel compared to a wiki. • What *reader interests* does the text assume? e.g. interpretations it anticipates/fails to anticipate.

In Kettle Moraine, Wisconsin the 'Create' school has literally taken down the walls that used to divide classrooms. Over a hundred students work together in a beautifully designed open space with lounges, round working tables, and discussion pods. The teachers' office is in the centre of things, a quiet glassed space.

The Scholar learning platform keeps this number of students closely connected with their teachers and each other as they write, and students hold discussions in Scholar's 'Community' webspace – a cross between a blog, Facebook and Twitter. One student has noted: 'In the legacy classroom, only one person could talk at a time, but on Scholar, more than one person can talk; they can branch out and share their voices.'

Students also do multimedia web writing in Scholar's 'Creator' area, incorporating live links, uploaded images, embedded videos, audio and even sometimes datasets or maths. Every work goes through stages of drafting, peer review, revision and finally publication to each student's web portfolio. Teacher Jessica Harroun said of this process: 'It's facilitating peer feedback and collaborative knowledge production. These kids are finding the resources and suddenly they become curators of all these web sources – the synthesis alone, is just amazing.'

In the era of social media, teachers are looking for platforms such as Scholar to engage their students in a more connected peer-to-peer environment, and to give them the opportunity to represent their knowledge using a full range of contemporary media. The business of writing is being transformed, not just in English language arts, but also science, social studies and other subject areas.

Table 10.5: The writing process

	Basic writing processes	Multimodal, digital and social writing
Phase 1: *Plan*	Sometimes called 'prewriting', this is the phase where the writer acquaints themselves with the writing task: • Carefully examine the writing prompt. • Choose a topic (if the prompt leaves scope for that). • Research, take notes. • Create an outline.	• It is very helpful for students to have a writing rubric, presented to them in language that is accessible to them, so they have a clear understanding of expectations of a high-quality text. Rubrics should spell out clearly what is expected in a particular text type or genre, such as information, argument or narrative texts. If there is going to be peer review, rubrics should have a tone that is prospective and constructive – looking forward, and suggesting the kinds of feedback that might be helpful to the writer. (See Figure 10.16.) • When working in a digital writing space, writers can use outline tools to create section headings and subheadings. These reflect the overall design of the text. These could stay visible in non-fiction texts, or may later be removed for the final versions of a text – for instance, invisible headings to mark stages of narrative development. (See Figure 10.17, right-hand side.) • The writer can put notes, ideas, and media objects under the heading in each section. (See Figure 10.17, left-hand side.) • If it's to be a multimodal text, writers should collect images, media objects, weblinks that will be useful to them as they write. (See Figure 10.17, left-hand side.)
Phase 2: *Draft*	The writer then creates a first, complete version of the text: • Write a rough draft. • Reread the draft, refining its flow and logic. • Proofread and copy edit (spelling, grammar, punctuation, appropriate word use etc.).	• It is a good idea for the writer to save the version of their work that contains headings, notes and media, then create a new version for their draft. They can then delete the notes and media in this new version as they are incorporated into the text, but they still have the original notes to go back to, if they wish. (See Figure 10.18.) • Use checker tools in digital writing programs: spelling, grammar, synonyms. (See Figure 10.19.) • The writer should check the rubric to be sure they have addressed expectations of good writing in this text type or in relation to standards set out in the curriculum. (See Figure 10.16.)

(continued)

Table 10.5: The writing process (*continued*)

	Basic writing processes	Multimodal, digital and social writing
Phase 3: *Review*	Then, the writer might show their writing to a peer, critical friend or teacher for feedback.	• Some writing software supports anonymous or open peer review. (See Figures 10.20, 10.21, 10.22 and 10.23.) • Some writing software also supports peer, self and teacher annotations. (See Figure 10.24.)
Phase 4: *Revise*	This feedback will then prompt the writer to create a final draft, taking on board the feedback they have received: • Make major revisions to structure, flow and logic. • Proofread and copy edit the final draft. • Reflect on the writing experience in a writer's diary.	• Writing software might also support self-review, where the student examines the rubric again, and reflects on which comments and suggestions have been most helpful, and the ways in which they have revised their work based on peer and/or teacher feedback. (See Figure 10.25.)
Phase 5: *Publish*	Finally, the writer's work is made available to an audience, so others can read it – in a class book, for instance, or posted to a class noticeboard.	• e-Portfolios are ideal for publishing multimodal works to the Web. (See Figure 10.26.) • Once they are shared, published works are available for post-publication discussion.

Figure 10.16 In the prewriting stage
While the student writer drafts (on the left) they see the rubric (on the right) created by the teacher or the curriculum resource developer to address the writing standards. A rubric that has been designed for self-reflection and peer review should be written so that it is clear and accessible to the writer. It should also have a prospective and constructive orientation, rather than the retrospective perspective and judgmental tone of summative assessment rubrics.

Figure 10.17 Starting the draft

On the right, the writer creates headings for sections and subheadings. They drag-and-drop headings up and down the structure tool, and pull them left or right to create different levels of heading. This provides them a way to plan their work, and easily redesign the plan as the work evolves. On the left, the writer makes notes and includes media. They are very careful to mark the quote so they don't accidentally plagiarise text they may want to quote directly. And, while they are there, they include a footnote reference so they don't forget where this quote came from, also avoiding interruption of their drafting process that would happen if they had to go looking for it again. They save this outline + notes version for their records (they may find it helpful to go back to this), and create a new version for their full draft.

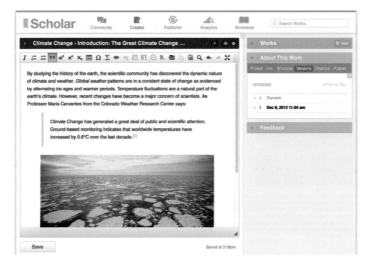

Figure 10.18 Producing a well-formed draft

Now in a new version, the writer creates a well-formed draft, ready for peer and/or teacher feedback.

Figure 10.19 Using a checker tool

Most digital writing environments have spelling and grammar checkers that highlight things that are wrong with the text – but often they are not wrong. This checker makes change suggestions – here, it says that 'African-American' is often spelled with a hyphen, but this is not necessarily the case. And it suggests that 'the whole' is a more complex expression than it need be, and that just 'the' might do, but the writer may well want the strong emphasis. Language checkers (spelling, grammar and synonym suggestion tools) should be regarded as no more than tools for thought, rather than measures of what is 'correct' in writing.

Figure 10.20 The review stage

A place where peer, teacher and self-reviews can be written, including rating levels (the slider), and space to write an explanation.

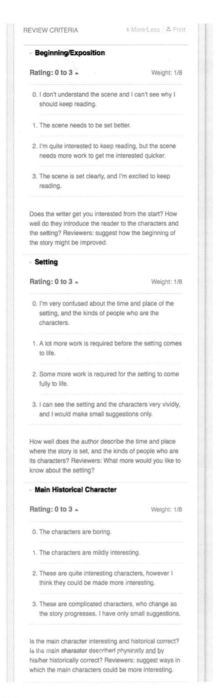

REVIEW CRITERIA   ± More/Less | ⚑ Print

- **Beginning/Exposition**

Rating: 0 to 3 ▴   Weight: 1/8

0. I don't understand the scene and I can't see why I should keep reading.

1. The scene needs to be set better.

2. I'm quite interested to keep reading, but the scene needs more work to get me interested quicker.

3. The scene is set clearly, and I'm excited to keep reading.

Does the writer get you interested from the start? How well do they introduce the reader to the characters and the setting? Reviewers: suggest how the beginning of the story might be improved.

- **Setting**

Rating: 0 to 3 ▴   Weight: 1/8

0. I'm very confused about the time and place of the setting, and the kinds of people who are the characters.

1. A lot more work is required before the setting comes to life.

2. Some more work is required for the setting to come fully to life.

3. I can see the setting and the characters very vividly, and I would make small suggestions only.

How well does the author describe the time and place where the story is set, and the kinds of people who are its characters? Reviewers: What more would you like to know about the setting?

- **Main Historical Character**

Rating: 0 to 3 ▴   Weight: 1/8

0. The characters are boring.

1. The characters are mildly interesting.

2. These are quite interesting characters, however I think they could be made more interesting.

3. These are complicated characters, who change as the story progresses. I have only small suggestions.

Is the main character interesting and historical correct? Is the main character described physically and by his/her historically correct? Reviewers: suggest ways in which the main characters could be more interesting.

Figure 10.21 Review ratings

Clear specification of the rating levels not only helps the writer and the reviewer to think clearly about their judgement. It also helps with inter-rater reliability, meaning that even peers can be supported to make judgements about writing that are on average as good as an expert or the teacher.

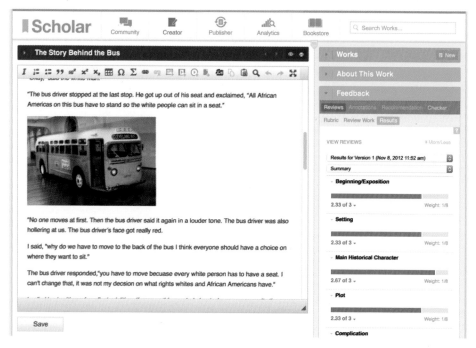

Figure 10.22 Receiving a rating
The writer receives and overall rating on their draft work from peer reviewers.

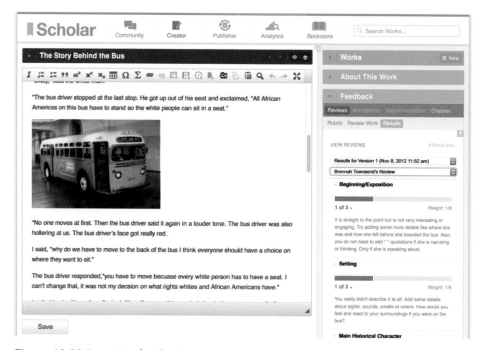

Figure 10.23 Receiving feedback
And here is the feedback the writer has received from one reviewer (an anonymous review, but this is the teacher view, so the name is visible.)

Figure 10.24 Viewing annotations

In-text annotations, coded by change type. Again, this was anonymous but you can see the name because it's the teacher view. In a cloud computing environment, many can comment on the same piece of writing at the same time, and even when anonymous, the writer can ask in response, 'what do you mean by that?', and a discussion might follow.

Figure 10.25 The revision stage

This student writer has just started a self-review.

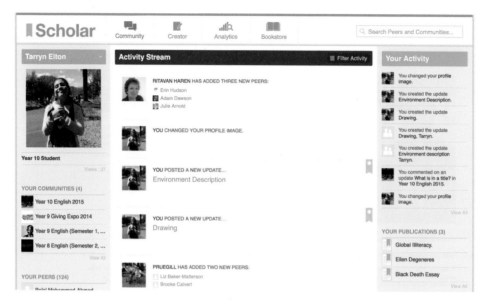

Figure 10.26 An e-Portfolio
See links to 'Your Publications' on the right-hand side of the screen.

Figure 10.27 At the 'Create' school

See literacies.com Web Writing in Practice

Writing as a complex cognitive and social learning process

Learning to write is not simply a five-stage linear process, starting with a plan and ending with a published work. It is socially, linguistically and cognitively much more complex than that. Indeed, writing is a multifaceted dialectic, a series of backwards-and-forwards plays between the individual writer and social dialogue about the work; the text itself and reflection on the design elements of the text; and cognition and metacognition, or thinking about thinking. We have provided examples of some of these plays in Table 10.6. In the Scholar writing environment, by way of example, we have the writer's individual work on the left and social

Table 10.6: Phases in the writing process

	Social writing	Metalanguage, design grammar	Cognition and metacognition
Phase 1: *Plan*	Thinking about my writing ↔ researching social sources for my writing	Creating notes and an outline ↔ working with a rubric that explicitly names the design features of an effective and powerful text	Rough draft that addresses a specific topic or themes ↔ thinking in general terms about that text type or kind of disciplinary practice that is represented in writing (e.g. writing science or history)
Phase 2: *Draft*	My writing ↔ change suggestions from computer checking tools	Drafting the text ↔ reflection about text type with the help of a rubric	Writing about something ↔ thinking about how to think about that something
Phase 3: *Review*	Looking at other people's writing ↔ offering them feedback	Reading a text ↔ structured reflection and feedback on the text using a rubric	Reading something substantive (on an information topic, a story) ↔ commentary on the underlying thinking
Phase 4: *Revise*	Looking at my own writing ↔ reflecting on peer and/or teacher feedback	My own writing ↔ analysis of commentary by others expressed in terms of design analysis	Revising my thinking as reflected in the draft ↔ considering others' thinking about my thinking.
Phase 5: *Publish*	Looking at my finished version ↔ writing a self-review; also, reading published texts ↔ discussion of published texts	Finished writing ↔ reflections on the design process	My thinking, revised ↔ self-reflection on how my thinking developed

↔ stands for the recursive relationship between the two, connected learning actions.

dialogue about the work on the right; we have the text on the left and consideration of the design of the text on the right; and we have cognition (the specific topic or theme in the text) on the left and metacognition, or thinking theoretically and abstractly on the right.

In every phase, writing involves a complex social and cognitive play, illustrated in Table 10.7. These processes are recursive. Learning to write, one of the most complex of all human representations and cognitive capacities, is, phase by phase, a task learned by cycling backwards and forwards across the text as it develops. This process is enriched by social interaction involving feedback from a variety of perspectives.

Table 10.7: Social and cognitive interactions in writing

My writing, writing as an *individual* activity	*Social* dialogue and feedback around writing: e.g. peers and teachers
Something specific, the *empirical* thing I am writing about in a factual text, or the particular participants and setting in a narrative	Generalisations, or *theoretical* reflection: e.g. about the nature of writing, the disciplinary content of the writing.
Text	Explicit reflection on the *design* of the text
Cognition, or representations of concrete thinking (in narratives, arguments, information texts etc.)	*Metacognition,* or reflections on the conditions of knowing, processes of thinking and representing that thinking
These things happen on the *left–hand side* of the *Scholar* screen	On the *right-hand side* of the *Scholar* Screen you'll be able to find these social and cognitive plays happening many strong writing pedagogies

See literacies.com Learning Modules.

See literacies.com #edtech Literacies Applications.

Summary

Multiliteracies design analysis	Systemic-functional grammar	Transformational-generative grammar	Traditional grammar
What do the meanings refer to? (To refer)	Ideational meaning (field)		Parts of speech
How do the meanings connect the people in the action and the people who are communicating? (To dialogue)	Interpersonal meaning (tenor)	Deep structures → particular meanings	Syntax
How does the overall meaning hold together? (To structure)	Textual meaning (mode)	Surface structures → particular meanings	Style
How are the meanings shaped by where they are located? (To situate)	Context and culture		Pragmatics
Whose purposes and interests are these meanings designed to serve? (To intend)	Culture Purpose		Rhetoric

Didactic writing pedagogy	Authentic writing pedagogy	Functional writing pedagogy	Literacies pedagogy and design analysis
Traditional grammar: • Learning to apply grammar and spelling rules • Composition • Vocabulary building	**Process writing:** • Learning to write by doing a lot of writing, without having to learn rules explicitly • Authentic text production	**Genre pedagogy:** • Explicit teaching of knowledge about genre, text and grammar through cycles of building field, deconstruction, modelling and independent construction of text	**Design elements:** Being able to name and consider the meaning choices you make as you write Writing process: 1. *Plan* 2. *Draft* 3. *Review* 4. *Revise* 5. *Publish*

Knowledge processes

experiencing the known

1. In terms of the writing pedagogies described in this chapter, how would you describe your own experience of learning to write? Which approaches have you personally found most effective?

experiencing the new

2. Read a highly scripted 'direct instruction' writing lesson. What do you find appealing or alienating about this approach to learning to write?

analysing critically

3. Debate the proposition that an authentic approach to writing (e.g. process writing) is the most effective path to early writing for (low-progress) students from poor and disadvantaged families. In preparation, read sample texts of proponents of both sides in this debate.

conceptualising by naming

4. As you work through this chapter, keep a running log of concepts about language. Define these concepts in a glossary. Perhaps this could take the form of a collaborative wiki, in which different students:

   a. name and define a concept
   b. provide examples
   c. suggesting teachable moments when this concept might be used in learning to write.

conceptualising with theory

5. Create a concept map linking the terms defined in the previous activity.

analysing functionally

6. Take a paragraph of written text. In groups of four, have one person apply the concepts of traditional grammar, transformational-generative grammar, systemic-functional grammar and multiliteracies design analysis to the text. Now compare the results. What insights can be gained from each approach? What aspects of each approach would be more or less useful for students learning to write?

applying appropriately

7. Develop a lesson plan that illustrates the way the concepts of design analysis can be used to help explain the way a written text serves its purposes. This could be a peer-reviewed learning module created in Scholar.

CHAPTER 11

Making visual meanings

Overview

This chapter explores the ways in which we make **visual meanings**. It offers a design analysis of the visual mode for the purposes of literacies learning and teaching. We will refer to two types of visual meanings or images. Perceptual images are the things that you see with your body's eye – your vision. Mental images are the things you see in your mind's eye – your envisionings. The world does not just present itself for us to simply see. Our minds make visual sense of the world through what we call perceptual imaging. We can also envision things that we cannot for the moment see by using our imaginations. Growingly aware babies make sense of the world first by seeing it and making mental images, only later learning words for what they see. Those without sight do the same thing through what they hear and feel. In fact, all humans work with mental images of the world. In this chapter, we outline the similarities and differences between visual images and language. The similarities in these two symbolic ways of making meaning allow us to refer to the same things in language or in a visual image. There are also important differences. Visual images and words can never be quite the same. This chapter also gives examples of classrooms in which teachers engage their learners in meaning-making texts that move between images and writing. These experiences highlight the power of synaesthesia, the process of shifting from one mode to another, and integrated, multimodal learning.

Visual meanings: Meanings made through images

Visual representation and communication

Word and image: making the connections

Written meaning has been privileged over visual meaning for a long while. Writing has certainly been regarded as more powerful than image since the rise of print culture and mass-institutionalised schooling. This situation began to change in the 20th century with the rise of new media, including photography, photolithographic printing, radio and television. In its own way, each of these media offered an alternative or supplement to writing as a way of recording meanings and communicating messages across distances.

In the second half of the 20th century, there were repeated laments about a supposed decline in reading, which was attributed to the rise of visual media, such as television and comics, along with pleas to return to books. Children learned the superiority of writing over image as they progressed from the 'picture books' for early readers to 'chapter books'. Apparently, more advanced readers no longer needed visual prompts in the form of illustrations. Older children may have chosen in their free time to read images connected with text in popular media, such as comics, but comics would never be used for literacy work in school. Picture books and comics were frowned upon as a limited, educationally unhelpful alternative to 'real reading'. As children worked their way through school, the disciplines of literacy and art became more and more rigidly separated. Literacy was regarded as essential and more 'academic', while the subject of 'art' was optional and oriented more to the acquisition of craft or trade skills.

See literacies.com Kress and van Leeuwen on Images and Writing.

Meanwhile, in some of the most influential academic theories of human communication and society, a parallel sentiment was expressed through the 'linguistic turn', in which language was taken to frame everything in our worlds of meaning and social interaction (Rorty 1992). In this view, all that is meaningfully real in the world is so because it is named or labelled by language. Language creates all meaning. Our consciousness is considered to be structured like a language. As a consequence, our higher cognitive functions, such as reasoning and problem-solving, are thought to be exclusively shaped by and expressed through language; for instance, as we categorise things by naming them with words and make connections between words through the linguistic logic of syntax. That is, something only exists meaningfully from a human perspective when it is named in language.

See literacies.com Arnheim on the Neglect of Images.

A number of aspects of our contemporary social and communications environments suggest we should now redress this longstanding bias towards written language. One factor we have discussed at various places in this book is the intrinsic multimodality of everyday communications in the era of digital media. Indeed, we may now be entering an era that W. J. T. Mitchell (1986) calls 'a pictorial turn'. Another factor is the greater effectiveness of a literacies pedagogy that supports shifting between different modes, or synaesthesia.

See literacies.com Mitchell on the 'Pictorial Turn'.

In this chapter we discuss how we mean in and through images, using the same framework for design analysis that we applied to written language in the previous chapter. We want to show how we can mean the same things in language and image. A word and a picture might refer to the same mountain or the same person, for instance. In Table 11.1, we apply the same design analysis to visual meanings that we introduced for written meanings in Chapter 10 (Table 10.4). To see the parallels, compare these two tables.

See literacies.com Kalantzis and Cope, Analysing the Designs of Images.

We examine some challenging aspects of the theory of images and the psychology of perception, focusing on the differences as well as the similarities between making meaning using images and making meaning using text. But first, some practical examples of multimodal learning in classrooms where teachers are successfully bringing together written and visual meanings.

Multimodal literacies

Pip teaches in Year/Grade 6 at a small rural school. Many of the children in her class come from relatively poor families. We see here how multimodal literacy learning has entered her classroom and, in particular, how she links writing with image-making to enable her students to understand the way texts were designed, as well as what they mean.

To engage their full attention for the challenging literacy goals she has set, she develops a sequence of 22 lessons in which students create interest-based 'passion projects'. One student chooses dance, and another chooses trucks. She has the students create websites about their projects, and eventually publishes articles about their passions into a class newspaper. Guided by the instructional framework she has chosen – the Multiliteracies pedagogy – they research their chosen topics in depth, going to a wide variety of sources: reading books, searching the World Wide Web, bringing materials from home. Together they examine the **visual design** of websites, contrasting them with the design of books and creating concept maps that capture the main presentational concepts in web design. She also has the students consider the design of newspapers (masthead, dateline, byline, captions, images, diagrams), comparing print and online editions (Kalantzis, Cope & Cloonan 2010: 76–84).

Visual design: The process of creating visual meanings, combining various visual design elements

Table 11.1: A grammar of visual meaning

Reference
What do the meanings refer to?
	• How have *particular things*, such as people, places, actions, processes and objects, been depicted by using:
	
	  ◦ line? (outline, defining features, length, angle, intersection, direction).
	  ◦ form? (shape, size, volume).
	  ◦ colour? (hue, density or brightness/dullness, tone or lightness/darkness).
	  ◦ Answer these questions:
	  ◦ What persons are referred to – *who?* (e.g. a cartoon of a particular person)
	  ◦ What places are referred to – *where?* (e.g. on a map, in a photograph)
	  ◦ What times are referred to – *when?* (e.g. the hands of a clock, day/night, seasons, auras of the future/contemporary/historical, timelines and charts)
	  ◦ Which objects of interest are referred to – *what?* (e.g. an advertisement for a gym, a diagram of leg muscles)
	
	• How have *general concepts* or kinds of things been depicted? (e.g. an icon such as a plane on a 'to the airport' sign, a diagram showing how something-in-general works, such as a human heart)
	
	• How have the *characteristics* of these things been depicted, including:
	
	  ◦ qualities? (e.g. perspective and proportion tells of 'large', blurring tells of 'fast')
	  ◦ quantities? (e.g. numbers, one/some/many, less/more/most)
	
	• How have the *relations* between things been depicted, including:
	
	  ◦ part/whole?
	  ◦ possession? (an attribute or something owned)
	  ◦ proximity? (e.g. near/far, juxtaposition/separation)
	  ◦ similarity/dissimilarity? (e.g. sameness/contrast, continuity/discontinuity)

Dialogue
How do the meanings connect the people who are interacting?
	• How are people or things *connected as actors* in the image:
	
	  ◦ by the *placement* of picture elements? (e.g. centre/margins, foreground/background, actor/goal, eyelines in images of people, focal planes of detachment/engagement)
	  ◦ by the depiction of *movement and change?* (e.g. trajectories, vectors, direction, interaction between picture elements, cause/effect)
	
	• How is *the viewer connected* to the image by:
	
	  ◦ the *kind of message?* (e.g. information sign versus a command sign)
	  ◦ the *positioning of the viewer?* (e.g. perspective, angles, vanishing points, framing, degree of detachment/involvement, such as eyelines of pictured people in relation to the viewer)

(continued)

Table 11.1: A grammar of visual meaning (*continued*)

Structure *How does the overall meaning hold together?*	• How are the picture elements *arranged?* (e.g. composition, foregrounding/backgrounding, framing or defining edges) • How is the image *sectioned?* (e.g. left/right; top/bottom, centre/margin, dispersed/centred focus) • How do the picture elements form *an integrated whole?* (e.g. similarities/contrasts, regularity/irregularity, symmetry/asymmetry, perspective and translating three dimensions into two) • What does the image *point out?* (e.g. prominence, figure/ground) • *How realistically* are ideas or information are depicted in the image? (e.g. naturalistic or realistic depictions of concrete things versus caricature; sketch or diagram versus iconic or abstract representation of ideas or feelings) • How are images *chained?* (e.g. in an exhibition, a comic, the pictures in a children's storybook, a slideshow, a video) • How do *media* shape the image? (e.g. production and reproduction materials and technologies: brushstrokes in a painting, lines in a drawing, the viewfinder of a camera)

Situation
How are the meanings shaped by the context of their location?
	• What is the *location* of the image, how does it point to its surroundings, and how do its surroundings point to it? (e.g. the painting in the gallery, the map in the travel guidebook book)
	  ◦ What *visual references* does the image use:
	  ◦ to *things in the world?* (e.g. visual analogies, metaphors, imagery)
	  ◦ to *other images?* (e.g. style conventions, motifs from other images, remixing, collage)
	• What is the *genre* of the image, or similarities with a type or style or method of image making? (e.g. abstract expressionist painting, documentary film making)

Intent
Whose interests do these meanings serve?
	• What is the *position of the image-maker?*
	  ◦ What is the *stance* of the image-maker? (e.g. foregrounding-backgrounding, how the image is designed to make its point)
	  ◦ What has the image-maker *included and excluded?* (e.g. framing and perspective that includes some things and leaves other things out, selective presentation of visual information)
	  ◦ Whose *interests* does the image support? (e.g. an advertiser selling something or a scientist trying to persuade using a diagram depicting scientific facts)
	• What is the *position of the viewer?*
	  ◦ How does the image-maker attempt to *engage* or get the attention of the viewer? (e.g. where the viewers might be when they see the image, what they might be expected to notice first, the mental images they may be expected to bring to the image)
	  ◦ Where is the *viewer placed* (e.g. power perspectives, such as looking up/looking down, appearances of objectivity and truth claims in the form of direct frontal or perpendicular views, such as plans and plans)
	  ◦ What *interpretation* does the image suggest for the viewer? (e.g. the positioning of the viewer, things constructed as more/less salient, the purpose or argument of the image)

Figure 11.1 Pip's passion project class

Here is Pip reflecting on the students' experience:

> We've got a wide range of children within this room ... Not all children have access
> to a computer at home, so there's been lots of planning for that concept naming and
> being able to understand that this is a 'hyperlink', or this is a 'font' ... identifying
> these features and concepts that they need to be able to use and need to be able to
> name ... being able to articulate what the concept is and then learn what does this
> do ... The critical analysis has been a really big part of looking at the webpages [and]
> newspapers for example and identifying features, they've been quite critical as to
> why they've chosen a particular background colour or animation, or does that font
> work with that particular coloured background. The children are very good at that
> now and they use the language very easily, very comfortably ... We've applied what
> we've learnt in creating our own web pages, each child now has their own personal
> profile, which is on the school intranet ... including the hyperlink to their passion
> project (Cloonan 2010a: 213).

Pip is describing a deceptively different world from that of traditional literacy
learning: similar insofar as there is still a good deal of reading and writing to be
done, but different, too, as students develop a way to describe and apply the visual
as well as textual design of multimodal texts.

 See literacies.com Pip's Website Work.

Now we're in Sue Gorman's Year/Grade 3 class, where the children are viewing
and reading Ursula Dubsoarsky's book *Rex*. They look at the cover of the book and,
in a Think-Pair-Share activity, predict what it might be about (Rex is a colourful lizard). They look for lizard videos on the Web. They explore 'picturing' words as they
read the book and look at the pictures. They compare close-up pictures with long
shots, and different angles in pictures. They take some photos (Figure 11.2). Then

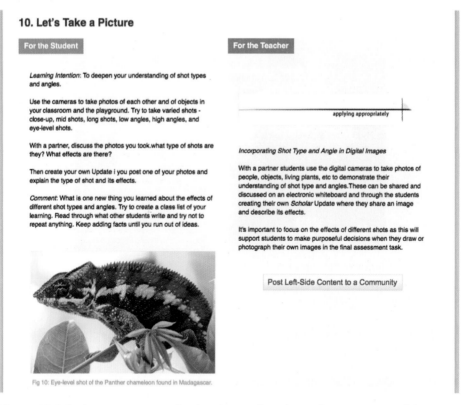

10. Let's Take a Picture

For the Student

Learning Intention: To deepen your understanding of shot types and angles.

Use the cameras to take photos of each other and of objects in your classroom and the playground. Try to take varied shots - close-up, mid shots, long shots, low angles, high angles, and eye-level shots.

With a partner, discuss the photos you took. what type of shots are they? What effects are there?

Then create your own Update i you post one of your photos and explain the type of shot and its effects.

Comment: What is one new thing you learned about the effects of different shot types and angles. Try to create a class list of your learning. Read through what other students write and try not to repeat anything. Keep adding facts until you run out of ideas.

For the Teacher

applying appropriately

Incorporating Shot Type and Angle in Digital Images

With a partner students use the digital cameras to take photos of people, objects, living plants, etc to demonstrate their understanding of shot type and angles. These can be shared and discussed on an electronic whiteboard and through the students creating their own *Scholar* Update where they share an image and describe its effects.

It's important to focus on the effects of different shots as this will support students to make purposeful decisions when they draw or photograph their own images in the final assessment task.

Post Left-Side Content to a Community

Fig 10: Eye-level shot of the Panther chameleon found in Madagascar.

Figure 11.2 Exploring camera angles (Rex by Ursula Dubosarsky Learning Module, Scholar)

they begin to write a factual text about something quite different, a recount in a week of their life, using picturing language and including images that use different camera angles and perspectives to describe things in different ways.

 See literacies.com van Haren and Gorman, 'Rex' by Ursula Dubosarsky.

Moving on to a Year/Grade 5 class, the students are focusing on the differences between information and narrative texts. Their starting point is *Wolves*, by Emily Gravett. Here's a narrative perspective: A wolf has a spine-tingling howl. A beautifully drawn picture captures the feeling perfectly. Here is a fact from an information website: 'A wolf is a hunter.' A photograph of a wolf illustrates it hunting. The students research wolves online. They read Emily Gravett's charming book. They compare and contrast the similarities and differences between the ways in which words and images are used to support narratives and information texts. They then choose a story text (such as book they like or know well) and write an illustrated information text that addresses the same theme as the story (Figure 11.3).

 See literacies.com van Haren and Gorman, Can a Wolf and a Rabbit Live Happily Ever After?

8. Project Information and Draft: A Multimodal Text

For the Student

Fig. 8: Wolf Love

Learning Intention: To start my writing project and to use the rubric to identify what is important to include.

Project Name: Weaving an Information Text into a Picture Book

Description: Find a narrative/picture book. Perhaps it could be a favorite one from when you were younger. You could also go to the library and find one. Think about the main topic that it covers and research information that could accompany it. Then write an information text to align with the images in the picture book.

This where you start your writing project by checking your Notifications and clicking on the "Work Request". The link will take you to Creator where you can start writing. Clicking on the "Work Request" is very important so that the work that you create is connected to the project that your teacher has set up.

You should look in the "About This Work" to find out more information

For the Teacher

applying appropriately

When we ask students to apply their knowledge through a report, essay, PPT or multimedia presentation, or in the case of this writing project, to create an information text, they have to be able to move beyond responding, to creating and becoming knowledge producers. "Analysing functionally" and "Analysing critically" provides them with the tools to do this.

Negotiate the task with students as they may have some original ideas on how they could innovate on the text. Support students to research their topics by providing access to electronic and print based resources. Story boards might also provide another scaffold.

As students begin to draft their work, encourage them to use the Structure Tool to organize and outline their texts. The images in the picture book should help them to create an outline. The Structure Tool supports students to develop an initial structure for their text, including notes based on their background knowledge. As they continue to research, they add more notes, refine the elements of their text, and draft new versions, transforming their notes into well written text.

Students should also refer to the rubric as a guide as they write in Creator. If necessary, look through the rubric with students.

For first time users of *Scholar*, the following Overt Instruction Updates from *The Writer's Toolkit: Strategies for Writing in the New Media* may be useful to post to Community:

- How to Write in Scholar
- Using the Rubric and Checker
- Planning Using the Structure Tool

Figure 11.3 Writing an information text, inspired by a story (Wolves Learning Module, Scholar)

Next, to Prue Gill's Year/Grade 8 class, where students are exploring haiku poetry. They read and view the picture book *Wabi Sabi* by Mark Reibstein with artwork by Ed Young. The learners research the design features of the genres of 'haibun' and 'haiku'. They compare literal and inferential meanings, in the text as well as in the images. They explore concepts of harmony, balance and colour in both text and image (Figure 11.4). Finally, they write and illustrate a haiku poem.

See literacies.com van Haren and Gill, Wabi Sabi: Intercultural Meaning Making.

Perceptual and mental images

Words and images

Words, phrases and sentences collect, represent and communicate our thoughts. So do images, but in a different way. We want to explore the parallels between linguistic concepts and visual concepts and also the differences, starting with representation (when we make sense of what we see in the world) and following with

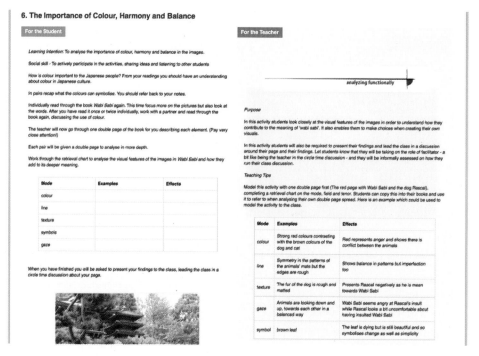

Figure 11.4 Colour, harmony and balance in text and image (Wabi Sabi Learning Module, Scholar)

communication (the visual messages we may choose to create in order to express our meanings).

An image is a visual likeness, a resemblance to some thing, idea or feeling. You might say to yourself: 'I've seen this mountain or that person before, in my real-life experience, or in an image presented to me that I have interpreted to be this mountain or that person. It is also a difference, a distinction I have made between mountain and sea, person and animal, or this mountain and that other mountain, and this person and that other person.'

After a while, a young child learns about the qualities of 'mountain-ness' or 'animal-ness' so that, when they encounter a mountain or animal like none other they have seen before, they are able to recognise what it is because they have developed a visual concept of mountain or animal. So far, images are working very much like language. The child is making sense of the world, doing some cognitive or thinking work on the world, and the result in representational terms is a meaning. It is revealing that the word 'idea' comes from the Greek word 'to see', underlining the very close connection between conceptualising and visualising (Mitchell 1986: 5).

We want to make a fundamental distinction between two kinds of visual representation or making visual meaning for oneself: *perceptual images* (seeing things with the body's eye, or 'vision'), and *mental images* (seeing things in the mind's eye, or 'envisioning').

Perceptual images

Perceptual images involve a direct, material and bodily encounter with meanings in the world. Light passes through the eye's cornea and lens, projecting an inverted image onto the retina at the back of the eye. In the human eye, 60 or more different types of cells process many types of optical information. One and a half million cells connect these receptors into the optic nerve. A person's field of focused vision is quite small, centred on a part of the retina where the photoreceptor cells – specialised cells that detect light – are most dense. Six muscles rotate the eyeball in a number of distinct patterns, 100 000 times per day, taking one small jump at a time and then coming to a stop to focus – making several such jumps across every line when reading, for instance. However, you do not see with your eyes. You see with your brain.

Perceptual images: Making sense of something that is immediately seen

Tiny electrical impulses from the optic nerve reach 100 cell types in an area of the brain called the visual cortex, selectively responding to colour, depth, space, motion, orientation and other aspects of vision. From here, signals are carried all over the brain, with different kinds of information being combined and recombined in 100 or more locations across the brain to create a single percept (the mental image of this mountain, or that person). Cognitive scientists call this mental interconnectedness 'binding'. The process takes time, probably about a quarter of a second to see a recognisable object that has just entered one's perceptual field.

Why do we see this mountain or that person? The world does not simply present itself to us. It requires our selective attention. There is always so much around us that we cannot take it all in. So we have learned to focus on what matters to our purposes in each moment. For example, we do not see each tree on the mountain or every hair on the person's head, though of course we could focus on one tree or one hair if that proved to be of interest to us. In other words, to see meaningfully we need to choose what we think we need to see, or want to see. We need to get ourselves to a scene, then choose a sequence of focal points for attention among the infinite range of possibilities in that scene (Koch 2004).

In his analysis of the psychology of pictorial representation, Gombrich (1960 (2000): xxvii, 5, 7) explains that, without the filtering device of selective attention, we would be overwhelmed by the stimulae in every scene and every image. Sartre (1940 (2004): 9) calls this an 'overflowing in the world of things', an 'inexhaustible richness' in what can be seen in any field of perception at any one time. This is why our visual attention has to be selective. Seeing is a process of choosing parts of what we can see, and directing our attention to these. We look out for things that are going to be meaningful to us. We only notice things that are meaningful. For this moment of seeing, the rest of what might have been seen is practically irrelevant. It remains unnoticed. This is how visual perception may be considered to be understood as an act of cognition – a mental process of knowing. Our attention may be considered to be an intention to see, an attentional interest, a kind of agency.

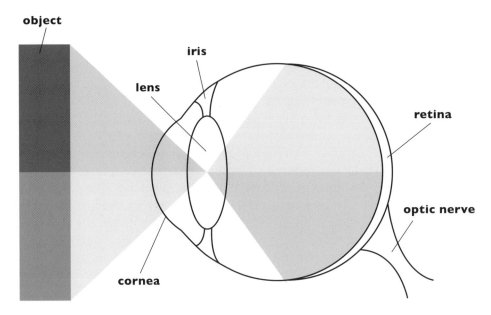

Figure 11.5 Human vision

Visual perception is a process of making things out using one's eyes and brain. It is also a complex cultural process, only possible when you have learned the arts of perceptive attention of your culture. That is, your culture teaches you what to look out for.

Take the strange cultural idea of a car, something inconceivable before the 20th century. It must have wheels – an essential characteristic of 'carness' – but from the front or the rear the wheels may not be visible as distinctively round objects. However, although it looks totally different from a car side-on, you are still able to see it as a car (Figure 11.6). It may be close or a long way away, but whichever

Figure 11.6 The idea of a car

it is, we adjust our vision to fit our expectations about the usual size of cars. We may look at a model car very close up and large, while nevertheless knowing we can't drive in it. Have a look at the images in Figure 11.7, from classic texts on the psychology of perception, and consider the ways in which visual meaning is made from these images based on the pre-existing visual meanings you as a viewer bring to the process of perception.

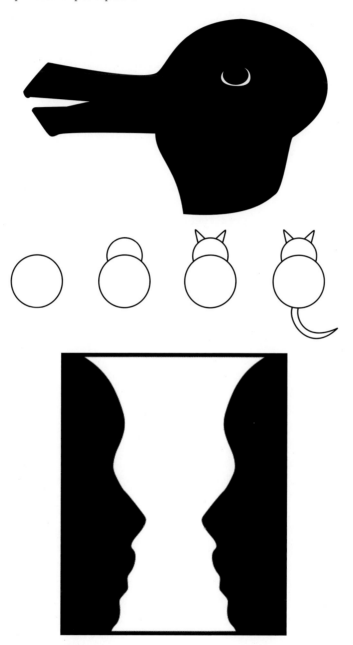

Figure 11.7 The psychology of perception. A duck or a rabbit? When does a circle become a cat? Figure and ground: a vase or two faces?

Children learn to see objects such as cars, ducks, rabbits and cats and get to know what they are and do before they have words for these objects. Vision is not what we see, as if the world could simply present itself to us. It is what we learn to see because we have made the things we see meaningful to ourselves. We learn vision before we learn language and, as a consequence, language is to a substantial degree a creature of vision. Language is layered on top of vision.

As babies, before we even learn our first words, we experience a vast and multi-dimensional world of meaningful visual perceptions. Our first thinking is visual. We learn to see people, things, movements, colours, spaces and distances. Human babies learn to see – they are not born with all their visual abilities. In the first two months of life, babies learn to narrow their focus to see one particular thing at a time, to separate it as a distinguishable thing from all else they can see. People born blind and whose vision has been restored by surgery as adults cannot see, because it is too late for them to learn to see in a way that distinguishes meaningful things in their field of vision. We can only learn at a young age the profound and complex cognitive capacity that is visual perception. Blind people use other resources to form mental images that make sense of the world to them, which they learn to align with sighted people's mental images.

Perception is a mental act of recognition and a process of making a judgement about what exists in a field of vision. How, then, do we make sense when we see? We see things that resemble other things (this mountain is not that mountain but it has some common characteristics of mountain-ness). We see things because they are different from other things (where this mountain meets the sea). We see things because they are near other things (a mountain makes sense in contrast to the sky). We may group what we see when the things we are seeing are visually continuous, and separate them when they are discontinuous. We see shapes that have an inside and an outside. We may see proximity as a kind of belonging (for instance, I can see you close by me, driving in the same car), and distance as a kind of not belonging (I can see you in the distance, near the mountain, getting into a car). None of these things simply exist to be seen. We have learned from our experience that these are meaningful visual distinctions to make. They work for us, preventing us from getting run over by cars and helpfully allowing us to distinguish mountains from people.

Just because we have had to learn to see these things, it does not mean they are figments of our perceptual imaginations. They really, materially exist. In fact, it is a peculiarity of visual perception, and one that makes it quite unlike language, that the thing we are seeing has to be present for us both internally to our bodies (our seeing) and externally in material reality at the same time (something seen). There has to be an external visible object for us to be able to see it; and we can only see it because we are able to make some sort of internal cognitive sense of what we are seeing.

Not that what we see is necessarily true. Our bodily experience tells us that, much of the time, our perceptual cognition serves us well. Sometimes, however, our continued attentive perception tells us that our initial perceptions should be changed when we fail to notice something that turns out to be important, or when our senses seem to play tricks on us, or when someone creates a deceptive or distorted visual effect in order to pursue their interests. For example, we think we see our friend walking by and then we realise it only looked like our friend because of their shape and size, but it was really a stranger. Or we thought a bowl of creamy white substance was ice-cream and, but then discover it is frozen yogurt once we taste it.

Mental images

Mental images are very different from perceptual images. They are images of things you can't for the moment see. Of course, mental images often have a common ground in perceptual images because they come from memories of perception. You can use mental images to recall to mind this mountain when you're no longer there, or that person now they are no longer with you. You can only do this because you remember this mountain and that person as former perceptual experiences.

Mental images: Images in a person's mind of things that they can't for the moment see

The cognitive processes for the formation of mental images are completely different from perceptual images. And what you can do with them is different. This mountain is not visible now because you're not there anymore. This person is not with you at the moment. But you can remember having seen that person. Or you may have never seen them in person, but you have seen their picture. Or, even more remarkably, you can envision them without ever having seen them or a picture of them, just from words that describe them. This is what happens as you read a novel that graphically describes a 'tall, serious-looking woman, wearing a bright red coat'. You can imagine by conjuring up a mental image that does not exist in reality. But you cannot see things that do not exist in visible reality. This is a fundamental difference between perceptual and mental images.

See literacies.com McGinn on Seeing with the Body's Eye and the Mind's Eye.

Perceptual images can only happen in the present. However, mental images can recall the past. As mental images become the stuff of memory, they can consist of a 'still' image (a matter of simultaneity, things that exist together in a mental image) or a 'moving' sequence of images (which are episodic or temporal, visualising things one after another, such as a walk through a park). Memory of mental images allows us to relive the past in our minds. However, these images are necessarily a reduced, abbreviated and altered version of the past. They consist of only those things you have paid attention to. There is always more to be seen in a perceptual image, but a mental image begins and ends with what you can recall (Koch 2004: 187, 194).

The object of perceptual images is present (the mountain is actually in front of you or a person is actually with you), but the object of mental images is absent (the person or mountain is only a memory). In perceptual images you can always look further into things you have so far left unattended. You notice a particular tree on the mountain or a hair on the person's head that all of a sudden catches your attention. But in mental images you can only see things that are focal to your interest, intention and attention. Perception can be informative, because you can always discover new seeable things. However, although mental images can present no new information, you can still reanalyse the information you have already committed to memory. Visual perceptions try to insist on their real-world truthfulness, but mental images are the stuff of a greater speculative tentativeness, a kind of reflective wondering. These are very different types of meaning agency. They entail different kinds of meaning-engagement with the world (McGinn 2004: 19–29).

Table 11.2: Perceptual compared to mental images

Perceptual images	Mental images
• Seeing things with the body's eye	• Envisioning things with the mind's eye
• Finding meaning in a scene	• Creating meaning from memory
• Selective attention, seeing some aspects of a scene whose actual, seeable aspects are infinite	• Being only able to see what you recall in your mind's eye, an abbreviated and selective version of reality
• Happening in the here and now	• Recalls the past
• Focusing attention on a present object	• Focusing attention on an absent object
• A mental act of recognition	• Mental act of remembering and imagining
• The real world	• Imagination and speculation

Imagination

Because mental images refer to a world that does not presently exist within the immediate field of vision of the meaning-maker, they allow us to imagine. In this way, to use Sartre's terms, our consciousness is able to free itself in part from a particular, momentary, spatially confined reality (Sartre 1940 (2004)). This, he argues, is the psychological and anthropological basis of human freedom, from the smallest freedoms to shift attention (for instance, to look at something else in your field of vision) or to move in a space or to undertake an action (such as picking something up) – all the way through to the largest freedoms to envision different worlds, utopias even.

 See literacies.com Sartre on the Imaginary.

So we can see there are some very significant differences between perceptual and mental images. No such fundamental distinction can be made about meaning-work using language. Language is made of very similar symbolic and mental stuff, whether we directly encounter it (through hearing or reading) or use it to think. Seeing is closely connected to the world; mental images are what you have left in your mind when you are not seeing something. Words are always like mental images. They are never like seeing. Wherever language is encountered, or however it is used by the human mind, it is always one step removed from the reality to which it refers. Language is always an abstract symbol system made up of mental concepts. Images, however, can be both things that are seen and mental concepts. While mental images are like language in some respects, perceptual images are the product of a direct engagement with the material world. That is, the mental image of mountain is not the mountain itself, but its memory in the mind. Similarly, the word 'mountain' only makes sense if you remember that it is the label for the real thing in the world.

Why do we need to know these distinctions? It is vital to understand that written language is not natural in any way. It is a human artefact. It has been produced for a purpose at a particular time in human history, and in the scale of our species' existence, not so long ago. In our times, the visual is assuming a new significance as a way of expressing meaning. This is why we are concerned to explore 'literacies' in the plural. To us, as literacies educators, the everyday and human-cognitive parallels and differences between written and visual meanings are of utmost importance.

The visual design process

Visual communication

Visual communication is a process of image-making, in which we create images for use in our interactions with others. Communication occurs when others represent those meanings to themselves as a consequence of visual perception, or remember as mental images things they have seen. Paintings, photographs, pages, advertisements, diagrams, drawings, maps, plans of buildings and computer screens are all examples of visual communication.

> **Visual communication:** An image that has been made to communicate a meaning with another person

Several things make visual communications in some ways like mental images. The image-maker is never able to represent the whole world that had been in their visual field, the original seeing upon which their image is based. They offer instead a perspective, based on the interest that shaped their original visual perception, what they saw as a result of their attentional focus, their way of seeing. Visual images are inevitably selective. They are always partial and incomplete pictures of what can be seen in a visual field. The photographer frames an image, deliberately leaving some things out while attentively including other things. The painter does not capture every detail in a scene, just those that will make their visual point. Sometimes the image-maker's visual point is the most abstract of feelings or general expression of an idea. The cartoonist captures only the distinctive features of a person's face or body, and the barest minimum at that. The plan of a building captures only the way objects are related and the dimension of a defined space.

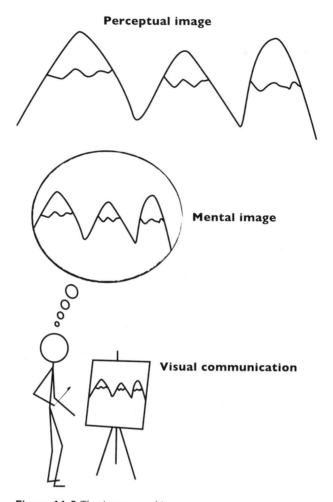

Perceptual image

Mental image

Visual communication

Figure 11.8 The image-making process

Visual communications are in these respects very like mental images. Often, in fact, pictures are created not from life and immediate perception, but from mental images – hence the envisioning of a yet-to-be-constructed building in a plan and rendering, or a painting of an imagined place. Even the life portraitist works from a sequence of mental images, looking up to see, then painting the canvas on the basis of their immediately preceding mental image or memory. Or the photographer is motivated to frame a scene in a particular way by a mental image of the photograph they want to create. In this sense, visual communications are not just reproductions of a person's visual perceptions. They are also acts of envisioning, acts of **imagination**.

Imagination: A capacity to create mental images of possible as well as actual things

Later on, a viewer may come onto the scene. They encounter the work of visual communication as their perceptual image; a painting of the mountain, let's say. No matter how hard they look, they can never see everything that the creator of the object of visual communication left in their image, intentionally or unintentionally,

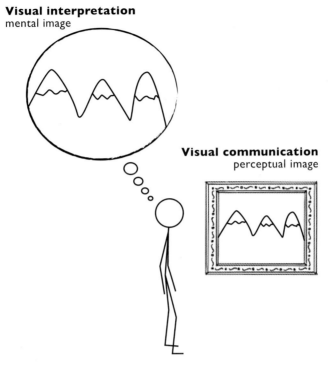

Figure 11.9 Visual communication and interpretation

not every brushstroke, not every little detail. In this sense, the image has the same overflowing fullness that all perception has. The viewer's inevitable perceptual selectivity shapes their interpretation, the sense they make of an image as they make sense of it for themselves.

As they can never see the whole picture at once, the viewer also follows a visual navigation path, looking at one point in the image then another, gathering information from the image as their eyes move around, from centre to margins, left to right, top to bottom, depending on their predispositions and habits of perception, or the aspects of the image that initially and then later attract their attention. This is how the viewer interprets an object of visual communication as a perceptual image. The viewer is always guided by the image-maker's selectivity. However, the viewer also uses their own selectivity and has to put in additional work if they are, using Gombrich's words, 'to collaborate with the artist and to transform a piece of coloured canvas into a likeness of the visible world' (Gombrich 1960 (2000): 290).

Then they look elsewhere, or they leave the perceptual field in which the image is present. Their interpretation remains with them as a mental image, with all the reductions and simplifications, and all the biases of selective interest that mental images inevitably entail. They remember something, but not everything, of the picture of the mountain. The image was selective in the first place, based on the image-maker's attentive interest. Now the viewer of the image adds another layer of selectivity, or interpretation of the image.

This does not mean, however, that meaning is arbitrary, and that I only ever see what I want to see and no more. Our sociable species is always interested in the other person's purposes. We want to appreciate what the artist is trying tell us about the mountain – after all, they seem to like that mountain so much that they took the trouble to paint it. We want to see things that others have seen, and at least get a sense of the way they have seen things. So we are always trying to interpret and understand what the meaning-designer intended because we want to understand who they are, what they are trying to tell us, and what they want with us. In these ways, looking at an image of a mountain is quite different from looking at a real mountain. Visual communication always involves this kind of person-to-person exchange of meaning. As we view the image, we are interpreting the person as much as we are interpreting the mountain.

Visual design

How, then, do we make visual meanings? The Multiliteracies notion of 'design' provides an alternative to older and simpler world-is-just-what-you-see theories of learning. These older theories suggest that the world presents itself to us through our sense of sight and that we simply learn what the world is from what we see. In such views, we are creatures of our sense perceptions. According to these theories, we know because of what we have seen. We are, humanly, what we have seen. This theory of knowledge is also called 'empiricism'. Human beings, in this view, are born empty vessels that get filled by the things they observe. Not that this is untrue; it's just that we take an active, perspective-filled interest in seeing. We are as much a product of our meaning-designing nature as we are products of what we have seen.

 See literacies.com John Locke on Empirical Knowledge.

The 'design' notion highlights the fact that, in every act of visual perception, and in the making of every mental image, we add something of ourselves. The artist sees aspects of a mountain she wants to communicate. The gallery-goer sees aspects of the artist's painting he thinks interesting or attractive.

 See literacies.com Gombrich on the Psychology of Imaging.

Developing the discussion we began in Chapter 8, we now explore how visual meanings are made, under three headings.

(Available) designs

We encounter visual designs, in nature and constructed by people. These appear in our perceptual fields every day, visual message-prompts that have been intentionally or unintentionally made for us in nature or by others. We use these as resources for visual representation. They shape our ways of seeing (visual representation) and ways of making images (visual communication). They create mental images for us that influence our subsequent seeings. They help our seeing as we learn to direct our attention in one way or another. They also provide us with media, methods, styles, habits and orders of value for the designing work we are about to do.

Designing

When we see, we create meanings for ourselves from the field of visual perception and our inherited repertoire of remembered visual designs. Our attention is drawn to certain things within the infinite detail of visible things in a visual field. Our attention wanders, from one thing to another, in a visual navigation path that we more or less consciously create by positioning our eyes and bodies. When we see, we design our meanings. No two people can ever see the same things in quite the same way. Every perceptual image is to some degree a unique product of our designing agency.

Then, once we are no longer there, our mental images remain. Another layer of agency is added to the selectivity of original perception: the selectivity of what we remember, or the reworking of these rememberings as we rethink what we saw, or even the imagination we create as we recombine resources for meaning to envision things that we know are not what we saw.

These can even be new envisionings of possible worlds. That is, we use visual resources for representation, making transformative meanings for ourselves. We may also apply these meanings for ourselves in the design of new images. This is also how mental images further transform the perceived world, and the perceiver.

 See literacies.com Merleau-Ponty on Perception and Imagination.

When, in human bodily existence, does meaning-as-design begin? Babies can see as soon as their images of the world come under their voluntary control. This is when they become meaning-agents, well before they can speak, let alone read or write. Babies learn to be meaning-designers when they see, and language adds new layers onto this initial cognitive experience, this first experience of themselves as meaning-makers. For example, they get to know their carers, the sight of food and the visible effects of grasping objects.

Not that our perceptions and images are stable, or that they don't need adjusting. When we see the world, it always a provisional 'seeing as'. As we do more seeing, we may want to revise our perceptions. As we reflect further on our mental images, we may want to revise our memories of what we thought we saw. Did our former perceptions, on careful reflection or re-seeing, serve us as well as they might? Were we influenced by mental images from our life experience in such a way that we did not see things that, on closer observation, we may have wanted to see from the start, but initially missed? Did our imagination produce illusions that proved to be delusions? Were the human-made images we encountered skewed to serve the interest of the visual communicator? Which visual resources produce what effects on which audiences? Might revision of our perceptions or mental images be warranted? This process of adjustment is the basis of learning, of making changes to the meanings we had formerly made, or supplementing these meanings as seems necessary.

(The re-)designed

Now visual experience and imagination re-enters the world. The transformations of perception and mental imaging find their way into the images we make.

Perception and mental images (visual representations) have resulted in the making of objects that re-enter the world of meaning when they appear in the perceptual field of others (visual communications).

These in turn become the objects of interpretation, leaving mental images that are available resources for the making of new visual meanings. In every act of visual meaning-making, the world is changed. These changes are the stuff of both teaching and learning.

Figure 11.10 Visual meaning-making

Visual design in the classroom

Children, Gunther Kress reminds us, learn to draw before they write, and writing is a kind of drawing (Kress 1997). Children's first designs of meaning on a page are images, and from here they progress to writing, a transition that is supported by image juxtaposed with writing.

Written language and image are two forms of visual representation that can reinforce one another to communicate messages, emotions or ideas. As children learn to make meaning in writing and images, they need to understand how visual elements create meaning in combination with language. They need to understand how visual and verbal meanings interact to complement each other in a text. They also need to understand how words and pictures can be juxtaposed to contradict,

Figure 11.11 Mama, Dada and me (two-year-old)

challenge or subvert one another, by separating and countering meaning. Many curricula around the world (e.g. Australia, Canada, Netherlands, Singapore, South Africa, United Kingdom and United States) include the interpretation of images in a broader concept of literacy that extends to reading, viewing and composing multi-modal texts. In the Australian Curriculum, for example, visual knowledge is a key aspect of literacy in content area learning, essential for:

> interpreting still and moving images, graphs, tables, maps and other graphic representations, and understanding and evaluating how images and language work together in distinctive ways in different curriculum areas to present ideas and information in the texts they compose and comprehend (ACARA 2015d).

Now, for some more examples of classrooms where knowledge of the visual is applied to the design of writing and visual images in literacies learning.

Mary Brennan is working with 25 first-graders as they design visual and written meanings about an issue in their local community. Mary gathers her children around her and shows her the front page of a newspaper. 'Grandma Ruth's' face gazes sadly; she is about to lose her house to a new development in the area. This is a design for meaning that she brings into the classroom as an 'available resource' for students' later learning.

'She looks very old and sad,' says one student. And another: 'Maybe she needs help. Maybe the photographer wants people to help her, so he made her look like she was staring at us, wanting us to talk to her.'

Here we find another powerful available resource for meaning – the visual meanings children bring to the class to support their understanding that the image represents 'old' and 'sad'. They even bring an interpretation of the kind of communicative interaction with the newspaper audience suggested by the way the photographer has designed the image.

The children are not just reading a story on the front page of a newspaper. They are also reading the story's defining image, and the interests of the photographer in framing the image the way she did. They are reading the gestural meanings in Grandma Ruth's bodily presentation in the image. The children bring with them, in other words, designs for visual meaning based on their previous understandings of images and the meanings they have made in their real-world visual experiences. These are a powerful resource for further learning.

Mary continues her questioning: 'Why do you think the photographer chose this particular picture? Why do you think it's on the front page of the paper right now, in December, right before the holidays?'

This is the beginning of a sequence of activities that eventually connect the class with the reporter who had written the story for the newspaper and with local government authorities.

The children research the issue further.

'Google it,' 'Click here,' 'You have to download first,' 'Bookmark it,' 'What's the Web address?' 'Where's the homepage?' and 'Look on the desktop.' The students become immersed in the hybrid text-image language of the screen as they immerse themselves in still more resources for meaning.

This prepares them to create multimodal images of their own, drawn and typed on the computer, voices of support for Grandma Ruth. Here we transition from immersion in available designs to the process of designing.

'We love Grandma Ruth and we care,' was Kenny's message. Lizzy said: 'Grandma Ruth should have a choice!'

Mary then puts all the images together into a PowerPoint presentation and sends it to the newspaper (Figure 11.12). The reporter writes back, telling the children how moved Grandma Ruth has been and how appreciative of receiving such wonderful support from the children and others who have written. Here the children's designs enter the world of 'the designed': visual and written meanings that are produced for the world and that may influence subsequent meanings in the world. The reporter promises she will email them when the next story is published, after the court hearing that is coming up in a few weeks (Crafton, Brennan & Silvers 2007: 512–14).

Half a world away, in a 'nursery' classroom for four-to-six-year-olds in Volos, Greece, a class is creating a multimodal text about water conservation. The students look at a newspaper article and a leaflet about water conservation, distributed by the local water supply company. These are available resources for meaning. As the students' designing work begins, they combine a number of modes of

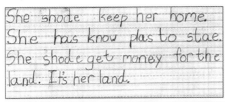

She shode keep her home.
She has know plas to stae.
She shode get money for the
land. It's her land.

Love. and care
we wish you had your home
We care
No t fair to you

Let her kepe it or give the mony to her. The
Gevmet said to rek it. Pipoale shode hlp her.

January 2005

Dear Ms. Spak,

We are a first grade class at XXXXX Elementary
School in XXXXX. We have been following your
stories about Grandma Ruth Molenkamp. In Social
Studies we have learned about needs and wants. We
understand that a home is a basic need for Grandma
Ruth. We also understand that basic needs for all of us
include love and care. We want to send a message to
Grandma Ruth that we care about her problem.

We are also learning about what it means to live in
a democracy and the responsibilities of being good
citizens. We are wondering why Grandma Ruth isn't
being given a choice. Why will she get a new house
if she wants her old one? Why is a developer going to
build her a new house and build other houses on her
land? It seems like all those houses should be hers. It
seems like a big problem. We do think it's a good thing
that people are trying to help. We are hoping that people
really listen to Grandma Ruth and care about her. We
do!

Sincerely,

Mrs. Brennan & the 1st-grade class in Room 17

Figure 11.12 Multimodal early literacies

meaning to create posters, including drawings, photographs, handwritten words
and typed and cut-out words.

Here are several of the posters they produced, expressing complex understandings visually. The first emotively opposes the presence or absence of water by jux-
taposing two panels describing each scenario (depicted in Figure 11.13). The second
shows ways in which water can be saved. The third is informative about the uses
of water. The children show they are able to read and write symbols, graphs, logos
and maps. The key motifs are 'water', coded blue, and 'life', coded green. They label
image with text in an informative way. These become complete and complex multimodal texts, remarkably sophisticated in their knowledge content and manipulation of communicative media for children not yet writing conventional sentences.
The finished works then enter the world as 'the designed', posted to the wall of the
classroom (Papadopoulou & Christidou 2004).

These are just two examples of classrooms where the design of writing and
visual images are brought together in the literacies learning process. To recap:

- Students are exposed to 'available designs' in the form of written and visual
  meanings.
- They do 'designing' as they create visual and written meanings of their own.
- And the products of their learning experiences are 'designed' multimodal
  texts that now enter the learner's world of experienced meanings.

Figure 11.13 Greek nursery school water poster

Visual design analysis

Making visual meaning

Visual meanings are not only one of the first designs of meaning that we learn as we represent the world to ourselves and learn to communicate. They are also closely connected with tactile modes (seeing things as you make sense of their feeling) and gestural modes (seeing meaningful bodily movements as made by others, and seeing your own gestures). You can only apprehend the spatial through perceptual images. Our existences are always and inevitably multimodal.

Reading and writing are also visual experiences, though as cognitive practices of representation and communicating, they are quite different from making meaning in images. However, to the extent that the sources of reading and writing are images, language frequently becomes a very image-like thing. We have very image-like writing – take, for instance, descriptions in words that attempt to portray something that is seen. We have metaphors, which are one way of describing a thing by the way it looks like something else. 'I have a mountain of work' uses a visual metaphor to conjure up the enormity of the tasks I have in front of me. Metaphors pack multifaceted meanings into a word or phrase that represents a mental image. The description or the metaphor is never quite like the perceptual image or the mental image, but it does the best that can be done in words to

Figure 11.14 Young child drawing

create an equivalent mental image. At these points, we find convenient locations for synaesthesia, or switching from one mode of meaning to another.

How, then, are meanings made in visual communications? What are the building blocks of visual meaning? In one sense, they are the same as the building blocks of all other modes of meaning. The same range of meanings that can be made in written or oral language can also be made in images. But the ways they are made are quite fundamentally different – so different, in fact, that visual meanings can only ever be roughly parallel to linguistic and other meanings.

Paths to synaesthesia: making connections between visual and other modes of meaning

Bringing image and other meanings into the literacies classroom

In a survey of the use of information and communications technologies to support early childhood Multiliteracies learning, Harrison, Lee, O'Rourke and Yelland

(2009) report that early childhood approaches that focus on literacy more narrowly understood as reading and writing, such as worksheets and phonics, tend to focus on children's individual needs and deficits, rather than their strengths. However, an approach that balances reading and writing with drama, dance, construction, visual arts and access to a range of digital technologies tends 'to see the children as curious, creative, capable and multiliterate with many existing experiences and skills that could be further extended at school' (at 471).

Rachel, a 'prep' or kindergarten teacher, reports to researcher Anne Cloonan about the ease with which younger learners were able to operate multimodally and synaesthetically:

> I've realised that I've made assumptions about the children's learning. I've realised that there are much deeper layers to learning, [such as] being aware before of visual literacies … I have found that I can look at it at a much deeper level, and I'd never have unpacked pictures to that level before, I'd never have dreamt of doing something like that with Prep children and what's really blown me away is that this age group of children are more able to take this on board than some of the children I work with in other areas of the school. I've worked with a literacy support group in [Years/Grades] 3 and 4 and I've tried to use the same ideas and it's harder for them to take on board. They've got to actually unlearn to focus on the alphabetic literacy and learn that it's fine to use all those other [modes] that are there to support them in the meaning … The Preps' language and understanding [of this] is much deeper or they're much more willing to use that [metalanguage] or demonstrate [their multimodal expression] (Cloonan 2010a: 173–4).

 See literacies.com Early Multimodal Literacies.

Moving on to the elementary or primary school, Hassett and Curwood (2009) describe the practice of multimodal learning using a picture book, *Arnie the Doughnut*. The teacher has students analyse the ways in which word meanings are expressed through the typesetting, the way the images present meanings that are in the text and also sometimes not in the text, and the multiple perspectives created with talk bubbles and author commentary. Using these ideas, each member of the class creates a page about their favourite food for the whole class book. Meanwhile, in her class in Singapore, Alicia looks at tourist brochures and videos promoting the city with a critical eye to their visual design. Why, she asks, are the commercial buildings foregrounded in the images rather than the public housing blocks (Tan, Bopry & Guo 2010)? In Norway, Erstad, Gilje and de Lange (2007) describe the ways in which children in two Norwegian schools remix image and text downloaded from the internet. And in Australia, Year/Grade 1 students use a magnifying glass and digital microscope to observe the life cycle of chickens. They save the projected images and record an online commentary on the VoiceThread platform to accompany their visual record of the developing chicks (Walsh 2010). These are just a few instances of different places where teachers are working with learners on multimodal literacies.

See literacies.com Callow on Multimodal Texts in Everyday Classrooms.

In the literacies classroom, as exemplified in the cases above, it is important for learners to be able to describe the visual design elements with which they are working – they need a metalanguage for making visual meaning (Cloonan 2011), just as they need to have words to describe the sound–writing relationships of text (the 'alphabetic principle') and the way sentences and whole texts are structured to make written meaning.

Parallels and differences between the visual and other modes

Different modes of meaning have the capacity to refer to the same kinds of things. However, the representational and communicative potentials of each mode are unique unto themselves. In other words, between the various modes, there are not only powerful parallels that allow for translation of meanings from one mode to another (describing a scene in words, or painting a picture of the same scene) but also differences that are so profound that the meanings can never be quite the same. (There's always something different about the description in words and the painting – you will always learn something not said in the one mode when you see the same meaning represented in the other mode.)

On the parallel side, a grammar of the visual can explain the ways in which images work like language. For instance:

- Action expressed by verbs in sentences may be expressed by vectors in images ('The car is *driving* down the street').
- Locative prepositions in language ('near', 'behind') are like foregrounding or backgrounding in images.
- Comparatives in language ('larger', 'shinier') are like sizing and juxtaposition in images.
- The 'given' and the 'new' English clause structures are like left/right placement in images (or at least in the cultures of left-to-right reading, writing and viewing) (Kress 2000c).

Children have natural synaesthetic capacities, and rather than build upon and extend these, didactic school literacy attempts to separate them to the extent even of creating different subjects or disciplines – literacy in one cell of the class timetable and art in another (Caughlan 2008). It is important to the learning process that visual and written modes of meaning are so powerfully parallel.

However, they are also irreducibly and helpfully different. The image will never convey the same mix of information as the written text. The parallels make synaesthesia possible. The differences make it necessary. Meaning expressed in one mode cannot be directly or completely translated into another. The movie can never be the same as the novel. The parallelism allows that the same things can be depicted in different modes, but the meaning is never quite the same.

In fact, some of the differences between the modes are quite fundamental. Writing (along the line, sentence by sentence, paragraph by paragraph, one page after the next) sequences the elements of a meaning in time. Because you read along the line, the most common kind of written meaning tends to have a 'first this', 'then that' and 'finally this' kind of pattern. Writing tends to favour the genres of recount, exposition and narrative. However, still image positions elements according to the logic of simultaneous space, and so favours the genre of informational display – this goes beside that. Writing's intrinsic temporality, its ordering of meaning into time sequences, orients it to causality (this leads to that). However, by contrast, still image orients it to location (for instance, scenes and maps).

This is not to say that writing can't describe space in a simultaneous moment of time. Nor that image can't 'do' both time and causation. It's just that often we may choose a diagram over a written description because it conveys a meaning about space more effectively. Or we may choose a written recount because it conveys a meaning about time more effectively. For instance, when we are reporting on a science experiment, we could in theory say everything we needed in images, such as diagrams and photographs of the experiment, or in written text, such as a scientific explanation. However, we use a complementary mix of image (diagram and photographs) to represent the spatial relationships of the components of the experiment (the instruments, the materials involved) and words to describe the sequence of activities, causality and effects.

Another example: it would be absurd and probably impossible to try to put all the spatial information in a map into words, but the time-sequenced narrative of directions, how to get from point A to point B, does translate nicely. It tells you

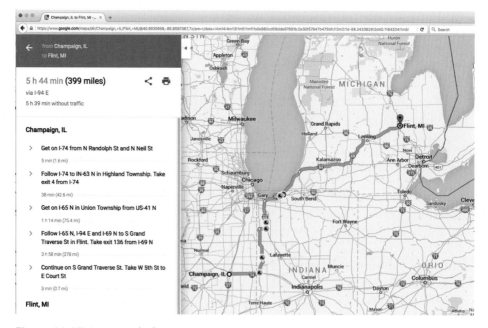

Figure 11.15 A map with directions

less than a map, but it tells you enough to be able to get from A to B. Having directions plus a map makes things even clearer, because you can supplement one mode of meaning with the other. A map represents space. Directions happen in time. Put the two together and you can visualise where you are going, as you are going.

So on the one hand, there are profound parallels between modes of meaning – so profound, in fact, that just about everything that can be said in one mode can also be said in another. However, different modes make for more practical and useful choices for meaning-making in different circumstances. Some modes, in other words, make a better choice for meaning some kinds of things, at some times, than others. Put different modes together and the result is powerfully integrated, multimodal meaning.

Written language, for instance, is open to a wide range of possible visualisations in words, or rich descriptions of scenes. In reading, however, you are taken along a line where the meaning-maker tells you what to see in your mental image of a scene, and in the order in which they present it. If you finally see an image that has previously been described to you in words, the former meaning becomes filled in with a whole range of additional visual meanings that no amount of wording could have conjured up in your mind's eye. Visuals communicating the same scene, by contrast, require different cognitive or thinking processes. Onus is placed on the viewer to create order (time, causation, purpose, effect) by arranging elements that are perceptually complete from the moment the viewer starts to look at the image (Kress 2003).

Reading and viewing, in other words, require different kinds of interpretation. They demand different forms of transformational effort and kinds of psychological processes as you represent the meanings to yourself in your mind's eye. They are fundamentally different ways of knowing and learning the world – knowing and learning the same world, but through different and complementary ways of meaning.

Table 11.3: Written and visual meanings compared

Written meanings	Visual meanings
Reading or writing along the line, one thing after the other	Seeing the whole picture, all at once
The reader follows the writer	The viewer looks across the image in their own way, starting with what first captures their attention
Particularly good at representing time and causal connections	Particularly good at representing space at one moment in time

The parallels between modes of meaning are the reason why we can describe a picture in words, or turn a novel into a movie, or turn a plan into a building. This paradoxical mix of parallelism between image and text (common design elements) and incommensurability (unique design elements, so image and text can never convey exactly the same information in quite the same way) between modes of meaning is the basis of the pedagogy of Multiliteracies.

Multimodal literacies and synaesthesia make for powerful learning in a number of ways. One of these is that some learners may be more comfortable in one mode than another. This may be their preferred mode of representation and communication – what comes to them easiest, what they are good at, the mode in which they best express the world to themselves and themselves to the world. One person may prefer to conceive a project as a list of instructions, while another envisages a flow diagram. The parallelism means that you can do a lot of the same things in one mode that you can do in the next.

Then, even though the starting point for meaning may be in one favoured mode, a learner may extend their representational repertoire by shifting from a favoured mode to a less comfortable but equally useful one. Powerful learning may result. If the words do not make sense the diagram might, and then the words may start to make sense. We can make the parallelism (common design elements) work to help learning. However, the incommensurability (unique design elements) of modes can work for us pedagogically, too. The words make sense because the picture conveys meaning that words could never (quite, or in a completely satisfactorily way) do. The memory and learning process is reinforced when moving from visual to oral and written. Conscious mode-switching makes for more powerful and relevant learning.

Synaesthetic learning: classroom examples

Jon Callow (2006) describes the ways in which students analyse politicians' promotional materials. This is another case of visual meeting gestural design – sorting a range of photos into:

> categories such as friendly/unfriendly, trustworthy/untrustworthy; sorting according to the purpose for which they might be used, e.g. for a fashion advertisement, an information book or family holiday photos; viewing and sorting images according to the use of angles to create power relationships, and shot at a distance to suggest intimacy or detachment.

The students then apply these analytical skills to:

> deconstructing a political pamphlet by annotating the various features such as the title, type of photos, type of information included, as well as the type of written texts that were included, such as testimonials (Callow 2006: 16).

Finally, they design a pamphlet of their own, as if they were running to be the environmental officer in their school. Callow asks a student, Joanne, about the kind of images people use in various design situations:

> **Joanne:** Well, it depends on their character and what they are like. If they were, like, a good person they would choose a friendly shot, and if they wanted to seem dominant and powerful, they would have a close up shot or a mid shot looking powerful.

Researcher: What if they weren't a very nice person, do you think they would put some nasty looking shots in?

Joanne: No, they want to appeal to you.

Researcher: Ok, so even it they weren't a nice person, they'd probably use what sort of shots do you think?

Joanne: They'd probably try putting friendly pictures or, if they couldn't, powerful pictures.

Researcher: Why would they put friendly pictures, because they are trying to do what?

Joanne: They are trying to attract you and persuade you to vote for them (Callow 2006: 20).

See literacies.com Making a Political Brochure.

Figure 11.16 Making a political brochure

Mary Neville (2008) describes the atmosphere in another classroom, this one using digital videos to tell stories. Along with a visiting film-maker, the teacher has set up a part of the literacy classroom as a film 'production house'.

[They] transformed ... a classroom atmosphere and arrangement of traditionally 'doing school' with desks, exercise books and a blackboard ... The classroom didn't seem to shape the learning, rather the multimodal texts gave the impression of shaping a 'green space' in the classroom where desks and blackboard were irrelevant and other 'open space' sites for discussion and filming equipment were located for creative innovation. 'My students and I really enjoyed being involved in this project [said the teacher]. It gave them a context in which to engage, intellectually, with some really higher order thinking. It gave them a sense of purpose and focus – a way of channelling their collaborative intellectual efforts into a single and fairly complex intent. It was stimulating for us all, not only because of the nature of the content, but also because it required new skills and competencies. It's hard to put all that into words – you have to be there and listen to their conversations and appreciate the complexity of how these 11 and 12 year old kids were thinking and behaving' … The data suggest that the pedagogical effectiveness [of this teacher's] classroom was related to increased cognitive, transformational opportunities for students linked to the inclusion of a video 'production house' [with a] focus on the real world of film production … A pedagogical concentration on the 'how' of multimodal text production provided students with 'insider' knowledge. This pedagogical concentration had links to teachers knowing the discourse of the social practices surrounding multimodality (Neville 2008): 88–9, 91–2, 133–4).

In secondary schools, we find teachers attempting to transform the traditional English literature curriculum in more engaging ways. Margaret Mackey provides a Canadian perspective on the application of a TV sitcom, *Felicity*, to traditional literature learning. She examines the connections teenagers make between the television program and the book that extended its narrative in contentious ways, the question of spin-off merchandising, the possibilities for written interpretive dialogue in online chatrooms, and the phenomenon of fan fiction in which viewers construct alternative narrative scenarios with the characters (Mackey 2003).

Now we move to a school in the remote tropical north of Australia, at Bamaga, near the most northerly tip of Cape York. Most of the students at the school are Torres Strait Islanders, and here we are going to describe a cross-curriculum early literacy and science class. We will use the Learning by Design pedagogical labels to describe some of the learner activities in this unit of work. The teacher is interested to explore germination of seeds, so asks the children how coconut trees grow – this connects with their experience, because lying on the beach right near the school are coconuts that have fallen off trees, some of which have roots sprouting from one end and shoots from the other (experiencing the known). They use the Torres Strait Kriol or everyday names for these things ('sid', 'sut', 'rut'). 'What do we call the parts of the sprouting coconut?' the teacher asks (conceptualising by naming: seed, root, shoot).

The students draw pictures of germinating coconuts, and label the different parts in Torres Strait Kriol. Then the teacher asks: 'How do new coconuts grow?' The students explore the way in which the roots go down into the ground, and the shoots reach up for light. She then asks the students to analyse the dangers of falling coconuts and what happens when they are all collected. Will this mean no more coconut trees? (analysing critically). Then they visit the local council to find out how coconut trees are managed and how new trees are grown and planted (experiencing the new). Finally, they write up their multimodal reports, describing in sentences how coconuts germinate and supplementing this with a scientific drawing. On facing pages in their books, they write this scientific text in Kriol (experiencing the known) and scientific English (experiencing the new, for these students whose home language is Kriol).

Left-hand page (Kriol)	Right-hand page (Scientific English – not shown here)
Tide i Tazde 10t October.	Today is Thursday 10th October.
Da rut i go antan [with spelling correction by the teacher to reflect the sound of this word in Kriol more accurately], da sut i go antap.	The root goes down, the shoot goes up.

Now we encounter a secondary English teacher, Douglas, working with his students on creative, multimedia 'text responses' to the Robert Drewe novel *The Shark Net*. One of the main characters in this book is a serial killer, Cooke, the last person to have been hung in Western Australia. Drewe autobiographically weaves his own experience of this time with a reconstruction of the Cooke story. Douglas' lesson and in particular his student Kate's response is described by researchers McClenaghan and Doecke (2010: 230):

Figure 11.17 Early childhood science literacies

> Kate creates a video in the style of a music clip, using 'Little Red Riding Hood' by Bowling for Soup. This song conveys a sense of the vulnerability of the young women Cooke murdered.

Kate changes the lyrics, putting different words up on the screen while the song is playing, thus making connections between Cooke's story and Drewe's. The song starts with 'Who's that I see walking in these woods?' The words up on the screen are: 'Who's that I see walkin' askew?' 'Why, it's Little Red Riding Hood!' (song) 'Why it's little Robert Drewe!' (words on screen). Later she presents the point of view of one of the victims with these words: 'Little Cottesloe Lass, I don't think that you should continue walking in my wood alone.' She enlisted her brother's help to make the video by filming him moving through shadows and darkness. The video consists of camera shots that are oblique and suggestive: dark shadows against a fence, silent feet creeping up the barely lit steps leading up to a house.

The researchers analyse the ways in which Kate uses image to perform the interpretive function historically carried by the written essay, melding techniques and motifs and using remixed and newly created images from popular culture. 'As a form of text response, this artefact reconstructs the imaginative world of *The Shark Net* using the popular cultural resources available (most notably the genre of the music video clip) to convey a vivid impression of how Kate has interacted with this text' (McClenaghan & Doecke 2010: 232).

These are just a few striking examples, among many, of the ways in which teachers around the world are using and analysing the design of visual meanings in their literacies classes. Importantly, they demonstrate the power and effect of students making multimodal meanings, and of synaesthesia, or moving between one mode and another.

See literacies.com Learning Modules.

See literacies.com #edtech Literacies Applications.

Summary

Perceptual images: making sense of things that we see *Mental images:* envisioning things we cannot see just now		
	Visual meaning is like written and oral meaning:<ul><li>It refers to people and things.</li><li>It represents interactions between people, and things.</li><li>It is composed in coherent ways.</li><li>It connects with its context.</li><li>It has social purposes and effects.</li></ul>*Visual meaning is not like written and oral meaning:*<ul><li>The reader has a wider choice of reading paths.</li><li>Meaning is more simultaneous/spatial than logical/temporal.</li></ul>	
		Multimodality: Meaning has always been expressed in multiple and mixed modes, but more so today in the digital media. *Synaesthesia:* Mode-shifting is a powerful way to make sense of things, and a way of learning.

Knowledge processes

experiencing the known

1. What are your favourite images? Choose an image you like. What is it that appeals to you about the image?

analysing functionally

2. Analyse the image using the analysis of design elements provided in this chapter.

experiencing the new

3. Read your detailed design analysis to a fellow student who has not seen the image to which you are referring, or give them the analysis to read. Ask them what they imagine. Now show them the image – how is the image like and unlike what they had imagined from the description? What does this tell you about the relationships between perception and mental images, and the extent to which meanings in images can be translated into writing, and vice versa?

conceptualising by naming

4. Take related pages in Wikipedia dealing with the physiology and psychology of vision, perception and imagination. Create an illustrated glossary of the key terms.

conceptualising with theory

5. Create a concept map linking the key terms in 'the psychology of perception'.

analysing critically

6. Read the opening chapter of a novel that is also available in a movie version you have not seen. How are visual meanings framed in language? What textual devices are used to depict image in words? Now watch the opening scenes of the movie. What do you find surprising or not surprising? How are the devices different? How is the text different? How and why is your interpretation of the meaning of the narrative in the movie similar to and different from the novel?

7. Analyse a child's drawing or information poster using the Multiliteracies framework for design analysis.

applying appropriately

8. Design a learning activity for students at a defined level that explores the potential of synaesthesia. You may wish to use the online Learning by Design lesson planner at L-by-D.com or any other lesson planning software you choose. Write an exegesis that explains your choice of texts. Discuss how different students might learn in different ways as they move between text and image. How will you assess learning outcomes?

applying creatively

9. Create a personal image (i.e. an image you have designed yourself) using visual, or visual-verbal media applying principles of visual design.
10. Apply your multimodal literacies understandings to designing a unit of work in another subject area, such as history, social studies, science or mathematics.

CHAPTER 12

Making spatial, tactile and gestural meanings

Overview

This chapter will explore three more important modes of meaning. Spatial meanings are framed by shape, proximity and movement. Tactile meanings capture our interactions with objects. Gestural meanings are bodily expressions, ranging from hand and arm movement, to facial expressions, to bodily presentations, such as clothing, to body language. These modes of meaning are closely interconnected and offer productive connections to oral and written meanings in multimodal literacies environments.

Learning through spatial, tactile and gestural meanings

In their Year/Grade 4 learning module, Lauren Hasler, David Livingstone and Marissa Owens' students read *Lin Yi's Lantern*, written by Brenda Williams and illustrated by Benjamin Lacom. 'Lin Yi's mother has sent him to the local market to buy food for the Moon Festival, but what he really wants is a red rabbit lantern,' states the book's blurb. 'Will he barter well enough to be able to buy one?' The class sets about re-designing the book as a drama that the students will act, transferring the narrative from the written and visual mode into the spatial (the set), tactile (the props) and gestural (the acting) modes. The narrative remains the same across the modes, but the mode of its communication is different. In this way, the students explore the notion of drama and develop a metalanguage to describe the distinctive features of drama, including setting, scene, dialogue, dramatic gestures, props and performance.

See literacies.com Gorman, Livingstone, Hasler and Owens, Lin Yi's Lantern.

Now to Year/Grade 7, where Keteurah Gill and Kim Smith have created a shadow puppetry learning module for their design and technology classes. The students begin watching a number of video clips of shadow puppets in various countries and cultures (experiencing the new). They analyse these video clips, exploring the ways in which gestures are represented, and the actions and emotions that these gestures are designed to communicate. Examining the gestural grammar of the puppets more closely, they interrogate aspects of colour, including line, shape, tone and texture (conceptualising by naming). Next they consider the processes for making the shadow puppets, including chiselling, drilling, filing, joining and sanding (analysing functionally). Finally each student makes a shadow puppet (applying appropriately) and groups of students write and perform plays in which their puppets appear (applying creatively).

See literacies.com Gorman, Livingstone, Hasler and Owens, van Haren, Keteurah Gill and Kim Smith, Chinese Shadow Puppetry in Woodwork.

Spatial meanings

The meanings of spaces and flows

Our **spatial meanings** are shaped in the places we inhabit, real and virtual, the way we move around in them and what we do in them. We see space and we also feel and manipulate objects in space, so spatial meanings are closely connected to visual and tactile meanings.

Spatial meaning: The way meanings are shaped by structures and landscape, and the flows or patterns of human movement through these spaces

Figure 12.1 Researching and creating shadow puppets (Chinese Shadow Puppetry in Woodwork Learning Module, Scholar)

We live and move about in space. We can do things in space. This moving and doing is episodic; it takes time and happens in spatially framed sequences. The scope of this movement is influenced by the way spaces have been designed by people, or in the case of natural spaces, the meaning we attribute to the space, such as natural beauty, or scientific interest.

Table 12.1: A grammar of spatial meaning

Reference
What do the meanings refer to?
	• How have *particular spaces* been presented, in plan or in reality? (e.g. edges, boundaries, volumes, topographical features of a building or a landscape)
	
	  ◦ *How is the movement or positioning of people influenced by the space? (e.g. flows, places of momentary stillness)*
	  ◦ *How is location referred to? (e.g. placement, proximity/distance)*
	  ◦ *How is time referred to? (e.g. time/space transpositions, such as a five-minute walk, a one-day drive)*
	  ◦ *How are things positioned in space? (e.g. a picture on a wall, an icon on a screen)*
	
	• How have *abstract elements or general concepts* been defined? (e.g. symbols used on plans or to help navigate around a space)
	
	• How are the *characteristics* of space defined? (e.g. quantities and qualities of size or scale, continuity/repetition, more/less)
	
	• How are *spatial relations* defined? (e.g. part/whole, possession, joining/not joining, sameness/contrast)

Dialogue *How do the meanings connect the people who are interacting?*	• How are *spatial elements* related? (conventions of front/back, points of entry/points of destination, outside views/inside views) • How are the *connections between persons, spaces and objects* configured? (e.g. ground level, floor levels, viewing heights) • How is *movement* anticipated and directed? (e.g. navigation paths in walkways, roads, train lines, flight paths) • How is the *user positioned*? (e.g. the point of view constructed for the viewer, perspective, degree of detachment/involvement)
Structure *How does the overall meaning hold together?*	• How are the *spatial elements arranged*? (e.g. in a whole architectonic space or landscape, where one space ends and other starts, how the spaces are engineered to hold together or how they cohere) • How is the space *sectioned*? (e.g. left ↔ right; top ↔ bottom, centre ↔ margin). • What does the space *point out*? (e.g. prominent/hidden aspects or functions)

↔ stands for 'and'.

(continued)

Table 12.1: A grammar of spatial meaning (*continued*)

	• How does the space form an *integrated whole*?
	• How are multiple spaces *chained*? (e.g. rooms in a building, buildings in a streetscape, cities in a landscape)
	• How is the space defined by its *media*? (e.g. construction materials)
Situation *How are the meanings shaped by the context of their location?*	• What is the *location* of the space? How does it point to its surroundings and its surroundings point to it? (e.g. settings assumed or referred to that are beyond the space; for instance, a tree in a cityscape compared to a tree in a forest)
	• How does the space *integrate or differentiate* its insides and its outsides? (e.g. warm/cool, bright/dark, open/secure, publicness/privacy, enclosure/vista, divided/open)
	• What does the space assume about the *field of movement* of its users? (e.g. the functional or aesthetic expectations they may bring to the space, or spatial restrictions by social role, such as in prisons and banks)
	• What *references* does the space make? (e.g. spatial metaphors, such as 'this luxury store is like a rich person's house', or battlements around prisons)
	• What resemblances and differences in overall composition does the space have with *other spaces* and space-making traditions (e.g. design motifs, building types, landscape forms)
Intent *Whose interests do these meanings serve?*	• How is space structured around certain *priorities*? (e.g. housing versus transport)
	• How is the space selectively configured to support a position or affirm a *role or stance*? (e.g. the visible/the hidden, the public/the private, the lockable/the unlockable, its presences/absences, foregrounding-backgrounding, suggestive navigation paths, how the space is designed for certain social practices)
	• Whose *interests* does the space support? (e.g. the shopping mall compared to the park)
	• What *range of alternatives for action* does the space suggest for the user? (e.g. from the positioning of different types of user, such as cooks, waiters and patrons in a restaurant)

Different spaces are designed for doing different things – for example, houses, schools, prisons, libraries, offices, places of worship, factories or theatres and electronic screens. They have different locations, different insides and outsides, and different internal designs. We move about them in different ways. Enter the lecture theatre, sit and listen, exit the lecture theatre. Go through the front door of the house, to the kitchen to cook, to the living room to watch television, to bed to sleep.

 See literacies.com Bachelard on the Poetics of 'House'.

Spaces shape flows. Flows are the ways in which we move through spaces. Different spaces are designed to serve different purposes, and these differences are the reasons for the flows – from bedroom to kitchen, from home to school, from the dairy section to the cereals section in the supermarket, from neighbourhood to holiday destination, from one area in a social networking site to another. Spaces have meanings based on their functions, and these meanings and functions have been designed by people. If places are something like a vocabulary of spatial meaning (neighbourhoods, rooms, drawers, webpages), flows are their syntax (meaningful sequences of movement).

 See literacies.com Whyte on the Social Life of Small Urban Spaces.

Spatial meanings may not even involve flows. They may just be meaningful continuities or discontinuities. An absence here may be defined by presences elsewhere. I am free and at home because I am not in prison and have never been to prison. I am on the beach on holiday now, as distinct from being at work in the office. The meaning of a space, in other words, is also often defined by its similarity with, or difference from, another space. Meaningful differences may prompt flows. For instance, cheap labour in one place may make it a convenient location to create manufactured goods for people who can afford them and who live in a different place. Flows are created by the magnetic forces of spatial difference.

We make sense of spaces, and not just humanly made spaces, but also natural spaces (such as natural landscapes that appear pristine because of the relative lack of human intervention, but where we make meaning based on walking paths or maps that direct our attention to interesting or beautiful sights). Our representations of space – the spatial meanings we make for ourselves – may consist of direct sensations of being in space, or imaginations of spatial possibility, from ordinary prospects of living better to the fantastic imaginary spaces of science fiction. We make mental maps of where we have been and where we are going. We draw plans in our heads, or we may put them on paper or draw them on a computer. We envision journeys and create itineraries. These are all acts of spatial representation or cognition.

Spatial communication includes giving directions, making maps, drawing plans, creating models and diagramming flows. It also involves constructing buildings, arranging the furniture in a room, creating parks, making paths, creating transport

Figure 12.2 A spatially framed social space

Figure 12.3 A tracking plan showing the ways six different people moved around a shop. (Each 'bounce' is a focal point of attention.)

infrastructure and building information transmission channels. The interpretation of these spaces is in their use, the meanings people make of spaces as they do things in them. And, in the nature of designing, every moment of spatial communication creates a new meaning for its user and the space. A shopping centre is not a casino, but no two people will move about in a shopping centre or a casino in quite the same ways for quite the same reasons or to quite the same effect. People design their spatial meanings, transforming the meaning of the space for themselves.

See literacies.com Weishar on Going Shopping.

Tactile meanings

The meanings of bodily sensations

Our definition of **tactile meaning** includes the closely connected bodily sensations of touch, taste and smell. We are able to feel temperature, pressure, texture and pain through our sense of touch. We are able to distinguish bitter, sweet, sour, salty and savoury through our sense of taste, distinguishing chemical differences between solid and liquid substances. However, our primary organ of taste, the tongue, can also feel in a touch-like way: temperature, texture and piquancy (it's

> **Tactile meaning:** The meanings of bodily sensations of touch, taste and smell

chilli-hot!). Meanwhile, our sense of smell can detect chemical differences between gaseous substances, through hundreds of meaning distinctions compared to the mere five distinctions available to taste. When we eat and drink, taste, smell and touch operate and integrate to form a complex panoply of meanings.

The metaphorical power of tactile meanings across all modes is remarkable. Consider how our repertoire of ideas of feeling would be diminished if we could not colour aspects of experience with words such as 'hot', 'warm', 'cool', 'cold', 'rough', 'smooth', 'painful', 'bitter', 'sweet' and 'sour'. We experience these primal tactile meanings all the time. The experience of tactile meaning is integral to our meaning systems, including language. Tactile meanings connect to the intimate world of our feelings. All our meanings, as Lackoff and Johnson say, are deeply and invariably embodied (Lakoff & Johnson 1980 (2003)).

Infants make the most fundamental of all meanings for life in a tactile, gestural, spatial, audio and visual world before they learn to speak and, later, to read and write. They make sense of the available designs in their tactile world, and they represent that world to themselves and begin to make meanings for themselves by touching things, holding things and moving things about. A toddler may move a stick through the air and imagine it to represent a plane. They may hold a stuffed animal and imagine it to be a friend.

With toys and other objects, young children begin to take control of their world. They begin to design and redesign the conditions of their immediate existence. As a result, they develop capacities that are basic to all meanings for all of life. They develop a sense of agency – that they can act with effect – along with a sense of interconnectedness with useable and meaningful objects; a sense of order among the objects in the world; a sense of interconnection with others through different kinds of touch that may express affection or anger; a sense that the meanings of

Table 12.2: A grammar of tactile meaning

Reference
What do the meanings refer to?
	• What is the *material form* of the object? (e.g. how it feels, how it is distinguishable from other objects, by being moveable/immovable, touchable/untouchable)
	
	   ◦ *Does it indicate a particular person? (e.g. a child's favourite toy)*
	   ◦ *Does it indicate a particular location? (e.g. a saucepan on a kitchen bench, a pen on desk)*
	   ◦ *How is time referred to? (e.g. something that feels new or old)*
	   ◦ *What particularities distinguish the object? (e.g. its function, a bowl compared to a saucepan)*
	   ◦ *What general concept does an object represent? (e.g. a knife/cutting, a soft toy/friendship)*
	   ◦ *What are the tangible characteristics of the object? (e.g. touch, taste, smell)*
	
	• What *tangible relations* are there in the object? (e.g. part/whole, possession, joining/not joining, sameness/contrast)

Dialogue *How do the meanings connect the people who are interacting?*	• How does the object *connect with people* in a meaningful way? (e.g. how objects are configured by their use or aesthetic appeal) • How is *use* anticipated and directed? How is the *user* positioned?
Structure *How does the overall meaning hold together?*	• How is the *object structured*? What is its internal order? (e.g. the relation of components, inside/outside, visible/hidden) • How does the object *work*? (e.g. the interactions of components and the effects of these interactions) • How is the object *sectioned*, and multiple sections *chained*? (e.g. the parts of the object and how they are interconnected) • How is the object defined by the *materials* from which it is made? (e.g. affordances/constraints)
Situation *How are the meanings shaped by the context of their location?*	• How/where is the object *located*? How does it *point to* its surroundings (e.g. different kinds of tables in different kinds of rooms; a keyboard in relation to a computer in relation to a desk) • How does the setting of the object *anticipate patterns of use*? (e.g. times of use, places of use, mobility of the object, different kinds of use in different contexts) • How does the object fit into the *whole universe of meaningful things*, from the highly local to the global? (e.g. how it works as a type object) • What *kind of object* is it? What are its resemblances and differences compared to other objects?

(continued)

Table 12.2: A grammar of tactile meaning (*continued*)

Intent *Whose interests do these meanings serve?*	• How is the object structured around certain *priorities*? • How is the object selectively designed or used to support a position or affirm a *role or stance*? (e.g. a gift/loan, something for free/a commodity for purchase) • Whose *interests* does the object support (e.g. private profit/an object in the public 'commons') • What are its *ancillary effects*? (e.g. environmental, social, cultural, economic) • What *range of alternatives for action* does the object offer, such as the different kinds of people whose roles and identities it may support? (e.g. flexible/inflexible, restrictive/expansive, open/closed).

tangible sensations can be communicated to others and interpreted (or misinterpreted) by others; a sense of subjectivity or projection of feelings; and a sense of whole self in the world (Stern 1985). Caregivers and peers touch babies and young children. Children incessantly handle objects. These are foundational aspects of the formation of the meaning universe of the infant.

We start meaning these foundational things in tactile, gestural and spatial ways, and keep meaning them in these ways for the rest of our lives. The main thing that language adds to tactile meaning after the age of about 18 months is to support a kind of conscious reflexivity that is only found in human communication and cognition. More than that, this conscious reflexivity comes to the other modes of meaning at the same time as language. It is not unique to language.

Conversely, language in its humanly meaningful entirety can be represented and communicated through touch, for instance with **Braille**.

Braille: A tactile form of writing for those who are sight-impaired

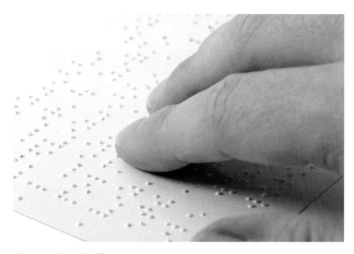

Figure 12.4 Braille

Tactile representation and communication involve direct bodily engagement with the material world. (Vision and hearing, by comparison, are engagements at a distance.) To illustrate how this happens, we will focus on the tactile meaning of objects. We're not interested in the objects alone, but also in the meanings we make of the objects. We live with distinguishable things, which we sometimes pick up, feel, hand to someone or locate in a position. We use objects: wearing shoes, driving a car, cutting with a knife, putting food in our mouths. We do things with objects and this doing makes us who we are – an avid walker, a terrible driver or a good cook.

We can create mental anticipations of the use of objects in our mind's eye or modelled on the templates of cultural tradition (tactile representations): how I will use this kitchen implement, how I will handle the ball in this game, how I will put on this item of clothing, how I will use a pen or a brush to create a picture. And we can make or place things for others' benefit, which they will use according to their interpretations of the meaning of the object (tactile communications) – the scrubbing brush left by the sink, the sports equipment left on the shelf, the clothes put away in the wardrobe or the pen left on the desk. These meanings are fundamental to our human natures. There can be no separable worlds of objectivity (truth-in-things) and subjectivity (our sense of ourselves) because we are in such direct contact with things that they have become virtually a part of ourselves (Krippendorf 2006). Shoes and cars, for instance, afford us mobility that becomes part of our natures, integral to our very existence. For many of us, these objects have become indispensable to the meanings of our lives. They are transformative.

One distinctive feature of our species is its capacity to represent and communicate meanings using objects that are direct tactile extensions of ourselves. Tangible things are objects available to us, resources for tactile meaning. We design or make meanings with and through them, be that in big ways by invention or in small ways by the subtle peculiarities of our use. And we leave traces of our designing in the world in the form of the objects we have left or the ways we have been seen to use them. These are the sources of the unique human species capacity to create an artefactual world from nature (Miller 2010).

These extensions to our bodies allow us to travel, to cook and to eat. Our communications media consist of objects that enable us to make meanings across time and distance. They are props for the enactments in the action sequences of human life (Suchman 2007). They are integral props in our social practices of meaning (Scollon 2001).In fact, no less than language, our human capacities to make meanings and transform the world with objects is a distinctive feature of our species. Indeed, tactile meaning can cover much the same range of meanings as language. We can silently do meaningful things with objects, or we can speak about the same things, or we can represent them visually, or we can do all of these things together, multimodally. Tactile meaning is every bit as transformative of the world as language, and just as important to our natures as thinking and learning creatures.

Not that objects always serve us in the ways we mean them to. We may have a car as an extension of our bodily selves, but we can be hurt by that car in an accident, or we can suffer from the effects of pollution, or we can be distressed by the ugliness of parking lots and motorways. Objects can oppress us. They can assault our senses in ways we do not necessarily want, or even sometimes anticipate. Objects can sometimes come to have a disturbingly alienating life of their own. Even though we humans are responsible for their design and production, our interpretations of them can change when we see discordant meanings emerge; for instance, the device that works badly or the object that is an ugly intrusion on our lives.

These interpretations might include interventions to change the meaning effects of certain objects; for example, by mounting road safety campaigns, putting pollution-control devices in our cars, and using public transport instead of driving or needing parking space. We don't just talk about these things. We transform our world by doing and using these things in our everyday lives with objects.

See literacies.com Scollon on Mediated Discourse.

Children, toys and tactile learning

Children start to apply symbolic meaning to objects and spaces from about the same time as they learn to speak. The table is draped with a blanket, and its inside becomes a play house, with pillows and empty containers as furniture. The cardboard box is imagined to be a pirate ship. In these ways, as Gunther Kress argues, children take objects and spaces – 'what is at hand' – and design meanings. They play cars, and shops, and hospitals, and schools (Kress 1997). They configure objects in space and attribute meaning to these objects and their configuration; and in so doing they transform the meanings of these objects for themselves (representation) and for or with their playmates (communication). Their actions leave the world of meaning transformed.

See literacies.com Lillian Katz on Play and Disposition.

Whether children do this with toys, literally representing the object of their meaning, or with found objects, the transformation is equally profound. A box can be configured as a car: a remarkable act of symbolising imagination. However, to imagine a configuration of meanings around a toy car is just as transformative: it's going from point X to point Y in the child's spatial imagination, with a certain driver and certain passengers for certain purposes. The difference between the toy and the box is somewhat like the difference between abstract expressionism, where a lot has to be read into the represented object, and landscape painting, in which the processes of referring are more literal. Both are meaning-transformative, and equally powerfully.

Pippa Stein and Denise Newfield describe the work of Tshidi Mmabolo, Ntsoaki Senja and Thandi Makhabela, who teach first and second grade at

Olifantsvlei Primary School, a school bordering informal settlements or 'squatter camps' on the edge of Johannesburg, South Africa. The 'fresh stories' project engages the children in multimodal pedagogies that bring together three-dimensional objects, creating images, performing, speaking and writing. Through these media, the project encourages the children to use these modes of expression to speak to their lives and cultural experiences. Stein and Newfield continue the story:

> The children began by drawing self-selected characters from their neighbourhoods who would form the basis of the characters for their stories. In preparation for the next stage, which involved making three-dimensional figures of these characters, the teachers made a papier-mâché mixture for them which collapsed into a kind of porridge. When the children came to make their figures, the mixture had 'turned into a puddle'. The children then turned to their teachers and said, 'Don't worry, We'll make our own figures' and, within a few days, they had brought to school a collection of extraordinary doll-like figures which they had constructed from the resources available to them in their environments – various forms of waste material such as plastic bags in different colours; coke bottles filled with stones and sand; pieces of dishcloth; scraps of materials including cardboard, paper, buttons, wire, and old stockings.
>
> One of these dolls was made by a seven year old girl who lives in a shack next to a rubbish dump on the outskirts of Johannesburg. Her doll was made out of a Coke bottle (its body), bubble wrap (its flowing clothes) and an old plastic bag (its head and doek/scarf). ... Another doll was also made from a Coke bottle only this time it had been filled with stones and an old stocking had been delicately and artfully wound around it. Yet another doll was the matriarch who carries her power in the multiple folds of cloth which encircle her weighty frame: a real 'ballabosta' ...
>
> Many of these dolls and figures are transformed traditional objects where the children have drawn on materials and designs which are part of African fertility doll making culture. These 'fertility dolls' are usually small, anthropomorphic figures fabricated by women, for young girls and women.
>
> A traditional doll has a characteristic body shape and cloth, beads and skins are central to its design. Such dolls have specific cultural, symbolic and identity functions, relating to women's fertility and marriage rituals. What is so interesting about the children's doll-like figures, however, is how they had at their disposal (through their families, histories, cultural memories and available people in the community) a range of representational resources for constructing these figures (the available designs), within an urban informal settlement, and how they had redesigned these figures to suit their own needs (to make characters for a story to be told at school) (Stein & Newfield 2002: 5–6).

Here we see at work a process of making tactile meaning, rich in cultural association. Most importantly, we see a move to symbolisation, a conceptual process where something 'stands for' something else. This is cognitively equivalent to

Figure 12.5 A 'pillow car'

Figure 12.6 Making dolls in a South African school

symbolisation using language or two-dimensional visual image. Tactile meaning-making can be a powerfully engaging and effective learning activity. It can also be a basis for synaesthesia, as students mode-shift from tactile to visual and linguistic modes as part of multimodal literacies learning.

Gestural meanings

Representation and communication of gestural meaning

If tactile meanings are expressed through the body – touching, tasting or smelling objects – **gestural meanings** are made through bodily appearances, movement and positioning. Gestural meanings include body location, hand and arm movement, facial expressions and gaze. They are insepara-ble from what we do to sculpt the appearance of our bodies with clothing, hairstyles, make-up, jewellery and body modification, which we for this reason are also going to consider to be gestural.

Gestural meaning: Meanings involving bodily presence or movement

 See literacies.com Miller on the Sari.

Gestural meanings are matters both of representation (remembering or think-ing ahead by rehearsing gestural meanings in one's mind's eye, or interpreting the gestural meanings of others) and of communication (making a gestural meaning that another person may interpret as meaningful). To use an expression of Goff-man's, gestural meanings are unavoidably 'given off' (Goffman 1959: 2). When any two people are in each other's presence, or for that matter when a sole person senses their own presence, there is a gestural meaning. In other words, oral and written meanings may happen every now and then, but gestural meanings are always there in a multilayered panoply of meanings.

 See literacies.com Goffman on the Presentation of Self.

Gestural meaning can take a number of quite distinct forms, which we will group into bodily configuration, gesticulation and signing.

Bodily configuration is about:

Bodily configuration: A kind of gestural meaning that involves body spacing, body movement and gaze

- body spacing, orientation and posture (where gestural mean-ing meets spatial meaning;often called 'proxemics')
- bodily movement (feelings of motion, another way in which the gestural meets the spatial; often called 'kinaesthesia')
- gaze (where gestural meets visual meaning); facial expres-sions; touching, clothing and designing other body appear-ances (where the gestural meets the tactile).

These translate into whole patterns of interaction situated in broader social meanings, called 'frames' (Goffman 1974). Examples of frames of action include doctor/patient (medical frames), performers/audience (theatrical frames), and circle time/teacher talk time (educational frames) (Miller 2010: 49). Gestural

Table 12.3: A grammar of gestural meaning

Reference
What do the meanings refer to?
	• What is the *particular* meaning of a gesture? What is its distinguishable form? (e.g. hand movement, body positioning and movement, posture, facial expression, gait, direction of gaze, fashion, makeup, hairstyle etc.)
	
	   ◦ *How is personality referred to? (e.g. dress, demeanour)*
	   ◦ *How is space and dimension referred to? (e.g. near/far)*
	   ◦ *How is time referred to? (e.g. fast/slow movement, beat)*
	   ◦ *How is an object represented gesturally? (e.g. mime)*
	   ◦ *What general concept does a gesture represent? (e.g. 'stop')*
	   ◦ *How are characteristics represented? (e.g. size, repetition)*
	   ◦ *How are relations represented? (e.g. connection/ disconnection)*

Dialogue *How do the meanings connect the people who are interacting?*	• How does the gesture *position the gesture-maker?* • How might another person be expected to interpret the gesture? How does gesture affect the interpersonal relations between participants? (proxemics e.g. doctor/patient, teacher/student, priest/congregation, touching)
Structure *How does the overall meaning hold together?*	• How is the *gesture structured*? (e.g. the phases of a gesticulation: preparation, stroke, retraction; or a sentence in deaf sign language) • What are its internal components and how do they *combine* to make meaning? (e.g. strongly/weakly integrated, action sequences, patterns of gesture across a social interaction – for instance, purchasing a cup of coffee, sending someone up, role play, dance, theatre) • How is a pattern of gesture and sequence of gestures *integrated*? (e.g. demeanour, deportment, behaviour: formal/informal, anger/warmth, a stranger/friendship/intimacy) • What are its perceptible *ways of referring* (e.g. literal or iconic tracing of a movement, pointing to something, abstract-iconic representation, naturalism/performance, spontaneous/premeditated, conscious/unconscious) • How is the gesture defined by its *bodily features and materials*? (e.g. facial expressions or clothing)
Situation *How are the meanings shaped by the context of their location?*	• How is the gesture *framed* by its context of situation? (e.g. uniforms, pointing) • How does the gesture connect into a universe of *gestural resemblances* (e.g. styles, fashion, forms of decorum (e.g. effeminate/masculine, politeness/rudeness)?

(continued)

Table 12.3: A grammar of gestural meaning (*continued*)

Intent	
Whose interests do these meanings serve?	• How does the gesture indicate certain *priorities* on the part of the person making the gesture?
	• How does the gesture selectively support a position or affirm a *role or stance*? (e.g. happiness/sadness, power/equality, sincerity/insincerity)
	• Whose *interests* does the gesture support, and to what extent is this at the expense of other interests? (e.g. concealment/transparency, bodily aura, magic tricks)
	• How do constellations of gestural meaning express *feeling* and *identity*? (e.g. pretentiousness/authenticity, hierarchy/equality)

designs can be spontaneous and relatively unconscious (in everyday social interaction) or premeditated (mimicry, role-playing, dance, theatre).

Gesticulation consists of movements of the hands and arms that accompany talking, or mental images of talking, or recordings of talking. Gesticulation is deeply integrated with oral meanings. McNeill shows how oral meaning and gesticulation are two sides of a common cognitive process (McNeill 1992). We 'conduct' our speech in a way that is somewhat like a conductor and the orchestra. The 'preparation' for a gesticulation begins with the start of a spoken phrase, the 'stroke' at the emphatic point in its meaning structure, and the 'retraction' representing its end (Kendron 2004). (McNeill and Kendron, both prominent contemporary analysts of gesticulation, use the word 'gesture' to describe what we call 'gesticulation'. We want to use the word 'gesture' more broadly, in order to group the three closely connected kinds of bodily meaning: bodily configuration, gesticulation and signing.)

Gesticulation: A kind of gestural meaning that involves movements of the hands and arms to accompany talking

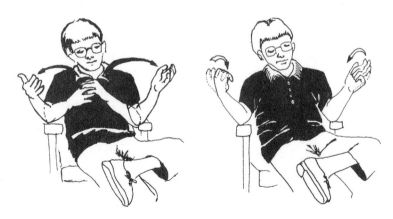

Figure 12.7 Analysing gesticulation

Gestural signing is abstract symbol-making that need not happen at the same time as speech. In fact, it mostly happens as an alternative to speech when, for a variety of reasons, speech is not present. For example, we all use gestural signs based on shared interpretations of their meanings: 'stop' or 'slow down' with the hands; the nodding of 'yes' and the head-shaking of 'no'; the 'thumbs up' of liking; the 'up yours' of insulting; or pointing to the head in a particular way to indicate that someone is 'crazy'. We make these signs in the hope that other people will more or less share our interpretations of the symbolic meaning of these signs. Gestural signing can reach symbolic heights equal to spoken language, as evidenced in deaf sign languages, for instance, or the sign languages used by Walpiri women in Australia when they are sworn to silence to mourn the death of a relative.

> **Gestural signing:** Gestures that represent and communicate abstract symbols, including the sign languages of those who are hearing-impaired

Figure 12.8 Examples from American sign language

The differences between gesticulation and gestural signing are important, to the extent in fact of needing to regard these as distinct gestural meaning systems. Gesticulation is spontaneous and much of the time relatively unconscious; signing is premeditated and highly conscious.

Gesticulation can be highly idiosyncratic, a matter of personal style. It is not conventionalised. Signing, however, is highly conventionalised, which means that the relationships of gesture to meaning are relatively stable from one person to the next. We all know the 'stop' gesture. People speaking a common deaf language use the same gestural signs as their peers in order to be intelligible to each other. Gesticulation adds information to speech. Signing mostly happens instead of speech.

See literacies.com McNeill on Gesture.

Understanding the nature of gesture is an invaluable part of a literacies teacher's repertoire. Bodily configuration and gesticulation have always been a part of drama as a literary form, and theatre as a disciplinary interest of language teaching and learning. Today, however, video is a widely used recording medium, and one that in its nature captures complex gestural forms. Writing used to be the primary mode of communication across time and distance, a mode of meaning that removed gesture. Video can easily and inexpensively serve the same function. With video come gestural meanings that require careful crafting for effective communication, and equally careful interpretation of gesture on the part of the viewer. Finally, the abstract sign systems of everyday gesture prefigure and replicate key cognitive aspects of symbolisation generally, taken to extraordinarily elaborate lengths in deaf languages – lengths, in fact, as broad as spoken language.

Paths to synaesthesia: making connections between spatial, tactile, gestural and other modes of meaning

Body talk

Ruth Moodie explains the 'body talk' unit she has created for the five- and six-year-olds in her classroom. Children re-enact a narrative from a book they have been reading, in body and speech, and the teacher records their performances. They name gestures, poses and the auras that come with particular stances. As they reinterpret the written text, they develop 'a common language to describe and explore gesture, feelings and meaning' (Moodie 2004). Here she discusses the visual concept of 'angle' in the images presented in illustrated fairy tales, and describes her experience working with early literacy learners to develop a visual grammar.

> I try to make sure I'm connecting with the children's experiences by ... continually making those links explicit, ... conceptualising ... for example with deconstructing and reconstructing the pictures [in the fairy tale books] and the meaning. I had to give them a language to do that ... The amusement of me lying down [on the classroom floor] taking a photo of [Child X] was to get that angle ... now one word they really know is 'angle'. [By taking photographs of each other from different angles the students have developed] ways of using the language and the skills to look at things critically ... then working out well why is this picture a better picture? Should we use this one? What makes that one more powerful? It's getting them to use that language, or use those understandings to frame their ideas ... getting them to apply their knowledge ...
>
> I found talking with other teachers that sometimes people say this is just good teaching practice and that's really true; it is good teaching practice, it's what we've

always done but, once again I think we're doing it at a more explicit level. I would never have spent three weeks unpacking pictures and fairytales like I have this time but I think the time and effort really shows in the sorts of things the kids are doing. Before I would have maybe spent a session on it and assumed that the knowledge was there and assumed that they'd take it on board but not see the evidence in a really, really deep way like I'm seeing now. … [The students are now] making links in their reading, I'm seeing it across other areas too, in other settings, other activities that they do, they're maintaining that knowledge because it's very strong and they're using that [knowledge of] design in the way they draw their characters too … they bring their own meaning to it … you see the power of the visual literacy coming through (Cloonan 2010a: 183, 180).

See literacies.com Moodie on Body Talk

Figure 12.9 Body talk unit

Figure 12.9 (*continued*)

In a 'Body Tracings' project designed by David Andrew and Joni Brenner in South Africa, 10-year-old students work in pairs to make traced, life-size self-portraits. They need to trust someone to trace their body outline, a genuinely collaborative exercise in which the gestural is translated into the visual. David Andrew explains:

> In the practice of making these texts, students are encouraged to draw on the notion of 'artists' sensibilities', to experiment with the idea of 'makeshiftness', which comes about through making shifts across modes, materials and media in a kind of less-anxious creativity which does not insist on knowing the path beforehand, but acknowledges that the next step might be an unexpected one.

The results were a series of images that translated bodily gesture and movement into image:

> bodies are twisting, dancing, skating, playing, dribbling balls. ... In these visual texts, we see students engaging in narratives of self, which in the practice of making, are felt, considered, imagined, and dreamed (cited in Stein & Newfield 2003: 2847).

Andrew and Brenner comment that these representational activities, '[these] profoundly intimate projections of self into the public gaze, have the effect of debating, contesting and challenging the language of deficit in South Africa that surrounds the capabilities of poor children' (Stein & Newfield 2003: 2848).

Figure 12.10 Self-portraits

Drama

Teaching in an Australian primary/elementary school, Margery Hertzberg describes the effect of dramatising a novel, Diana Kidd's *Onion Tears*. The children discuss the differences between reading the book and improvised 'acting out' of scenes.

> **Rob:** Well, if you're just reading the book and you see Nam-Huong being teased, you don't really get the feel of the book, but if you're doing drama about it then you really know how she's feeling about it.
>
> **Jake:** ... you can understand it 'cause you're the one who's like in the shoes sort of and you're the one who's doing it. ...
>
> **Kate:** Just that we can do the things we do in class the same through drama, like we can learn through drama and do those activities through drama ... You ... use as much body and facial expression as you want to so people watching us can see who our characters are ... This way [drama] is better because you can by the expression on your face and the way you're sitting and moving around people can tell how you feel ...
>
> **John:** Because it, like, helps you in reading, writing. Helps you understand heaps of stuff that you never understand, as well as if you don't do drama. Usually, like, when you read books you don't understand it but when you're doing drama you understand why they're feeling and how (Hertzberg 2001: 4, 6).

Moving on to an illustration from a high-school literature classroom, Stephanie Power Carter discusses an interaction about gesture between two African American students. The class has been undertaking a video analysis of *Huck Finn*. Their observations take them on a reflective tangent about the nature of gestural meaning. Here, they build an 'interpretative frame' that helps them connect with the gestural imagery of the video. The researcher is speaking with one of these students, Natonya.

> **N:** Many people like uh, Black African-American men of course, then some, some White, Whites, male and female, and everything, they say we all have these little, funky look or whatever. I mean –
>
> **SC:** When we say 'we', you mean ...
>
> **N:** The, Black African-American females.
>
> **SC:** Okay.
>
> **N:** Um, and it's like when, every time we like see something we don't like, or somebody say something to us, we roll our eyes or, twitch our lip or something like that, you know? And it's like, we have this so-called attitude, that we get and everything, which, some people say we sensational. You know? And so, it's like uh. And, and it's like many, many Black African-American females have they own, face expression, either when they mad, when they don't like something, when somebody say something to them and they don't like it, you know what I'm saying? And so ... (Carter 2006: 354).

In a final illustration, Jason Goulah describes a Japanese language learning experience during an exchange visit to Japan for secondary students from the United States. They are creating video 'uncommercials', or short narratives about the length of a commercial.

> The first uncommercial begins with the essential question *risouteki nu kuni ha nani wo sum beki desuka* [What should ideal countries do?] raining down a black screen. It then shows a male student as a weak and thirsty country in a convenience store (a mix of the inn's kitchen and a real convenience store) trying to buy a soft drink. The store clerk, another male student, makes an X gesture with his arms and then makes the Japanese gesture for money (the OK gesture used in America turned upside down). The thirsty student/country gestures with shrugged shoulders and arms spread outward from the body, palms up to indicate that he has no money. Then a female student/country/customer, coughing and standing behind the weak student/ customer, buys him the drink, placing yen on the counter. The poor student/country thanks her and drinks the beverage as the girl coughs more pronouncedly and asks the clerk for medicine. But the clerk again makes an X with his arms. The camera flashes to the poor, thirsty country's pocket, in which he has a cup labelled kusuri [medicine]. The poor student/country gives the wealthy but sick student/country the medicine. She drinks it and they smile, both refreshed, and leave. As they leave, the camera flashes to another female student/country walking. She trips and falls to the ground and the two customers/countries rush to save her like superheroes. Then the answer to the essential question showers down a black screen: *risouteki na huni ha mazushii kuni wo tetsudau beki desu* [Ideal countries should help poor countries]. In this uncommercial, music plays in the background, but there are no audible voices. Except for the essential question, its answer, and kusuri [medicine] written on the cup, there is no text (Goulah 2007: 68).

These are vivid examples of classrooms where teachers are having students work in gestural, spatial and tactile modes of meaning. The power of their learning is as much in their capacity to switch modes as in the profound aspects of meaning that they are able to name and enact in each of the modes. Put simply, multimodality helps learning, including learning the mode that is the traditional focal point of literacy learning in the singular – the written mode.

Multimodal literacies learning

Clearly, all our modes of meaning are deeply and irretrievably interconnected, even though we can identify discrete meaning systems at work – written, visual, spatial, tactile, gestural, audio and spoken. As we have seen in the case of gesture, there are also systems within systems – bodily configuration, gesticulation and symbolic signing. Traditionally, literacy teaching and learning tried to separate language from the other modes of meaning, or at least, it tried as best it could. The fact is that it couldn't, or at least not terribly well and not without artificially forcing the point. Of course, some practices, such as drama and theatre, which were part of the canon of literacy pedagogy, have always brought written and spoken language

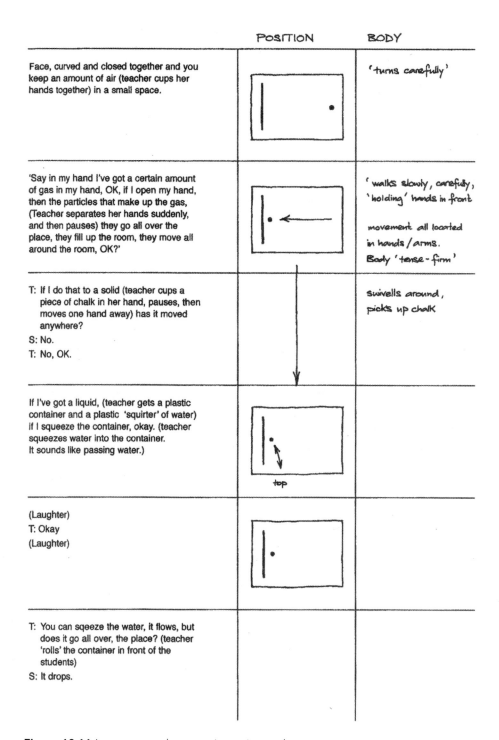

Figure 12.11 Language and gesture in a science class

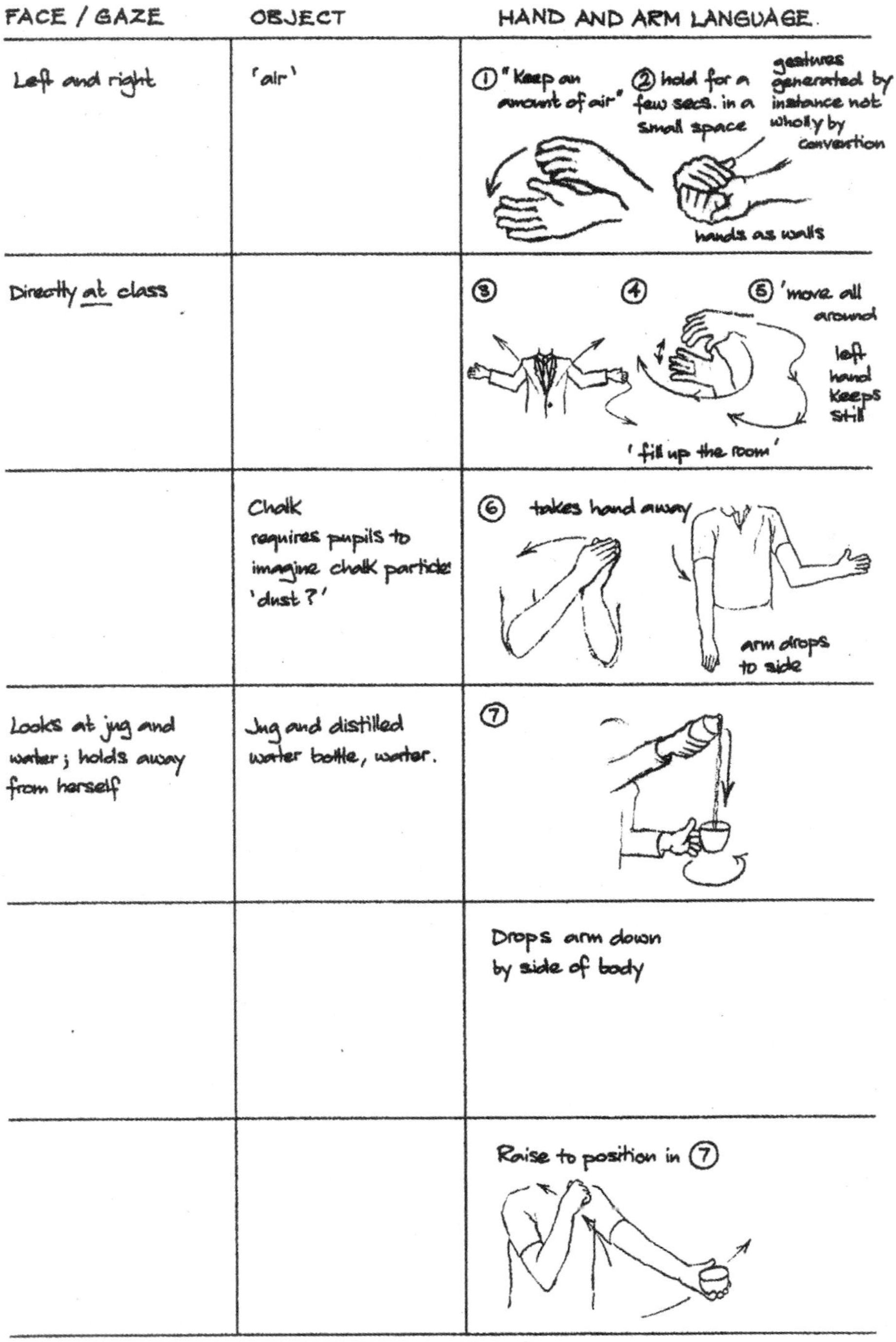

FACE / GAZE	OBJECT	HAND AND ARM LANGUAGE
Left and right	'air'	① "Keep an amount of air" ② hold for a few secs. in a small space gestures generated by instance not wholly by convention hands as walls
Directly <u>at</u> class		③ ④ ⑤ 'move all around left hand keeps still ' fill up the room '
	Chalk requires pupils to imagine chalk particle 'dust?'	⑥ takes hand away arm drops to side
Looks at jug and water; holds away from herself	Jug and distilled water bottle, water.	⑦
		Drops arm down by side of body
		Raise to position in ⑦

Figure 12.11 (*continued*)

into a systematically taught connection with spatial and gestural meanings. So does early childhood learning, with its focus on visual, spatial, tactile and gestural expression as an integral aspect of the learning process, including learning to read and write.

See literacies.com Kress on Multimodality in the Science Classroom.

Two important conclusions can be drawn from this analysis. Firstly, each meaning mode is capable of the full range of human meaning. As adult meaning-makers we use many modes of meanings together, simultaneously, or side by side, or meaning one way or another. And if access to one meaning mode is for some reason restricted or removed, by sensory disability for instance, the full range of human meanings is still available to us through the complete substitution of the other modes. If we have sight impairment we can learn the whole of written language in Braille. If we are hearing-impaired, we can learn the whole of spoken language in signing.

Secondly, instead of dividing modes off from each other we need to bring them closer together, recognising that synaesthesia is a powerful path to learning how to mean. If we can't quite mean something fully one way, we can perhaps mean it better in another. If something needs to be understood more deeply, we can always find another mode of meaning or combination of modes to add depth. We do that simply by adding the perspective of another mode. For, as much as the modes are parallel to each other in their meaning potentials, as much as they cover the same range of thinkable and communicable things, they do their expressing in very different ways.

See literacies.com Learning Modules.

See literacies.com #edtech Literacies Applications.

Summary

Spatial meanings	Tactile meanings	Gestural meanings
• Shapes, sizes and proximities in places • Bodily movement and space • Perceived and imagined spaces • Physical and virtual spaces	• Sensations and feelings: touch, smell, taste • Interacting with objects and tools • The physicality and materiality of media used in representation and communication	• Bodily configuration: spacing, orientation, posture, gaze, facial expressions, clothing • Gesticulation: hand and arm movements • Signing: symbolic meanings conveyed in gesture

Knowledge processes

experiencing the known

1. Describe an incident in which you have been involved where body talk conveyed powerful meanings. Perhaps you might consider a moment of cross-cultural misunderstanding based on a misreading of body language.

experiencing the new

2. Write a short overview of a deaf sign language project or Braille. Discuss the dimensions of multimodal meaning in humans.

analysing functionally

3. 'Parse' a home improvement television show for the design elements of spatial meaning or a cooking show for the design elements of tactile meaning.

analysing critically

4. Conduct a toy analysis, either by watching a small child use a toy, or taking a toy and projecting the tactile meanings you anticipate will occur during children's play. How does tactile learning with toys contribute to children's capacities to make meaning?

applying appropriately

5. Apply the design analysis terminology introduced in this chapter to a traditional drama lesson.

applying creatively

6. Create a plan for a sequence of lessons that explore spatial, tactile and gestural modes of meaning. You may wish to use the Scholar platform to create a learning module.

CHAPTER 13

Making audio and oral meanings

Overview

Audio and oral meanings share the sense of hearing as the primary medium of reception. **Audio meanings** range from ambient or background sounds in our environment, to sounds that have symbolic meaning, and to the complex meanings represented in music. **Oral meanings** carry with them the basic qualities of audio meanings as we modulate volume and pitch in the sounds of speaking. Despite the important connections, there are large and significant differences between the ways in which language is formed in the oral and written modes. These differences are what motivates mode-shifting in communications and learning, not just between oral and written meanings, but across the full range of modes of meaning.

Audio meanings: Meanings made in sound, including ambient and deliberately made sounds and music

....

Oral meaning: Language as represented in speech

....

Learning audio and oral meanings

Sue Gorman, Tayla Zanotto and Mike Aspden are working with their Year/Grade 1 students to investigate sound and light. In this multimodal learning module, 'Good Vibrations', as well as developing their multimodal literacies students are exploring scientific concepts of sound, light waves, sources, vibration, pitch and reflection. To begin a discussion of sounds and words, the class reads *Night Noises* by Mem Fox, considering words such as 'quack', 'click' and 'ring' that are written the way they sound (experiencing the new). The class creates a word wall of sound words (conceptualising by naming). They classify sound types (conceptualising with theory). They then begin to create objects designed to make certain kinds of sound, discussing also the range of sounds made by various musical instruments (analysing functionally). They watch a video without sound, reflecting on the kinds of sound effects that they would expect in the video. Then they listen to the video without watching it, trying to align the audio cues to what they have seen (analysing critically). Finally, they create a sound-only role play (applying creatively).

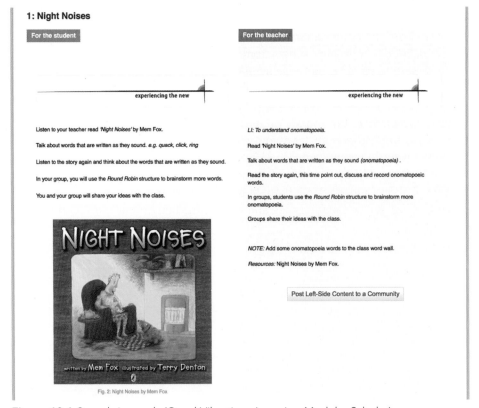

Figure 13.1 Sounds in words (Good Vibrations Learning Module, Scholar)

See literacies.com Good Vibrations, Gorman, Zanotto and Aspden.

Now, we're in a Year/Grade 5 class with Rita van Haren, Kylie Libbis, Sue Gorman and Jenny Loudon. In their learning module 'Singing Together, Giving Together', students sing together in class, while developing musical concepts of pitch, tempo and rhythm, and examining the ways in which these overlay the poetic form of lyrics. What happens to the meaning of a song, when its pitch, tempo and rhythm are changed? In what ways are lyrics oral, but also, in what ways are they more characteristic of a written text?

See literacies.com Singing Together, Giving Together, van Haren, Libbis, Gorman and Loudon.

And in a final example for the moment, 'soundscapes', a learning module by Bill Miller and Rita van Haren for their Grade/Year 7 music and literacies classes, explores the ambient sounds around us – the textures and timbres of soundscapes. The students listen to Vivaldi's *Four Seasons*, then some of the works of John Cage. They go on to create a musical composition that translates ideas from soundscape into musical form.

See literacies.com Miller and van Haren, Soundscapes.

These examples give a sense of the range of exciting interdisciplinary activities that students can undertake in multimodal literacies. But now for the theory …

Audio meanings

Representation and communication in sound

The human sense of hearing captures sounds that come through air pressure waves. The human ear is capable of detecting loudness in these waves (amplitude) and pitch (frequency). The human capacity to hear is within a very particular range. The upper limits of loudness are defined by a point at which the effect is hearing loss. Low frequencies are also perceptible by touch in the form of vibrations.

Table 13.1: A grammar of audio meanings

Reference *What do the* *meanings refer to?*	• What is the *particular meaning* of the rhythm, pitch, volume, tempo, texture or directionality of a sound? (e.g. a bell ringing, a voice heard over background noise)
	◦ How is a *person* noticeable in the sounds they make? (e.g. the sound of walking, breathing)
	◦ How is *time* referred to? (e.g. tempo, rhythm)

(continued)

Table 13.1: A grammar of audio meanings (*continued*)

	○ How is *place* referred to? (such as sound distance and directionality e.g. the sound in relationship to the conditions of its transmission and hearing) ○ How is an *object represented* by its distinctive sound? (e.g. a shower compared to an keyboard) • What *general concept* does a sound represent? (e.g. a doorbell, a car horn) • How is are the *characteristics* of the meaning represented in sound? (e.g. volume, pitch, texture) • How are *relations* represented in sound? (e.g. foreground/background sounds)
Dialogue *How do the meanings connect the people who are interacting?*	• How do sounds *position the sound-maker?* (e.g. a door opening, a steak frying) • How might another person *interpret the sound?* (e.g. information, a warning)
Structure *How does the overall meaning hold together?*	• How is the *audio meaning structured?* What constitutes completeness/incompleteness? (such as a piece of music or entering-starting and leaving ending a soundscape e.g. a song, a movement, a symphony; the sounds of the street/the sounds of the store) • What are its internal components and how do they *combine* to make meaning? (such as sound sequence e.g. notes to bars to whole pieces of music) • How is does an integrated set of sounds *cohere?* (e.g. musical scales, keys) • What are the perceptible *ways of referring?* (such as literal sound likeness/abstract-symbolic reference e.g. a door bell compared to car horn) • What *media* are used to make the sound? (e.g. voice, musical instrument, sounds incidental to the use of an object)
Situation *How are the meanings shaped by the context of their location?*	• How is sound *framed* by its context of situation? (e.g. incidental sound/focused sounds, prominent sounds/ambient sounds, such as sound effects in a movie, elevator music, online music, live music performed in an auditorium) • How does an audio meaning connect into a *universe of sounds?* (such as soundscapes, musical keys, musical genres e.g. major/minor musical keys, baroque/reggae genres)
Intent *Whose interests do these meanings serve?*	• How do sounds or constellations of sounds establish certain *priorities*? (e.g. warnings, mood in musical keys) • Whose *interests* does the audio meaning serve? (e.g. ambient store music) • What *affinities* does it express or suggest? (e.g. serious/easy listening music)

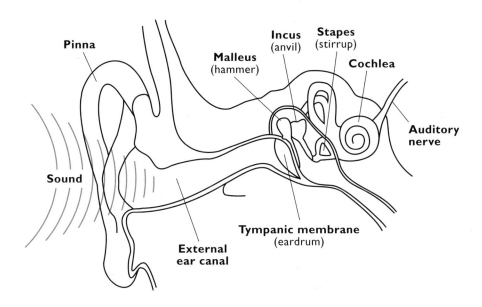

Figure 13.2 The ear

Signal processing begins in the inner ear. Sound perception may be masked by other sounds – for instance, an audible sound that may be heard because it is covered by a more prominent sound.

Our audio meanings begin with the similarities and contrasts that are created by rhythm, pitch, volume, tempo, texture and directionality. Everyday soundscapes, music and speech are distinct systems of audio meaning, closely related to each other. We do not simply hear the sounds of our environment, music and speech. We learn to make sense of them based on their meanings (audio representation) – the sound of a bell ringing, or mood music in a store, for instance. We make sounds that have meanings for others to interpret (audio communication), such as warning sounds with a car horn, or music that evokes particular feelings (Ball 2010).

 See literacies.com Ball on Meanings in Music.

We also record and transmit sounds for communication at a later date or across time (Chanan 1995).

 See literacies.com Chanan on the Invention of Recording.

Music and multimodal literacies

Ryan Rimmington teaches music in a Chicago secondary school. His learning module 'Multicultural Choral Connections' takes his students through a sequence of activities that not only include explorations of the characteristic audio mode of music, but quite consciously and directly link audio with other modes of meaning. In the audio mode, he has students listen to music, rehearse it, perform it and then listen to recordings of music representing the ethnic diversity of the school and broader communities.

However, this is not without shifting between audio and other modes to create a fuller and deeper sense of the meanings embodied in the music. In the written mode, the students read and write music reviews, create definitions of specific technical terms, explore sight/singing strategies to connect the melody line with the lyrics, and post blog entries reflecting on their learning experiences. In the oral mode, students discuss the way in which the feeling of a cultural expression is represented through its music, plan their rehearsal strategies, and discuss the finer points of performance after listening to recordings. In the visual mode, they read musical notation, design concert program notes and explore visual metaphors in music. In the spatial mode, they configure the space for a public performance. In the gestural mode, they discuss the modes of expression to accompany the choral performance and the role of the conductor. And in the tactile mode, they explore the connections between instruments and sound in performance. The final performance captures musical nuances across five different cultural traditions. To support this multimodal intervention, the music teacher enlists the expertise and support of teachers from the foreign language department in the school and the history department.

Historically, the subject of music separated this variety of audio meaning-making from subjects that dealt with other modes. Art dealt with the visual mode, for instance, and literacy the written mode. Here we can see a powerfully synaesthetic learning environment at work in which students shift between modes of meaning to add depth to their learning of music.

Oral meanings

How speaking is different from writing

Oral communication uses the elemental audio qualities of volume and pitch to configure a range of meaning as wide as that of each of the other modes. Oral representation takes the form of listening, or interpreting the meanings in the oral language one hears. Oral communication takes the form of speaking, or making an audible linguistic utterance that another person may hear.

We have put oral meaning last in our discussion of modes for a reason. In our circle diagram (Figure 13.3), oral meaning, as well as having audio meaning as its obvious immediate neighbour, has written language for its other immediate neighbour. This is the point where we started to discuss each of the modes of representation and communication in Chapter 9. However, we have kept this discussion about oral meaning as far away from the discussion of written meaning as possible because we want to argue that oral language and written language are deceptively different. When schools teach phonics, it is on the assumption that

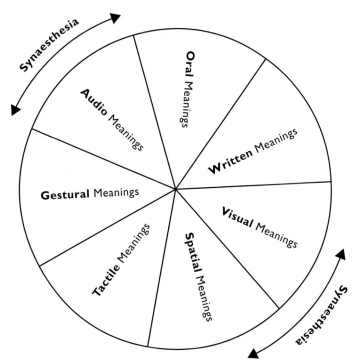

Figure 13.3 Modes of meaning

learning to write and read in alphabetic languages is foundationally a business of learning sound–letter correspondences. However, we want to argue that oral and written meanings are so importantly different from each other that they are no more closely related than any two of the other modes of meaning.

Here are some common misconceptions about the connection between speaking and writing, misconceptions that we need to interrogate carefully as we consider the question of learning 'literacy' in the singular as much as 'literacies' in the plural.

First misconception: writing is a transcription of the sounds of speech. However, no writing captures the full range of meanings to be found in sound. Writing has to compensate by creating quite different ways to capture meanings carried in sounds – such as emphases with underlining or italics, or queries with question marks. The exact form and degree of oral meaning is difficult to transcribe into writing. No matter how hard writing tries to capture an oral meaning, it can never quite succeed. It can do something roughly equivalent or broadly similar, but never quite the same thing. In any event, the sound transcription business is made all the more confusing by the phonic complexities we described in Chapter 9, and is irrelevant to literacies in logographic languages such as Chinese.

The second misconception is that written language is a different wording for the same meanings that happen in oral language. We know that a spontaneous oral description of something, if fully and accurately transcribed, will look very

Table 13.2: A grammar of oral meanings

Reference
What do the meanings refer to?
	• What are the distinctive *audible features* of the speech? (e.g. rhythm, stress, tempo, pausing and pitch: rising, falling, dipping, peaking)
	
	  ◦ How is a *person* connected in speech? (e.g. I am speaking, I am listening, I am saying or hearing something about a person)
	  ◦ How is *time* referred to? (e.g. live speech in the present, recorded speech to be heard in the future)
	  ◦ How is *place* referred to? (e.g. live speech here, recorded or transmitted speech played somewhere else)
	  ◦ How are things referred to? (e.g. the spoken words for things)
	  ◦ What *general concept* does speaking refer to?
	  ◦ How are *characteristics* referred to? (emphases, intonation e.g. happiness/sadness, anger/even temper, fear, surprise, sarcasm)
	  ◦ How are *relations* represented? (e.g. phrasing)

Dialogue *How do the meanings connect the people who are interacting?*	• How does the *speech configure* the persons involved? (e.g. a lecture, a conversation) • What *kinds of connections* do the audible sounds of speech establish between participants? (e.g. a statement, a question, a command) • What *patterns of emphasis* are established within spoken meaning units? (e.g. stress of the focal meaning-point or new information)
Structure *How does the overall meaning hold together?*	• How are the *units of speech* marked by audio variation? (such as by pause and pitch e.g. beginning/ends of oral information units) • How do sound units *cohere*? (e.g. syllables, utterances – note phonemes have no meaning in-themselves) • How are meaningful *sound variations chained*? (such as prosody, poetics e.g. metre, rhyme) • What are the *audible ways of referring* in speech (such as literal/symbolic e.g. the sound resemblance of onomatopoeia) • How is the oral meaning *expressed*? (e.g. spoken or whispered close up/shouted from a distance, speech with/without mechanical amplification, live/recorded speech)
Situation *How are the meanings shaped by the context of their location?*	• How is speech *framed* by the context of its situation? (e.g. a one-on-one conversation, a group discussion, a monologue, talking to oneself) • How does the oral quality of an utterance fit into a wider framework of *alternative modes of speaking*? • What larger *patterns of oral meaning* does the utterance fit into by its overall modes of resemblance/difference (e.g. accents, dialects)
Intent *Whose interests do these meanings serve?*	• How does speech reflect or establish *role differentials*? (e.g. tones of expertise, condescension, power) • Whose *interests* does this way of speaking serve? (e.g. tones of pleading, haranguing, ordering) • What *affinities* does it express or suggest by its tone? (e.g. serious, playful)

different from a 'well-written' paragraph describing the same thing. However, what is the difference between a paragraph description of a scene and a photograph of the same scene? The two are referring to one scene but, the ways in which they present the information are different. Because the meaning modes are different, the meanings can never be quite the same. The difference between speaking and writing is just as great.

Oral and written meanings are, of course, connected through language. For this reason, in referring to the same things meanings in oral and written languages may be parallel. But they are never quite the same. In fact, there are equally powerful connections between oral and audio meanings because they share hearing as a primary sense medium, and written and visual meanings because they share visual perception as a primary sense medium.

Oral and written meanings compared

What, then, are the differences between oral and written meanings?

We are going to analyse the differences on the basis of two archetypical forms: spontaneous live speech and carefully formed writing, such as an essay or a letter. There are also intermediate forms, such as speaking-like-writing (for instance, a lecture being given without notes) and, particularly important today, writing-like-speaking (such as a text message or a conversation in a chat room). We will discuss these later. However, before we get to these hybrid, oral–written crossover forms, we want to disentangle the features that make the two modes significantly different.

We are going to argue that these differences in meaning between the written and oral modes are so significant that the two modes are typically used to mean different things.

For a start, there are important differences in the processes of the design of oral language and the design of written language that leave their traces in the text or, in the case of writing, have particular ways of hiding their traces. On first impression, speaking seems messier, full of 'ums', 'ahs' and phrases such as 'I mean to say'. There are many false starts as you reframe an idea, revising choices of wording or diction or grammar after you have heard yourself say them the first time. Speaking often sounds like a kind of 'thinking aloud'.

Writing, by comparison, seems to be better-formed language because it is more methodically and consciously made. However, the writing process involves at least as many changes to recover missteps as speaking, and nowadays keyboarding makes these changes easier than ever. In fact, it is probably an even messier process than speaking, at least in the initial drafting. The main difference with writing is that we hide these traces of the process of construction of meaning because we have time to create a polished final draft, with initial formulations revised. Signs of the making of text are out of sight, and their details also out of mind, by the time a keyboarded text is finished.

Whether we are speaking or writing, we are always making our choices of words and selecting combinations of words for meaning. We are always consciously weighing up in our own minds what we have just said, the words that have just come out. It's just that we do this in completely different ways for speaking and writing, and this results in completely different kinds of text. These conscious processes of making on-the-fly changes are unavoidably audible in the case of speaking, but can be made invisible in the case of writing because the writing process is such that we can hide them. This is why, if we were to transcribe every word, sound and pause that comes out of our mouths, it would seem to be very poor writing. Indeed, we may be tempted to think it poor language because it comes out as poor writing. But it is not. That would be to judge speech by the measure of writing.

Indeed, there is not much point in transferring speech directly to writing, and linguists in the subfield of phonetics are the only ones who ever seriously try. Neither speaker nor listener picks up things that the speaker might change if they were put in carefully formed writing. When a person is asked to recall what another person has just said, they usually can't remember it verbatim. They remember ideas, not wordings. Their response is always a paraphrase, not a repetition. This is because a listener follows the meanings, not the words. A listener doesn't notice the repetitions, hesitations and revisions – except when they signify something (like the speaker's state of uncertainty, or difficulty with an idea – things, incidentally, that writing largely erases).

The business of transcribing speech to writing does not highlight the inadequacies of speech, such as 'errors' that are corrected or left uncorrected. It shows the vast differences between speech and writing, in which there are no errors but just on-the-fly changes as the speaker thinks aloud about their meanings. This is a normal process of meaning-making in which listeners don't hear things that are irrelevant to meaning. The analogy in writing would be you, the reader, seeing the text you are reading now, not as the carefully crafted text that you see in front of you but as a replay of the sequence of keystrokes from which it was constructed. This would distract you from the meaning while typos are corrected, words changed, phrases moved around and ideas rethought. You, the reader, don't need that. It is irrelevant to the sense you may make of this text. As a listener, your cognitive process of interpretation of speech edits out irrelevant, cursory revisions because your focus is not on the meanings-of-the-words but on the meanings-to-you.

For these reasons, and many more, transcribing speech produces poor writing because it has none of the qualities that make writing a mode of meaning that is importantly different from speech. These differences start with the way that each is made. Writing/reading and speaking/listening are profoundly different kinds of communication, representation and cognitive processes. To learn to write you need to learn to think differently, not just recognise the sounds of written words.

Writing is unable to capture the full, audible dimensionality of intonation, accent and dialect. A comma can never tell you how poignant the pause, a question mark how insistent the question, nor underlining how stressed the emphasis. Tonic prominence or sound emphasis tells you the point of a sentence (given information/the subject), contrasted in a word cluster with audibly more prominent new information/the predicate. In written English you can only tell the prominence of a new idea because it is located at the end of the clause, but you can't easily tell how prominent it is, or detect nuances of prominence at other points in the clause. No matter how hard we try, we can't translate the subtle and profound nuances of oral language into writing. Linguists do try, using obscure phonetic notations, but even their best attempts never capture every aspect of meaning conveyed by speech. When we speak, we are able to mean differently. Although there are parallels that allow us to shift mode, we can never mean in quite the same ways, or even mean quite the same things.

There are also important differences in the ways speaking and writing are explicit. In oral conversation, the language points to 'I' or 'you', 'this' or 'that', 'here' or 'there', 'today' or 'yesterday', which are all relative to the speaking participants, their time and their place. These things do not have to be explicitly named, because they are an integral part of the multimodal meaning event – its situation. They are evident in the spatial, visual, gestural and tactile meanings surrounding speech in its moment of utterance.

Writing, however, first has to name 'I', 'you', 'this', 'that', 'here', 'there', 'today' and 'yesterday' before these words can be used, so the reader knows what they are referring to. In speaking, the reference can point directly to a shared context. In writing, pointing words mostly have to point to another, more explicit word in the text – a previously mentioned name of a person, thing, place or time, for instance. The difference is fundamental. Speaking is tied to the here and now. Writing, however, is in its very nature dislocated from context. This is another way in which, even though oral and written meanings want to talk about the same thing, they need to say it in a quite different way.

The differences, moreover, go even deeper. Oral and written meanings are not only different ways of passing messages (communicating); they are different ways of thinking (representation). To show how deep these differences can be, we will reproduce an oral 'translation' by the linguist Michael Halliday of some text from *Scientific American* magazine (see Table 13.3).

Already, simply in the transcription, Halliday's translation has lost much that makes oral language different, such as the running revisions that would have been heard in the speech, its intonation, its pauses and its hesitations. He has also put the spoken text in sentences and paragraphs, where speech has strings of phrases and clauses that run on. Kress calls these 'information units' (Kress 1993: 175–6). Sentences and paragraphs only happen in written language.

See literacies.com Halliday on Speaking.

However, it is not this that Halliday wants to highlight by comparing these texts. The very wordings and word relations of language change. Speech uses more words than writing to make an equivalent meaning. Speech uses shorter clauses and more of them (Halliday 2002: 327–35). Writing is more dense, more synoptic, with less redundancy. Speech strings information units one after the other, connecting them with words that link roughly equivalent things (such as 'and', 'or', 'then')

Table 13.3: Halliday's comparisons between written meaning and oral meaning

Written meaning: a text from *Scientific American*	Oral meaning: Halliday's 'translation' into (somewhat more) oral language
Private civil actions at law have a special significance in that they provide an outlet for efforts by independent citizens. Such actions offer a means whereby the multiple initiatives of the private citizens, individually or in groups, can be brought to bear on technology assessment, the internalisation of costs and environmental protection. They constitute a channel through which the diverse interests, outlooks and moods of the general public can be given expression. The current popular concern over the environment has stimulated private civil actions of two main types.	One thing is especially significant, and that is that people should be able to bring private civil actions at law, because by doing this independent citizens can become involved. By bringing these actions, whether they are acting as individuals or in groups, private citizens can keep on taking the initiative; they can help to assess technology, they can help to internalise costs, and they can help to protect the environment. The general public, who want all kinds of different things, and who think and feel in all kinds of different ways, can express all these wants and thoughts and feelings by bringing civil actions at law. At present, people are concerned about the environment; so they have been bringing quite a few private civil actions, which have been mainly of two kinds.
• More dense • More synoptic • Less redundancy • Uses nominalisations – packing an idea that might have been a whole spoken clause into a noun or a noun phrase inside a written clause • Needs to be explicit to make sense to strangers or people not present • Uses pronouns that cross-reference subjects, places and action • More likely to choose the third person to refer to events • Dislocated from context • Uses passive voice more • Has an aura of objectivity • Is inclined to represent the world more as a product	• More words than writing to make an equivalent meaning • Shorter clauses and more of them • Strings information units one after the other • Connects bits of information with words that link roughly equivalent things • Does not have to refer to subjects, time and place explicitly because all are present and assumed • Can get away with leaving the things it is referring to implicit • Focuses on the here and now • Uses the active voice more • Has an aura of subjectivity • Is inclined to represent the world more as a process

Source: Halliday (2002: 330).

and logical connectives that link things where a difference needs to be highlighted (such as 'until', 'as', 'to', 'because', 'if', 'to', 'which'). Writing, on the other hand, uses a process called nominalisation, or packing an idea that might have been a whole spoken clause into a noun or a noun phrase inside a written clause. In the example above, 'People should be able to bring' in the oral text becomes 'provides an outlet' in the written text. 'They can help to internalise costs' in the oral text becomes 'the internalisation of costs' in the written text. In other words, writing performs the logical task of connecting ideas in a way quite different from speaking. Each is just as intricate as a meaning-design. It is just that they are very different kinds of intricacy. These are signs that their modes of reasoning are entirely different. They are different ways of seeing the world and thinking about the world.

The full range of human meaning can be expressed in speaking and writing (and also in each of the other modes). This is how mode-shifting is possible. This is how we can mean about the same things in parallel ways in different modes. However, what we mean can never be quite the same. For instance, speaking often ends up being less explicit than writing. The characteristic ways of referring in speech are made clearer by the stance of the speaker, the speaker's connection with other participants and the level of certainty that the speaker wants to express about their knowledge. This is partly because a lot can go without saying in speaking because of the manifest presence of the participants in time and space, their real-time, live co-location. Even though it is not explicitly stated, what is said is clear because so much is obvious. If you eavesdrop on a conversation between two people on a bus or in a restaurant, it is often very hard to work out what they are talking about because you don't share their understanding of all the reference points for all the 'thems', 'theres' and 'thises' they are saying.

Speaking is also full of statements such as 'I think', 'In my opinion', 'I'm sure', 'you see?' and 'you know?', which make the interactive stance of the participants much clearer than is mostly the case for writing. Speech will also more often use the active voice, in which who is doing what to whom is directly stated. ('I went to the party yesterday, and there were lots of other people there as well.') In these and other ways, speaking makes the interest-laden role of the speaker-as-meaning-maker more explicit.

A writer, on the other hand, is more likely to choose the passive voice, and is also more likely to choose third person to refer to events. ('Yesterday's party was well attended.') The writer may be referring to the same thing as a speaker, but in writing they tend to create the impression that objects and events have a life of their own. This is why writing has an aura of objectivity while speaking has an aura of subjectivity.

Writing, explains Halliday, is inclined to represent the world more as a product; speaking more as a process. Speech is more spun out, flowing, choreographic and oriented to events (doing, happening, sensing, saying, being). It is more process-like, with meanings related serially. Writing is dense, structured, crystalline and oriented towards things (entities, objectified processes). It is product-like and tight, with meanings related as components (Halliday 2002: 344, 350).

Writing is not only designed to cross distances in time and space between the point of its writing and the points of its reading. It also creates a sense of distance through its aura of objectivity. Of course, this is more a rhetorical effect, an impression you are expected to get, than a reality. Writers want you to think they are speaking facts or true opinions, but they really have a lot invested personally and subjectively just to be writing. People design writing and transform the world with it to no less effect than speakers do.

Speakers, by comparison, are more explicit about their subjective, immediate, here-and-now connection with their meanings. 'You know, I reckon …', they may characteristically frame a statement. It is hard for them not to express their personal investment in what they are saying.

Writers, however, can create a sense that the writing speaks objectively; that its contents are true and factual. If I were speaking, I might say, 'I agree with all the scientists who mostly say that global warming has been caused by humans,' but if I were writing a scientific paper I might say, 'Overwhelming scientific evidence supports the thesis that climate change is a by-product of human settlement.' This is how I imbue 'I agree', which is just my opinion, with the authority of 'scientific evidence'. I'm still agreeing, but I'm making my mere opinion sound more like serious science. Nothing is totally objective. We always have interests and every utterance is an expression of those interests. However, I can use writing to create the impression of objectivity, to cloak my interest in the voice of an authority that is greater than my own.

We can talk about the same things in writing and speaking, but by choosing one mode or the other we can also mean in importantly different ways. By meaning in such different ways, writing and speaking end up meaning different things. Because they are able to mean different things, they are used for different purposes at different times and in different places. We choose to speak or to write in one context or another because, for the moment, it is more apt to our meaning-intent. We choose the one mode or the other because we think it will work better for our purposes. The choices we make, to speak or to write, are a consequence of peculiarities in the design of each mode. These peculiarities are not only about how we can mean, but about what we can mean.

Paths to synaesthesia: crossovers between oral and written meanings

Writing-like speech and speech-like writing

There are, however, a number of crossover spaces: times when speech acts more like writing and times when writing acts more like speech.

Take the case of writing-like speech. A lecturer may speak from schematic notes instead of reading a script. Or an expert may give answers to questions in a radio or television interview. The spoken texts that the lecturer or the expert utters will be somewhat writing-like, at least compared to how they may speak about the same issues with a friend over a drink. The lecturer and the expert sound educated in the lecture theatre or the interview because they have imported some of the characteristic grammatical forms of writing into their speech. It makes it sound as if they are speaking objective truths. It makes them seem authoritative. Ong calls this secondary orality, or orality that has been influenced by literacy (Ong 1982). However, no matter how hard they may try, these speakers' meanings are still irreducibly oral. If they were faithfully written down, and not edited as interview or lecture transcripts mostly are, you would always be able to tell that they were transcribed from spoken language.

Now to take the other kind of crossover case, the case of speech-like writing. Direct quotes and theatrical dialogue are two ways to try to capture the nuances of spoken language. But, of course, they never quite do. Personal letters are in their design somewhat closer to speech than a formal memo, but that is only a matter of degree. Writing a diary is a kind of talking to oneself, but its text is nothing like the language of silently talking to oneself. These are examples of writing that try hard to capture the characteristic meanings of orality, but they are still irreducibly written meanings, regardless. Even the most personal letter is not like real talking, and no theatrical script is like any conversation that may really happen in the world.

Here is a famous piece of speech-like writing, a paragraph from Mark Twain's *Huckleberry Finn*, which captures some of the lilt of everyday speech of Mississippi communities in the 19th century.

> Sometimes we'd have the whole river all to ourselves for the longest time. Yonder was the banks and the islands, across the water; and maybe a spark – which was a candle in a cabin window – and sometimes on the water you could see a spark or two – on a raft or a scow, you know; and maybe you could hear a fiddle or a song coming over from one of them crafts. It's lovely to live on a raft. We had the sky, up there, all speckled with stars, and we used to lay on our backs and look up at them, and discuss about whether they was made, or only just happened – Jim he allowed they was made, but I allowed they happened; I judged it would have took too long to make so many. Jim said the moon could a laid them; well, that looked kind of reasonable, so I didn't say nothing against it, because I've seen a frog lay most as many, so of course it could be done. We used to watch the stars that fell, too, and see them streak down. Jim allowed they'd got spoiled and was hove out of the nest.

As writing, on some measures, it is at times ungrammatical. However, it's still writing, a hybrid form which from sentence to sentence weaves between attempting to be like speech and then not.

Across the range of writing-types, some genres are somewhat closer to the distinctive features of speech than others, even though they are still characteristically written. A written personal recount, for example, can have features characteristically closer to speech than writing. ('First I did this, then I did that …'.) Many of the most powerful written genres have the aura they do precisely because they are more distant from speech – such as scientific articles or legal contracts. Writing 'readable' popular science or 'plain English' contracts imports some of the design features of speaking into the written text. We may receive this as 'chatty' reader-friendliness, but these remain irreducibly written texts. In any event, it takes a scientist or a lawyer who can also read and understand the 'hard stuff' to make the translation. When power is put on display, it will sound more like writing. But when a writer wants to downplay or bridge power discrepancies, they will push their writing in the direction of speaking.

Today's media environment is also full of these kinds of hybrid, crossover forms. Emails are more like speaking than traditional business letters. Text messages are less formal than telegrams were in their day. Instant messaging has many of the characteristics of speaking. A blogger sounds more like they are speaking to you than a traditional magazine writer or journalist. Grammar checkers warn us against using the passive voice. Professionals who write instruction manuals or legal documents are told to make their communications 'user-friendly'.

Meanwhile, more important things happen in speaking today than they ever did before. Scientific as well as academic articles are spoken in video on the Web as well as academic articles. Business strategy is articulated as a slideshow voice-over as well as business reports. Decisions are conveyed in team meetings and not just in memos. There are fewer old-fashioned newsreaders on television and radio speaking from flawlessly written texts of objective events, and more people expressing strongly voiced opinions in distinctively oral ways. Oral meanings are becoming more powerfully important parts of our everyday lives.

See literacies.com Speaking Like Writing.

These developments are connected deeply to the sensibilities of our time, such as the way we now seem to value perspective over information and how, in an egalitarian spirit, we often want to downplay hierarchy and power. They are the practical reasons why today's literacies must focus not just on writing in its classical forms, but on speaking as well. This is also why literacies educators need to focus on mode-shifting. Practically speaking, we go backwards and forwards between speaking and writing more than ever. Furthermore, of great importance today are the hybrid in-between forms in which one mode influences the other while never erasing its fundamental differences.

Classroom discourse in old and new media, in speaking and writing

One very interesting example of a crossover space between speaking and writing is classical oral classroom discussion compared to written discussion in web forums and social media activity streams. Both are forms of discussion, but this is where the similarity ends – the two are remarkably different. In this case, new media has taken a traditionally oral mode, and recreated in the written mode.

In her pathbreaking book, *Classroom Discourse,* Courtney Cazden characterises the classical pattern of classroom discussion as Initiate-Respond-Evaluate (I-R-E) (Cazden 2001). Here's the classical pattern:

Figure 13.4 Hands up!

Teacher initiates: 'What's the furthest planet from the sun in the Solar System?'

Students respond: (Members of the class shoot up their hands, and one responds, a proxy for all the others:) 'Pluto.'

Teacher evaluates: 'Yes, that's correct!' (Or an alternative ending: 'No, that's wrong, does someone else know the answer?')

Now let's look at the discussions that happen in a web activity stream. They're the same in this respect – this is a class discussion space that enacts the classic discursive Initiate-Respond-Evaluate pattern. And it's utterly different, in the following ways.

1. *Everyone responds.* In classical I-R-E, one person is proxy, answering for all. Instead, in new media discussions potentially everyone responds. In fact, there can be an expectation that everyone must respond. The result: a silent classroom that in classical classroom discourse would have been chaotically noisy, or where the class would have to wait an interminably long time for more or all to give their response.

2. *Lowered barriers to response.* Here's a rough rule of thumb – in classical I-R-E, it's usually the wrong person who responds first with the proxy answer – the student who has the confidence to shoot up their hand first or early, or the person who the teacher can rely upon to have the anticipated answer. In new media written discussions (we'll use the Scholar example here), the initiation happens in an 'update', and the response in a 'comment' on that update. In our research, students have told us that simply having a few extra moments to look over their response before they press the 'submit comment' button reduces their anxiety to participate (Cope & Kalantzis 2013).

3. *When everyone responds, learner differences become visible and valuable.* In the classical I-R-E scenario, it is not practicable to get answers from everyone. The expectation is that there is one answer because the person answering for the rest of the class must act as proxy for the others. This becomes an exercise in guessing the answer that the teacher expects. In asking the question, they

must have had something particular in mind. If only one person is going to answer, it must mean there is only one answer. But is Pluto really a planet? And if it is, might there be other small planets? The definition of planet is not so simple. Most things are interesting enough for there to be more than one answer, or differently nuanced answers, or different examples that students might give to illustrate a point based on personal interest and experience. In the Scholar community dialogue dialogue, for example, the univocal response of the proxy in classical I-R-E becomes polyvalent. Distinctive identities and voice come through. Students soon start discussing these differences, addressing each other by beginning their comment, for example, with @Juan, or @Maritsa. If classical I-R-E erases the differences, now they become visible and valued as a resource for intellectual dialogue. Also, anxieties to participate and voice one's own view are reduced as others' responses start to come through.

4. *This is highly engaging.* Classical I-R-E is boring – listening to the teacher ask a question and to another student give an answer. The cognitive load is suboptimal. Reading lots of answers is much more engaging. Instead of one answer, there may be as many as there are members of the community, and more. In the era of intensive Facebook and Twitter feeds, the cognitive load is about right. And there is a social stickiness in the visibility of the discussion – you stay engaged because others will be reading and responding to your updates and comments.

5. *The read/write mix and the participation mix is right.* Heritage classrooms had students listening more than speaking, reading more than writing. Like the participatory social media, e-learning environments such as Scholar offer a balance of read/write, and an expectation of active participation that resonates with the spirit of our times. Also, the text of the discussion is deceptively different from oral language. Halliday contrasts the grammars of orality and writing in the ways already characterised in this chapter – speaking is linear, redundant and made up of strings of clauses; writing is in sentences, concise and carefully composed in a non-linear, backwards and forwards process (Halliday 1989). Looking back over a comment, and editing it before submitting, moves part way from the grammar of speaking to the grammar of writing – and towards 'academic literacy'.

6. *We can break out of the four walls of the classroom and the cells of the timetable.* In these kinds of new media environments, there is no difference between in-person, synchronous classroom discussion and at-a-distance, asynchronous discussion. And there are useful intermediate permutations – 'Finish the discussion tonight,' or 'Not at school today? No problem, participate anyway.'

7. *Anyone can be an initiator.* It's not only the teacher who can start a classroom discussion. If the teacher choses to open this setting in their e-learning environment, students can make updates too – and this can include any number of media objects, including image, sound, video and dataset.

8. *A new transparency, learning analytics and assessment.* Whereas discussions in the traditional classroom were ephemeral, online discussions are for-the-record. In the new I-R-E where everyone responds, every response can be seen, and the responses can be parsed using learning analytics (frequency of engagement,

extent of engagement, language level, discussion network visualisations, and myriad other measures). If you are not participating, it will be visible to others and your teachers. It will show up in your results.

Figure 13.5 Classroom discussion in Scholar

 See literacies.com Written Classroom Discussion in New Media.

Synaesthesia and learning

There are profound educational reasons why we would want to bring the oral and oral–written mode-shifting back into literacies, and these are connected with the concept of synaesthesia. Mode-shifting can be used as a strategy for learning. We can mean a house in a mental image, we can mean it in a written description. We may ask a learner to draw the house, then write a description of the house. Both meanings refer to the same thing, but in completely different ways. They end up as different meanings about the same thing. So it is with speaking and writing. We may ask a student to talk about a house, and then write about it. The oral and the written texts are as different from each other as the visual and the written. However, the mode-shifting will have been helpful to learning. Making meaning about the house through the one mode helps us form the meaning in the other. It also adds something to the developing overall, multimodal meaning of the house.

Early literacy teachers have naturally, and as a matter of course, used synaesthetic strategies to support the development of reading and writing skills. Phonics is itself a stratagem using synaesthesia, in its most powerfully effective moments exploring the subtle and deceptively intricate nexus between sound as heard and sound as represented in writing. To ease the mode-shift from the oral to the written, early reading often carries the cadences of speaking onto the printed page.

Rhada Iyer describes a case of mode-shifting in an early literacy classroom. In pairs, students read fairy tales to each other, focusing on the sound of these stories as told – its tone, its stress and its emphases. They then begin a multimodal composing process to create their own fairy tale, a collage of the tales they have read. The teacher storyboards the overall story with the whole class. Students create various pages using a painting program, which the teacher then compiles into a whole-class digital story presented in PowerPoint. The story is titled 'The Great Big Enormous Carrot'.

> Once upon a time Pinocchio planted a carrot seed. 'Grow little carrot seed. Grow sweet. Grow strong,' he said.
>
> The carrot grew big and sweet and strong. 'I'm going to pull up this great big enormous carrot,' he said. BUT he could not pull it up.
>
> Pinocchio called Rapunzel to help.
>
> Rapunzel called the Three Little Pigs to help.
>
> The Three Little Pigs called the Big Bad Wolf to help.
>
> The Big Bad Wolf called Cinderella to help.
>
> Cinderella called The Ugly Duckling to help.
>
> The Ugly Duckling called Sleeping Beauty to help.
>
> Sleeping Beauty called Jack and the Beanstalk to help.
>
> Jack and the Beanstalk called the Woodcutter to help.
>
> They pulled and **Pulled and Pulled**.
>
> Up came the carrot at last!
>
> They took the carrot home and made a great big carrot cake for dessert.

The oral source of fairy stories remains in the repetition and the typography ('BUT' and '**Pulled and Pulled**'). The students then perform the story orally for each other and their parents. 'Audio design', concludes Iyer, 'was closely examined along with gestural design, to train students to deliver the text with suitable effect to their audience' (Iyer 2006: 25–33).

In Soweto, South Africa, we find Robert Maungedzo teaching his Year/Grade 10 and 11 students. 'Teaching literature was frustrating for Robert', report Stein and Newfield. 'Students did not read the set books – most did not even have the books. Robert tried to help them to pass the final examinations by lecturing to them on the books' themes and characters.' One of his students said to him one day: 'We are wasting our time at school because people who are educated are unemployed and those who are driving posh cars are the criminals.' Robert says this prompted him to do some 'soul searching'. He decided to explore multimodal teaching, to provide a pathway from the rich oral experiences of his students to the world of the written word.

Robert's students had prescribed for them a novel written by South African author Bessie Head, about a woman Margaret, of 'mixed race' and who teaches in Botswana. Her mother has died in childbirth and her body lies unwashed on the hospital floor because the nurses refuse to wash someone of her Masarwa tribe.

> When Robert asked his learners to draw rather than discuss key scenes in the novel, the novel sprang to life for them. According to Robert, one mode of semiotic production led to another. The students drew pictures, sang songs and performed plays. They explained that in their culture songs are sung to ease the pain, and that acting is cathartic: 'sometimes we run out of words, but not out of body language,' they said ... At the end of the year, in the final Matric examination, the results showed a dramatic improvement; out of 140 candidates, only one failed the English Second Language examination (Stein & Newfield 2002: 9).

Robert went on to explore in greater depth the oral tradition of African 'praise poems', a ritualistic way in which black South Africans introduce or identify themselves and their situations. Thando, a student in Robert's class, has now written 81 poems, including 'Soweto for Young Freaks'. As Stein and Newfield explain:

> It has the edgy contemporary feel of kwaito (a current popular music genre) and tsotsitaal (a multilingual street language), and catches both the glamour and danger of life in the fast lane. It is, in spite of its irony, a celebration of the ghetto and makes a contribution to the archive of writing on township life.

Translations appear in square brackets.

> **Soweto ... Soweto for Young Freaks**
> In Soweto there are no birds to sing in the sky
> They ate them all up.
> In Soweto there are no cocks to wake you up
> 'cause we had them for thanksgiving
> In Soweto there are no longer horses to ride
> because Basotho ba djile.
> [because the Basotho people have eaten them up]
> But in Soweto we have AK47 to sing
> But in Soweto we have screams to wake you up
> But in Soweto we have stolen cars to ride

Figure 13.6 Soweto

> Because amajita a shaisile.
> [because gangsters have made a killing]

Another student, Sonnyboy, writes:

> My Tsonga praise poem induced me to know my roots. I was like a tree without
> roots, a brook without a source. ... I think this is the most precious thing I have ever
> done in my life. Since I began schooling I have never had an opportunity to discover
> my talents and gifts ... It's like I was fortified in knowledge and understanding (Stein
> & Newfield 2003: 2844).

Stein and Newfield conclude: 'Robert has characterised his experiences as a journey, beginning with the Station of Reluctance, travelling to the Station of Uncertainty, and then arriving at the Station of Agency.'

In a final example of the oral meanings, we take a journey with Michael Newman
to a high school in Queens, New York. Here he examines the oral vernacular genre
of rap cipher, or improvised, round-robin rhyming. In narrower understandings,
laments Newman, rap would not be considered 'literacy'. This school, however, recognised it as a powerful mode of oral meaning, of enormous power in a wider view
of multiliteracies. Its practices meld hip-hop music with graffiti art (called 'writing'),
break dancing ('b-boying'), and DJing ('turntablism'). 'Cherub' is a member of the rap
crew 'squad Innumerable' who attend this small public secondary school, 'Urban
Arts Academy'. Here is the beginning of a 121 'verse' (line) improvisation by Cherub.

> Yao Yao Hey yo,
> Yeah Cherub blasts past everyone

Proud with all around me.

Like my name is the sun.

Number one.

Breaking out all the charts

Cherub is guaranteed to spit a dart

right through your heart.

Appear in the dark

When the night comes.

Cherub always the rhyme never done.

My style flow consistently

Ain't nobody

in this vicinity

fuck with me.

'cause I can't count back from three.

And you can see how easily

I crush MCs

'cause I flow consistently.

Cherub, huh, that cat that lyrically

rip rappers in half; you know their name.

Remember this: it gonna be the same

ten years from now, but right now, fear this style.

Cause Cherub, huh, gonna freestyle (Newman 2005: 405).

Compared to the underground rap scene to which Cherub and his friends belong, Newman explains that this 'squad' was considered, to some degree, an artefact of the school. Some said their rap work at school was 'just a class'. Others, however, said it was the only reason they were still at school. A few of the artists had gone on to create a production company with a website, offering MP3s for download (Newman 2005).

These are striking examples of teachers exploring to their fullest the differences between oral and written modes of meaning and using synaesthesia, or mode-shifting, as the basis for a powerful, multimodal pedagogy.

All meaning is intrinsically, unavoidably, always, humanly, multimodal. So writing cannot happen without some visualisation, nor without saying things to yourself in oral meaning as you translate these meanings into writing. Multimodal, synaesthetic learning brings these processes to consciousness. It discusses explicitly the relation of the design elements across each mode. It gets the students to make their meanings in one mode then another. There is cognitive power in both these moves. It also encourages the metacognition intrinsic to creating meanings about meaning, and a depth of learning that comes of making meaning in one mode, then another.

These are the fundamentals of literacies in the plural.

See literacies.com Learning Modules.

See literacies.com #edtech Literacies Applications.

Summary

Audio and oral meanings	Written meanings, by comparison
• Carried by the sense of hearing, and in this respect closely connected with audio meaning	• Carried by the sense of seeing, and in this respect closely connected with visual meaning
• Hesitations, revisions and reframings on-the-fly	• Carefully measured revisions, invisible to readers
• Strings of ideas, a linear flow	• Hierarchical structuring of ideas (e.g. title, sections, paragraphs, sentences, clauses)
• Referring to shared context, outside of the text (today, you, here)	• Referring to explicitly named context internal to the text ('she' refers to Valetta, who has been already named in the text)
Crossover oral–written meanings	
• Spoken verse and story	• Quoted direct speech
• Music lyrics	• Email
• Theatre dialogue	• Text and instant messaging
• Technical talk: talking (a bit) like writing	• Social networking posts

Knowledge processes

experiencing the known

1. Create an audio log for a day or part of one of your days. What alerts and warnings do you encounter in a day? What ambient sounds do you experience? What meanings do you attribute to these sounds?

experiencing the new

2. Listen to several pieces of music from an unfamiliar genre, with or without words. What feelings or meanings does the music evoke for you? Explain the associations you make.

conceptualising by naming

3. Create a comparison table contrasting the distinctive features of oral language with those of written language. Give examples of each feature.

analysing critically

4. Examine some contemporary crossover oral–written texts, such as email or text messages. What features of oral language do they have? What are the advantages and dangers of these kinds of communication? Compare with older, more formal genres such as a business letter or a telegram.

applying appropriately

5. Record a person speaking impromptu about a topic. Transcribe what they say. (What challenges did you experience in the transcription?) Now turn this text into formal writing. (What changes did you need to make? How are the meanings of the oral and written texts similar and different?)

analysing functionally

6. Take a formal written text, such as a science report. Analyse the design elements of this text that make it different from spoken language.

applying creatively

7. Plan a learning experience that moves students between oral and written language, and that does so in such a way that it highlights the differences as well as making the most of the parallels.

PART D

The 'how' of literacies

CHAPTER 14

Literacies to think and to learn

Overview

We begin this chapter by exploring the similarities and differences between communication in humans and other animals. One key difference is our human capacity to apply symbols to meanings in the world, and to connect symbols with each other into symbol systems. Symbols represent general things – the concept of 'dog' as distinct from this dog, Fido. Although young children learn the word 'dog' at a young age, it is not until they are older that they use the word as a concept. Conceptualisation can also occur in the other modes – for instance, in visual or gestural meanings. All academic disciplines use literacies as a basis for communicating knowledge, and also for learners to represent knowledge to themselves in their thinking. Literacies, for this reason, are the most basic of all basics in education.

Literacies and cognitive development

Human thinking compared to other thinking in animals

Animals other than humans can also think and communicate. However, no other animals have our species' peculiar representational capacities (the way we make meanings for ourselves) and communicative capacities (the way we make meanings for others). Nor do they have our thinking capacities.

Thinking and literacies are inseparable. Adult humans think through the representational systems that are literacies. Without these systems they could not think, or at least they could not think in the ways that are characteristically human. In children, for this reason, learning literacies and developing thinking capacities are inseparable. Literacies are absolutely a 'basic' of education. In fact, they are the most basic of basics. Once again, we mean literacies in the plural, not just reading and writing.

To help us draw a borderline between human and non-human thinking and communication, we are going to turn to a philosopher and an ape. The ape first. Kanzi is a bonobo (a small species of chimpanzee) who lives in a reserve outside Atlanta, Georgia. He learned to use abstract symbols to communicate almost by accident when researchers Duane Rumbaugh and Sue Savage-Rumbaugh attempted, unsuccessfully, to teach his mother. Because the young animal was closely attached to his mother and with her all the time, after a time the researchers realised that Kanzi was beginning to pick up some of the things they were trying to teach the mother.

Eventually, Kanzi was able to identify symbols and photographs and understand simple sentences in English, even in unique combinations that he had not heard before, such as 'Put the soap on the apple'. However, he could not handle more complex constructions, such as embedded clauses; an example might be 'Put the soap on the apple that I put on the table', where the 'that …' clause is used to distinguish the particular apple to which the speaker is referring. Nor did he learn to show any higher-level, self-reflexive awareness to be found in constructions such as 'I think' or 'I feel'.

Kanzi eventually learned some elementary visual, written and oral symbol recognition skills. However, the fact remained that he came from a species that has never symbolised spontaneously or passed on symbols from generation to generation (Deacon 1997; Donald 2001). In other words, although he could be taught some elementary aspects of symbolisation, he did not belong to a species that could ever do this for itself. In this respect, humans are hugely different from all other animals, even though we share many neurobiological fundamentals with other animals. Our brains and nervous systems are remarkably similar to those of other animals, particularly primates. However, our literacies – our multifarious literacy capacities – make us really different.

See literacies.com Kanzi Learns Language.

Literacies and human cognition

A substantial literature in cognitive science, psychology and pedagogy connects language learning with cognitive development. However, as our concern is literacies in the plural, we also want to highlight parallel developments of sophisticated thinking capacities in and through other modes, such as visual symbolisation; these are developments of the same cognitive order as those that occur in language.

As the child grows and acquires language, words describing things that happen to be beside each other in the world (the particular chairs and tables that are parts of their lives) turn into concepts, which allow for generalisation and abstraction of higher-order, adult thinking. An example is the idea of a chair or a table as a kind of abstract function, such that when you see quite different-looking chairs and tables, you nevertheless recognise them as the same kinds of things, and also connected to superordinate, organising concepts, such as 'dining-room set' and 'furniture'. This is cognitive work involving words. In the visual and spatial modes, we create similarly abstract concepts when we draw diagrams and plans so as to capture aspects of the seen world. These developments in linguistic, visual, spatial and other thinking capacities are parallel and complementary.

See literacies.com Piaget on the Language and Thought of the Child.

In order to explore the unique nature of these literacies, we now turn to a philosopher, Charles Sanders Pierce. He makes a distinction between three kinds of connection that representations – or signs – make with the world: icon, indicator and symbol (Pierce 1998). Animal communication uses icons and indicators, but not symbols except in rare, very limited and quite unnatural cases, such as that of Kanzi.

Meaning 1: icon

The first kind of sign is an **icon**, or likeness of a particular thing.

- A picture is not the thing; it is a representation of a thing through a likeness.
- The word 'woof' is not my dog barking; it is a representation of how my dog barks through a likeness of the way my dog barks. In language, iconic meaning is called 'onomatopoeia'.
- A plan of a particular building or a map of a space is not the building or the space itself; it is a likeness of that building or space.
- A gesture that imitates a person's demeanour is not the demeanour itself, but represents the meaning of that demeanour through likeness.

Icon: A signifier that stands for something in the world (a signified), where the connection is made by the likeness of the sign to its signified

An icon is a sign that stands for the particular thing to which it refers by way of mimicry, copying or imitation.

Meaning 2: indicator

A second kind of sign is an **indicator** or index, where there is a direct 'pointing to' connection between a sign and the world to which it refers.

Indicator: A signifier that stands for something where the connection is made by pointing to a particular thing

- A thermometer points to the temperature, a clock to the time, and a signpost to a place.
- The words 'Julius Caesar' point to a person.
- The gesture pointing 'over there' refers to something you can see.
- Laughing and grunting are indicative meanings.
- When an animal makes an alarm call to warn its fellows that it has seen a predator, it is engaged in this indicative or indexical kind of communication.

Indicators are signs that point to something specific.

Meaning 3: symbol

The third type of meaning identified by Pierce requires a kind of thinking that only humans can engage in, and that only humans can pass on from generation to generation – creating meaning with **symbols**. (Kanzi learned to use symbols in a limited way, but only because he had been taught in unusual circumstances. He had no way of teaching what he had learned to another bonobo.)

Symbol: A signifier that refers to a general meaning

- Word symbols; these offer no immediate or direct clues as to their particular meanings. We say 'give', 'bird', 'marriage'; each word is a symbol of an idea or thing, and the word itself does not point to anything other than what we as humans have learned it means. The word, says Pierce (1998: 9), 'does not show us a bird, nor enact before our eyes a giving or a marriage, but supposes that we are able to imagine those things, and have associated the word with them'. Nor does the word as a concept point to anything specific in the world. There are millions of instances of giving, birds and marriages in the world. These may appear to be quite different at first glance, yet all of them share some quite complex essential meaning characteristics.
- Visual icons, such as international signs; keys in diagrams; works of art that represent not just a particular thing, but a generalisable idea; or colours that stand for things.
- Objects that stand for things, such as sacred objects that stand for religious concepts; functional objects that stand for different kinds of action.
- Gestures that convey general messages, such as shaking or nodding your head to say yes/no, or using your hands to say stop/go.
- Sounds that represent signals, such as a doorbell or a car horn; or that evoke atmospheres, such as music.

Symbols also form systems in which one meaning comes to be defined, not just in terms of what it represents in the world, but in relation to other meanings in the meaning system (chairs + tables = dining-room set).

The meaning of a symbol is purely a matter of convention or social agreement. It is a creature of rule or habit, or common custom. For instance, we've learned what words mean and for practical everyday purposes we live by this social agreement. So, when we encounter a speaker of another language whose conventions we don't know, we need to resort to iconic and indicative meanings to communicate in some rudimentary ways. A considerable amount of language is symbolic, because much of the time a word refers to a kind of thing ('dog'), rather than pointing to a specific thing ('Fido'). Images can also be symbolic, such as a coat of arms, a logo or the symbols used in electrical circuit diagrams or in the key of a building plan or map. So can objects, such as a wedding ring, or the coloured wrapping paper of a gift; spaces, such as religious spaces, or the interior decoration of bedrooms compared to bathrooms and living-rooms; and gestures, such as nodding one's head as a 'yes', or a priest's garb, or etiquette, or ceremonial protocol.

 See literacies.com Deacon on the Symbolic Species.

The meaning behind a symbol we call a **concept**. A symbol has a general meaning, referring not to something specific but to a kind of thing. The cognitive processes underlying the use of symbols we call **generalisation**, abstraction or conceptualisation.

Concept: The meaning behind a symbol, as represented in a person's mind

A sign conveys to the mind an idea about a thing. To mean is to think. Animals can mean and think. Animals, however, cannot create and use symbols except in strange cases such as Kanzi's, and even then only in a limited way. All animal thinking is merely about applying and manipulating icons and indicators.

Generalisation: A cognitive process of applying a symbol to delineate the essential features of a group or class of things

In human thinking, we use a mixture of icons, indicators and symbols. Not only do symbols connect to the world in this cognitively peculiar way; they also refer to the world in a process of conceptualisation. Further, they connect with each other into systems of meaning; symbols gain their sense through their connections with each other within a symbolising system. For example, we learn to recognise dogs and distinguish them from cats – something much harder than you would think. Even the most sophisticated computer imaging systems still cannot do this reliably. This aspect of conceptualising refers to something outside of the symbol system. However, there is another important aspect to conceptualising, and that is to build systematic relations between concepts, to construct the symbol system itself. So, for example, we also learn that dogs are a kind of animal, and that animals are a kind of life. We learn that there are many kinds of dogs, and that some of the characteristics of dogs are shared with other animals, and that these characteristics make them mammals.

This process of conceptualising is one in which symbols are connected to each other by their 'sense'. Their meaning is determined not only by the reference to the world, but by their relation to each other within the symbolising system – the symbolic language of biological taxonomy, or the functional relations of the symbols on electrical circuit diagrams, for instance (Deacon 1997).

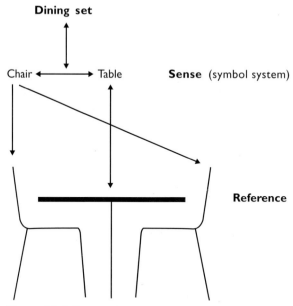

Figure 14.1 Connecting concepts

Designing meaning

Human babies are born into the world with an astounding dependence on their social environment. No animal is less capable when it is born. Then, unlike any other animal, they inherit powerful symbolic systems from the fellow members of their species with which they can make meaning of the world (representing it to themselves) and make meanings with each other (communication). Japanese babies learn Japanese. German babies learn German. Hearing-impaired babies learn the symbols of sign language.

Sense: Symbol-to-symbol meanings

Reference: Symbol-to-world meanings

These symbol systems make meaning of the world to which they refer by classifying, grouping, categorising, generalising and abstracting things that are seen, felt and used in everyday life. They also create internal symbol-to-symbol or concept-to-concept sense. In other words, symbolising has two fundamental and closely connected dimensions: symbol-to-symbol **sense** and symbol-to-world **reference**. Babies don't work out the meaning of the world for themselves; they inherit meanings that have evolved in the literacies or symbol systems they inherit.

These remarkable conceptualising capacities mean that we humans inherit powerful meaning-making systems (see the discussion of '(Available) designs' in Chapter 8). However, this is not a static inheritance in which we simply 'assimilate' and 'accommodate' – to use Swiss psychologist and philosopher Jean Piaget's terms – what we have been given by the culture that surrounds and precedes us. It is a powerful system that allows us to recombine meanings and make sense of the world in ways that are never exactly the same.

Take the case of language. With just a few thousand memorable words, and perhaps a few hundred types of logical and grammatical connectives, we can make an infinity of meanings. We are given a profound symbolic toolkit by our cultures, a repertoire of design elements, and then we spend our lives recombining or re-designing these to make meanings that have never been made before, or at least, not in quite the same way (in Chapter 8, we called this 'Designing'). The recombinations are always new. So we don't just inherit evolved sign systems. We also contribute to their further evolution ('The (re-)designed' in Chapter 8). This, too, makes humans a species like no other. We are a species with the capacity to create new meanings. To the extent that we can make our own meanings, we are in charge of our own destinies. We are also uniquely responsible for our own destinies and the destiny of the ecological space we inhabit.

Cognitive development in children

The Russian psychologist of child language learning, Lev Vygotsky, traces the dynamic of the process of language acquisition, learning and conceptual thinking. He starts with language, analysing the word as 'the [most basic] unit of verbal thought' (Vygotsky 2012: 6). He is particularly interested in words which, to use Pierce's terminology, have a symbolic character. This kind of word:

> does not refer to a single object, but to a group or to a class of objects. Each word is therefore already a generalisation. Generalisation is a verbal act of thought and reflects reality in quite another way than sensation and perception reflect it (Vygotsky 2012: 6).

For example, 'dog' is a generalisation; 'Fido' is not. In fact 'dog', when used to refer to just one dog (my dog, or that dog over there), is not a symbol and does not require conceptual thinking of the kind Vygotsky is referring to. How then does the child learn to conceptualise through words-as-symbols?

The initial stages of a child's linguistic-cognitive development, Vygotsky argues, are characterised by undirected extension of the sign to inherently unrelated objects linked subjectively and by chance in the child's perception. Language and thought are characterised by highly unstable, 'unorganised congeries', or 'heap[s]' – 'inherently unrelated objects linked by chance in the child's perception' (Vygotsky 2012: 117–18). Tables happen to be associated with chairs because they are near each other. The words will meet adult language because they may refer to the same things, but they do not have the conceptual character that they are later to acquire in adult language. When a young child uses the word, they mean something specific: this table. When an adult is looking through a furniture website, they are applying the concept of table as a kind of furniture. They are using the same word as the child, but their cognitive operations are different.

In the next stage, the child begins to think in what Vygotsky calls 'complexes' – a crucial intermediate step on the way to the following stage of conceptual thinking. The child begins to make logical connections. However, 'in a complex, the bonds between its components are *concrete and factual* rather than abstract and logical' (Vygotsky 2012: 120). Complex meaning is a process of the agglomeration of things and the association of these with words. Vygotsky (2012: 125) notes that 'a complex does not rise above its elements as does a concept; it merges with concrete objects that compose it'. For example, the child uses the word 'dog' to describe a kind of animal with a number of specific associations.

Vygotsky identifies a number of sub-steps in this stage, representing types of complexes that more or less follow one another in order of development. At the start, the child means through associative complexes, rather like giving a 'family' name to a group of individuals regularly linked in everyday experience. For example, dogs and cats are referred to as 'animals'. Then, things that differ are put into collections where they are associated by contrast rather than similarity. The connection in a collection complex is the participation of objects in the same practical operation. For example, the child puts together different animals in a play zoo or farm.

Later, chain complexes involve the linking of objects, such as coloured blocks of different shapes, but the attribute for linkage keeps changing. Chain complexes are inherently unstable, too, as the child adds more blocks to the group, first on the basis of shape, but later on the basis of colour. An example would be:

> [A] child's use of *quah* to designate first a duck swimming in a pond, then any liquid, including the milk in his bottle; when he happens to see a coin with an eagle on it, the coin also is called a *quah*, and then any round, coin-like object. This is a typical chain complex – each new object included has some attribute in common with another element, but the attributes undergo endless changes (Vygotsky 2012: 136).

Then, in a diffuse complex, the child focuses on attributes that unite adjacent elements and successively adds elements, potentially *ad infinitum*: from triangle to trapezoid, to square, to hexagon, to semicircle, to circle.

Complex thinking: Thinking that represents and associates particular things

Finally, the child comes to use what Vygotsky calls pseudo-concepts, when their **complex thinking** coincides with an adult concept. For example, by complex association a child may put a group of triangles together and use the same word as the adult concept of 'triangle' to describe the same thing that the adult would. The child, in other words, ends up with what is operationally a concept, but has used complex thought to get there. In pedagogical terms, the pseudo-concept is tremendously important because it shows the way in which adult language of a generalising, theoretical nature is imported into the child's language even before they can use words conceptually. As Vygotsky (2012: 128) states:

> [C]omplexes corresponding to word meanings are not spontaneously developed by the child: The lines along which a complex develops are predetermined by the meaning a given word already has in the language of adults.

This coincidence of words and the concepts to which they refer, Vygotsky points out, often means that forms of adult thought are incorrectly assumed to be present in children. On the contrary, the reality of mutually intelligible adult–child meaning occurs in spite of a much more significant cognitive gap than the mere commonality of words might lead the communicants to believe. The adult may mean 'dog' as a concept: a kind of animal unlike a cat. The child, meanwhile, means 'this dog, Fido' and 'that cat, Ginger'.

Yet the coincidence works pedagogically. Children learn by having words put into their mouths, so to speak – words that tease their perceptions into shape, words that gradually impose a culturally inherited meaning on the world, words that mould **cognition** through its various phases of thinking in complexes towards adult conceptual thinking. Adult language supplies children with words whose full generalising power is not realised until later childhood. Vygotsky (2012: 134–5) explains:

> **Cognition:** Capacities to think, which in humans but not other animals include capacities to represent the world in symbol systems such as language, visual imagery and gesture

> [A]t the complex stage, word meanings as perceived by the child refer to the same objects that the adult has in mind, which ensures understanding between child and adult, but that the child thinks the same thing in a different way, by means of different mental operations.

Towards conceptual thinking

After complexes, evidence of a final major stage in the development of child thought is to be found when words are used as fully-fledged concepts. **Conceptual thinking** involves using words to abstract; to single out defining elements that categorise events, people or objects under a single word; to unite and separate; to analyse and synthesise. Fido is a dog, and a dog is a kind of mammal, and mammals are kinds of vertebrates, and vertebrates are kinds of animals, and animals are different from plants.

> **Conceptual thinking:** Thinking that represents and connects generalisations

> Complex thinking begins the unification of scattered impressions; by organising discrete elements of experience into groups, it creates a basis for later generalisations. But the advanced concept presupposes more than unification. To form such a concept it is also necessary *to abstract*, *to single out* elements, and to view the abstracted elements apart from the totality of the concrete experience in which they are embedded. ... In the actual development of the child's thinking ... generalisation and abstraction ... are closely intertwined (Vygotsky 2012: 144–5).

Initially, a child can demonstrate that they know what a concept can do by translating it into concrete language. Vygotsky (2012: 148) notes that 'Even [the most] abstract concepts are often translated into the language of concrete action: "*Reasonable* means when I am hot and don't stand in a draught."' In the first steps of conceptual thinking, the child 'will form and use a concept quite correctly in a concrete situation, but will find it strangely difficult to express that concept in words' (Vygotsky 2012: 150). The greatest difficulty is encountered when, having grasped the abstract concept, the child needs to reapply it to a new concrete situation.

Concepts do not only refer to the world in abstract, generalising ways; for example, when, having seen many dogs, you encounter a breed you have not seen before but nevertheless recognise it as a dog. Concepts also refer to each other in a symbolic system: knowing that dogs are kinds of mammals, as are cats, but not fish, but that fish are also animals. Or, in Vygotsky's (2012, 183–4) example:

> A child learns the word *flower*, and shortly afterwards the word *rose*; for a long time the concept 'flower', though more widely applicable than 'rose', cannot be said to be more general for the child. It does not include and subordinate 'rose' – the two are interchangeable and juxtaposed. When 'flower' becomes generalised, the relationship of 'flower' and 'rose', as well as of 'flower' and other subordinate concepts, also changes in the child's mind. A system is taking shape.

So, although a child knows the meanings of the words 'rose' and 'flower' for the purposes of interacting with adults, these words do not yet have the conceptualising capacities that they do in adult thought.

This has important implications for pedagogy. The direct teaching of concepts, the transmission of received generalisations, Vygotsky (2012: 159) says, is 'impossible and fruitless'. He further elaborates upon this point:

> A teacher who tries to do this usually accomplishes nothing but empty verbalism, a parrot-like repetition of words by the child, simulating a knowledge of the corresponding concepts but actually covering up a vacuum (at 159).

This is one of the occupational hazards of didactic teaching – to drill abstract definitions and rules without the child internalising what they mean. Instead, Vygotsky (1978, 1986) stresses the developmental role of play, learning by doing under the guidance of an adult, the negotiated nature of adult–child interaction, and the relationship of received generalisations to practical experiences. Learning needs to ease children through complex thinking and towards conceptualisation. Gradually, complex thinking transforms itself into conceptual thinking.

Table 14.1: Vygotsky's stages of cognitive development

Congeries	Heaps of inherently unrelated objects linked by chance in the child's perception
Complexes	When the child begins to make logical connections between the particular things they perceive
Concepts	Words that can generalise about kinds of things in the child's experience

See literacies.com Vygotsky on Thought and Language.

Literacies for learning

Learning in the 'zone of proximal development'

Learning occurs in what Vygotsky calls a **zone of proximal development**. Such a zone is determined by:

> the distance between the actual development level as determined by independent problem solving and the level of potential development as determined through problem solving under adult guidance or in collaboration with more capable peers (Vygotsky 1978: 86).

Zone of proximal development: A zone of learning in which students operate beyond their level of cognitive capacity, but with adult scaffolding – for instance, the teacher is using concepts, but as yet the student can only think in complexes or pseudo-concepts

This suggests that pedagogy offers a kind of 'scaffolding' in which a teacher 'lends' consciousness to children who do not have consciousness to reason on their own. The teacher orchestrates student performance of tasks the children would not be able to do by themselves (Bruner 1986).

Cognitively, the productive relationship of pseudo-concepts to concepts is one important instance of this process at work. The child is not able to think conceptually, but orders the world through a language 'borrowed' from adults that coincides empirically with adult concepts and thus foreshadows these concepts. The role of inherited symbol systems is clear here. Intellectual scaffolds point towards conceptualisation in the very symbols that surround children, even when they are still using these symbols in complex rather than conceptual modes of thought.

> The zone of proximal development defines those functions that have not yet matured but are in the process of maturation, functions that will mature tomorrow but are currently in an embryonic state (Vygotsky 1978: 86).

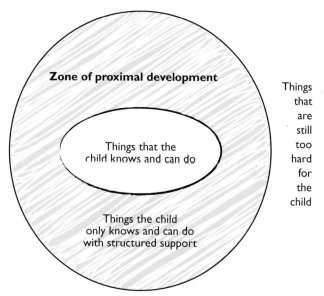

Figure 14.2 The zone of proximal development

'Constructivist' theories of learning

Vygotsky distinguishes his view of learning from the 'constructivist' theory of his contemporary, Jean Piaget. Constructivist theories serve as a key founda-tion of authentic pedagogies. In the constructivist view, the learning mind is a self-assembling system. When a child reaches a certain stage of development – as linked to biological maturation – the mind 'constructs' meanings in, and of, the world appropriate to that stage. The child connects their meanings to the world by assimilating new experiences to their existing conceptual frames, or accommodating or changing those conceptual frames to accord with new ex-perience (Piaget 2002). For Piaget, biological development frames the conditions for learning from experience.

> [T]here are biological factors linked to the ... maturation of the nervous system. These factors, which doubtless owe nothing to society ... [are] decisive in the devel-opment of cognitive functions ... [F]rom the biological point of view, the stages ... show a 'sequential' character (each being necessary to the following one in a con-stant order). ... [T]his would naturally suppose a certain constancy or uniformity of development regardless of the social milieu within which individuals are formed (Piaget 1971: 46–7).

Such a view tends to place the individual, self-constructing child at the centre of its account of the development of thought.

Vygotsky, by contrast, attributes much more to social learning. He observes that children talk out loud to themselves, copying the language of adults, before they internalise the thought embodied in this language into inner speech, or silently talk to themselves. In other words, we learn to think through language and also, we would add, through symbolic thinking using other modes, including visual, spa-tial, tactile and gestural. We acquire our thinking capacities to a significant degree through the tools for thinking embodied in our capacities for representation and communication, and not just by virtue of biological maturation or by every child reinventing the wheel of meaning. This is a kind of mind-sharing, transferring cul-turally acquired species memories and understandings from one generation to an-other.

Vygotsky (1978: 89–91) explains how this occurs in the case of language:

> Language arises initially as a means of communication between the child and the people in his environment. Only subsequently, upon conversion to internal speech, does it come to organise the child's thought, that is, become an internal mental function. ... We propose that an essential feature of learning is that it creates the zone of proximal development; that is, learning awakens a variety of internal de-velopmental processes that are able to operate only when the child is interacting with people in his environment and in cooperation with his peers. Once these pro-cesses are internalised, they become part of the child's independent developmental achievement. From this point of view, learning is not development; however, prop-erly organised learning results in mental development and sets in motion a variety

of developmental processes that would be impossible apart from learning. Thus, learning is a necessary and universal aspect of the process of developing culturally organised, specifically human, psychological functions. ... [T]he most essential feature of our hypothesis is the notion that developmental processes do not coincide with learning processes. Rather, the developmental process lags behind the learning process; this sequence then results in zones of proximal development. ... Therefore, it becomes an important concern of psychological research to show how external knowledge and abilities in children become internalized.

Reflecting on an earlier period in his career, the influential educator Jerome Bruner notes that his constructivist views had tended to mean learning on one's own, or in Piaget's words, 'learning by inventing'.

My model of the child in those days was very much in the tradition of the solo child mastering the world by representing it to himself in his own terms. In the intervening years I have come to increasingly recognise that most learning in most settings is a communal activity, a sharing of the culture. It is not just that the child must make his knowledge his own, but that he must make it his own in a community of those who share his sense of belonging to a culture (Bruner 1986: 127).

When later he took a view more like Vygotsky's, says Bruner (1986: 132), he realised:

that conceptual learning was a collaborative enterprise involving an adult who enters into dialogue with the child in a fashion that provides the child with hints and props that allow him to begin a new climb, guiding the child in next steps before the child is capable of appreciating their significance on his own.

The role of literacies in learning

Literacies learning comes at a crucial stage in the child's internalisation of adult, symbolic-conceptual learning frameworks. The shift from complex to conceptual thinking happens simultaneously in oral language, written language, visual imaging and the other modes of meaning as well. For instance, contrary to the assumptions of authentic pedagogy's theories of learning to write, in Vygotsky's (2012: 191–2 view, 'the development of writing does not repeat the developmental history of speaking'. Even the 'minimal development' of writing 'requires a high level of abstraction'. For example, the child must 'disengage himself from the sensory aspect of speech and replace words by images of words' as well as 'take cognisance of the sound structure of each word, dissect it, and reproduce it in alphabetical symbols'. Writing, thus, 'requires deliberate analytical action on the part of the child' (Vygotsky's 2012: 192).

The motives for writing, moreover, are far from 'authentic' or 'natural', even if these words are accepted as accurate descriptions of the ways in which children's oral language in their first years expresses their immediate needs and interests. Writing is 'more abstract, more intellectualised, further removed from immediate needs' (Vygotsky 2012: 192). In fact, this detachment goes as deep as the discrepancy between thinking in the language of 'inner speech' (imported as a tool for thinking from the oral language learned as a child) and the language of writing.

> Inner speech is almost entirely predicative because the situation, the subject of thought, is always known to the thinker. Written speech, on the contrary, must explain the situation fully in order to be intelligible. The change from maximally compact inner speech to maximally detailed written speech requires what might be called deliberate semantics – deliberate structuring of the web of meaning (Vygotsky 2012: 193).

Obviously, children start to write long before they have the cognitive capacity to employ the full resource of a 'deliberate semantics'. At its highest levels, this resource includes planning and drafting. However, the fact that writing instruction starts when the cognitive capacities upon which writing is ultimately based are only at a rudimentary stage of development is evidence that cognitive capacity 'does not precede instruction' but rather 'unfolds in a continuous interaction with the contributions of instruction' (Vygotsky 2012: 195). Accordingly, 'grammar' is of 'paramount importance for the mental development of a child' because it cultivates the deliberate, abstract and analytical forms of thinking through language that are peculiar to writing (Vygotsky 2012: 194). These forms of thinking are then imported back into adult speaking, and particularly the 'speaking-like-writing' that we have discussed in Chapter 13 (see 'Making audio and oral meanings').

We want to extend Vygotsky's notion of 'deliberate semantics' from writing to literacies in the plural. As well as in writing, learners can also conceptualise and think abstractly using image, gesture and space. We think multimodally. In fact, it may often be the case that we can think more powerfully when we represent our meanings in multiple modes. And we can learn to think more effectively and efficiently by representing the world in writing, then image, then in speaking – in whatever order or mix may seem appropriate to a particular knowledge representation, or whichever starting point seems to work best for a particular learner. We can think things through in parallel but necessarily different ways in different modes. We think through these modes. As for reading and writing, literacy in this narrow sense alone does not mean you will necessarily think better.

Research by Scribner and Cole (1981) into readers and writers of the West African Vai script demonstrates this. Comparing the cognitive skills of Vai who could write in their first language with those who couldn't, they found no significant differences. There were differences, however, for those who had become literate through formal schooling, with its peculiarly generalising conceptual frameworks of disciplinary understanding. Formal schooling, not literacy itself, was the variable that influenced cognition.

Developing 'metarepresentations'

In the old days of didactic literacy, one of the moves of formal schooling was to teach grammar – a metalanguage that described some of the logic of language. We've already explored the limitations of this idea in its traditional guise. However, there is one thing we want to keep as we move from literacy to literacies in the plural, and that is a space for what we want to call **metarepresentations** or representations about representation. 'Dog' is a symbol that represents a kind of animal, but to call 'dog' a 'noun' is to use a symbol to describe the kind of symbol that 'dog' is. 'Noun' is a metasymbol or metarepresentation. We want to use metarepresentations like these to describe the way literacies work, across a number of different modes. Metarepresentations are one of a number of helpful tools for learning literacies.

Metarepresentation: Meanings about meaning; symbols that describe symbol systems, such as grammar, visual keys and musical notation

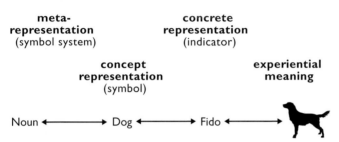

Figure 14.3 From experience to metarepresentation

Metarepresentation is no more than a process of identifying design elements in representations (literacies to think) and communications (literacies to pass on messages). It is a tool for uncovering the principles of order and organisation in literacies: how they work, who they work for, why they work for them. The aim of metarepresentation is not that you learn definitions and rules (like old-fashioned grammar rules), but that you learn how to 'unpack' texts by developing and applying a conceptual framework (however represented, in words, diagrams and so on) that explains the design of that text. Let's say the text is a website. In that case, you would develop a metarepresentation of the visual, written and perhaps also audio design elements of the site. You might do this in words, or you might do it by using systems or network diagrams.

One of the arguments for using metarepresentations as a path for learning is a simple case of efficiency. By the time they come to school, children have meaning-making resources in the forms of complex thinking through words, images, space, gesture and the like. The most efficient way to support children in the multifaceted, multistep and gradual process of transitioning from complex thinking to conceptual thinking is to build upon and extend the foundation of complex thinking that they bring to school. When children come to school they are already on a path to conceptualising, so why not use that imminent capability and nurture it as a more efficient way than immersion alone? School, after all, has to cover a staggering amount of intellectual ground with resources that are always being squeezed to the limit. Using conceptualisation, generalisation and abstraction is a convenient short-cut. It is a way of concentrating reality, a way of encapsulating patterns of regularity, so that a few generally applicable things can be learned instead of a lot of particular things.

The strangeness of school

Here we encounter a strangeness in schooling; an unnatural peculiarity of its manner of speaking about the world. Here is Vygotsky (1986: 86) again:

> The mind faces different problems when assimilating concepts at school and when left to its own devices. When we impart systematic knowledge to the child, we teach him many things that he cannot directly see or experience.

School has some unique ways of connecting its meanings to the world that are decidedly inauthentic, at least compared to the child's everyday experiences outside school. Schooling is founded on what Vygotsky calls 'scientific concepts': 'nouns' and 'integers' and 'atoms'. Unlike everyday natural language, which for the child mostly points to concrete things in their immediate field of interest, thought founded upon scientific concepts is 'guided by the use of words as the means of actively centering attention, of abstracting certain traits, synthesising them, and symbolising them by a sign' (Vygotsky 1962: 81).

Exophoric reference: Reference to something outside a social situation or a text, shown, for example, in schooling's peculiar way of speaking about anything and potentially everything in the outside world

School learning, moreover, can and does refer to everything in the world (languages and histories and geographies and natural environments), but mostly does so at a distance and in a distancing kind of way. The inevitable 'schoolishness' of classroom discourse is characterised by Courtney Cazden as very different from the other discourses of a child's life. She introduces and develops the concept of **exophoric reference**, or reference to things that are external to school and at a distance from school.

> When school language use is called *decontextualised*, it is generally because talk refers less often than it does at home to one kind of context: the physically present situation to which exophoric (pointing) reference can be made. But the learning difficulties inherent in classroom discourse are due less to that loss, and more to the many implied, but often unstated, references to another kind of context: the words of other oral and written texts (Cazden 2001: 74–5).

To this, we would add the elaborate visual modes of conceptualisation in the scientific diagram, the audio modes of musical notation, the gestural modes of drama and video story, and so on. This phenomenon, says Cazden (2001), culminates in academic discourse – 'the special ways of talking expected in school'. Because classroom discourse is so different from the child's common sense, it is the role of the teacher to help students to recontextualise, to construct contexts actively in the mind (Cazden 2001). This strange character of classroom discourse parallels, in linguistic and intellectual terms, the peculiarity of literacies in general. Recording and re-presentation of non-present meanings can occur in writing, but also today in various other readily available digital forms of recording: speech, music, video recordings of gesture, photograph, drawing, graph, diagram, and the like. Classrooms can use these expanded literacies to refer to an outside world. The representation of the world by schooling is intrinsically the stuff of literacies.

See literacies.com Cazden on Classroom Discourse.

Towards the 'reflective consciousness' of adult cognition

Taking this argument one step further, it is clear that the 'scientific concepts' that Vygotsky is also talking about are not just concepts that refer to the world, but ones that make sense by defining each other, a syntax of abstraction, the structure of disciplines in which nouns are defined within the disciplinary schema of grammar, integers within mathematics, and atoms within chemistry. Cognitively, Vygotsky (2012) says that the long journey that children make into this sort of conceptual thinking eventually takes them to another cognitive plane, that of 'reflective consciousness' and a new 'awareness of the activity of the mind – the consciousness of being conscious' (at 180). Then, scientific concepts developed through the practices of schooling are 'transferred to everyday concepts, changing their psychological structure from the top down' (at 183).

> For the young child, to think means to recall; but for the adolescent, to recall means to think. Her memory is so 'logicalised' that remembering is reduced to establishing and finding logical relations; recognising consists in discovering that element which the task indicates has to be found (Vygotsky 1978: 51).

Literacies, then, help us to learn to think in new ways – ways that evolve to be characteristic of adult cognition. As they learn literacies, children do not reinvent the meaning of the world for themselves. Nor do they come to understand the world because this understanding has been pre-wired into their brains. They come to understand the meaning of the world as a consequence of a good deal of representational work. However, the answers that come to them are written into the meanings of the objects (tables and computers), spaces (parks and classrooms), gestures (nodding 'yes' and shrugging shoulders for uncertainty), words (naming kinds of persons, actions or things; connecting kinds of persons, actions or things conceptually) and images (visual symbols). They are born into a world drenched with the inherited meanings of particular life forms or cultures.

The mind is an essentially social product, a cultural inheritance (Bereiter 2002; Gee 1992). The sense children make of the world is a sense that they find in the world; designs of meaning laid out as the written, visual, spatial, tactile, gestural and oral meanings they encounter. In the words of Leontyev (2009: 202):

> Man does not know the world like a Robinson Crusoe making independent discoveries on an uninhabited island. He assimilates the experience of preceding generations of people in the course of his life; that happens precisely in the form of his mastering of meanings and to the extent that he assimilates them. Meaning is thus the form in which the individual man assimilates generalised and reflected human experience.

This social learning occurs through forms of activity or action. Children grow up in an environment in which they learn to use the conceptual meanings of their culture, be those physical objects in the form of tools or the symbolic objects of language or images (Wertsch 1991; Wertsch 1998).

 See literacies.com Gee on Academic Language and New Literacies.

Literacies as extensions of mind

Not only are literacies a medium for thinking. They also represent an ever-present extension of memory and personal thinking, overcoming its limitations.

Literacies are a social mnemonic or aide-memoire – a social memory outside of our individual minds that, as children grow, become an essential supplement to adult minds. Literacies are knowledge that we can always reach when not re-membered by a process of 'looking up' – asking someone else who knows, reading a written text, finding a recorded image, reminding ourselves by passing through a spatial prompt (like the way we remember things walking down the aisles of a super-market, or remembering a complex route), or replaying a piece of audio (replaying a piece of music, reaching a doorbell). In these ways, literacies are conceptual artefacts by means of which our thinking and acting capacities extend well beyond the stuff of our brains.

Literacies are the accumulated, collective, distributed and essentially human intelligence. They are the products of communities. They are the glue that binds communities. They are ever-present and always-needed social extensions of our personal minds.

Literacies across the curriculum

The notion of 'literacy across the curriculum' is not a new one. It has arguably, however, come into sharper focus in more recent years as renewed attention is being paid to this concept. This concentration upon literacy across the curriculum is, for example, evident in the curriculum documents currently informing educa-tional practice in both the United States and Australia. Within these documents, a focus on literacy across the curriculum is foregrounded, albeit with varying ex-plicitness. Literacy is positioned as integral to the various subject areas – with 'discipline-specific literacies' or 'curriculum literacies' residing within these. These documents, again in varying degrees of specificity, bear the traces of recognition that each subject area has its own systematic ways of writing, thinking and rep-resenting their work; each subject has a specific range of 'ways' that need to be understood (Kress 1985). It is also evident that literacy is considered to be the work of all teachers; that the responsibility for the teaching and learning of literacy sits with all teachers regardless of the context within which they work, regardless of the subject area or discipline they teach. *All teachers are literacy teachers.* It is to the curriculum documents 'at play' within each of these locales that this chapter will now briefly turn its attention.

Firstly, to the United States and its Common Core Standards (the title of the source document is *Common Core State Standards for English Language Arts and Literacy in History/Social Studies, Science and Technical Subjects* (CCSS 2010). Within the 'Introduction' of the source document, it is noted that 'the Standards set requirements not only for English language arts (ELA) but also for literacy in history/social studies, science, and technical subjects' (CCSS 2010: 3). It is stated that an 'interdisciplinary approach to literacy' is supported by the Standards detailed (CCSS 2010: 4). Two 'Key Design Considerations' – as relevant to the discussion here – are identified. These are an attendant focus on the adoption of 'an integrated model of literacy' and a 'shared responsibility for students' literacy development' (CCSS 2010: 4).

Shifting to Australia, in its nationally adopted Australian Curriculum there is clear articulation and explicit endorsement of a literacy across the curriculum approach. Literacy is conceptualised and presented in a three-fold manner within the curriculum documentation, namely a 'Strand' within the Australian Curriculum: English, a set of 'requirements' in the subject areas (or disciplines) represented in this curriculum, and a 'General Capability' (see Figure 2.5 in Chapter 2). It is upon the latter that we will now direct our focus.

The General Capabilities section of the Australian Curriculum provides a 'Background' that acknowledges the theoretical and pedagogical positions espoused within the national curriculum and commentary on this in relation to literacy per se and literacy teaching and learning in the curriculum areas. This Background states:

> The definition of literacy in the Australian Curriculum is informed by a social view of language that considers how language works to construct meanings in different social and cultural contexts. … This view is concerned with how language use varies according to the context and situation in which it is used. There are important considerations for curriculum area learning stemming from this view because, as students engage with subject-based content, they must learn to access and use language and visual elements in the particular and specific ways that are the distinctive and valued modes of communication in each learning area. They need to learn how diverse texts build knowledge in different curriculum areas, and how language and visual information work together in distinctive ways to present this knowledge (ACARA 2015b).

As already indicated, the General Capabilities section of the Australian Curriculum explicitly identifies – that is, 'marks out' and 'names' – 'Literacy across the Curriculum' as a dedicated topic. This section asserts:

> Literacy presents those aspects of the Language and Literacy strands of the English curriculum that should also be applied in all other learning areas. …
>
> [T]he explicit teaching of literacy … is strengthened, made specific and extended in other learning areas as students engage in a range of learning activities with significant literacy demands. These literacy-rich situations are a part of learning in all curriculum areas. Paying attention to the literacy demands of each learning area ensures that students' literacy development is strengthened so that it supports subject-based learning. This means that:

- all teachers are responsible for teaching the subject-specific literacy of their learning area
- all teachers need a clear understanding of the literacy demands and opportunities of their learning area
- literacy appropriate to each learning area can be embedded in the teaching of the content and processes of that learning area (ACARA (2015c).

See literacies.com Freebody on Literacy across the School Curriculum.

Literacies learning across the curriculum

Before we go on to explore the theoretical dimensions of academic literacies, we look at some practical examples of multimodal literacies across the curriculum. Our first stop is Aly Allpress, Bianca Parkin, Robyn Kiddy and Sharon De Rooy's pre-kindergarten classes. The children are learning about how plants

Figure 14.4 Creating and documenting a garden (Growing to Give Learning Module, Scholar)

grow. They begin by discussing what they already know about gardens (experiencing the known). They read stories about gardens. They visit some vegetable gardens, where they have the gardeners explain what they are doing (experiencing the new). They talk about how plants grow (analysing functionally). They draw some pictures of things to be found in gardens, which the teacher labels (applying appropriately). Then they create their own garden (applying appropriately).

See literacies.com Allpress, Parkin, Kiddy and De Rooy, Growing to Give.

Next we find ourselves in Christopher Antram, Rita van Haren and Dean Dudgeon's Year/Grade 3 classes, working now on the learning module 'What's with the Weather?' The students read some stories with weather themes (experiencing the new). They explore how the weather is measured (conceptualising with theory in mathematics and science). They build a weather station, collect weather data and write a weather report (applying appropriately). They then analyse a weather disaster (analysing critically), and write this up as an information report (applying creatively).

See literacies.com Antram and Dudgeon, What's with the Weather?

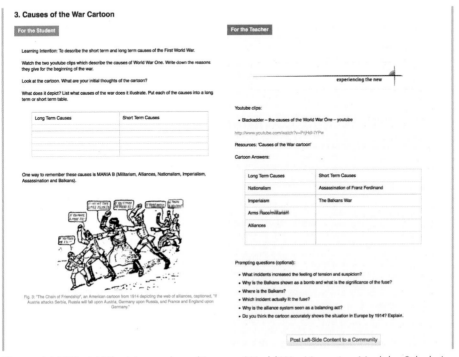

Figure 14.5 World War 1 in words and images (World War I Learning Module, Scholar)

Moving to a Year/Grade 9 History class, Prue Gill, Laura Hicks, Jennifer Nott and Rita van Haren have created a learning module that explores World War 1. They look at the configuration of the opposing powers on maps. They look at cartoons from the time that attempt to explain the causes of the war. They investigate the meanings of 'nationalism', 'imperialism', 'militarism' and 'alliance'. They look at posters encouraging men to enlist and read diaries from the time. They write and peer review a research paper on the causes of the war, including images and quotes from primary sources.

 See literacies.com Gill, Hicks and Nott, World War 1.

Finally for now, we are in a Year/Grade 9 Mathematics class with Rita van Haren and Ed Cuthbertson, exploring the mathematical concept of probability using multimodal literacies strategies. The class watches some narrative clips from films where improbable things happen, such as *Fight Club, 21* and *Bangkok Insurance*. Students play a probability game, 'pig'. They rank a number of things across a scale of impossible, to unlikely, to even chance, to certain: whether it will rain tomorrow, whether their favourite sports team will win at least one of the next three matches, and so on. They then go on to translate these approximate descriptions of probability in language into formal mathematical representations. They calculate the odds of winning a lottery. In pairs, they make a short video explaining concepts of probability to a lay person. They then write and peer review a project that discusses probability in society, such as gambling, insurance, or weather forecasting.

 See literacies.com Cuthbertson on Probability.

What is happening in these classes, where literacies are such a powerful tool for learning, across all curriculum areas?

Representing and communicating academic meanings

So far in this book, when we speak of literacies, we have mainly been referring to the work that is done in the subject area of English or language arts. However, literacies are – as alluded to in the preceding section – the raw material of every other subject area. In a very ordinary way, the curriculum is communicated to learners through multimodal texts – the images and writing in a heavily illustrated textbook or web resource, the oral language and gesture of a teacher, the showing and telling of small group work, the diagrams or models that students make and the writing they do. If learners do not master these modes of communication, they will not succeed at school. As students learn, they use the tools of literacies to help them think and act. Every subject is a site of literacies learning, and learning literacies is about learning to think and act in the ways that are characteristic of that subject area.

The reason why this is important is that school subjects represent the world in peculiar ways, ways that are in some respects quite different from everyday, ordinary representations. They frame their knowledge in different ways from more casual, everyday knowledge. We are going to call these 'technical' or 'academic' forms of knowledge and meaning-representation. This difference is for a reason: the knowledge we value in a doctor, lawyer, electrician, plumber, teacher or social worker is written into the peculiar ways of making meaning of each of these occupations – the texts they have read, the diagrams they use, the way they interact with objects, the way each kind of person speaks with their colleagues. This means their knowledge is more perceptive and useful in some important ways than the language of untrained people when they speak about any of these subjects. The technical, academic kinds of representation that we learn in school subjects and in further education embody ways of thinking and also create particular kinds of people.

Literacies in science

'Science', according to Latour and Woolgar (1986: 41), is 'the process whereby an ordered account is fabricated from disorder and chaos'. This may be something of an overstatement, because everyday life is not so chaotic that we can't make sense of it. The words of our language order everyday experience quite effectively; our language helps us learn to know that dogs and cats are kinds of animals. However, in the nature of 'natural language', the language we use in everyday life, there is often imprecision and ambiguity, which academic language cannot afford because it seeks to know the world in a more carefully focused way (Bowker & Star 2000). Academic language generates deeper insights than can be provided to us in the impressionistic language of everyday life. Take the classification system of modern biology, for instance.

Here is a piece of theory that links abstract concepts to each other:

Species are groups of biological individuals that have evolved from a common ancestral group and, over time, have separated from other groups that have also evolved from this ancestor. So, to take the example of our own species: a species, for instance, 'sapiens', is a member of a genus, homo. Hence the formal Latin naming scheme creates the phrase 'homo sapiens'. The species homo sapiens:

is a member of a family (hominids)
is a member of an order (primates)
is a member of a class (mammals)
is a member of a phylum (vertebrates)
is a member of a kingdom (animals).

By careful classificatory work, evolutionary scientists have recently shown that the concept 'fish' no longer works as a unifying category, even though of course it still does in our everyday language – fish, more or less, are creatures that have a familiar shape and live in water.

However, a lot of things live in water, and the shapes of fishes can be greatly varied. The systematic analysis of evolutionary variations in recent decades has

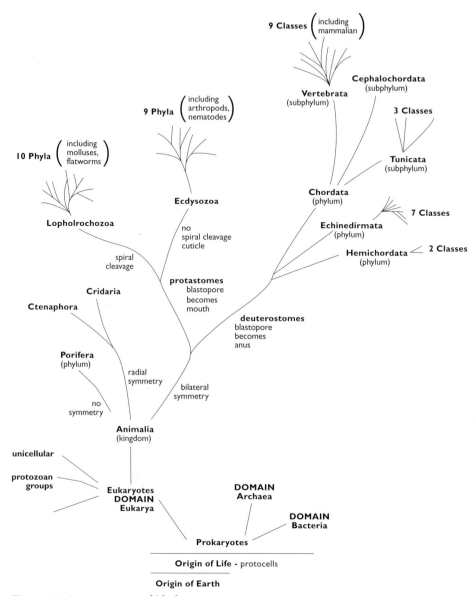

Figure 14.6 A taxonomy of life forms

shown that lungfish, salmon and cows all share a common ancestor, but lungfish and cows share a more recent common ancestor than lungfish and salmon. So, lungfish are more closely related to cows than to salmon, and the commonsense idea of fish leads us to draw a wrong scientific conclusion (Yoon 2009). We may represent this more scientific knowledge about lungfish and cows in writing (as we have here), in taxonomic diagrams, or in juxtaposed, labelled photographs of fossils. And when we do, we are representing knowledge in a way that brings about different kinds of understanding than those possible in everyday life. The literacies are different, and the thinking is different.

Figure 14.7 A lungfish

Here are some ways in which **academic literacies** are different:

- They involve systematic construction of mental models that categorise factual instances (the lungfish in this photograph) and link them with generalising concepts (species, genus), which define concepts by a range of variable characteristics, and which build theories by explaining the relations between concepts.
- They create chains of evidential reasoning that connect documentation of concrete, empirical realities (narratives of observation or photographs, for instance) with the concepts and theory (Abi-El-Mona & Abd-El-Khalick 2006).
- They require learners to monitor their own thinking, always self-questioning veracity and identifying possible fallacies in the meanings or sense being made.

Academic literacies: The ways in which meanings are expressed in the various discipline areas – science, history, social studies, art etc.

In the case of written language, linguists have attempted to analyse some of the peculiar aspects of the academic language in which formal knowledge is packaged. They have done this because if you don't master this language you won't succeed as you move to higher levels of learning in the secondary school and beyond.

Gee (2004a) offers these two sentences, the first typical of everyday speaking; the second typical of academic writing:

1. Hornworms sure vary a lot in how well they grow.
2. Hornworm growth exhibits a significant amount of variation.

Here are some changes that have occurred in the transition from the first sentence to the second.

- The verbs 'vary' and 'grow' have been transformed into nouns – a process called 'nominalisation' in which actions are turned into abstract things.
- Next, a verb with descriptive content ('vary') has been replaced by a generic verb of appearance that connects abstract things ('growth' and 'variation').
- The end point of a hornworm's development ('how well') has been replaced by a term related to the measures of science ('significant amount').
- The first sentence tells you something of its creator's attitude to the subject ('sure'), but the second does not.

In this transition, Gee (2004a: 16–17) concludes that:

> some things are lost – concrete things such as hornworms and empathy for them; [and] changes and transformations as dynamic, ongoing processes … Some things gained are abstract ideas and relations among them; traits and the quantification and categorisation of traits; and evaluation from within a specialised domain.

Children in school are not taught the language of science explicitly. But by being exposed to the language of science while doing science, they learn its literacies, and so learn the ways of thinking embedded in those literacies.

(Lemke 1990: 21) comes to similar conclusions about the language of science:

> There is a lot of use of the passive voice, of abstract nouns in place of verbs, of verbs of abstract relation (e.g. be, have, represent) in place of verbs of material action. It also has its preferred figures of speech, like analogy, and rhetorical patterns (e.g. Thesis-Evidence-Conclusion). It also works through a variety of activity structures, whether triadic dialogue, ordinary question-and-answer, lecture, or summary monologues, or many others. It even has its own special forms of written texts: laboratory notes, reports of experiments, theoretical treatises, and so on.

Such are the representational and communicative raw materials of science and learning science. Science is no more and no less than the peculiarities of its literacies. According to Lemke (2004: 34): 'Science is the great enterprise of paying attention to the kinds of meanings that require us to go beyond natural language'. This is also how science becomes something bigger than experience, perspective and voice; a body of social knowledge institutionalised and 'objectified' in the shared meanings communicated in scientific texts of various kinds – scientific books, articles, videos, demonstrations.

See literacies.com Halliday and Martin on the Language of Science.

Increasingly today, science is communicated multimodally (Alvermann 2004; Lemke 1998). Science learning today, as Gunther Kress and his colleagues show, moves between written text, diagram, image, gesture, action, model and speech (Kress, Jewitt, Ogborn & Tsatsarelis 2014). According to these researchers, all modes 'produce meaning in themselves and through their intersection or interaction with each other' while different modes 'make meaning in different ways and to produce different meaning-making potentials' (at 18, 21) Each mode has certain 'affordances' – that is, possibilities or potentials and limitations or constraints. So, which should we use at any particular point of time?

> 'Are the modes specialised to function in particular ways? Is speech, let's say, best for this, and image best for that?' ... Is the structure of an electronic circuit best represented in writing or in image? Is this aspect of the topic of blood circulation best handled using the model of the human body, an abstract image, gesture, or a particular combination of these? (Kress, Jewitt, Ogborn & Tsatsarelis 2014: 1–2, 207).

How can we most effectively develop the ways of thinking of science by mode-shifting, or synaesthesia?

Between the lifeworld and academic literacies

School is the site of transition from everyday ways of making meaning to more academic literacies. We call this everyday world the 'lifeworld' – a place where knowing and meaning go on all the time, but a different kind of knowing and meaning from that of formal, disciplinary or expert knowledge. The lifeworld is a place where we intuitively know that this goes with that, because it does so habitually without our even having to think about it much – fish at the seaside or fish on the dinner table.

These are embedded meanings, a world of meanings and assumptions so deeply shared with those around us that they mostly do not bear mentioning. This is a place where the world does with some justification seem flat, and the older Lamarckian explanations of evolution in which creatures adapt to environmental circumstances seem to be more immediately understandable than Darwinian ones, which explain evolution in terms of natural selection (Williams 2009). It is a world of complex thinking, rather than conceptual thinking – to return to Vygotsky's distinction – which not only works for children, but also for practical purposes for most adults for most of the time as they go about doing the ordinary things that constitute their daily lives.

However, our knowledge and our meanings in the lifeworld have their limitations. Our immediate conceptions may prove, on closer examination, to be misconceptions, from the way the earth seems flat to the word 'fish'. Vygotsky describes the underlying psychological processes as children adopt adult ways of thinking, starting to use adult language in more adult-like ways. It's not that the natural language and everyday ways of thinking of the lifeworld are completely wrong, because within a limited frame of reference, our experience of 'ground' and 'floor' and 'plane' may lead us to an intuitive existential sense of the planar nature of living, which is not itself wrong. It's just that science can supplement these immediately apprehended realities with a revised and more complicated view. Knowledge is a work in progress. Learning is a process of deepening and broadening the casual, circumstantial ways of meaning and knowing in the lifeworld. It means meaning and thinking in the characteristic ways of knowledgeable people such as teachers, researchers, professionals or well-versed amateurs.

The disciplinary knowledge of schooling and its academic ways of expressing meaning are connected to the lifeworld, for sure. In fact, there is nothing in the lifeworld to which disciplinary knowledge and school learning does not, or cannot, refer. And the purpose of all knowledge is to take it back to the lifeworld, to enhance our lives and contribute to the lives of others. However, as we have seen here, disciplinary knowledge and **academic meanings** refer to the lifeworld from a distance and in quite particular ways – different from the ways of representing meaning characteristic of the lifeworld itself. Of course, there's no question of whether one of these ways of knowing and meaning is better than the other. The only question is how they may be productively connected; how two complementary ways of knowing and meaning may work best together; and how we may shunt backwards and forwards between the one and the other.

Academic meanings: The processes of representation and communication of meanings in formal knowledge disciplines

Table 14.2 traces the move from everyday **lifeworld meanings** to the academic meanings of disciplined knowledge, through knowledge processes that happen in the classroom – an idea briefly mentioned several times in this book and explored in depth in Chapter 3, 'Literacies pedagogy'.

Lifeworld meanings: Everyday, casual ways of speaking and thinking about things

Science literacies in practice

In Malaysia, Ambigapathy Pandian and Shanthi Balraj have used the knowledge processes as the core pedagogical device in a science literacy project, 'Sense about Science', spanning five states in which teachers created 48 'learning elements' or modules of work covering topics as varied and as important to Malaysia's environment as rainforests, succession and conservation of mangrove swamps, conservation of energy, water conservation, the greenhouse effect and global warming, endangered ecosystems, practising the three R's (reduce, reuse and recycle), ozone depletion, environmental pollution, deforestation, eutrophication, force and pressure, the methods of controlling industrial waste disposal, air pollution, and the abiotic and biotic components of the environment. In a context where teachers are 'more inclined towards using the chalk and board method' and students often 'turn to memorising facts', the modules attempted to traverse a broader range of knowledge processes (Pandian & Balraj 2010: 305).

In one unit, on water pollution (and the activities were not in this order – we summarise them in this order here for clarity's sake), experiencing activities included collecting evidence and images of pollution in the local waterways, documenting water uses and the consequences of pollution, collecting water samples and carrying out an experiment to determine pollution levels. Conceptualising activities included looking up print and web material to find the key concepts, defining terms such as 'pollution', 'conservation', 'biochemical oxygen demand', and drawing concepts together into scientific generalisations about water pollution.

Table 14.2: Transforming everyday knowledge into disciplined knowledge

Lifeworld meanings, everyday knowledge	→ Knowledge processes in education →	Academic meanings, disciplined knowledge
Unspoken life stories, personal past experiences, conversations recalled, mental images, intuitive senses, tacit or commonsense understandings, unarticulated emotions	Experiencing the known	Articulating personal stories, reflecting on the influence of past experiences, self-conscious reflection on voice, insight and awareness into emotions and feelings, locating the sources of self and identity
New experiences, the feeling of being in a new or unfamiliar context, incidental perceptions	Experiencing the new	Focused observation, methodical examination of perceptions, inductive reasoning, experimentation, recording, measurement, corroborating perceptions with others
The ways all words and symbols make sense of experience by grouping things	Conceptualising by naming	Categorising, classifications, drawing distinctions, developing criteria for categorisation, defining
The ways all words and symbols are connected into clusters of meaning	Conceptualising with theory	Developing theories, making models
The ways in which we are often needing to explain things to ourselves or others	Analysing functionally	Reasoning and explanation: logic, inference, prediction, hypothesis, deduction; statements whose logical consistency can be demonstrated
Our sense of our own interests and purposes, our instinctive wariness of the interests and power plays of others	Analysing critically	Examination of interests, motives and ethics, wary scepticism, metacognitive reflection, explicit recognition of one's own beliefs, justifying opinions and beliefs to oneself and others
The pragmatics of getting things done, routines, habits	Applying appropriately	Procedural knowledge application
Things we do that turn out differently than expected, or which come together in surprising ways	Applying creatively	Transformative, creative, innovative, knowledge transfer

Analysing activities included a report on the experiment, which comprised a statement, hypothesis, variables, apparatus and materials, technique, procedure and results. Applying activities included creating a slide presentation, writing a letter to the editor of a local newspaper about water pollution in the neighbourhood (andsuggesting solutions), and creating a short video on how humans pollute water. Pandian and Balraj (2010: 310) conclude:

Compared to traditional classroom writing practices that use paper-based media, writing and producing screen images, visuals and graphics require[d] a whole new set of skills that involve inquiry, reading, speaking and writing abilities in new ways.

The teachers also found they had created an experience of science literacies that could properly be called 'doing science' (Pandian & Balraj 2010).

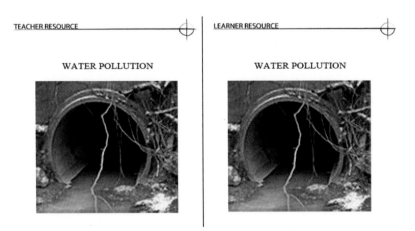

Figure 14.8 Learning Science

And to Australia now, where Beryl Exley and Allan Luke (2009) describe another science unit, 'Micro-organisms: Good or Bad?', taught in a multi-age class of seven- to ten-year-olds. Once again, the activities were not in this order, but during analysing activities students were introduced to a role-play drama in which two bumbling 'scientists' were each seeking knowledge about micro-organisms for very different purposes: one to take control of the world with the dangerous organisms, and the other to do good with the helpful ones. During experiencing activities, the two teachers role-playing the scientists could be asked questions online about micro-organisms. During conceptualising activities, a scientist parent spoke directly to science concepts as he had students examine micro-organisms under a microscope. Also, the teacher gave students an explicit explanation of how to control a computer animation program to represent biological processes graphically. During applying activities, students wrote a hortatory exposition on the topic, and developed a multimedia presentation for a public audience of parents, carers and siblings followed by a community ballot to decide which scientist would have access to the learners' knowledge and which would be banished from practising science forever.

Shifting attention now to a more 'broad-brush' example of science literacies in practice, we look again to Australia. Here, Stephen Ritchie and Louisa Tomas engaged in extensive work with primary and secondary school teachers and students on an online science writing project that saw students involved in the production of 'hybridised narratives' that integrated a socio-scientific issue – namely, biosecurity – referred to by Ritchie and Tomas (2012, 2013) as 'BioStories'. A chief aim of this venture was 'to engage students imaginatively in activities designed to improve their scientific literacy' (Ritchie & Tomas 2012: 213; Ritchie & Tomas 2013; Tomas 2012); while also acknowledging the 'growing recognition that there is value in engaging students in writing to learn science activities that move beyond the traditional scientific genres taught in schools' (Tomas 2012: 24; see also Prain 2006; Prain & Hand 1996a, 1996b, 1999).

As an online science writing project, a dedicated BioStories website was established. This website housed links to online resources (for example, technical information produced on government-approved websites) and short story templates and guidelines for use by the teachers and students. It provided a medium in which students could upload their stories for peer and formative teacher review – with the hope that such review would facilitate the refinement of their stories by students. Here, students could also share the stories constructed by others; 'read a diverse range of narrative styles and about different topics' (Ritchie & Tomas 2012: 217). Furthermore, it enabled the fostering of a sense of community – of a 'science' community and its learners. Ultimately, the website provided a platform for the publication of the students' stories.

Hybridised writing is a 'writing-for-learning' strategy (Prain & Hand 1999: 158). It refers to a 'diversified' approach to writing that involves 'crossing borders' (a term attributed to Aikenhead (1996)) between formal writing of technical information and everyday language conventions with which students are comfortable (Prain 2006). Such a pedagogical approach, as Prain (2006: 186) notes, 'incorporates the capacities of everyday and vernacular language in learning the languages of science'. It is founded on the premise that 'students should use a more diversified range of writing types, both formal and informal, to acquire science literacy as well as knowledge of, and particular attitudes towards, science inquiry' (Prain 2006: 181).

In undertaking the production of their hybridised narratives, students were required to 'transform scientific information on important issues for their communities from government websites [as provided on the dedicated website] into narrative text suitable for a lay reader', to 'transform technical information about biosecurity into narrative storylines that could be understood by the general public' (Ritchie & Tomas 2012: 213, 214). A series of three tasks – organised as Parts A, B and C – were framed around the hybridised narrative title of 'Crikey'. With regard these tasks, as Ritchie and Tomas (2013: 387) explain: 'three writing tasks were developed, progressively fading out the scaffolding such that the final task was an open-written task'. Such scaffolding, of the hybridised writing tasks, came by way of the provision of short story templates that detailed a specific scenario to which the students were required to respond in constructing their narratives. The details of the three tasks are presented below.

Part A   Students' writing involved the completion of a conversation between two central characters – an expert with a novice – about an allocated biological incursion (e.g. tilapia) that has affected Australian ecosystems. Students were provided with a short story template and required to complete their narrative in view of the scenario detailed. An extract from the short story template pertaining to this writing task is provided in Figure 14.9.

Figure 14.9 Part A short story template – 'Crikey'!

Part B   Students' writing involved the completion of a narrative wherein they adopted the role of an expert. The focus of the narrative was upon the possible consequences of an incursion (e.g. varroa mite) yet to affect Australia. Again, students were required to construct their narrative in view of a given scenario as detailed in a short story template provided.

Part C   This was an open-ended task, whereby students chose to write their own hybridised story involving any of the ideas they had garnered from their own stories or from those of other students as shared on the dedicated website. In completing this final narrative in the 'Crikey' series, students were free to choose their own biological incursion as the focus of their text, create their own characters, situate the narrative within a setting of their own choosing, and develop their own plot. Scaffolding, through the provision of a short story template, was removed.

While the BioStories project involved, specifically, the 'online' production (via a website) of hybridised 'narratives' that integrated the socio-scientific concept of 'biosecurity' as suitable for a 'lay reader' or 'the general public', we note the opportunities afforded more broadly by such an enterprise. Such an approach could be adapted and applied to engage students in a range of modes; to have students involved in the production of a variety of hybridised text types or genres and for a range of audiences; and to engage students in the exploration of a gamut of science-related concepts and issues – and, indeed, concepts or issues relevant to the raft of subject or curriculum areas.

CRIKEY!

Since Steve Irwin's fatal encounter with a stingray in 2006, September 4 is usually a sad day for Jennifer. On this particular spring day, strolling between biology lectures at Uni, Jennifer fondly remembered her first meeting with the legendary environmentalist, affectionately know around the world as the *Crocodile Hunter* ...

Suddenly, there was a commotion at one of the checkpoints. A customs officer was trying to persuade a reluctant passenger to part with some prohibited plants he had brought with him from the US.

'You know,' Steve started as he watched the passenger try to argue his way out of trouble, 'biosecurity and quarantine are so important to our country. We know how devastating it has been for our vulnerable ecosystems when [Species X, e.g. tilapia] got into the country somehow; it ruined [[Y] **native ecosystem or agricultural industry, e.g. local waterways**],' he explained.

'How on earth could something like that have such a terrible impact?' Jennifer asked.

'Well,' Steve continued energetically ...

Your task: Write 200–250 words in order to complete the story. Your teacher will allocate you one of the following scenarios, from which to insert [**the relevant X and Y**] into the storyline above. Be sure to research your biological incursion by exploring the associated websites and reading the scientific information, before completing Part A. Your story must be **informative** and **include scientific information**. Remember, using the biological incursion allocated to you, Steve is trying to help Jennifer understand the importance of quarantine. In the conversation that you complete between the characters, aim to address the following information:

- what the biological incursion is
- its country of origin
- how it entered Australia
- the problems it caused or continues to cause for native ecosystems or agricultural industries (i.e., its impacts)
- the difficulties scientists and farmers face controlling the pest, or how the pest was brought under control.

Source: Tomas (2012).

See literacies.com Learning Modules.

See literacies.com #edtech Literacies Applications.

Summary

Animal thinking, non-human		Human thinking	
• Iconic	• Iconic		
• Indicative	• Indicative		
	• Symbolic		
	Younger children's thinking	Older children's thinking	
	• In complexes	• Conceptual	
	Children's learning	Academic disciplines	
	• In a 'zone of proximal development', transitioning from complex to conceptual thinking	• Representation and communication of formal disciplinary meanings • Exophoric reference: about anything in the outside world • Metarepresentation: meanings about meanings that make learning more efficient and effective	

Knowledge processes

experiencing the new

1. Research communication in one species of animals. Create a table that analyses the similarities and differences between communication in humans and communication in other mammals.

conceptualising with theory

2. On the basis of the previous activity, write a theory of the differences between human thinking and the thinking of your chosen animal species.

conceptualising by naming

3. Define complex and conceptual thinking, and provide examples of each.

experiencing the known

4. What does Vygotsky mean by 'zone of proximal development'? Describe one particular instance when you were struggling to learn new concepts. What did it feel like? What scaffolds got you through? How did you learn?

5. Read summaries or overviews of the work of Piaget and Vygotsky in Wikipedia or some other introductory source. What are the most obvious similarities and differences between their work?

6. Select two lesson plans – one from the English/language arts subject area and one from the science subject area. Examine each of these lesson plans and consider the types of literacies – or repertoire of literacy practices – required of students in fulfilling the lesson objectives/outcomes.

7. Locate a recent 'news' article with scientific content. Once you have done so, undertake the work that we call upon our students to do when we engage them in critical literacy pedagogy (see Chapter 7, 'Critical literacies pedagogy'). That is, undertake 'interrogative' work, and ask the following questions of the text:

- What is the subject matter or topic?
- Why might the author have written this text?
- Who is the intended audience? How do you know?
- What worldview and values does the author assume that reader holds? How do you know?
- What knowledge does the reader need to bring to this text in order to understand it?
- Who would feel 'left out' in this text, and why; and is it a problem? Who would find that the claims made in this text clash with their own values, beliefs or experiences?
- How is the reader 'positioned' in relation to the author (e.g. as a friend, as an opponent, as someone who needs to be persuaded, as invisible, as someone who agrees with the author's views)?
- Are there 'gaps' or 'absences' or 'silences' in this text? If so, what are they? For example, is there a group of people missing who logically should be included? Are different groups talked about as though they belong to the same, seamless group? Does the author write about a group without including *their* perspective on things or events?

applying appropriately

8. Take a particular topic within a particular discipline area. Describe the ways in which literacies are essential to learning that topic.

applying creatively

9. Design a unit of work in science that focuses on concept development, and uses the resources of multimodal meaning as fully as possible. You may wish to create a Learning Module in Scholar.

CHAPTER 15

Literacies and learner differences

Overview

In this chapter, we are going to explore the range of learner differences that impact upon literacies learning. We outline concepts with which to classify and interpret these differences among learners. We discuss, in general terms, how we approach learner differences in relation to literacies learning. Then we explore in depth two particularly important dimensions of learner difference: age and other-language background.

The effects of difference in literacies learning

The demographics of social groups

In the schools of today, the differences between learners are more visible and in-sistent than ever. We are going to start with a frame of reference that we call group **demographics**, the visible realities in the form of distinguishable social groupings. After that, we are going to suggest that this is only the beginning of the story – learner differences are deeper and more subtle than these categories at first glance suggest.

Demographics: The social-scientific task of classifying social groups for the purposes of statistical analysis and program design

A litany of terms is conventionally used to describe and catego-rise differences in human populations called 'demography' – sex, gender, social class, disability, race, ethnicity. However, each of these terms is fraught with ambiguities and complexities.

Table 15.1: Demographic dimensions of learner differences

Material differences (access to resources)	*Class:* access to economic resources, household, employment and social status
	Locale: neighbourhoods and regions with differential social resources
	Family: relationships of domesticity and cohabitation
Corporeal differences (of the body)	*Age:* child development, life phases and peer dynamics
	Race: historical and social practices based on interpretations of phenotypical difference
	Sex and sexuality: the bodily realities of masculinity, femininity and varied sexualities
	Physical and mental abilities: spectrums of bodily and cognitive capability
Symbolic differences (human meanings)	*Language:* first and second language learners, and differences in dialect and social language
	Ethnos: national, ethnic, indigenous and diasporic identities
	Gendre: identities based on gender and sexual orientation

Material differences and literacies learning

Material differences are the result of variable access to resources, from grinding poverty to great wealth. Socio-economic differences that have an impact on access to such things as food, health, shel-ter, safety and information have a marked effect in student per-formance, including in the areas of reading and writing, as well

Material differences: Factors that affect people's access to social resources, such as socio-economic class, locale or neighbourhood and family circumstances

as literacies in a broader sense, as the basis for learning across all subject areas. The difference can be as striking as this: researchers estimate that the children of professionals are exposed to 42 million words of talk and 15000 different words in the first four years of life; this is compared to 13 million words of talk and 5000 unique words for children in poor families (Marulis & Neuman 2010). Put simply, if you are poorer you are less likely to do well in literacy tests, and less likely to do well at school.

This demographic reality has been the foundation of major programs in compensatory education since the second half of the 20th century. In the United States, President Lyndon B. Johnson introduced the Elementary and Secondary Act in 1965 as an aspect of his 'War on Poverty'. Under Title 1 of this law, the federal government was authorised to distribute special funding to schools with a high proportion of low-income children, as defined by the census. In 2001, the first major legislative initiative of the George W. Bush presidency, in collaboration with Senator Edward Kennedy, was the reauthorisation of this law under the new name 'No Child Left Behind'. In Australia, the Whitlam Government established the Schools Commission in 1973, one of whose most significant programs was the Disadvantaged Schools Program. These programs form a common pattern of compensatory education, which started in many countries in the second half of the 20th century and were originally part of the broader idea of a 'welfare state'. These programs required significant public investment.

Researcher Victoria Purcell-Gates tells the story of Jenny and her son Donny. Neither Jenny nor her husband, 'Big Donny', can read or write. They are poor whites living in a city in the mid-west of the United States. The young Donny is in second grade, but cannot read and can only write his name. The family, in Purcell-Gates' words, lives in 'a world without print'. Working with Donny in a university-based literacy centre, the researcher encountered a child who was 'either frightened of being wrong or had absolutely no idea of how to begin' and 'absolutely refused to experiment with writing beyond the letter level'. She also describes the enormous differences between oral and spoken language, and particularly spoken language, unaffected by literacy. 'I *knew* she [Jenny] was ignorant as soon as she opened her mouth!' said one of Donny's teachers in the local school. Purcell-Gates concludes that:

> [The maxim] 'the rich get richer and the poor get poorer' ... was never so true as when used to describe the educational possibilities of children from well-educated, highly literate homes as compared with equally bright and promising children from homes with no books, low levels of literacy use, and parents unable to or unaware of how they can support their children's schooling (Purcell-Gates 1995: 75, 164, 197).

See literacies.com Purcell-Gates on the Differences between Oral and Literate Culture.

Basil Bernstein is an education thinker whose work explores the reasons why working-class children do not as a rule perform as well at school as children from more affluent backgrounds. He theorises that one underlying difference is the

Figure 15.1 President Johnson signs the Elementary and Secondary Act with his childhood schoolteacher, Kate Loney, sitting at his side

range of linguistic codes accessible to learners. Working-class children are immersed in the lifeworld experience of what he calls 'restricted code' (Bernstein 1990). Restricted code is based on shared assumptions and common experience. It points to specific things in this context in the manner of indicative thinking, to use a term we introduced in the previous chapter. These are not meanings that stand on their own. They are context-dependent. They are only meaningful for people in that context – the family, the community, the informal person-to-person conversation.

Middle-class children, in addition to restricted code, have also been exposed to the 'elaborated code' characteristic of literacy and schooling. This, by comparison, is explicit. Its meanings are intelligible to strangers. It is conceptual, generalising and abstracting. It involves speaking that is more like writing. It is the code of people immersed in the culture and cognitive practices of print. This is why working-class children do not do so well at school. School speaks a language that is foreign to them.

See literacies.com Bernstein on Elaborated and Restricted Codes.

Table 15.2: Bernstein's Theory of Codes

Restricted code	• Implicit meanings, based on shared assumptions and common experience, which are hard for strangers to understand
	• Indicative thinking, referring to specific things
	• The oral culture of the family, the community, and informal, person-to-person conversation
Elaborated code	• Explicit meanings, which are intelligible to strangers
	• Conceptual and abstract thinking, referring to general things
	• Speaking that is often like writing
	• The code of people immersed in the culture and cognitive practices of print

Not that things always have to be this way, or are this way for everyone. Education and literacy can also be a site of social mobility. Literacy researcher Kathryn Au tells her own life story starting with her grandmother, Hew Ngim Moi, born in Hong Kong, who never learned to read or write. She moved to Hawaii as a child, but did not go to school there because education was considered unnecessary for girls. When the truant officers came around, Chinese families hid girls who were not going to school. As an adult, she worked in the family store where she could read prices and a few labels, but nothing more. However, she also took a great interest in her children's education – including the education of her daughters.

> I [Au] cannot remember a time when I did not think of schooling as a precious commodity, so family members must have instilled this into me at an early age ... I grew up believing that education would be the key to my own success in life (Au 2011: 6).

Here we see the close interconnection of material and symbolic factors in the demographics diversity – the economic resources of social class, the culture and resources of a locale, and the dynamics of family that is the poverty and wealth of individual and communities. The educational outcomes are by no means inevitable, even if much of the time a combination of class, locale and family context conspires to mean that learners from materially less well-off settings are struggling against greater odds and do not do as well at school as students from more affluent contexts. Challenging conditions also at times provide a motivation to use education as an opportunity, as a path to social mobility. We cannot and should not rely on this dynamic, however.

Corporeal differences in literacies learning

Corporeal differences: Bodily differences and the meanings given to these differences including age, race, sex/ sexuality and physical and mental abilities

Corporeal differences refer to one's bodily capacity. Key dimensions that affect literacies learning are age, race, sex and sexuality, and physical and mental abilities. We will address age differences in detail later in this chapter.

Race consists of the meanings historically ascribed to physical appearances and the lifeworlds of groups that are racially defined.

Race is not a scientific category and there are more differences within groups of people called 'a race' than between groups labelled as 'races'. In Chapter 7 we discussed the work of the linguist William Labov, who identified differences in African American English that produced difficulties for African American students in schools that were ill-prepared to deal with these differences. Historically, there have been structural responses to people categorised as different by powerful groups of people in society. These responses – for example, slavery, nationalism, segregation, apartheid and ethnic cleansing – have restricted the lifeworld opportunities of less powerful people and resulted in degrees of marginalisation and injustice. Much of the time, the issues that lead to these responses are what we call 'symbolic'; that is, involving the meaning-making systems of language and culture. However, when these coincide with phenotypical groupings ('phenotype' is a technical word to describe visible physical characteristics), it is impossible to ignore the history of racism, discrimination and systemic inequality based on the classification 'race'.

Sex and sexuality are corporeal differences that affect one's physical presence, and relationships to the other and same sex. If literacies are a learning space that deal with human meanings, it is hard for sexual differences and sexuality not to be a pervasive topic – from the old Dick and Jane readers, to Shakespeare, to contemporary literatures or movies that explore modern dilemmas of sexual difference and sexuality – in ways that some people may at times find disquieting.

Physical and mental abilities are another major area affecting literacies learning. With appropriate educational support, degrees of hearing and sight abilities need have no impact at all on a learner's capacity to mean and to learn. In the case of hearing impairment, oral language can be fully replaced by the gestural mode of communication of deaf sign language. And in the case of visual impairment, written language can be fully substituted in the tactile mode with Braille.

Other physical and mental differences also require specialist programs for learners to reach their full personal capacity as makers and interpreters of meaning. Dyslexia is a neurobiological condition that specifically affects a student's capacity to read and write. It is not a sign of low intelligence. In fact, quite the contrary: many outstandingly brilliant people have been dyslexic, from Michelangelo to Einstein. Common aspects of the condition include difficulties in distinguishing phonic symbols, the creation of sounds from writing, writing directionality and speed of visual-oral response. Signs of the condition may include delays in speaking, letter reversal or mirror writing and difficulties in decoding words by analysing the alphabetical representation of their sounds and spelling.

In order to cater to the needs of students with a wide range of abilities, the principle of 'universal design for learning' suggests the creation of flexible, multimodal and synaesthetic learning environments (CAST 2011). Barriers to learning are reduced when the range of learning capacities of learners is designed into the instructional environment, tools and materials. For instance, in the context of literacies using digital media, all written text and images should be representable in spoken words, and written meanings should be supplemented with oral meanings. Providing and supporting multiple literacies has been shown to be a powerful way to promote the effective inclusion of students with disabilities into learning environments (Westby 2010).

In a Multiliteracies activity at the E. C. Drury School for the Deaf in Ontario, Canada, storytellers from the local deaf community explain to elementary students how they got their sign names, using the local Ontario dialect of American Sign Language (ASL). William explains how he got his name, a clawed V hand shape in an arc across his chin, associated with the sign 'strong'. He also explains how, although the children of deaf parents were often given sign names after other family members, names were also given to them by other deaf children at school, based on some individual trait. When he was at school, ASL was banned in the classroom. The teacher videos the storytelling so the class can go back over and carefully examine the signs William and the other storytellers use. Then the students create videos telling their own sign name stories, recording multiple drafts and getting feedback from other students between each draft. The result is a powerful series of multimodal identity texts (Snoddon 2010).

Symbolic differences in literacies learning

Some speakers benefit from the privileged position of the language they speak. Speakers of the official, national language find school easier and are more likely to succeed than immigrant speakers of minority languages, or speakers of 'non-standard' dialects, or speakers of indigenous languages in places that have been colonised in the past. Language and cultural marginalisation often come together.

Karen Martin is a Noonuccal woman, a literacy researcher at Queensland University of Technology and an Indigenous educator whose ancestral 'Country' is now called Stradbroke Island, Australia. She creates an image that tells the story of her ancestral relatedness to her country. The story tells narratives of space, place and the lived connections of people to Country. Her text is at once science, history, culture and spirituality.

'In terms of a Multiliteracies design framework,' says Martin, 'the example demonstrates how the visual and the spatial are powerful literacies in their own right.' She goes on to explain how a Multiliteracies approach is more effective for Indigenous Australian students:

> A Multiliteracies approach acknowledges and is inclusive of the representation of information in a number of ways that incorporate the visual, spatial, gestural, linguistic and the audio. When these design elements are not in place for Aboriginal students, programs and practices become obsessed with 'filling up' the perceived lack of cultural knowledge and experiences on the part of Aboriginal students, families and homes, as a means to replace their 'bad' English. Such models ... persistently ignore or give superficial attention to the ways in which knowledge is acquired, confirmed, and expressed by Aboriginal people – in other words, ignoring Aboriginal worldviews and knowledges and hence, Aboriginal literacies ... Multiliteracies pedagogy gives promise to the teaching of Aboriginal students through its wider definition of literacy and the recognition of social and historical contexts (Martin 2008: 59).

Figure 15.2 Minjerripah (Stradbroke Island), by
Karen Martin

Mario Lopez-Gopar describes Multiliteracies learning in an indigenous community school in Oaxaca, Mexico. In a video recording made by the students, a Triqui
girl and her mother share the meaning of an indigenous garment called a huipil.
According to the Triquis, the garment is full of life and symbolic of metamorphosis.
The wearer's head is the sun, the caterpillar is represented by red lines and the
butterfly it becomes, by different designs on these lines. Death is represented at the
bottom, but that is not the end because the huipil continues, as does life. Lopez-
Gopar concludes: 'the Multiliteracies Framework recognises not only that the artist
behind the huipil is the author, but also that many indigenous groups are literate
even when they do not know the alphabet'. They 'can read the weather and know
exactly when to plant; they are able to read plants and create different medica-
tions; they can read the natural clock by simply looking at the position of the sun'
(Lopez-Gopar 2007: 168–9).

Gender and 'gendre' are key areas of **symbolic difference** that
affect learners' literacies outcomes. Gender consists of the cultural meanings ascribed to the corporeal differences of sex. Gendre is a broader concept, which includes gender but also includes
aspects of sexuality. With this concept comes a recognition of the
range and complexity of identities and connected cultural practices that overlie the biological realities of sex and sexuality.

**Symbolic
differences:** Differences in
cultural and social meanings
including language, ethnicity,
gender identities and sexual
orientation.

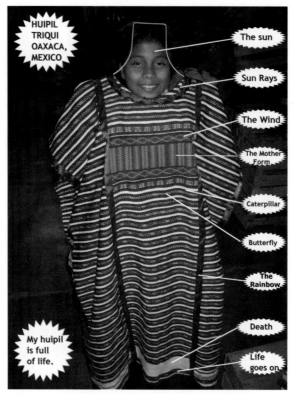

Figure 15.3 A Triqui girl explains the meaning of her huipil

Historically, schooling may have been biased towards boys and heterosexual masculinity – the heroes of children's stories, the family roles in children's readers, the heterosexual relationships of love stories, the great men of history, the scientific and mathematical learning that was a prerequisite for many professional men's jobs, and the applied technology learning for boys destined to be tradespeople. Girls got less schooling, were less represented in higher education, and were trained to be good mothers and housewives in 'domestic science'.

By the beginning of the 21st century, the educational outcomes of boys and men seem to have been reversed. Much of the time girls were doing better in many school subjects than boys, and particularly in literacy, as reflected in conventional assessments. While more girls were succeeding in 'boys' subjects' such as mathematics and science, fewer boys were succeeding in humanities subjects. By the end of school, more women were securing entry into areas of professional education that were traditionally the preserve of men, such as law and medicine. Meanwhile, the numbers of men who were entering lower-paying and historically female professions such as teaching were not equalising to the same degree. The result today is that there are more women studying in higher education than men. Meanwhile, male youth suicide rates have soared, and violence and crime remain predominantly male. Some have viewed this as evidence of a cultural crisis in masculinity.

Researchers rightly warn us not to rush to stereotypical generalisations, because boys from more affluent circumstances still outperform girls from poorer circumstances (Alloway 2007). And although boys, instead of reading, may be playing more video games, many of which are grounded in male identities, such as first-person shooter games and car racing games, girls are in some respects missing out on the level and intensity of engagement with new media that today's boys experience (Gilbert & Gilbert 1998). Also, there is a broad range of gender identities and shades of sexuality across boys and girls. Different boys and girls respond to learning and literacies curricula in different ways.

Jane Kenway and Helen Nixon describe a Multiliteracies practice in the form of a history project, which had been moved from a print-based to a computer-based setting. Jim and Theo were creating a series of screens that involved not just reading and writing on the screen but interacting with it gesturally and orally – pointing at the things they were seeing and creating, and talking about them. Kenway calls this:

> relating to the screen ... a noticeably physical set of bodily dispositions [and] ways of holding their bodies ... Here the boys acted-out, zoomed in, jumped about, waved their arms, sang and chanted and provided a running commentary ... [T]he boys' performance was notable for the way it made reference to scenarios and narratives from popular media culture and used similar technical conventions such as multi-voiced voice-over narration and sound effects ... As has been observed in computer game play, the boys made ... connections between semiotic modes (Kenway & Nixon 1999: 470).

From group demographics to the complexities of learner differences

Already in the examples we have examined above, we can get a sense of the complexities of learner differences. Although group demographics can tell us a lot about a child's background and can often help patterns of educational outcome, nothing is as simple as demographic classifications such as male–female, affluent–poor and black–white.

Problems with group demographics

For a start, the more we become aware of learner differences, the more unmanageable the list of group classifications becomes – the subtleties of dis/ability, the catalogue of countless different ethnic groups, the proliferation of subtly nuanced distinctions of sexuality and gender, and the distinctions of language background and language use in different social contexts. In classrooms, teachers today often feel they need to have knowledge of an impossible-to-manage encyclopedia of differences.

Add to this the internal complexity in any one demographically defined group. In fact, the closer we look at differences in stance, self-identification and behaviour within any demographically defined group, we discover that these are almost always greater than the average difference between groups. Indeed, the categories of gross demographics can easily lead to stereotypical generalisations – about Chinese learning styles, boys' interest in reading and writing, or the likely consequences of socio-economic disadvantage for literacies learning, for instance. Many individuals fall outside the norm. Some students in disadvantaged groups do succeed; background is not all-determining. Indeed, at times a student's 'disadvantaged' background is the basis for their particular resilience, their peculiar success. Sometimes, even, the terms of demographic grouping become invidious labels, implying a deficit on the part of the student, when in fact they may be an opportunity upon which to build constructive learning experiences. And still other children from seemingly privileged backgrounds suffer from emotional problems linked to family crises and alienation.

Differences also intersect. They are never things in themselves. Rather, they are always complex, multilayered realities in which each aspect of material, corporeal and symbolic difference is deeply overlaid with other aspects, forming an integrated whole. For any individual, the specific mix of group demographic dimensions is sometimes so specific that they end up belonging to the tiniest of minorities. Throwing quite different people together into one of the larger categories may also do a disservice to the actual needs and interests of particular people in specific contexts. The list of demographic classifiers, in other words, is all too neat. The groups are not separate; they are overlapping, simultaneous, multilayered. Every individual represents a peculiar conjunction of dimensions of difference, a unique mix of group or community experiences.

See literacies.com Bereiter on Kinds of Diversity.

Lifeworld attributes and learning

The **lifeworld** consists of the things you end up knowing without having to think how you came to know them. It is the way you end up being without ever having consciously decided to be that way. The lifeworld is not particularly explicit. It is a set of habits, behaviours, values and interests that go without saying in a particular context. The lifeworld goes without saying because it has come without saying. It is made up of things that seem so obvious to insiders that they don't need saying. Knowledge of the lifeworld does not have to be taught in a formal way. You learn how to be in the lifeworld just by living in it, and this learning is mostly so unconscious that it is rarely even experienced as learning. The lifeworld is the ground of our existence, the already-learned and continuously-being-learned experience of everyday life. It is also the site of our subjectivity and identity and the source of our motivation. It is intuitive, instinctive and deeply felt.

This is what learners bring to a learning setting. It is the background to their learning – the kind of learner they have become through the influence of their

Lifeworld: The everyday life of individuals in communities

family, their local community, their friends, their peers and the particular slices of popular or domestic culture with which they identify. It is a place where the learner's everyday understandings and actions seem to work, and so much so that their active participation is almost instinctive – something that requires not too much conscious or reflective thought. The lifeworld is what has shaped them. It is what they unreflectively like and dislike. It is who they are and an identity they carry with them in all other contexts.

Table 15.3: Lifeworld attributes

		Examples
Narrative	The stories of a person's life, their experiences, their background, their life history.	Family cultures Life experiences
Persona	Identity, grounded both in the quirks of 'personality' traits and the experiences people have had as part of a larger social history. Persona captures the kind of person you envision yourself to be, what you style yourself as and how you present yourself. It may be affected or unarticulated. It may be conscious, semi-conscious or unconscious. Persona may be manifest in gesture and the various modes of presentation of self, such as fashion, ways of speaking or modes of interaction.	Interpersonal styles Languages spoken
Affinity	Attachments to groups or worldviews – for instance, the infinitely varied shades of religious or non-religious identifications, and political or apolitical alignments. Affinity may also be to products or material objects; or games or sports; or aesthetics or styles. You are what you associate yourself with, and what that association stands for. Affinity captures an extraordinary variety of senses of connection, from personal beliefs and attitudes, to membership of networks, to more formal connections with groups.	Values Interests Political stance Social values Contacts and networks Local, regional, national and international links Employment sector
Orientation	The ways in which people connect into new and unfamiliar contexts on the basis of their preferred ways of knowing (e.g. by immersion in the facts or by big-picture abstraction), their ways of learning (e.g. experiential or conceptual), their ways of speaking of particular things (e.g. technical or applied discourses) and their ways of relating to people	Thinking style Communication style Disposition Sensibilities Demeanour Intersubjective style

See literacies.com Gee on Social Languages.

Narrative, persona, affinity and orientation are key lifeworld attributes. Using these categories to explore learner differences focuses on the specificities of a particular person's life experience. It is a way to account for internal group variations. It allows us to identify the unique intersections of every person's group-and history-related position. Gutiérrez and Rogoff call these 'linguistic and cultural-historical repertoires' (Gutiérrez & Rogoff 2003). Importantly also, this approach asks these questions of every learner, thus getting away from the sometimes only-perfunctory list of equity groups.

Learning succeeds or fails to the extent that it engages the varied subjectivities of learners. Engagement produces opportunity, equity and participation. Not engaging produces failure, disadvantage and inequality. The dilemma for teaching is that, no matter how much filtering is done according to the demographic categories (by age, or gender, or ethnicity, for instance) from person to person, learners invariably remain different.

See literacies.com Delpit on Language Diversity and Learning.

Differentiated instruction: Pedagogical approaches that cater for learner differences by offering a range of activity options and modes of meaning

Education, then, needs to start with an engagement with difference far deeper than the demographics of social groups. So the challenge is: how do we engage all learners in classrooms of deep difference? In other words, how do we do diversity?

Following are five principles and practices for **differentiated instruction** in literacies that addresses learner diversity.

Differentiated literacies instruction 1: the idea of design

The Multiliteracies approach provides a number of concepts and pedagogical strategies to support learner differences. The first is the 'design' idea that we introduced in Chapter 8. Didactic literacy teaching tends to assume that language is just one set of rules to be learned and that modes of good expression are to be acquired from well-written or literary texts. It spawns a one-size-fits-all curriculum, assuming or intending to create cultural uniformity. The teacher talks to the middle of the class, the textbook assumes every learner is on the same page at the same time, and the test is 'standardised' to a single measure of learner outcomes. This is a reproduction model of literacy. Into the reader go author meanings; out of their learning comes correct comprehension of the meaning of the text. Into the writer go rules and models of good writing; and out come well-written texts.

The 'design' proposition is quite different. Every student brings to the class a repertoire of 'available designs' of meaning across a number of modes – the things they have read, heard and seen as a part of their lifeworld and previous educational experiences. From learner to learner, no two experiences of 'available designs' can ever be quite the same. These may be supplemented by new designs offered by the teacher – different kinds of written, oral, visual, gestural and other texts. The student then undertakes the process of 'designing'. They interpret the new texts the teacher has given them, and no two interpretations will ever be quite the same. They create a new text – in writing, video, recorded voice and the like. And once more, no two texts will be the same, representing the student's reworking of design elements from their lifeworld and the particular educational experiences. As students share their designs, either as collaborators on joint texts or as readers of other students' texts, student work re-enters the world of meaning and learning as 'the designed' – artefacts that can enter the cycle of meaning as new 'available designs'. This is a model of literacies learning that recognises diversity, voice and constant change rather than uniformity, regimentation and enforced stability.

Kris Gutiérrez describes the space we here call 'designing' as a 'third space', located between the primary space of lifeworld experience and informal learning, on the one hand, and on the other, a secondary space of formal school learning. Here, she adapts Vygotsky's notion of 'zone of proximal development', which we introduced in the previous chapter. Vygotsky considers this space more narrowly as a site of cognitive development in which children move with teacher and other adult support from complex to conceptual thinking. Gutiérrez expands the zone of proximal development as an intermediate cultural space in which students make connections between the meanings they make in out-of-school spaces and the meanings of school literacy and learning (Gutiérrez 2008).

Differentiated literacies instruction 2: multimodality

Some students may 'get' a meaning in written words, some in a diagram, others in a gestural and tactile demonstration, others in an oral explanation. Some may have a talent or passion for drawing, others for video, others for podcasting, others for crafting words on a blog, still others for concept mapping. Students need to be able to express themselves in the ways they feel most comfortable. However, they also need to be encouraged to move beyond their comfort zones, into modes of communication with which they are less familiar, learning their techniques and their technologies. However, the most powerful learning starts with expression of meaning in the modes that come most easily.

James Green is a social studies teacher in a school serving immigrant and working-class families in California. He is teaching a Year/Grade 7 world history class, required of all students in California, covering a period from the Roman Empire to the Industrial Revolution and beyond. This is an enormous stretch of time and requires students to do a lot of reading. To make the subject matter more compelling, he involves the students in role-plays, discussions and art projects. He shows videos, and has the students search the Web and look up a variety of books. He makes connections between past and present. The class discusses whether there are parallels between the Crusades and present-day terrorism. When investigating the agricultural revolution, he has the students explore where the food in the local supermarket comes from and how it got there. Wanting the students to understand the nature and processes of history, he has the class work on an oral history project. Here, students record parents and family members, learning how to develop historical questions and frame historical interpretation. These oral histories are then presented in the form of digital storytelling, and when completed, shared with parents (Cummins, Brown & Sayers 2007: 149–65).

Differentiated literacies instruction 3: knowledge processes

Using the pedagogical terminology introduced in Chapter 3, some 'knowledge processes' are particularly well suited to bringing diversity into the literacies classroom. In 'experiencing the known' students are prompted to bring into the classroom texts that are familiar to them or of interest to them, and encouraged to introduce perspectives, experiences and knowledge from their social worlds. In 'analysing critically', students reflect on their own and others' perspectives and interests as reflected in the texts. And in 'applying creatively', students take new ideas and capacities to communicate and apply them in creating and communicating real-world texts.

These kinds of pedagogical moves create avenues in the curriculum for learners to express who they are in all its subtlety and richness. This is a way to value what they already know. Such a learning environment opens a window onto student identities and helps teachers and fellow students figure out what makes them 'tick'. By honouring their lifeworlds as places of valid and relevant knowledge, these knowledge processes create a sense of belonging that is central to inclusive education. African American educational theorist and researcher Gloria Ladson-Billings calls this culturally relevant teaching (Ladson-Billings 2001). In the case of the 'knowledge process' notion specifically, Keiju Suominen describes the effect of this kind of pedagogical openness as a kind of personalisation: 'although the learning [is] designed by the teacher for the entire class, the nature of the activities work[s] to personalise the learning for each student' (Suominen 2009: 126–7).

Researcher Jim Cummins describes the work of three students in a Year/ Grade 7–8 literacy classroom in Canada. Kanta and Sulmana had arrived in Toronto in Year/Grade 4 and were reasonably fluent in English, but Madiha had arrived more recently and was still in the early stages of English language acquisition. In an integrated social studies and language unit, they created a bilingual text, 'The New Country'. They researched and wrote the story over a period of several weeks, writing it in English, but discussing it in Urdu. Later they translated the English text into written Urdu. 'In a "typical" classroom', Cummins concludes, 'Madiha's ability to participate in a Grade 7 social studies unit would have been severely limited by her minimal knowledge of English. ... However, following simple changes to the social structure of the classroom, Madiha was enabled to express her intelligence, feelings and identity .... She contributed her ideas and experiences to the story, participated in discussions about how to translate vocabulary, ... and shared in the affirmation that all three students experienced with the publication of their story in print and on the ... web' (Cummins 2009 : 50–1). Cummins calls this 'transformative Multiliteracies pedagogy', a process that activates students' prior knowledge and constructs an image of the student as 'intelligent, imaginative and linguistically talented' (Cummins 2006; Cummins 2009; Cummins & Early 2011).

Differentiated literacies instruction 4: alternative navigation paths

A Multiliteracies pedagogy does not require that every learner is on the same page at the same time. For instance, in the era of blended e-learning delivery, individual students or groups of students might be working over different units of work or 'learning modules' at any one time. Or learners will be able to negotiate to change the sequence of knowledge processes so they start with an activity type with which they are most comfortable. Some students, for instance, might prefer big-picture 'conceptualising' before they immerse themselves in 'experiencing'; others the reverse. Or they will be able to negotiate preferred modes of expression of meaning. Some learners may prefer to video an oral story before they attempt to create the story as a written text.

A key area for the creation of alternative navigation paths pivots on distinctions of 'disability'. Some students may not be doing well at school for reasons related to corporeal differences: cognitive issues, visual or audio impairment, autism, ADHD, dyslexia and the like. Early identification, intervention and progress monitoring will help them achieve to the best of their abilities. Many students are also falling behind for a variety of reasons related to the material and symbolic conditions of their lives, not disability.

To address this range of differences, tiered intervention strategies are developed, one of which is called 'Response to Intervention' (Buffum, Mattos & Weber 2009). At a first tier, children whose performance is below expected at that age level are catered for in the mainstream curriculum as the teacher differentiates instruction to meet their needs and to optimise their progress. The teacher constantly evaluates how these students are performing and provides them with learning tasks that are within their zone of proximal development. At a second tier of intervention, supplementary teaching is provided one-to-one or in small groups by a specialist literacy coach, speech therapist or teacher's aide. Typically, such interventions might occur several times per week for periods of half an hour or an hour. A third tier of intervention is more intensive, requiring one or two sessions per day for a period of two to three months, according to an individualised plan that sets goals, describes strategies and plans assessment. Trained special education teachers are required for this level of intervention.

See literacies.com Response to Intervention.

'Reading Recovery' is an example of an intervention strategy for early literacy learners. Developed by New Zealander Marie Clay, Reading Recovery aims to assist students struggling with learning to read in daily one-on-one lessons for approximately 20 weeks. In each session, a child rereads yesterday's book, examines some words and their phonemic make-up for a few minutes, composes and writes a story, reassembles a story as a puzzle from its parts, and is introduced to a new reading book, which they start to read. The teacher makes on-the-fly responses to areas of difficulty and maintains daily records, identifying specific areas in which the child is struggling with text (Clay 1998; Clay 2005).

See literacies.com Marie Clay on Reading Recovery.

Differentiated literacies instruction 5: creating a learning environment of productive diversity

When learner lifeworlds are so varied, diversity of knowledge, experience and perspective becomes a learning resource. Students benefit from the varied texts their peers bring to the classroom from among the 'available designs' of their lives. Learning activities highlight and value the varied knowledge and experiences that learners are able to contribute. Learners also benefit from the diverse perspectives, opinions and worldviews, not only because this introduces them to a wider range of curriculum content, but also because it demonstrates the important role of interpretation in all meaning-making.

Collaborative Reasoning is a strategy developed by Richard Anderson and his colleagues at the Center for the Study of Reading at the University of Illinois. In small groups, and with minimal intervention on the part of teachers, children discuss story, or information books that they are reading. They think out loud as they engage in argumentation and reasoning about the text – the moral dilemma that a character faces in a storybook, or an environmental problem that a natural science information book poses, for instance (Clark, Anderson, Kuo, Kim, Archodidou & Nguyen-Jahiel 2003). As a reading pedagogy, Collaborative Reasoning involves oral response to written text (what in the Multiliteracies theory we would call synaesthesia), topic selection and turn-taking in the context of presentation of one's own opinion, and reflection on the multiple possibilities for meaning in a text, which are neglected in ABCD tests of 'comprehension'. Students also learn to appreciate the different interpretations and insights that different people bring to a text.

In fact, the text is most powerfully interpreted through the synthesis of multiple perspectives.

Developed by Annemarie Palinscar and Ann Brown, initially also while they were at the University of Illinois, Reciprocal Teaching is a strategy for interpreting the meaning of a text. It prompts students to clarify meanings (including decoding words and exploring vocabulary), predict (or bring one's background knowledge to bear on the meaning of a text), question (or demonstrate self-awareness about how the reader is making sense of the text) and summarise (discriminating aspects of the text that are of greater or lesser significance to its meaning). The pedagogy is dialogical, at first between teacher and students as the method is learned, then between learners in small-group Reciprocal Teaching sessions (Palinscar & Brown 1984). Once again, the principles of productive diversity come into play – as group members combine their knowledge for the purposes of clarification, bringing their varied life experiences together in the interpretative task of predicting meaning, and assigning significance to different aspects of the text.

A 'workshop' approach to writing begins with generating ideas about the topic students will write on, with a focus in language learning on topics that are meaningful to learners' own lives. Teachers then workshop the developing text with students, exploring their intended meanings and assisting them to express these meanings. Finally, the finished text – in Multiliteracies' terms, the 'redesigned' – is shared with the whole class and published (Fletcher & Portalupi 2001). Here, too, the diversity of student voices is supported and highlighted.

Learning-knowing is most powerful when the invariably diverse perspectives of students are deliberately introduced into the classroom and used as a resource for learning. This is the basis for learning and knowledge ecologies that are very different from traditional 'transmission' models of pedagogy, which are generic and uniform. The broader educational outcome of a more diverse and inclusive approach to literacies learning is the development of kinds of people who have the capacity to negotiate deep diversity and navigate change. They can engage in sometimes difficult dialogues; they can compromise and create shared understandings; and they can comfortably extend their cultural and knowledge repertoires into new areas. They are tolerant, responsible and resilient in their differences. The key questions for educators, then, is how to support the learning of this kinds of people as they learn to express themselves and learn to communicate with others.

Age differences and literacies learning

Literacies and child development

Children learn to make meanings in a developmental progression. A child's capacity to mean is linked to their physiological growth and cognitive development from infancy to adulthood – a phenomenon we have termed 'corporeal differences' of age. Learners with physical or mental disabilities may reach a developmental stage later than others, or in ways not recognisable to conventional school cultures.

In literacies development, the meanings children make are invariably multi-modal, despite the most rigorous attempts of didactic literacy pedagogy to separate the written mode as a separately learned subject area. Here we present an overview of five steps of development that are explicitly multimodal. This is based on well-established stages of reading and writing development, supplementing these analyses with multimodal literacies and the processes of mode-shifting, or synaesthesia – we have adapted and extended Clay and Chall (Chall 1983; Clay 2001). However, one important difference between our perspective and the conventional literacy progression is that, being multimodal, our stages start earlier. We recognise that significant early meanings are made in modes other than writing. These are important precursors to reading and writing, in some respects cognitively equivalent to reading and writing, and essential supports in learning to read and write.

Before we run through these steps, some words of caution. Firstly, things do not always come first for all children – some children do well at some things earlier than might be expected, but at other things later. Moreover, we want to be wary of finely grained stage analyses such as 'reading age', which consider a single number to be meaningful and assume that a number can be as specific as a one-year timeframe. Learning to mean is so multifaceted and so variable that there can be no adequate substitute for a detailed and specific analysis of the range of capacities of a particular child at a particular time. Moreover, waiting for a significant discrepancy in reading age in relation to chronological age to show up can often mean leaving potential learning problems until they are too late.

See literacies.com Chall on Stages of Reading Development.

Initial literacies

Initial literacies bridge the all-important gap between home and school: a more troublesome gap for some learners than others. We cluster these three steps because together they constitute the first significant transition into literacies. In fact, this transition represents a crucial transformation in the young human person as a meaning-maker, and also as a person ready to settle into academic learning in a formal educational setting.

Developing academic literacies

Considerable attention is focused on initial literacies as a site where some learners do better at literacies and schooling than others. However, equally important is another major and often neglected transition, which we characterise here as a shift from complex to conceptual meaning-making. Here we apply and extend the distinction made by Vygotsky that we introduced in Chapter 14. James Gee and others talk about the 'fourth grade' slump, in which students who may have made it through the transition to initial literacies quite successfully start to perform poorly as academic expectations are ratcheted to a higher level (Gee 2004b: 18, 36).

Table 15.4: Stages of development of initial literacies

Step 1: Literacies awareness Before and starting school (approximate age 3–5), the child:	• writes and draws as scribble, and explains what it 'says' (synaesthesia involving written, visual, oral and gestural meanings) • recognises that there are distinguishable parts to images and written words (e.g. alphabets, numerals and other symbols), and knows there is a difference between writing and pictures (written and visual) • recognises that there are patterns in print and image (written and visual) • knows some letters and that there are sounds connected with them (written, oral and audio) • can read along with an adult reading a picture book or screen, pointing to the relevant part of a picture when the adult reads a corresponding word or phrase (gestural, visual and oral) • can watch a story or informational narrative in print, screen or other renderings for a sustained period of time because it carries meanings for them (audio, oral and visual)
Step 2: Beginning literacies During a first year at school (approximate age 5), the child:	• can write their name and draw a self-portrait (visual and written) • uses oral language to describe pictures (oral and visual) • knows the connection between pictures, symbols and written text (written and visual) • can read many letters, some words, a short sentence (written and oral) • points to words while sounding (written, oral and audio) • understands directionality in writing: left-right, top-down, read left page first, turn-right-page (spatial, visual and written) • understands beginning and end in video (audio, oral, visual)
Step 3: Early literacies In the first and second years of school (approximate age 5–6), the child:	• can draw distinguishable things, multiple picture elements and one or more word labels (visual and written) • can read stories with phonemically simple words supported by visual mnemonics pointing to the meaning of those words (oral, visual and written) • can point to words along a line as they read along with an adult (oral and written) • knows that written text does not contain the same information as accompanying pictures (visual and written) • can tell a spoken story (audio and oral) • can recount the content of a video (visual, oral and audio) • can write and illustrate a story of one or several sentences (visual and written) • has good motor control, such as turning the pages of a book, or scrolling on a smartphone or e-book reader (gestural and written)

Table 15.5: Stages of development of academic literacies

Step 4: Moving into complex meaning-making In the lower primary/ elementary school (approximate ages 6–9), the child:	• uses strategies of association to decode temporarily unintelligible parts of an image or written text, such as guessing from context (written, oral, visual) • changes and revises text and image, or re-enacts gesture, sound, spatial movement or tactile demonstration (any and all modes) • can name design elements of a text and can name design elements in any and all modes • understands levels of chunking of ideas and their interconnection, such as images in image sets, acted-out gesture sequences, words in sentences in paragraphs, headings and chapters (any and all modes) • can draw progressively more realistic images (visual) • can use media such as a digital camera to create images and insert into a text (visual and written) • can record and play back sound and video (audio, oral and gestural) • is able to navigate website and electronic reading devices (spatial, written, visual) • is able to identify interests, perspectives and purposes in a text (any and all modes)
Step 5: Moving into conceptual meaning-making From mid primary/ elementary to middle school (approximate ages 9–13), the child:	• can independently investigate written and visual meaning representations; e.g. dictionaries, encyclopedias, web searches, screen menus (written, visual and spatial) • knows how to add new words, visual meanings, gestures and sounds to their meaning repertoire (any and all modes) • can theorise design elements; e.g. define 'metarepresentation' terms and explain terms in relation to each other (any and all modes) • can use and create conceptual images using symbols and keys such as maps, plans, diagrams and other non-realistic conceptual imagery (visual) • can present structured information using styles, outlines or menus (written and visual) • can identify multiple and alternative perspectives, voices, interests and purposes within a text or between parallel texts (any and all modes) • can present information, make an argument or tell a story with affect (written, oral and visual) • is able to create navigational architectures characteristic of the internet and electronic reading devices including nesting, cross-linking and tagging (spatial, visual, written)

Different language backgrounds and literacies learning

Varieties of EAL/D learners or ELLs

We classify language as a kind of symbolic difference. Specifically, language involves the quite different experiences of making meaning in the oral and written modes. Students face a disadvantage when they come to school with a first or home language that is not the main language of instruction. In terms of demographic grouping, in Anglophone countries these students are categorised as speakers of English as an Additional Language or Dialect (EAL/D) or English Language Learners (ELLs).

However, like all such demographic categories, these labels often obscure extraordinary internal diversity within the category (Gutiérrez & Orellana 2006). There can be big differences between low-wage, low-skill migrants and business or professional migrants. There can be big differences between people who come from countries where English is taught little and countries where it is taught to all students (such as the countries of Northern Europe) or where English is the lingua franca (such as India). There can be big differences between the typical life and language experiences of legal migrants, refugees and undocumented migrants. There can be big differences between migrants of all kinds and historically marginalised indigenous groups, who may or may not continue to speak their indigenous language, a creole or a dialect, at home. There can be big differences between foreign and local-born children, and between children who have arrived at an English language school for the first time at different ages. There can also be a range of subtle linguistic variations – whether the learner is already literate in a first language, whether they are already bilingual or monolingual, the similarity or dissimilarity of language structures and writing systems, and varied patterns of interference with English (transferring phonic, grammatical and other logics from their first language into English). In other words, a large demographic category is no substitute for careful analysis of particular life experiences and language capacities.

Moreover, adding to the complexity of age levels is another series of levels of competence in English, based on the amount and forms of exposure. The amount of exposure is not simply a matter of how long a child has been in an English-speaking country; it is also their levels of exposure to English. They may come to school having been born in the country but never speaking English because all their family and community interactions, and perhaps their preschool too, were exclusively in the home language. On the other hand, they may have had bilingual exposure in all these settings, playing with neighbours, speaking with different family members, or attending an English-language preschool. And, in the case of older children, there is also a question of forms of exposure: how much exposure to academic language they have had, either in their first language or in English.

Social and academic languages

Jim Cummins is a leading researcher of language development in bilingual learners. He describes two major phases in second language learning. The first is learning a **social language** ('basic interpersonal communicative skill'). This may take one to two years for a learner with little or no prior knowledge of English. The second is learning academic language ('cognitive academic language proficiency'), which may take five years or more (Cummins 2000). Social languages occur in situations such as conversations with English language peers and in other informal social settings. Here, oral-linguistic meanings are highly context-embedded, supported by the signs of spatial arrangement, gesture and intonation. The grammar of social language is typically that of oral communication, and its vocabulary consists of short, high-frequency words. **Academic language**, by contrast, is less easy to make sense of from contextual clues. It uses the grammar of writing, including, for instance, more complex forms of passive voice and embedded clauses, and its vocabulary consists of longer, less frequent and more conceptually abstract terms.

Social language: The ordinary way of speaking in the lifeworld

Academic language: The more abstract and conceptual ways of representing meanings in writing and other modes in formal educational settings

A serious problem for older speakers of EAL/D or older ELLs is that they may have begun the transition from social to academic language in their first language in their country of origin. Then they move, and their conceptual development is interrupted because academic subjects are in an unfamiliar language. For the moment at least, all their language learning efforts need to go into mastering social language. Second language learners tend to fall behind in their general learning progression if their needs in this transition phase are left unattended, and often find it very hard to catch up. Many educators recommend bilingual education to reduce this disadvantage, in which students continue in a transitional phase to learn key academic subjects in their first language or learn in both languages in parallel.

Another strategem is to make greater use of multimodality, so that conceptual academic learning is supported by other modes (Ng 2006). For instance, a report of a science experiment may have students video the experiment in both their first language and English (image, gesture and oral language), create and label a diagram bilingually and draw up a table of results with bilingual row and column heads. Then, using academic language, perhaps the most challenging part will be to write up hypotheses and results as continuous text. However, a strategy of embedding academic English in multimodal and multilingual documentation will help ESL learners.

Steps to bilingualism

The steps bilingual learners will take as they learn to learn in a second language will vary enormously according to age. However, EAL/D learners or ELLs entering school in the phase of emerging academic literacies may develop in English language competence through the steps laid out in Table 15.6.

Table 15.6: Steps to bilingualism

Step 1: Beginning school in a second language (years one and two) The child:	• becomes a competent user of social language and basic conversational capacities on everyday topics in the second language • is able to use basic academic language terminology orally in first and second languages, with gestural and visual supports • continues academic learning at a level appropriate to their age in the first language
Step 2: Beginning to use academic language in the second language (years two to five) The child:	• is able to use academic language with multimodal, context-embedded and bilingual supports, demonstrating an equivalent conceptual grasp of an academic discipline area to monolingual peers • develops in their capacity to use academic language in their first language to the level of competence expected in schools teaching in that language
Step 3: Bilingual academic language (years two to five) The child:	• becomes competent in academic language in the second language to the level of native speakers at the same grade level • maintains parallel academic language capacities in their first language appropriate to their grade level

The access principle

Two foundational principles underlie teaching for bilingual learners: the principle of access and the principle of diversity.

Access has traditionally meant access to the dominant language of society and to educational opportunities when that language is the primary language of instruction in schools. In the era of didactic pedagogy, access was provided through a sink-or-swim immersion approach. Just teach all the students in the class English, and in the same way, and access will be provided to all. This was the theory or, when unarticulated, just the practice. It was the primary approach to language diversity among learners in the era of assimilation. It was how all learners would, with the help of schooling and for their own good, be made the same.

In the second half of the 20th century, specialist English as a Second Language approaches (as this area was then known) and Transitional Bilingual methods were developed, including special classes for students who did not speak English or speak it well. The old, assimilationist approach was shown to have resulted in disturbing patterns of inequality. Here are some of the specialist access models that were introduced:

- *EAL/D or ELL* teaching provided in separate, intensive, 'sheltered' classes. It may take a traditional, didactic approach focusing on the formalities of pronunciation, vocabulary, grammar and error correction. Or it may take a more authentic, communicative approach in which teacher and student are

involved in simulated social interactions and students are immersed in authentic uses of the language, such as cinema.

- *Classroom-Embedded EAL/D or ELL* instruction in which mainstream teachers, literacy coaches or bilingual teachers' aides focus on academic content, team teaching with mainstream teachers as they work beside students on the language of their school subjects. At more advanced levels, this approach to EAL/D or ELL teaching is often called English for Academic Purposes.
- *Transitional Bilingual Education* in which students are assisted into English by being offered temporary bilingual teaching of the English language and other academic subject areas. This may involve bilingual teaching of whole classes, or the use of bilingual teachers' aides to support individual students or small groups of students in mixed classes.

The diversity principle

A second principle – the principle of diversity – should also inform the education of speakers of languages other than English in contexts and schools where English is the dominant language or language of instruction. According to this principle, first languages are of value as a meaning-making resource, a cultural resource and a resource for learning. Examples of programs exemplifying the principle of diversity include:

- *Heritage Language Education*, which minimally aims at the maintenance of so-cial competence in the learner's home language for the purposes of ethnic identity, family connectedness, community cohesion, cultural preservation, and social and cultural relationships in diasporic communities. Heritage language programs are often offered as supplementary school subjects, or outside regular school hours by ethnic community organisations (Arvanitis, Kalantzis & Cope 2014).
- *Dual Language Education*, or two-way bilingual immersion with the goal of developing full bilingual academic language competence across a num-ber of subject areas. In an ideal scenario, a balanced number of students who are native speakers of the first language are included in each class (Soltero 2011).

Approaches to the teaching of second language learners of English have fre-quently become highly politicised around variations of the access and diversity themes. Some believe that the only legitimate pedagogical aim is to provide all students with access to the dominant national language via monolingual im-mersion and formal EAL/D or ELL teaching. Anything else, they believe, is to invite dangerous social division and to suggest to immigrants that they do not need to assimilate fully into the society they have joined. This has been the ral-lying cry of the 'English Only' movement in a number of Anglophone countries. In California this reached a crescendo in 1998 when a referendum banned bilin-gual education, replacing it with a one-year intensive English immersion model. In Australia it resulted in the policy changes limiting the teaching of Aboriginal languages in the Northern Territory to the last hour of the day. Researchers have shown that the consequences have sometimes been dire for students whose first language is not English (Gutiérrez, Asato, Pacheco, Moll, Olson, Horng, Ruiz, Garcia & McCarty 2002).

However, the principles of access and diversity need not be at odds with each other. Programs that focus on access to the dominant language need not be offered at the expense of the principle of diversity. And programs whose focus is diversity can provide important paths for access to the dominant language, including its academic language in formal educational settings. Jim Cummins finds substantial evidence to support the claim that bilingual students who continue to learn in both languages at school perform better than students whose social and cognitive development is hindered by sudden immersion in a language in which they are not natively competent. Cummins' (2000: 175) research shows that:

> continued academic development of both languages conferred cognitive/linguistic benefits, whereas less well developed academic proficiency in both languages limited children's ability to benefit cognitively and academically from interaction with their environment through those languages.

This explains why second language learners often fall further and further behind in their overall academic performance, even after they have become visibly competent in 'social language' forms of English (Cummins 2000: 175). In addition, learning academic forms of the first language creates an invaluable resource for learners in a multilingual and globalised world, providing the basis for interactions in this language in later life in professional, commercial, educational and other public settings.

See literacies.com Cummins on Bilingual Education.

Transformative multilingual learning

Lisa Taylor and her fellow literacies researchers take us into a Toronto kindergarten in a multilingual community. The children are native speakers of Tamil, Urdu, Punjabi, Gujarati, Hindi and Cantonese. The teacher, a Farsi speaker, has devised a beginning literacy activity in which family members are invited to become expert partners in their children's biliteracy development. Each of the children locates their family migration histories on a map of the world. They write their names in English and their first language and place them on the map. Then they talk about their family origins, and their favourite foods and activities. The students dictate their responses orally, which the teacher and aides transcribe into English, one book per child. The students then take these identity books home with requests for the collaboration of parents or other family members – to add other information and photographs, and to translate the written text so the books are fully bilingual. When the task is completed, the books are scanned, so they can be shared with other family members, at home and abroad.

Here Taylor, Bernhard, Garg and Cummins (2008: 280–1) describe the experience of one student, Sarah, who is fluent in Cantonese even though her parents speak more English at home than Cantonese:

> Before the project, a particular configuration of circumstances prevented Sarah's grandmother from contributing to her literacy development, despite the deep bond between them ... When Sarah brought home her initial draft of her book with drawings and English captions to be translated into Chinese, the challenge inspired an unprecedented three-generational collaboration).

As Sarah's mother explains: 'The biggest advantage that I really enjoyed about this whole project was the sense of interaction between Sarah and my mother-in-law and myself.' Taylor and her colleagues conclude:

> [This] points to the transfigured, unique roles family members can play as partners in children's Multiliteracies development, within a curriculum and school environment centred in the dynamic cultural flows and multiple communities of practice intersecting in students' life pathways (at 289).

It can be argued that dedicated, specialist second language programs and bilingual education programs are expensive and not feasible when the mix of learners is not optimal. However, around the world we find numerous examples of literacies innovation like the one Taylor and colleagues describe.

In a Greek primary school, we find first and second language learners involved in the creation of a multimodal and multilingual album of popular theatre from the countries of various students in the class, Greek and non-Greek (Katsarou 2009). We encounter a Grade 8 Multiliteracies project in New York City's Chinatown in which students explore Chinese American history and identity through a digital gothic and hip-hop cartoon web project (Walsh 2009). In Burkina Faso, West Africa, a Multiliteracies approach to bilingual learning has produced improved school outcomes at the same time as increasing the recognition and status of the local language, Mooré (Lavoie 2008). Bin and Freebody analyse the mix of modes, genres and voices in an early literacy program in China (Bin & Freebody 2010). In South Africa, teachers explore the possibilities of multimodal learning to support literacies learning in a multilingual society (Newfield, Stein, Rumboll, Meyer, Badenhorst, Drew, Mkhabela, Benyon & McCormick 2001). Lam explores the text-messaging literacies of an adolescent Chinese immigrant girl in the United States (Lam 2009). On the islands of the Torres Strait, between Australia and Papua New Guinea, a Year/Grade 6–7 project created and aired a bilingual radio commercial addressing the critical local medical issue of diabetes (Osborne & Wilson 2003). And in Greece again, students from immigrant language groups create hybrid texts, drawing on two familiar resources: folk tales from different countries and advertisements (Sakellariou 2007).

Back in Canada, teachers at Coppard Glen Public School have their students create dual-language stories, drawing on family resources and supported by bilingual dictionaries. In the words of one teacher:

[A]s a student, I remember, only too vividly the trauma of walking into a class where I didn't understand much of what went on, of being very afraid, bewildered and deskilled. My rich resource of my first language accumulated over 13 years [had] suddenly been rendered redundant. Children in these situations are left to 'sink or swim'. I do not want that to happen to my students in my class or in my school (Giampapa 2010: 415).

In order to achieve the twin goals of access and diversity, literacies pedagogies need to be fully aware of the language diversity of learners in a world of extraordinary global movement: a deeply multilingual world. Language differences also need to be understood in their complexity and their variation from one child to the next. These differences should be affirmed and used as building blocks rather than considered a deficit. Far from creating problems for teachers, they should be regarded as a resource for learning in a learning community of productive diversity.

See literacies.com Cummins et al. on the Multilingual Classroom.

See literacies.com Learning Modules.

See literacies.com #edtech Literacies Applications.

Summary

Learner differences	Lifeworlds	Differentiated literacies instruction
Material differences	• Family cultures	*Strategy 1:* considering every learner as a *designer* of unique meanings, based on their lifeworld experiences and interests
Class	• Life experiences	
Locale	• Interpersonal styles	
Family	• Languages spoken	*Strategy 2:* opening the scope of literacies learning to include a broader range of *multimodal meanings* supports a broader range of learners to succeed
Corporeal differences	• Values	
	• Interests	
Age	• Political and social stances	
Race		*Strategy 3:* offering a more varied range of *knowledge processes* or activity types supports a broader range of learners
Sex and sexuality	• Contacts and networks	
Symbolic differences	• Local, regional national and international links	
Language		*Strategy 4:* supporting alternative *navigation paths* means that not every student has to be on the same page at the same time
Ethnos	• Employment sector	
Gendre	• Thinking styles	
	• Communication styles	*Strategy 5:* creating a learning environment of *productive diversity* means that diversity becomes a positive resource for learning instead of a deficit or a problem
	• Dispositions	
	• Sensibilities	
	• Demeanour	
	• Intersubjective styles	*Strategy 6:* tracking *performance* and *outcomes* as you go and recalibrating instruction as required to meet learning goals

Knowledge processes

experiencing the known

1. Write your literacies learning autobiography, linking your successes and challenges in learning a range of literacies to the categories of material, corporeal and symbolic differences described in this chapter.

experiencing the new

2. Research and write a short overview of the history of compensatory education in the country or state where you live.

conceptualising by naming

3. Define the various categories of disability. Describe the ways in which each disability impacts upon literacies learning, and suggest the ways in which specialist approaches to literacies learning or a general multimodal approach can support learning for students with this particular disability. One suggested way to address this question is to create a wiki in which each person addresses these issues for one particular area of disability.

analysing critically

4. Examine media and web reports of the debates around 'English only' and 'bilingual education'. How are these debates connected to anxieties about immigration and globalisation? Write a blog post that argues the case that the objectives of 'access' and 'diversity' need not be incompatible.

applying creatively

5. Create a unit of work that uses multimodal and bilingual methods to assist second language learners in their transition from social to academic language. You may choose to use to create a learning module in Scholar.

CHAPTER 16

Literacies standards and assessment

Overview

This chapter introduces the idea of **standards**, which specify expected learning outcomes at different levels of learning across a variety of subject areas – literacy or literacies, for instance. Assessments measure student outcomes against these standards. The chapter contrasts the fundamental assumptions and processes of standards or achievement assessments with intelligence assessments. It then goes on to explore the differences between diagnostic versus formative and summative assessments, norm-referenced versus criterion-referenced or self-referenced assessments, and select response versus supply response assessments. Finally, we explore the possibilities of bringing formative assessment (providing direct feedback to learners) closer to summative assessment (providing a retrospective view of what learners have achieved), particularly in new-media learning environments.

Standards (educational): Statements of expected learning outcomes in a particular subject area at a particular level of learning

Literacies standards

The idea and practice of 'standards'

Educational standards are statements of expected learning outcomes in particular subject areas at particular grade or year levels. Here is an example of a statement from the US Common Core State Standards; it is the Writing Standard for Grade 7 provided within the Standards for English Language Arts.

1. Write informative/explanatory texts to examine a topic and convey ideas, concepts, and information through the selection, organization, and analysis of relevant content.
    a. Introduce a topic; organize ideas, concepts, and information, using strategies such as definition, classification, comparison/contrast, and cause/effect; include formatting (e.g., headings), graphics (e.g., charts, tables), and multimedia when useful to aiding comprehension.
    b. Develop the topic with relevant facts, definitions, concrete details, quotations, or other information and examples.
    c. Use appropriate transitions to clarify the relationships among ideas and concepts.
    d. Use precise language and domain-specific vocabulary to inform about or explain the topic.
    e. Establish and maintain a formal style.
    f. Provide a concluding statement or section that follows from the information or explanation presented (CCSS 2010: 42).

And here is an example from the Australian Curriculum: English (the Achievement Standard for Year 3):

> By the end of Year 3, students understand how content can be organised using different text structures depending on the purpose of the text. They understand how language features, images and vocabulary choices are used for different effects.
>
> They read texts that contain varied sentence structures, a range of punctuation conventions, and images that provide extra information. They use phonics and word knowledge to fluently read more complex words. They identify literal and implied meaning connecting ideas in different parts of a text. They select information, ideas and events in texts that relate to their own lives and to other texts. They listen to others' views and respond appropriately using interaction skills.
>
> Students understand how language features are used to link and sequence ideas. They understand how language can be used to express feelings and opinions on topics. Their texts include writing and images to express and develop, in some detail, experiences, events, information, ideas and characters.
>
> Students create a range of texts for familiar and unfamiliar audiences. They contribute actively to class and group discussions, asking questions, providing useful feedback and making presentations. They demonstrate understanding of grammar and choose vocabulary and punctuation appropriate to the purpose and

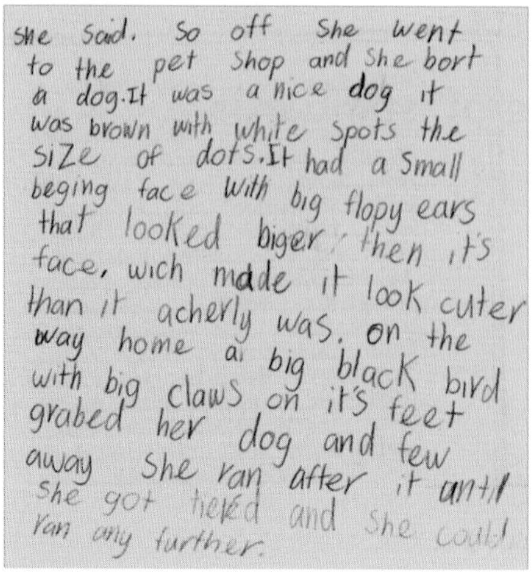

She said. So off She went to the pet shop and she bort a dog. It was a nice dog it was brown with white spots the size of dots. It had a small beging face with big flopy ears that looked biger, then it's face, wich made it look cuter than it acherly was. on the way home a big black bird with big claws on it's feet grabed her dog and few away She ran after it until she got tiered and she could ran any further.

Annotations

Uses vocabulary effectively to describe events and characters, for example 'a small begging face with big floppy ears'.

Uses a range of simple, compound and complex sentences.

Spells many words accurately and uses visual and sound – letter knowledge to attempt unknown words, for example 'bart' (bought), 'acherly' (actually).

Uses past tense verbs including action verbs (grabbed), relating verbs (had), speaking verbs (said) and sensing verbs (thought).

Annotation summary

This work sample demonstrates understanding of the typical structure and features of a narrative text, although it seems to lack a reasonable resolution (conclusion) and a title. The work sample shows knowledge of some characteristic features of traditional narrative tales such as 'once upon a time'. It has a logical sequence of events and effectively builds a credible main character. As a first draft the work sample still needs editing, with more careful attention to paragraphing, punctuation, spelling and presentation.

Figure 16.1 An annotated Year 3 narrative work sample, Australian Curriculum: English

context of their writing. They use knowledge of letter-sound relationships including consonant and vowel clusters and high-frequency words to spell words accurately. They re-read and edit their writing, checking their work for appropriate vocabulary, structure and meaning. They write using joined letters that are accurately formed and consistent in size (ACARA 2015g).

The standards approach sets learning objectives, with benchmarks for expected learner achievement at various grade or year levels. These are cast at a high level of generality, leaving teachers to fill out the curriculum with specific learning content, activities and assessments in order for their students to meet these learning objectives. Standards focus on performance rather than learning facts and rules – which, in the case of literacy, means certain forms of competence, not just as a communicator, but as someone who uses literacy for representation or thinking. What students can do is an indicator of what they know – and the focus now is on that doing, or performance, rather than older ideas of 'understanding'.

The reason for the move towards standards since about the 1980s has been partly political – to make it clear to teachers, parents and the community that the highest of standards are expected. The context is a 'knowledge society' and 'knowledge economy' in which high levels of communicative and cognitive skill are required in more jobs and in a wider range of social settings. The aim of the standards is to set ambitious objectives that increase the quality of education for more students. Making core standards common to all schools in a state or a nation is also designed to be an assurance of equality; an assurance that, no matter which school you attend, the expectations are the same and that, if the expectations are not met, schools and society are accountable. And finally – a pragmatic consideration – if a child moves from one school to another within the state or country where a shared set of standards applies, the work that they do and the level of learning expected should be more or less the same.

 See literacies.com Fuhrman on the Origins of the Standards Movement.

Assessing standards

The standards movement represents a sea change in some of the most basic assumptions about learner differences and the appropriate objectives of learning. To illustrate this, we will contrast standards-based **achievement assessment** with an older tradition of **intelligence testing**. In fact, as we will see, this form of testing actually addressed the same things we are interested in: 'literacies' in the plural, including representation as well as communication, although with quite different assumptions from today's focus on standards.

Achievement assessment: Testing what students have learned on the assumption that all students without cognitive disabilities are capable of comparable performance

Lewis Terman, a professor of psychology at Stanford University, brought the idea of intelligence testing to the United States in 1916, modifying Alfred Binet's work in France to create the Stanford-Binet Intelligence Test. The test is still in use today, though it is used much less widely than in the heyday of intelligence testing, and mainly now for diagnostic purposes in the case of students with disabilities. Terman's first mass application of the test was to over a million army recruits during World War 1. Those who did well in the test were considered to be worthy material for officer training.

Intelligence testing: Testing of mental capacities on the assumption that these are, to a relevant degree, a product of heredity

The most significant part of Terman's approach was the interpretation he put on the source of intelligence. It was, for him, natural or innate – a quality of the person. This idea he extended from the army tests to education of children in school. Education, he thus deduced, could not hope to produce the same results for children with different native intelligence. Naturally 'gifted' children therefore needed to have education appropriate to their social potential and destiny. For less naturally intelligent children, there was no point in teaching them more than they were capable of learning, given their native abilities. Once these tests were applied, it just so happened that the poor, immigrants, blacks and women did not do well on them. This was proof, it seemed, that their native intelligence was lower. In scoring intelligence, children were spread along a normal distribution or 'bell' curve, with most performing at average IQ (intelligence quotient) levels, a few exceptionally well and a few exceptionally poorly.

IQ tests have mostly fallen from fashion. Not even defenders of the tests claim that there are native differences in intelligence between different demographic groups (Mackintosh 1998: 271). There are only rare exceptions, and these are among the few raised by those who still object strongly to standards-based curriculum

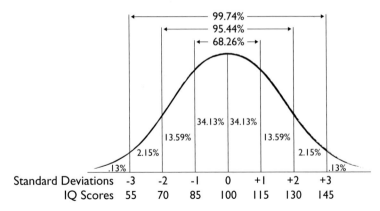

Figure 16.2 The IQ bell curve

and assessment (Gottfredson 2009). Mostly educators account for the differences between learners measured by intelligence in terms of social conditions and opportunities, or disability. A celebrated study by Risley and Hart made a comparison of the number of words that preschool children heard per hour. Children from families on welfare heard 600 words per hour on average, but children from families with professionals in employment heard over 2000. Little wonder, then, that such children would demonstrate greater 'intelligence' (Risley & Hart 1995).

Today, 'interactionist' theory closely connects genetic potentials with environmental influences. Shenk (2010: 18) sums up the research upon which this theory is founded in these terms:

> There is no genetic foundation that gets laid before the environment enters in; rather, genes express themselves strictly in accordance with the environment ... We do not inherit traits directly from our genes. Instead, we develop traits through the dynamic process of gene–environment interaction.

According to Shenk, the more complex the trait – such as cognitive and communicative performance capacities – the less likely there is direct genetic inheritance that is relevant in any sense.

Standards reflect a paradigm shift in our thinking as educators, and one that meshes with our contemporary understandings of learner diversity. There is no inheritable or natural reason why groups or individuals should underperform at school, with the exception of those with cognitive disabilities. It is not unreasonable to expect all learners to be able to achieve the same outcomes at a particular learning level, and these can be described in standards.

This is not to say that IQ tests do not measure some interesting and worthwhile things. It is just that they bring with them some anachronistic, scientifically unfounded and today ethically unacceptable baggage. Alongside the Stanford-Binet tests, perhaps the test most used today is the Wechsler Intelligence Scale for Children. If we choose to ignore the word 'intelligence' and all its hard-to-avoid connotations, much of the test might be considered an assessment of a

Table 16.1: Standards-based and intelligence assessments compared

Standards assessment	Intelligence testing
Assessment of performance	Assessment of native ability
Provides evidence of things you can do	Searches for evidence of, and makes inferences about, something in your head
Assessment of a wide range of specific things a learner can do; e.g. in the case of literacy, communicating by writing an informational text	Assessing one thing: 'g', or 'general intelligence'
Performance statements relative to a performance standard and a learning level; e.g. 'advanced', 'proficient', 'basic'	A single number, average IQ = 100
Absolute or criterion-referenced measures: you can perform to a standard that is appropriate for your age, or you can't and more should be done to support your learning	Norm-referenced measures: spreading a population across a normal distribution curve so half the population is always performing below average
Standards represent the high expectations of education experts and communities	Intelligence is what the test happens to find in the population it tests
Every child who is not disabled cognitively can be expected to achieve a particular learning level	Children can never do better than their native ability
Assumption of growing social equality, assisted by education	Assumption of inevitable social inequality, with education providing learning appropriate to different students' life destinies

type of Multiliteracies – not just a person's native ability to make meaning with language, but the meanings they have learned to make in a multimodal way using words, images and space. For example, it has a 'Verbal Comprehension Index' that includes naming pictures, searching for similarities between objects or written concepts and the meanings of texts or social situations. Clearly, what is being measured in this index is much more than use of verbal skills. There is also a 'Perceptual Reasoning Index' that involves analysing visual and spatial patterns, matrix reasoning to complete a picture, and visual conceptualisation (Flanagan & Kaufman 2009: 7, 29).

In other words, tests like these might be used to assess students' Multiliteracies capabilities, so long as no assumptions are made about innate intelligence or any preconceptions applied about how learners and their scores should be spread across a distribution curve.

Such tests also remain helpful for identifying students in need of special education – so long as no assumptions are made about the limits of an individual's 'natural' potentials, even for students with cognitive disabilities. In fact, far from proving the heritability of intelligence, the widespread application of these tests for over a century shows a phenomenon called the 'Flynn effect' after the man who discovered it – that average intelligence has steadily gone up over the century (Flynn 2007). It's not that humans become more intelligent naturally, because biological evolution could not possibly have worked as fast as this. Rather, more and more children have become better earlier in their lives at the socially acquired capacities that IQ tests actually measure. In other words, our social conditions are changing and, with these changes, children's Multiliteracies capacities are growing.

Literacies assessment

The purposes of assessment

We can assess learners in a number of ways, from a number of different perspectives, and at different points in the learning process (Pellegrino, Chudowsky & Glaser 2001; Popham 2008; Wiliam 2011). Following are three classical assessment types, based in three different assessment purposes (see Figure 16.3):

Diagnostic assessment: Assessment designed to find out what students know in order to design learning activities appropriate to their needs

Formative assessment: Assessment that provides learners with feedback on what they are learning

Summative assessment: Assessment that tells learners, teachers, administrators, parents and other interested stakeholders what students have learned

- **Diagnostic assessment** – to find out what learners already know and still need to learn. Assessment preparatory to learning, for teachers.
- **Formative assessment** – to give learners feedback on their learning, as they learn. Assessment integrated with and for learning, for learners. The orientation of formative assessments is prospective (looking forward to further learning on the current curriculum content) and constructive (specific advice on how to extend what you currently now, or complete a task).
- **Summative assessment** – to find out what students have learned, after they are supposed to have learned it. Assessment of learning, for learners, teachers and parents. The orientation of summative assessment is retrospective (looking back over an area of learning that has been completed) and judgemental (coming to a generalised conclusion about how well you have done, such as B+, or 68%).

We do these various kinds of assessment for a number of reasons:

- to support student learning by providing useful 'before, during and after' information to learners
- to inform parents and friends of what students have been learning at school, and report on their progress
- to inform teachers about what has been successfully taught and what they still need to teach
- to provide differentiated information about individual students so their learning programs can be customised to meet every learner's particular needs

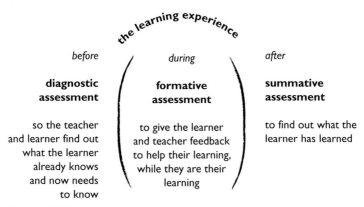

Figure 16.3 Assessment perspectives

- to provide information about the relative achievements of different demographic groups in order to address patterns of underachievement and possible discrimination
- to provide educational administrators with information about the effectiveness of individual teachers – controversially at times, because student outcomes are strongly related to the social contexts from which learners come and the resources available in schools
- to provide school systems with information about the effectiveness of whole schools, rewarding effective schools or schools that are making progress towards improved learner outcomes, or sanctioning schools that are not
- to serve political purposes in the ongoing public discussion of whether resources devoted to education are being well spent.

Norm-, criterion- and self-referenced assessments

On what measure do we gauge student learning? There are three major measures: norm-referenced, criterion-referenced and self-referenced.

- **Norm-referenced assessments** spread learners across a bell curve (see Figure 16.4). They are like IQ tests in this respect – however, in a standards-based regime, norm-referenced tests are not supposed to be measuring native intelligence, just where you are compared to others in reaching the standard. Still, it has hard for students, teachers and parents to avoid the take-away lesson, even in a standards-based curriculum, that the scores reflect natural differences between those who are smart by nature, and those who are not so smart. The problem with forcing students across a bell curve like this is it enforces an intrinsic logic whereby you have to have some students judged not smart at all, and many who are pronounced mediocre, for the few to appear to excel. In a standards-based regime, the ones who appear not very smart today may be

Norm-referenced assessment: Assessment that compares students and statistically judges relative excellence, mediocrity and failure

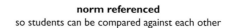
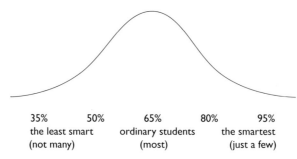

norm referenced
so students can be compared against each other

35%	50%	65%	80%	95%
the least smart		ordinary students		the smartest
(not many)		(most)		(just a few)

Figure 16.4 Norm-referenced assessment (scores on the horizontal axis, the number of students getting each score on the vertical axis)

as smart as the smartest in a few months when they have covered more of the curriculum – but by that time they may still be judged not smart because by then the 'smart ones' are even further ahead. Because inequality is structured into the bell curve, it's hard if not impossible to move along the curve. However, having cautioned the dangers of norm-referenced assessments, they can still be useful to teachers, highlighting different levels of student achievement at any particular time as measured against the objectives of standards-based curriculum. The comparison can show the teacher who is ready to move on, and who is not. This is particularly useful in self-paced, personalised, and adaptive learning environments.

Criterion-referenced assessment: Assessment that measures mastery of an area of knowledge or a skill

• **Criterion-referenced assessments** are an ideal solution in standards-based curricula (see Figure 16.5). A standard needs to be achieved. All students can achieve this standard. The only difference between students is that some may have already achieved the standard (the criterion), while others are still

criterion referenced
to check that all students have met a learning criterion

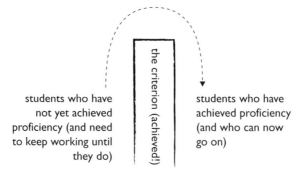

the criterion (achieved!)

students who have not yet achieved proficiency (and need to keep working until they do)

students who have achieved proficiency (and who can now go on)

Figure 16.5 Criterion-referenced assessment

working to achieve it. Such assessments are part of a longstanding and honourable tradition of 'mastery learning' (Block 1971). Whereas norm-referenced assessment institutionalises failure, criterion-referenced assessment is a no-failure educational paradigm. The only exception might be students with disabilities, but even in this case it is highly problematic to assume that they can never reach a particular criterion, because with specialist intervention, it may be possible.

- **Self-referenced assessments** measure a learner's progress over time. They are closely related to criterion-referenced assessments, tracing the achievement of target standards over time (see Figure 16.6). Where norm-reference tests might demonstrate no progress (a student seemingly stuck at something like a B+, or 68%), we can see progress over time by documenting successive achievement of criteria, irrespective of whether an individual student is achieving these criteria sooner or later than their peers.

Self-referenced assessment: An assessment measure that describes an individual learner's progress

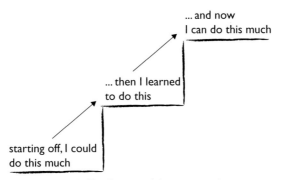

self referenced
following a learner's progress over time

... and now
I can do this much

... then I learned
to do this

starting off, I could
do this much

Figure 16.6 Self-referenced (or progress) assessment

Testing controversies

Testing has become a larger part of school life since the last decades of the 20th century. There are more systems-mandated tests. Students spend more time taking tests. And teachers spend more class time preparing their students for tests. Nearly always, these are norm-referenced, summative assessments.

As a consequence, assessment has become a site of fierce debate. Some people advocate strongly for more assessments because they create an outcomes-focused culture of accountability for teachers and schools. Standards clarify what should be learned; the test related to standards tells learners, teachers, school administrators, parents and the wider community what has actually been learned.

Others, however, have argued that the tests – or at the very least the kinds of tests we have today – create new problems while doing no better than meeting old educational requirements. We're going to focus for a moment upon these problems, before looking at some of the best assessment practices.

See literacies.com Kohn on Standardised Testing.

Perhaps most important among the criticisms is that, although testing is about learning, it is different from learning in a number of important ways. As a consequence, tests test what tests test rather than what has been actually learned. Testing is a game, and a quite strange game at that. Some people learn to play the game well, others do not.

There are two types of game in conventional tests, and these are called 'select response', such as the ABCD answers of a reading comprehension test, and 'supply response', such as a piece of writing provided in response to a prompt. In select response tests, you choose from among alternatives offered by the test-maker: multiple choice, true/false, matching words and the like. Only one response is correct, and the other items are called 'distractors'. They have been deliberately created by the test-maker as plausible answers that may seem correct, but are in fact incorrect. The distractors are, if you like, designed to trick you into giving a wrong answer. You have to have learned your work thoroughly to give the precisely correct answer. In this game, there are some peculiar ways of getting to the right answer that every teacher teaches their students – for instance, first eliminate the answers that are most likely to be wrong; then, when you get to the last two, try to work out the carefully placed trap in the second last option.

The advantage of select response tests is that you can get a clear score. The opinions of the person marking the test are irrelevant. There can be no disagreements between test-markers about the subtle and qualitative differences that are an inevitable part of **supply response assessments** such as essays. Select response tests are also quick and easy to mark, particularly when you have a lot of students taking the test. Computers can automatically score large numbers of selected response tests cheaply, whether the responses are pencil-to-paper marks or directly entered into a computer terminal.

Supply response assessment: Assessment that asks students to give open-ended responses to questions or prompts

However, there is nothing like a select response test in the real world of literacies, or the real worlds of communication, representation and knowledge. This is a strange game, having to navigate the attempted trickery of the test-maker. The test-maker can only intend one answer to each question; that's the main rule of the game, and although the other things may seem right at first, they are actually there because they are, from the point of view of the test-maker, wrong.

In the field of literacy, select response tests of reading are the main forms of assessment because they are cheap and easy to administer. In class, students can even be given the answers to mark their own work, or they can do a test on the computer. Of course, these tests do give us a reasonable sense of what the students have understood of the text they have read, or at least what they can recall of the text in short-term memory.

However, they also present a number of problems. They cannot allow for different interpretations of the meaning of the text. The questions try to get at what the test-maker thinks the author really said, as if that could be so clear and not a matter of interpretation. Some things are clear. Q: 'When did the action happen?' A: 'It was Wednesday.' But these are usually not the most important parts of the text. If you didn't notice it was Wednesday because it was not crucial to the story, and you reach this question in your test, you can scan back over the text looking for days of the week; but this is not something an author is ever likely to have expected you to do as a normal part of enjoying their story. The most interesting and important questions cannot be answered in a selected response test – 'Do you think Hamlet was a hero or a coward?' – because they are matters for interpretation, and do not have right or wrong answers. So multiple choice reading tests focus on small and discrete things, rather than on the larger and more significant questions about the overall structure, meaning and purpose of a text.

See literacies.com Wagner on What We Need to Assess Today.

Moreover, although **select response assessments** are used extensively today as a matter of convenience, they are rather different in their emphasis from the spirit and letter of curriculum standards. These do not focus on facts, theories and specific knowledge contents; rather they focus on higher-order skills, such as performance of complex communicative tasks, reading for deeper meanings and interpretation of textual purposes. Much of the time these kinds of tests simply do not align well with the standards (Beach 2011). The standards may recommend a broad focus. The tests, though, assess a narrower way of thinking. This means that teachers often spend time focusing on narrow test preparation instead of addressing the often broader and more interesting expectations of the standards.

Select response assessment: Assessment that expects students to give right and wrong answers

Supply response tests ask students to provide a short or extended answer to a question or prompt – from a phrase or sentence to an extended essay or report. This is less of a strange game than selected response, because these texts can be more like real-world texts. They are not so unlike the kinds of communicative performance required in many workplace and communicative settings.

However, supply response assessments require time-consuming human assessment, and this can be very variable depending on what standards the assessor sets – whether they are a 'hard' or an 'easy' marker. Consistency between markers can be improved with assessment rubrics, which clearly specify the aspects of a successful response to a kind of task at a particular level of learning. However, even then, in high-stakes assessments where educational placement and one's life's destiny are in the balance, careful, time-consuming and expensive processes of 'moderation' (comparing samples of marking) and statistical adjustments of 'inter-rater reliability' (adjusting the scores of different markers up or down based on their marking habits) are required.

See literacies.com The NAEP Rubric.

One of the unfortunate consequences of the cost of supply response assessment is that, in the area of literacy, multiple choice comprehension tests are most often used. At times, they even become a proxy for literacy, as if they could be a sign of broader literacy skills. In reality, they mostly measure just one very narrow aspect of reading, and that is short-term memory of hard-to-dispute specifics mentioned in a text. It is an irony indeed that today's assessments focus on the more receptive literacy skill of reading ('Did you understand correctly what the reader said?') than the more productive skill of writing, when today in workplaces as well as in other community settings we are expected to be contributors and participants more than passive receptors of information, perspectives and knowledge. This is not to mention the neglect of assessment of multimodal and new media texts.

The literacy testing we have today, its critics argue, does not necessarily nurture ways of thinking required for a future of work and community life that will increasingly value creativity, innovation, problem-solving, collaboration and risk-taking. These tests have also been criticised for the focus on in-your-head, individualised knowledge, when more and more knowledge is situated, contextual and socially embedded. When you need to know something specific, you don't have to have remembered it, because you can look it up on the Web or ask an expert. Much of the knowledge and many of the human capabilities that are most relevant today are instances of what the educational standards are designed to measure: problem-solving where the answers are never unequivocal; coming to modulated conclusions that are beyond yes/no dichotomies; knowledge that makes a different sense when contextualised in other knowledge and social systems; and knowledge created in social collaborations. This is an era when the questions we have to face are at times complex and ambiguous, the facts contestable, and the theories open to interpretation.

Moreover, there is now a considerable body of evidence to support the contention that an obsession with testing produces a narrowing of curriculum (Au 2009; Nichols & Berliner 2007; Ravitch 2010). The quality of students' learning experiences has been questioned when teachers focus their efforts on test success, particularly when a lot of effort is put into students close to critical score thresholds to the neglect of students significantly below these thresholds. And despite all the hopes, the promise of greater accountability for educational outcomes is often not realised in reality (Ryan 2008).

A final significant criticism of today's testing regimes is their focus on summative assessment from a managerial perspective, and relative neglect of diagnostic and formative assessment design to directly support student learning. Research shows that 'situated assessment' in the form of regular and multiple forms of

feedback produces enhanced learning outcomes (Black & Wiliam 1998; Greeno 1998; OECD Centre for Educational Research and Innovation 2005; Popham 2011; Wiliam 2011).

New media, new learning, new assessments

In Part B of this book, we introduced you to Sophia, Mary, Kosta and Vincent, children we accompanied on the journeys we took into different literacy pedagogies. Just as improbably, we are going to introduce you to two more children, Delphine and Pascale, working in Scholar – the web writing environment we have been developing and trialling in classroom research at the University of Illinois. We provided screenshots of examples of doing literacies in Scholar in Chapter 10.

Delphine and Pascale are 14-year-old science students. Their science teacher, Ms Homer, has developed a learning module on the subject of forest ecosystems for delivery to her students through Scholar. Scholar is a ubiquitous learning tool, which means Delphine can access her work anywhere, any time, through any networked device – her laptop, in the school library, at home, through her mobile phone, on her e-book reader. Scholar uses social networking technologies, based in 'cloud computing' infrastructure and 'social networking' software. It reflects a shift away from the highly individualistic world of 'personal computing' that became the dominant paradigm in the third quarter of the 20th century, to the socially and collaboratively focused paradigm of 'interpersonal computing' of the 21st century.

Technically, this means that the work you are doing on your device is moved from 'my hard disk' to a shared server space. Socially, it means that the chaotically unordered world of documents and emails is replaced by a collaboration-friendly working environment of interconnected works and well-supported connectivity. Documents are gone. Emails are gone. In their place are 'works' – coherent texts with a beginning, middle and end that is focused on an idea, captured perhaps in a title, a description and semantic tags to assist discovery. The 'work' does not have the kind of sharp beginning and end that a document does. In your workspace you may have many works in progress. Each work has parts, and you can reshape your work by recombining the parts, and moving the parts from one work to another. In other words, there will be lots of stuff in your workspace, and the way you form and reform works is seamless and continuous, until such time as you have your work in a publishable condition.

This is also a deeply multimodal space. The first generation of digital technologies ghettoised modes of meaning into different software programs and different document types: writing in word-processing programs and files, image in various kinds of image capture and rendering programs, and video and audio in spaces of their own, too. The first generation of web publishing spaces did the same thing: writing in blogs and wikis, image in various gallery sites, audio on podcasting sites, videos on internet television sites. The environment in which Delphine now works allows her to type text, but also to position an image or video taken on a phone, audio recorded on her computer, or a file that can be executed by another software program, such as a three-dimensional drawing, an animation, or a database file.

Delphine starts her work. She creates an initial plan of the parts of her work, the things she wants to cover in a report she is writing on forest ecosystems – its title, and possible section subheadings. She researches the topic on the web. She participates in class and group discussions on the main concepts, typing rough notes into the relevant sections in the first draft of her work. With her class, she takes an excursion to a forest, including its very informative visitors' centre. She records the voice of the guide on her phone, which she also uses to take pictures of some very clear diagrams on display there. During the walk that she and her classmates take through the forest, she makes several small videos of some of its interesting aspects. When she gets home that night, she uploads her images, notes and audio files into the draft of her report, putting them roughly in the sections where they fit.

Next day at school, Delphine starts a new draft of her work. She does this because she wants to be able to go back to the old, rough draft in case there are things she deletes in the redrafting that she later changes her mind about and wants to access again. Her teacher also suggests that the group in which she sits write a joint report, rather than four singly authored reports. Delphine agrees to take the lead in this process, inviting another member of her group, Pascale, to be a collaborator in a jointly written work. The collaborator role she invites Pascale to have is 'creator', because he will also be an author. Pascale then moves material from his first drafts into the shared draft that Delphine first created, now a version with two authors instead of just one.

Ms Homer, by the way, is already involved as their 'publisher', because she has requested them to undertake this work in Scholar and will publish the final work to the class website at the same time as each of the students' portfolio sites. A publisher is a special kind of collaborator on a work. Also, another kind of collaborator will later get involved, called a 'contributor'. This kind of collaborator does not get their name mentioned as a creator, but provides one kind of help or another, such as proofreading and annotating change suggestions on a full draft of the report, or writing a review that provides general advice for rewriting.

The writing work undertaken by Delphine, Pascale and their classmates happens in two parallel spaces. The work is on the left-hand side of the screen, where the creators type their text and where they place their images, video, sound and other digital material. 'About the work' appears on the right-hand side of the screen, where various social interactions occur, including, for instance, the teacher's work request. (Ms Homer tells the class what she wants them to do, including the steps they are to take in her 'project' plan.) This 'about the work' space also includes a variety of other kinds of social interaction, including a running instant message conversation between the authors, proofreaders making comments and change suggestions, and others giving overall reviews. All kinds of people might get involved with these different kinds of social interactions about the work, including peers, the teacher, parents, experts or any other type of 'critical friend'. These are social supports or scaffolds for student work. They all involve, as we shall soon see, kinds of assessment.

So a very social and collaborative environment has been set up for Delphine's and Pascale's work; much more so than the environments of didactic pedagogy ever were, and a far more supportive collaborative environment for her writing than was the case in the era of 'personal computing'. In fact, 'real writing' was always a well-ordered social process like this. For instance, an author writing a book worked with an agent, a publisher, copy editors and the like, and a journalist worked alongside the editor, copy editors and other people involved in the business of producing a magazine or newspaper. The place where Delphine, Pascale and their classmates are now working brings many of the old sociabilities of writing into the classroom of the digital era. Therefore, Delphine and Pascale are now well set on a path to write their science report, 'The Ecosystem of Parkville Forest'.

Delphine and Pascale are now busy at work with their web search of supporting information about forests and theories about ecosystems; uploading the pictures and videos from the visit to the forest reserve; laboratory analysis of the sample leaves they collected; a debate about the carbon cycle; and writing a scientific report on the forest in the 'Work' pane in Scholar.

They decide which parts of the report each will write, and develop a connecting theoretical narrative, report on evidence and add images taken on the trip to the forest, as well as those taken from various information sources, duly credited. They draw and label diagrams, create internal and external hyperlinks and credit sources of information

Delphine and Pascale are now ready to post a first draft for feedback. They ask a friend and their parents to read their draft and give them comments based on the assessment rubric Ms Homer has created. This rubric links to the science standards.

Delphine and Pascale face a dilemma when they get somewhat conflicting advice about their overall text structure from their parents and peers. However, they chat with them online, seek Ms Homer's advice and finally make their own decision about structure, which they record in the 'dialogue' tool. They then rewrite the draft of their report based on this feedback.

Next, they post their completed draft ready for anonymous peer review, as required by Ms Homer at this stage in her project design. The peer reviewers, Delphine and Pascale's classmates, make qualitative comments and achievement-level ratings against each of the criteria in Ms Homer's rubric. This provides them with useful formative assessment feedback, as well as scores from each reviewer.

Delphine and Pascale now finish rewriting their text, also rating the usefulness of the raters' reviews and how helpful they were, thus contributing to the raters' scores as raters. Incidentally, Delphine and Pascale both have excellent accumulated ratings as raters, which means that their reviews are weighted as more likely to be reliable and constructive when they assess their peers. Ms Homer then moderates these scores. She also considers their progress between the initial full draft and the final, post-review draft.

They now submit their final report to Ms Homer, who considers it complete and also feels that Delphine and Pascale have diligently incorporated those reviewer comments that were relevant. Ms Homer also notices from the log that, although Delphine contributed a few more words than Pascale, the parts Pascale did took him longer. Finally, with all this information, their assessment analytics dashboard assigns them scores on a number of criteria, slightly different for each of the two students, given their varied contribution to the final report. Then Ms Homer publishes their report to both their web portfolios and the class portfolio.

Let's return now to the five-phase analysis of the writing process that we offered in Chapter 10, to see where formative assessment enters the process.

- *Phase 1: Plan.* The assessment rubric is available to the students from the beginning of the writing process and is framed in terms that are accessible to learners. It provides them with a metalanguage describing design elements that helps them to plan their text.
- *Phase 2: Draft.* While learners are drafting, they can refer to the assessment rubric. They might also seek frequent small pieces of formative feedback from spelling, grammar and synonym suggestion tools.
- *Phase 3: Review.* Next, learners offer peer reviews of each other's work, so distributing the assessment role more widely, and positioning the learners not just as receivers of assessment, but givers of assessment as well.
- *Phase 4: Revise.* Writers now receive assessment feedback to help them with their revision, representing a variety of peer and teacher perspectives.
- *Phase 5: Publish.* Before publication, writers might undertake self-assessments, reflecting on the progress they have made from draft to draft, and the role of formative assessment feedback in shaping the final work.

As a consequence, assessment is not just at the end, and it is not just a grade with a few comments from the teacher. Assessment questions are present all along. There are many small increments in the assessment process. Assessment is from many perspectives – such as peer, teacher and self. And it is of many kinds – such as machine feedback from checking software, numerical ratings on review criteria, comments against review criteria, and coded annotations.

An interesting consequence of having formative assessment in many small increments is that the quality of the final writing products is more consistent than it is in the case of one-off submission at the end for summative assessment. In this model of 'reflexive' assessment and pedagogy, peers get to see drafts of each other's work. They see published models in e-portfolios. They get specific advice on how to change their work at a stage in the writing process where they can still make significant changes. In this way, the teachers and learners work towards the ideals of criterion-referenced assessment and standards-based curriculum. Norm-based assessment, by contrast, sets out to spread learners over a standardised distribution curve of success, mediocrity and failure. In an ideal scenario, the processes of formative assessment will push the whole group towards a more similar, criterion-referenced outcome. This will ideally involve all students meeting learning objectives as articulated in the rubric (the criterion). In other words, it is possible, and at the very least desirable, that via these iterative means the whole class can achieve full 'mastery' as expressed in the objectives in the rubric and curriculum standard.

The key however is the quality of the learning scaffolds – the assessment rubric and the careful staging of the writing processes across a series of phases where there is recursive feedback in every phase. Students also need to learn something that is often called 'digital citizenship', or how to be a constructive collaborator in a learning environment where peer interactions are now such an important part of the process of formative assessment. Sometimes it takes a few cycles of peer feedback to learn to be this kind of a learner.

Literacies for assessment across the discipline areas

Traditional tests are very particular artefacts. We want to suggest that, in the computer-mediated student work environments of the near future, all assessment may be formative and that summative assessment is no more than a retrospective view of student achievement and progress. Assessments will be of everything students have done in the course of their learning. We saw how this happened in Ms Homer's class – a whole range of information, including peer as well as teacher scores, came together to create a final rating for their work; however, along the way Delphine and Pascale also received a lot of very useful feedback and were engaged productively with collaborators.

More than this, we want to suggest that the best way to represent student knowledge across all subject areas is in rich multimodal writing. The academic discipline areas require what we call 'complex epistemic performance'. The closest thing a student does to being a scientist is to write a scientific report, these days complete with images, diagrams, videos and maybe even a data set collated from observation work. Science is a complex performance. The report is a representation of that performance – in other words, it demonstrates all the aspects of the student's thinking (representation) and communicates that to reviewers: peers, parents, experts or teachers.

By comparison, an ABCD selected response test that asks about some isolated scientific facts gives us a limited window on 'understanding'. In practice, this kind of test only provides information about memory of fragments of facts, definitions and theories. And really, as the old cliché goes, even though they are technically in long-term memory, things learned in this way become quite forgettable.

However, multimodal science writing is the real thing. There is nothing more real than this, the representation and communication of your complex epistemic performance. Assessing science writing brings us closer to the practices of science and scientists, a crucial part of which is the task of reading and reporting upon science. The science hasn't happened until it has been written up by the scientist in the form of a journal article or a book. The science happens ultimately in its representation and communication. Getting closer to science as a practice involves building on and producing scientific texts.

And here is another example. The closest thing a student does to being a historian is to interview several elderly people, read some old newspapers, search historical source documents, read the interpretations of different historians, and then create a case that links their own interpretation of the past with evidence from the past. The student may include video or audio extracts from their interview in their historical argument, or archival images and links to sources. In the old regime of testing, we guessed at a student's understanding of the French Revolution when they answered the question correctly: 'D. The year was 1789.' Or when the student was asked (books closed!) to write an examination essay on the causes of the French Revolution, recalling all the facts they needed to support their case from memory, and perhaps some paraphrases of quotes – but, of course, there can be no real sources, no proper citations to sources or historians and no images in a closed-book test. However, multimodal history writing is the real thing. Reasoning from historical evidence and citing sources is what historians do. Today we can also present this evidence multimodally. So let's assess students' performance doing the real thing – historical reasoning illustrated and backed up with available evidence.

We want to make a distinction between the older ideas of assessment of understanding and a newer idea, consistent with the spirit of the curriculum standards, of assessments of knowledge representations. Instead of testing the things that can be recalled to memory in an examination, we assess knowledge representations (thinking things through in scientific reports or historical arguments) and knowledge communication (conveying to others clear messages about the knowledge the students have created). Instead of guessing at 'understanding' or things the students can keep in their heads until the test is over, we assess things that

Table 16.2: Knowledge representation and communication

Knowledge representations	Thinking things through – for instance, in scientific reports or historical arguments
Knowledge communication	Conveying clear messages for others about the knowledge you have created

they can do – such as being a scientist or a historian. Writing – and particularly the multimodal writing that is so accessible today – is the best way to represent most subject areas.

An edge case might be mathematics. But even there, mathematical notation is a form of writing. It requires grounding in the narrative of a problem, written explanations of reasoning, descriptions of conclusions, and visuals that demonstrate in a parallel mode the mathematical reasoning used. It is not possible to infer from the correct answer, 'C. The result is 42', that the student has fully understood the mathematics. We need a multimodal knowledge representation of their mathematics, not unlike those that mathematics practitioners such as engineers have to provide in real life.

Writing is thus both an integrative process of 'complex performance' (for instance, presenting evidence, reasoning and argumentation) and a uniquely powerful window into the substance of disciplinary practice (for instance, by representing the narratives of science practice through working hypotheses, literature consulted, theories tested, experiments undertaken and effects observed). If we can assess the writing that students do, we can get closer to the practices and ways of thinking that define the discipline they are undertaking. Complex performance means thinking and acting like a scientist or a historian or a journalist in a context of 'situated learning'. It requires higher-order thinking. It entails working with others to make knowledge in a 'community of practice'. It involves evidential reasoning and developing disciplinary arguments. These are typically social processes requiring, not so much individualised memory work, but rather a capacity to work with collaborating experts, search sources in the collective social memory, document and cite material used, and distinguish one's own reasoning from the reasoning of others.

 See literacies.com Kalantzis and Cope on New Media and New Assessments.

How do we assess this? In the example of Delphine and Pascale's science report, we have suggested an integrated process of formative and summative assessment, in which the summative assessment is a collection of multiple datapoints representing learning progress and achievement. The technology and expertise exist to make this an elegant exercise that focuses on a learner's productive capacities and their collaborative efforts.

Literacies assessment technologies

In didactic literacies pedagogy, the test is a peculiar artefact. It is in most respects different from the processes of learning – books are closed, interactions with others are forbidden, time is strictly delimited. It is retrospective and judgemental. At the end of a defined stretch of learning, the examinee answers questions created by a teacher or expert examiner, and the examiner uses the results to determine the extent of learning. Assessment artefacts include select response or item-based tests, and supply response assessment, such as short answers or an essay. In both of these methods of assessment, there have been significant technological advances in recent decades.

Select response tests were made machine-readable with the pen-and-paper 'bubble test' in the third quarter of the 20th century. Then, in the 21st century, the item-based test was moved onto the internet, with secure access from personal computers and laptops. Because these kinds of test are relatively cheap to mechanise, test-makers and administrators exert a great deal of influence around what is testable given the nature of the testing technologies. So, for instance, item-based reading comprehension tests become a proxy for literacy in general, often to the neglect of writing. It is a particular kind of reading at that – one that is able to elicit relatively straightforward yet frequently not crucial 'facts' from a text, but not meanings that require interpretation (which character do you relate to? which argument do you find the more powerful?).

In recent decades, psychometric techniques have grown in sophistication (and statistical obscurity), in order to measure comparative performance of learners as they undertake standardised assessment tasks. Computer-adaptive tests offer a group of students' questions that are continuously recalibrated to be at just the right level of difficulty for each student. A wrong answer means that the next question you are given to answer will be easier. A correct answer and the next question will be harder (Chang 2015). As well as reading comprehension, computer adaptive tests can also be used to test specific features of writing that can be judged to be right or wrong, such as grammar and vocabulary. Such tests have the effect of narrowing what counts as literacy for the purposes of assessment.

In the area of supply response assessments, natural language processing (NLP) techniques have been applied to the assessment of short-answer responses and extended pieces of writing, such as essays. NLP technology works like this: take a corpus of text, say 500 essays written for a test in a certain grade/year level. Have humans grade these tests, say on a four- or five-point scale. Then, as new essays are fed into the computer, NLP algorithms will make statistical comparisons between the human-graded texts and the new texts, and then assign a grade to the new texts. Research shows that the machine can be as accurate as a human grader (McNamara & Graesser 2012; Shermis 2014; Vojak, Kline, Cope, McCarthey & Kalantzis 2011).

Both of these assessment technologies, however, remain primarily retrospective and judgemental. They mostly do not provide feedback that a learner could constructively act upon going forward. They produce grades containing a general exhortation (implying 'well done!' or 'try harder!') but are not actionable in any specific ways. They position a student in a cohort without giving meaningful feedback about their own progress (because the progress of the whole norms away individual progress). They may be cheaper than the traditional tests of didactic literacy pedagogy, but they don't change its assessment logic. Indeed, these methods of mechanisation expand the scope of the testing process, meaning that students are subjected to more tests, and more frequently, and based by and large on didactic learning assumptions.

However, technologies of assessment have been developed to serve the peculiar needs of the social learning ecologies that are our classrooms and schools. We'll focus here mainly on the affordances of assessment using 'big data' and 'cloud computing' technologies (Cope & Kalantzis 2015b; Cope & Kalantzis 2015c). One particularly promising area for these technologies is formative assessment.

To reframe our earlier definition, formative assessment is assessment during and *for* learning, providing feedback to learners and their teachers which enhances their learning. Summative assessment is retrospective assessment *of* learning, typically a test at the end of a unit of work, a period of time, or a component of a program. There have been frequent laments that formative assessment has been neglected in the face of the rise of standardised, summative assessments as an instrument of institutional accountability (Armour-Thomas & Gordon 2013; Gorin 2013; Kaestle 2013; Ryan & Shepard 2008).

However, a new generation of embedded, formative assessments enabled by computer-mediated learning may reverse this imbalance (Behrens & DiCerbo 2013; Knight, Shum & Littleton 2013; Pea & Jacks 2014). Indeed, it is even conceivable that summative assessments could one day be abandoned, and even the distinction between formative and summative assessment. Take the practice of 'big data' in education, or the incidental recording of learning actions and interactions. In a situation where data collection has been embedded within the learner's workspace, it is possible to track back over every contributory learning action, to trace the microdynamics of the learning process, and analyse the shape and provenance of learning artefacts.

Here are some examples from the research and development work we have done to create the Scholar web learning environment (Cope & Kalantzis 2013). One of the assessment modes we use here is rubric-based review. In a traditional retrospective/judgemental perspective, an expert assessor assesses the work after it has been completed, asking questions such as 'did the creator of a knowledge work support the claims in their argument with evidence?'. In a prospective/constructive frame of reference, this can be reframed, addressing the same criteria of quality intellectual work after an initial draft. In this case, the same review criterion in a rubric might be suggestive: 'how might the evidence offered by the creator in support of their claims be refined or strengthened'? There can be multiple steps in this process, before a work is finally 'published'. And there can be multiple perspectives: peer review, self-review, teacher or expert review. We can also record and analyse computer-mediated discussions. We can take surveys of specific items of knowledge.

The difference in a cloud computing environment is simply logistical – many perspectives can be contributed to the same source text simultaneously, with rapid iteration from version to version. Then, it is possible to track the changes that have been made. This is a measure of progress rather than ends. It is also possible to evaluate social contributions as outputs as well as inputs. What emerges also is a phenomenon called 'crowdsourcing' where the 'wisdom of crowds' (Surowiecki 2004) is at least equal to the wisdom of experts. Indeed, our research shows that mean scores of several non-expert raters come close to those of expert raters, in

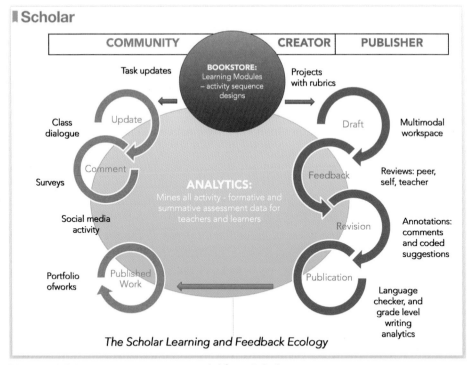

Figure 16.7 Literacies assessment model from Scholar

addition to the value of receiving rapid qualitative feedback from multiple perspectives (Cope, Kalantzis, Abd-El-Khalick & Bagley 2013). Clear rating level distinctions, accessible to learners, also increase inter-rater reliability among peers (Kline, Letofsky & Woodard 2013; McCarthey, Magnifico, Woodard & Kline 2014; Woodard, Magnifico & McCarthey 2013).

Another area of our work has been to apply natural language processing technologies, not for grading, but to provide feedback for learners. Within Scholar, we have created a 'Checker' tool that makes change suggestions, not only for grammar and spelling, but for synonyms as well. This tool presents alternatives that may or may not be correct, coded by change type (e.g. changing a complex expression to a simpler one, or informal vocabulary to that which is more formal/technical). We have also created an Annotations tool in which peers or teachers can make comments or suggestions, coded for suggestion type. We are now working to extend this by developing a crowdsourced training model where a learner accepting a machine or human change suggestion progressively trains the system, and these changes are contextualised to learning level, discipline area and topic (Cope, Kalantzis, McCarthey, Vojak & Kline 2011; Massung, Zhai & Hockenmaier 2013; Roth 2004).

And a final example: we have begun to apply semantic tagging technologies (Cope, Kalantzis, & Magee 2011) by means of which students can create diagrammatic representations of their thinking. This builds on a strong tradition of using computers for concept mapping (Cañas, Hill, Carff, Suri, Lott, Gómez, Eskridge,

Arroyo & Carvajal 2004; Chang, Sung & Lee 2003; Kao, Chen & Sun 2010; Liu 2002; Pinto, Fernandez-Ramos & Doucet 2010; Su & Wang 2010; Tzeng 2005). We have applied semantic mark-up technologies to formative assessment of written project work – interim self-assessment to clarify one's thinking, and peer assessment to provide feedback to others (Olmanson, Kennett, McCarthey, Searsmith, Cope & Kalantzis 2015).

See literacies.com Visualizing writing.

This represents a mix of machine assessment and crowdsourced human assessment, as well as linking technology and persons by applying machine learning and artificial intelligence methods so the system becomes smarter as more data are collected – smarter in the sense that, based on past patterns that have been analysed, the system can learn to provide progressively better feedback.

What we have been describing here is a learning environment where networked computers support intense human interaction and collective intelligence, in addition to machine feedback. There are a variety of data types: for instance, a qualitative comment by a peer against a review criterion, a language suggestion made by the machine, an annotation made by a peer, an answer to a select response question, a comment made in a class discussion. Every one of these is semantically legible in the sense that immediate, intelligible, actionable feedback is provided to the learner. And the datapoints are numerous: thousands and then millions for a student in an educational program; or for a teacher in a course over the duration of a unit of work; or a cohort of learners in a school over a period of weeks. Learning analytic processes can be used to produce progress generalisations at different levels of granularity, but it is always possible to drill down to specific programs and learners, all the way down to every and any of the semantically legible datapoints on which these generalisations are based. Now all our assessment is formative, and summative assessment is simply a perspective on the same data.

Our research and development work has led us towards two main conclusions. Firstly, assessment can now be readily embedded into learning, including even complex learning activities, such as writing, or writing to represent disciplinary knowledge. As a consequence, the traditional instruction/assessment distinction is blurred. Learning and assessment take place in the same time and space. Every moment of learning can be a moment of computer-mediated feedback. The grain size of these datapoints may be small and so numerous. Without these kinds of learning-analytic systems, recording so much detail and so many interactions would have almost entirely been lost to the teacher. For instruction and assessment to become one, however, every datapoint needs to be semantically legible, or learner-actionable feedback. In this way, every such datapoint presents to the learner a teachable moment. Such learning environments, where the distinctions between instruction and assessment are so blurred (Armour-Thomas & Gordon 2013), might require that we move away from the old assessment terminology, with

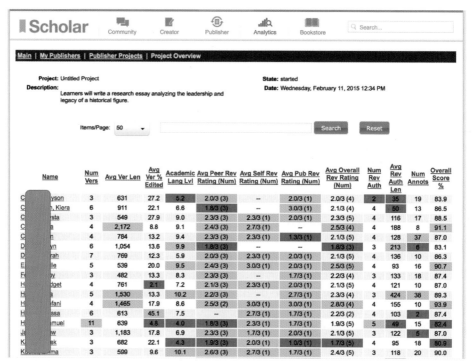

Figure 16.8 Writing analytics in Scholar

The columns from left to right: 1) the number of versions written by each student; 2) average version length; 3) percentage of change from version to version; in other words, the extent to which feedback led to a transformation of the text; 4) academic language level, expressed as a grade/year level; 5) average peer review rating, which we have shown in our research to be close to an expert rating; 6) average self-review rating, and ideally this will be close to a perfect score, with the students declaring that they have reached criterion; 7) average teacher rating; 8) average overall rating; 9) number of reviews authored; 10) average review length – because we want to recognise when students who have put a lot of effort into offering formative assessment feedback to their peers; 11) number of annotations; 12) an overall score based on 22 different kinds of datapoint. Green is one standard deviation above the norm, and red one standard deviation below, not because this analytics dashboard is about norm-referenced assessment, but so a teacher can see at a glance which students need support to bring their work up to criterion – and when they do, they can run the analytics again.

all its connotative baggage. Perhaps a notion of 'reflexive pedagogy' might replace the traditional differentiation of assessment from instruction.

Secondly, the distinction between formative and summative assessment may not need to be made in future. Semantically legible datapoints that are 'designed in' can serve traditional formative purposes (Black & Wiliam 1998; Wiliam 2011). They can also provide evidence aggregated over time that has traditionally been supplied by summative assessments. This is because when structured or self-describing data is collected at these datapoints, each point is a waypoint in a student's progress

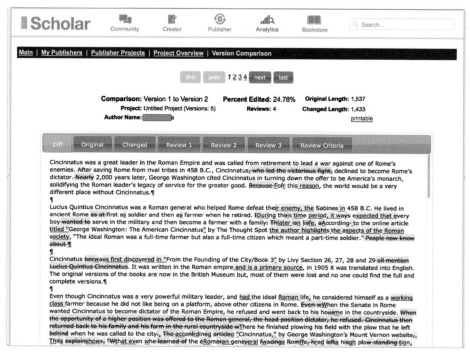

Figure 16.9 Drilling down into one student's work; here we get a finely grained view of a student's writing and formative assessment
Tabs from left to right: 1) highlights the changes between versions; 2) original version; 3) changed version; 4) review 1; 5) review 2; 6) review criteria.

map that can be analysed in retrospective progress visualisations. Why, then, would we need summative assessments if we can analyse everything a student has done to learn, the evidence of learning they have left at every datapoint? Perhaps, also, we need new language for this distinction? Instead of formative and summative assessment as different collection modes, designed differently for different purposes, we need a language of 'prospective learning analytics', and 'retrospective learning analytics', which are not different kinds of data but different perspectives and different uses for a new species of data framed to support both prospective and retrospective views.

 See literacies.com Learning Modules.

 See literacies.com #edtech Literacies Applications.

Summary

Standards

The expected outcomes of your learning in a particular subject area at a particular year or grade level

Assessment times and places	*Assessment types*
• Diagnostic – before you start learning • Formative – feedback as you are learning • Summative – after you have learned, a sign of what you have learned	• Selected response – with right and wrong answers • Supply response – with learner-constructed responses

Contemporary challenges

• To assess disciplinary and epistemic performance rather than rely on the strange game of tests

• To assess social cognition, or knowledge a student can access rather than just remember

• To assess metacognition, or a student's thinking about their thinking

• To provide more formative assessment and to link it more closely to summative assessment

Knowledge processes

experiencing the known

1. Write a reflection, based on your personal experiences, on the good and bad things about tests.

conceptualising with theory

2. Write an assessment rationale and glossary for a school website or parent handbook.

analysing functionally

3. Research the history of IQ testing. Stephen Jay Gould's *The Mismeasure of Man* is a very readable book on the subject (Gould 1981). Create a comparison table contrasting the approach and assumptions of intelligence testing with those of standards and achievement testing.

analysing critically

4. Research the alternative positions in today's highly politicised debates about assessment. Conduct a mock television interview or write a balanced newspaper report representing the different positions in the debate. It's too much or it's not enough? It's being done right or it should be done differently?

applying appropriately

5. Create a selected response quiz on a literacies topic, such as a reading comprehension test, or a test of literacies concepts. Identify 'correct' and distractor items. Consider the range of possible interpretations of your questions. Reflect on the challenges of constructing test items for selected response assessments.

applying creatively

6. Take a literacy standard that could require students to create a multimodal text. Create an innovative assessment that measures student performance in this standard.

References

Abi-EI-Mona, I. & Abd-EI-Khalick, F. 2006. Argumentative discourse in a high school chemistry classroom. *School Science and Mathematics*, 106(8), 349–61.

Abley, Mark. 2003. *Spoken Here: Travels Among Threatened Languages*. London: William Heinemann.

Adoniou, M. 2014. What should teachers know about spelling? *Literacy*, 48(3), 144–54.

Afflerbach, P., Pearson, D. & Paris, S. G. 2008. Clarifying differences between reading skills and strategies. *The Reading Teacher*, 61(5), 364–73.

Aikenhead, G. 1996. Science education: Border crossing into the subculture of science. *Studies in Science Education*, 27(1), 1–52.

Alloway, N. 2007. Swimming against the tide: Boys, literacies, and schooling, An Australian story. *Canadian Journal of Education/Revue Canadienne de l'Education*, 30: 582–605.

Alvermann, D. E. 2004. Multiliteracies and self-questioning in the service of science learning. In E. W. Saul (ed.), *Crossing Borders in Literacy and Science Instruction* (pp. 226–38). Arlington, VA: NSTA Press.

Anderson, L. W. & Krathwohl, D. R. 2001. *A Taxonomy for Learning, Teaching and Assessing: A Revision of Bloom's Taxonomy of Educational Objectives*. New York: Longman.

Anderson, R. C., Hiebert, E. H., Scott, J. A. & Wilkinson, I. A. G. 1985. *Becoming a Nation of Readers: The Report of the National Commission on Reading*. Champaign, IL: National Academy of Education.

Anderson, R. C. & Pearson, D. 1984. A schema-theoretic view of basic processes in reading comprehension. In D. Pearson (ed.), *Handbook of Reading Research* (pp. 255–92). New York: Longman.

Anstey, M. & Bull, G. 2006. *Teaching and Learning Multiliteracies: Changing Times, Changing Literacies*. Newark, DE: International Reading Association.

Apple, M. W. & Beane, J. A. 2007. *Democratic Schools: Lessons in Powerful Education* (2nd edn). Portsmouth, NH: Heinemann.

Armour-Thomas, E. &. Gordon, E. W. 2013. *Toward an Understanding of Assessment as a Dynamic Component of Pedagogy*. Princeton, NJ: The Gordon Commission.

Arnold, M. 1869. *Culture and Anarchy: An Essay in Political and Social Criticism*. Oxford: Project Gutenberg.

Aronowitz, S. & Giroux, H. 1991. *Postmodern Education: Politics, Culture and Social Criticism*. Minneapolis, MN: University of Minnesota Press.

Arvanitis, E., Kalantzis M. & Cope, B. 2014. Language policies in the context of Australian civic pluralism. In P. P. Trifonas & T. Aravossitas (eds), *Rethinking Heritage Language Education* (pp. 115–40). Cambridge, UK: Cambridge University Press.

Au, K. H. 2011. *Literacy Achievement and Diversity*. New York: Teachers College Press.

Au, W. 2009. *Unequal by Design: High-Stakes Testing and the Standardization of Inequality*. New York: Routledge.

Australian Curriculum, Assessment and Reporting Authority (ACARA). 2009. *Shape of the Australian Curriculum: English*. Retrieved from http://www.acara.edu.au/verve/_resources/australian_curriculum_-_english.pdf

—— (2015a). Australian Curriculum [version 8.1]. Retrieved from http://www.australiancurriculum.edu.au/

—— (2015b). Australian Curriculum, v.7.5 F–10 Curriculum, General Capabilities, Literacy – Background. Retrieved from http://v7-5.australiancurriculum.edu.au/generalcapabilities/literacy/introduction/background

—— (2015c). Australian Curriculum, v.7.5 F–10 Curriculum, General Capabilities, Literacy – Literacy Across the Curriculum. Retrieved from http://v7-5.australiancurriculum.edu.au/generalcapabilities/literacy/introduction/literacy-across-the-curriculum

—— (2015d). Australian Curriculum, v.7.5 F–10 Curriculum, General Capabilities, Literacy – Visual Knowledge. Retrieved from http://v7-5.australiancurriculum.edu.au/generalcapabilities/literacy/organising-elements/visual-knowledge

—— (2015e). Australian Curriculum, v. 8.1 F–10 Curriculum, Cross-Curriculum Priorities, Aboriginal and Torres Strait Islander Histories and Cultures. Retrieved from http://www.australiancurriculum.edu.au/crosscurriculumpriorities/Aboriginal-and-Torres-Strait-Islander-histories-and-cultures

—— (2015f). Australian Curriculum, v. 8.1 F–10 Curriculum, Cross-Curriculum Priorities, Asia and Australia's Engagement with Asia. Retrieved from http://www.australiancurriculum.edu.au/crosscurriculumpriorities/asia-and-australia-s-engagement-with-asia/overview

—— (2015g). Australian Curriculum, v. 8.1 F–10 Curriculum, English – Curriculum ('Australian Curriculum: English'). Retrieved from http://www.australiancurriculum.edu.au/english/curriculum/f-10?layout=1

—— (2015h). Australian Curriculum, v. 8.1 F–10 Curriculum, General Capabilities, Intercultural Understanding – Introduction. Retrieved from http://www.australiancurriculum.edu.au/generalcapabilities/intercultural-understanding/introduction/introduction

—— (2015i). Australian Curriculum, v. 8.1 F–10 Curriculum, General Capabilities – Introduction. Retrieved from http://www.australiancurriculum.edu.au/generalcapabilities/overview/introduction

Ayers, W. 2010. *To Teach: The Journey of a Teacher* (3rd edn). New York: Teachers College Press.

Ball, P. 2010. *The Music Instinct: How Music Works and Why We Can't Do Without It.* Oxford, UK: Oxford University Press.

Beach, R. W. 2011. Issues in analyzing alignment of language arts common core standards with state standards. *Educational Researcher,* 40(4), 179–82.

Beane, J. A. & Apple, M. W. 2007. The case for democratic schools. In M. W. Apple & M. W. Apple (eds), *Democratic Schools: Lessons in Powerful Education* (pp. 5–28, 14–19). Portsmouth, NH: Heinemann.

Behrens, J. T. & DiCerbo, K. E. 2013. Technological implications for assessment ecosystems. In E. W. Gordon (ed), *The Gordon Commission on the Future of Assessment in Education: Technical Report* (pp. 101–22). Princeton, NJ: The Gordon Commission.

Benkler, Y. 2006. *The Wealth of Networks: How Social Production Transforms Markets and Freedom.* New Haven: Yale University Press.

Bennett, W. 1984. *To Reclaim a Legacy: A Report on the Humanities in Higher Education.* Washington, DC: National Endowment for the Humanities.

Berdiansky, B., Cronnell, B. & Koehler, J. (1969). *Spelling-Sound Relations and Primary Form-Class Descriptions for Speech Comprehension Vocabularies of 6-9 Year Olds.* Los Alamitos, CA: Southwest Regional Laboratory for Educational Research and Development.

Bereiter, C. 2002. *Education and Mind in the Knowledge Age.* Mahwah, NJ: Lawrence Erlbaum.

Bernstein, B. 1990. Class, vodes, and control. *The Structuring of Pedagogical Discourse,* 4.

Bin, B. Z. B. & Freebody. P. 2010. Image, genre, voice, and the making of the school-literate child: Lessons from multiliteracy teaching in China. In D. R. Cole & D. L. Pullen (eds), *Multiliteracies in Motion: Current Theory and Practice* (pp. 42–58). London: Routledge.

Birkerts, S. 1994. *The Gutenberg Elegies: The Fate of Reading in an Electronic Age.* New York: Fawcett Columbine.

Black, P. & Wiliam, D. 1998. Assessment and classroom learning. *Assessment in Education,* 5, 7–74.

Blackburn, J. E. & Conrad Powell, W. 1976. *One at a Time, All at Once: The Creative Teacher's Guide to Individualized Instruction Without Anarchy.* Glenview, IL: Scott, Foresmanand Company.

Block, J. H. (ed.) 1971. *Mastery Learning: Theory and Practice*. New York: Holt Rinehart & Winston.

Bloom, A. 1987. *The Closing of the American Mind: How Higher Education Has Failed Democracy and Impoverished the Souls of Today's Students*. New York: Simon & Schuster.

Bloom, Harold. 1994. *The Western Canon: The Books and School of the Ages*. New York: Harcourt Brace & Company.

Boomer, G. 1982. *Negotiating the Curriculum: A Teacher–Student Partnership*. Sydney: Ashton Scholastic.

Boomer, G. & Davis, C. 1980. *Reading and Writing, Book 1*. Melbourne: Macmillan.

Bowker, G. C. & Star, S. L. 2000. *Sorting Things Out: Classification and its Consequences*. Cambridge, MA: MIT Press.

Bransford, J. D., Brown, A. L. & Cocking, R. R. 2000. *How People Learn: Brain, Mind, Experience and School*. Produced by NRC Commission on Behavioral and Social Sciences and Education. Washington, DC: National Academy Press.

Brown, A. L. & Campione, J. C. 1994. Guided discovery in a community of learners. In K. McGilly (ed.), *Classroom Lessons: Integrating Cognitive Theory and Classroom Practice* (pp. 229–70). Cambridge, MA: MIT Press.

Bruner, J. 1986. *Actual Minds, Possible Worlds*. Cambridge, MA: Harvard University Press.

Buffum, A., Mattos, M. & Weber, C. 2009. *Pyramid Response to Intervention*. Bloomington, IN: Solution Tree Press.

Callaghan, M. & Rothery, J. 1988. *Teaching Factual Writing: A Genre Based Approach* (Report of the Disadvantaged Schools Program Literacy Project). Sydney: NSW Department of Education.

Callow, J. 2006. Images, politics and multiliteracies: Using a visual metalanguage. *Australian Journal of Language and Literacy*, 29, 7–23.

Cañas, A. J., Hill, G., Carff, R., Suri, N., Lott, J., Gómez, G., Eskridge, T. C., Mario Arroyo & Carvajal, R. 2004. CMAPTOOLS: A knowledge modeling and sharing environment. In A. J. Cañas, J. D. Novak & F. M. González (eds), *Concept Maps: Theory, Methodology, Technology. Proceedings of the First International Conference on Concept Mapping*. Pamplona, Spain.

Carnine, D. W., Silbert, J., Kame'enui, E. J. Tarver, S. G. & Jungjohann, K. 2006. *Teaching Struggling and At-Risk Readers: A Direct Instruction Approach*. Upper Saddle River, NJ: Pearson.

Carter, R. & McCarthy, M. 2006. *Cambridge Grammar of English*. Cambridge, UK: Cambridge University Press.

Carter, S. P. 2006. 'She would've still made that face expression': The use of multiple literacies by two African American young women. *Theory into Practice*, 45, 352–8.

CAST. 2011. *Universal Design for Learning Guidelines: Version 2.0*. Wakefield, MA: National Center on Universal Design for Learning.

Caughlan, S. 2008. Advocating for the arts in an age of multiliteracies. *Language Arts*, 86, 120–6.

Cazden, C. B. 2001. *Classroom Discourse: The Language of Teaching and Learning*. Portsmouth, NH: Heinemann.

—— 2006. Connected learning: 'Weaving' in classroom lessons. In *'Pedagogy in Practice 2006' Conference*. University of Newcastle, NSW.

Chall, J. S. 1967 (1983). *Learning to Read: The Great Debate*. New York: McGraw-Hill.

—— 1983. *Stages of Reading Development*. New York: McGraw Hill.

Chanan, M. 1995. *Repeated Takes: A Short History of Recording and its Effects on Music*. London: Verso.

Chandler-Olcott, K. & Mahar, D. 2003a. Adolescents' anime-inspired 'fanfictions': An exploration of multiliteracies. *Journal of Adolescent and Adult Literacy*, 46(7), 556.

—— 2003b. 'Tech-savviness' meets multiliteracies: Exploring adolescent girls' technology-mediated literacy practices. *Reading Research Quarterly*, 38(3), 356–85.

Chang, H. H. 2015. Psychometrics behind computerized adaptive testing. *Psychometrika*, 80, 1–20.

Chang, K. E., Sung, Y. T. & Lee, C. L. 2003. Web-based collaborative inquiry learning. *Journal of Computer Assisted Learning*, 19, 56–69.

Childe, V. G. 1936. *Man Makes Himself*. London: Watts.

Chomsky, N. 1957. (2002). *Syntactic Structures*. Amsterdam: de Gruyter Mouton.

—— 1959. Review of *Verbal Behavior*, by B. F. Skinner. *Language*, 35, 26–58.

Christie, F. & Derewianka, B. 2008. *School Discourse: Learning to Write Across the Years of Schooling*. London: Continuum.

Christie, M. J. 1992. Grounded and ex-centric knowledges: Exploring Aboriginal alternatives to Western thinking. In *Conference on Thinking*. Townsville, QLD.

Clancy, S. & Lowrie, T. 2003. Pokemon meanings: Narrative constructions from multimodal texts. *International Journal of Learning*, 10(3), 1127–32.

—— 2005. Multiliteracies: New pathways into digital worlds. *International Journal of Learning*, 12(7), 141–5.

Clark, A.-M., Anderson, R., Kuo, L.-J. Kim, I.-H., Archodidou, A. & Nguyen-Jahiel, K. 2003. Collaborative reasoning: expanding ways for children to talk and think in school. *Educational Psychology Review*, 15, 181–98.

Clay, M. M. 1998. *By Different Paths to Common Outcomes*. York, ME: Stenhouse.

—— 2001. *Change Over Time in Children's Literacy Development*. Auckland: Heinemann.

—— 2005. *Literacy Lessons: Designed for Individuals*. Auckland: Heinemann.

Cloonan, A. 2010a. *Multiliteracies, Multimodality and Teacher Professional Learning*. Champaign, IL: Common Ground Publishing.

—— 2010b. Technologies in literacy learning: A case study. *e-Learning and Digital Media,* 7, 248–57.

—— 2011. Creating multimodal metalanguage with teachers. *English Teaching: Practice and Critique,* 10(4), 23–40.

—— 2015. Integrating by design: Multimodality, 21st century skills and subject area knowledge. In B. Cope & M. Kalantzis (eds), *A Pedagogy of Multiliteracies: Learning By Design.* London: Palgrave.

Cloonan, A., Kalantzis, M. & Cope, B. 2010. Schemas for meaning-making and multimodal texts. In T. Locke (ed.), *Beyond the Grammar Wars* (pp. 254–75). London: Routledge.

Cole, D. & Pullen, D. L. (eds). 2010. *Multiliteracies in Motion: Current Theory and Practice.* London: Routledge.

Comber, B., Thomson, P. & Wells, M. 2001. Critical literacy finds a 'place': Writing and social action in a low-income Australian grade 2/3 classroom. *The Elementary School Journal,* 101, 451–64.

Common Core State Standards Initiative (CCSS). 2010. *Common Core State Standards for English Language Arts and Literacy in History/Social Studies, Science, and Technical Subjects.* National Governors Association Center for Best Practices, Council of Chief State School Officers, Washington, DC.

Cook-Gumperz, J. 2006. Literacy and schooling: An unchanging equation? In J. Cook-Gumperz (ed.), *The Social Construction of Literacy* (pp. 19–50). Cambridge, UK: Cambridge University Press.

Cope, B. 1998. The language of forgetting: A short history of the word. In M. Fraser (ed.), *Seams of Light: Best Antipodean Essays* (pp. 192–223) Sydney: Allen & Unwin.

Cope, B. & Kalantzis, M. 1993. *The Powers of Literacy: Genre Approaches to Teaching Writing.* London and Pittsburgh: Falmer Press (UK edn) and University of Pennsylvania Press (US edn).

—— 1997a. *Productive Diversity: A New Approach to Work and Management.* Sydney: Pluto Press.

—— 1997b. White noise: The attack on political correctness and the struggle for the Western canon. *Interchange,* 28, 283–329.

—— 2000. Designs for social futures. In B. Cope & M. Kalantzis (eds), *Multiliteracies: Literacy Learning and the Design of Social Futures* (pp. 203 34). London: Routledge.

—— 2009. 'Multiliteracies': New literacies, new learning. *Pedagogies: An International Journal,* 4, 164–95.

—— 2013. Towards a new learning: The 'scholar' social knowledge workspace, in theory and practice. *e-Learning and Digital Media,* 10, 334–58.

—— (eds). 2015a. *A Pedagogy of Multiliteracies: Learning by Design.* London: Palgrave.

—— 2015b. Interpreting evidence-of-learning: Educational research in the era of big data. *Open Review of Educational Research,* 2, 218–39.

—— 2015c. Sources of evidence-of-learning: Learning and assessment in the era of big data. *Open Review of Educational Research,* 2, 194–217.

—— 2015d. The things you do to know: An introduction to the pedagogy of multiliteracies. In B. Cope & M. Kalantzis (eds). *A Pedagogy of Multiliteracies: Learning By Design.* London: Palgrave.

Cope, B., Kalantzis, M., Abd-El-Khalick, F. & Bagley, E. 2013. Science in writing: Learning scientific argument in principle and practice. *e-Learning and Digital Media,* 10, 420–41.

Cope, B., Kalantzis, M. & Magee, L. 2011. *Towards a Semantic Web: Connecting Knowledge in Academic Research.* Cambridge, UK: Woodhead Publishing.

Cope, B., Kalantzis, M., McCarthey, S. Vojak, C. & Kline, S. 2011. Technology-mediated writing assessments: Paradigms and principles. *Computers and Composition,* 28, 79–96.

Crafton, L. K., Brennan, M. & Silvers, P. 2007. Critical inquiry and multiliteracies in a first-grade classroom. *Language Arts,* 84, 510–18.

Crystal, D. 1997. *The Cambridge Encyclopedia of Language.* Cambridge, UK: Cambridge University Press.

—— 2000. *Language Death.* Cambridge, UK: Cambridge University Press.

—— 2005. *The Stories of English.* London: Penguin.

Cuban, L. 1993. *How Teachers Taught: Constancy and Change in American Classrooms, 1890–1990.* New York: Teachers College Press.

Cumming-Potvin, W. 2007. Scaffolding, multiliteracies, and reading circles. *Canadian Journal of Education,* 30, 483–507.

Cummins, J. 2000. *Language, Power and Pedagogy: Bilingual Children in the Crossfire.* Clevedon, UK: Multilingual Matters.

—— 2006. Multiliteracies and equity: How do Canadian schools measure up? *Education Canada,* 46, 4–7.

—— 2009. Transformative multiliteracies pedagogy: School-based strategies for closing the achievement gap. *Multiple Voices for Ethnically Diverse Exceptional Learners,* 11, 38–56.

Cummins, J., Brown, K. & Sayers, D. 2007. *Literacy, Technology and Diversity: Teaching for Success in Changing Times.* Boston: Allynand Bacon.

Cummins, J. & Early, M. 2011. *Identity Texts: The Collaborative Creation of Power in Multilingual Schools.* Stoke-on-Trent, UK: Trentham.

Dalley-Trim, L. 2012. Popular culture in the classroom: A plethora of possibilities. In R. Henderson (ed.), *Teaching Literacies in the Middle Years: Pedagogies and Diversity* (pp. 81–110). Melbourne: Oxford University Press.

Davies, A., Fidler, D. & Gorbis, M. 2011. *Future Work Skills 2020.* Phoenix: Institute for the Future, University of Pheonix Research Institute.

Deacon, T. W. 1997. *The Symbolic Species: The Co-evolution of Language and the Brain.* New York: W. W. Norton.

Delpit, L. D. 1988. The silenced dialogue: Power and pedagogy in educating other people's children. *Harvard Educational Review,* 58, 280–98.

Derewianka, B. 2001. Pedagogical grammars: their role in English language teaching. In A. Burns & C. Coffin (eds), *Analysing English in a Global Context: A Reader* (pp. 240–69). London and New York: Routledge Taylor & Francis Group.

Deutscher, Guy. 2006. *The Unfolding of Language: An Evolutionary Tour of Mankind's Greatest Invention.* New York: Henry Holt.

Dewey, J. 1902 (1956). *The Child and the Curriculum.* Chicago: University of Chicago Press.

—— 1915 (1956). *The School and Society.* Chicago: University of Chicago Press.

—— 1916 (1966). *Democracy and Education: An Introduction to the Philosophy of Education.* New York: Free Press.

—— 1938 (1963). *Experience and Education.* New York: Collier Books.

Dewey, J. & Dewey, E. 1915. *Schools of To-morrow.* New York: Dutton.

Diamond, J. 1999. *Guns, Germs and Steel: The Fates of Human Societies.* New York: W. W. Norton.

Dixon, R. M. W. 1972. *The Dyirbal Language of North Queensland.* Cambridge, UK: Cambridge University Press.

—— 1980. *The Languages of Australia.* Cambridge, UK: Cambridge University Press.

Donald, M. 2001. *A Mind So Rare: The Evolution of Human Consciousness.* New York: W.W. Norton.

Donnelly, K. 2008. English goes back to basics. *The Australian,* 17 October.

Duncan-Andrade, J. M. & Morrell, E. 2008. *The Art of Critical Pedagogy: Possibilities for Moving from Theory to Practice in Urban Schools.* New York: Peter Lang.

Engelmann, S. 1992. *War Against the Schools' Academic Child Abuse.* Portland, OR: Halcyon House.

Erstad, O., Gilje, A. & de Lange, T. 2007. Remixing multimodal resources: Multiliteracies and digital production in Norwegian media education. *Learning, Media, and Technology,* 32, 183–98.

Everett, D. L. 2005. Cultural constraints on grammar and cognition in Piraha: Another look at the design features of human language. *Current Anthropology,* 46, 621–46.

Exley, B. & Luke, A. 2009. Uncritical framing: Lesson and knowledge structure in school science. In D. Cole & D. L. Pullen (eds), *Multiliteracies in Motion: Current Theory and Practice* (pp. 17–41). London: Routledge.

Febvre, L. & Martin, H.-J. 1976. *The Coming of the Book.* London: Verso.

Flanagan, D. P. & Kaufman, A. S. 2009. *Essentials of WISC-IV Assessment.* Hoboken, NJ: Wiley.

Flesch, R. 1955. *Why Johnny Can't Read, and What to Do About It.* New York: Harper.

Fletcher, R. & Portalupi, J. 2001. *Writing Workshop: The Essential Guide*. Portsmouth, NH: Heinemann.

Flynn, J R. 2007. *What is Intelligence?* Cambridge, UK: Cambridge University Press.

Freebody, P. 2007. *Literacy Education in School Research: Perspectives from the Past, for the Future*. Camberwell, Vic.: ACER.

Freebody, P. & Luke, A. 1990. Literacy programs: Debates and demands in cultural context. *Prospect: Australian Journal of TESOL*, 5(7), 7–16.

Freire, P. 2015. *Pedagogy of the Oppressed* (30th anniv. edn) (trans. by M. Bergman Ramos). New York, NY: The Continuum International Publishing Group Inc.

Freire, P. & Macedo, D. 1987. *Literacy: Reading the Word and the World*. South Hadley, MA: Bergin & Garvey.

Fterniati, A. 2010. Literacy pedagogy and multiliteracies in Greek elementary school language arts. *International Journal of Learning*, 17, 319–50.

Gee, J. P. 1992. *The Social Mind: Language, Ideology, and Social Practice*. New York: Bergin & Garvey.

—— 2000. New people in new worlds: Networks, the new capitalism and schools. In B. Cope & M. Kalantzis (eds), *Multiliteracies: Literacy Learning and the Design of Social Futures* (pp. 41–66). London: Routledge.

—— 2004a. Language in the science classroom: Academic social languages as the heart of school-based literacy. In E. W. Saul (ed.), *Crossing Borders in Literacy and Science Instruction* (pp. 13–32). Arlington, VA: NSTA Press.

—— 2004b. *Situated Language and Learning: A Critique of Traditional Schooling*. New York: Routledge.

—— 2007. *Good Video Games + Good Learning: Collected Essays on Video Games, Learning and Literacy*. New York: Peter Lang.

—— 2010. *New Digital Media and Learning as an Emerging Area and 'Worked Examples' as One Way Forward*. Cambridge, MA: MIT Press.

Gellner, E. 1983. *Nations and Nationalism*. Ithaca, NY: Cornell University Press.

Giampapa, F. 2010. Multiliteracies, pedagogy and identities: Teacher and student voices from a Toronto elementary school. *Canadian Journal of Education*, 33, 407–31.

Gilbert, R. & Gilbert, P. 1998. *Masculinity Goes to School*. London: Routledge.

Giroux, H. 1987. Introduction: Literacy and the pedagogy of political empowerment. In P. Freire & D. Macedo (eds), *Literacy: Reading the Word and the World* (pp. 1–27). South Hadley, MA: Bergin & Garvey.

—— 1996. Slacking off: Border youth and postmodern education. In H. A. Giroux, C. Lankshear, P. McLaren & M. Peters (eds), *Counternarratives: Cultural Studies and Critical Pedagogies in Postmodern Spaces* (pp. 59–80). New York: Routledge.

—— 1997. *Channel Surfing: Race Talk and the Destruction of Today's Youth*. Houndmills, UK: Macmillan.

Goeke, J. L. 2009. *Explicit Instruction*. Upper Saddle River, NJ: Merrill.

Goffman, E. 1959. *The Presentation of Self in Everyday Life*. New York: Doubleday Anchor.

—— 1974. *Frame Analysis: An Essay on the Organization of Experience*. Cambridge, MA: Harvard University Press.

Gombrich, E. H. 1960 (2000). *Art and Illusion: A Study of the Psychology of Pictorial Representation*. Princeton, NJ: Princeton University Press.

Goodman, K. 1993. *Phonics Phacts*. Portsmouth, NH: Heinemann.

—— 1996. *Ken Goodman on Reading*. Portsmouth, NH: Heinemann.

—— 2005. *What's Whole in Whole Language*. Berkeley, CA: RDR Books.

Gorin, J. S. 2013. *Assessment as Evidential Reasoning*. Princeton, NJ: The Gordon Commission.

Gottfredson, L. S. 2009. Logical fallacies used to dismiss the evidence on intelligence testing. In R. P. Phelps (ed.), *Correcting Fallacies About Educational and Psychological Testing* (pp. 11–65). Washington, DC: American Psychological Association.

Goulah, J. 2007. Village voices, global visions: Digital video as a transformative foreign language learning tool. *Foreign Language Annals*, 40, 62–78.

Gould, S. J. 1981. *The Mismeasure of Man*. New York: W. W. Norton.

Graff, H. J. 1979. *The Literacy Myth: Literacy and Social Structure in the Nineteenth-Century City*. New York: Academic Press.

—— 1987. *The Legacies of Literacy: Continuities and Contradictions in Western Culture and Society*. Bloomington, IN: Indiana University Press.

Graves, Donald H. 1994. *A Fresh Look at Writing*. Portsmouth, NH: Heinemann.

—— 2002. *Testing is Not Teaching: What Should Count in Education*. Portsmouth, NH: Heinemann.

—— 2003. *Writing: Teachers and Children at Work*. Portsmouth, NH: Heinemann.

Greeno, J. G. 1998. The situativity of knowing, learning, and research. *American Psychologist*, 53, 5–26.

Gunning, T. G. 2008. *Creating Literacy Instruction For All Students*. Boston: Pearson.

Gutiérrez, K. D. 2008. Developing a sociocritical literacy in the third space. *Reading Research Quarterly*, 43, 148–64.

Gutiérrez, K. D., Asato, J., Pacheco, M., Moll, L. C., Olson, K., Horng, E. L., Ruiz, R., Garcia, E. & McCarty, T. L. 2002. 'sounding American': The consequences of new reforms on English language learners. *Reading Research Quarterly*, 37, 328–43.

Gutiérrez, K. D. & Orellana, M. F. 2006. The 'problem' of English learners: constructing genres of difference. *Research in the Teaching of English*, 40, 502–7.

Gutiérrez, K. D. & Rogoff, B. 2003. Cultural ways of learning: Individual traits or repertoires of practice. *Educational Researcher,* 32, 19–25.

Halliday, M. A. K. 1975. *Learning how to mean: Explorations in the development of language.* London: Edward Arnold.

—— 1989. *Spoken and Written Language,* Edited by F. Christie. Oxford: Oxford University Press.

—— 1998. Things and relations: Regrammaticalising experience as technical knowledge – stratification and metaphor, semogenic power of nominalisation, types of grammatical metaphor. In J. R. Martin & R. Veel. (eds), *Reading Science: Critical and Functional Perspectives on Discourses of Science* (pp. 185–236). London and New York: Routledge.

—— 2002. *On Grammar* (vol. 1) (edited by J. J. Webster). London: Continuum.

—— 2004. *An Introduction to Functional Grammar.* London: Hodder Arnold.

—— 2009. Context of culture and of situation. In J. J. Webster (ed.), *The Essential Halliday* (pp. 55–84). London and New York: Continuum.

Halliday, M. A. K. & Hasan, R. 1985. *Language, Context and Text: Aspects of Language in a Social-Semiotic Perspective.* Melbourne: Deakin University Press.

Harrison, C., Lee, L., O'Rourke, M. & Yelland, N. 2009. Maximising the moment from preschool to school: The place of multiliteracies and ICT in the transition to school. *International Journal of Learning,* 16(11), 465–74.

Harvey, S. & Goudvis, A. 2007. *Strategies that Work: Teaching Comprehension for Understanding and Engagement* (2nd edn). Portland, ME: Stenhouse Publishers.

Hass Dyson, A. 2001. Relational sense and textual sense in a US urban classroom: The contested case of Emily, girl friend of a ninja. In B. Comber & A. Simpson (eds), *Negotiating Critical Literacies in Classrooms* (pp. 3–18). Mahwah, NJ: Lawrence Erlbaum.

Hassett, D. D. & Scott Curwood, J. 2009. Theories and practices of multimodal education: the instructional dynamics of picture books and primary classrooms. *Reading Teacher,* 63, 270–82.

Hayes, C. W. & Bahruth, R., 1985. Querer es poder. In J. Hansen, T. Newkirk & D. Graves (eds), *Breaking Ground: Teachers Relate Reading and Writing in the Elementary School* (pp. 97–110). Portsmouth, NH: Heinemann.

Healy, A.H. (ed.). 2007. *Multiliteracies and Diversity in Education: New Pedagogies for Expanding Landscapes.* Melbourne: Oxford University Press.

Herndon, J. H. 1970. *A Survey of Modern Grammars.* New York: Holt, Rinehart & Winston.

Hertzberg, M. 2001. Using drama to enhance the reading of narrative texts. In *Australian Association for the Teaching of English.* Hobart, Tasmania.

Hirsch, E.D. 1988. *Cultural Literacy: What Every American Needs to Know.* New York: Vintage Books.

hooks, b. 1994. *Teaching to Transgress: Education as the Practice of Freedom*. New York: Routledge.

Hull, G. A. & Nelson, M. E. 2005. Locating the semiotic power of multimodality. *Written Communication*, 22(2), 224–61.

Humphrey, S., Droga, L. & Feez, S. 2012. *Grammar and Meaning*. Newtown, NSW: Primary English Teaching Association (Australia).

Iyer, R. 2006. Pedagogies of design and multiliterate learner identities. *International Journal of Learning*, 13: 25–33.

Jenkins, H. 2006a. *Confronting the Challenges of Participatory Culture: Media Education for the 21st Century*. Chicago: MacArthur Foundation.

—— 2006b. *Convergence Culture: Where Old and New Media Collide*. New York: New York University Press.

Kaestle, C. 2013. *Testing Policy in the United States: A Historical Perspective*. The Gordon Commission: Princeton, NJ.

Kalantzis, M. & Cope, B. 1993. Histories of pedagogy, cultures of schooling. In B. Cope & M. Kalantzis (eds), *The Powers of Literacy: A Genre Approach to Teaching Literacy* (pp. 38–62). London: Falmer Press.

—— 2006. On globalisation and diversity. Computers and Composition, 31: 402–11.

—— 2012. *New Learning: Elements of a Science of Education* (2nd edn). Cambridge, UK: Cambridge University Press.

—— 2013. On transformations: Reflections on the work of, and working with, Gunther Kress. In M. Böck & N. Pachler (eds), *Multimodality and Social Semiosis: Communication, Meaning-Making and Learning in the Work of Gunther Kress* (pp. 16–32). London: Routledge.

Kalantzis, M., Cope, B. & Cloonan, A. 2010. A multiliteracies perspective on the new literacies. In E. A. Baker (ed.), *The New Literacies: Multiple Perspectives on Research and Practice* (pp. 61–87). New York: Guildford.

Kao, G. Y., Chen, K & Sun, C. 2010. Using an e-learning system with integrated concept maps to improve conceptual understanding. *International Journal of Instructional Media*, 37, 151–61.

Katsarou, E. 2009. A multiliteracy intervention in a contemporary 'mono-literacy' school in Greece. *International Journal of Learning*, 16, 55–65.

Kendron, A. 2004. *Gesture: Visible Action as Utterance*. Cambridge, UK: Cambridge University Press.

Kenway, J. & Nixon, H. 1999. Cyberfeminisms, cyberliteracies, and educational cyberspheres. *Educational Theory*, 49, 457–74.

Kirschner, P. A., Sweller, J. & Clark, R. E. 2006. 'Why minimal guidance during instruction does not work: An analysis of the failure of constructivist, discovery, problem-based, experiential, and inquiry-based teaching. *Educational Psychologist*, 41, 75–86.

Kitson, L., Fletcher, M. & Kearney, J. 2007. Continuity and change in literacy practices: A move towards multiliteracies. *Journal of Classroom Interaction*, 41, 29–41.

Kline, S., Letofsky, K. & Woodard, B. 2013. Democratizing classroom discourse: The challenge for online writing environments. *e-Learning and Digital Media*, 10, 379–95.

Knight, S., Shum, S. B. & Littleton, K. 2013. Epistemology, pedagogy, assessment and learning analytics. In *Third Conference on Learning Analytics and Knowledge (LAK 2013)* (pp. 75–84). Leuven, Belgium: ACM.

Knobel, M. 1998. Critical literacies in teacher education. In M. Knobel & A. Healy (eds), *Critical Literacies in the Primary Classroom* (pp. 89–111). Newtown, NSW: Primary English Teaching Association (Australia).

Koch, C. 2004. *The Quest for Consciousness: A Neurobiological Approach*. Engelwood, CO: Roberts and Company.

Kress, G. 1985. *Linguistic Processes in Sociocultural Practice*. Geelong, Vic.: Deakin University.

—— 1993. *Learning to Write*. London: Routledge.

—— 1997. *Before Writing: Rethinking the Paths to Literacy*. London: Routledge.

—— 2000a. Design and transformation: New theories of meaning. In B. Cope & M. Kalantzis (eds), *Multiliteracies: Literacy Learning and the Design of Social Futures* (pp. 153–61). London: Routledge.

—— 2000b. *Early Spelling: From Convention to Creativity*. London: Routledge.

—— 2000c. Multimodality. In B. Cope & M. Kalantzis (eds), *Multiliteracies: Literacy Learning and the Design of Social Futures* (pp. 182–202). Melbourne: Macmillan.

—— 2003. *Literacy in the New Media Age*. London: Routledge.

—— 2009. *Multimodality: A Social Semiotic Approach to Contemporary Communication*. London: Routledge.

Kress, G., Jewitt, C., Ogborn, J. & Tsatsarelis, C. 2014. *Multimodal Teaching and Learning: The Rhetorics of the Science Classroom*. London: Bloomsbury.

Krippendorf, Klaus. 2006. *The Semantic Turn: A New Foundation for Design*. Boca Raton, FL: Taylor & Francis.

Labov, William. 1972. *Language in the Inner City: Studies in the Black English Vernacular*. Philadelphia: University of Pennsylvania Press.

Ladson-Billings, Gloria. 2001. *Crossing Over to Canann: The Journey of New Teachers in Diverse Classrooms*. San Francisco, CA: Jossey-Bass.

Lakoff, G. & Johnson, M. 1980 (2003). *Metaphors We Live By*. Chicago, IL: University of Chicago Press.

Lam, W. S. E. 2009. 'Multiliteracies on instant messaging in negotiating local, translocal, and transnational affiliations: A case of an adolescent immigrant. *Reading Research Quarterly*, 44, 377–97.

Lankshear, C. & Knobel, M. 2006. *New Literacies: Everyday Practices and Classroom Learning* (2nd edn). Maidenhead, UK: Open University Press.

—— 2008. Digital literacy and the law: Remixing elements of Lawrence Lessig's ideal of 'free culture'. In C. Lankshear & M. Knobel (eds), *Digital Literacies: Concepts, Policies and Practices* (pp. 279–306). New York: Peter Lang.

Latour, B. & Woolgar, S. 1986. *Laboratory Life: The Construction of Scientific Facts.* Princeton, NJ: Princeton University Press.

Lavoie, C. 2008. Developing multiliteracies through bilingual education in Burkina Faso. *Educational Research and Reviews, 3,* 344–50.

Lemke, J. L. 1990. *Talking Science: Language, Learning and Values.* Westport, CN: Ablex.

—— 1998. Multiplying meaning: Visual and verbal semiotics in scientific text. In J. Martin & R. Veel (eds), *Reading Science* (pp. 87–113). London: Routledge.

—— 2004. The literacies of science. In E. W. Saul (ed.), *Crossing Borders in Literacy and Science Instruction* (pp. 33–47). Arlington, VA: NSTA Press.

Leontyev, A. N. 2009. An outline of the evolution of the psyche. In M. Cole (ed.), *The Development of Mind* (pp. 137–244). Pacifica, CA: Marxists Internet Archive.

Levi-Strauss, C. 1955 (1976). *Triste Tropiques.* Harmondsworth, UK: Penguin.

—— 1966. *The Savage Mind.* Chicago: University of Chicago Press.

Lewis, M. P. 2009. *Ethnologue: Languages of the World.* Dallas, TX: SIL International.

Liu, E. Z. F. 2002. Incomas: An item bank based and networked concept map assessment system. *International Journal of Instructional Media, 29,* 325–35.

Lopez-Gopar, M. E. 2007. Beyond the alienating alphabetic literacy: Multiliteracies in indigenous education in Mexico. *Diaspora, Indigenous, and Minority Education, 1,* 159–74.

Luke, A. & Freebody, P. 1997. Shaping the social practices of reading. In S. Muspratt, A. Luke & P. Freebody (eds), *Constructing Critical Literacies: Teaching and Learning Textual Practice* (pp. 185–225). Cresskill, NJ: Hampton Press.

—— 1999. A map of possible practices: Further notes on the four resources model. *Practically Primary,* 4(2), 5–8.

Macken, M., Kalantzis, M., Kress, G., Martin, J. R.Cope, B. & Rothery, J. 1990. *A Genre-Based Approach to Teaching Writing, Years 3–6, Book 2: Factual Writing: A Teaching Unit Based on Reports About Sea Mammals.* Sydney. Directorate of Studies, NSW Department of Education.

Mackey, M. 2003. Television and the teenage literate: Discourses of 'Felicity'. *College English, 65,* 389–410.

Mackintosh, N. J. 1998. *IQ and Human Intelligence.* Oxford, UK: Oxford University Press.

Martin, J. R. 1986. *Writing to Mean: Teaching Genres Across the Curriculum.* Bundoora, Vic.: Applied Linguistics Association of Australia.

—— 1992. *English Text: System and Structure*. Philadelphia: John Benjamins.

—— 1993. Life as a noun: Arresting the universe in science and humanities. In M. A. K. Halliday & J. R. Martin (eds), *Writing Science: Literacy and Discursive Power* (pp. 221–67). London; Washington, DC: The Falmer Press.

—— 1997. Analysing genre: Functional parameters. In F. Christie & J. R. Martin (eds), *Genres and Institutions: Social Processes in the Workplace and School* (pp. 3–39). London: Cassell Academic.

Martin, K. 2008. The intersection of Aboriginal knowledges, Aboriginal literacies, and new learning pedagogy for Aboriginal students. In A. Healy (ed.), *Mulitiliteracies and Diversity in Education: New Pedagogies for Expanding Landscapes* (pp. 58–81). Melbourne: Oxford University Press.

Marulis, L. M. & Neuman, S. B. 2010. The effects of vocabulary intervention on young children's word learning: A meta-analysis. *Review of Educational Research*, 80, 300–35.

Massung, S., Zhai, C. & Hockenmaier, J. 2013. Structural parse tree features for text representation. In *IEEE Seventh International Conference on Semantic Computing*. Irvine, CA.

Mayer, J. S. 1990. *Uncommon Sense: Theoretical Practice in Language Education*. Portsmouth, NH: Heinemann.

McCarthey, S. J., Magnifico, A., Woodard, R. & Kline, S. 2014. Situating technology-facilitated feedback and revision: The case of Tom. In K. E. Pytash & R. E. Ferdig (eds), *Exploring Technology for Writing and Writing Instruction* (pp. 152–70). Hershey, PA: IGI Global.

McClenaghan, D. & Doecke, B. 2010. Multiliteracies: Resources for meaning-making in the secondary English classroom. In D. R. Cole & D. L. Pullen (eds), *Multiliteracies in Motion: Current Theory and Practice* (pp. 224–38). London: Routledge.

McGinn, C. 2004. *Mindsight: Image, Dream, Meaning*. Cambridge, MA: Harvard University Press.

McLaren, P. 2015. *Life in Schools: An Introduction to Critical Pedagogy in the Foundations of Education* (6th edn). Boulder, CO: Paradigm Publishers.

McLaughlin, M. & DeVoogd, G. L. 2004. *Critical Literacy: Enhancing Students' Comprehension of Text*. New York: Scholastic.

McMahon, W. 2009. *Higher Learning, Greater Good: The Private and Social Benefits of Higher Education*. Baltimore, MD: Johns Hopkins University Press.

McNamara, D. S. & Graesser, A. C. 2012. Coh-Metrix: An automated tool for theoretical and applied natural language processing. In P. M. McCarthy & C. Boonthum-Denecke (eds), *Applied Natural Language Processing: Identification, Investigation and Resolution* (pp. 188–205). Hershey, PA: IGI Global.

McNeill, D. 1992. *Hand and Mind: What Gestures Reveal About Thought*. Chicago: University of Chicago Press.

McWhorter, J. 2001. *The Power of Babel: A Natural History of Language*. New York: Perennial.

Meyer, R. J. 2002. *Phonics Exposed: Understanding and Resisting Systematic Direct Intense Phonics Instruction*. Mahwah, NJ: Lawrence Erlbaum.

Miller, D. 2010. *Stuff*. Cambridge, UK: Polity.

Mills, K. A. 2006. Mr Travelling-at-will Ted Doyle: Discourses in a multiliteracies classroom. *Australian Journal of Language and Literacy*, 29(2), 132–49.

—— 2010. *The Multiliteracies Classroom*. Bristol, UK: Multilingual Matters.

—— 2015. Doing digital composition on the social web: Knowledge processes in literacy learning. In B. Cope & M. Kalantzis (eds), *A Pedagogy of Multiliteracies: Learning By Design*. London: Palgrave.

Mitchell, W. J. T. 1986. *Iconology: Image, Text, Ideology*. Chicago: University of Chicago Press.

Montessori, M. 1912 (1964). *The Montessori Method*. New York: Schocken Books.

—— 1917 (1973). *The Montessori Elementary Material*. New York: Schocken Books.

Moodie, R. 2004. Body talk. *Australian Screen Education*, 35, 56–8.

Morgan, L. 2010. Teacher professional transformation using learning by design: A case study. *E-Learning and Digital Media*, 7, 280.

Murray, D. M. 1982. *Learning by Teaching: Selected Articles on Writing and Teaching*. Montclair, NJ: Boynton/Cook.

Neville, M. 2008. *Teaching Multimodal Literacy Using the Learning by Design Approach to Pedagogy*. Melbourne: Common Ground.

New London Group. 1996. A pedagogy of multiliteracies: Designing social futures. *Harvard Educational Review*, 66(1), 60–92.

Newfield, D., Stein, P., Rumboll, F. Meyer, L., Badenhorst, C., Drew, M., Mkhabela, T., Benyon, A. & McCormick, T. 2001. Exploding the monolith: Multiliteracies in South Africa. In M. Kalantzis & B. Cope (eds), *Transformations in Language and Learning: Perspectives on Multiliteracies* (pp. 121–52). Melbourne: Common Ground.

Newman, M. 2005. Rap as literacy: A genre analysis of hip-hop ciphers. *Text*, 25, 399–436.

Ng, J. 2006. Enhancing literacy skills through the multiliteracies teaching approach. *International Journal of the Humanities*, 3, 13–22.

Nichols, S. L. & Berliner, D. C. 2007. *Collateral Damage: How High Stakes Testing Corrupts America's Schools*. Cambridge, MA: Harvard University Press.

OECD Centre for Educational Research and Innovation. 2005. *Formative Assessment: Improving Learning in Secondary Classrooms*. Paris: Organisationfor Economic Co-operation and Development.

Olmanson, J., Kennett, K., McCarthey, S., Searsmith, D., Cope, B. & Kalantzis, M. 2015. Visualizing revision: Leveraging student-generated between-draft diagramming data in support of academic writing development. *Technology, Knowledge and Learning*, November, DOI: 10.1007/s10758-015-9265-5.

Olson, D. R. 1998. *The World on Paper: The Conceptual and Cognitive Implications of Writing and Reading.* Cambridge, UK: Cambridge University Press.

Ong, W. J. 1958. *Ramus, Method and the Decay of Dialogue.* Cambridge, MA: Harvard University Press.

—— 1982. *Orality and Literacy: The Technologizing of the Word.* London: Methuen.

Osborne, B. & Wilson, E. 2003. Multiliteracies in Torres Strait: A Mabuiag Island state school diabetes project. *Australian Journal of Language and Literacy,* 26, 23.

Palinscar, A. S. & Brown, A. L. 1984. Reciprocal teaching of comprehension-fostering and comprehension-monitoring activities. *Cognition and Instruction,* 1, 117–75.

Pandian, A. & Balraj, S. 2010. Driving the agenda of learning by design in science literacy in Malaysia. *E-Learning and Digital Media,* 7(3), 301–16.

Papadopoulou, M. & Christidou, V. 2004. Multimodal text comprehension and production by preschool children: An interdisciplinary approach of water conservation. *International Journal of Learning,* 11, 917–27.

Paris, S. 2005. Reinterpreting the development of reading skills. *Reading Research Quarterly,* 40(2), 184–202.

Paris, S. G. & Stahl, S. A. (eds). 2005. *Children's Reading Comprehension and Assessment.* Malwah, NJ: Lawrence Erlbaum Associates.

Pea, R. & Jacks, D. 2014. *The Learning Analytics Workgroup: A Report on Building the Field of Learning Analytics for Personalized Learning at Scale.* Stanford, CA: Stanford University.

Pellegrino, J. W., Chudowsky, N. & Glaser, R. 2001. *Knowing what Students Know: The Science and Design of Educational Assessment.* Washington, DC: National Academies Press.

Piaget, J. 1923 (2002). *Language and Thought of the Child.* London: Routledge.

—— 1971. *Psychology and Epistemology: Towards a Theory of Knowledge.* Harmondsworth, UK: Penguin.

Pierce, C. S. 1998. What is a sign? In The Pierce Edition Project (ed.), *Selected Philosophical Writings, Volume 2 (1893–1913)* (pp. 5–10). Bloomington, IN: Indiana University Press.

Pinto, M., Fernandez-Ramos, A. & Doucet, V. 2010. Measuring students' information skills through concept mapping. *Journal of Information Science,* 36, 464–80.

Plato. c. 399–347 BCE. Phaedrus. In J. M. Cooper (ed.), *Compete Works.* Indianapolis, IN: Hackett.

Popham, W. J. 2008. *Transformative Assessment.* Alexandria, VA: ASCD.

—— 2011. *Classroom Assessment.* Boston MA: Pearson.

Prain, V. 2006. Learning from writing in secondary science: Some theoretical and practical implications. *International Journal of Science Education,* 28(2–3), 179–201.

Prain, V. & Hand, B. 1996a. Writing and learning in secondary science: Rethinking practice. *Teaching and Teacher Education*, 12(6), 609–26.

—— 1996b. Writing to learn in the junior secondary science classroom: Issues arising from a case study. *International Journal of Science Education*, 18(1), 117–28.

—— 1999. Students' perceptions of writing-to-learn in secondary school science. *Science Education*, 83(2), 151–62.

Purcell-Gates, V. 1995. *Other People's Worlds: The Cycle of Low Literacy*. Cambridge, MA: Harvard University Press.

Ramachandran, V. S. 2011. *The Tell-Tale Brain*. New York: W. W. Norton.

Ranker, J. 2007. Designing meaning with multiple media sources: A case study of an eight-year-old student's writing processes. *Research in the Teaching of English*, 41(4), 402–34.

Ravitch, D. 2010. *The Death and Life of the Great American School System: How Testing and Choice are Undermining Education*. New York: Basic Books.

Ravitch, D. & Finn, C. 1988. *What Do Our 17 Year-Olds Know?* New York: Harper & Row.

Raymond, Eric. 2001. *The Cathedral and the Bazaar: Musings on Linux and Open Source by an Accidental Revolutionary*. Sebastapol, CA: O'Reilly.

Risley, T. R. & Hart, B. 1995. *Meaningful Differences in the Everyday Experience of Young American Children*. Baltimore, MD: Paul H Brookes Pub.

Ritchie, S. M. & Tomas, L. 2012. Hybridized writing for scientific literacy: Pedagogy and evidence. In R. M. Gillies (ed.), *Pedagogy: New Developments in the Learning Sciences* (pp. 213–26). New York, NY: Nova Science Publishers.

—— 2013. Designing an innovative approach to engage students in learning science: The evolving case of hybridized writing. In L. V. Shavinina (ed.), *The Routledge International Handbook of Innovation Education* (pp. 385–95). Oxon, UK: Routledge.

Rorty, R. 1992. *The Linguistic Turn: Essays in Philosophical Method*. Chicago: Chicago University Press.

Rose, M. 1993. *Authors and Owners: The Invention of Copyright*. Cambridge, MA: Harvard University Press.

Rosowsky, A. 2005. Just when you thought it was safe: Synthetic phonics and syncretic literacy practices. *English in Education*, 39, 32–46.

Roth, D. 2004. Learning based programming. In L. C. Jain & D. Holmes (eds), *Innovations in Machine Learning: Theory and Applications*. Springer-Verlag.

Rugg, H. & Shumaker, A. 1928. *The Child-Centered School: An Appraisal of the New Education*. Yonkers, NY: World Book Company.

Ryan, K. E. 2008. Fairness issues and educational accountability. In K. E. Ryan & L. A. Shepard (eds), *The Future of Test-Based Educational Accountability* (pp. 191–208). New York: Routledge.

Ryan, K. E. & Shepard, L. A. 2008. *The Future of Test-based Accountability*. New York: Routledge.

Sakellariou, A. 2007. Combined teaching of folk tale and advertisement: An application of the pedagogy of multiliteracies to the teaching of a second language. *International Journal of Learning*, 14, 231–8.

Sapir, E. 1921. *Language: An Introduction to the Study of Speech*. New York: Harcourt Brace.

Sartre, J.-P. 1940 (2004). *The Imaginary: A Phenomenological Psychology of the Imagination*. London: Routledge.

Schoenfeld, A. H. & David Pearson. P. 2009. The reading and math wars. In G. Sykes, B. Schneider & D. N. Plank (eds), *Handbook of Education Policy Research* (pp. 560–80). New York: Routledge.

Schultz, B. D. 2007. 'Feelin' what they feelin': Democracy and curriculum in Cabrini Green. In M. W. Apple & J. A. Beane (eds), *Democratic Schools: Lessons in Powerful Education* (pp. 62–82). Portsmouth, NH: Heinemann.

Scollon, R. 2001. *Mediated Discourse: The Nexus of Practice*. London: Routledge.

Scott, Foresmanand Company. 1951. *Dick and Jane: We Play*. New York: Grossat & Dunlap.

Scribner, S. & Cole, M. 1981. *The Psychology of Literacy*. Cambridge, MA: Harvard University Press.

Searle, J. R. 2002. End of the revolution. *New York Review of Books*, 49, 28 February.

Shenk, D. 2010. *The Genius in All of Us: Why Everything You've Been Told About Genetics, Talent and IQ is Wrong*. New York: Doubleday.

Shermis, M. D. 2014. State-of-the-art automated essay scoring: Competition, results, and future directions from a United States demonstration. *Assessing Writing*, 20, 53–76.

Shor, I. 2009. What is critical literacy? In A. Darder, M. P. Baltodano & R. D. Torres (eds), *The Critical Pedagogy Reader* (2nd edn) (pp. 282–304). New York: Routledge.

Smith, F. (2004). *Understanding Reading: A Psycholingustic Analysis of Reading and Learning to Read* (6th edn). Mahwah, NJ: Lawrence Erlbaum.

Snoddon, K. 2010. Technology as a learning tool for ASL literacy. *Sign Language Studies*, 10, 197–213.

Snow, C. E., Burns, S. M. & Griffin, P. 1998. *Preventing Reading Difficulties in Young Children*. Washington, DC: National Academy Press.

Snyder, I. 2008. *The Literacy Wars: Why Teaching Children to Read and Write is a Battleground in Australia*. Sydney: Allen & Unwin.

Soltero, S. W. 2011. *Schoolwide Approaches to Educating ELLs: Creating Linguistically and Culturally Responsive K-12 Schools*. Portsmouth, NH: Heinemann.

Stein, P. 2001. Classrooms as sites of textual, cultural and linguistic reappropriation. In B. Comber & A. Simpson (eds). *Negotiating Critical Literacies in Classrooms* (pp. 151–69). Mahwah, NJ: Lawrence Erlbaum.

Stein, P. & Newfield, D. 2002. Agency, creativity, access and activism: Literacy education in post-apartheid South Africa. In M. Kalantzis, G. Varnava-Skoura & B. Cope (eds), *Learning for the Future* (pp. 155–65). Melbourne: Common Ground.

—— 2003. Recovering the future: Multimodal pedagogies and the making of culture in South African classrooms. *International Journal of Learning,* 10, 2841–50.

Stern, D. L. 1985. *The Interpersonal World of the Infant: A View from Psychoanalysis and Developmental Psychology.* New York: Basic Books.

Su, C. Y. & T. I. Wang. 2010. Construction and analysis of educational assessments using knowledge maps with weight appraisal of concepts. *Computers and Education,* 55, 1300–11.

Suchman, L. 2007. *Human-Machine Reconfigurations.* Cambridge, UK: Cambridge University Press.

Suominen, K. 2009. Students learning by design: A study on the impact of learning by design on student learning. School of Education, RMIT, Melbourne.

Surowiecki, J. 2004. *The Wisdom of Crowds: Why the Many Are Smarter than the Few and How Collective Wisdom Shapes Business, Economies, Societies and Nations.* New York: Doubleday.

Tan, J. P.-L. 2007. Closing the gap: A multiliteracies approach to English language teaching for 'at-risk' students in Singapore. In A. Healy (ed.), *Multiliteracies and Diversity in Education: New Pedagogies for Expanding Landscapes.* Melbourne: Oxford University Press.

Tan, L., Bopry, J. & Guo, L. 2010. Portraits of new literacies in two Singapore classrooms. *RELC Journal: A Journal of Language Teaching and Research,* 41, 5–17.

Taylor, L. K., Bernhard, J. K., Garg, S. & Cummins, J. 2008. Affirming plural belonging: Building on students' family-based cultural and linguistic capital through multiliteracies pedagogy. *Journal of Early Childhood Literacy,* 8, 269–94.

The Economist Intelligence Unit. 2014. *The Learning Curve: Education and Skills for Life 2014 Report.* Pearson Australia.

Thompson, E. P. 1971. The moral economy of the English crowd in the eighteenth century. *Past and Present,* 50, 76–136.

Tomas, L. 2012. Writing narratives about a socioscientific issue: Engaging students and learning science. *Teaching Science,* 58(4), 24–8.

Tompkins, G., Campbell, R., Green, D. 2012. *Literacy for the 21st Century: A Balanced Approach.* Pearson Australia.

Tzeng, J. Y. 2005. Developing a computer-based customizable self-contained concept mapping for taiwanese history education. In P. Kommers & G. Richards (eds), *Proceedings of World Conference on Educational Multimedia, Hypermedia and Telecommunications* (pp. 4105–11). Chesapeake, VA: AACE.

Unsworth, L. 2001. *Teaching Multiliteracies Across the Curriculum: Changing Contexts of Text and Image in Classroom Practice.* Buckingham, UK: Open University Press.

van Haren, R. 2015. Engaging learner diversity through learning by design. In B. Cope & M. Kalantzis (eds), *A Pedagogy of Multiliteracies: Learning By Design.* London: Palgrave.

Vojak, C., Kline, S. Cope, B. McCarthey, S. & Kalantzis, M. 2011. New spaces and old places: An analysis of writing assessment software. *Computers and Composition,* 28, 97–111.

Vygotsky, L. S. 1934 (1986). *Thought and Language.* Cambridge, MA: MIT Press.

—— 1962 (1978). *Mind in Society: The Development of Higher Psychological Processes.* Cambridge, MA: Harvard University Press.

—— 1962. *Thought and Language.* Boston: MIT Press.

—— 1978. *Mind in Society: The Development of Higher Psychological Processes.* Cambridge, MA: Harvard University Press.

—— 1986. *Thought and Language.* Cambridge, MA: MIT Press.

—— 2012. *Thought and Language.* Cambridge, MA: MIT Press.

Walsh, C. S. 2009. The multi-modal redesign of school texts. *Journal of Research in Reading,* 32(1), 126–36.

Walsh, M. 2010. Multimodal literacy: What does it mean for classroom practice? *Australian Journal of Language and Literacy,* 33(3), 211–39.

Weishar, J. 1992. *Design for Effective Selling Space.* New York: McGraw-Hill.

Wertsch, J. V. 1991. *Voices of the Mind.* Cambridge, MA: Harvard University Press.

—— 1998. *Mind as Action.* New York: Oxford University Press.

Westby, C. 2010. Multiliteracies: The changing world of communication. *Topics in Language Disorders,* 30, 64–71.

Whorf, B L. 1956. *Language, Thought and Reality: Selected Writings of Benjamin Lee Whorf.* Cambridge, MA: MIT Press.

Wiliam, D. 2011. *Embedded Formative Assessment.* Bloomington, IN: Solution Tree Press.

Williams, J. 2009. Managing student conceptions about evolution using the integration of multiliteracies in the classroom. *Teaching Science,* 55(1), 10–14.

Windschitl, M. 2002. Framing constructivism in practice as the negotiation of dilemmas: An analysis of the conceptual, pedagogical, cultural, and political challenges facing teachers. *Review of Educational Research,* 72, 131–75.

Woodard, R., Magnifico, A. & McCarthey, S. 2013. Supporting teacher metacognition about formative writing assessment in online environments. *e-Learning and Digital Media,* 10, 442–70.

Yoon, C. K. 2009. *Naming Nature: The Clash Between Instinct and Science.* New York: W. W. Norton.

Index